Political Concepts

POLITICAL CONCEPTS
A READER AND GUIDE

Edited by
Iain MacKenzie

EDINBURGH UNIVERSITY PRESS

Selection and editorial material
© Iain MacKenzie, 2005. The texts are
reprinted by permission of other publishers;
the acknowledgements on pp. 675–9
constitute an extension of this copyright page.

Edinburgh University Press Ltd
22 George Square, Edinburgh

Typeset in Sabon and Gill Sans
by TechBooks, New Delhi, India, and
printed and bound in Great Britain by
Antony Rowe Ltd, Chippenham, Wilts

A CIP record for this book is available from
the British Library

ISBN 0 7486 1677 2 (hardback)
ISBN 0 7486 1678 0 (paperback)

The right of the contributors to be
identified as authors of this work
has been asserted in accordance with the
Copyright, Designs and Patents Act 1988.

CONTENTS

ANALYTICAL TABLE OF CONTENTS

ACKNOWLEDGEMENTS

I am deeply indebted to the contributors to this collection for their patience and persistence as well as for the analytical rigour and stylistic clarity they have all brought to the often murky waters of conceptual analysis in politics. The breadth, depth and pertinence of their essays, alongside their careful and often inventive choices of the selected readings, are really what bring this collection to life. The staff at Edinburgh University Press are also deserving of the highest praise for their patience with me and the good-humoured and careful way they oversaw the production of this book. In particular, Nicola Carr, who initially pitched the idea of this collection to me (too long ago for me to mention in decency), is clearly everything one could hope for in a commissioning editor: creative, responsive, critical and unswervingly friendly. Anna, Kathryn and Sam have been and continue to be my inspiration in life and their love and support through the many stages of this project have been invaluable in seeing it to completion. This book is dedicated to my mother and father: Margaret and Angus.

NOTES ON THE CONTRIBUTORS

Ruth Abbey is a senior lecturer in the Department of Politics and International Relations at the University of Kent. She is the author of *Nietzsche's Middle Period* (Oxford University Press, 2000) and *Philosophy Now: Charles Taylor* (Acumen, 2000) and the editor of *Contemporary Philosophy in Focus: Charles Taylor* (Cambridge University Press, 2004). In addition she has published numerous journal articles. Her research and teaching interests focus on contemporary political theory, with special reference to liberalism and feminism.

Patrick Bernhagen is a lecturer in the Department of Politics and International Relations at the University of Aberdeen. He has written numerous articles on the political power of business, globalisation, and citizen participation in various journals including *Contemporary Politics* and *Political Studies*.

Christopher J. Berry is Professor of Political Theory, Department of Politics, University of Glasgow. He is an elected Fellow of the Royal Society of Edinburgh and the author of five books and many academic articles in intellectual history and political theory. He is currently writing a book on the philosophical anthropology of politics.

Christian Brütsch teaches politics in the Institute for Political Science at the University of Zurich.

Phillip Cole is Reader in Applied Philosophy at Middlesex University. He has written about the problems of boundaries in moral and political theory, most recently on nation-state borders in *Philosophies of Exclusion: Liberal Political Theory and Immigration* (Edinburgh University Press, 2000).

Sylvie Delacroix is a lecturer in Kent University, teaching constitutional law and philosophy of law. She is now the Evelyn Green Davis Fellow at the Radcliffe Institute for Advanced Study, Harvard University, where she is researching her next book, provisionally titled *Religious Absolutism and Secular Normativity*. She is the author of *Legal Norms and Normativity: A Genealogical Enquiry* (forthcoming).

Stephen Elstub has recently completed his PhD on deliberative and associational democracy at the University of Sheffield. He is currently lecturing and tutoring in political theory, British politics and social policy at both the University of Sheffield and Sheffield Hallam University. His main areas of interest are democratic theory, liberalism and civil society.

Paul Graham is a lecturer in political theory at Glasgow University. His present research focuses on the role moral reasons play in stabilising a political order. He is completing a book provisionally entitled *Liberal Stability*, as well as a book on John Rawls.

Kieran Laird is currently a sessional lecturer in the School of Politics and International Studies at Queen's University of Belfast. His research interests include the connections between the neurology and philosophy of mind and political theory.

Debbie Lisle is a lecturer in politics and international studies at Queen's University Belfast. Her research examines the intersections between international relations, cultural studies and tourism. She has published work on travel writing, tourism, airports and war films.

Adrian Little is lecturer in political theory at the University of Melbourne. He is the author of *The Political Thought of Andre Gorz* (Routledge, 1996), *Post-Industrial Socialism: Towards a New Politics of Welfare* (Routledge, 1998), *The Politics of Community: Theory and Practice* (Edinburgh University Press, 2002) and *Democracy and Northern Ireland: Beyond the Liberal Paradigm?* (Palgrave Macmillan, 2004).

Alice Ludvig is a lecturer in political science and a research assistant at the University of Vienna. She teaches gender in political theory and selected methods in political science. Her research covers citizenship and nationality, comparative politics and Black feminism.

John McGovern teaches politics at the University of East London. He is the co-author of *Theories of the Modern State* (forthcoming, Edinburgh University Press, 2006).

Iain MacKenzie teaches political theory at the University of Kent. He is the author of *The Idea of Pure Critique* (Athlone, 2004).

James Martin is Senior Lecturer in Politics at Goldsmiths College, University of London. He is the author of *Gramsci's Political Analysis* (Macmillan, 1998) and various articles and chapters on Italian political thought and on poststructuralist discourse theory. He is co-author (with Steve Bastow) of *Third Way Discourse* (Edinburgh University Press, 2003) and has co-edited (with Terrell Carver) *Palgrave Advances in Continental Political Thought* (Palgrave Macmillan, 2005).

Robert Porter is a research associate in the Media Studies Research Institute, University of Ulster. His forthcoming book, *Ideology: Explorations in Contemporary Social, Political and Cultural Theory*, will be published by the University of Wales Press.

Birgit Schippers is a lecturer in politics at St Mary's University College Belfast. She has recently completed her PhD thesis on the notion of marginality in the ideas of Julia Kristeva and Judith Butler. Her areas of interest include French feminism, citizenship, identity politics and poststructural and psychoanalytic models of politics.

David Stevens is a lecturer in politics at the University of Nottingham.

Mark Anthony Wenman is currently a teaching fellow in the School of Politics at the University of Nottingham, and has recently completed his Ph.D. in the Government Department at the University of Essex. He has published a number of articles on poststructuralism, pluralism and the political.

Nathan Widder is a lecturer in political theory at the University of Exeter. His teaching and research focus on issues of identity, power, and knowledge, which he has examined through engagements with both contemporary philosophy and the history of Western thought. He is the author of *Genealogies of Difference* (Urbana, 2002).

Stephen de Wijze teaches political theory at the University of Manchester. He is currently working on a book concerning John Rawls and political liberalism.

GENERAL INTRODUCTION
WHAT ARE POLITICAL CONCEPTS?

Iain MacKenzie

INTRODUCTION

Arguably, to think at all is to think conceptually: that is, to deploy generalities that survey particular cases by way of connecting and synthesising those cases but also by way of establishing differences or differentiating between the particularities as well. If we take the example of 'the state', this political concept brings together a number of particular forms of political organisation under one conceptual banner – nation-states, nascent or emerging states, democratic states and so on – but it also implies that we differentiate 'the state' from other forms of political organisation – communities, nations, supra-national organisations etc. I began with 'arguably', however, because already the general claim is packed full of assumptions that we shall see need to be unpacked and refined: Is a concept always a generality? Can we have concepts that express particulars, for example 'particularity' itself? Are we assuming already that concepts are the product of thinking by individuals and that 'individuals' here really means 'individual human beings endowed with certain capacities for thought'? What exactly is the relationship between the connective and the differentiating requirements of conceptual thinking; in what way do concepts link some things together and exclude others from their survey of any set of cases? Continuing the example of 'the state', what *exactly* is it that links different kinds of organisation under this umbrella concept and what *exactly* is it that allows us to differentiate states from other political formations? Moreover, what *exactly* do we imply about conceptual thinking in general when we make such links and distinctions? Already, therefore, we can see that to think about concepts in general is to *think about thinking in general* and this is no straightforward matter.

Of course, the task of this volume is to present a series of key *political* concepts, so we need only be concerned with a subset of concepts: those that refer directly to the realm of politics. This, however, is both a help and hindrance. It is a help because it limits the scope of our enquiries to a list of broadly familiar concepts, by which I mean concepts that we employ commonly in our everyday lives whenever we engage directly or indirectly in political life. As such, we have an intuitive benchmark established for much of our thinking about political concepts, namely that our understanding of them should accord with our experiences of taking part in the world of politics, at least to some degree. But this caveat, 'at least to some degree', also expresses one of the key hurdles that must be overcome in thinking conceptually about politics: namely, that we must not be led astray by our intuitive understanding of particular political concepts and political concepts in general, into a series of dead ends that reveal more about our biases and prejudices than they do about our capacity to think conceptually – rigorously, analytically, creatively – about the political world. In order to avoid these dead ends and in order to keep our focus on political concepts, we must walk a fine line between purely abstract 'thinking about thinking' and simply reinforcing our political biases by thinking that political concepts can be analysed *without* thinking about what they imply about our conceptual understanding of the world and our relationship to it, in the most general sense.

There are two principal ways of treading this fine line. First, we must conduct in-depth studies into the nature and meaning of the concepts that make up our everyday grasp of political life. This is the task of the main body of this book in that each of the introductory essays and selected readings expresses the complexities surrounding and suffusing many of the concepts that shape our understanding of politics. Second, we must ask ourselves, as we read through all the material on particular concepts, 'what are political concepts?' so that we can always maintain a certain critical distance on the assumptions that guide our thinking about any particular concept. This general question, therefore, can be split into others that will help our navigation through the seas of conceptual political thinking: What does argument X about concept Y reveal about writer Z's approach to political concepts in general? Do the different perspectives on concept Y that make up the debates surrounding it express different assumptions about political concepts in general, in which case can the debates be resolved, refined or removed by thinking about politics at the level of political concepts in general? Are there some concepts – ideology, for example – which necessarily express this general level of discussion and some – equality, for example – which do so but only indirectly, and if this is the case, are there different kinds of political concept or, perhaps less dramatically, concepts that relate to political life in quite starkly different ways?

Within these general remarks and guiding questions there is one key element that must always be at the forefront of our concerns as we try to tread the fine line involved in thinking conceptually about politics. We must always remember that the phrase 'political concepts' already contains a concept within it, namely 'the political'. (Arguably, the idea of 'concept' is also already a concept, such that there are two concepts expressed within the phrase, but the quagmire of reflection and analysis that this gets us into can be neatly side-stepped for the purposes of this volume!) The point is this: in thinking about *political* concepts as a sub-set of concepts in general we have already conceptualised, implicitly for the most part, what we mean by 'the political'. Bringing to light the different conceptualisations of 'the political' that inform our grasp of particular political concepts is one of the key aims of this text. Moreover, thinking conceptually about 'the political' is one of the key features that differentiates students of politics (from the A-level student to the most 'esteemed' professor of the discipline, from the reflective participant in politics to the informed policy-makers shaping our global institutions) from unreflective participants in political life (similarly occupying all areas of the political realm) who assume implicitly a definition of 'the political' and who also assume that whatever definition guides their thinking about politics is so obvious as to be unquestionable. To think conceptually about politics, therefore, is not just to think about the concepts that we use in political life; it is also to think conceptually about 'the political' itself. In all good political analysis there is a constant interplay between the analysis of particular political concepts like 'justice', 'power', 'multiculturalism' and 'globalisation' and the analysis of 'the political' itself.

POLITICAL CONCEPTS: A MULTIDIMENSIONAL APPROACH

As these introductory remarks make clear, it is not sufficient to think of political concepts as simple one-dimensional phenomena that can be straightforwardly defined in order that the 'real' business of getting on with political analysis and reform of our political institutions (assuming they are in need of reform) can begin. Rather, as students of politics, we need to work in parallel; the analysis of political life – its dynamism, its institutions, its histories and the possibilities for its future – must be conducted with a constant eye on the many different dimensions of the concepts we employ in these analyses. But if this is the case, then we need to have a preliminary grasp of the multidimensional nature of political concepts so that we can keep these dimensions in mind as we conduct our analyses and so that the vitality and vibrancy of political studies can be conveyed at its most general level; in the hope, perhaps, that all the different kinds of students of politics who may use this book will be inspired to reflect upon, and maybe even provide, answers that have yet to be given to the guiding question of this introduction: 'what are political concepts?'.

The first, and perhaps most obvious, dimension of political concepts is that they should *reflect* political reality. When we think about a political concept like 'globalisation' we tend to assume that it 'works' as a concept precisely because it provides insight into the nature of current political realities. Political concepts, we might argue, should act like mirrors to the world of politics, representing the realities of that world to our minds so that we can grasp that reality 'in our heads'. This reflective dimension of political concepts, however, needs to be treated with some caution as it carries with it a number of assumptions about conceptual thinking in general that may be overly simplistic. As the example of globalisation makes clear, in reflecting political 'realities' we must be wary of assuming that those realities are unchanging. Indeed, the vibrancy and dynamism of political realities, their tendency to change over time and mutate in different contexts, is precisely what makes the study of politics such a lively and engaging pursuit. Of course, while few would hold that the reality described by political concepts is unchanging and immutable, many would still argue that the main function of political concepts is to reflect and describe the *changing* realities of political life: globalisation is a relative newcomer to the conceptual scene in politics because the processes it reflects are new and emerging realities of political life. But is this 'reflective' dimension of political concepts the whole, or even the main part, of the story about political concepts?

As the essay on globalisation in this volume makes clear, it is not simply a reflective or a descriptive concept: it is also an *evaluative* one. Political reality is not just reflected through concepts; it is evaluated through concepts, that is, students of politics use concepts to assess the reality as they see it by giving it value (or not). Even where the main focus of the analysis is descriptive, by virtue of using concepts evaluations are made: is any given feature of global political life part of this 'thing' we call 'globalisation' or not? By evaluating what is worthy of inclusion under a conceptual banner and what is not, we are already moving beyond any simple account of concepts as purely or simply reflective or descriptive. We might be tempted at this stage to invoke the famous philosophical distinction between 'is' and 'ought' to distinguish different kinds of political concepts: those that merely reflect the political world as it is and those that evaluate this reality by asking how it ought to be. In this way, moreover, it might be tempting to say that we should distinguish conceptual definition – globalization is X, therefore reality Y is included and reality Z is not – from conceptual evaluation – globalization is X, therefore it is 'good' or 'bad' etc. As such, it could be said, we can distinguish between two senses of 'evaluation' – the evaluation of what counts as a salient feature of the concept and the evaluation of the concept against some standards which dictate how we ought to respond to the reality being described. But, at least when dealing with political concepts, this distinction is extremely hard and maybe even impossible to maintain.

As argued above, every attempt to think conceptually about politics already involves a definition, at least implicitly, of what counts as 'the political'. In this light, the notion that we can distinguish the two different senses of 'evaluation' just discussed begins to look rather thin. As soon as we invoke a conceptual definition that is supposed to reflect political realities we have already made an evaluation about how 'the political' itself ought to be conceived. Behind every political 'is' there is already a political 'ought' by virtue of invoking political concepts at all. It might be said that this is putting the matter too starkly, that there is indeed broad agreement about what constitutes 'the political' realm and that this can be distinguished from a number of other realms without much controversy: family life, economic life, religious life and so on. But, as is now commonly recognised within political studies, this manoeuvre is no longer tenable. If we have learned anything from the history of debates surrounding political concepts it is that whenever there is even a temporary agreement within the literature about the nature of politics in general this is immediately called into question and the fundamental battles about what 'the political' actually is begin again. In recent times, one can think of the interventions of feminist political theorists in this way; the often cosy assumptions of mainstream/male-stream political thinkers have been and continue to be shattered by revealing their implicit and explicit patriarchal construction of the political. For many feminists, indeed, we can say that the attempt to define 'the political' as it actually *is* – say, an arena in which rational individuals compete for scarce resources – has masked claims about what it *ought* to be – namely, that all who engage in politics ought to have the qualities of 'competitiveness', 'individualism' and 'rationality', where these are defined in peculiarly 'masculine' ways.

That said, this does not mean that we should give up on the guiding intuition that political concepts do have and should have some bearing on the realities of the political world. If we take the example of the concepts that open this collection – justice, liberty, equality and rights – we can see that all these explicitly evaluative concepts gain their prescriptive force from having a plausible and compelling descriptive dimension to them. Indeed, the very nature of their prescriptive force usually emanates from the insightful diagnoses thinkers who deal with these concepts make about political realities. Our wish to see a 'just' world where 'liberty' is fostered, 'equality' attained and our 'rights' respected would be merely empty theorising were it not for the descriptions of injustices, infringements of liberty, inequalities and abuses of our rights; descriptions that make a claim to reflect the present realities of political life. It is with this in mind, that it is preferable to talk of the different dimensions within political concepts rather than to talk of different kinds of political concepts for different kinds of political analysis.

But do these two dimensions – the reflective and the evaluative – exhaust the multi-dimensional make-up of political concepts?

A problem that has beset both our reflective and our evaluative thinking about politics is the persistent sense that both these dimensions are abstract from the lived experience of being in the political world. Thinking from a perspective that prioritises the descriptive dimension of political concepts has, at times, tended to create an overly academic language of politics suffused with concepts that generalise our experiences as political actors to the point where we feel they no longer adequately represent that experience. Similarly, overly prescriptive evaluations of how we ought to organise our political life are often presented as if they are impositions upon the way we conduct our political lives, impositions emanating from the 'ideal' world of enquiries into the rational meaning of certain concepts that make untenable demands upon us as 'real' political actors. Clearly, a technical, specialised language of political studies is defensible as an integral part of gaining insight into the complex mechanisms of political life and, what is more, the gains to our understanding made by way of such academic languages testify in support of this defence. It is also certainly the case that the rational interrogation of what we mean by many of the core political principles that guide our sense of how we ought to conduct our political affairs has had and continues to have enormous impact on clarifying our thinking, removing prejudices and criticising our all-too-often unquestioned assumptions about 'the right thing to do' in political life. Accepting these views, however, does not necessarily remove or assuage our sense that much of the conceptual work in political studies has little to offer when it comes to getting *inside* our experience of life as political actors. It is not so much that political thinkers do not aim to do this – they clearly do, almost without exception – but that they often unconsciously prioritise the two dimensions of political concepts just addressed (the reflective and evaluative) over and above two other important dimensions of political concepts, dimensions I shall call the *effective* and the *affective*.

The *effective* dimension of political concepts is this: thinking conceptually about politics does not only reflect political realities, nor simply provide evaluations of how we ought to organise political life; it can actually effect a change in the political world itself. At one level, this is quite obvious: to think of the global political order as made up of nations, for example, can change the ways in which certain political groups respond to that order; some may seek to claim nationhood so as to gain acceptance within the global arena, some may respond by citing nations as the political bodies that are deemed to oppress them such that any member of a given nation becomes a 'legitimate target' in a war of liberation, as it might be perceived. This dimension of conceptual analysis is not simply one of reflecting political reality, nor of simply evaluating it against core political principles; rather, it is a dimension that actually changes the reality of the situation, for some at least, and brings about changes in how our core political principles are to be understood. At another level, the effective dimension of political concepts is rather more complicated. To say that concepts can have an effect in the make-up of the political world is to include our conceptual thinking in the causal chains that construct the dynamism of the political itself. In this way, the image of the impartial researcher of politics studying political life 'at a distance', as it were, is one which cannot be held onto for very long. At the very least, it demands a careful and rigorous analysis of what may remain of the ideal of 'impartiality' once we recognise the effect of political concepts on the political world. At most, it may lead us to conclude that 'impartial' political research is merely a pipe-dream from a long-gone age of Enlightenment. Whatever view one takes, and there are plenty of options between these two positions, what we may think of as the distance between political concepts and political reality is eroded by virtue of the concepts we deploy being agents that bring about change in that which we are trying to study in the first place.

Closely allied to this dimension is the *affective* dimension of political concepts. Political concepts do not simply bring about change in the world that we are studying; they can also bring about change in 'us', as students of politics (meaning anyone who reflects upon the political, not just those students that are at school, college or university 'studying politics'). Perhaps the best way of explaining this affective dimension is to think of it as a change of perspective. As those who encounter the work of Karl Marx or Simone de Beauvoir for the first time (to give just two possible examples from a potentially infinite list) often testify, they emerge from reading their work with a different view of the world. In a literal and profound sense, their perspective on the world has changed: new realities emerge, old realities disappear, concepts they once held dear are now no longer important and new concepts take their place. However, for those of us who have some sense of this experience, it is not just a change of perspective on a world assumed to have its own reality 'out there', it is a change of how the world *feels* to us as political actors; it is a change that manifests itself as a transformation in how the world *affects* us, as felt from 'the inside', as it were. Indeed, the image of a political reality that exists 'out there' coupled with a view of that reality from 'inside our heads' begins to look like an insufficient metaphor to express our 'embeddedness' in the world of politics and the 'embodiment' of the world of politics in us. The power of political concepts, therefore, does not just derive from their ability to reflect reality, to guide our evaluation of that reality or to effect change in political reality itself; it also derives from their capacity to transform our most intimate affections – how we feel about those around us, the communities we inhabit, the institutions that shape so much of our lives and so much more.

However, even bringing our *thinking about political thinking* to this most intimate level does not exhaust the different dimensions of political concepts. Implicit within much of the discussion so far has been the idea that political concepts have a *critical* function. Even within the reflective dimension of conceptual thinking this is evident: concepts are defined in ways that challenge other definitions of the concept (or other related concepts) and as such challenge what is deemed to be the reality of the situation. But equally the critical dimension of political concepts is not the sole preserve of academics criticising each other's definitions, it is also a matter of deploying concepts that foster a critical attitude to the organisations and formations that make up the political world itself. Moreover, if we accept the idea that political concepts have an effective and an affective dimension to them as well, then the critical dimension is not simply a matter of theorising critically about politics and then putting that critical theory into practice, as this implies the very distance between 'the political' and our thinking about it that was found wanting. More plausibly, the critical dimension of political concepts is one that traverses the theory/practice divide such that our political theories are always already embedded within our political practices and our political practices are always already embodied versions of our theoretical perspectives on what counts as political and how the political functions. Indeed, to put it in the terms used throughout this discussion, the critical dimension is precisely this interplay of and interaction between the reflective, evaluative, effective and affective dimensions. As we think about politics, using (amongst others) the concepts gathered in this collection and being guided by the authors of the essays and the selected readings, we engage critically with the concepts by thinking in these four dimensions simultaneously: To what extent, if any, does concept X really reflect political reality? How should we evaluate the different arguments being made in support of concept X? To what extent does concept X bring about changes in the way the political world operates? How do the discussions surrounding concept X affect the way I and others may interact with the world of politics?

In pursuit of answers to these critical questions, it is tempting to suppose that there must be a priority given to one over the others so that a foundation for one's critical endeavours can be secured. It may be supposed that, whatever the difficulties, we must prioritise the guiding intuition that concepts reflect reality or, alternatively, that the main task of political analysis is the evaluation of reality in the name of a better future to come. Once the multidimensional nature of political concepts is exposed, however, then the hard task of trying to justify why one dimension is more important or foundational than any other has to be addressed. It is not that this is an impossible task or that answers could not be given to prioritise as well as differentiate the dimensions of political concepts; rather it is that all too often discussions of what we mean when we talk of political concepts are carried out without consideration of one or more of these dimensions. One of the main aims of this introduction, therefore, is to ask of readers, just as they will be asked to suspend hasty judgements about the meaning of the concepts in this collection, that they suspend any hasty judgements about the meaning and nature of political concepts in general; thinking about politics requires a good grasp of the intricacies of political concepts and thinking about political concepts *as* political concepts requires a good grasp of what we mean by 'the political' and what is involved in thinking about thinking.

THE STRUCTURE OF THIS BOOK

The key feature of this text it that it provides, almost uniquely amongst the literature on political concepts, both original and insightful introductory essays that survey the main debates surrounding a concept and a number of key readings from leading scholars in the respective field reprinted from elsewhere but chosen by the contributors to accompany their essays. Taken together, the essays and the readings throughout the book provide both an invaluable overview into the vibrant and vital nature of contemporary political analysis and exemplary instances of the intricacies involved in constructing conceptual debates within political studies. The exact relationship between the introductory essay and the accompanying readings has been left to the contributors to determine but they fall into broadly two camps: those essays that establish a context for the readings that follow and those that refer directly to the readings so as to guide the reader through the arguments. Both approaches involve decisions about what to include and what not to include and it is important that the reader is aware of this so as to encourage a critical perspective on the essays and readings and so as not to assume that the selected readings are the only ones that need to be tackled in thinking about any particular concept. With this critical perspective in place, however, readers will find in all the contributions insights, arguments and debates that will happily fill their conceptual tool-box as long as they continue to think about politics.

The book is structured in five parts. Each part is designed to reflect broad family resemblances among its members as it is expected that readers who intend to study 'justice' will move easily on to 'liberty', 'equality' and rights', just as those that wish to know about 'ideology' will find much of resonance in 'discourse', 'difference' and 'the body politic'. That said, conceptual thinking in general does not come in parts and it is important that readers who use the parts as guides also peek beyond the boundaries that they establish and follow not just the guidance they will find in the essays and readings towards concepts in other parts but their own intuitions and gut-feelings as well. It is often by 'thinking outside the box' – or 'thinking outside the part' in this case – that creative and innovative work takes place. The brief editor's introduction to each part both explains the rationale for the grouping within parts and suggests ways in which the reader may want to link these concepts with others in the collection. Another way of reflecting upon the connections within and between parts is to look at the 'questions for discussion' that immediately follow each essay. They have been chosen to encourage reflection upon the essay that precedes them but also to encourage cross-fertilisation of conceptual debates throughout the collection.

It would be presumption of the worst kind to try to summarise the issues raised by the twenty contributors to this collection and the thirty-seven authors of the selected readings for the purpose of introducing this book (a sentiment that in part explains the meta-conceptual feel of the body of this general introduction). In place of such a summary I would rather offer some advice and reveal what I hope may emerge from following it. My advice to the reader is to dive into the riches of these texts by beginning with whatever concept seems most pressing for your own concerns and then to follow the leads around the text as you find them. My hope is that you will then find your way to reading the whole book and to garnering the subtle and rigorous insights to be found on every page. In that way, you may acquire not just a reader and guide to political concepts but an invaluable tool-kit for unlocking the complexities of the contemporary political world.

PART I
POLITICAL PRINCIPLES

INTRODUCTION

The concepts discussed in this part are the guiding political principles that have come to dominate contemporary political thinking. Whatever one's view of the make-up of the political world – whether one thinks of politics in terms of individuals competing for scarce resources, or economic classes at war with each other, or different genders constructing the realm of the political differently, and so on – there is an almost inexorable pull within one's analysis to ask if the current situation and any future forms of political organisation can meet the demands of justice, of maximising liberty and equality and of ensuring the fundamental rights of all. Of course, that these political principles are now at the core of political thinking should not blind us to two obvious facts. First, and with the exception of justice, which can claim to have been a central preoccupation of political thinking since its inception (at least in the western tradition), these principles are relative newcomers on the scene, at least as principles that our political thinking ought to follow. That is, the tradition of thinking about liberty, equality and rights as political principles is distinctly modern, and their status as virtually unassailable principles of political thinking is distinctly contemporary. Even justice, with its foundational role in political thought, has only recently been brought back to the centre of political life, largely thanks to the work of John Rawls. Secondly, the meaning and relative value of each of these political principles is deeply contested within political life and thought. As each of the essays and readings in this part deftly points out, there is actually very little agreement on the meaning and relative value of these principles beyond the polemical point that they are generally thought to be principles to which we should adhere. In many respects, it is this paradoxical position that provides the fuel that drives the engine of political thinking: we agree about so much in contemporary political thought and yet we agree about so little of what this basic consensus actually entails. Put like this, we are forced to enquire into the nature of political dis/agreements in general and the pursuit of institutions and apparatuses which can facilitate agreement or ensure that our disagreements do not forestall our ability to live together. As such, and this is to mention just a few connections that can be made, the concepts of democracy, human nature, ideology and power are never far away from the intricate analyses of what exactly we mean when we talk about justice, liberty, equality and rights and how we ought to weigh up the relative demands that each of these principles makes upon our political thinking.

I

JUSTICE[1]

David Stevens

INTRODUCTION

Imagine that I have some doughnuts to share amongst the students in my class. I give three to Alice, two to Bert, none to Claude, and one each to the rest of the class. There are no doughnuts left. When Claude says, in response to this act of distribution, that it is unjust, we understand the sort of complaint he is making. Whilst the details of Claude's objection might be unclear, the *type* of claim being made is a familiar one. It signals, most likely, a sense of unfairness Claude feels. Perhaps he views the distribution as arbitrary. Maybe Claude thinks there are relevant considerations to be taken into account when distributing, and these have been ignored or confused. For a distribution of doughnuts to be just it must not make arbitrary distinctions between people. In this sense we can be said to have an understanding of the *concept* of justice.

How we flesh out what counts as arbitrary distinctions – the content of the concept – is a different matter, and here things get more complicated. If asked to explain why the distribution was unjust, Claude might claim that doughnuts ought to be distributed equally because this reduces envy. But what if Bert objects to Claude's egalitarian principle of distribution on the grounds that doughnuts ought to be distributed according to need? An equal distribution ignores the fact that the need of some is greater than the need of others. Bert needs more doughnuts than Claude, therefore he should be allocated more. Alice might offer a different view: that doughnuts ought to be distributed on the basis of enjoyment. Most people like doughnuts so they should each get one. Alice is a true connoisseur and will derive far more pleasure from extra doughnuts. Claude, not particularly liking doughnuts, will receive little pleasure from any amount of doughnuts, and should not therefore get any.

Alice, Bert, and Claude all have a shared understanding of the concept of justice. When it comes to distributing doughnuts they all agree that the resulting state of affairs should be just, but they simply disagree as to what constitutes a just state of affairs. That is, they all offer different, and competing, *conceptions* of justice.

It is the enterprise of expounding and defending different conceptions of justice that lies at the heart of contemporary political philosophy. The concept of justice – specifically social justice – has come to dominate political thought over the past few decades. Questions of social justice – how a political community should distribute its scarce resources between individuals with competing claims – have subsumed nearly the entire spectrum of political concerns and concepts. Concepts such as rights, liberties and equality have been sucked into justice's sphere of influence. Justice, to borrow a phrase, is where the action is.

The concept itself has always been important to political theory, at least since Plato penned his *Republic* over two millennia ago. But, until recently, it was only one political concept amongst others. The rise of justice to its place of prominence in political thought is due largely to John Rawls's *A Theory of Justice* (1971, rev. ed. 1999). Rawls's work brought new analytical and philosophical techniques and tools to bear on the subject of justice, shedding new light on an old problem. Rawls opens *A Theory of Justice* by observing the importance of justice as the primary political virtue: 'justice is the first virtue of social institutions', and that 'laws and institutions no matter how efficient and well-arranged must be reformed and abolished if they are unjust' (Rawls 1999b: 3). If a society is unjust then any other praiseworthy features of it are of secondary worth. Historians tell us that Hitler's Germany developed a remarkably efficient set of public institutions and services. The fact that the trains ran on time, however, in no way justifies or mitigates the massive injustices perpetrated by the Nazi regime. If justice is this central to politics then it deserves considerable attention.

In contemporary political philosophy virtually all roads lead back to Rawls. The question of where to begin an examination of the various debates about justice is therefore a simple one. We shall focus our attention on the task of excavating the Rawlsian foundations of the subject. We shall examine the basics of Rawls's view, including his proposed principles of justice and his hypothetical device, the original position. This will allow us to consider two main opposing lines in the battle over justice. These are lines that share certain similarities, but exist at different ends of the political spectrum. Surveying all the different issues that have arisen from the burgeoning literature on the subject of justice would be an impossible task. The positions considered here, however, provide a foundation for understanding the myriad of arguments that have been made over the past few decades.

The example with which we began contains at least three important features that are analogous to questions of social justice. First, there is a limited set of resources to be distributed. There is no abundance of doughnuts from which the students can help themselves without exhausting that supply. If there were, then questions of justice would not arise. This limited supply of goods is part of what David Hume ([1739] 1978) called 'the circumstances of justice'. According to Hume it is 'only from the selfishness and confin'd generosity of men, along with the scanty provision nature has made for his wants, that justice derives its origins' ([1739] 1978: 495). The idea is that the need for principles of justice arises because of an innate propensity to satisfy one's own interests, coupled with a limited supply of resources such that we cannot all have everything we want.

Second are the principles of justice themselves. Alice, Bert and Claude all offer different principles. These principles are the *outcomes* of a conception of justice. They are intended to govern the distribution of whatever resources are at stake. The third feature is the need for a process or *method* for judging between competing principles. Why should we prefer Bert's suggestion to Alice's, or vice versa? How do we tell a superior view of justice from an inferior one?

Rawls's own conception of justice – what he calls 'justice as fairness' – contains all these elements. It recognises the circumstances of justice, offers principles for governing the distribution of resources in society, and provides a mechanism for defending those principles as appropriate. Let us begin, then, with the outcomes. Justice as fairness offers two principles of justice:

> First Principle: Each person is to have an equal right to the most extensive system of equal basic liberties compatible with a similar system of liberty for all [The Equal Liberty Principle].
> Second Principle: Social and economic inequalities are to be arranged so that they are both: (a) to the greatest benefit of the least advantaged [The Difference Principle], and (b) attached to offices and positions open to all under conditions of fair equality of opportunity [The Fair Equality of Opportunity Principle]. (Rawls 1999b: 302)

A society is just, according to Rawls, when its basic structure – its social, economic and political institutions, as well as its constitution – manifests these two principles. The first principle governs the distribution of various rights and liberties within society, such as rights to vote and take public office (political liberties), freedom of association and worship (freedom of conscience), rights protecting the freedom and integrity of the individual, and rights associated with the rule of law, such as protection from arbitrary arrest. All citizens, under this principle, have an equal set of these civil and political freedoms.

The second principle, which has two parts, governs the distribution of such resources as occupational and educational opportunities, as well as the other goods that arise from these, most notably wealth and income. The first principle is lexically prior to the second principle (and the fair equality of opportunity principle is lexically prior to the difference principle), meaning that the rights and liberties guaranteed under the first principle have priority and cannot be traded off for gains in opportunities or wealth provided by the second principle. Taken together, these rights, liberties, opportunities and other goods, such as wealth, income and the social bases of self-respect, form what Rawls calls *primary social goods*. These are the 'things' that get distributed within a society; they form the *currency* of social justice. Rawls's own list is supposed to represent a truncated set of goods that all individuals require in life, regardless of their specific plans, beliefs or ambitions. The correct currency for social justice has been widely contested.[2] Though the differences between the various views are important, there exist more general issues about distribution that apply to them all. We shall concentrate our attention on these more general issues.

EQUALITY AND PRIORITY

Let us begin with Rawls's difference principle, because this raises the question of on what *basis* goods should be distributed. The difference principle governs the distribution of wealth and income within a society. It holds that departures from a baseline of equality are justifiable if this would make everyone better off. For example, allowing inequalities might incentivise talented citizens to work harder and produce more wealth which can, in turn, be used to raise the standard of living of others. Rawls's primary concern here is with those who are in the worst-off group in terms of wealth and income. Under any inegalitarian distribution the difference principle requires that the worst-off group be placed in the best possible position (through such mechanisms as redistributive taxation schemes and so on).

Rawls is no strict egalitarian. Rather, this type of principle is best described as *prioritarian* because of the priority it gives to a specific group (the worst off) in the distribution process. The differences between prioritarianism and egalitarianism stem from what their defenders view as being the most important consideration. For egalitarians the important consideration is often that of how each person's level of advantage compares with the level of other people. Egalitarianism is, then, a comparative view of justice. By contrast, prioritarianism is concerned with absolute, rather than relative, levels of advantage. What is important is that those who are worst off are as well off as they can be in absolute terms. Derek Parfit writes that prioritarians 'do of course think it bad that some people are worse off. But what is bad is not that these people are worse off than *others*. It is rather that they are worse off than *they* might have been' (2000: 104; emphasis in original).

On this view, benefits to the worst off simply matter more. Rawls's difference principle embodies this concern by allowing departures from equality, but in so doing, requires that the position of the worst off be maximised. To see this imagine a society comprised, for the sake of simplicity, of just two social classes (Groups A and B). The economic system can be arranged in several different ways, such that three resulting distributions of income (represented by numerical levels) are possible across those groups. This can be represented thus:

	Group A	Group B	Total
Distribution 1	100	100	200
Distribution 2	100	170	270
Distribution 3	120	140	260

Under D1 both groups are equally well off. However, either D2 or D3, though unequal, can make both groups better off. Maintaining D1 in the face of the other two possibilities suffers from the defect that this would mean holding people's levels of resources back – what is often termed 'levelling down'. Indeed, D2 makes society, as a whole, much better off than it would be under D1. For utilitarians this is attractive, because what is of primary importance to them is that people are better off (how these benefits are distributed across people is a secondary consideration). However, the difference principle supports D3 over D1 and D2 because D3 makes the worst-off group the best off it can be from the available options. What is important is not primarily the total amount of goods in society, nor the relative relationship between groups, but the issue of who gets what, in particular what the worst-off group gets (in absolute terms).

But why should we accept these principles and all they entail? What reasons are there for thinking it more urgent to benefit the worst off? Such questions lead us neatly to a discussion of the method component of a conception of justice.

THE ORIGINAL POSITION

When Alice, Bert and Claude offer different principles for distributing doughnuts, how can we decide between them? Each, no doubt, has its merits, but is it possible to rank these merits so that a particular principle can be selected as the most appropriate? One immediate stumbling block is the role that self-interest often plays in our deliberations about justice. If we possess a marketable talent then we might prefer a conception of justice that is not heavily redistributive because we are likely to earn a lot of money. Our own interests, that is, have the potential to skew our deliberations, and if this happens then it is likely that we will never agree upon a single conception. In order to achieve agreement we need to clear any damaging bias out of the way. The dominant trend has been to try and achieve a level of *impartiality* in our deliberations that enables the securing of such an agreement.

Rawls suggests one way of achieving this. If we are to deliberate about justice in a fair manner, then we must abstract from those features of our selves, or exclude knowledge, that would make our decisions partisan. Rawls's hypothetical device, the original position, attempts exactly this. According to Rawls, sound principles of justice are ones that 'free and rational persons concerned to further their own interests would accept in an initial position of equality as defining the fundamental terms of their association' (1999b: 5). The original position models this initial situation of equality. It is a device for thinking in a hypothetical way about justice.

When we think about justice from within the original position we are placed behind what Rawls calls a 'veil of ignorance'. The veil hides certain pieces of knowledge from us. We do not know such things as our class position, level of intelligence, talents or disabilities, family background, or our conception of the good life (our beliefs about what gives our life meaning and value). Without access to this knowledge, Rawls argues, we are able to reach agreement on principles of justice for distributing social resources (primary social goods). This stems from the *impartiality* that the veil creates. Partiality requires information (think here of anonymised exam scripts: removing names from scripts combats any possible partiality on the part of examiners) and this is excluded by the veil.[3]

At the foundations of the original position is a view of fairness common to many (broadly) egalitarian thinkers, namely, that no one should be worse off through no *fault* of their own. Fault, luck, and responsibility are key elements in much recent work on social justice. The point of social justice for such theorists is to neutralise the contingencies of the world. We have no control over which family or social group we are born into, nor over the raw natural talents or disabilities that we might possess. These things are simply matters of brute luck; we cannot be said to deserve them or be held responsible for them. We should not, therefore, be advantaged or disadvantaged because of them – they are morally arbitrary features – so it is the purpose of social institutions to neutralise the effects of luck. Whilst the natural distribution of these things is not, in itself, just or unjust, the way that institutions treat them can be. Rawls explains: 'Aristocratic and caste societies are unjust because . . . the basic structure of these societies incorporates the arbitrariness found in nature. But there is no necessity for men to resign themselves to these contingencies' (1999b: 102).

Constrained by the conditions of the original position we will supposedly select Rawls's two principles. The criterion for adjudicating between competing principles is what Rawls terms 'maximin', or maximising the minimum position.[4] If we do not know which group in society we belong to then we should, Rawls argues, choose as though we might end up at the very bottom of the social strata. Given that the decision over which principle to select will dictate all our life chances, a certain level of risk-averse decision-making seems warranted. This offers an answer to the earlier question of why we should prioritise the position of the worst off. We prioritise the worst-off position to make sure it has sufficient in absolute terms, just in case we happen to be in the worst-off group when the veil is lifted.

Rawls's reasoning has received much critical attention. The debates have followed two main lines. The first is whether the two principles of justice would be chosen in the original position. Rational choice-based critiques question whether maximin is the appropriate criterion or whether we should gamble, in conditions of uncertainty, on not being in the worst-off group. Similarly, commentators such as Thomas Nagel (1979) have questioned the *absolute* priority given to the worst off in Rawls's reasoning. Nagel wonders whether other considerations might sometimes outweigh the urgency of benefiting the worst off. For example, a significant gain for the best-off group (and no gain for the worst-off group) would be sacrificed by such an absolute criterion for a tiny gain for the worst-off group (and no significant gain for the better off).[5]

The second line of criticism takes issue with the construction of the original position itself. One common view is that the characteristics excluded by the veil of ignorance are the very things that make us who we are. As individuals, we are simply the sum of our cultural, religious and familial parts. Take those away, as the original position requires, and there is no 'self' left to do any choosing. This unencumbered self has no basis on which to make decisions about justice. That Rawls believes we will choose his principles of justice betrays, this criticism suggests, an attempt to smuggle a non-neutral view of what constitutes a good life into a supposedly neutral process.

Rawls has attempted to rebut such objections by stressing the hypothetical nature of the original position (1993b: 22–9). Nevertheless, there is something to this line of criticism, and the emphasis on the sociocultural origins of the 'self' lives on in the writings of multiculturalists and defenders of the politics of difference.

What is important here, however, is not the details of the original position, but the idea that it is supposed to represent. The purpose of this device is to secure *agreement* – or *agreeableness*, since the agreement is only hypothetical – on principles of justice. Without such agreement the state runs the risk of losing its legitimacy. If a framework of justice is imposed on a society where a significant proportion of its population rejects it, then those people are being coerced. The search for principles that are acceptable to all is a long-standing tradition in political theory, and the one that currently dominates the field. Rawls's original position is one possible device for trying to achieve that consent. More recent attempts have jettisoned the contrived circumstances of the original position but retained the need for impartiality in the contractualist method of constructing principles of justice. For Thomas Scanlon (1982, 1998, 2003), and more recently, Brian Barry (1995), the agreement on principles is to be secured by searching for principles that no one could reasonably reject. Scanlon develops his view in terms of morality rather than justice, but his statement of the position is instructive: 'An act is wrong if its performance under the circumstances would be disallowed by any system of rules for the general regulation of behaviour which no one could reasonably reject as a basis for informed, unforced general agreement' (1982: 110).

Much turns here on what would count as reasonable grounds for rejecting a principle. Reasonableness, as a virtue of citizens who seek agreement on principles of justice, has been the focus of contractualist efforts to move the justice debate forward whilst maintaining the concern for legitimacy and toleration of difference. But what about views that reject this foundation of justice in agreement? The idea of natural rights provides an alternative position from which to start discussions of justice. We shall turn to consider one variant of that view next.

Nozick and the violation of property rights

The views examined so far regard justice as compensating for undeserved disadvantages. But is this 'no fault' view of justice warranted? One concern is that it glosses over the fact that the goods being distributed are already owned. Taking goods from one person to give to another, even in the name of justice, might reasonably be thought to violate the rights of the original owner.

This is a line pursued most forcefully by Robert Nozick in *Anarchy, State, and Utopia* (1974). Nozick claims the preoccupation with matching distributive outcomes to preconceived patterns, typical of views like Rawls's, neglects a set of already existing freedoms and ownership rights. When the state removes goods from an individual it rides roughshod over those rights and freedoms. Instead, Nozick argues, justice should be concerned with the historical development of a distribution. As long as no coercion or fraud exists in the process of transferring goods, then a distribution is just.

To illustrate how distributive schemes violate freedom Nozick invokes his potentially devastating Wilt Chamberlain example. Nozick invites us to pick our ideal distribution. Let us assume, for simplicity, we pick an egalitarian one (the difference principle would also suffice). Call this distribution D1. Next, Nozick asks us to imagine that in this society there is a basketball player – Wilt Chamberlain – who is very much in demand. Knowing this, Wilt contracts with his team that 25 cents be added to the price of admission to his games. This 25 cents goes directly to Wilt. Over the course of a season one million fans gladly pay the extra 25 cents to see Wilt play. Wilt rakes in $250,000. The resulting distribution (D2) is now remarkably inegalitarian.

We cannot object to D1 because we chose it. But how can we object to D2 either, when all that has happened is that the people in D1 have chosen how to spend 25 cents of their money? Maintaining our preferred pattern would mean preventing individuals in our egalitarian society from using their resources – even very small amounts – as they wish. Any activity that upsets the pattern would have to be prohibited. Nozick assumes that our intuitions will baulk at restricting freedom this much. Suddenly our egalitarian society is looking less than ideal. Either we allow inequality to develop or we trample freedom.

The analogy with distributive justice is obvious. When the state taxes us it interferes with our rights to control our resources. Nozick puts the point forcefully: 'Taxation of earnings from labor is on a par with forced labor' (1974: 169). There would be something unsavoury about a society that forced us to do our jobs at gunpoint. But why is taking the earnings of n hours' labour any different to taking the same number of hours from the person? The upshot of this is that 'no end-state principle or distributional patterned principle of justice can be continuously realized without continuous interference with people's lives' (Nozick 1974: 163).

If correct then this devastates schemes of justice like Rawls's. The illegitimacy of redistributive mechanisms, such as taxation, means that the state can have no role in the provision of public goods and services, such as healthcare, education, welfare benefits, public transport and the like. All things currently provided by the state would have to be provided by voluntary private schemes. The only legitimate state becomes a minimal one – one that protects the system of contracts that underpin the unfettered market. This libertarian doctrine gained much currency in the 1980s, forming the ideological backbone of the New Right governments of Ronald Reagan and Margaret Thatcher. The effects of its attempt to divorce welfare from the state are still being felt today.

Nevertheless, Nozick's example, if not his wider theory, suffers from a defect that makes this type of position less convincing than initially thought. Notice that the Wilt example contains a cunning sleight of hand. Nozick invites us to pick a *distribution* of resources, and then shows how liberty decimates it. But this misrepresents most theories of distributive justice.[6] The Rawlsian-type view does not promote particular distributional patterns. Instead, it proposes rules or principles for the organisation of *institutions*. Once the institutions are set up according to the dictates of justice, whatever distribution of goods arises from them is just. Such views are procedure rather than outcome driven. The Wilt example elides this distinction. We pick a distribution and Nozick covertly installs a set of capitalist rules on top of it. It is unsurprising, therefore, that absolute rights over property subvert an egalitarian distribution. However, once aware of the distinction we can insist on picking egalitarian institutions and rules to go with our preferred distribution. If citizens truly desired an egalitarian distribution then it seems reasonable to assume that they would also desire institutions that uphold it. This might include redistributive taxation schemes to maintain a particular pattern of distribution. Nozick gives no reason for thinking this not to be the case, he simply assumes capitalist motivations and rules. There is no reason to think that the intuitions of twentieth-century capitalist societies are representative of human nature as a whole.

THE SITE OF DISTRIBUTIVE JUSTICE

What this does draw our attention to, however, is the different levels or sites at which principles of justice apply. Rawls's principles apply to the basic structure of society, and not to the actions of individuals or non-state bodies. Many thinkers follow Rawls in this. Rawls writes in his work on global justice:

> The principles of justice for the basic structure of a liberal democratic society are not...fully general principles. They do not apply to all subjects: not to churches or universities, or even to the basic structures of all societies. And they also do not hold for the Law of Peoples, which is autonomous. (1999a: 85–6)

This delineation of autonomous spheres is, again, something that is attributable to Rawls. Liam Murphy writes: 'Though Rawls's conception of the difference between political justice and personal ethics now seems very much the mainstream view, it is a significant innovation in political philosophy' (1998: 252–3). Prior to Rawls, this strict separation was non-existent. Indeed, utilitarianism – the dominant view of ethics before Rawls – makes no such distinction. Its principle of happiness maximisation applies at the levels of individual action, political institutions and public policy. It might assist theorists to limit principles of justice to institutions – the basic structure – but a simple desire is not sufficient to warrant such a demarcation. The boundaries between spheres cannot be drawn arbitrarily, or merely according to convenience. In order to countenance different principles for different spheres, we must be able to point to some relevant difference between those spheres that legitimises their separate treatment. The relevant difference, for Rawls, is as follows:

> The basic structure is the primary subject of justice because its effects are so profound and present from the start. The intuitive notion here is that the structure contains various social positions and that men born into different positions have different expectations of life determined, in part, by the political system as well as by economic and social circumstance. (1999b: 7)

The criteria, then, are the profound effects of these institutions on our lives, and that they are present from the beginning of our lives. As various commentators have pointed out, it is unclear exactly *which* institutions meet these criteria. Rawls himself is ambiguous here. Three examples should make this problem clear.

First, feminists have long pointed out the profound effects of the family on the lives of its members. 'The personal is political' is a well-known feminist dictum. The family can be a significant site for the oppression of women. It would certainly seem to meet Rawls's criteria for inclusion within the basic structure. Susan Moller Okin (1989) has noted Rawls's ambivalence about the family, and has herself argued for its inclusion. However, intrusion into the family is something that liberal theorists have typically resisted. The unwillingness to completely dismantle the public–private distinction is founded in a desire to tolerate things like diverse family arrangements (for example, ones based on religious beliefs). Including the family in the basic structure would mean intervening in it to ensure its organisation in accordance with principles of justice. This has led some feminist thinkers to abandon the justice approach to political morality as inadequate because of its failure to address the issue of the family.[7]

The second example is the market. This, again, seems to meet the criteria for inclusion within the basic structure. Yet including it means the economic actions of individuals (for example, what job to take) would be subject to regulation by the principles of justice. This would break down the distinction between political institutions and personal ethics as the site of distributive justice. Instead, theorists like Rawls prefer to restrict the principles to institutions that regulate the market, thus excluding everyday economic decisions from the basic structure, and allowing individuals to act in self-interested ways within the confines of those institutions. This allows individuals to be economic egoists, but within a structure regulated by a redistributive principle such as the difference principle.

Critics such as G. A. Cohen (1997) find this dual position perverse. If talented individuals in a Rawlsian society really do support the principles of justice, then why would they demand greater economic remuneration? Cohen writes:

> Either the relevant talented people themselves affirm the difference principle or they do not. That is: either they themselves believe that inequalities are unjust if they are not necessary to make the badly off better off, or they do not believe that to be a dictate of justice. If they do not believe it, then their society is not just in the appropriate Rawlsian sense, for a society is just, according to Rawls, only if its members themselves affirm and uphold the correct principles of justice. (1997: 8)

The only other response the talented have to justify their greater economic reward is that it is necessary in order to benefit the worst off. Much turns on the meaning of 'necessary'. It is likely that 'necessary' actually means an *unwillingness* to work for less. The talented themselves make it necessary. If it is unwillingness then the bind remains: how can they claim to believe in the difference principle, but demand remuneration that runs contrary to its aim?

> Talented people who affirm the difference principle would find those questions hard to handle. For they could not claim, *in self-justification*, ...that their high rewards are necessary to enhance the position of the worst off, since...it is they themselves who *make* those rewards necessary, through their own unwillingness to work for ordinary rewards as productively as they do for exceptionally high ones, an unwillingness which ensures that the untalented get less than they otherwise would. (Cohen 1997: 9; emphasis in original)

If this is correct, then principles of justice reach beyond institutions and into our daily decision-making.

The third example is global justice. Rawls sees global politics as distinct from domestic state institutions and justice. In his recent work (1999a) he has argued that certain principles of justice do apply at the global level, but these are different to those that apply within states. Importantly, no global equivalent of the difference principle – a requirement to distribute resources to the world's poor – exists. Rawls's justification is that there is no global basic structure that would qualify it for inclusion under his two principles of justice.

This claim seems dubious – out of touch with the reality of world politics. Such global 'institutions' as the European Union, the World Trade Organization, the World Bank and the International Monetary Fund indicate the existence of a global basic structure. These institutions often outweigh the effects a domestic basic structure has on the life of its citizens. As globalisation theorists point out, the global basic structure shapes domestic regimes, and pervades many aspects of our lives. Indeed, recent international political protests have been aimed at the unaccountability of institutions and organisations that have a more profound effect on our lives than do many domestic institutions. This would seem to make the global basic structure – contra Rawls's intentions – the legitimate site of social justice.

If any of these claims for inclusion are correct, and there are good reasons for thinking they might be, then liberal egalitarian conceptions of justice such as Rawls's are too narrow in their focus. Principles of justice might not be restricted in their application to legally coercive state institutions, but might extend to international organisations, the family and our individual choices within those institutions.

CONCLUSION

Our job of unpacking the concept of justice has taken us through several different views and conceptions. We have explored some of the basic ideas within the view of justice that pioneered the revival of interest in the subject – Rawls's justice as fairness – in particular the difference principle and the original position. These features have spawned a multitude of reactions and counter-reactions in the debate over justice. Of all the possible lines of opposition we have considered two of the strongest and most well known: the libertarian challenge and the critique of the site of justice. The Rawlsian response to the libertarian critique – that justice is concerned with institutions, not distributions *per se* – opens the view up to criticism about the delineation of the basic structure.

These basic positions do not exhaust the justice debate; rather, they represent its foundations. Much of the recent work within the field of social justice builds upon these important interventions. A good grounding in the aims, assumptions and content of these views provides an invaluable roadmap for steering a course through the layers of often complex and detailed arguments of contemporary political thought.

QUESTIONS FOR DISCUSSION

- Does the fact that I would agree to a set of principles of justice under specific conditions mean that I am in fact bound by those principles? Or do hypothetical contracts have no moral force?
- Is impartiality really necessary for achieving justice?
- Is it possible to bring liberty and equality into harmony, or do they always pull in opposite directions?
- Is justice fully compatible with democracy, or are there some areas in which democratically made decisions should have no purchase?

NOTES

1. I thank Christopher Woodard for his excellent comments on an earlier draft of this essay.
2. For a detailed treatment of the currency of social justice – the 'equality of what?' question – see Stephen De Wijze's essay in this volume.
3. I owe this example to Chris Woodard.
4. It is important to note that the original position is not the only method Rawls proposes for reaching agreement on his two principles of justice. The device of the original position is merely representative of Rawls's driving idea that principles of justice should match, or cohere with, our considered convictions on such matters. This is a process, or moral method, termed 'reflective equilibrium'. Rawls argues that we can arrive at the same principles of justice by building upon our shared intuitions about the arbitrary allocation of goods. I mention this to offset the criticism that maximin is too closely related to the difference principle to do any serious work. For the non-original-position route to the two principles see Rawls (1999b), sections 12–13. For an accessible reconstruction of this argument see Barry (1989: 217–234) and Kymlicka (2002: 57–60).

5. As illustration consider the following example:

	Group A	Group B	Total
Distribution 1	100	100	200
Distribution 4	101	110	211
Distribution 5	100	160	260

Rawls's reasoning supports the rejection of D5 (a significant gain for the better off, but no gain for the worst off) in favour of a marginal gain for the worst off, but which does not significantly improve the amount of social good in the society. The inability to consider such possibilities strikes commentators such as Nagel as too restrictive.

6. More precisely, it misrepresents most liberal egalitarian conceptions of justice. As G. A. Cohen has pointed out, Nozick's position is more troubling for some Marxian views because, unlike liberal theories, they do not restrict principles of justice to the basic structure. See Cohen (1995: 144–64).

7. See, for example, Gilligan (1982).

JOHN RAWLS
EXTRACTS FROM *A THEORY OF JUSTICE*

JUSTICE AS FAIRNESS

[. . .]

The role of justice

Justice is the first virtue of social institutions, as truth is of systems of thought. A theory however elegant and economical must be rejected or revised if it is untrue; likewise laws and institutions no matter how efficient and well-arranged must be reformed or abolished if they are unjust. Each person possesses an inviolability founded on justice that even the welfare of society as a whole cannot override. For this reason justice denies that the loss of freedom for some is made right by a greater good shared by others. It does not allow that the sacrifices imposed on a few are outweighed by the larger sum of advantages enjoyed by many. Therefore in a just society the liberties of equal citizenship are taken as settled; the rights secured by justice are not subject to political bargaining or to the calculus of social interests. The only thing that permits us to acquiesce in an erroneous theory is the lack of a better one; analogously, an injustice is tolerable only when it is necessary to avoid an even greater injustice. Being first virtues of human activities, truth and justice are uncompromising.

These propositions seem to express our intuitive conviction of the primacy of justice. No doubt they are expressed too strongly. In any event I wish to inquire whether these contentions or others similar to them are

John Rawls (1999), *A Theory of Justice*, rev. ed., Oxford: Oxford University Press.

sound, and if so how they can be accounted for. To this end it is necessary to work out a theory of justice in the light of which these assertions can be interpreted and assessed. I shall begin by considering the role of the principles of justice. Let us assume, to fix ideas, that a society is a more or less self-sufficient association of persons who in their relations to one another recognize certain rules of conduct as binding and who for the most part act in accordance with them. Suppose further that these rules specify a system of cooperation designed to advance the good of those taking part in it. Then, although a society is a cooperative venture for mutual advantage, it is typically marked by a conflict as well as by an identity of interests. There is an identity of interests since social cooperation makes possible a better life for all than any would have if each were to live solely by his own efforts. There is a conflict of interests since persons are not indifferent as to how the greater benefits produced by their collaboration are distributed, for in order to pursue their ends they each prefer a larger to a lesser share. A set of principles is required for choosing among the various social arrangements which determine this division of advantages and for underwriting an agreement on the proper distributive shares. These principles are the principles of social justice: they provide a way of assigning rights and duties in the basic institutions of society and they define the appropriate distribution of the benefits and burdens of social cooperation.

Now let us say that a society is well-ordered when it is not only designed to advance the good of its members but when it is also effectively regulated by a public conception of justice. That is, it is a society in which (1) everyone accepts and knows that the others accept the same principles of justice, and (2) the basic social institutions generally satisfy and are generally known to satisfy these principles. In this case while men may put forth excessive demands on one another, they nevertheless acknowledge a common point of view from which their claims may be adjudicated. If men's inclination to self-interest makes their vigilance against one another necessary, their public sense of justice makes their secure association together possible. Among individuals with disparate aims and purposes a shared conception of justice establishes the bonds of civic friendship; the general desire for justice limits the pursuit of other ends. One may think of a public conception of justice as constituting the fundamental charter of a well-ordered human association.

Existing societies are of course seldom well-ordered in this sense, for what is just and unjust is usually in dispute. Men disagree about which principles should define the basic terms of their association. Yet we may still say, despite this disagreement, that they each have a conception of justice. That is, they understand the need for, and they are prepared to affirm, a characteristic set of principles for assigning basic rights and duties and for determining what they take to be the proper distribution of the benefits and burdens of social cooperation. Thus it seems natural to think of the concept of justice as distinct from the various conceptions of justice and as being specified by the role which these different sets of principles, these different conceptions, have in common.[1] Those who hold different conceptions of justice can, then, still agree that institutions are just when no arbitrary distinctions are made between persons in the assigning of basic rights and duties and when the rules determine a proper balance between competing claims to the advantages of social life. Men can agree to this description of just institutions since the notions of an arbitrary distinction and of a proper balance, which are included in the concept of justice, are left open for each to interpret according to the principles of justice that he accepts. These principles single out which similarities and differences among persons are relevant in determining rights and duties and they specify which division of advantages is appropriate. Clearly this distinction between the concept and the various conceptions of justice settles no important questions. It simply helps to identify the role of the principles of social justice.

[. . .]

The subject of justice

Many different kinds of things are said to be just and unjust: not only laws, institutions, and social systems, but also particular actions of many kinds, including decisions, judgments, and imputations. We also call the attitudes and dispositions of persons, and persons themselves, just and unjust. Our topic, however, is that of social justice. For us the primary subject of justice is the basic structure of society, or more exactly, the way in which the major social institutions distribute fundamental rights and duties and determine the division of advantages from social cooperation. By major institutions I understand the political constitution and the principal economic and so- cial arrangements. Thus the legal protection of freedom of thought and liberty of conscience, competitive markets, private property in the means of production, and the monogamous family are examples of major social insti- tutions. Taken together as one scheme, the major institutions define men's rights and duties and influence their life-prospects, what they can expect to be and how well they can hope to do. The basic structure is the primary sub- ject of justice because its effects are so profound and present from the start. The intuitive notion here is that this structure contains various social posi- tions and that men born into different positions have different expectations of life determined, in part, by the political system as well as by economic and social circumstances. In this way the institutions of society favor cer- tain starting places over others. These are especially deep inequalities. Not only are they pervasive, but they affect men's initial chances in life; yet they cannot possibly be justified by an appeal to the notions of merit or desert. It is these inequalities, presumably inevitable in the basic structure of any society, to which the principles of social justice must in the first instance apply. These principles, then, regulate the choice of a political constitution and the main elements of the economic and social system. The justice of a social scheme depends essentially on how fundamental rights and duties are assigned and on the economic opportunities and social conditions in the various sectors of society.

The scope of our inquiry is limited [...]. [...] I am concerned with a special case of the problem of justice. I shall not consider the justice of institutions and social practices generally, nor except in passing the justice of the law of nations and of relations between states. Therefore, if one supposes that the concept of justice applies whenever there is an allotment of something rationally regarded as advantageous or disadvantageous, then we are interested in only one instance of its application. There is no reason to suppose ahead of time that the principles satisfactory for the basic structure hold for all cases. These principles may not work for the rules and practices of private associations or for those of less comprehensive social groups. They may be irrelevant for the various informal conventions and customs of everyday life; they may not elucidate the justice, or perhaps better, the fairness of voluntary cooperative arrangements or procedures for making contractual agreements. The conditions for the law of nations may require different principles arrived at in a somewhat different way. I shall be satisfied if it is possible to formulate a reasonable conception of justice for the basic structure of society conceived for the time being as a closed system isolated from other societies. The significance of this special case is obvious and needs no explanation. It is natural to conjecture that once we have a sound theory for this case, the remaining problems of justice will prove more tractable in the light of it. With suitable modifications such a theory should provide the key for some of these other questions.

[...]

The original position and justification

I have said that the original position is the appropriate initial status quo which insures that the fundamental agreements reached in it are fair. This fact yields the name 'justice as fairness'. It is clear, then, that I want to say that one conception of justice is more reasonable than another, or justifiable with respect to it, if rational persons in the initial situation would choose its principles over those of the other for the role of justice. Conceptions of justice are to be ranked by their acceptability to persons so circumstanced. Understood in this way the question of justification is settled by working out a problem of deliberation: we have to ascertain which principles it would be rational to adopt given the contractual situation. This connects the theory of justice with the theory of rational choice.

If this view of the problem of justification is to succeed, we must, of course, describe in some detail the nature of this choice problem. A problem of rational decision has a definite answer only if we know the beliefs and interests of the parties, their relations with respect to one another, the alternatives between which they are to choose, the procedure whereby they make up their minds, and so on. As the circumstances are presented in different ways, correspondingly different principles are accepted. The concept of the original position, as I shall refer to it, is that of the most philosophically favored interpretation of this initial choice situation for the purposes of a theory of justice.

But how are we to decide what is the most favored interpretation? I assume, for one thing, that there is a broad measure of agreement that principles of justice should be chosen under certain conditions. To justify a particular description of the initial situation one shows that it incorporates these commonly shared presumptions. One argues from widely accepted but weak premises to more specific conclusions. Each of the presumptions should by itself be natural and plausible; some of them may seem innocuous or even trivial. The aim of the contract approach is to establish that taken together they impose significant bounds on acceptable principles of justice. The ideal outcome would be that these conditions determine a unique set of principles; but I shall be satisfied if they suffice to rank the main traditional conceptions of social justice.

One should not be misled, then, by the somewhat unusual conditions which characterize the original position. The idea here is simply to make vivid to ourselves the restrictions that it seems reasonable to impose on arguments for principles of justice, and therefore on these principles themselves. Thus it seems reasonable and generally acceptable that no one should be advantaged or disadvantaged by natural fortune or social circumstances in the choice of principles. It also seems widely agreed that it should be impossible to tailor principles to the circumstances of one's own case. We should insure further that particular inclinations and aspirations, and persons' conceptions of their good do not affect the principles adopted. The aim is to rule out those principles that it would be rational to propose for acceptance, however little the chance of success, only if one knew certain things that are irrelevant from the standpoint of justice. For example, if a man knew that he was wealthy, he might find it rational to advance the principle that various taxes for welfare measures be counted unjust; if he knew that he was poor, he would most likely propose the contrary principle. To represent the desired restrictions one imagines a situation in which everyone is deprived of this sort of information. One excludes the knowledge of those contingencies which sets men at odds and allows them to be guided by their prejudices. In this manner the veil of ignorance is arrived at in a natural way. This concept should cause no difficulty if we keep in mind the constraints on arguments that it is meant to express. At any time we can enter the original position, so to speak, simply by following a certain procedure, namely, by arguing for principles of justice in accordance with these restrictions.

It seems reasonable to suppose that the parties in the original position are equal. That is, all have the same rights in the procedure for choosing principles; each can make proposals, submit reasons for their acceptance, and so on. Obviously the purpose of these conditions is to represent equality between human beings as moral persons, as creatures having a conception of their good and capable of a sense of justice. The basis of equality is taken to be similarity in these two respects. Systems of ends are not ranked in value; and each man is presumed to have the requisite ability to understand and to act upon whatever principles are adopted. Together with the veil of ignorance, these conditions define the principles of justice as those which rational persons concerned to advance their interests would consent to as equals when none are known to be advantaged or disadvantaged by social and natural contingencies.

[. . .]

THE PRINCIPLES OF JUSTICE

[. . .]

Two principles of justice

I shall now state in a provisional form the two principles of justice that I believe would be chosen in the original position. In this section. I wish to make only the most general comments, and therefore the first formulation of these principles is tentative. As we go on I shall run through several formulations and approximate step by step the final statement to be given much later. I believe that doing this allows the exposition to proceed in a natural way.

The first statement of the two principles reads as follows.

> First: each person is to have an equal right to the most extensive basic liberty compatible with a similar liberty for others.
>
> Second: social and economic inequalities are to be arranged so that they are both (a) reasonably expected to be to everyone's advantage, and (b) attached to positions and offices open to all. There are two ambiguous phrases in the second principle, namely 'everyone's advantage' and 'equally open to all'.

[. . .]

By way of general comment, these principles primarily apply, as I have said, to the basic structure of society. They are to govern the assignment of rights and duties and to regulate the distribution of social and economic advantages. As their formulation suggests, these principles presuppose that the social structure can be divided into two more or less distinct parts, the first principle applying to the one, the second to the other. They distinguish between those aspects of the social system that define and secure the equal liberties of citizenship and those that specify and establish social and economic inequalities. The basic liberties of citizens are, roughly speaking, political liberty (the right to vote and to be eligible for public office) together with freedom of speech and assembly; liberty of conscience and freedom of thought; freedom of the person along with the right to hold (personal) property; and freedom from arbitrary arrest and seizure as defined by the concept of the rule of law. These liberties are all required to be equal by the first principle, since citizens of a just society are to have the same basic rights.

The second principle applies, in the first approximation, to the distribution of income and wealth and to the design of organizations that make use of differences in authority and responsibility, or chains of command. While the distribution of wealth and income need not be equal, it must be to everyone's advantage, and at the same time, positions of authority and offices of command must be accessible to all. One applies the second principle by holding positions open, and then subject to this constraint, arranges social and economic inequalities so that everyone benefits.

These principles are to be arranged in a serial order with the first principle prior to the second. This ordering means that a departure from the institutions of equal liberty required by the first principle cannot be justified by, or compensated for, by greater social and economic advantages. The distribution of wealth and income, and the hierarchies of authority, must be consistent with both the liberties of equal citizenship and equality of opportunity.

It is clear that these principles are rather specific in their content, and their acceptance rests on certain assumptions that I must eventually try to explain and justify. A theory of justice depends upon a theory of society in ways that will become evident as we proceed. For the present, it should be observed that the two principles (and this holds for all formulations) are a special case of a more general conception of justice that can be expressed as follows.

> All social values – liberty and opportunity, income and wealth, and the bases of self-respect – are to be distributed equally unless an unequal distribution of any, or all, of these values is to everyone's advantage.

Injustice, then, is simply inequalities that are not to the benefit of all. Of course, this conception is extremely vague and requires interpretation.

As a first step, suppose that the basic structure of society distributes certain primary goods, that is, things that every rational man is presumed to want. These goods normally have a use whatever a person's rational plan of life. For simplicity, assume that the chief primary goods at the disposition of society are rights and liberties, powers and opportunities, income and wealth. (Later on in Part Three the primary good of self-respect has a central place.) These are the social primary goods. Other primary goods such as health and vigor, intelligence and imagination, are natural goods; although their possession is influenced by the basic structure, they are not so directly under its control. Imagine, then, a hypothetical initial arrangement in which all the social primary goods are equally distributed: everyone has similar rights and duties, and income and wealth are evenly shared. This state of affairs provides a benchmark for judging improvements. If certain inequalities of wealth and organizational powers would make everyone better off than in this hypothetical starting situation, then they accord with the general conception.

Now it is possible, at least theoretically, that by giving up some of their fundamental liberties men are sufficiently compensated by the resulting social and economic gains. The general conception of justice imposes no restrictions on what sort of inequalities are permissible; it only requires that everyone's position be improved. We need not suppose anything so drastic as consenting to a condition of slavery. Imagine instead that men forego certain political rights when the economic returns are significant and their capacity to influence the course of policy by the exercise of these rights would be marginal in any case. It is this kind of exchange which the two principles as stated rule out; being arranged in serial order they do not permit exchanges between basic liberties and economic and social gains. The serial ordering of principles expresses an underlying preference among primary social goods. When this preference is rational so likewise is the choice of these principles in this order.

In developing justice as fairness I shall, for the most part, leave aside the general conception of justice and examine instead the special case of the two principles in serial order. The advantage of this procedure is that from the first the matter of priorities is recognized and an effort made to find principles to deal with it. One is led to attend throughout to the conditions under which the acknowledgment of the absolute weight of liberty with respect to social and economic advantages, as defined by the lexical order of the two principles, would be reasonable. Offhand, this ranking appears extreme and too special a case to be of much interest; but there is more justification for it than would appear at first sight. Or at any rate, so I shall maintain. Furthermore, the distinction between fundamental rights and liberties and economic and social benefits marks a difference among primary social goods that one should try to exploit. It suggests an important division in the social system. Of course, the distinctions drawn and the ordering proposed are bound to be at best only approximations. There are surely circumstances in which they fail. But it is essential to depict clearly the main lines of a reasonable conception of justice; and under many conditions anyway, the two principles in serial order may serve well enough. When necessary we can fall back on the more general conception.

The fact that the two principles apply to institutions has certain consequences. Several points illustrate this. First of all, the rights and liberties referred to by these principles are those which are defined by the public rules of the basic structure. Whether men are free is determined by the rights and duties established by the major institutions of society. Liberty is a certain pattern of social forms. The first principle simply requires that certain sorts of rules, those defining basic liberties, apply to everyone equally and that they allow the most extensive liberty compatible with a like liberty for all. The only reason for circumscribing the rights defining liberty and making men's freedom less extensive than it might otherwise be is that these equal rights as institutionally defined would interfere with one another.

Another thing to bear in mind is that when principles mention persons, or require that everyone gain from an inequality, the reference is to representative persons holding the various social positions, or offices, or whatever, established by the basic structure. Thus in applying the second principle I assume that it is possible to assign an expectation of well-being to representative individuals holding these positions. This expectation indicates their life prospects as viewed from their social station. In general, the expectations of representative persons depend upon the distribution of rights and duties throughout the basic structure. When this changes, expectations change. I assume, then, that expectations are connected: by raising the prospects of the representative man in one position we presumably increase or decrease the prospects of representative men in other positions. Since it applies to institutional forms, the second principle (or rather the first part of it) refers to the expectations of representative individuals. As I shall discuss below, neither principle applies to distributions of particular goods to particular individuals who may be identified by their proper names. The situation where someone is considering how to allocate certain commodities to needy persons who are known to him is not within the scope of the principles. They are meant to regulate basic institutional arrangements. We must not assume that there is much similarity from the standpoint of justice between an administrative allotment of goods to specific persons and the appropriate design of society. Our common sense intuitions for the former may be a poor guide to the latter.

Now the second principle insists that each person benefit from permissible inequalities in the basic structure. This means that it must be reasonable for each relevant representative man defined by this structure, when he views it as a going concern, to prefer his prospects with the inequality to his prospects without it. One is not allowed to justify differences in income or organizational powers on the ground that the disadvantages of those in one position are outweighed by the greater advantages of those in another. Much less can infrigements of liberty be counterbalanced in this way. Applied to the basic structure, the principle of utility would have us maximize the sum of expectations of representative men (weighted by the number of persons they represent, on the classical view); and this would permit us to compensate for the losses of some by the gains of others. Instead, the two principles require that everyone benefit from economic and social inequalities. It is obvious, however, that there are indefinitely many ways in which all may be advantaged when the initial arrangement of equality is taken as a benchmark. How then are we to choose among these possibilities? The principles must be specified so that they yield a determinate conclusion.

NOTE

1. Here I follow H. L. A. Hart, *The Concept of Law* (Oxford, The Clarendon Press, 1961), pp. 155–9.

G. A. COHEN
EXTRACTS FROM 'WHERE THE ACTION IS: ON THE SITE OF DISTRIBUTIVE JUSTICE'

I

In this paper I defend a claim which can be expressed in the words of a now familiar slogan: the personal is political. That slogan, as it stands, is vague, but I shall mean something reasonably precise by it here, to wit, that principles of distributive justice, principles, that is, about the just distribution of benefits and burdens in society, apply, wherever else they do, to people's legally unconstrained choices. Those principles, so I claim, apply to the choices that people make *within* the legally coercive structures to which, so everyone would agree, principles of justice (also) apply. In speaking of the choices that people make *within* coercive structures, I do not include the choice whether or not to comply with the rules of such structures (to which choice, once again, so everyone would agree, principles of justice (also) apply), but the choices left open by those rules because neither enjoined nor forbidden by them.

[. . .]

In defending the claim that the personal is political, the view that I oppose is the Rawlsian one that principles of justice apply only to what Rawls calls the 'basic structure' of society. Feminists have noticed that Rawls wobbles, across the course of his writings, on the matter of whether or not the family belongs to the basic structure and is therefore, in his view, a site at which

G. A. Cohen (1997), 'Where the Action is: On the Site of Distributive Justice', *Philosophy and Public Affairs*, 26:1.

principles of justice apply. I shall argue that Rawls's wobble on this matter is not a case of mere indecision, which could readily be resolved in favor of inclusion of the family within the basic structure: that is the view of Susan Okin,[1] and, in my opinion, she is wrong about that. I shall show (in Section V below) that Rawls cannot admit the family into the basic structure of society without abandoning his insistence that it is to the basic structure only that principles of distributive justice apply. In supposing that he could include family relations, Okin shows failure to grasp the *form* of the feminist critique of Rawls.

II

[. . .]

My criticism of Rawls is of his application of the difference principle. That principle says, in one of its formulations,[2] that inequalities are just if and only if they are necessary to make the worst off people in society better off than they would otherwise be. I have no quarrel here with the difference principle itself,[3] but I disagree sharply with Rawls on the matter of *which* inequalities pass the test for justifying inequality that it sets and, therefore, about how *much* inequality passes that test. In my view, there is hardly any serious inequality that satisfies the requirement set by the difference principle, when it is conceived, as Rawls himself proposes to conceive it,[4] as regulating the affairs of a society whose members themselves accept that principle. If I am right, affirmation of the difference principle implies that justice requires (virtually) unqualified equality itself, as opposed to the 'deep inequalities' in initial life chances with which Rawls thinks justice to be consistent.[5]

It is commonly thought, for example by Rawls, that the difference principle licenses an argument for inequality which centers on the device of material incentives. The idea is that talented people will produce more than they otherwise would if, and only if, they are paid more than an ordinary wage, and some of the extra which they will then produce can be recruited on behalf of the worst off.[6] The inequality consequent on differential material incentives is said to be justified within the terms of the difference principle, for, so it is said, that inequality benefits the worst off people: the inequality is necessary for them to be positioned as well as they are, however paltry their position may nevertheless be.

Now, before I mount my criticism of this argument, a *caveat* is necessary with respect to the terms in which it is expressed. The argument focuses on a *choice* enjoyed by well-placed people who command a high salary in a market economy: they can choose to work more or less hard, and also to work at this occupation rather than that one, and for this employer rather than that one, in accordance with how well they are remunerated. These well-placed people, in the foregoing standard presentation of the argument, are designated as 'the talented', and [. . .] I shall so designate them throughout my criticism of the argument. Even so, these fortunate people need not be thought to be talented, in any sense of that word which implies something more than a capacity for high market earnings, for the argument to possess whatever force it has. All that need be true of them is that *they are so positioned that, happily, for them, they do command a high salary and they can vary their productivity according to exactly how high it is.*

[. . .]

Now, for the following reasons, I believe that the incentives argument for inequality represents a distorted application of the difference principle, even though it is its most familiar and perhaps even its most persuasive application. Either the relevant talented people themselves affirm the difference principle or they do not. That is: either they themselves believe that inequalities are unjust if they are not necessary to make the badly off better off, or they do not believe that to be a dictate of justice. If they do not believe it, then their society is not just in the appropriate Rawlsian sense, for a society is just, according to Rawls, only if its members themselves affirm and uphold the correct principles of justice. The difference principle might be appealed to in justification of a government's toleration, or promotion, of inequality in a society in which the talented do not themselves accept it, but it then justifies a public policy of inequality in a society some members of which – the talented – do not share community with the rest:[7] their behavior is then taken as fixed or parametric, a datum vis-à-vis a principle applied to it from without, rather than as itself answerable to that principle. That is not how principles of justice operate in a just society, as Rawls specifies that concept: within his terms, one may distinguish between a just society and a just government, one, that is, which applies just principles to a society whose members may not themselves accept those principles.

So we turn to the second and only remaining possibility, which is that the talented people do affirm the difference principle, that, as Rawls says, they apply the principles of justice *in their daily life* and achieve a sense of their own justice in doing so.[8] But they can then be asked why, in the light of their own belief in the principle, they require more pay than the untalented get, for work that may indeed demand special talent, but which is not specially unpleasant (for no such consideration enters the Rawlsian justification of incentives-derived inequality). The talented can be asked whether the extra they get is *necessary* to enhance the position of the worst off, which is the only thing, according to the difference principle, that could justify it. Is it necessary *tout court*, that is, independently of human will, so that, with all the will in the world, removal of inequality would make everyone worse off? Or is it necessary only insofar as the talented would *decide* to produce less than they now do, or not to take up posts where they are in special demand, if inequality were removed (by, for example, income taxation which redistributes to fully egalitarian effect[9])?

Talented people who affirm the difference principle would find those questions hard to handle. For they could not claim, *in self-justification*, at the bar of the difference principle, that their high rewards are necessary to enhance the position of the worst off, since, in the standard case,[10] it is they themselves who *make* those rewards necessary, through their own unwillingness to work for ordinary rewards as productively as they do for exceptionally high ones, an unwillingness which ensures that the untalented get less than they otherwise would. Those rewards are, therefore, necessary only because the choices of talented people are not appropriately informed by the difference principle.

Apart, then, from the very special cases in which the talented literally *could* not, as opposed to the normal case where they (merely) would not, perform as productively as they do without superior remuneration, the difference principle can justify inequality only in a society where not everyone accepts that very principle. It therefore cannot justify inequality in the appropriate Rawlsian way.

Now, this conclusion about what it means to accept and implement the difference principle implies that the justice of a society is not exclusively a function of its legislative structure, of its legally imperative rules, but also of the choices people make within those rules. The standard (and, in my view, misguided) Rawlsian application of the difference principle can be modeled as follows. There is a market economy all agents in which seek to maximize their own gains, and there is a Rawlsian state that selects a tax function on income that maximizes the income return to the worst off people, within the constraint that, because of the self-seeking motivation of the talented, a fully equalizing taxation system would make everyone worse off than one which is less than fully equalizing. But this double-minded modeling of the implementation of the difference principle, with citizens inspired by justice endorsing a state policy which plays a tax game against (some of) them in their manifestation as self-seeking economic agents, is wholly out of accord with the (sound) Rawlsian requirement on a just society that its citizens themselves willingly submit to the standard of justice embodied in the difference principle. A society that is just within the terms of the difference principle, so we may conclude, requires not simply just coercive *rules*, but also an *ethos* of justice that informs individual choices. In the absence of such an ethos, inequalities will obtain that are not necessary to enhance the condition of the worst off: the required ethos promotes a distribution more just than what the rules of the economic game by themselves can secure.

To be sure, one might imagine, in the abstract, a set of coercive rules so finely tuned that universally self-interested choices within them would raise the worst off to as high a position as any other pattern of choices would produce. Where coercive rules had and were known to have such a character, agents could choose self-interestedly in confidence that the results of their choices would satisfy an appropriately uncompromising interpretation of the difference principle. In that (imaginary) case, the only ethos necessary for difference principle justice would be willing obedience to the relevant rules, an ethos which Rawls expressly requires. But the vast economics literature on incentive-compatibility teaches that rules of the contemplated perfect kind cannot be designed. Accordingly, as things actually are, the required ethos must, as I have argued, guide choice within the rules, and not merely direct agents to obey them. (I should emphasize that this is not so because it is *in general* true that the point of the rules governing an activity must be aimed at when agents pursue that activity in good faith: every competitive sport represents a counterexample to that generalization. But my argument for the conclusion stated above did not rest on that false generalization.)

III

There is an objection which friends of Rawls's *Theory of Justice* would press against my argument in criticism of his application of the difference principle. The objection is that my focus on the posture of talented producers in daily economic life is inappropriate, since their behavior occurs within, and does not determine, *the basic structure* of society, and it is only to the latter that the difference principle applies.[11] Whatever people's choices within it may be, the basic structure is just provided that it satisfies the two principles of justice. To be sure, so Rawls acknowledges, people's choices can themselves be assessed as just or unjust, from a number of points of view. Thus, for example, appointment to a given job of candidate A rather than candidate B might be judged unjust, even though it occurs within the rules of a just basic structure.[12] But injustice in such a choice is not the sort of injustice that the Rawlsian principles are designed to condemn. For, *ex hypothesi*, that choice occurs within an established basic structure: it therefore cannot affect the justice of the basic structure itself, which is what, according to Rawls, the two principles govern. Nor, similarly, should the choices with respect to work and remuneration that talented people make be submitted for judgment at the bar of the difference principle. So to judge those choices is to apply that principle at the wrong point. The difference principle is a 'principle of justice for institutions'.[13] It governs the choice of institutions, not the choices made within them. The development of the second horn of the dilemma argument [. . .] misconstrues the Rawlsian requirement that citizens in a just society uphold the principles that make it just: by virtue of the stipulated scope of the difference principle, talented people do count as faithfully upholding it, as long as they conform to the prevailing economic rules *because* that principle requires those rules.

Call that 'the basic structure objection'. Now, before I develop it further, and then reply to it, I want to point out that there is an important ambiguity in the concept of the basic structure, as that is wielded by Rawlsians. The ambiguity turns on whether the Rawlsian basic structure includes only coercive aspects of the social order or, also, conventions and usages that are deeply entrenched but not legally or literally coercive. I shall take the phrase 'basic structure', as it appears in the basic structure objection, as denoting *some* sort of structure, be it legally coercive or not, but whose key feature, for the purposes of the objection, is that it is indeed a structure, that is, a framework of rules within which choices are made, as opposed to a set of choices and/or actions.[14] Accordingly, my Rawlsian critic would say, whatever structure, precisely, the basic structure is, the objection stands that my criticism of the incentives argument misapplies principles devised for a structure to individual choices and actions.

In further clarification of the polemical position, let me make a background point about the difference between Rawls and me with respect to the site or sites at which principles of justice apply. My own fundamental concern is neither the basic structure of society, in any sense, nor people's individual choices, but the pattern of benefits and burdens in society; that is neither a structure in which choice occurs nor a set of choices, but the upshot of structure and choices alike. My concern is *distributive justice*, by which I uneccentrically mean justice (and its lack) in the distribution of benefits and burdens to individuals. My root belief is that there is injustice in distribution when inequality of goods reflects not such things as differences in the arduousness of different people's labors, or people's different preferences and choices with respect to income and leisure, but myriad forms of lucky and unlucky circumstance. Such differences of advantage are a function of the structure *and* of people's choices within it, so I am concerned, secondarily, with *both* of those.

[. . .]

In discussion of my claim [. . .] that social justice requires a social *ethos* that inspires uncoerced equality-supporting choice, Ronald Dworkin suggested[15] that a Rawlsian government might be thought to be charged with a duty, under the difference principle, of promoting such an ethos. Dworkin's suggestion was intended to support Rawls, against me, by diminishing the difference between Rawls's position and my own, and thereby reducing the reach of my criticism of him. I do not know what Rawls's response to Dworkin's proposal would be, but one thing is clear: Rawls could not say that, to the extent that the indicated policy failed, society would, as a result, be less just than if the policy had been more successful. Accordingly, if Dworkin is right that Rawlsian justice requires government to promote an ethos friendly to equality, it could not be for the sake of making society more distributively just that it was doing so, *even* though it would be for the sake of making its distribution more *equal*. The following threefold conjunction, which is an inescapable consequence of Rawls's position, on Dworkin's not unnatural interpretation of it, is strikingly incongrous: (1) the difference principle is an egalitarian principle of distributive justice; (2) it imposes on government a duty to promote an egalitarian ethos; (3) it is not for the sake of enhancing distributive justice in society that it is required to promote that ethos. Dworkin's attempt to reduce the distance between Rawls's position and my own threatens to render the former incoherent.

[. . .]

V

I now provide a more fundamental reply to the basic structure objection. It is more fundamental in that it shows, decisively, that justice requires an ethos governing daily choice that goes beyond one of obedience to just rules,[16] on grounds which do not, as the preliminary reply did, exploit things that Rawls says in apparent contradiction of his stipulation that justice applies to the basic structure of society alone. The fundamental reply interrogates, and refutes, that stipulation itself.

A major fault line in the Rawlsian architectonic not only wrecks the basic structure objection but also produces a dilemma for Rawls's view of the subject[17] of justice from which I can imagine no way out. The fault line exposes itself when we ask the apparently simple question: what (exactly) *is* the basic structure? For there is a fatal ambiguity in Rawls's specification of the basic structure, and an associated discrepancy between his criterion for what justice judges and his desire to exclude the effects of structure-consistent personal choice from the purview of its judgment.

The basic structure, the primary subject of justice, is always said by Rawls to be a set of institutions, and, so he infers, the principles of justice do not judge the actions of people within (just) institutions whose rules they observe. But it is seriously unclear *which* institutions are supposed to qualify as part of the basic structure. Sometimes it appears that coercive (in the legal sense) institutions exhaust it, or, better, that institutions belong to it only insofar as they are (legally) coercive.[18] In this widespread interpretation of what Rawls intends by the 'basic structure' of a society, that structure is legible in the provisions of its constitution, in such specific legislation as may be required to implement those provisions, and in further legislation and policy which are of central importance but which resist formulation in the constitution itself.[19]

The basic structure, in this first understanding of it, is, so one might say, the *broad coercive outline* of society, which determines in a relatively fixed and general way what people may and must do, in advance of legislation that is optional, relative to the principles of justice, and irrespective of the constraints and opportunities created and destroyed by the choices that people make within the given basic structure, so understood.

Yet it is quite unclear that the basic structure is *always* thus defined, in exclusively coercive terms, within the Rawlsian texts. For Rawls often says that the basic structure consists of the *major* social institutions, and he does not put a particular accent on coercion when he announces *that* specification of the basic structure.[20] In this second reading of what it is, institutions belong to the basic structure whose structuring can depend far less on law than on convention, usage, and expectation: a signal example is the family, which Rawls sometimes includes in the basic structure and sometimes does not.[21] But once the line is crossed, from coercive ordering to the non-coercive ordering of society by rules and conventions of accepted practice, then the ambit of justice can no longer exclude chosen behavior, since the usages which constitute informal structure (think, again, of the family) are bound up with the customary actions of people.

'Bound up with' is vague, so let me explain how I mean it, here. One can certainly speak of the structure of the family, and it is not identical with the choices that people customarily make within it; but it is nevertheless impossible to claim that the principles of justice which apply to family structure do not apply to day-to-day choices within it. For consider the following contrast. The *coercive* structure arises independently of people's quotidian choices: it is formed by those specialized choices which legislate the law of the land. By contrast, the non-coercive structure of the family has the character it does only because of the choices that its members routinely make. The constraints and pressures that sustain the non-coercive structure reside in the dispositions of agents which are actualized as and when those agents choose to act in a constraining or pressuring way. With respect to coercive structure, one may fairly readily distinguish the choices which institute and sustain a structure from the choices that occur within it.[22] But with respect to informal structure, that distinction, though conceptually intelligible, collapses extensionally: when A chooses to conform to the prevailing usages, the pressure on B to do so is reinforced, and no such pressure exists, the very usages themselves do not exist, in the absence of conformity to them.

Now, since that is so, since behavior is *constitutive* of *non*-coercive structure, it follows that the only way of protecting the basic structure objection against my claim that the difference principle condemns maximizing economic behavior (and, more generally, of protecting the restriction of justice to the basic structure against the insistence that the personal, too, is political) is by holding fast to a purely coercive specification of the basic structure. But that way out is not open to Rawls, because of a further characterization that he offers of the basic structure: this is where the discrepancy adverted to in the second paragraph of this section appears. For Rawls says that 'the basic structure is the primary subject of justice because its effects are so profound and present from the start'.[23] Nor is that further characterization of the basic structure optional: it is needed to explain why it *is* primary, as far as justice is concerned. Yet it is false that only the *coercive* structure causes profound effects, as the example of the family once again reminds us.[24] Accordingly, if Rawls retreats to coercive structure, he contradicts his own criterion for what justice judges, and he lands himself with an arbitrarily narrow definition of his subject matter. So he must let other structure in, and that means, as we have seen, letting chosen behavior in. What is more, even if behavior were not, as I claim it is, constitutive of non-coercive structure, it will come in by direct appeal to the profundity-of-effect criterion for what justice governs. So, for example, we need not decide whether or not a regular practice of favoring sons over daughters in the matter of providing higher education forms part of the *structure* of the family to condemn it as unjust, under that criterion.[25]

Given, then, his stated rationale[26] for exclusive focus on the basic structure – and what *other* rationale could there be for calling it the *primary* subject of justice? – Rawls is in a dilemma. For he must either admit application of the principles of justice to (legally optional) social practices, and, indeed, to patterns of personal choice that are not legally prescribed, *both* because they are the substance of those practices, *and* because they are similarly profound in effect, in which case the restriction of justice to structure, in any sense, collapses; or, if he restricts his concern to the coercive structure only, then he saddles himself with a purely arbitrary delineation of his subject matter. I now illustrate this dilemma by reference to the two contexts that have figured most in this paper: the family, and the market economy.

Family structure is fateful for the benefits and burdens that redound to different people, and, in particular, to people of different sexes, where 'family structure' includes the socially constructed expectations which lie on husband and wife. And such expectations are sexist and unjust if, for example, they direct the woman in a family where both spouses work outside the home to carry a greater burden of domestic tasks. Yet such expectations need not be supported by the law for them to possess informal coercive force: sexist family structure is consistent with sex-neutral family law. Here, then, is a circumstance, outwith the basic structure, as that would be coercively defined, which profoundly affects people's life-chances, *through the choices people make in response to the stated expectations, which are, in turn, sustained by those choices.*[27] Yet Rawls must say, on pain of giving up the basic structure objection, that (legally uncoerced) family structure and behavior have no implications for justice in the sense of 'justice' in which the basic structure has implications for justice, since they are not a consequence of the formal coercive order. But that implication of the stated position is perfectly incredible: no such differentiating sense is available.

John Stuart Mill taught us to recognize that informal social pressure can restrict liberty as much as formal coercive law does. And the family example shows that informal pressure is as relevant to distributive justice as it is to liberty. One reason why the rules of the basic structure, when it is coercively defined, do not by themselves determine the justice of the distributive upshot is that, by virtue of circumstances that are relevantly independent of coercive rules, some people have much more power than others to determine what happens *within* those rules.

The second illustration of discrepancy between what coercive structure commands and what profoundly affects the distribution of benefits and burdens is my own point about incentives. Maximinizing legislation,[28] and, hence, a coercive basic structure that is just as far as the difference principle is concerned, are consistent with a maximizing ethos across society which, under many conditions, will produce severe inequalities and a meager level of provision for the worst off, yet both have to be declared just by Rawls, if he stays with a coercive conception of what justice judges. And that implication is, surely, perfectly incredible.

Rawls cannot deny the difference between the coercively defined basic structure and that which produces major distributive consequences: the coercively defined basic structure is only an instance of the latter. Yet he must, to retain his position on justice and personal choice, restrict the ambit of justice to what a coercive basic structure produces. But, so I have (by implication) asked: why should we *care* so disproportionately about the coercive basic structure, when the major reason for caring about it, its impact on people's lives, is *also* a reason for caring about informal structure and patterns of personal choice? To the extent that we care about coercive structure because it is fateful with regard to benefits and burdens, we must care equally about the ethi that sustain gender inequality, and inegalitarian incentives. And the similarity of our reasons for caring about these matters will make it lame to say: ah, but only the caring about coercive structure is a caring about *justice*, in a certain distinguishable sense. That thought is, I submit, incapable of coherent elaboration.

NOTES

1. Okin is singularly alive to Rawls's ambivalence about admitting or excluding the family from the basic structure: see, e.g. her '*Political Liberalism*, Justice and Gender', *Ethics* 105, no. 1 (Oct. 1994): 23–4, and, more generally, her *Justice, Gender and the Family* (New York: Basic Books, 1989), Chapter 5. But, so far as I can tell, she is unaware of the wider consequences, for Rawls's view of justice in general, of the set of ambiguities of which this one is an instance.
2. See 'incentives, inequality, and community', in Grethe Peterson, ed., *The Tanner Lectures on Human Values*, Vol. 13 (Salt Lake City: University of Utah Press, 1992), p. 266, n. 6 (this article is henceforth referred to as 'incentives'), for four possible formulations of the difference principle, all of which, arguably, find support in *A Theory of Justice* (Cambridge, Mass.: Harvard University Press, 1971). The argument of the present paper is, I believe, robust across those variant formulations of the principle.
3. I do have some reservations about the principle, but they are irrelevant to this paper. I agree, for example, with Ronald Dworkin's criticism of the 'ambition-Insensitivity' of the difference principle: see his 'What is Equality? Part 2: Equality of Resources', *Philosophy & Public Affairs*, 10, no. 4 (Fall 1981): 343.

4. 'Proposes to conceive it': I use that somewhat precious phrase because part of the present criticism of Rawls is that he does not succeed in so conceiving it – he does not, that is, recognize the implications of so conceiving it.
5. *A Theory of Justice*, p. 7.
6. This is just the crudest causal story connecting superior payment to the better off with benefit to the worst off. I adopt it here for simplicity of exposition.
7. They do not, more precisely, share *justificatory community* with the rest, in the sense of the italicized phrase that I specified at p. 282 of 'Incentives'.
8. 'Citizens in everyday life affirm and act from the first principles of justice'. They act 'from these principles as their sense of justice dictates' and thereby 'their nature as moral persons is most fully realized'. (Quotations drawn from, respectively, 'Kantian Constructivism in Moral Theory', *The Journal of Philosophy*, 77, no. 9 (Sept. 1980): 521, 528, and *A Theory of Justice*, p. 528.)
9. That way of achieving equality preserves the information function of the market while extinguishing its motivational function: see Joseph Carens, *Equality, Moral Incentives, and the Market* (Chicago: University of Chicago Press, 1981).
10. See 'Incentives', p. 298 *et circa*, for precisely what I mean by 'the standard case'.
11. For a typical statement of this restriction, see, John Rawls, *Political Liberalism* (New York: Columbia University Press, 1993), pp. 282–3.
12. See the first sentence of Sec. 2 of *A Theory of Justice* ('The Subject of Justice'): 'Many different kinds of things are said to be just and unjust: not only laws, institutions, and social systems, but also particular actions of many kinds, including decisions, judgments, and imputations' (*ibid*, p, 7). But Rawls excludes examples such as the one given in the text above from his purview, because 'our topic . . . is that of social justice. For us the primary subject of justice is the basic structure of society' (*ibid.*).
13. *A Theory of Justice*, p. 303.
14. The contrast between structure and action is further explained, though also, as it were, put in its place, in the Endnote to this article.
15. At a seminar in Oxford, in Hilary Term of 1994.
16. Though not necessarily an ethos embodying the very principles that the rules formulate [. . .]. Justice will be shown to require an ethos, and the basic structure objection will thereby be refuted, but it will be a contingent question whether the ethos required by justice can be read off the content of the just rules themselves. Still, [. . .] the answer to that question is almost certainly 'Yes'.
17. That is, the subject matter that principles of justice judge. I follow Rawls's usage here (e.g. in the title of Lecture VII of *Political Liberalism*: 'The Basic Structure as Subject'; and cf. n. 12 above).
18. Henceforth, unless I indicate otherwise, I shall use 'coercive', 'coercion', etc. to mean 'legally coercive', etc.
19. Thus, the difference principle, though pursued through (coercively sustained) state policy, cannot, so Rawls thinks, be aptly inscribed in a society's constitution: see *Political Liberalism*, pp. 227–30.
20. Consider, for example, the passage at pp. 7–8 of *A Theory of Justice* in which the concept of the basic structure is introduced:

> Our topic . . . is that of social justice. For us the primary subject of justice is the basic structure of society, or more exactly, the way in which the major social institutions distribute fundamental rights and duties and determine the division of advantages from social cooperation. By major institutions I understand the political constitution and the principal economic and social arrangements. Thus the legal protection of freedom of thought and liberty of conscience, competitive markets, private property in the means of production, and the monogamous family are examples of major social institutions. . . . I shall not consider the justice of institutions and social practices generally. . . . [The two principles of justice]

may not work for the rules and practices of private associations or for those of less comprehensive social groups. They may be irrelevant for the various informal conventions and customs of everyday life; they may not elucidate the justice, or perhaps better, the fairness of voluntary cooperative arrangements or procedures for making contractual agreements.

I cannot tell, from those statements, what is to be included in, and what excluded from, the basic structure, nor, more particularly, whether coercion is the touchstone of inclusion. Take, for example, the case of the monogamous family. Is it simply its 'legal protection' that is a major social institution, in line with a coercive definition of the basic structure (if not, perhaps, with the syntax of the relevant sentence)? Or is the monogamous family itself part of that structure? And, in that case, are its typical usages part of it? They certainly constitute a 'principal social arrangement', yet they may also count as 'practices of private associations or . . . of less comprehensive social groups', and they are heavily informed by the 'conventions and customs of everyday life'.

Puzzlement with respect to the bounds of the basic structure is not relieved by examination of the relevant pages of *Political Liberalism*, to wit, 11, 68, 201–2, 229, 258, 268, 271–2, 282–3, and 301. Some formulations on those pages lean toward a coercive specification of the basic structure. Others do not.

21. See the final paragraph of Sec. 1 of this chapter.
22. For more on structure and choice, see the Endnote to this article. Among other things. I there entertain a doubt about the strength of the distinction drawn in the above sentence, but, as I indicate, if that doubt is sound, then my case against Rawls is not weakened.
23. *A Theory of Justice*. p. 7.
24. Or consider access to that primary good which Rawls calls 'the social basis of self-respect'. While the law may play a large role in securing that good to people vulnerable to racism, legally unregulable racist attitudes also have an enormous negative impact on how much of that primary good they get.

    But are the profound effects of the family, or of racism, 'present from the start' (see the text to n. 23)? I am not sure how to answer that question, because I am unclear about the intended import, here, of the quoted phrase. Rawls probably means 'present from the start of each person's life': the surrounding text at *Theory*, p. 7 supports this interpretation. If so, the family, and racial attitudes, certainly qualify. If not, then I do not know how to construe the phrase. But what matters, surely, is the asserted profundity of effect, not whether it is 'present from the start', whatever may be the sense which attaches, here, to that phrase.
25. Note that one can condemn the said practice without condemning those who engage in it. For there might be a collective action problem here, which weighs heavily on poor families in particular. If, in addition to discrimination in education, there is discrimination in employment, then a poor family might sacrifice a great deal through choosing evenhandedly across the sexes with whatever resources it can devote to its children's education. This illustrates the important distinction between condemning injustice and condemning the people whose actions prepetuate it.
26. See the text to n. 23 above.
27. Hugo Adam Bedau noticed that the family falls outside the basic structure, under the coercive specification of it often favored by Rawls, though he did not notice the connection between non-coercive structure and choice that I emphasize in the above sentence: see his 'Social Justice and Social Institutions', *Midwest Studies in Philosophy*, 3 (1978): 171.
28. That is, legislation which maximizes the size of the primary goods bundle held by the worst off people, given whatever is correctly expected to be the pattern in the choices made by economic agents.

2

LIBERTY

Patrick Bernhagen

Introduction

The *Declaration of the Rights of Man and of Citizens* by the National Assembly of France in 1789 stipulated that the 'end of all political associations is the preservation of . . . Liberty'. Earlier in history, liberty features as a central motive in the political theories of Aristotle and Cicero in classic antiquity, and later in Niccolò Machiavelli's Renaissance republicanism. And more recently, the peaceful revolutions that brought about the fall of the authoritarian regimes in central and eastern Europe and the former Soviet Union were driven by the desire of the people to live in freedom. Indeed, we may safely speak of liberty as the supreme value in liberal societies and in Western political thought.[1]

Yet despite the importance people attach to it, some have ascribed little more than an instrumental value to freedom, suggesting that freedom is good because, where it prevails, other highly prized things will be promoted. For the utilitarian philosophers of the nineteenth century, for example, liberty was interesting to the extent that it allows people to achieve maximum happiness. More recently, Ronald Dworkin found that it is not so much liberty itself that liberals really value, but things like justice, equality, or some list of rights such as the rights to freedom of worship, of expression and of association, but to which they misleadingly refer as liberty (1977: 266–78). In the tradition of Jean-Jacques Rousseau's democratic republicanism, by contrast, liberty is all about participation in government and is as such worthy in its own right. For contemporary civil-liberties and human-rights advocacy groups such as Amnesty International (2004) or Freedom

House (2004), furthermore, freedom serves as a yardstick for evaluating the performance of governments and entire countries. These groups regularly assess the successful (or otherwise) implementation of various civil and political liberties – including freedom of assembly, freedom of expression and belief, and free choice of occupation – in countries around the world.

Despite such nearly universal acclaim, politicians and political theorists alike find it difficult to agree on, firstly, what exactly liberty is and, secondly, which political practices, programmes and institutions are best suited for protecting and increasing freedom. Adherents of left-wing, social-democratic welfare politics, for instance, have justified the creation of the welfare state out of a concern for liberty, while neo-liberal economists and conservative politicians invoke liberty when arguing the case for its demolition. We will return to this contradictory theme further on. At this point it is useful to emphasise that we are concerned with political or social freedom, as opposed to philosophical freedom. The grand debates concerning freedom in the philosophical sense are about freedom of the will *versus* philosophical necessity; they are concerned with the question of whether humans possess 'free will' or whether their states of mind and actions are entirely determined by causal forces that are part of the natural order.[2] Social or political freedom, by contrast, is concerned with the interactions between human beings, and with the rules and institutions that are designed to shape these interactions.

LIBERTY VERSUS LICENCE

In its simplest sense, freedom means to do what one wants. In the words of Bertrand Russell (1952: 169), 'freedom in its most abstract sense means the absence of external obstacles to the realisation of desires'. The focus on wants and desires in this formulation can have peculiar consequences for how we think about freedom. If freedom is the power to satisfy wants, then one way to enlarge freedom would be to manipulate people's wants. In this sense, a happy slave can be freer than a frustrated citizen. A different position was taken by T. H. Green ([1888] 1991: 21), for whom freedom is 'a positive power or capacity of doing or enjoying something *worth doing or enjoying*' (emphasis added). This view implies the possibility that people may desire doing things that are *not* worth doing, or, conversely, that people may fail to recognise what *is* worth doing and therefore remain unfree. From this perspective, as Martin Hollis (1997: 150) points out, happy slaves are unfree because they could not satisfy wants which they do not have!

Green's concept of freedom suggests, furthermore, that the distinction between things that are 'worth doing' and those that are not may be *morally* relevant for what we mean by liberty. The drafters of the French *Declaration of the Rights of Man and of Citizens* actually built this criterion into their definition of liberty. For them, 'Political Liberty consists in the power of doing *whatever does not injure another*' (emphasis added). Following the French revolutionaries, we can look at liberty as a 'right' or entitlement: liberty means acting within one's rights, while acting outside these rights would be *licence*. Taken to the extreme, this position can lead to the view that liberty corresponds to the power to do all the things, and only those things, that are positively sanctioned by a given belief system, such as the Judeo-Christian-Islamic set of values, for instance, or whatever happens to be permitted under the law in a given country. The problem with such a rights-based definition of liberty is that, by using it, we deprive ourselves of a standard by which we can judge whether a particular right or entitlement promotes or restricts people's freedom.

John Stuart Mill's definition of liberty, by contrast, is unconstrained from any concern for the interests of others. For Mill ([1859] 1969: 15), 'the only freedom which deserves the name is that of pursuing our own good in our own way'. Because he devised such a non-moralised, rights-neutral definition of freedom, Mill added a standard for justifying restrictions on individual liberty. According to his 'harm principle', the only valid justification for restricting individual freedom is to prevent harm to others (Mill [1859] 1969: 12). It should come as little surprise that what is to count as 'harm to others' is then itself fiercely disputed. One way of avoiding this minefield is to view liberty as an entitlement enjoyed equally by all people. After all, if liberty is thought to be a fundamental value, surely it must be one to which all human beings are entitled to an equal degree. According to John Rawls (1971: 60), 'each person is to have an equal right to the most extensive basic liberty compatible with a similar liberty for others'. Yet how are we to judge whether the amount of freedom enjoyed by you is similar to mine? And, if it is not, how can we rectify the situation?

To guarantee people's equal entitlements to freedom, institutions must be in place to prevent the liberty of some being invaded or unduly restricted by the actions of others. In this perspective, the law does not restrict liberty so much as defend or enlarge it. Traffic regulations, for instance, increase the freedom of those using the roads by enabling them to travel freely from *A* to *B* without constantly bumping into others. Socialists and modern liberals argue, moreover, that the principle of equal liberty points to the need to redistribute wealth and resources more equally in society. They claim that the welfare state enlarges freedom by empowering individuals and *freeing* them from the social evils that otherwise blight their lives – unemployment, homelessness, poverty, ignorance, disease, and so forth (Green [1888] 1991; Plant 1985). However, critics from the right have argued that this doctrine has given rise to new forms of unfreedom since, by justifying broader state powers, it robs individuals of control over their own economic and social circumstances, for example by levying higher taxes on high-income earners (Hayek 1960; Nozick 1974).

So far, we have encountered conflicting views on two analytically distinct issues of liberty: The first conflict is about whether liberty is about doing *what one wants*, or about doing *what is worth doing*. The second conflict is over whether collectively binding arrangements, such as those entailed in social-democratic welfare politics, enlarge or restrict liberty. Underlying these conflicting views are distinct conceptions of the nature of liberty, with some viewing liberty in a strictly negative sense as the freedom from interference by others, above all the state, while others portray liberty as the ability to be positively in control of one's own life plan. A precursor to this classification was first introduced by the French politician and theorist Benjamin Constant ([1819] 1988), who distinguished between the 'liberty of the moderns', by which he meant independence from government and from encroachment by others, and the 'liberty of the ancients', which refers to direct and collective participation in political life. In an influential adaptation of this theme, Isaiah Berlin (1969, see the extract reprinted in this volume) distinguishes two concepts of liberty, a *negative* one corresponding roughly to Constant's 'liberty of the moderns' and a *positive* one that is closer to the 'liberty of the ancients'.

NEGATIVE AND POSITIVE LIBERTY

Freedom in the *negative* sense is usually described as a realm of action unimpeded by external rules or interference by others (Berlin [1969] 2002: 122). It begins where politics ends, especially in what we conceive of as the 'private life' (Miller 1991: 3). This links freedom very closely to privacy, suggesting a distinction between a private or personal realm of existence and some kind of public world. Advocates of negative freedom often regard this private sphere of life, consisting largely of family and personal relationships, as a realm within which people can 'be themselves', without being told by others or the state what to do and how to do it.

The view of freedom as privacy is contested among feminist political theorists. Some endorse conceptions of privacy as tools for expressing ideals of independent decision-making with respect to sex, reproduction and family (Roberts 1991). Viewed in this way, privacy consists of freedom from unwanted physical observation or bodily contact. It also demands neutrality on the part of the state with respect to the free pursuit of different lifestyles and is inconsistent with privileging any one form of the family or of sexual relationships by the basic institutions of society (Cornell 1998: 180). However, privacy can also be seen as synonymous with the private sphere of home and family life – a context of traditional female subordination in dependent socio-economic, and sometimes violent, relationships. Here, governments cannot protect vulnerable citizens from abuse, exploitation and marital rape if high boundaries of legally and constitutionally sanctioned privacy surround the family (MacKinnon 1987: 100–2; Okin 1989: 124–33).

Advocates of negative freedom are often libertarians, who would like to see government restricted to a minimal role entailing little more than the maintenance of domestic order, personal security and, above all, the protection of private property against any threats ranging from taxation to industrial action to theft. According to Robert Nozick (1974), freedom is maximised in capitalist market economies, in which property in goods and services is exchanged according to the freely chosen preferences of men and women. Yet, upholding the concept of negative freedom does not necessarily lead people to favour cut-throat market capitalism and minimum state involvement in social and economic matters. Left-wing adherents of negative freedom are often willing to restrict freedom for the sake of other goals, such as equality or socio-economic security. They justify these restrictions by making a distinction between liberty and the *value* of liberty (see Plant 1985: 306–7). This distinction means that somebody who lacks the financial means to buy an expensive car is nevertheless perfectly free to do so, but because of their lack of money this freedom is of very little *value* to them. In this view, some restrictions of freedom, such as those implied in taxing the rich and giving to the poor, are then justified because they increase the value of freedom on the part of the poor.

It is questionable, however, whether freedom can be conceived of in purely negative terms in the first place, without any positive reference to the values and beliefs that are held in common by the members of a community. According to Charles Taylor (1979), we cannot make sense of judgements about the relative degrees of freedom enjoyed in different societies without evaluating the significance of actions to those who perform them, enabling us to distinguish restrictions that are without relevance for freedom altogether from others that are judged to be of greater and lesser importance. Such a distinction is implied in the notion of *positive* freedom, by which Berlin means the ability of 'being one's own master' (Berlin 1969: 131).[3] In this sense, positive freedom stands for self-determination as the absence of various constraints, both *external* ones such as an oppressive political regime or lack of resources, as well as *internal* obstacles, such as inner fears, compulsions or ignorance. At the level of the individual, positive liberty is equivalent to personal autonomy – a person's life is autonomous if it is to a considerable extent his/her own creation (Raz 1986: 369–70). This view of positive freedom brings us back to the modern liberal and social-democratic welfare politics mentioned above, but also raises important questions for feminists. For, how could a person be in charge of her own life without assurance of the means to stay alive and to feed her children? Consequentially, some feminists have stressed that for women to be fully free citizens, employment and childcare must be available, or people must have access to the basic necessities of life (Held 1984: 136–8).

At the level of society, positive liberty can be equated with democracy. Democracy has been described as the adaptation of individual autonomy to the fact that human beings rarely live in isolation (Dahl 1989: 89). As people seek satisfactory lives by living in association with others, they inevitably make collective arrangements that regulate how people interact with each other peacefully and that are binding on all members of society. The problem, then, is to discover a way by which the members of society may make such collectively binding decisions and still govern themselves. As was famously claimed by Rousseau ([1762] 1973: 190–2), democratic government is just the solution to that problem. This view of liberty also underlies the republican tradition, which equates liberty with *non-domination*. For republicans, to be a free person is to be a citizen of a self-governing, free political community (Pettit, 1997).

Other conceptions of positive liberty go further and entail richer notions of self-mastery or self-realisation, moral or 'inner' freedom, higher levels of rationality, or the collective ends of society. Green ([1888] 1991: 23), for instance, defined freedom as the ability of people 'to make the most and best of themselves', and as 'the liberation of the powers of all men equally for contributions to a common good'. Note that in identifying legitimate goals ('the best', 'a common good'), this notion of positive liberty leads us straight back to the non-neutral distinction of worthy *versus* unworthy activities, and thereby to the issue of liberty *versus* license. Such references to higher ends have often been used to justify paternalism and coercion, professed to help people discover what they 'really want', and, if necessary, 'force them to be free' (Rousseau [1762] 1973: 194). The Stalinist systems of central and eastern Europe and the former Soviet Union are cases in point. In the west, accusations of perverting positive liberty into a totalitarian concept of the common good have been directed at communitarians, who deem it neither desirable nor possible that people freely revise their life plans independently from the social contexts and traditions in which they live.[4] For Berlin, positive liberty is the root of tyranny, as it can easily be used to justify the destruction of negative freedom in the name of the 'higher' value of positive liberty.

We can go further and ask whether the distinction between negative and positive freedom is a meaningful one in the first place. This point has been made by Gerald MacCallum, who suggests there is only one concept of liberty and that is best understood as always one and the same triadic relation between a *person*, an intended *action* and what he calls a *'preventing condition'* (MacCallum 1967: 314). Freedom, in this view, is always of someone, from something, to do, have or be something. Disputes about the nature of freedom are, according to MacCallum, really disagreements over the proper range and meaning of one or more of the three variables, in particular of the last one – what is to count as an obstacle, impediment or interference. The next section explores some of these disputes.

RESTRICTIONS TO FREEDOM: INTERFERENCE, COERCION AND CONSTRAINTS

If somebody points a gun at my head and forces me to perform a certain action, such as handing over my wallet, there is little doubt they thereby restrict my freedom to do as I please. Likewise, physical obstruction literally makes an option physically impossible for a person. Coercive laws make some options ineligible, or at least significantly less eligible. All of the above reduce freedom by narrowing a person's range of options. But if need forces a person to accept employment for a very low wage, does it mean that anyone has restricted his/her freedom?

One way to think about restrictions of freedom is as *interference*. The notion of interference is integral to Berlin's concept of negative freedom, for whom being free means not being interfered with by others. Berlin is not very clear, however, about whether freedom can be restricted only by the deliberate acts of other human beings, and whether there must be a direct connection between the act and the restriction to count as interference (Berlin 1969: 122–3). Friedrich Hayek, for his part, is less ambiguous in this regard. For him, restrictions of freedom take place through *coercion* – a state of affairs in which one person is made into an instrument of another's will, which 'implies both the threat of inflicting harm and the intention thereby to bring about certain conduct' (Hayek 1960: 133). By contrast, any impediments to people's action resulting from market transactions, including hiring and firing in the labour market, are not the result of the action of a restraining human agent, because they are usually neither intended nor foreseen. Therefore, according to Hayek, the rules of capitalism and private property do not restrict freedom. The freedom of the worst off is no more diminished by their lack of resources than it is by their lack of any other endowments, such as the ability to fly like a bird or to perform miracles. This view is also fervently endorsed by Nozick. At the same time, however, Nozick (1974: 163) maintains that any restriction on a person's right to private property, such as taxing people's assets or regulating their use, constitutes an interference with their freedom.

For G. A. Cohen (1991), by contrast, a lack of money inevitably carries with it a lack of freedom, even if we identify freedom in the strictly negative sense as the absence of interference. According to Cohen, there is a fundamental difference between money and other endowments, such as beauty, intelligence or physical strength, because a property distribution is itself a distribution of rights of interference. As Cohen explains elsewhere,

> If *A* owns *P* and *B* does not, then *A* may use *P* without interference and *B* will, standardly, suffer interference if he attempts to use *P*. *But money serves, in a variety of circumstances (and, notably, when A puts P up for rent or sale), to remove that latter interference. Therefore*

> *money confers freedom, rather than merely the ability to use it*, even
> if freedom is equated with absence of interference (2001: 13; original
> emphasis).

According to Cohen, a sum of money is equivalent to a licence to perform
a variety of actions, like, for example, visiting one's sister in Glasgow; or
taking home, and wearing, the sweater on the counter at Selfridges (2001:
19–20). Money exchange operates through a system of constraint that even
in ordinary discourse we conceptualise as freedom and unfreedom. Goods
for which one has to pay are not 'free', and the level of constraint is clearly
less the more money one has (Hyland 1995: 133). And this constraint is itself
ultimately backed with legal sanctions, enforceable by the very physical
coercion by the police of anyone who dares to transgress the boundaries of
private property.

In order to uphold the view that freedom has little to do with money,
libertarians such as Nozick tend to switch to a definition of freedom in terms
of the exercise of one's rights. In this view, the interference by the police
with somebody trying to grab the sweater at Selfridges without paying for
it does not actually affect their freedom, because they had no right to do so.
However, as we saw above when discussing the distinction between liberty
and licence, saying that people should be free to do what they have a right
to do is of little help. Ultimately, this rights-based definition of freedom can
mean that the heavy travel restrictions imposed on citizens of the communist
societies in central and eastern Europe and the former Soviet Union did not
restrict their freedom. After all, according to the law of these countries they
had no 'right' to travel freely to western countries. On any rights-neutral
definition of freedom, by contrast, it remains a fact that, if one lacks the
capacity to travel as a result of a lack of money, one is just as *unfree* to travel
as if one had the money but travelling was prohibited by the government
(Cohen 2001).

The unfreedom that results from a lack of money in market societies
does not stop here. The need to earn money makes it necessary for most
people to enter into employment contracts. In entering the employment
contract, employees agree to give up their freedom to do as they please for
the duration of the working day, and instead commit to obey the orders of
their boss (Cohen 1983). Note that this necessity is not equally given for
everyone. Those who, for whatever reason, say because they won the lottery
or because they were born into a wealthy family, already have enough money
to enjoy the freedom not to work at all. And if you have sufficient means to
afford excellent education, you may still have to take on a job, but it will
no longer have to be *any* job. Instead, you will enjoy a significant degree of
freedom of choice regarding your career path. Moreover, the kind of job one
is able to get as a result of a good education will quite likely involve greater
freedom regarding the way in which one carries out one's duties. Thus, the

unequal distribution of money in combination with the capitalist institution of the employment contract can actually lead to the diminution of freedom.

This result becomes glaringly obvious with respect to one particular aspect of poverty – homelessness – that highlights the connection between the freedom to *be somewhere* and freedom to *do something*. As Jeremy Waldron (1993a: 316) points out, if one is not free to be in a certain place, one is not free to do anything at that place. It follows that a person who is not free to be in any place – something that is true for homeless people most of the time – is not free to do anything at all. And to the extent that homeless people are increasingly prohibited from performing necessary and essentially human activities, such as eating, sleeping or urinating, in the only remaining places where they have hitherto been tolerated to do so – public parks, subway stations or the side entrances of town halls and department stores – they are made comprehensively unfree.

FREEDOM, DOMINATION AND DISCURSIVE BIAS

While historically the doctrine of equal liberty has been a liberating formula, feminist political theorists have frequently viewed it with scepticism, suspecting that the very philosophical foundations of modern liberal societies systematically privilege men. Carole Pateman, for example, has discerned a deep-seated male bias in the universalist mode in which the social contract theories of Grotius, Hobbes, Locke, and Pufendorf are cast. According to Pateman, while the commonwealth founded by the social contract in these theories has been conceived in terms of the free consent of free individuals, this contract was simultaneously a *sexual* contract that subordinated women to men. Freedom for male citizens depended on patriarchal right, which has been premised on the subordination of wives, female domestic servants and prostitutes. An obvious example is the husband's conjugal right, which until very recently ensured that husbands own the sexual property in their wives' persons (Pateman 1988: 124).

As a result, the free, individual, reasoning subject of modern western political philosophy is implicitly male, while women's role in society is still to a great extent associated with the realm of necessity characterised by the 'natural' duties of family life and reproduction (Okin 1989: 110–33). For this reason, feminists have viewed with scepticism the traditional republican distinction between the public realm (*res publicae*), in which free males, whose property and economic status convey citizenship, participated in collective government, and the private realm (*res privatae*), where wives, children, slaves and servants lived as subordinate ancillaries to male protagonists. In the extract reproduced in this volume, Wendy Brown (1995) shows how dualisms such as those of *freedom* and *nature*, *public* and *private*, *autonomy* and *dependence*, *rights* and *needs*, *contract* and *consent* are the building blocks of liberal discourse. It turns out that the more highly valued term of each pair is systematically associated with masculinity and the less valued with femininity. Liberalism itself then appears as a discourse of male dominance (Brown 1995: 141). This inbuilt bias becomes visible in the context of reproduction. As Patricia Smith (1993: 14) observes, while it is generally not found unusual that a woman's decision as to whether and when she will have a baby is governed to a large extent by *man*-made legal arrangements, it is inconceivable that any issue that comparably affected the basic individual freedom of any man would not be under his control in a free society.

If the problem of gender bias is less one of blatant discrimination than of patriarchy as an all-encompassing worldview, the solution will be not so much the absence of discrimination, but rather the presence of power (Kymlicka 2002: 383). Drucilla Cornell, for example, argues the case for affirmative powers against sexual harassment as an example of freedom as active empowerment. Women's effective empowerment in this sense would involve the abandonment of existing presumptions of female blame in favour of the effective demand to be free from sexual harassment (Cornell 1998). Indeed, the point can be made that the more formally free the institutional or legal setting, the deeper women's vulnerability can be and the more male power is masked (MacKinnon 1987: 15). For that reason, freedom of contract in civil society is a target for feminist critique reminiscent of the socialist critique of that same legal institution. Socialist critics of the employment contract and feminist critics of the marriage contract alike have attacked the liberal claim that, if two individuals make a contract, the fact that the compact has been made is sufficient to show that it must have been freely willed (Pateman 1988: 57). Quite the opposite may be the case when a person agrees to a particular arrangement not because it accords with their desires but only because any alternative is totally unacceptable. As Cohen clarifies, 'At least usually, when a person says, "I was forced to do it. I had no other choice", the second part of the statement is elliptical for something like "I had no other choice worth considering"' (Cohen 1983: 4).

CONCLUSION

Since the demolition by the philosophers of the Enlightenment of 'naturally' ordained privilege, liberty can only mean equal liberty for all. And while it is extremely difficult to determine just how equally or unequally liberty is distributed among people, we can in principle identify and challenge sources of relative or absolute unfreedom. Now that the blatant unfreedoms known from feudal serfdom or fascist dictatorship are no longer problems to be reckoned with – at least in the wealthy industrialised countries of the West such optimism may be justified – feminist and socialist political theorists sharpen our view for more covert, but no less important, restrictions on the freedom of certain groups of people: those that are neither male nor well heeled. In countries of mixed ethnic make-up, we will often have to add ethnic minorities to the list of groups that suffer unnecessary restrictions of freedom.

Liberty is not a dichotomous condition that is either present or absent, as in the case of somebody being either a free person or a slave. As I have attempted to elucidate in this chapter, liberty is a multidimensional phenomenon that can be gradually decreased or increased along one or more of these dimensions. The dimensions of freedom most pertinent to people's lives in liberal democratic societies concern (1) the resources necessary to lead a free and self-determined life; (2) the structural constraints and biases that systematically undermine the freedom of some people more than others; and (3) the cultural, discursive or ideological constraints on the freedom of the individual. Concerning (1), to the extent that in capitalist market economies money confers freedom, a person becomes freer with every additional pound in their pocket. On the level of structural constraints (2), socialists have drawn our attention to the system of private property and market exchange as a system for the distribution of rights of interference and non-interference. The way we organise production and reproduction in society, furthermore, has been shown to systematically undermine women's freedom to be the authors of their own life plans. The insistence of feminist and socialist critics of liberalism, finally (3), that the problem of freedom was contained in the social relations declared 'unpolitical' in liberal discourse, highlights the extent to which the public/private distinction is an ideological aspect of subordination in societies in which white, propertied men dominate other groups. The laws regulating property, contracts and criminal offence, and ultimately the very market system itself, are *man*-made institutions that allocate freedom according to more or less consciously designed principles. These institutions only work smoothly, however, if they enjoy the acquiescence of those who lose out in terms of their personal freedom. Historically, it was only when real possibilities for alternatives were spelt out that happy slaves ceased to be happy, contented housewives withdrew their consent, and the poor stopped applauding the rich for enjoying the freedoms they were deprived of themselves.

QUESTIONS FOR DISCUSSION

- Some feminist theorists argue that the formal freedoms granted in liberal society actually undermine the freedom of women. What do they mean by that?
- In a market society, can a person be free without having money?
- Politicians should not try to distribute income and wealth more equally, because egalitarian welfare politics underline liberty. Do you agree?
- Can it ever be morally legitimate to limit the freedom or liberty of people that hold and propagate extremist views (e.g., neo-Nazis or religious fundamentalists)?

NOTES

1. Following the majority of writers on the subject, I use the terms 'freedom' and 'liberty' interchangeably (see for example Berlin 1969: 121).

2. See Hollis (1997: 154–70) for an introduction to the problem of philosophical freedom.

3. On closer inspection of Berlin's 'Two Concepts of Liberty' it turns out that there is a plurality of different concepts hidden underneath the umbrella term 'positive liberty', and the state of the literature in this respect is generally very pluralistic, to say the least. In Berlin's account alone we come across numerous different meanings of 'positive liberty'. As David Miller (1991: 10) points out, these involve fundamental ambiguities, confusions and inconsistencies in Berlin's account of liberty, which, however, partly correspond to similar disarray in the writing of some of the advocates of positive freedom, notably in the aforementioned essay by T. H. Green ([1888] 1991).

4. To assess for yourself whether or not these accusations are justified, consult Kymlicka (2002: 228–44) or Kenny (2003) for informative introductions to the debate on communitarianism.

ISAIAH BERLIN
EXTRACTS FROM 'TWO CONCEPTS
OF LIBERTY'

THE NOTION OF NEGATIVE FREEDOM

I am normally said to be free to the degree to which no man or body of men interferes with my activity. Political liberty in this sense is simply the area within which a man can act unobstructed by others. If I am prevented by others from doing what I could otherwise do, I am to that degree unfree; and if this area is contracted by other men beyond a certain minimum, I can be described as being coerced, or, it may be, enslaved. Coercion is not, however, a term that covers every form of inability. If I say that I am unable to jump more than ten feet in the air, or cannot read because I am blind, or cannot understand the darker pages of Hegel, it would be eccentric to say that I am to that degree enslaved or coerced. Coercion implies the deliberate interference of other human beings within the area in which I could otherwise act. You lack political liberty or freedom only if you are prevented from attaining a goal by human beings.[1] Mere incapacity to attain a goal is not lack of political freedom.[2] This is brought out by the use of such modern expressions as 'economic freedom' and its counterpart, 'economic slavery'. It is argued, very plausibly, that if a man is too poor to afford something on which there is no legal ban – a loaf of bread, a journey round the world, recourse to the law courts – he is as little free to have it as he would be if it were forbidden him by law. If my poverty were a kind of disease which prevented me from buying bread, or paying for the journey round the world or getting my case heard, as lameness prevents

Isaiah Berlin (1969), 'Two Concepts of Liberty', in *Four Essays on Liberty*, Oxford: Oxford University Press.

me from running, this inability would not naturally be described as a lack of freedom, least of all political freedom. It is only because I believe that my inability to get a given thing is due to the fact that other human beings have made arrangements whereby I am, whereas others are not, prevented from having enough money with which to pay for it, that I think myself a victim of coercion or slavery. In other words, this use of the term depends on a particular social and economic theory about the causes of my poverty or weakness. If my lack of material means is due to my lack of mental or physical capacity, then I begin to speak of being deprived of freedom (and not simply about poverty) only if I accept the theory.[3] If, in addition, I believe that I am being kept in want by a specific arrangement which I consider unjust or unfair, I speak of economic slavery or oppression. The nature of things does not madden us, only ill will does, said Rousseau.[4] The criterion of oppression is the part that I believe to be played by other human beings, directly or indirectly, with or without the intention of doing so, in frustrating my wishes. By being free in this sense I mean not being interfered with by others. The wider the area of non-interference the wider my freedom.

This is what the classical English political philosophers meant when they used this word.[5] They disagreed about how wide the area could or should be. They supposed that it could not, as things were, be unlimited, because if it were, it would entail a state in which all men could boundlessly interfere with all other men; and this kind of 'natural' freedom would lead to social chaos in which men's minimum needs would not be satisfied; or else the liberties of the weak would be suppressed by the strong. Because they perceived that human purposes and activities do not automatically harmonise with one another, and because (whatever their official doctrines) they put high value on other goals, such as justice, or happiness, or culture, or security, or varying degrees of equality, they were prepared to curtail freedom in the interests of other values and, indeed, of freedom itself. For, without this, it was impossible to create the kind of association that they thought desirable. Consequently, it is assumed by these thinkers that the area of men's free action must be limited by law. But equally it is assumed, especially by such libertarians as Locke and Mill in England, and Constant and Tocqueville in France, that there ought to exist a certain minimum area of personal freedom which must on no account be violated; for if it is overstepped, the individual will find himself in an area too narrow for even that minimum development of his natural faculties which alone makes it possible to pursue, and even to conceive, the various ends which men hold good or right or sacred. It follows that a frontier must be drawn between the area of private life and that of public authority. Where it is to be drawn is a matter of argument, indeed of haggling. Men are largely interdependent, and no man's activity is so completely private as never to obstruct the lives of others in any way. 'Freedom for the pike is death for the minnows';[6]

the liberty of some must depend on the restraint of others. Freedom for an Oxford don, others have been known to add, is a very different thing from freedom for an Egyptian peasant.

This proposition derives its force from something that is both true and important, but the phrase itself remains a piece of political claptrap. It is true that to offer political rights, or safeguards against intervention by the State, to men who are half-naked, illiterate, underfed and diseased is to mock their condition; they need medical help or education before they can understand, or make use of, an increase in their freedom. What is freedom to those who cannot make use of it? Without adequate conditions for the use of freedom, what is the value of freedom? First things come first: there are situations in which – to use a saying satirically attributed to the nihilists by Dostoevsky – boots are superior to Pushkin; individual freedom is not everyone's primary need. For freedom is not the mere absence of frustration of whatever kind; this would inflate the meaning of the word until it meant too much or too little. The Egyptian peasant needs clothes or medicine before, and more than, personal liberty, but the minimum freedom that he needs today, and the greater degree of freedom that he may need tomorrow, is not some species of freedom peculiar to him, but identical with that of professors, artists and millionaires.

What troubles the consciences of Western liberals is, I think, the belief, not that the freedom that men seek differs according to their social or economic conditions, but that the minority who possess it have gained it by exploiting, or, at least, averting their gaze from, the vast majority who do not. They believe, with good reason, that if individual liberty is an ultimate end for human beings, none should be deprived of it by others; least of all that some should enjoy it at the expense of others. Equality of liberty; not to treat others as I should not wish them to treat me; repayment of my debt to those who alone have made possible my liberty or prosperity or enlightenment; justice, in its simplest and most universal sense – these are the foundations of liberal morality. Liberty is not the only goal of men. I can, like the Russian critic Belinsky, say that if others are to be deprived of it – if my brothers are to remain in poverty, squalor and chains – then I do not want it for myself, I reject it with both hands and infinitely prefer to share their fate. But nothing is gained by a confusion of terms. To avoid glaring inequality or widespread misery I am ready to sacrifice some, or all, of my freedom: I may do so willingly and freely; but it is freedom that I am giving up for the sake of justice or equality or the love of my fellow men. I should be guilt-stricken, and rightly so, if I were not, in some circumstances, ready to make this sacrifice. But a sacrifice is not an increase in what is being sacrificed, namely freedom, however great the moral need or the compensation for it. Everything is what it is: liberty is liberty, not equality or fairness or justice or culture, or human happiness or a quiet conscience. If the liberty of myself or my class or nation depends on the misery of a number of other human beings, the system which promotes this is unjust and immoral. But if I curtail or lose my freedom in order to lessen the shame of such inequality, and do not thereby materially increase the individual liberty of others, an absolute loss of liberty occurs. This may be compensated for by a gain in justice or in happiness or in peace, but the loss remains, and it is a confusion of values to say that although my 'liberal', individual freedom may go by the board, some other kind of freedom – 'social' or 'economic' – is increased.

[. . .]

Freedom in this sense is not, at any rate logically, connected with democracy or self-government. Self-government may, on the whole, provide a better guarantee of the preservation of civil liberties than other regimes, and has been defended as such by libertarians. But there is no necessary connection between individual liberty and democratic rule. The answer to the question 'Who governs me?' is logically distinct from the question 'How far does government interfere with me?' It is in this difference that the great contrast between the two concepts of negative and positive liberty, in the end, consists.[7] For the 'positive' sense of liberty comes to light if we try to answer the question, not 'What am I free to do or be?', but 'By whom am I ruled?' or 'Who is to say what I am, and what I am not, to be or do?' The connection between democracy and individual liberty is a good deal more tenuous than it seemed to many advocates of both. The desire to be governed by myself, or at any rate to participate in the process by which my life is to be controlled, may be as deep a wish as that for a free area for action, and perhaps historically older. But it is not a desire for the same thing. So different is it, indeed, as to have led in the end to the great clash of ideologies that dominates our world. For it is this, the 'positive' conception of liberty, not freedom from, but freedom to – to lead one prescribed form of life – which the adherents of the 'negative' notion represent as being, at times, no better than a specious disguise for brutal tyranny.

THE NOTION OF POSITIVE FREEDOM

The 'positive' sense of the word 'liberty' derives from the wish on the part of the individual to be his own master. I wish my life and decisions to depend on myself, not on external forces of whatever kind. I wish to be the instrument of my own, not of other men's, acts of will. I wish to be a subject, not an object; to be moved by reasons, by conscious purposes, which are my own, not by causes which affect me, as it were, from outside. I wish to be somebody, not nobody; a doer – deciding, not being decided for, self-directed and not acted upon by external nature or by other men as if I were a thing, or an animal, or a slave incapable of playing a human role, that is, of conceiving goals and policies of my own and realising them. This is at least part of what I mean when I say that I am rational, and that it is my reason that distinguishes me as a human being from the rest of the world. I wish, above all, to be conscious of myself as a thinking, willing, active being, bearing responsibility for my choices and able to explain them by reference to my own ideas and purposes. I feel free to the degree that I believe this to be true, and enslaved to the degree that I am made to realise that it is not.

The freedom which consists in being one's own master, and the freedom which consists in not being prevented from choosing as I do by other men, may, on the face of it, seem concepts at no great logical distance from each other – no more than negative and positive ways of saying much the same thing. Yet the 'positive' and 'negative' notions of freedom historically developed in divergent directions, not always by logically reputable steps, until, in the end, they came into direct conflict with each other.

One way of making this clear is in terms of the independent momentum which the, initially perhaps quite harmless, metaphor of self-mastery acquired. 'I am my own master'; 'I am slave to no man'; but may I not (as Platonists or Hegelians tend to say) be a slave to nature? Or to my own 'unbridled' passions? Are these not so many species of the identical genus 'slave' – some political or legal, others moral or spiritual? Have not men had the experience of liberating themselves from spiritual slavery, or slavery to nature, and do they not in the course of it become aware, on the one hand, of a self which dominates, and, on the other, of something in them which is brought to heel? This dominant self is then variously identified with reason, with my 'higher nature', with the self which calculates and aims at what will satisfy it in the long run, with my 'real', or 'ideal', or 'autonomous' self, or with my self 'at its best'; which is then contrasted with irrational impulse, uncontrolled desires, my 'lower' nature, the pursuit of immediate pleasures, my 'empirical' or 'heteronomous' self, swept by every gust of desire and passion, needing to be rigidly disciplined if it is ever to rise to the full height of its 'real' nature. Presently the two selves may be represented as divided by an even larger gap; the real self may be conceived as something wider than the individual (as the term is normally understood), as a social 'whole' of which the individual is an element or aspect: a tribe, a race, a Church, a State, the great society of the living and the dead and the yet unborn. This entity is then identified as being the 'true' self which, by imposing its collective, or 'organic', single will upon its recalcitrant 'members', achieves its own, and therefore their, 'higher' freedom. The perils of using organic metaphors to justify the coercion of some men by others in order to raise them to a 'higher' level of freedom have often been pointed out. But what gives such plausibility as it has to this kind of language is that we recognise that it is possible, and at times justifiable, to coerce men in the name of some goal (let us say, justice or public health) which they would, if they were more enlightened, themselves pursue, but do not, because they are blind or ignorant or corrupt. This renders it easy for me to conceive of myself as coercing others for their own sake, in their, not my, interest. I am then claiming that I know what they truly need better than they know it themselves. What, at most, this entails is that they would not resist me if they were rational and as wise as I and understood their interests as I do. But I may go on to claim a good deal more than this. I may declare that they are actually aiming at what in their benighted state they consciously resist, because there exists within them an occult entity – their latent rational will, or their 'true' purpose – and that this entity, although it is belied by all that they overtly feel and do and say, is their 'real' self, of which the poor empirical self in space and time may know nothing or little; and that this inner spirit is the only self that deserves to have its wishes taken into account.[8] Once I take this view, I am in a position to ignore the actual wishes of men or societies, to bully, oppress, torture them in the name, and on behalf, of their 'real' selves, in the secure knowledge that whatever is the true goal of man (happiness, performance of duty, wisdom, a just society, self-fulfilment) must be identical with his freedom – the free choice of his 'true', albeit often submerged and inarticulate, self.

This paradox has been often exposed. It is one thing to say that I know what is good for X, while he himself does not; and even to ignore his wishes for its – and his – sake; and a very different one to say that he has *eo ipso* chosen it, not indeed consciously, not as he seems in everyday life, but in his role as a rational self which his empirical self may not know – the 'real' self which discerns the good, and cannot help choosing it once it is revealed. This monstrous impersonation, which consists in equating what X would choose if he were something he is not, or at least not yet, with what X actually seeks and chooses, is at the heart of all political theories of self-realisation. It is one thing to say that I may be coerced for my own good, which I am too blind to see: this may, on occasion, be for my benefit; indeed it may enlarge the scope of my liberty. It is another to say that if it is my good, then I am not being coerced, for I have willed it, whether I know this or not, and am free (or 'truly' free) even while my poor earthly body and foolish mind bitterly reject it, and struggle with the greatest desperation against those who seek, however benevolently, to impose it.

This magical transformation, or sleight of hand (for which William James so justly mocked the Hegelians), can no doubt be perpetrated just as easily with the 'negative' concept of freedom, where the self that should not be interfered with is no longer the individual with his actual wishes and needs as they are normally conceived, but the 'real' man within, identified with the pursuit of some ideal purpose not dreamed of by his empirical self. And, as in the case of the 'positively' free self, this entity may be inflated into some super-personal entity – a State, a class, a nation, or the march of history itself, regarded as a more 'real' subject of attributes than the empirical self. But the 'positive' conception of freedom as self-mastery, with its suggestion of a man divided against himself, has in fact, and as a matter of history, of doctrine and of practice, lent itself more easily to this splitting of personality into two: the transcendent, dominant controller, and the empirical bundle of desires and passions to be disciplined and brought to heel.

Notes

1. I do not, of course, mean to imply the truth of the converse.
2. Helvétius made this point very clearly: 'The free man is the man who is not in irons, not imprisoned in a gaol, nor terrorised like a slave by the fear of punishment.' It is not lack of freedom not to fly like an eagle or swim like a whale. *De l'esprit*, first discourse, chapter 4.
3. The Marxist conception of social laws is, of course, the best-known version of this theory, but it forms a large element in some Christian and utilitarian, and all socialist, doctrines.
4. *Émile*, book 2: vol. 4, p. 320, in *Oeuvres complètes*, ed. Bernard Gagnebin and others (Paris, 1959–95).
5. 'A free man', said Hobbes, 'is he that … is not hindered to do what he has a will to.' *Leviathan*, chapter 21: p. 146 in Richard Tuck's edition (Cambridge, 1991). Law is always a fetter, even if it protects you from being bound in chains that are heavier than those of the law, say some more repressive law or custom, or arbitrary despotism or chaos. Bentham says much the same.
6. R. H. Tawney, *Equality* (1931), 3rd ed. (London, 1938), chapter 5, section 2, 'Equality and Liberty', p. 208 (not in previous editions).
7. 'Negative liberty' is something the extent of which, in a given case, it is difficult to estimate. It might, prima facie, seem to depend simply on the power to choose between at any rate two alternatives. Nevertheless, not all choices are equally free, or free at all. If in a totalitarian State I betray my friend under threat of torture, perhaps even if I act from fear of losing my job, I can reasonably say that I did not act freely. Nevertheless, I did, of course, make a choice, and could, at any rate in theory, have chosen to be killed or tortured or imprisoned. The mere existence of alternatives is not, therefore, enough to make my action free (although it may be voluntary) in the normal sense of the word. The extent of my freedom seems to depend on (*a*) how many possibilities are open to me (although the method of counting these can never be more than impressionistic; possibilities of action are not discrete entities like apples, which can be exhaustively enumerated); (*b*) how easy or difficult each of these possibilities is to actualise; (*c*) how important in my plan of life, given my character and circumstances, these possibilities are when compared with each other; (*d*) how far they are closed and opened by deliberate human acts; (*e*) what value not merely the agent, but the general sentiment of the society in which he lives, puts on the various possibilities. All these magnitudes must be 'integrated', and a conclusion, necessarily never precise, or indisputable, drawn from this process. It may well be that there are many incommensurable kinds and degrees of freedom, and that they cannot be drawn up on any single scale of magnitude. Moreover, in the case of societies, we are faced by such (logically absurd) questions as 'Would arrangement X increase the liberty of Mr A more than it would that of Messrs B, C and D between them, added together?' The same difficulties arise in applying utilitarian criteria. Nevertheless, provided we do not demand precise measurement, we can give valid reasons for saying that the average subject of the King of Sweden is, on the whole, a good deal freer today [1958] than the average citizen of Spain or Albania. Total patterns of life must be compared directly as wholes, although the method by which we make the comparison, and the truth of the conclusions, are difficult or impossible to demonstrate. But the vagueness of the concepts, and the multiplicity of the criteria involved, are attributes of the subject-matter itself, not of our imperfect methods of measurement, or of incapacity for precise thought.

8. '[T]he ideal of true freedom is the maximum of power for all members of human society alike to make the best of themselves', said T. H. Green in 1881. Apart from the confusion of freedom with equality, this entails that if a man chose some immediate pleasure – which (in whose view?) would not enable him to make the best of himself (what self?) – what he was exercising was not 'true' freedom: and if deprived of it, he would not lose anything that mattered. Green was a genuine liberal: but many a tyrant could use this formula to justify his worst acts of oppression.

WENDY BROWN
EXTRACTS FROM *STATES OF INJURY: POWER AND FREEDOM IN LATE MODERNITY*

LIBERALISM'S FAMILY VALUES

[. . .]

I want to argue, first, that liberalism is premised on and perpetuates a sexual division of labor, the actual powers of which are obscured by the terms of liberal discourse. Yet I also want to argue that liberal discourse produces subjects without regard to their 'social positioning' by other discourses of gender, class, and race. In this regard, liberalism both produces and positions gendered subjects whose production and positioning it disavows through naturalization (an ideological moment) *and* produces abstract, genderless, colorless sovereign subjects (a more discursive moment), whose sovereignty and abstract equality contend uneasily with the discourses marking relative will-lessness and inferiority according to socially marked attributes.

[. . .]

Within liberal discourse itself, there is both an expressly gendered and a generic strain, the former often subterranean and surfacing only at points at which the family, heterosexuality, maternity, or sexual violence is explicitly at issue. Yet the generic or gender-neutral strain, while wielding substantial force, overlooks the extent to which subjects are interpellated and positioned as gender, and it is in this regard that liberalism 'misdescribes' or ideologically obscures the extent to which its subjects are shaped

Wendy Brown (1995), *States of Injury: Power and Freedom in Late Modernity*, Princeton: Princeton University Press.

and positioned by a sexual division of labor and a sex difference that liberal discourse presumes to transcend. The gendered ideological moments of liberalism, then, pertain on the one hand to essentializing gender as difference; on the other, to glossing the social power of gender formation with generic or neutral language.

[. . .]

If the social order presumed by liberalism is itself pervasively gendered, representing both a gendered division of labor and a gendered division of the sensibilities and activities of subjects, we should expect to find this gendering as well in the terms defining the interests, activities, and political freedom of the subject in civil society, the political subject of liberalism. The remainder of this essay outlines the ways in which the constitutive terms of liberal political discourse depend upon their implicit opposition to a subject and set of activities marked 'feminine', and at the same time obscure both this dependence and this opposition.[1] The discussion proceeds by identifying constitutive dualisms in liberal discourse and then discerning how the power of the dominant term in the dualism is achieved through its constitution by, dependence upon, and disavowal of the subordinate term. Tracking how the second term is pushed out of the first in the latter's claim to primacy and power permits an understanding of how these dualisms are operations not merely of division or distinction but dominance – male dominance – at the heart of liberal discourse.

[. . .]

Liberty–Necessity. Liberty, which denotes the sovereignty of the liberal subject, marks the freedom to *do* what one *desires*, the freedom to discover and pursue one's interests where the law does not interfere. Insofar as liberalism premises our liberty on a relatively unencumbered will – the possibility of choosing – and a domain of free movement – the possibility of acting – liberty signifies our sovereignty in both a subjective and a worldly sense. We are considered to have liberty when we have choices and when we have the capacity to exercise our deliberative faculty. The opposite of liberty is therefore not slavery but will-lessness and/or constraint. Just as equality is premised upon overcoming inequality but is not its opposite, liberty is what liberates us from the condition of slavery or political subjection but is not its opposite. Liberal liberty's opposite is encumbrance, constraint, by necessity: barriers to deliberating, choosing, or acting. If we are free when we have free will, when the will desires and is free to act on its own behalf, we are unfree when we are without desire or aim on the one hand, and weighed down, constrained by necessity, and lacking choice or freedom of movement on the other.

Within almost any sexual division of labor in history, women have been encumbered by the bonds of necessity and the stigma of ontological immanence. Bound over time to relationships they are born to honor and tend, confined spatially to caretaking and labor in the household, women are also bound symbolically to the work their bodies are said to signify; in this sense, they are without the mark of subjective sovereignty, the capacity to desire or choose. This is what Simone de Beauvoir names 'the worst curse that was laid upon woman ... biologically destined for the repetition of Life',[2] Indeed, the 'pro-choice' language of reproductive politics aims at giving women the status of choosing rather than immanent beings; in seeking to emancipate us from both semiotic and physical constraints of the female body, it asserts our right to share the voluntarist premises of liberal freedom with men. And much of the political language opposing abortion aims to deny women precisely this right, insisting either that a woman should not have such liberty in the first place, or that she necessarily loses this liberty when her body's 'natural processes' take over, when she is *taken over* by her nature, by nature, by necessity, by another.[3] A similar rehearsal of women's relative consignment to her body transpires in political and legal arguments about rape and sexual harassment, where the question of women's own desire and self-determination remains a question so long as 'consent' and 'incitement' are the terms through which the sexual (non)agency of women is brokered. The character of argument in both domains reveals the gendered characteristics of liberal freedom, the extent to which the sexual and reproductive liberty of men is premised upon an immanent and constrained other.

A formulation of liberty that has as its opposite immanence, necessity, encumbrance, and external nature is not, of course, the only possible formulation of human freedom.[4] It is, rather, a notoriously bourgeois but now also evidently gendered formulation, and a formulation that depends upon and enforces a gendered division of labor in which women are encumbered while men are free, in which encumbrance and subjection by the body function as the permanent constraint on freedom. This formulation of liberty, and the identification of the liberal subject with it, requires that someone somewhere be fully bound by necessity, while others eschew this responsibility, thereby institutionally securing the unfree nature of such responsibility. In liberal discourse, of course, the domain of avowed and naturalized encumbrance is the private, familial, sexual, and reproductive domain(s), the domains through and within which women are marked and positioned as women. The sphere of liberty, the sphere of civil society, is defined historically against feudal ties of encumbrance and relationality, ties that persist, as the Filmer–Locke quarrel reminds us, in the familial domain, the domain of patriarchalism now divested of political standing.

The liberal formulation of liberty is thus not merely opposed to but premised upon encumbrance; it is achieved by displacing the embodied, encumbered, and limited nature of existence onto women, a displacement that occurs discursively and practically through a set of assigned activities, responsibilities, and emotional attributes. Insofar as this formulation of liberty *requires* the existence of encumbered beings, the social activity of those without liberty, it can never be fully universalized. A liberty whose conceptual and practical opposite is encumbrance cannot, by necessity, exist without it; liberated beings defined as unencumbered depend for their existence on encumbered beings, whom their liberty in turn encumbers. In this regard, liberalism would seem to tacitly sustain rather than break with the explicit belief of the ancient citizens of Athens: some must be slaves so that others might be free.[5]

Autonomy–Dependency/Dependents. The autonomous self and psyche of the liberal subject, whose liberty we have just considered, also derives from and inscribes a gendered sexual division of labor. The autonomy of the liberal subject has three aspects.

First, this subject, which is expressly civil rather than familial, moves about freely in civil society. He is not encumbered by conflicting responsibilities or demands elsewhere, he does not have dependents attached to him in civil society, making claims on him, surviving directly by his hand. This dimension of autonomy refers to the absence of immediate constraints on one's entry into and movement within civil society, and it contrasts directly with women's encumbrance by familial responsibilities that limit her movement into and within civil society.

Second, the liberal subject is autonomous in the sense that he is presumed capable of providing for himself; he is not conceived as dependent on others for survival or protection. Ontologically naturalized, this dimension of autonomy is facilitated by the state in its provision of collective protection and its establishment of an individual's rights not to be infringed upon by others. This dimension of autonomy also contrasts with the condition of women when they are engaged in child raising, with a culture of naturalized and legitimate violence against women, and with the construction of women as inherently emotionally dependent or needy.

The third feature of the liberal subject's autonomy pertains to a presumed self-interest and self-orientation. The subject of liberalism drawn for us by Hobbes and Locke as well as contemporary liberals and bourgeois economists is presumed to have an identity and bearing of diffident, acquisitive self-regard. Needless to say, this figure of self-interest and self-orientation is quite at odds historically with what men have wanted women to be, with what women were allowed to be, with what families have required of women, and with what women have been socially constructed to be.

These three aspects of the autonomy of the liberal subject correspond to three ways in which that subject is gendered masculine. That subject is, first, drawn in opposition to women's activity, responsibility, character, experience, and the expectations placed upon her. Indeed, the autonomous woman – the childless, unmarried, or lesbian woman – is within liberalism a sign of disordered society or nature gone awry on the one hand, or of individual failure to 'adapt to femininity' on the other. Second, the autonomous subject of liberalism requires a large population of nonautonomous subjects, a population that generates, tends, and avows the bonds, relations, dependencies and connections that sustain and nourish human life. Indeed, as Adam Smith himself knew, and worried about at length in *The Theory of Moral Sentiments*, a world of unrelieved autonomous individuals is an unlivable world: it offers no bases for association and connection other than utilitarian or instrumental ones. As Durkheim and later Habermas added, such a culture is not simply undesirable but is, rather, impossible to the extent that it lacks an internal principle of cohesion. In Durkheim's formulation, market contracts require precontractual sensibilities and relations (truth telling and honor) for their viability; in Habermas's account, mass participation in a capitalist workforce depends on motivations induced by precapitalist social formations – religious, cultural, and familial – all of which capitalism weakens in the rationalizing course of its development. Finally, the putative autonomy of the liberal subject partakes of a myth of masculinity requiring the disavowal of dependency, the disavowal of the relations that nourish and sustain this subject. Male autonomy constituted in opposition to dependency and immediate responsibility for dependents is achieved by displacing both onto women, thus sustaining the fantasy of a creature who is self-sufficient and self-made from birth to death.

Put another way, the autonomous liberal subject is a fantastic figure, born into and existing wholly in the realm of civil society, who disavows the relations, activities, and subjects that sustain him in civil society from their sequestered place in the family. This creature is not only fantastic, however, but ultimately dependent: the 'autonomous' subject depends on the subjection of the 'dependent' ones for emotional and physical sustenance. Consequently, efforts by women to assume such autonomy are often maligned as selfish, irresponsible, or, more to the point, simply 'unfeminine'. If liberal autonomy were universalized, the supports upon which it rests would dissolve.

Insofar as it operates within these terms, liberal feminism finds itself in the position either of arguing for women's right to autonomous personhood, thereby joining men in the disavowals and repudiating the relations, dependents, and dependency for which women have been made responsible, or arguing for female 'difference', thereby reifying the effects of this economy. Neither approach challenges the gendered division between public and private that locates civic autonomy in opposition to the family, sexuality, and reproduction. Neither approach challenges the liberal antinomy between autonomy and dependence/dependents by articulating a formulation of autonomy in the context of connection or by replacing permanent hierarchies of dependence with mutual, partial, or contingent dependencies.

[. . .]

To the extent that many elements of women's subordination are tied to a division of labor that does not require all biological women to occupy the position assigned their gender, the emancipation of particular women can be 'purchased' through the subordination of substitutes. Put differently, the gendered terms of liberal discourse solicit the production of a bourgeois feminism that emancipates certain women to participate in the terms of masculinist justice without emancipating gender as such from those terms. In short, gender and class converge here, as every middle- and upper-class woman knows who has purchased her liberty, personhood, and equality through child care and 'household help' provided by women earning a fraction of their boss's wage.

Notes

1. Feminine here has no transcendent or essential referent but rather refers solely to the sexual division of labor that converts itself into a gendered ontology.
2. *The Second Sex*, trans. H. M. Patshley (New York Random House, 1952). p. 72.
3. Here, of course, familiar associations appear between nature-accessity-woman on one side and human-liberty-man on the other. What also appears is an interesting paradox of human liberty: signified by mind, actualized by body, it can be confounded by either.
4. Some will discern a convergence between my account of liberal freedom and existential formulations of freedom. And I do mean to suggest that they share masculinist, even misogynist premises – precisely those for which de Beauvoir's *Second Sex* has often been criticized Here is de Beauvior:

   > Every time transcendence falls back into immanence, stagnation, there is a degradation of existence into the '*en-soi*' – the brutish life of subjection in given conditions – and of liberty into constraint and contingence. This downfall represents a moral fault if the subject consents to it; if it is inflicted upon him, it spells frustration and oppression. In both cases it is an absolute evil. Every individual concerned to justify his existence feels that his existence involves an undefined need to transcend himself, to engage in freely chosen projects.
   >
   > Now what preculiarly signalizes the situation of woman is that she – a free and autonomous being like all human creatures – nevertheless finds herself living in a world where men compel her to assume the status of the other. They propose to stabilize her as object and to doom her to immanence since her transcendence is to be overshadowed and forever transcended by another ego [*conscience*] which is essential and sovereign (pp. xxxiii–xxxiv)

   De Beauvoir's argument does not question the terms of liberty from which woman as Other has been excluded; in particular, it does not identify the masculinism of a formulation of liberty that ontologically positions woman as its antithesis. Rather, her argument calls for woman's recognition as 'a free and autonomous being like all other human creatures' such that she can be assimilated to this formulation of liberty, a call that falters at the site of the body.
5. Recall that Hannah Arendt lamented modernity's inability to sustain what she took to be 'the Greeks' appreciation of this truism. See *The Human Condition* (Chicago: University of Chicago Press, 1958), pp. 50–73.

3

EQUALITY

Stephen de Wijze

Introduction

Kurt Vonnegut's short story 'Harrison Bergeron' begins with an account of a truly equal society.

> The year was 2081, and everybody was finally equal. They weren't only equal before God and the law. They were equal every which way. Nobody was smarter than anybody else. Nobody was better looking than anybody else. Nobody was stronger or quicker than anybody else. All this equality was due to the 211th, 212th, and 213th Amendments to the Constitution, and the unceasing vigilance of agents of the United States Handicapper General. (Vonnegut 1979: 19–25)

This equality comes at a very high price since it requires, among other things, the handicapping of all talented individuals. In order to prevent natural inequalities disturbing this egalitarian ideal of social life, the thought processes of the intelligent are disrupted while the beautiful are forced to wear hideous masks. The athletic and agile are handicapped so that they hold no physical advantage over the average person. Equality stands as the all-important dominant social value, one which takes precedence over all others. Consequently, in order to create and maintain this ideal, the state needs to prevent physical, mental, aesthetic, social and economic differences between persons by a continual and massive interference with our individual liberties and the exercise of our natural talents. Of course, Vonnegut's satire is mocking those who call for a crude notion of 'equality of outcome' and with it the required 'levelling down' to achieve this goal. But Vonnegut is also forcefully pointing out that when we try too strenuously to achieve one value, in this case equality, we end up violating other values such as 'individual liberty'. Worse still, we destroy those differences that make individual beings valuable and interesting.

There can be no doubt that the value of equality has been central to our political discourse over the last 250 years. Alongside 'liberty', 'equality' stands as one of the great and pervasive political values over which many hundreds of thousands have fought and died. A perfunctory glance at the epoch-defining political texts of modern and contemporary times demonstrates just how central the issue of equality has been. The American Declaration of Independence as far back as July 1776 begins with the now well-known claim: 'We hold these truths to be self-evident, that *all men are created equal . . .*' (emphasis added). In France thirteen years later in 1789, the Declaration of the Rights of Man and of the Citizen insists: 'Men are born and remain *free and equal in rights . . .*' (emphasis added). More recently the United Nations' Universal Declaration of Human Rights shows a deep concern with the notion of equality throughout the document, claiming that 'all human beings are born free and *equal* in dignity and rights' (emphasis added), and later makes explicit references to equality before the law, equal pay for equal work, equal access to public goods and so on. But paradoxically, despite its ubiquitous acceptance in liberal democratic states, during the last two decades equality has become the most controversial of the great social ideals. The decline of the traditional socialist parties in western Europe (despite the election of centre-left parties in many countries across Europe) has resulted in a triumph for the views of the centre-right, which advocate a freer market and less state intervention in the lives of citizens. With the fall of the Soviet Union, and the advent of the 'third way' in politics with centre-left governments such as Tony Blair's New Labour and Gerhard Schröder's Social Democrats, talk of the need for social equality is often perceived as the 'politics of envy', based on old tired notions of class warfare, or, worse still, a political view wedded to demonstrably flawed policies which have failed to improve the lives of the poor. Traditional left-wing parties now talk of 'increasing opportunities for all' rather than effecting redistribution by taxing the rich. They insist that the value of equality has not been rejected but must now be re-examined in the context of the 21st century. The goal of social equality must now be pursued in a contemporary setting of globalisation and necessary pragmatic policies that transcend old stultifying ideologies.

However, what is abundantly clear from the recent debates on the notion of equality is that, notwithstanding its central place in all serious discussions concerning justice, it remains an essentially contested concept. This is despite the fact that there is near-universal agreement that a just liberal democratic state must treat all its citizens with *equal* concern and respect.

However, there are no definitive or uncontroversial answers about the meaning and implementation of the value of equality in such a society. The debate remains very much alive and central to the work of both practising politicians and political theorists today, as it was hundreds of years ago. A great deal of the debate around the notion of equality tries to answer the question of whether a society ought to ensure that all its citizens enjoy more than equal basic political and legal rights. Serious political theorists and politicians do not contest this minimum requirement (at least not in western democratic societies) and it is seen by many as a necessary, but not sufficient, condition of real (or substantive or meaningful) equality. Real equality requires (depending on one's view of what 'equality' means) compensation for social and natural disadvantages through a significant redistribution of material goods, equal access to important institutions and, in countries where everyone is above the poverty line, the deliberate reduction of the gap between the richest and poorest members of society. When expressed as a *formal condition*, the ideal of social equality would garner near-universal agreement and it could take the following formulation:

> Equality requires that people who are *similarly* situated (in morally *relevant* respects) should be treated *similarly*.

However, once we seek to give substance to this claim, the enormous difficulties begin. Everything hinges on just how we are to understand the terms '*similarly*' and '*relevant*', and here achieving universal agreement is very difficult to obtain, and some would argue, well-nigh impossible.

For someone trying to understand and form an educated judgement on the centrality and importance of equality in political discourse as political rhetoric, or in historic documents, or in the endless philosophical discussions, this task requires clarity on three important general questions. They are:

1. Why is the notion of equality important to us?
2. What exactly does it mean to be equal in a political/social context and how do we measure this equality *vis-à-vis* others in society?
3. Does the value of equality necessarily take precedence over other important political and social values such as, for example, liberty and efficiency, and is it applicable across all the spheres or dimension of human existence?

If we can make some headway in finding answers to these questions, we will have gone a long way in making sense of an important and pervasive, yet extremely slippery, notion. The remainder of this essay examines each of these questions in turn.

WHY IS EQUALITY IMPORTANT TO US?

Since it is uncontroversial that in the early 21st century the value of equality matters to us a great deal in the political/social context, the urgent question that needs answering is why. The answers to this question help in preparing the analysis of other related concerns, such as what exactly we mean by equality and how it stands in relation to other important values. Our deep concern with equality in western democracies is often traced to a Judaeo-Christian religious heritage which views all human beings as equal in the eyes of God. Political theorists have developed this idea, and the values it promotes, in various ways and their contemporary articulation takes a secular form. It is not possible to pursue the very many strands of argument offered to demonstrate the importance of equality, but I intend to briefly examine two main groups, each of which follows a general motif under which a variety of arguments of a similar type are made. The first concerns arguments that seek to show that the value of equality arises from certain facts about human beings, while the second group derives the importance of equality from our beliefs, or strong intuitions, concerning the necessary and minimal conditions required for any conception of justice and fairness in a political community. What is striking about both these general groups of argument is that they fail to make a watertight case for why equality ought to be the central and pre-eminent value in the way we organise our social and political lives.

The arguments from 'common humanity'

This group of arguments supports the conclusion that all persons ought to be treated equally given the incontestable facts about common or shared human characteristics (material and/or spiritual). The argument form is as follows: X Y Z . . . all share common characteristics/capacities/attributes A B C . . . therefore X, Y and Z ought to be treated equally. When theorists talk of our 'common humanity' they variously evoke, either individually or collectively, a number of different characteristics such as our common spiritual needs, or our ability to speak a language, or our capacity to develop and use tools, or our embeddedness in a society and culture, or our clear and obvious vulnerability to the great evils of illness, pain, death, homelessness and starvation. Some theorists take a slightly different path by insisting that equality matters because all human beings uniquely share certain moral capacities and attributes. These capacities must not be understood as simply contingent abilities such as intelligence or bravery or resoluteness (which human beings clearly do not share equally) but rather moral capacities which make all human beings, to use Immanuel Kant's terminology, 'ends in themselves': free and rational wills with interests who are able to develop a conception of justice and a conception of the good life. These claims about our 'common humanity' stand as justification for the conclusion that the value of equality ought to be central to social and political issues.

However, this form of argument suffers from at least one fatal flaw. It commits what is commonly known as the 'naturalistic fallacy' by deriving an evaluative conclusion (people *ought* to be treated equally) from factual premises (people share certain non-moral characteristics). We might indeed all concur that persons share a common humanity, that they share certain essential characteristics and capacities, and need protection from the calamitous natural events and the terrible actions of fellow humans, without agreeing that this stands as a justification for the moral requirement of social equality. We could agree with the facts but then legitimately ask: why does this mean that we need to be treated or that we should distribute social and economic goods equally? There always remains a logical gap between the facts of human existence and human capacities and the set of values we ought to adopt concerning the just and moral treatment of human beings. To logically arrive at the conclusion that all persons *ought* to be treated equally we would need to begin with a normative claim already present within the premises of such an argument, a premise that states something of this kind: 'If persons all share common capacities/characteristics etc. then they *ought* to be treated equally.' However to slip in a premise of this sort is to stipulate that very conclusion which we are seeking to discover by examining the facts of our common humanity. In short, we commit the fallacy of *petitio principii* (or 'begging the question'), where we assume that very conclusion which we have set out to justify or prove.

The argument from impartiality

A second form of argument for equality arises from a concept that is very widely (perhaps universally) considered to be central to any conception of justice and fairness, namely that of impartiality. The requirement of impartiality arises from our ability as moral beings to abstract from personal circumstances and interests to appreciate that, from the point of view of justice and fairness, all persons are of equal importance and moral worth. Placing impartiality as central to any conception of justice *ipso facto* imports egalitarian considerations which some would argue encompass social welfare distribution among other things. Why is this the case? The reason lies in the implicit concern for equality encapsulated by the notion of impartiality. To act impartially requires that we treat all persons alike, as not favouring one over the other unless there is a good reason to do so. In short, impartiality requires us to treat all persons as equally worthy of our concern and respect. However, to do this implies a need to treat all people equally where possible, and importantly, it places the onus on those advocating inequality to show why such departures are justified. If we accept that people are similar in their basic needs and desires, and that in general rational people will satisfy their important needs before their less important ones, then by invoking the principle of diminishing marginal utility (DMU),[1] we can conclude that a bundle of resources will benefit a poor person to a far greater extent than it would a rich person. The corollary is also true. By taking resources from the rich, there is a far less adverse effect on them than if the same resources were taken from the poor. Consequently, from an impartial perspective, if everyone is to be given the maximum benefits compatible with like benefits for all, the DMU dictates that a redistribution of material wealth must continue until we achieve a society where the distribution of goods has achieved a maximum aggregate utility. And this kind of society is necessarily an egalitarian one.

Unfortunately, this argument is deeply flawed despite its initial plausibility. It relies on problematic presuppositions such as the claim that the utility functions of all persons are the same and that they all derive the same (or similar) utility from their goods. However, the most worrying aspect of the argument is that the DMU is assumed to be an appropriate way of distributing all goods irrespective of what they are. However, this is clearly not so with a generic instrument of exchange such as money. The almost limitless versatility of money makes it quite possible that it does not follow the same marginal decline in utility as, for example, beer consumption. More money may mean greater opportunities and with this greater enjoyment and utility.

Given the problems with the previous arguments, perhaps the defence of equality is best done by simply insisting that it is a strong conviction that feels or seems *intuitively* right and just. When we are faced with large inequalities in wealth, our deeply held moral instincts tell us that this state of affairs is self-evidently wrong *in itself* and no further explanation is possible or required. When we examine our intuitions, we find it morally objectionable that some people enjoy, for no good reason, a greater share of economic benefits than others. These intuitions are not mere prejudices but reflect an important, deeply held belief about the nature of society and the importance of each and every individual member. Yet this approach won't do either. Even strong and heartfelt intuitions that inequality is morally offensive are indeed often based on ignorance, misconceptions or sheer bias. And what are we to say to those who hold equally strong and heartfelt convictions that inequalities are not wrong? Are they simply mistaken? And if so, how could we prove this? To answer these questions would require a justification for the value of equality that does not rely on an intuition-based argument. What is more, it may be that we are misinterpreting our intuitions so that what is really troubling about differences in levels of wealth is not the mere fact that some have more than others, but that some people do not have *enough* to live a decent life. If this is the correct interpretation of the intuition, then what we should be aiming to provide is a sufficiency rather than equality of resources for all.

EQUALITY OF OPPORTUNITY

As Vonnegut's satirical vignette makes clear, the ideal of equality of outcome is utopian. Given that people have differing talents, circumstances, characters and interests, it seems that seeking to ensure that we all conform to a mean or average requires unacceptable interference that clashes with other cherished values such as liberty or efficiency. So if it is impossible (not to mention undesirable) to obtain a society where there is equality of outcome, what notion of equality ought we to properly pursue? In western democratic societies, the form of equality that is widely sought and strongly defended is that of equality of opportunity. As we shall see, in the end this form of equality may not be achievable either but it certainly remains the politically dominant notion held out as the desirable and achievable form of equality, and indeed the foundation for justice in liberal democratic societies. In the standard political usage, equality of opportunity requires that all persons in a society have an equal chance or prospect of securing the important social and political goods in the society, goods which although limited are very widely desired. Individuals need these goods so that they will be able to pursue their own view of the good life within the constraints of a just society. Typically we think that at the very least, all persons must have an equal opportunity to avail themselves of educational and political goods, and that the social positions of prestige, authority and great financial reward should be open to everyone without prejudice. Equal opportunity does not imply that we will all achieve the same level of social, economic or political affluence. The differences among individuals in the final distribution of goods depend on how *individual talent* and *hard work* are used to make the most of the opportunities available.

However, it is this last claim about the importance of individual talent and hard work which immediately raises many intractable problems for the notion of 'equality of opportunity'. The reason is that theorists hold different views on whether our talents are a matter of luck (and so irrelevant from a moral point of view), or an essential property of our personal identity and hence not the proper subject of distributive justice. Furthermore, some theorists insist that if the government removes all *formal* (that is legal) barriers to compete for social, political and educational goods, then that is all that is required (indeed all that is possible) to ensure equality of opportunity. This approach ensures that the society will enable individuals to overcome, for example, the blatant deleterious effects of racism, sexism, ageism and so on. Yet this position, often described as 'formal equality of opportunity' (or 'careers open to talents') is strongly denounced by many egalitarians as unfair and inadequate to its task as it places unjust burdens on the disadvantaged in society, whose social and economic backgrounds make competition with the more fortunate very difficult indeed. It also fails to acknowledge and combat some of the subtle effects of prejudice in society since it assumes that simply removing legal barriers will suffice to remove discrimination. The analogy evoked is one that compares formal equality of opportunity to a marathon race that allows everyone to enter but does nothing to ensure that everyone starts at the same place. Some fortunate individuals begin the race well ahead of their rivals and hence gain an unfair advantage, and with it a disproportionate share of the prizes to be won. This inequality is perpetuated through the generations, where the rich and/or politically and socially connected are able to provide opportunities to their children, which further undermines the goal of achieving real equality in the society.

So if formal equality of opportunity fails to achieve equality, what ought we to strive for in its place? One answer is to try to take into account and compensate for those factors which are arbitrary from a moral point of view, yet have a profound effect on how people lead their lives and achieve their goals and vision of the good life. In short, we must aim to achieve a 'real (sometimes referred to as 'substantive' or 'fair') equality of opportunity'. The idea can be expressed simply as follows. Real equality of opportunity seeks to mitigate *arbitrary* differences between individuals resulting from accidents of birth, bad luck or any other natural and social contingencies. Roughly speaking, the aim is to ensure that all individuals with similar abilities should have similar life chances. To this end, society needs to ensure that all individuals receive adequate social and economic resources to be able to compete fairly with others. Social class, financial resources, political affiliations, family background ought not to affect their ability to enter and make full use of the society's social and political institutions. Again, this position is quite different from the rejected equality of outcome vision that we dismissed as impossible and undesirable. The final distribution of goods and resources in the society will differ from individual to individual but this difference will be the result of hard work or talent (as it is with the formal equality of opportunity position) after having removed unfair advantages by levelling the playing field. To continue the analogy of the marathon race, real equality of opportunity will strive to ensure that all individuals begin the race from the same starting line and none of the participants will be unfairly burdened or handicapped by a lack of the appropriate running equipment or diet and so on.

However, as attractive as this position initially seems, critics raise some difficult questions which illustrate instabilities that threaten to seriously undermine this view. Why, for example, shouldn't we view raw intelligence as arbitrary from a moral point of view? No one chooses to be clever or gifted or talented, just as no one chooses to be born white or female or into an impoverished family. These natural attributes greatly affect whether or not we will be successful in pursuing our goals and vision of the good life. If I wish to become an expert in pure mathematics, this goal is impossible unless I have a talent for manipulating abstract ideas. Similarly, if I am born with a genetic coding that limits my height to no more than 5 feet 2 inches, then I am very unlikely to succeed as a professional basketball player. In a world where my competitors will be well over six feet tall, my being so short will effectively prevent me from achieving greatness in this sport. The point to stress here is that natural talents are no less (in fact arguably more) important for success than, say, wealth and social connections. And if this is indeed the case, then the doctrine of real equality of opportunity needs to acknowledge that since the lack of natural talents is also arbitrary from a moral point of view, then justice requires some form of government compensation. Those less talented individuals need assistance or, alternatively, the state could level down and penalise those who are talented to remove unfair advantage. But the former position seems impossible (can a government compensate for, say, lack of intelligence, or lack of curiosity?) while the latter attempt to level down is deeply undesirable (think of Vonnegut's vignette). The problem goes even further than the above suggests. Those who advocate real equality of opportunity seek to make sure that only hard work and talent ought to make the difference to how the distribution of social and economic goods eventually pans out. Yet if our talents are a matter of luck, then why not insist that our motivations (say to work hard, put up with hardships and so on) are also largely a factor of luck? If I just happen to have the right kind of temperament that enables long periods of concentration allied to a deep natural curiosity, this would give me an enormous advantage over those who lack similar attributes. Does real equality of opportunity require that these differences also be compensated? If the answer is yes, then we no longer have a clear notion of what makes someone an individual who is unique and deserving of praise or censure. We seem to have slid unwittingly into a position which we initially rejected; namely, a position which in effect espouses the view that the only fair outcome in society is an equality of outcome. However if the answer is no, then advocates of real equality of opportunity must explain why natural talents and attributes are exempt from compensation, given their enormous effect and the fact that their possession is a matter of luck.

EQUALITY OF WHAT?

For those who champion real equality of opportunity, a further important question needs attention. Given that equality is a core value and involves more than just ensuring that everyone has the same formal rights, it is necessary to be clear on what exactly constitutes the currency of egalitarian justice. To put it another way, are those who advocate real equality of opportunity clear about what the government ought to measure and provide to citizens so that they are in a position to compete fairly with others in the society? In virtue of what, then, ought people to be equal in order to have real equality of opportunity?

There have been two main schools of thought on how to respond to this question. Although there are differences within each school (and some theorists who wish to combine the two in some way), they have been variously labelled as the welfarists and the resourcists. The former approach argues that in deciding on how to measure the well-being of a person (and by implication the amount of goods that will be needed to ensure equality of opportunity), it is necessary to focus on individual subjective preferences. To put it rather crudely, we are well off when our preferences are, by and large, satisfied and badly off if they are frustrated or thwarted. Welfarists can come in many stripes, from those who are essentially concerned with a person's subjective experiences such as happiness or pain (conscious-state theorists) while others focus on welfare as a matter of preference satisfaction (success theorists).[2] Utilitarian Egalitarianism, for example, is a welfarist approach, with its stress on redistributing goods in terms of the principle of diminishing marginal utility to maximise the utility of goods within the population. The resourcists, on the other hand, seek to offer a list of socio-economic goods, which individuals would have at their disposal and be able to use as they see fit. Whatever level of satisfaction each person finally obtains from these resources is neither here nor there in deciding on the issue of equality of opportunity, provided everyone began with, or had access to, the same list of things. Perhaps the best-known resourcist position is represented by the work of John Rawls with his list of 'social primary goods'.

Unfortunately both the welfarists and the resourcists face serious problems. Let us examine the welfarists' claims first to see why this is the case. Recall that welfarists look to individual subjective preference satisfaction as the indicator of well-being. However, to adopt this method immediately gives rise to an extremely difficult problem and it is not clear if welfarists have any persuasive response. Given that for the welfarist well-being is measured by preference satisfaction, then they face the intractable problem of how to contend with two categories of persons; namely, those with expensive tastes and those with physical or mental handicaps. We have strong intuitions about what fairness demands in each of these cases, yet the welfarists are at a loss to offer any justification for these views. Why, for example, should society provide extra resources to those who have expensive tastes when others can achieve the same preference satisfaction with far fewer and more modest amounts of resources? Welfarists need a reason to deny compensating expensive tastes yet there doesn't seem to be one if preference satisfaction is indeed what is central to knowing whether real equality of opportunity is possible. My need for copious amounts of caviar and champagne will require satisfaction just like your more moderate need for beer and sandwiches, because what is important here is the satisfaction of my preferences, not their justification.[3] The opposite intuition about compensating the handicapped poses a slightly different problem for welfarists. Although the proffering of more resources for those with handicaps seems eminently right and proper (and it can be justified by seeking to ensure parity of preference satisfaction for those with disabilities), the problem arises in cases where the handicaps are so severe that it is either impossible to deliver the level of resources needed or the level required is so high that it severely depletes the resources available for others. Here we face the problem of not having sufficient resources to achieve equal preference satisfaction and with it real equality of opportunity.

Perhaps the resourcist position offers a better alternative for cashing out the currency of egalitarian justice. They reject preference satisfaction for lists of goods which individuals would need in order to pursue whatever they decide would be the good life. Rawls for example offers a loosely linked list of 'social primary goods', those things or resources 'that every rational man is presumed to want' (Rawls 1971: 62). While natural primary goods include health, intelligence and vigour (attributes which we obtain very largely as a matter of luck), the social primary goods (those things which are communally created and society is able to distribute) are self-respect, opportunities, income/wealth and liberty.[4] These social primary goods are linked in that you cannot enjoy the benefits of one without a substantial amount of the others. An individual's amount of the social primary goods offers a standard of relative advantage in the society. The more primary goods I possess, the better I am able to achieve my particular vision of human excellence and a worthwhile life. Of course we need not adopt Rawls's list (or we could adapt it)[5] but the essential resourcist move is to move away from measuring preference satisfaction to examining basic resources needed by human beings if they are to thrive in the society.

However, despite overcoming the problems faced by welfarists, resourcists face some problems of their own which cast doubt on the efficacy of this approach. Firstly, it is not clear how we decide on what constitutes the appropriate bundle of resources. Rawls's list, for example, does not include important social goods such as guaranteed leisure time or having a sense of, and affiliation to, a community.[6] This may result in a bias against some conceptions of human excellence and consequently his list of social primary goods faces the charge of being inappropriate or unfair as a basis for redistributive justice. In short, any list, unless extraordinarily and unrealistically broad, would face the charge of unfairness towards some views of the good life. Secondly, even if a list could be universally agreed upon, any capability-based assessment of a person's position in society fails to account for the fact that people use goods differently. Simply having a bundle of resources does not mean that I have the requisite abilities to change the resources into welfare. A disabled person would not be able to convert resources into welfare as efficiently as an able-bodied person. Consequently, the resourcist position does not provide the basis for all individuals in the society to enjoy real equality of opportunity.[7]

COMPLEX EQUALITY

The discussion so far has highlighted many of the problems associated with defining, justifying and measuring equality. Central to this debate has been the implicit assumption that to ensure equality it is necessary to identify the dominant social good (or set of goods) to be redistributed among the population in order to achieve this aim. Michael Walzer identifies this assumption with attempts to establish a 'regime of simple equality' and he argues that it is a deeply flawed presupposition, due to its simplistic understanding of what equality consists in. If we accept the simple equality view then we face the insoluble problem of how to maintain equality in the society once people begin to use their goods and talents to achieve their disparate goals. What is more, a simple equality account inevitably runs up against the problem of how to incorporate other cherished social values, especially when the imposition of equality serves to seriously undermine them. For example, too much equality has a deleterious effect on individual liberty and vice versa. Vonnegut's concern with what is required in order to achieve an equality of outcome, and the difficulties with the doctrine of real equality of opportunity, largely arise from the attempt to make equality the overriding social value so that it becomes necessary to try and compensate for many of our attributes and talents, which are simply a matter of good or bad luck.

Walzer insists that equality is possible but it needs to be a complex notion which takes into account the different spheres or domains of people's lives. According to Walzer, 'equality is a complex relation of persons, mediated by the goods we make, share, and divide among ourselves; *it is not an identity of possessions*. It requires then, a diversity of distributive criteria that mirrors the diversity of social goods' (Walzer 1997: 495; emphasis added). The *normative or moral core* of his theory of complex equality contains two main features. Firstly, all distributable social goods are divided into distinct spheres governed by their own unique distributive principles. These principles determine the allowable inequalities in each sphere and no attempt is made to apply the specific principle across the different spheres. Secondly, any inequalities in one sphere *ought never* to intrude into, and dominate, distribution in other spheres (at least not in societies that differentiate these spheres). This approach is radically different from advocating any simple single egalitarian formula such as those we have been searching for in the previous sections. Any one social good, say money or financial wealth, ought not to dominate other spheres, such as that of education, since to do so constitutes a form of tyranny. The sphere of education, for example, may distribute educational goods in terms of ability and diligence, and if the use of wealth distorts this distributional understanding then the money is being used illegitimately and this ought to be stopped.

But how do we know what these distributional principles are for each specific sphere such as wealth, education, politics and so on? Walzer argues that since all distributable goods are *social* goods, we need to examine the particular relationships and understandings that those who make, distribute and consume the goods have developed in their co-operative social behaviour over time. These relationships will develop from the particular understandings of the value of such goods in that particular society and in the relevant social sphere. Consequently, there is no set of primary or basic goods that apply across all conceivable moral and material worlds. The meaning of goods, how they are appropriately distributed, needs to be understood against the relevant background of what it means to those who make them and those who want them. For example, depending on what it is being used for, a common item such as bread can be seen as merely a mundane everyday form of food or as a highly symbolic religious symbol or medium of exchange. These social meanings are historical in character and within a particular distributive sphere provide a certain set of criteria and arrangements for their just and proper distribution. When these distributional criteria are violated or one social good is used inappropriately in another sphere, then the result is tyranny. Wealth, for example, cannot be used legitimately to buy other human beings, or to buy love and friendship or divine grace or educational honours and so on. These are, in Walzer's term, 'blocked exchanges'. The differences in spheres within society and the principles governing them are the proper subject of sociology or anthropology. Political philosophy has nothing to contribute at this level. The key philosophical insight to take away from an understanding of complex equality is that this notion is complex and distribution of social goods properly varies in different spheres. Complex equality 'establishes a set of relationships such that domination is impossible' (Walzer 1997: 496). Although there will certainly be unequal distribution within spheres, the advantage such inequalities might give across the spheres is prevented. Given that individuals hold different ideals, goals, talents and aspirations, a complex equality results and this prevents the dominance of some citizens by others due to their possession of a substantial amount of one particular social good.

Attractive as Walzer's account of complex equality may appear, it faces some difficult issues. Firstly, it seems that although a great deal depends on a unified social meaning for the important social goods within the spheres, it is not clear how to arrive at such common meanings. The interpretation of the relevant commitments and understandings already embedded in shared social meanings might be highly controversial, especially in a complex multicultural society such as Britain or the USA. Consequently, it is not at all clear how any such disagreement would be resolved. Secondly, even if a shared meaning of the distributive principles were to be agreed upon, there is still the issue of their authenticity and legitimacy. A particular culture or society may merely reflect a history of class struggle and domination by a ruling class or external culture. Social meanings may for historical purposes have ignored a particular gender, or certain religious group, or race, or those with different sexual orientation and so on. And whatever the principles used in each sphere, how can we be certain that all (or even that the vast majority) consent to them? In short, Walzer's relativistic approach faces the problems common to all such accounts, namely, the lack of an independent universal standard against which to judge the claims made by groups concerning the appropriateness of certain principles. The idea of complex equality, then, rests on an unsupportable presupposition that social meanings are clear and evident to all members of the society.

CONCLUSION

Our attempt to understand the important and widely held value of political equality has come full circle. We began by seeking to understand why this political value has been so important to us over the last few hundred years and still continues to dominate political thinking among theoreticians and practitioners today. This search did not result in a definitive answer. We then examined the notion of 'equality of opportunity' since it is the dominant view of what we ought to be striving for in liberal democratic societies, and found that there remains a deep disagreement over whether to strive for a 'formal' or 'real' formulation. What is more, if we opt for real equality of opportunity, then we need to be clear about what constitutes the currency of egalitarian justice. In short, we need to answer the 'equality of what' question. Finally, we examined Walzer's account of 'complex equality', which rejected the presupposition that there ought to be an egalitarian distribution of one dominant social good in society. Although his account has initial plausibility, it also suffers from some serious problems. All in all, then, although most politicians and political theorists remain strongly committed to the value of political equality, our understanding and justification of this notion remains worryingly unsatisfactory. Along with liberty and other important political values, it seems destined to remain an essentially contested concept provoking an endless debate over what the notion involves in terms of redistribution and its place *vis-à-vis* other cherished social values. Perhaps Isaiah Berlin was right to insist that political values remain irreducibly plural given the complexity of human society, human aspirations and the very wide diversity of conceptions of the good life. As he succinctly puts it:

> Equality may demand the restraint of the liberty of those who wish to dominate; liberty – without some modicum of which there is no choice and therefore no possibility of remaining human as we understand the word – may have to be curtailed in order to make room for social welfare . . . , to allow justice and fairness to be exercised. (Berlin 1990: 12)

So it seems that perhaps the best we will be able to achieve, the best we can hope for, is a pragmatic balancing of different important values, of which equality undoubtedly remains one of the most cherished and controversial.[8]

QUESTIONS FOR DISCUSSION

- Is equality a core notion for any conception of justice?
- Is real equality of opportunity possible for all?
- Does an increase in liberty reduce equality (and vice versa), or can both of these political values happily co-exist in a just society?
- Does the notion of equality for all persons raise problems for a communitarian view that gives priority to the community over the individual?

NOTES

1. The principle of diminishing marginal utility (DMU) states that for the consumer of goods or services, the marginal utility or value to the consumer of that good or service decreases as the amount of consumption of the good increases, all things being equal. In other words, total utility increases more and more slowly as the quantity consumed increases.
2. Problems can arise if we distinguish between 'relative' (achieving particular goals) and 'overall' (achieving life goals) success. It might be necessary to compensate those who reach difficult particular goals at the cost of achieving overall success and vice versa.
3. This point isn't resolved by claiming that tastes are voluntary and hence do not apply since Welfarist theory does not make this distinction nor can it. Our tastes are a combination of enculturation, genetics and luck.
4. Rawls maintains that these 'social primary goods' are loosely indexed and that the most important social primary good is self-respect. See Rawls (1971: 90–5).
5. Rawls's index of social primary goods could be substituted, for example, by Ronald Dworkin's auction option. To ensure a fair initial distribution of goods in society Dworkin argues for equality of resources. Equal division is achieved by means of an imaginary *auction*. The allocation of resources must pass the *envy test*. 'No division of resources is an equal division if, once the division is complete, any immigrant would prefer someone else's bundle of resources to his own bundle.' This procedure also prevents the arbitrariness of a unilateral division since every person constructs and bids for their own bundle. Dworkin distinguishes between *brute* and *option* luck and proposes an idea of insurance to compensate for the former.
6. Rawls does add leisure time to his list of primary goods in his later work. See Rawls (2001: 179).
7. While Rawls and Dworkin adopt Resourcist positions, some theorists seek to combine the insights of both the welfarists and the resourcists. Amartya Sen, for example, argues for equal capabilities, which is essentially the ability to change resources into welfare. Gerry Cohen argues for 'equal access to advantage', roughly similar to Sen's position in that it seeks to ensure that individuals have an equal ability to transform resources into welfare. See Cohen (1989a). Cohen argues that Dworkin's equality-of-resources approach fails to live up to its egalitarianism by neutralising the effects of brute luck. He further argues that Dworkin should be concerned with disadvantages whatever their form and so should advocate an 'equal access to advantage' approach, where 'advantage' is understood to include access to welfare and resources. See also Sen (1997).
8. I am indebted to Jeremy Barris and Colin Farrelly for comments on an earlier draft.

KURT VONNEGUT
'HARRISON BERGERON'

The year was 2081, and everybody was finally equal. They weren't only equal before God and the law. They were equal every which way. Nobody was smarter than anybody else. Nobody was better looking than anybody else. Nobody was stronger or quicker than anybody else. All this equality was due to the 211th, 212th, and 213th Amendments to the Constitution, and the unceasing vigilance of agents of the United States Handicapper General.

Some things about living still weren't quite right, though. April, for instance, still drove people crazy by not being spring-time. And it was in that clammy month that the H-G men took George and Hazel Bergeron's fourteen-year-old son, Harrison, away.

It was tragic, all right, but George and Hazel couldn't think about it very hard. Hazel had a perfectly average intelligence, which meant she couldn't think about anything except in short bursts. And George, while his intelligence was way above normal, had a little mental handicap radio in his ear. He was required by law to wear it at all times. It was tuned to a government transmitter. Every twenty seconds or so, the transmitter would send out some sharp noise to keep people like George from taking unfair advantage of their brains.

George and Hazel were watching television. There were tears on Hazel's cheeks, but she'd forgotten for the moment what they were about.

Kurt Vonnegut (1979), 'Harrison Bergeron', *Welcome to the Monkey House*, St Albans: Triad/Granada.

On the television screen were ballerinas.

A buzzer sounded in George's head. His thoughts fled in panic, like bandits from a burglar-alarm.

'That was a real pretty dance, that dance they just did', said Hazel.

'Huh?' said George.

'That dance – it was nice', said Hazel.

'Yup', said George. He tried to think a little about the ballerinas. They weren't really very good – no better than anybody else would have been, anyway. They were burdened with sashweights and bags of birdshot, and their faces were masked, so that no one, seeing a free and graceful gesture or a pretty face, would feel like something the cat dragged in. George was toying with the vague notion that maybe dancers shouldn't be handicapped. But he didn't get very far with it before another noise in his ear radio scattered his thoughts.

George winced. So did two out of the eight ballerinas.

Hazel saw him wince. Having no mental handicap herself, she had to ask George what the latest sound had been.

'Sounded like somebody hitting a milk bottle with a ball peen hammer', said George.

'I'd think it would be real interesting, hearing all the different sounds', said Hazel, a little envious. 'All the things they think up'.

'Um', said George.

'Only, if I was Handicapper General, you know what I would do?' said Hazel. Hazel, as a matter of fact, bore a strong resemblance to the Handicapper General, a woman named Diana Moon Glampers. 'If I was Diana Moon Glampers', said Hazel, 'I'd have chimes on Sunday – just chimes. Kind of in honor of religion'.

'I could think, if it was just chimes', said George.

'Well – maybe make 'em real loud', said Hazel. 'I think I'd make a good Handicapper General'.

'Good as anybody else', said George.

'Who knows better'n I do what normal is?' said Hazel.

'Right', said George. He began to think glimmeringly about his abnormal son who was now in jail, about Harrison, but a twenty-one-gun salute in his head stopped that.

'Boy', said Hazel, 'that was a doozy, wasn't it?'

It was such a doozy that George was white and trembling, and tears stood on the rims of his red eyes. Two of the eight ballerinas had collapsed to the studio floor, were holding their temples.

'All of a sudden you look so tired', said Hazel. 'Why don't you stretch out on the sofa, so's you can rest your handicap bag on the pillows, honeybunch'. She was referring to the forty-seven pounds of birdshot in a canvas bag, which was padlocked around George's neck. 'Go on and rest the bag for a little while', she said. 'I don't care if you're not equal to me for a while'.

George weighed the bag with his hands. 'I don't mind it', he said. 'I don't notice it any more. It's just a part of me'.

'You been so tired lately – kind of wore out', said Hazel. 'If there was just some way we could make a little hole in the bottom of the bag, and just take out a few of them lead balls. Just a few'.

'Two years in prison and two thousand dollars fine for every ball I took out', said George. 'I don't call that a bargain'.

'If you could just take a few out when you come home from work', said Hazel. 'I mean – you don't compete with anybody around here. You just sit around'.

'If I tried to get away with it', said George, 'then other people'd get away with it – and pretty soon we'd be right back to the dark ages again, with everybody competing against everybody else. You wouldn't like that, would you?'

'I'd hate it', said Hazel.

'There you are', said George. 'The minute people start cheating on laws, what do you think happens to society?'

If Hazel hadn't been able to come up with an answer to this question, George couldn't have supplied one. A siren was going off in his head.

'Reckon it'd fall all apart', said Hazel.

'What would?' said George blankly.

'Society', said Hazel uncertainly. 'Wasn't that what you just said?'

'Who knows?' said George.

The television program was suddenly interrupted for a news bulletin. It wasn't clear at first as to what the bulletin was about, since the announcer, like all announcers, had a serious speech impediment. For about half a minute, and in a state of high excitement, the announcer tried to say, 'Ladies and gentlemen——'

He finally gave up, handed the bulletin to a ballerina to read.

'Thats all right——' Hazel said of the announcer, 'he tried. That's the big thing. He tried to do the best he could with what God gave him. He should get a nice raise for trying so hard'.

'Ladies and gentlemen——' said the ballerina, reading the bulletin. She must have been extraordinarily beautiful, because the mask she wore was hideous. And it was easy to see that she was the strongest and most graceful of all the dancers, for her handicap bags were as big as those worn by two-hundred-pound men.

And she had to apologize at once for her voice, which was a very unfair voice for a woman to use. Her voice was a warm, luminous, timeless melody. 'Excuse me——' she said, and she began again, making her voice absolutely uncompetitive.

'Harrison Bergeron, age fourteen', she said in a grackle squawk, 'has just escaped from jail, where he was held on suspicion of plotting to overthrow the government. He is a genius and an athlete, is under-handicapped, and should be regarded as extremely dangerous'.

A police photograph of Harrison Bergeron was flashed on the screen – upside down, then sideways, upside down again, then right side up. The picture showed the full length of Harrison against a background calibrated in feet and inches. He was exactly seven feet tall.

The rest of Harrison's appearance was Halloween and hardware. Nobody had ever borne heavier handicaps. He had outgrown hindrances faster than the H-G men could think them up. Instead of a little ear radio for a mental handicap, he wore a tremendous pair of earphones, and spectacles with thick wavy lenses. The spectacles were intended to make him not only half blind, but to give him whanging headaches besides.

Scrap metal was hung all over him. Ordinarily, there was a certain symmetry, a military neatness to the handicaps issued to strong people, but Harrison looked like a walking junkyard. In the race of life, Harrison carried three hundred pounds.

And to offset his good looks, the H-G men required that he wear at all times a red rubber ball for a nose, keep his eyebrows shaved off, and cover his even white teeth with black caps at snaggle-tooth random.

'If you see this boy', said the ballerina, 'do not – I repeat, do not – try to reason with him'.

There was the shriek of a door being torn from its hinges.

Screams and barking cries of consternation came from the television set. The photograph of Harrison Bergeron on the screen jumped again and again, as though dancing to the tune of an earthquake.

George Bergeron correctly identified the earthquake, and well he might have – for many was the time his own home had danced to the same crashing tune. 'My God——' said George, 'that must be Harrison!

The realization was blasted from his mind instantly by the sound of an automobile collision in his head.

When George could open his eyes again, the photograph of Harrison was gone. A living, breathing Harrison filled the screen.

Clanking, clownish, and huge, Harrison stood in the center of the studio. The knob of the uprooted studio door was still in his hand. Ballerinas, technicians, musicians, and announcers cowered on their knees before him, expecting to die.

'I am the Emperor!' cried Harrison. 'Do you hear? I am the Emperor! Everybody must do what I say at once!' He stamped his foot and the studio shook.

'Even as I stand here——' he bellowed, 'crippled, hobbled, sickened – I am a greater ruler than any man who ever lived! Now watch me become what I *can* become !'

Harrison tore the straps of his handicap harness like wet tissue paper, tore straps guaranteed to support five thousand pounds.

Harrison's scrap-iron handicaps crashed to the floor.

Harrison thrust his thumbs under the bar of the padlock that secured his head harness. The bar snapped like celery. Harrison smashed his headphones and spectacles against the wall.

He flung away his rubber-ball nose, revealed a man that would have awed Thor, the god of thunder.

'I shall now select my Empress!' he said, looking down on the cowering people. 'Let the first woman who dares rise to her feet claim her mate and her throne!'

A moment passed, and then a ballerina arose, swaying like a willow.

Harrison plucked the mental handicap from her ear, snapped off her physical handicaps with marvellous delicacy. Last of all, he removed her mask.

She was blindingly beautiful.

'Now——' said Harrison, taking her hand, 'shall we show the people the meaning of the word dance? Music!' he commanded.

The musicians scrambled back into their chairs, and Harrison stripped them of their handicaps, too. 'Play your best', he told them, 'and I'll make you barons and dukes and earls'.

The music began. It was normal at first – cheap, silly, false. But Harrison snatched two musicians from their chairs, waved them like batons as he sang the music as he wanted it played. He slammed them back into their chairs.

The music began again and was much improved.

Harrison and his Empress merely listened to the music for a while – listened gravely, as though synchronizing their heart-beats with it.

They shifted their weights to their toes.

Harrison placed his big hands on the girl's tiny waist, letting her sense the weightlessness that would soon be hers.

And then, in an explosion of joy and grace, into the air they sprang!

Not only were the laws of the land abandoned, but the law of gravity and the laws of motion as well.

They reeled, whirled, swiveled, flounced, capered, gamboled, and spun.

They leaped like deer on the moon.

The studio ceiling was thirty feet high, but each leap brought the dancers nearer to it.

It became their obvious intention to kiss the ceiling.

They kissed it.

And then, neutralizing gravity with love and pure will, they remained suspended in air inches below the ceiling, and they kissed each other for a long, long time.

It was then that Diana Moon Glampers, the Handicapper General, came into the studio with a double-barreled ten-gauge shotgun. She fired twice, and the Emperor and the Empress were dead before they hit the floor.

Diana Moon Glampers loaded the gun again. She aimed it at the musicians and told them they had ten seconds to get their handicaps back on.

It was then that the Bergerons' television tube burned out.

Hazel turned to comment about the blackout to George. But George had gone out into the kitchen for a can of beer.

George came back in with the beer, paused while a handicap signal shook him up. And then he sat down again. 'You been crying?' he said to Hazel.

'Yup', she said.

'What about?' he said.

'I forget', she said. 'Something real sad on television'.

'What was it?' he said.

'It's all kind of mixed up in my mind', said Hazel.

'Forget sad things', said George.

'I always do', said Hazel.

'That's my girl', said George. He winced. There was the sound of a rivetting gun in his head.

'Gee – I could tell that one was a doozy', said Hazel.

'You can say that again', said George.

'Gee——' said Hazel, 'I could tell that one was a doozy'.

JOHN H. SCHAAR
EXTRACTS FROM 'EQUALITY OF OPPORTUNITY, AND BEYOND'

I

Equality is a protean word. It is one of those political symbols – liberty and fraternity are others – into which men have poured the deepest urgings of their hearts. Every strongly held theory or conception of equality is at once a psychology, an ethic, a theory of social relations, and a vision of the good society.

Of the many conceptions of equality that have emerged over time, the one that today enjoys the most popularity is equality of opportunity. The formula has few enemies – politicians, businessmen, social theorists, and freedom marchers all approve it – and it is rarely subjected to intellectual challenge. It is as though all parties have agreed that certain other conceptions of equality, and notably the radical democratic conception, are just too troublesome to deal with because they have too many complex implications, too broad a scope perhaps, and a long history resonant of violence and revolutionary fervor. Equal opportunity, on the other hand, seems a more modest proposal. It promises that the doors to success and prosperity will be opened to us all yet does not imply that we are all equally valuable or that all men are really created equal. In short, this popular and relatively new concept escapes many of the problems and pitfalls of democratic equality and emphasizes the need for an equal opportunity among men to develop and be paid for their talents, which are of course far from being equal.

John H. Schaar (1967), 'Equality of Opportunity, and Beyond', in J. Roland Pennock and John W. Chapman (eds), *Equality*, New York: Atherton Press.

The doctrine itself is attractively simple. It asserts that each man should have equal rights and opportunities to develop his own talents and virtues and that there should be equal rewards for equal performances. The formula does not assume the empirical equality of men. It recognizes that inequalities among men on virtually every trait or characteristic are obvious and ineradicable, and it does not oppose differential evaluations of those differences. Nor is the formula much concerned with complex chains of normative reasoning: it is practical and policy-oriented. In addition, equal opportunity is not, in principle, confined to any particular sector of life. It is held to be as applicable to politics as to law, as suitable for education as for economics. The principle is widely accepted as just and generous, and the claim is often made that application of the principle unlocks the energies necessary for social and economics progress.

Whereas this conception of equality answers or evades some questions, it raises others. Who is to decide the value of a man's talents? Are men to be measured by the commercial demand for their various abilities? And if so, what happens to the man whose special gifts are not recognized as valuable by the buying public? And most important, is the resulting inequality, based partly on natural inequalities and partly on the whims of consumers, going to bury the ideal of democratic equality, based on a philosophy of equal human worth transcending both nature and economics?

These are serious questions, and it is my intention in this essay to probe their deeper meanings, as well as to clarify some major assumptions, disclose the inner spirit, and explore some of the moral and political implications of the principle of equal opportunity.

II

The first thing to notice is that the usual formulation of the doctrine – equality of opportunity for all to develop their capacities – is rather misleading, for the fact always is that not all talents can be developed equally in any given society. Out of the great variety of human resources available to it, a given society will admire and reward some abilities more than others. Every society has a set of values, and these are arranged in a more or less tidy hierarchy. These systems of evaluation vary from society to society: soldierly qualities and virtues were highly admired and rewarded in Sparta, while poets languished. Hence, to be accurate, the equality of opportunity formula must be revised to read: equality of opportunity for all to develop those talents which are highly valued by a given people at a given time.

When put in this way, it becomes clear that commitment to the formula implies prior acceptance of an already established social-moral order. Thus, the doctrine is, indirectly, very conservative. It enlists support for the established pattern of values. It also encourages change and growth, to be sure, but mainly along the lines of tendency already apparent and approved in a given society. The doctrine is "progressive" only in the special sense that it encourages and hastens progress within a going pattern of institutions, activities, and values. It does not advance alternatives to the existing pattern. Perhaps we have here an example of those policies that Dwight D. Eisenhower and the theorists of the Republican Party characterized as the method of "dynamic conservatism".

If this argument is correct, then the present-day "radicals" who demand the fullest extension of the equal-opportunity principle to all groups within the society, and especially to Negroes and the lower classes, are really more conservative than the "conservatives" who oppose them. No policy formula is better designed to fortify the dominant institutions, values, and ends of the American social order than the formula of equality of opportunity, for it offers *everyone* a fair and equal chance to find a place within that order. In principle, it excludes no man from the system if his abilities can be put to use within the system. We have here another example of the repeated tendency of American radicals to buttress the existing framework of order even while they think they are undermining it, another example of the inability of those who see themselves as radical critics of the established system to fashion a rhetoric and to formulate ends and values that offer a genuine alternative to the system. Time after time, never more loyally than at the present, America's radicals have been her best conservatives.

Before one subscribes to the equality-of-opportunity formula, then, he should be certain that the dominant values, institutions, and goals of his society are the ones he really wants. The tone and contents of much of our recent serious literature and social thought – thought that escapes the confines of the conservative–radical framework – warn that we are well on the way toward building a culture our best men will not honor. The facile formula of equal opportunity quickens that trend. It opens more and more opportunities for more and more people to contribute more and more energies toward the realization of a mass, bureaucratic, technological, privatized, materialistic, bored, and thrill-seeking, consumption-oriented society – a society of well-fed, congenial and sybaritic monkeys surrounded by gadgets and pleasure-toys.

Secondly, it is clear that the equal-opportunity policy will increase the inequalities among men. In previous ages, when opportunities were restricted to those of the right birth and station, it is highly probable, given the fact that nature seems to delight in distributing many traits in the pattern of a normal distribution, and given the phenomenon of regression toward the mean, that many of those who enjoyed abundant opportunities to develop their talents actually lacked the native ability to benefit from their advantages. It is reasonable to suppose that many members of ascribed elites, while appearing far superior to the ruck, really were not that superior in actual attainment. Under the regime of equal opportunity, however, only those who genuinely are superior in the desired attributes will enjoy rich opportunities to develop their qualities. This would produce, within a few generations, a social system where the members of the elites really were immensely superior in ability and attainment to the masses. We should then have a condition where the natural and social aristocracies would be identical – a meritocracy, as Michael Young has called it.[1]

Furthermore, the more closely a society approaches meritocracy, the wider grows the gap in ability and achievement between the highest and the lowest social orders. This will happen because in so many fields there are such huge quantities of things to be learned before one can become certified as competent that only the keenest talents, refined and enlarged by years of devoted study and work, can make the grade.[2] We call our age scientific, and describe it further as characterized by a knowledge explosion. What these labels mean from the perspective of equalitarianism is that a handful of men possess a tremendous fund of scientific knowledge, while the rest of us are about as innocent of science as we have always been. So the gap widens: the disparity between the scientific knowledge of an Einstein and the scientific knowledge of the ordinary man of our day is greater than the disparity between a Newton and the ordinary man of his day.

Another force helps widen the gap. Ours is an age of huge, complex, and powerful organizations. Those who occupy positions of command in these structures wield enormous power over their underlings, who, in the main, have become so accustomed to their servitude that they hardly feel it for what it is. The least efficient of the liberal-social welfare states of our day, for example, enjoys a degree of easy control over the ordinary lives of its subjects far beyond the wildest ambitions of the traditional "absolute" rulers. As the commanding positions in these giant organizations come to be occupied increasingly by men who have been generously endowed by nature and, under the equal-opportunity principle, highly favored by society, the power gap between the well- and the poorly-endowed widens. The doctrine of equality of opportunity, which in its origins was a rather nervous attempt to forestall moral criticisms of a competitive and inequalitarian society while retaining the fiction of moral equality, now ironically magnifies the natural differences among men by policies based on an ostensibly equalitarian rationale. The doctrine of equal opportunity, social policies and institutions based on it, and advances in knowledge all conspire with nature to produce more and more inequality.

This opens a larger theme. We untiringly tell ourselves that the principle of equality of opportunity is a generous one. It makes no distinctions of worth among men on any of the factitious grounds, such as race, religion, or nationality, that are usually offered for such distinctions. Nor does it set artificial limits on the individual. On the contrary, it so arranges social conditions that each individual can go as high as his natural abilities will permit. Surely, nothing could be fairer or more generous.

The generosity dissolves under analysis. The doctrine of equal opportunity, followed seriously, removes the question of how men should be treated from the realm of human responsibility and returns it to "nature". What is so generous about telling a man he can go as far as his talents will take him when his talents are meager? Imagine a footrace of one mile in which ten men compete, with the rules being the same for all. Three of the competitors are forty years old, five are overweight, one has weak ankles, and the tenth is Roger Bannister. What sense does it make to say that all ten have an equal opportunity to win the race? The outcome is predetermined by nature, and nine of the competitors will call it a mockery when they are told that all have the same opportunity to win.

The cruelty of the jest, incidentally, is intensified with each increase in our ability to measure traits and talents at an early age. Someday our measuring instruments may be so keen that we will be able to predict, with high accuracy, how well a child of six or eight will do in the social race. Efficiency would dictate that we use these tools to separate the superior from the inferior, assigning the proper kinds and quantities of growth resources, such as education, to each group. The very best training and equipment that society can afford would, of course, go to those in the superior group – in order to assure equality of opportunity for the development of their talents. It would seem more generous for men themselves to take responsibility for the matter, perhaps by devising a system of handicaps to correct for the accidents of birth, or even by abandoning the competitive ethic altogether.

Three lines of defense might be raised against these criticisms of the equality-of-opportunity principle.

It might be replied, first, that I have misstated the principle of equal opportunity. Correctly stated, the principle only guarantees equal opportunity for all to *enter* the race, not to *win* it. That is certainly correct: whereas the equal-opportunity principle lets each individual "go as high as his natural abilities will permit", it does not guarantee that all will reach to the same height. Thus, the metaphor of the footrace twists the case in that it shows fools, presumably deluded by the equal-opportunity doctrine, trying to stretch hopelessly beyond their natural reach. But there is no reason to think that fat men who foolishly compete against Roger Bannister are deluded by a doctrine. They are deluded because they are fools.

These reservations are entirely proper. The metaphor of the footrace does misrepresent the case. But it was chosen because it also expresses some features of the case which are often overlooked. The equal-opportunity principle probably does excite a great many men to dreams of glory far beyond their real capabilities. Many observers of American life have pointed to the frequency of grand, bold, noble "first acts" in the drama of American life, and the scarcity of any "second acts" at all. The equal-opportunity principle, with its emphasis on success, probably does stir many men to excesses of hope for winning and despair at losing. It certainly leaves the losers with no external justification for their failures, and no amount of trying can erase the large element of cruelty from any social doctrine which does that. Cases like that of the footrace, and our growing ability to measure men's abilities, makes it clear that the equal-opportunity principle really is not very helpful to many men. Under its regime, a man with, say an Intelligence Quotient of ninety, is given equal opportunity to go as far as his native ability will take him. That is to say, it lets him go as far as he could have gone without the aid of the doctrine – to the bottom rung of the social ladder – while it simultaneously stimulates him to want to go farther.

Secondly, it might be argued that the equality-of-opportunity principle need not be interpreted and applied, as it has been in this treatment, within a setting and under the assumptions of social competitiveness. The principle could be construed as one that encourages the individual to compete against himself, to compare what he is with what he might become. The contest takes place between one's actual and potential selves, rather than between oneself and others.

This is an interesting, and hopeful, revision of the principle. It would shift the locus of judgment from society to the individual, and it would change the criteria of judgment from social utility to personal nobility. This shift is possible, but it would require a revolution in our present ways of thinking about equality, for those ways are in fact socially oriented and utilitarian. Hence, this defense against the criticisms is really no defense at all. It is irrelevant in the strict sense that instead of meeting the specific charges it shifts the question to a different battleground. It is an alternative to the existing, operative theory, not a defense of it. In fact, the operative doctrine, with its stress on overcoming others as the path of self-validation, is one of the toughest obstacles in the way of an ethic of personal validation through self-transcendence. The operative doctrine specifies success as the test of personal worth, and by success is meant victory in the struggle against others for the prizes of wealth and status. The person who enters wholeheartedly into this contest comes to look upon himself as an object or commodity whose value is set, not by his own internal standards of worth but by the valuations others placed on the position he occupies. Thus, when the dogma of equal opportunity is effectively internalized by the individual members of a society, the result is as humanly disastrous for the winners as for the losers. The winners easily come to think of themselves as beings superior to common humanity, while the losers are almost forced to think of themselves as something less than human.

The third defense is a defense, though not a strong one. It consists in explaining that the metaphor of the footrace oversimplifies the reality that is relevant to an appraisal of the equal-opportunity principle. What actually, occurs in a society is not just one kind of contest but many kinds, so that those who are not good at one thing need only look around for a different contest where they have a better chance of winning. Furthermore, there is not just one prize in a given contest but several. Indeed, in our complex and affluent society, affairs might even be so arranged that everyone would win something: there need be no losers.

This reply has some strength, but not enough to touch the basic points. Although there are many avenues of opportunity in our society, their number is not unlimited. The theory of equal opportunity must always be implemented within a set of conventions which favors some potentialities and discourages others. Persons who strive to develop potentialities that are not admired in a given society soon find their efforts tagged silly, or wrong-headed, or dangerous, or dysfunctional. This is inherent in any society, and it forms an insurmountable barrier to the full development of the principle of equal-opportunity. Every society encourages some talents and contests, and discourages others. Under the equal-opportunity doctrine, the only men who can fulfill themselves and develop their abilities to the fullest are those who are able and eager to do what society demands they do.

There is, furthermore, a hierarchy of value even among those talents, virtues, and contests that are encouraged: the winners in some contests are rewarded more handsomely than the winners in other contests. Even in a complex society, where many contests take place, and even in an affluent society, where it might seem that there had to be no losers, we know full well that some awards are only consolation prizes, not the real thing, and a bit demeaning to their winners. When the fat boy who finishes last in the footrace gets the prize for "best try", he has lost more than he has won.

The formula of equality of opportunity, then, is by no means the warm and generous thing it seems to be on first view. Let us now examine the doctrine from another perspective.

III

The equal-opportunity principle is widely praised as an authentic expression of the democratic ideal and temper. I shall argue, to the contrary, that it is a cruel debasement of a genuinely democratic understanding of equality. To argue that is also to imply, of course, that a genuinely democratic conception of equality is not widely held in the United States.

The origins and development of the principle are enough to throw some doubt on its democratic credentials. Plato gave the principle its first great statement, and he was no democrat. Nor was Napoleon, who was the first to understand that the doctrine could be made the animating principle of the power state. In the United States, the Jacksonian demand for equal rights was assimilated by the Whigs and quickly converted into the slogan of equal opportunity. It soon won a secure place in popular political rhetoric. Whig politicians used the slogan to blunt popular demands for equality – interpreted as "levelling equality" – while defending the advantages of the wealthy.

This argument from origins is, of course, merely cautionary, not conclusive, but other, more systematic considerations, lead toward the same conclusion.

The doctrine of equality of opportunity is the product of a competitive and fragmented society, a divided society, a society in which individualism, in Tocqueville's sense of the word,[3] is the reigning ethical principle. It is a precise symbolic expression of the liberal-bourgeois model of society, for it extends the marketplace mentality to all the spheres of life. It views the whole of human relations as a contest in which each man competes with his fellows for scarce goods, a contest in which there is never enough for everybody and where one man's gain is usually another's loss. Resting upon the attractive conviction that all should be allowed to improve their conditions as far as their abilities permit, the equal-opportunity principle insists that each individual do this by and for himself. Thus, it is the perfect embodiment of the Liberal conception of reform. It breaks up solidaristic opposition to existing conditions of inequality by holding out to the ablest and most ambitious members of the disadvantaged groups the enticing prospect of rising from their lowly state into a more prosperous condition. The rules of the game remain the same: the fundamental character of the social-economic system is unaltered. All that happens is that individuals are given the chance to struggle up the social ladder, change their position on it, and step on the fingers of those beneath them.

A great many individuals do, in fact, avail themselves of the chance to change sides as offered by the principle of equality of opportunity.[4] More than that, the desire to change sides is probably typical of the lower and middle classes, and is widely accepted as a legitimate ethical outlook. In other words, much of the demand for equality, and virtually all of the demand for the kind of equality expressed in the equal-opportunity principle, is really a demand for an equal right and opportunity to become unequal. Very much of what goes by the name of democratic sentiment – as that sentiment is molded within the framework of an individualistic, competitive society and expressed in the vocabulary of such a society – is really envy of those who enjoy superior positions combined with a desire to join them.[5]

This whole way of thinking leads effortlessly to the conclusion that the existence of hierarchy, even of oligarchy, is not the antithesis of democracy but its natural and necessary fulfillment. The idea of equality of opportunity assumes the presence of a mass of men of average talents and attainments. The talents and attainments of the superior few can be measured by comparison with this average, mass background. The best emerge from the democracy, the average, and set themselves over it, resting their position securely on the argument from merit and ability. Those on top are automatically justified because they owe their positions to their natural superiority of merit, not to any artificial claim derived from birth, or wealth, or any other such basis. Hence, the argument concludes, the workings of the equal-opportunity principle help the democracy discover its own most capable masters in the fairest and most efficient way. Everybody gains: the average many because they are led by the superior few; the superior few because they can legitimately enjoy rewards commensurate with their abilities and contributions.

So pervasive and habitual is this way of thinking today that it is virtually impossible to criticize it with any hope of persuading others of its weaknesses. One is not dealing with a set of specific propositions logically arrayed, but with an atmospheric condition, a climate of opinion that unconsciously governs articulate thought in a variety of fields. Something like this cluster of opinions and sentiments provides the framework for popular discussion of the origins and legitimacy of economic inequality. We are easily inclined to think that a man gets what he deserves, that rewards are primarily products of one's talents and industry, secondarily the consequences of luck, and only in small part the function of properties of the social-cultural structure. Somewhere around three-fourths of all personal wealth in the United States belongs to the richest fifth of our families. There is no evidence, in the form of major political movements or public policies, that this distribution shocks the American democratic conscience – a fact suggesting that the American conscience on this matter simply is not democratic but is, rather, formed by the rhetoric of equal opportunity. Similarly, the giant public and private bureaucracies of our day could not justify for a minute their powers over the lives of men if the men so used did not themselves believe in the justness of hierarchy based on merit – merit always defined as tested competence in a special subject matter, tested mastery of a special skill or craft. Most modern writers on the theory of democracy accept this argument for elitism and point out happily that no serious moral or political problems arise so long as avenues for the movement of members into and out of the hierarchies are freely provided. The principle of equal-opportunity, of course, does just that.

The basic argument is not new. What is new is the failure to appreciate the profoundly anti-democratic spirit of the argument. This failure is the specific novelty of the "democratic" thought and sentiment of our day, and it makes today's democrats as amenable to domination as any men have ever been. It is only necessary to persuade the masses (usually an easy task) that the hierarchs possess superior merit and that anyone (one naturally thinks of himself at this point) with the requisite ability can join them.

All that can be said against this orientation is that a genuinely democratic ethic and vision rejects oligarchy *as such*. The democrat rejects in principle the thesis that oligarchy of merit (special competence) is in some way different in kind from oligarchy of any other sort, and that this difference makes it nobler, more reasonable, more agreeable to democracy, than oligarchies built on other grounds. The democrat who understands his commitment holds oligarchy itself to be obnoxious, not merely oligarchy of this or that kind.

The argument for hierarchy based on merit and accomplished by the method of equal opportunity is so widespread in our culture that there seems no way to find a reasonable alternative to it. We automatically think that the choice is either-or: *either* hierarchy and orderly progress *or* anarchy and disorderly stalemate. But that is not so. It is hardly even relevant. The fact that it is thought to be so is a reflection of the crippling assumptions from which modern thought on these matters proceeds. It is thought that there must be hierarchies and masses, elites and non-elites, and that there can be no more democratic way of selecting elites than by the method of equal opportunity. The complexity of affairs demands elites; and democracy and justice require selection of those elites by merit and equal opportunity.

Of course there must be hierarchy, but that does not imply a hierarchical and bureaucratic mode of thinking and acting. It need imply no more than specialization of function. Similarly, the fact that complexity demands specialization of function does not imply the unique merit and authority of those who perform the special functions. On the contrary: a full appreciation of complexity implies the need for the widest possible diffusion of knowledge, sharing of views, and mutual acceptance of responsibility by all members of the affected community.

Of course there must be organization, and organization implies hierarchy. Selection of the hierarchs by the criterion of merit and the mechanism of equal opportunity seems to reassure the worried democrat that his values are not being violated. But hierarchy may or may not be consonant with the democratic spirit. Most of today's democratic thinkers soothe themselves on this question of democracy and organization with the assertion that everything that can be done is being done when organizations permit factions, provide channels of consultation, and protect individual rights by establishing quasi-judicial bodies for hearing and arbitrating disputes. Certainly these guarantees are valuable, but they have little to do with making organizations democratic. They are constitutionalist devices, not democratic ones.

Before there can be a democratic organization, there must first be a democratic mentality – a way of thinking about the relations among men which stresses equality of being and which strives incessantly toward the widest possible sharing of responsibility and participation in the common life. A democratic orientation does not grow from and cannot coexist with the present bureaucratic and "meritorian" ethic. It is an alternative to the present ethic, not an expansion or outgrowth of it. When the democratic mentality prevails, it will not be too hard to find the mechanisms for implementing it.

NOTES

1. Michael Young, *The Rise of the Meritocracy*, London: Thames and Hudson, 1958.
2. Success is a function of both inborn talent and the urge to do well, and it is often impossible to tell which is the more important in a particular case. It is certain that the urge to do well can be stimulated by social institutions. How else can we account for Athens or Florence, or the United States?
3. *Democracy in America*. New York: Vintage, 1945, vol. 2, pp. 104–5.
4. Some civil rights leaders are suspicious of open enrollment plans to combat *de facto* segregation for precisely this reason.
5. "The greatest obstacle which equality has to overcome is not the aristocratic pride of the rich, but rather the undisciplined egoism of the poor". Proudhon, as quoted in James Joll, *The Anarchists*, Boston: Little, Brown, 1964, p. 67.

4

RIGHTS

Ruth Abbey

INTRODUCTION

The discourse of human rights dominates politics in the westernised world.[1] Be it in the arena of domestic politics, in relations between states or in the increasing intersections between intra- and interstate politics, players turn to the language of rights to find a way of expressing their claims for resources, recognition or simply for the entitlement to act upon their desires and achieve their aims without interference. As Richard Bellamy observes, 'political debate is currently suffused by the language of rights. All the main political parties, most pressure groups and individuals of almost every ideological persuasion make their demands and define our identity as citizens in terms of rights' (2000: 162). This chapter critically explores the meaning of rights. It asks what rights are, largely by considering the role they play in some current liberal theorising about politics. To this end, the work of John Rawls, Will Kymlicka and Richard Rorty is outlined. Some reservations about the dominance of rights discourse are expressed, and along the way examples are drawn from contemporary social and political issues in westernised societies to illustrate some of the strengths and weaknesses of rights discourse.

WHAT ARE RIGHTS?

At its barest minimum, a right is a legally enforceable claim, usually made upon the state by an individual who belongs to that state. The claim might be directed against another individual, an institution, or even the state itself. But no matter who or what the claim is directed against, it is made upon the state because the state has, since the advent of the Westphalian system in the seventeenth century, been seen as the ultimate guarantor of rights. As Max Weber indicated, the state is that entity which 'successfully claims the *monopoly of the legitimate use of physical force* within a given territory' (1948: 78, emphasis in original). With such resources for coercion at its disposal, the state can thus ensure, if anyone can, that rights claims are respected. Yet the state is Janus-faced, able to use its huge power to infringe upon individuals' rights as well as to uphold and enforce them. Hence Jack Donnelly's paradoxical description of the state as 'principal violator and essential protector' of individual rights (2003: 35; compare Beetham 1999: 136). When the question of what rights are is approached in this way, it becomes apparent that rights differ from the other political principles discussed in this section of the book, for justice, liberty and equality are irretrievably normative concepts. Rights, rather than being inherently normative, provide a mechanism for summarising and conveying normative claims and for protecting and promoting valued goods.

It is not difficult, however, to think of the many ways in which this rather spare depiction of a right can be complicated. Sometimes groups, rather than individuals, claim rights for themselves. Some individuals or organisations claim rights for non-human creatures or entities – think of animal-rights activists or wilderness conservation groups. Some individuals or groups appeal above the state for the recognition of their rights: indigenous minority groups might take cases against their governments to the International Court of Justice, for example. Some individuals belong to no state, yet even those who lack the usual mechanisms for claiming rights are not thought of as devoid of rights altogether.[2] As this latter observation suggests, we tend to think of humans as rights-bearers simply by virtue of being human, irrespective of their membership of a state. This approach, which grows out of the natural-rights tradition, makes rights theoretically independent of actually existing political arrangements. Indeed, the belief that humans are inherently entitled to certain rights can become the yardstick by which actually existing political arrangements are judged and found wanting.[3] From this perspective, the idea of rights is inherently normative.

As these remarks suggest, although the legalistic depiction of a right offered above is not wholly incorrect or misleading, the notion of rights is much less straightforward. It could be argued that part of the expansion of rights discourse in the modern era has seen rights coming to be thought of as primarily normative, and only secondarily or derivatively legal, claims. On an everyday level, we claim 'rights' to all sorts of things that could not be legally enforced. In ordinary life, we typically invoke a right to something as a means of conveying its importance. Labelling something good or desirable as a 'right' lends it a certain moral weight.

This tendency to endow particular claims to goods with moral weight by invoking the language of rights points to a tension between the legal and the normative aspects of rights. Originally a right, as an entitlement that could be retrieved through legal means, was accorded to individuals in recognition of the normative gravity of the thing being promised or protected by that right. In the work of one of the seminal theorists of liberalism, John Locke ([1690] 1963), individuals are said to have a natural and inalienable right to life, liberty and property because these are seen as essential to human well-being. Making something a right was, then, a sign of its moral significance. However, over the centuries this process has expanded and some would say exploded, so that it now seems that the only way to convey the importance of a good is to transform it into a right. Whereas originally something was made a right because of its normative importance, we now signify a thing's normative importance by making it a right. I would argue that the possibility of rights discourse expanding in this way to cover any and every desirable thing is inherent in the universalism and abstraction of the discourse itself. Because human rights are said to belong to individuals simply by virtue of their being human, the logic of human rights knows no political or geographic borders. And because the language of human rights originally promised rights to abstractions such as liberty and happiness, there are no necessary or obvious ethical limits on what can be claimed as a right (compare Beetham 1999: 137–8).

There are other ways in which the question of what a right is can be approached. It is, for example, customary to distinguish different generations of rights, with the first generation consisting of traditional civil and political rights, the second of social, economic and cultural rights, while the third embraces developmental and environmental rights, rights to self-government and rights for indigenous minorities (see Orend 2002: 110). Another approach is to ask about the relationship between rights and duties, with reflections on whether every right claimed by one person has a correlative duty that must be executed by another or others (Orend 2002, ch. 5; see also Raz 1986: 170–6; Waldron 1993: 16, 25; O'Byrne 2003: 47–9). A third debate that is commonly raised about rights is how universal they are. Does the language of human rights speak to concerns that exist in all cultures, or is it a quintessentially western phenomenon?[4]

The approach to rights adopted in this chapter focuses on the role rights play within some current liberal theorising about politics. This is not to imply that liberal theorists are the only proponents of human rights: on the contrary, many other approaches to politics accord rights an important place.[5] Liberal theories provide the focal point for this discussion of rights for two main reasons. The first is that in a chapter of this size, it would be impossible to consider with any justice the role played by rights in every contemporary theory of politics. Indeed, nothing short of a book-length treatment could hope to do justice to the various approaches to rights that prevail in contemporary political theory. The second major rationale is that liberalism, in both theory and practice, has been the key engine for the articulation and propagation of rights claims in the modern era. The language of human rights began with seventeenth-century social-contract thought, in particular that of Locke,[6] and has expanded ever since. In so far as other approaches to politics incorporate the language of rights, it is largely as a response to the perceived inadequacies and lacunae of liberalism. Liberalism is, in short, the 'mother' of all human-rights discourses, and it is thus to an examination of the role rights play in some contemporary debates within and around liberalism that we turn.

JUSTICE AS FAIRNESS

'Citizens of a just society are to have the same basic rights' (Rawls 1999b: 60).

The work of John Rawls provides the obvious place to begin any presentation of rights thinking in contemporary liberal theory.[7] Rawls is widely considered to be the most influential liberal thinker of the twentieth century. His work represents for many a watershed in political theory in the English-speaking world, for he is typically seen to have instituted a new era in political thought by combining a normative outlook with a highly systematic and architectonic approach to politics (see Wolff 1998: 118–20; Martin 2003: 499). There are three major stages in Rawls's work: the first is represented by *A Theory of Justice*, published in 1971 (rev. ed. 1999), the second by *Political Liberalism*, published in 1993,[8] and the third by *The Law of Peoples* in 1999. For the purposes of this chapter, the similarities between *A Theory of Justice* and *Political Liberalism* are more important than any differences, because Rawls carries over the two principles of justice articulated in the former to the latter work.[9] In *The Law of Peoples*, Rawls asks to what extent the theory of justice adduced in the two previous works is relevant for an understanding of relations between states. He posits respect for certain basic human rights as one of the necessary criteria for liberal states recognising the legitimacy of non-liberal ones. These human rights are a sub-set of the basic rights he believes that citizens in a just society will enjoy (Rawls 1999a: 3–10). Of these three works, *A Theory of Justice* has also been most influential thus far. For this reason, and because, of the three, it pays the most attention to the question of rights, this work will command most of our interest.

Rawls portrays his project in *A Theory of Justice* as an attempt to revive the social contract tradition of thinking about politics. In this tradition, which stretches back to Thomas Hobbes and includes Locke, Jean-Jacques Rousseau and Immanuel Kant,[10] the very existence of social and political life needs to be accounted for, and this is typically done by reference to the interests individuals have in interaction with others and in the creation of government. Social-contract theorists conceive of social and political life as if it were a contract among partners, a sort of deal or agreement by which both or all sides bind themselves to certain things in return for certain benefits (Rawls 1999b: 4). As Rawls says, 'a society is a cooperative venture for mutual advantage . . . social cooperation makes possible a better life for all than any would have if each were to live solely by his own efforts' (1999b: 4).

Social-contract thinkers thus tend to be concerned with how the existence of the state can be justified, and why individual citizens should feel obliged to respect the state's legitimacy and obey its rulings. An appeal to the value of rights plays a major role in answering these questions, for the idea is that only an entity as powerful as the state can ensure that individual rights are respected. Rights, in turn, protect fundamental goods for individuals. At a more symbolic level, it should come as no surprise that when the legal ideal of a contract freely entered into by equal parties for their mutual advantage becomes the central metaphor for social relations, a belief in entitlements that individuals can claim from one another and have legally enforced via the state should assume significance.

What lends Rawls's theory of justice its architectonic flavour is that it applies to 'the basic structure of society', which comprises a society's major institutions: its political constitution, its economy and property laws and the family (Rawls 1999b: 7). As Rawls says:

> The guiding idea is that the principles of justice for the basic structure of society are the object of the original agreement. They are the principles that free and rational persons concerned to further their own interests would accept in an initial position of equality as defining the fundamental terms of their association. These principles are to regulate all further agreements; they specify the kinds of social cooperation that can be entered into and the forms of government that can be established. (1999b: 11)

A just society is characterised by two major principles. The first is the equal-liberties principle, which holds that everyone has an equal entitlement to the most extensive basic liberty in so far as this is compatible with the liberty of others. The sorts of freedom to which people in a just society should have equal access are the traditional civil and political freedoms of liberalism. These include freedom of conscience, assembly, association, speech, worship, freedom to vote and stand for public office and freedom from arbitrary arrest. Rawls calls these 'the equal liberties of citizenship' (1999b: 61). His understanding of liberty comports fairly closely with the traditional negative conception of liberty, according to which freedom means the absence of external interference. As Rawls says, 'persons are at liberty to do something when they are free from certain constraints either to do it or not to do it and when their doing it or not doing it is protected from interference by other persons' (1999b: 202).

So far, so liberal. Yet Rawls's contractors care not just about the distribution of liberty in society but also about the distribution of other primary goods, such as material assets. Rawls proposes that the contractors' second principle of justice would be what he calls the difference principle. This operates on the assumption that rational individuals who were entering into a social contract would only do so if certain key social goods were distributed in a way that was to their advantage. It is further assumed that these things should be equally distributed unless it could be shown that unequal distribution would benefit the worst off. If social goods, such as incomes, were made unequal because this would benefit the worst off, Rawls adds that the positions to which these incomes are attached must be allocated on the basis of equal opportunity: all suitably qualified persons in society should have an equal chance of competing for and winning these (1999b: 61). Thus inequalities in the distribution of primary social goods are compatible with justice if it can be shown that these inequalities redound to the benefit of all (Rawls 1999b: 62).

Rawls insists upon the lexical ordering of these two principles, meaning that that which is number one takes first priority. The ranking of the principles is not indifferent or interchangeable: the first principle – that of equal liberties – cannot be sacrificed to benefit the second – the difference principle. So even if the worst off in society were to be advantaged by reducing the fundamental liberties outlined in the first principle of justice, this would not be acceptable. Because they are lexically ordered, the first principle has top priority and it must be satisfied before attending to the requirements of the second principle of justice. The only thing that can qualify a person's claim to liberty is, therefore, that it impinges upon equal liberty for others. As Rawls sees it, liberty can only be sacrificed for the sake of liberty: an individual's freedom can only be curtailed if it threatens the freedom of another individual (1999b: 40–5, 64–5).

Despite the fact that the index to *A Theory of Justice* contains no entry for rights (see also Martin 1985: vii–viii), rights play a crucial role in the Rawlsian picture. This lacuna could illustrate either how pervasive rights are in Rawls's thought or how taken for granted the notion of rights is in the liberal outlook.[11] Rawls makes it clear several times that rights derive from the two principles of justice (1999b: 4, 5, 6, 10, 11 and passim), and the major function of rights is to guarantee that the basic liberties are equally available to all. Rights and liberties are thus among the 'chief primary goods at the disposition of society' (Rawls 1999b: 62). The combined institutions of the basic structure 'define men's rights and duties and influence their life prospects' (Rawls 1999b: 7). In terms of the different generations of rights mentioned above, Rawls's theory of justice embraces both first and some second generation. The first principle of justice covers the standard first-generation rights while the second principle shows a strong regard for economic and social rights.[12]

Like Marxist and social-democratic thinkers, Rawls is aware of the possibility for interaction between these two generations of rights. As he says, 'the inability to take advantage of one's rights and opportunities as a result of poverty and ignorance, and a lack of means generally, is sometimes counted among the constraints definitive of liberty' (1999b: 204).[13] However, unlike Marxist and social democratic thinkers, he does not agree that civil and political rights and freedoms are diminished unless social and economic rights are respected. Were Rawls to concede that they were, he would be contradicting his own requirement of the lexical ordering of the two principles of justice, for he would be forced to concede that the first principle cannot be satisfied before attending to the second. Indeed, the full realisation of the first principle would become contingent upon the second, which would directly contravene their lexical ordering.

However, as we have seen, Rawls is not indifferent to the fair distribution of social and economic goods. In order to reconcile this concern with the lexical ordering of the two principles of justice, he distinguishes between equal liberty and the equal worth of liberty (1999b: 204–5). The first principle of justice is supposed to ensure equal liberty, while the second principle contributes to the equal worth of liberty by minimising the incidence of poverty, ignorance and other avoidable hardships. This attempt to preserve the lexical ordering by distinguishing between liberty and its worth might, upon scrutiny, prove to be untenable, but his insistence upon the ordering and the prioritising of first-generation civil and political rights is one of the things that makes Rawls's position ultimately a liberal one.[14]

Group-differentiated rights

'Now all the liberties of equal citizenship must be the same for each member of society' (Rawls 1999b: 204).

This question of what makes a position a liberal one is central for the work of Will Kymlicka. As we have seen, a key feature of Rawlsian liberalism is that the rights provided by a just society should be equally available to all. It is also assumed that individuals are the bearers of rights: there is no conception of groups or collective entities of any sort as claimants or holders of rights.[15] This assumption that rights can only be borne by individuals could, in turn, be explained by reference to the atomist ontology of not just social-contract thought, but of much thinking in the liberal tradition.[16] According to this ontology, the individual is the fundamental reality. Groups do not enjoy this foundational ontological status: they are derivative or secondary because they are forged and dissolved by the choices and actions of individuals. It would be foolish to accord rights to entities that can wax and wane in this way. Individuals, however, are ontologically secure: they will endure – or if they don't, rights will cease to be an issue! (Waldron 1993: 345–6, 367; Kukathas 1995). For many liberals there is also a political problem in according rights to groups. As our foray into Rawlsian thinking reveals, rights are designed to protect individual freedoms. Were groups to be given rights, they could use such rights to limit or threaten the freedom of individual members. This would contravene the whole rationale for rights in the first place.

In *Multicultural Citizenship: A Liberal Theory of Minority Rights*, Kymlicka tries to show that the idea of rights for minority groups can be made consistent with a liberal outlook.[17] Or rather, what Kymlicka proposes is that some rights for some minority groups can be reconciled with liberalism. One of the techniques used in his attempt to persuade his fellow liberals that they can accept the idea of minority rights is to demonstrate that rights formed part of the liberal outlook in the nineteenth and early twentieth centuries. Kymlicka thus points to liberal thinkers such as Leonard Hobhouse and liberal institutions such as the League of Nations and recommends that this legacy be not forgotten but recovered (1989: 3, 5; 1995: 2).

In order to understand why Kymlicka thinks that liberals can and should endorse the imputation of some rights to some minority groups, it is necessary to appreciate his thinking about the relationship between the individual, community and culture. Kymlicka reminds us that personal autonomy is one of the things that liberals value: they seek to build a society that will protect and promote this capacity. Culture precedes individual choice and makes it possible, providing a source of meaning and value for individuals. Culture is therefore an important context for the sort of informed, meaningful choice that liberals value and want to promote. So culture should matter to liberals because individual choice matters to them and culture shapes choices. 'Liberal values require both individual freedom and a secure cultural context from which to choose' (1989: 169, cf. 4; 1995: 83–4).

What Kymlicka provides thus far is simply an argument for the recognition of culture's importance for personal autonomy. However, he goes further and argues that particular cultures matter to particular individuals. Liberals need to acknowledge this because all individuals should have a sense that the choices they make are their own and not alien to or imposed upon them (Kymlicka 1995: 84–93). I would describe this as a concern with authenticity: what matters is not simply that individuals feel connected to some culture but that they feel connected to a culture that they can claim as their own. Kymlicka then considers what the implications are for a diverse society once we accept that culture is the milieu that makes individual choice meaningful. He argues that some minority groups or cultures within plural societies should be accorded rights so that their culture can be protected and their individual choices thereby made meaningful.

Kymlicka is not, however, suggesting that all minority groups with a cultural background different from the mainstream culture are entitled to such rights. Instead, he distinguishes between multinational and polyethnic states and defends rights for some groups in multinational states. A multinational state has one group or more of people who were either original inhabitants or part of its founding group. Countries such as Canada, the United States, Australia and New Zealand all have indigenous populations and thus fall into the category of multinational states. The status of such groups is different in Kymlicka's estimation from that of the ethnic minorities created via immigration. These latter groups contribute to a polyethnic state rather than a multinational one, and do not have the claims to group rights that national groups have. The basic rationale for this distinction among minority cultures is choice: Kymlicka works with the premise that immigrants elect to leave their homeland and make their life in another country. In doing so they voluntarily relinquish those parts of their culture that can't be carried with them. National groups, by contrast, did not make a choice to be eclipsed by or absorbed into another culture (Kymlicka 1995: 95–6).

Kymlicka is therefore suggesting that the different sources or causes of cultural pluralism invite different responses from the state. It is enough that immigrant groups be allowed to assimilate if they wish to, and be free from discrimination. Should they choose to continue some elements of their cultural life such as religious beliefs and practices, culinary and marriage customs, and so on, that is their prerogative. The government is under no obligation to assist or treat them in any way differently from other members of the population (Kymlicka 1995: 96–7). Kymlicka's defence of group-differentiated rights is therefore based on the idea that the cultural group to which you belong determines the sort of collective rights you can legitimately claim.

Just as only some groups are entitled to different rights, so they are entitled to claim only certain rights. In deciding which rights a minority culture can legitimately claim, Kymlicka distinguishes internal from external rights. When a group exercises internal rights, it tries to control the members of its group. When it exercises external rights, it tries to protect its culture from outside threats. Given that Kymlicka is articulating a liberal defence of minority rights, he cannot endorse internal rights. Any group that tried to limit its members' rights to free movement, to free exit from the group, to choose their marriage partners and so forth, would be trampling on long-standing individual rights.[18] The sort of external group rights that he wants to legitimate are directed against the threat posed by the dominant culture. These external, protective rights include things like language rights, education rights and so on. By claiming these rights, national groups can preserve their culture and thus enable meaningful individual choice for their members.

Kymlicka is thus suggesting that the characteristic liberal ways of dealing with social diversity, such as the affirmation of individual rights, the belief in state neutrality and the separation of the public and private spheres, are insufficient in multinational societies. He proposes some rights for some groups as a complement to the existing liberal mechanisms for accommodating diversity. Rawls emphasises how powerfully egalitarian his conception of justice as fairness is compared to other liberal approaches to justice (1993b: 51, 226 n. 36; 1999a: 14 n. 5). Yet whereas the Rawlsian image of the just society sees all individuals as being accorded the same rights, Kymlicka contends that a just society can promote egalitarianism by treating some of its members differently. Respecting equality can require special rights for minorities, because a seminal component of the equality that liberals care about is that all individuals can make free choices about their lives.

When viewed in terms of the different generations of rights, Kymlicka's work goes a step beyond Rawls's by showing a concern for cultural rights, which are part of the second generation, and for rights for indigenous minorities, which belong to the third generation. However, in taking both these steps, Kymlicka is anxious to demonstrate that he is treading a liberal path: group rights are intimately linked to culture, and culture matters because of the liberal respect for meaningful individual choice. As he declares when defining the 'liberal culturalist' position, 'there are compelling interests related to culture and identity which are fully consistent with liberal principles of freedom and equality, and which justify granting [some] special rights to [some] minorities' (2002: 339).[19]

RIGHTS WITHOUT FOUNDATIONS
'We have yet to consider what sorts of beings are owed the guarantees of justice' (Rawls 1999b: 505).

Like his fellow liberals, Richard Rorty is an enthusiast for human rights (1993: 115–16). But Rorty differs from many liberals in the way he goes about justifying and fostering individual rights. He complains that for too long, western thinkers have sought to defend human rights by reference to some uniquely human essence (1993: 114–15, 117). This is symptomatic of the wider trend in western philosophy to seek ahistorical and universal forms of knowledge which can be verified independently of human need, desire or inclination, which Rorty analysed and criticised in his first major work, *Philosophy and the Mirror of Nature*. In 'Human Rights, Rationality, and Sentimentality' he contends that the foundationalist approach to human rights is outmoded (1993: 116; cf. 117, 120, 128) and proposes a different way of encouraging the widening and deepening of the human-rights culture. As he says, 'we see our task as a matter of making our own culture – the human rights culture – more self-conscious and more powerful, rather than of demonstrating its superiority to other cultures by an appeal to something transcultural' (1993: 117).

A major problem confronting those who want to extend and deepen human rights is how to promote respect for the rights of others, even those who seem very different from, and perhaps repugnant to, oneself (Rorty 1993: 133). Rorty believes that the experience of the last two centuries indicates that 'a sentimental education' is the answer (1993: 133–4). Appealing to the emotions is more likely to promote sympathy and to encourage people to see others as like them in certain salient regards, as distinct from the traditional argument that as rational animals, all humans should be accorded certain rights (Rorty 1993: 118, 122). As Rorty puts it, 'the relevant similarities are not a matter of sharing a deep true self which instantiates true humanity, but are such little, superficial, similarities as cherishing our parents and our children' (1993: 129).

Sad and sentimental stories about the sufferings of particular others are more likely to move people to feel and act in ways that extend the community of rights-holders than are abstract, universalist philosophical arguments about the rationality or dignity of all human beings (Rorty 1993: 134). However, Rorty concedes that it is not a simple contest between reason and sentiment: material conditions also affect people's willingness to regard strange and different others as rights-bearers like themselves. Speaking of places like Europe and America, he posits a connection between moral progress on the one hand and the vast increase in wealth, learning and leisure on the other, over the last two centuries (1993: 121, 128). He explains this by saying that those who enjoy material security are less likely to feel threatened by others who are different, and are consequently more willing to consider them as similar in significant ways (1993: 128). Indeed, at one point Rorty even advances the strong claim that raising children who are personally secure and thus capable of sympathy is not just a necessary but a sufficient condition of the ever-wider dissemination of human rights: 'Producing generations of nice, tolerant, well-off, secure, other-respecting students ... in all parts of the world is just what is needed – indeed *all* that is needed – to achieve an Enlightenment utopia. The more youngsters like this we can raise, the stronger and more global our human rights culture will become' (1993: 127, emphasis in original). One entailment of this, not developed by Rorty in this lecture,[20] is that those concerned with moral education must keep a weather eye on the state of the economy as well.

This assertion of the sufficient conditions for the propagation of human rights is no doubt controversial, but as an historical-cum-empirical thesis it could be debated by considering whether violations or denials of human rights are typically perpetrated, supported or tolerated by those who are in some way materially deprived. Does the work of social psychologists bear out Rorty's claim that as people become more affluent they become more genuinely tolerant of difference? Or is this a passive tolerance made possible by the ability to insulate themselves from daily exposure to those who are not like them?

Another of the contentious features of Rorty's argument is more philosophical, deriving from the conception of selfhood that informs his claims and predictions about the achievement and extension of the human-rights culture. As evidenced above, Rorty contrasts the traditional foundational belief in 'a deep true self' with his preferred emphasis on 'little, superficial, similarities'. He gives 'cherishing our parents and our children'(1993: 129) as examples of these small, a superficial characteristics that people can come to see themselves as sharing with seemingly distant and different others. Yet it is hard to accept that regard for familial bonds is either a small or a superficial element of identity. It is of course true that not all people feel a deep or ongoing affection for their parents and/or children if they have any, but in such cases family bonds are typically replaced by strong friendships. To express it as generally as possible, Rorty could argue that the common capacity for an abiding concern with the well-being of significant others is the sort of thing that can heighten 'the sense of shared moral identity which brings us together in a moral community' (1993: 117). But this capacity seems like a major and profound part of a person's identity rather than a small and superficial one.

Although a conception of selfhood is only gestured at in this lecture, it receives a fuller treatment in Rorty's earlier work, *Contingency, Irony, and Solidarity*. There he operates with a similarly minimal view of the self, suggesting that it is a 'centreless web of beliefs and desires' (1989: 88). Beyond this minimal definition, selves are characterised, or thickened, by the sort of vocabulary they adopt for interpreting the world and themselves. From the sort of ironist perspective Rorty prefers, no vocabulary is final, or rather, the vocabulary one has when one dies becomes, *ipso facto*, the final one.

Rorty acknowledges the apparent difficulty of reconciling this ontology with his liberal political project of promoting and extending solidarity and a respect for the equality of human beings (1989: 88, 189). Here he tries to integrate them by adopting Judith Shklar's contention that liberals see cruelty as the greatest vice (Rorty 1989: 74, 192). Liberal ironists will try to minimise the harm, suffering and cruelty in human life not because they believe that these experiences violate any deep, true, human self but because they think things are better without harm, suffering and cruelty. Thus for Rorty's liberal ironist, 'recognition of a common susceptibility to humiliation is the *only* social bond that is needed . . . the ironist takes the morally relevant definition of a person, a moral subject, to be "something that can be humiliated"' (1989: 91, emphasis in original). Thence we return to the point made in the Oxford Amnesty lecture about the need to develop empathy or sympathy in human beings, so that they can recognise and be moved to action by the humiliation of others wherever and whenever it occurs (Rorty 1989: 93–4, 192).

Yet there seems to be some slippage between the resolutely a priori and minimalist view of the self and the liberal's sensitivity to the humiliable self. For it may be that when the liberal ironist asks the question 'What humiliates?' (Rorty 1989: 91), she comes up with a universal answer. As this intimates, Rorty could underpin his recommendations about generating support for human rights with something closer to the minimal universalism adduced by John Gray. As a pluralist, Gray is aware of the great variety of ways in which human beings can flourish, both within and across cultures. As a historicist, he is alive to the ways in which these change over time. Gray's approach can thus avoid the sort of uniform essentialism Rorty detects in the western philosophical tradition while accommodating Rorty's emphasis on the self's malleability (Rorty 1993: 115, 121). But Gray also identifies the shared and enduring ways in which humans can suffer. These include such things as starvation, torture, genocide and humiliation (Gray 2000: 110, 113–14, 120). This sort of minimal, largely negative universalism would seem to be consistent with Rorty's other claims about rights and identity, and could provide a more persuasive account of the basis for the promotion of human-rights culture than his own references to small and superficial similarities.[21]

<h2 style="text-align:center">RESERVATIONS ABOUT RIGHTS</h2>

While rights discourse has proven to be spectacularly attractive and successful as a language for debating political and social issues in westernised societies, several dangers inhere in the tendency, mentioned above, to convert all desiderata into rights. Firstly there is the threat of trivialisation: if everything desirable becomes a right, how do we distinguish grave matters like the *habeas corpus* entitlement of Article 9 of the Universal Declaration of Human Rights from the right to 'periodic holidays with pay' as asserted in Article 24 of that document? There is a very real sense in which the huge success of rights discourse could be self-undermining, because when so many desiderata become rights, the appeal to rights loses its normative gravity.[22]

Secondly, when rights discourse dominates, other vocabularies for depicting and discussing social and political conflicts and challenges are squeezed out. Yet not all things that are valuable for individuals, groups or society as a whole can be shoehorned into the discourse of rights (Patrick 2002). One size does not fit all: no single language can suit all the social and political problems that confront complex, plural societies. Complex, plural societies would be better served by having a range of discourses with which to discuss problems and possibilities.

A good illustration of the inherent unsuitability of rights discourse for some of the social challenges facing westernised societies comes with the issue of the rights of grandparents to see their grandchildren. While there could be genuine goods at stake for the children and the grandparents in this matter, rights discourse would seem to provide little headway in negotiating a problem like this, not least because the rights of parents can be invoked against those of grandparents, and the rights of children for or against those of grandparents, and so on ad infinitum. Another example of the poor fit between rights discourse and certain social problems comes with the attempts by some parents to genetically engineer children to act as 'saviour siblings' by providing genetic material needed to keep an existing older child alive. In this situation, the language of rights appeals immediately to those who would insist that because this is essentially a private matter, the state has no role in either preventing or promoting such choices. Yet even if this argument were accepted, the question remains whether the state should provide financial support for such expensive endeavours. If it did not, then the rights of wealthy individuals would be respected while those of poorer ones were violated. For many reasons then, the satisfactory discussion, let alone resolution, of this thorny question is unlikely to be assisted by recourse to the language of rights – be they the rights of the parents, of the existing child or the prospective, modified child.[23] These two illustrations also point to the ambiguous location of the family – on the one hand it is seen as a private institution and thus should be immune from governmental interference, yet on the other, when individuals are supposed to have rights as humans, they can in principle be invoked in any context and within any institution, including the family.

Another problem with this temptation to shoehorn everything into the discourse of rights is the risk that if something cannot be redescribed in the terms of rights discourse, it loses its valued status or can be easily dismissed by detractors. The issues revolving around conservation of the natural world and care for animals provide good illustrations of this problem: challenges that seem more suited to discussion in terms of humans' stewardship of the natural world[24] become instead questions of rights for hens and trees and are thus vulnerable to misrepresentation or ridicule.

Rawls seems ambivalent about this question of the reach of rights discourse. On the one hand, he explains that animals and the natural world more widely are not, in the first instance, covered by his theory of justice.[25] Yet this exclusion is not because these issues are seen to be outside morality: on the contrary, he believes that humans' relationship with the natural world is a moral question 'of the first importance' (1999b: 17, 504). From this we could infer the need for a whole other, non-rights-based, ethic for this significant area of human concern. Rawls certainly believes that humans have duties 'of compassion and humanity' (1999b: 512) to animals and the rest of nature. He also allows that his rights-based theory of justice might have to be modified once humans' relationship to the natural world becomes part of the moral mix. However, Rawls effectively defers the resolution of this matter to the distant future by saying that it relies upon the articulation of a metaphysical theory that correctly situates humans within nature (1999b: 512).[26] Yet deferring this question, perhaps indefinitely, does not deter him from predicting that if justice as fairness 'is sound as an account of justice among persons, it cannot be too far wrong when these broader relationships are taken into consideration' (1999b: 512).[27] It is unclear from this whether he means that once a metaphysical theory has located humans properly in the natural world, the theory of justice as fairness will remain largely unaffected as a prescription for intra-human relations, or whether it can simply be extended to non-human entities.

The implications of Rorty's thinking about rights for this question of their reach seem easier to infer. Shifting the focus of human-rights discourse away from a preoccupation with the essential qualities shared by all humans creates the potential for rights to apply to non-human entities. As Rorty says, 'nothing relevant to moral choices separates human beings from animals except historically contingent facts of the world, cultural facts' (1993: 116). Moreover, he suggests that some of the emotions that should be highlighted through a sentimental education are evinced by animals. The passage quoted above about the superficial similarities relevant to rights-holding are in Rorty's estimation 'similarities that do not interestingly distinguish us from many nonhuman animals' (1993: 129). His style of thinking about rights would seem then to veer away from anthropocentrism, and is therefore perhaps better characterised as seeking to extend rights culture, rather than human-rights culture.

Another set of problems with the ascendancy of rights discourse revolves around its impact on the conduct of democratic politics. Rights discourse inevitably fosters a juridical approach to politics. Rights retrieval typically occurs through the mechanism of the courts and involves an elite of professionals using specialist language to decide outcomes.[28] This legalistic model of politics can crowd out the sort of popular debate and discussion that many hold as vital to the conduct of democratic politics. A related problem here is that claims and counter-claims to rights tend to be expressed in zero-sum terms, which militates against the possibility of compromise. As Charles Taylor observes, rights language 'lends itself to extravagance and intransigence' (1986: 57). Once something is claimed as a right, it becomes difficult to justify its limitation. As he puts it, 'the very concept of a right seems to call for integral satisfaction, if it's a right at all; and if not, then nothing' (1995b: 284). The winner-take-all mentality of rights discourse can intensify social divisions by leaving the losing parties resentful, alienated and feeling that their cause has been deemed illegitimate by being declared unconstitutional.[29]

CONCLUSION

According to Michael Ignatieff, we have witnessed a rights revolution, with the language of rights being appealed to in ever more matters of contention across ever more areas of the globe. Rights are invoked to demand equality and to defend diversity.[30] In this chapter I have tried to indicate some of the attractions of rights discourse, and to point out some of its complexities as well as some of its shortcomings. Rights discourse stemmed from the liberal tradition of political thought and practice, and while most contemporary liberals continue to confirm the importance of rights, they cannot agree among themselves about the purposes, foundation or reach of rights, or even on who or what should be considered a rights-bearer. Rights discourse is thus both familiar and ubiquitous but challenging (and exciting) to theorise about at the same time.

QUESTIONS FOR DISCUSSION

- Is the spread of rights discourse a welcome development?
- Do rights need foundations?
- What is the relationship between rights and equality?
- Is rights discourse compatible with multiculturalism?

NOTES

1. The term 'westernised' rather than 'western' is used to convey a cultural process rather than a geographic location.
2. On this theme of justice for non-citizens, see O'Neill (2000).
3. See Freeman (2002: 7), Langlois (2004: 247). Frost (2002: 4–5) also provides a clear statement of this view.
4. Rawls argues that human rights are not peculiarly western but rather politically and culturally neutral (1993b: 69–70, 78; 1999a: 65). Donnelly claims that while human rights are western in origin, they are now universal (2003: 1–2, 61–4). For other treatments of this question, see Taylor (1999), Bell (2000), Freeman (2002: 101–21).
5. See, for example, Robert Nozick on libertarianism and natural rights, Bellamy on rights in the republican tradition, David Chandler on cosmopolitanism and Mervyn Frost on global civil society.
6. Cf. Donnelly (2003: 47) on Locke's pivotal role in this tradition. Rawls's depiction of the social-contract tradition begins with Locke rather than Thomas Hobbes. Hobbes's work is said to 'raise special problems' (Rawls 1999b: 11, n. 4) but these are not enumerated in *A Theory of Justice*. Belden Fields, however, identifies Hobbes, Locke's seventeenth-century predecessor, as the crucial philosophical source of rights discourse in the modern era. Hobbes is the first thinker to see rights as inhering in humans qua humans, and thus to give rights a secular, rationalist justification (Fields 2003: 10–13). Yet as Fields concedes, Hobbes is a rather ambiguous figure in the history of modern rights discourse, because the only natural right he imputes to human beings is that to self-preservation. As a social-contract theorist he makes rational consent by individuals the basis of the state's legitimacy, yet *Leviathan* defends the prerogative of the sovereign power over individual freedom on so many practical questions of state power. Locke is a less ambiguous figure because in the *Second Treatise of Government* he nominated three inalienable rights – those to life, liberty and property – and advocated rebellion against corrupt or overbearing governments. *A Letter Concerning Toleration* ([1689] 1990) also shows Locke to be an exponent of the freedom of conscience and practice in religious matters, although these religious liberties were not extended to Catholics or atheists. However, while I think that Locke comes closer than Hobbes to being the crucial philosophical source of rights discourse in the modern era, I do not think it would be correct to say of Locke what Fields does of Hobbes: that he provides a wholly secular justification for rights. See Waldron (2002).
7. As Jerome Shestack contends, 'no theory of human rights for a domestic or international order in modern society can be advanced today without considering Rawls's thesis [that the role of justice is crucial to understanding human rights]' (2000: 46).
8. Although Rawls's commentators typically depict *Political Liberalism* as his response to the massive attention, and criticism, received by *A Theory of Justice*, Rawls himself describes the second book as working through some of the problems and tensions inherent in the first. (Rawls 1993a: xix, n. 6. Cf. Rawls 1999a: 179).

9. Rawls (1993: xvi–xix, 177). Thomas Nagel suggests that the differences between the two works are not so significant (2003: 73), while Burton Dreben (2003) insists that they are.

10. Rawls (1999b: 11). The feminist liberal Susan Moller Okin seizes upon Rawls's inclusion of the family as one of the institutions constituting the basic structure. In this she sees Rawls's ambivalent legacy for feminists. On the one hand, including the family among the basic structure's constituents means that standards of justice must be applied to the family, and she welcomes this departure from much previous liberalism that consigned the family to the private realm and showed little interest in its dynamics or norms. However, having numbered the family among the components of the basic structure, Rawls effectively ignores it. Moreover, the assumption of a traditional, patriarchal family appears in section 44, where he posits the contractors in the original positions as heads of household, assumed to be male and willing and able to make principled decisions on behalf of their family members (Okin 1989: 89–109). See Nussbaum (2003) for an overview of feminist responses to Rawls.

11. It is also noteworthy that most of the literature linking Rawls with human rights discusses his 1999 work *The Law of Peoples* rather than *A Theory of Justice* or *Political Liberalism*.

12. Rawls has thus been read as providing a liberal defence of the welfare state. His theory of justice requires considerable government intervention in the economy; the state might, for example, provide public education, police the conduct of firms and guarantee a minimum social income. Fields describes Rawls's concern with the distribution of primary social goods as 'profoundly a human rights position' (2003: 135).

13. Jonathan Wolff illustrates their possible connection by the impact that greater wealth can have on participation in, and influence on, politics (1998: 124–5).

14. As Nagel puts it, 'the strict priority of individual rights and liberties over the reduction of social and economic inequalities is the true core of liberalism' (2003: 67). Kymlicka likewise claims that 'one way of differentiating liberalism just is that it gives priority to the basic liberties.' (2002, p. 56).

15. In his adumbration of the law of the peoples, Rawls allows that in well-ordered hierarchical societies, individuals can be accorded rights 'as members of estates and corporations, but not as citizens' (1993b: 70; 1999a: 68), but it is still persons who are the rights-holders, not the collective entities.

16. As Jack Donnelly observes, 'liberal visions of human rights . . . see group affiliations as largely irrelevant to the rights and opportunities that ought to be available to individuals' (2003: 206). For a fuller discussion of the atomist ontology of much liberalism, see Taylor (1985).

17. In this he is developing an argument sketched in his previous book, *Liberalism, Community, and Culture*.

18. As enshrined in Articles 13 and 16 of the Universal Declaration of Human Rights.

19. For a fuller discussion of the issues canvassed in this section, see Baumeister (2000: 26–35, 103–19).

20. Rorty does have more to say about the connection between economic progress and moral progress in his 1998 work, *Achieving Our Country*.

21. For a fuller depiction and a different critique of Rorty's position, see Langlois (1998).

22. Rawls acknowledges this problem, saying that some of the rights in the UDHR are human rights proper while others are better understood as 'liberal aspirations' and yet others 'presuppose specific kinds of institutions' (1993b: 228, n. 46; 1999a: p. 80, n. 23) Yet this seems like a wholly arbitrary distinction.

23. For a fuller discussion of the question rights and reproduction, see Warnock (2002).

24. To indicate just one possible alternative to rights discourse in this domain, Charles Taylor (1995a) suggests that the work of Martin Heidegger opens up a fruitful way of talking about human relations with the natural world.

25. For a fuller discussion of this, see Garner (2003).
26. By the time Rawls was sketching his argument about the extension of his theory of justice to the international realm twenty years later, 'the problem of what is owed to animals and the rest of nature' was still deferred (Rawls 1993b: 44. I could find no reference to this question in the 1999 extended version of *The Law of Peoples*).
27. This seems to contradict his earlier claim that how far the conclusions of justice as fairness 'must be revised once these other matters are understood cannot be decided in advance' (1999b: 17).
28. According to Freeman, 'the academic study of human rights has been dominated by lawyers... The field of human rights has become a technical legal discourse, and lawyers dominate it because they are the technical experts' (2002: 6; cf. 12).
29. Taylor (1998: 155). Some reservations about the relationship between rights and democracy are also expressed in Walzer (1981). See Bellamy (2000, ch. 9) for some other reservations about rights.
30. In *The Rights Revolution*, which began as the year 2000's contribution to the CBC's annual Massey lecture series, Ignatieff portrays Canada with its Charter of Rights and Freedoms, its multiculturalism, its recognition of some indigenous rights, and the issue of Quebec's status as a distinct society, as a microcosm of this movement.

JOHN RAWLS
EXTRACTS FROM *A THEORY OF JUSTICE*

[. . .]

The main idea of the theory of justice

My aim is to present a conception of justice which generalizes and carries to a higher level of abstraction the familiar theory of the social contract as found, say, in Locke, Rousseau, and Kant.[1] In order to do this we are not to think of the original contract as one to enter a particular society or to set up a particular form of government. Rather, the guiding idea is that the principles of justice for the basic structure of society are the object of the original agreement. They are the principles that free and rational persons concerned to further their own interests would accept in an initial position of equality as defining the fundamental terms of their association. These principles are to regulate all further agreements; they specify the kinds of social cooperation that can be entered into and the forms of government that can be established. This way of regarding the principles of justice I shall call justice as fairness.

Thus we are to imagine that those who engage in social cooperation choose together, in one joint act, the principles which are to assign basic rights and duties and to determine the division of social benefits. Men are to decide in advance how they are to regulate their claims against one another and what is to be the foundation charter of their society. Just as

John Rawls (1999), *A Theory of Justice*, rev. ed., Oxford: Oxford University Press.

each person must decide by rational reflection what constitutes his good, that is, the system of ends which it is rational for him to pursue, so a group of persons must decide once and for all what is to count among them as just and unjust. The choice which rational men would make in this hypothetical situation of equal liberty, assuming for the present that this choice problem has a solution, determines the principles of justice.

In justice as fairness the original position of equality corresponds to the state of nature in the traditional theory of the social contract. This original position is not, of course, thought of as an actual historical state of affairs, much less as a primitive condition of culture. It is understood as a purely hypothetical situation characterized so as to lead to a certain conception of justice.[2] Among the essential features of this situation is that no one knows his place in society, his class position or social status, nor does any one know his fortune in the distribution of natural assets and abilities, his intelligence, strength, and the like. I shall even assume that the parties do not know their conceptions of the good or their special psychological propensities. The principles of justice are chosen behind a veil of ignorance. This ensures that no one is advantaged or disadvantaged in the choice of principles by the outcome of natural chance or the contingency of social circumstances. Since all are similarly situated and no one is able to design principles to favor his particular condition, the principles of justice are the result of a fair agreement or bargain. For given the circumstances of the original position, the symmetry of everyone's relations to each other, this initial situation is fair between individuals as moral persons, that is, as rational beings with their own ends and capable, I shall assume, of a sense of justice. The original position is, one might say, the appropriate initial status quo, and thus the fundamental agreements reached in it are fair. This explains the propriety of the name 'justice as fairness': it conveys the idea that the principles of justice are agreed to in an initial situation that is fair. The name does not mean that the concepts of justice and fairness are the same, any more than the phrase 'poetry as metaphor' means that the concepts of poetry and metaphor are the same.

Justice as fairness begins, as I have said, with one of the most general of all choices which persons might make together, namely, with the choice of the first principles of a conception of justice which is to regulate all subsequent criticism and reform of institutions. Then, having chosen a conception of justice, we can suppose that they are to choose a constitution and a legislature to enact laws, and so on, all in accordance with the principles of justice initially agreed upon. Our social situation is just if it is such that by this sequence of hypothetical agreements we would have contracted into the general system of rules which defines it. Moreover, assuming that the original position does determine a set of principles (that is, that a particular conception of justice would be chosen), it will then be true that whenever social institutions satisfy these principles those engaged in them can say to one another that they are cooperating on terms to which they would agree if they were free and equal persons whose relations with respect to one another were fair. They could all view their arrangements as meeting the stipulations which they would acknowledge in an initial situation that embodies widely accepted and reasonable constraints on the choice of principles. The general recognition of this fact would provide the basis for a public acceptance of the corresponding principles of justice. No society can, of course, be a scheme of cooperation which men enter voluntarily in a literal sense; each person finds himself placed at birth in some particular position in some particular society, and the nature of this position materially affects his life prospects. Yet a society satisfying the principles of justice as fairness comes as close as a society can to being a voluntary scheme, for it meets the principles which free and equal persons would assent to under circumstances that are fair. In this sense its members are autonomous and the obligations they recognize self-imposed.

One feature of justice as fairness is to think of the parties in the initial situation as rational and mutually disinterested. This does not mean that the parties are egoists, that is, individuals with only certain kinds of interests, say in wealth, prestige, and domination. But they are conceived as not taking an interest in one another's interests. They are to presume that even their spiritual aims may be opposed, in the way that the aims of those of different religions may be opposed. Moreover, the concept of rationality must be interpreted as far as possible in the narrow sense, standard in economic theory, of taking the most effective means to given ends. I shall modify this concept to some extent [. . .] but one must try to avoid introducing into it any controversial ethical elements. The initial situation must be characterized by stipulations that are widely accepted.

In working out the conception of justice as fairness one main task clearly is to determine which principles of justice would be chosen in the original position. To do this we must describe this situation in some detail and formulate with care the problem of choice which it presents. These matters I shall take up in the immediately succeeding chapters. It may be observed, however, that once the principles of justice are thought of as arising from an original agreement in a situation of equality, it is an open question whether the principle of utility would be acknowledged, Offhand it hardly seems likely that persons who view themselves as equals, entitled to press their claims upon one another, would agree to a principle which may require lesser life prospects for some simply for the sake of a greater sum of advantages enjoyed by others. Since each desires to protect his interests, his capacity to advance his conception of the good, no one has a reason to acquiesce in an enduring loss for himself in order to bring about a greater net balance of satisfaction. In the absence of strong and lasting benevolent impulses, a rational man would not accept a basic structure merely because it maximized the algebraic sum of advantages irrespective of its permanent effects on his own basic rights and interests. Thus it seems that the principle of utility is incompatible with the conception of social cooperation among equals for mutual advantage. It appears to be inconsistent with the idea of reciprocity implicit in the notion of a well-ordered society. Or, at any rate, so I shall argue.

I shall maintain instead that the persons in the initial situation would choose two rather different principles: the first requires equality in the assignment of basic rights and duties, while the second holds that social and economic inequalities, for example inequalities of wealth and authority, are just only if they result in compensating benefits for everyone, and in particular for the least advantaged members of society. These principles rule out justifying institutions on the grounds that the hardships of some are offset by a greater good in the aggregate. It may be expedient but it is not just that some should have less in order that others may prosper. But there is no injustice in the greater benefits earned by a few provided that the situation of persons not so fortunate is thereby improved. The intuitive idea is that since everyone's well-being depends upon a scheme of cooperation without which no one could have a satisfactory life, the division of advantages should be such as to draw forth the willing cooperation of everyone taking part in it, including those less well situated. The two principles mentioned seem to be a fair basis on which those better endowed, or more fortunate in their social position, neither of which we can be said to deserve, could expect the willing cooperation of others when some workable scheme is a necessary condition of the welfare of all.[3] Once we decide to look for a conception of justice that prevents the use of the accidents of natural endowment and the contingencies of social circumstance as counters in a quest for political and economic advantage, we are led to these principles. They express the result of leaving aside those aspects of the social world that seem arbitrary from a moral point of view.

The problem of the choice of principles, however, is extremely difficult. I do not expect the answer I shall suggest to be convincing to everyone. It is, therefore, worth noting from the outset that justice as fairness, like other contract views, consists of two parts: (1) an interpretation of the initial situation and of the problem of choice posed there, and (2) a set of principles which, it is argued, would be agreed to. One may accept the first part of the theory (or some variant thereof), but not the other, and conversely. The concept of the initial contractual situation may seem reasonable although the particular principles proposed are rejected. To be sure, I want to maintain that the most appropriate conception of this situation does lead to principles of justice contrary to utilitarianism and perfectionism, and therefore that the contract doctrine provides an alternative to these views. Still, one may dispute this contention even though one grants that the contractarian method is a useful way of studying ethical theories and of setting forth their underlying assumptions.

Justice as fairness is an example of what I have called a contract theory. Now there may be an objection to the term 'contract' and related expressions, but I think it will serve reasonably well. Many words have misleading connotations which at first are likely to confuse. The terms 'utility' and 'utilitarianism' are surely no exception. They too have unfortunate suggestions which hostile critics have been willing to exploit; yet they are clear enough for those prepared to study utilitarian doctrine. The same should be true of the term 'contract' applied to moral theories. As I have mentioned, to understand it one has to keep in mind that it implies a certain level of abstraction. In particular, the content of the relevant agreement is not to enter a given society or to adopt a given form of government, but to accept certain moral principles. Moreover, the undertakings referred to are purely hypothetical: a contract view holds that certain principles would be accepted in a well-defined initial situation.

The merit of the contract terminology is that it conveys the idea that principles of justice may be conceived as principles that would be chosen by rational persons, and that in this way conceptions of justice may be explained and justified. The theory of justice is a part, perhaps the most significant part, of the theory of rational choice. Furthermore, principles of justice deal with conflicting claims upon the advantages won by social cooperation; they apply to the relations among several persons or groups. The word 'contract' suggests this plurality as well as the condition that the appropriate division of advantages must be in accordance with principles acceptable to all parties. The condition of publicity for principles of justice is also connoted by the contract phraseology. Thus, if these principles are the outcome of an agreement, citizens have a knowledge of the principles that others follow. It is characteristic of contract theories to stress the public nature of political principles. Finally there is the long tradition of the contract doctrine. Expressing the tie with this line of thought helps to define ideas and accords with natural piety. There are then several advantages in the use of the term 'contract'. With due precautions taken, it should not be misleading.

A final remark. Justice as fairness is not a complete contract theory. For it is clear that the contractarian idea can be extended to the choice of more or less an entire ethical system, that is, to a system including principles for all the virtues and not only for justice. Now for the most part I shall consider only principles of justice and others closely related to them; I make no attempt to discuss the virtues in a systematic way. Obviously if justice as fairness succeeds reasonably well, a next step would be to study the more general view suggested by the name 'rightness as fairness'. But even this wider theory fails to embrace all moral relationships, since it would seem to include only our relations with other persons and to leave out of account how we are to conduct ourselves toward animals and the rest of nature. I do not contend that the contract notion offers a way to approach these questions which are certainly of the first importance; and I shall have to put them aside. We must recognize the limited scope of justice as fairness and of the general type of view that it exemplifies. How far its conclusions must be revised once these other matters are understood cannot be decided in advance.

NOTES

1. As the text suggests, I shall regard Locke's *Second Treatise of Government*, Rousseau's *The Social Contract*, and Kant's ethical works beginning with *The Foundations of the Metaphysics of Morals* as definitive of the contract tradition. For all of its greatness, Hobbes's *Leviathan* raises special problems. A general historical survey is provided by J. W. Gough, *The Social Contract*, 2nd ed. (Oxford, The Clarendon Press, 1957), and Otto Gierke, *Natural Law and the Theory of Society*, trans. with an introduction by Ernest Barker (Cambridge, The University Press, 1934). A presentation of the contract view as primarily an ethical theory is to be found in G. R. Grice, *The Grounds of Moral Judgment* (Cambridge, The University Press, 1967).

2. Kant is clear that the original agreement is hypothetical. See *The Metaphysics of Morals*, pt. I (*Rechtslehre*), especially §§47, 52; and pt. II of the eassy 'Concerning the Common Saying: This May Be True in Theory but It Does Not Apply in Practice,' in *Kant's Political Writings*, ed. Hans Reiss and trans. by H. B. Nisbet (Cambridge, The University Press, 1970), pp. 73–87. See Georges Vlachos, *La Pensée politique de Kant* (Paris, Presses Universitaires de France, 1962), pp. 326–335; and J. G. Murphy, *Kant: The Philosophy of Right* (London, Macmillan, 1970), pp. 109–112, 133–136, for a further discussion.

3. For the formulation of this intuitive idea I am indebted to Allan Gibbard.

WILL KYMLICKA
EXTRACTS FROM *MULTICULTURAL CITIZENSHIP: A LIBERAL THEORY OF MINORITY RIGHTS*

FREEDOM AND CULTURE

The value of cultural membership

I have tried to show that people's capacity to make meaningful choices depends on access to a cultural structure. But why do the members of a national minority need access to their *own* culture?[1] Why not let minority cultures disintegrate, so long as we ensure their members have access to the majority culture (e.g. by teaching them the majority language and history)? This latter option would involve a cost to minorities, but governments could subsidize it. For example, governments could pay for the members of national minorities to learn about the majority language and history.

This sort of proposal treats the loss of one's culture as similar to the loss of one's job. Language training for members of a threatened culture would be like worker retraining programmes for employees of a dying industry. We do not feel obliged to keep uncompetitive industries afloat in perpetuity, so long as we help employees to find employment elsewhere, so why feel obliged to protect minority cultures, so long as we help their members to find another culture?

This is an important question. It would be implausible to say that people are never able to switch cultures. After all, many immigrants function well in their new country (although others flounder, and many return home).

Will Kymlicka (1995), *Multicultural Citizenship: A Liberal Theory of Minority Rights*, Oxford: Clarendon Press.

Waldron thinks that these examples of successful 'cosmopolitan' people who move between cultures disprove the claim that people are connected to their own culture in any deep way. Suppose, he says, that

> a freewheeling cosmopolitan life, lived in a kaleidoscope of cultures, is both possible and fulfilling.... Immediately, one argument for the protection of minority cultures is undercut. It can no longer be said that all people need their rootedness in the particular culture in which they and their ancestors were reared in the way that they need food, clothing, and shelter ... Such immersion may be something that particular people like and enjoy. But they no longer can claim that it is something that they need.... The collapse of the Herderian argument based on distinctively human *need* seriously undercuts any claim that minority cultures might have to special support or assistance or to extraordinary provision or forbearance. At best, it leaves the right to culture roughly on the same footing as the right to religious freedom. (Waldron 1992: 762)

Because people do not need their own culture, minority cultures can ('at best') claim the same negative rights as religious groups – that is, the right to non-interference, but not to state support.

I think Waldron is seriously overstating the case here. For one thing, he vastly overestimates the extent to which people do in fact move between cultures, because (as I discuss below) he assumes that cultures are based on ethnic descent. On his view, an Irish-American who eats Chinese food and reads her child *Grimms' Fairy-Tales* is thereby 'living in a kaleidoscope of cultures' (e.g. Waldron 1992: 754). But this is not moving between societal cultures. Rather it is enjoying the opportunities provided by the diverse societal culture which characterizes the anglophone society of the United States.

Of course, people do genuinely move between cultures. But this is rarer, and more difficult. In some cases, where the differences in social organization and technological development are vast, successful integration may be almost impossible for some members of the minority. (This seems to be true of the initial period of contact between European cultures and indigenous peoples in some parts of the world.)

But even where successful integration is possible, it is rarely easy. It is a costly process, and there is a legitimate question whether people should be required to pay those costs unless they voluntarily choose to do so. These costs vary, depending on the gradualness of the process, the age of the person, and the extent to which the two cultures are similar in language and history.[2] But even where the obstacles to integration are smallest, the desire of national minorities to retain their cultural membership remains very strong (just as the members of the majority culture typically value their cultural membership).

In this sense, the choice to leave one's culture can be seen as analogous to the choice to take a vow of perpetual poverty and enter a religious order. It is not impossible to live in poverty. But it does not follow that a liberal theory of justice should therefore view the desire for a level of material resources above bare subsistence simply as 'something that particular people like and enjoy' but which 'they no longer can claim is something that they need' (Waldron 1992: 762). Liberals rightly assume that the desire for nonsubsistence resources is so normal – and the costs of forgoing them so high for most people's way of life – that people cannot reasonably be *expected* to go without such resources, even if a few people voluntarily choose to do so. For the purposes of determining people's claims of justice, material resources are something that people can be assumed to want, whatever their particular conception of the good. Although a small number of people may choose to forgo non-subsistence resources, this is seen as forgoing something to which they are entitled.

Similarly, I believe that, in developing a theory of justice, we should treat access to one's culture as something that people can be expected to want, whatever their more particular conception of the good. Leaving one's culture, while possible, is best seen as renouncing something to which one is reasonably entitled. This is a claim, not about the limits of human possibility, but about reasonable expectations.

I think that most liberals have implicitly accepted this claim about people's legitimate expectation to remain in their culture. Consider Rawls's argument about why the right to emigrate does not make political authority voluntary:

> normally leaving one's country is a grave step: it involves leaving the society and culture in which we have been raised, the society and culture whose language we use in speech and thought to express and understand ourselves, our aims, goals, and values; the society and culture whose history, customs, and conventions we depend on to find our place in the social world. In large part, we affirm our society and culture, and have an intimate and inexpressible knowledge of it, even though much of it we may question, if not reject. The government's authority cannot, then, be freely accepted in the sense that the bonds of society and culture, of history and social place of origin, begin so early to shape our life and are normally so strong that the right of emigration (suitably qualified) does not suffice to make accepting its authority free, politically speaking, in the way that liberty of conscience suffices to make accepting ecclesiastical authority free. (Rawls 1993b: 222)

Because of these bonds to the 'language we use in speech and thought to express and understand ourselves', cultural ties 'are normally too strong to be given up, and this fact is not to be deplored'. Hence, for the purposes of developing a theory of justice, we should assume that 'people are born and are expected to lead a complete life' within the same 'society and culture' (Rawls 1993b: 277).

I agree with Rawls's view about the difficulty of leaving one's culture.[3] Yet his argument has implications beyond those which he himself draws. Rawls presents this as an argument about the difficulty of leaving one's political community. But his argument does not rest on the value of specifically political ties (e.g. the bonds to one's government and fellow citizens). Rather it rests on the value of cultural ties (e.g. bonds to one's language and history). And cultural boundaries may not coincide with political boundaries. For example, someone leaving East Germany for West Germany in 1950 would not be breaking the ties of language and culture which Rawls emphasizes, even though she would be crossing state borders. But a francophone leaving Quebec City for Toronto, or a Puerto Rican leaving San Juan for Chicago, would be breaking those ties, even though she is remaining within the same country.

According to Rawls, then, the ties to one's culture are normally too strong to give up, and this is not to be regretted. We cannot be expected or required to make such a sacrifice, even if some people voluntarily do so. It is an interesting question why the bonds of language and culture are so strong for most people. It seems particularly puzzling that people would have a strong attachment to a liberalized culture. After all, as a culture is liberalized – and so allows members to question and reject traditional ways of life – the resulting cultural identity becomes both 'thinner' and less distinctive. That is, as a culture becomes more liberal, the members are less and less likely to share the same substantive conception of the good life, and more and more likely to share basic values with people in other liberal cultures.

The Québécois provide a nice illustration of this process. Before the Quiet Revolution, the Québécois generally shared a rural, Catholic, conservative, and patriarchal conception of the good. Today, after a rapid period of liberalization, most people have abandoned this traditional way of life, and Québécois society now exhibits all the diversity that any modern society contains – e.g. atheists and Catholics, gays and heterosexuals, urban yuppies and rural farmers, socialists and conservatives, etc. To be a 'Québécois' today, therefore, simply means being a participant in the francophone society of Quebec. And francophones in Quebec no more agree about conceptions of the good than anglophones in the United States. So being a 'Québécois' seems to be a very thin form of identity.

Moreover, the process of liberalization has also meant that the Québécois have become much more like English Canadians in their basic values. Liberalization in Quebec over the last thirty years has been accompanied by a pronounced convergence in personal and political values between English- and French-speaking Canadians, so that it would now be 'difficult to identify consistent differences in attitudes on issues such as moral values, prestige ranking of professions, role of the government, workers' rights, aboriginal rights, equality between the sexes and races, and conception of authority' (Dion 1992: 99; cf. Dion 1991: 301; Taylor 1991: 54).[4]

In short, liberalization in Quebec has meant both an increase in differences amongst the Québécois, in terms of their conceptions of the good, and a reduction in differences between the Québécois and the members of other liberal cultures. This is not unique to Quebec. The same process is at work throughout Europe. The modernization and liberalization of Western Europe has resulted both in fewer commonalities within each of the national cultures, and greater commonalities across these cultures. As Spain has liberalized, it has become both more pluralistic internally, and more like France or Germany in terms of its modern, secular, industrialized, democratic, and consumerist civilization.

This perhaps explains why so many theorists have assumed that liberalization and modernization would displace any strong sense of national identity. As cultures liberalize, people share less and less with their fellow members of the national group, in terms of traditional customs or conceptions of the good life, and become more and more like the members of other nations, in terms of sharing a common civilization. Why then would anyone feel strongly attached to their own nation? Such an attachment seems, to many commentators, like the 'narcissism of minor differences' (Ignatieff 1993: 21; Dion 1991).

Yet the evidence is overwhelming that the members of liberal cultures *do* value their cultural membership. Far from displacing national identity, liberalization has in fact gone hand in hand with an increased sense of nationhood. Many of the liberal reformers in Quebec have been staunch nationalists, and the nationalist movement grew in strength throughout the Quiet Revolution and afterwards. The same combination of liberalization and a strengthened national identity can be found in many other countries. For example, in Belgium, the liberalization of Flemish society has been accompanied by a sharp rise in nationalist sentiment (Peterson 1975: 208). The fact that their culture has become tolerant and pluralistic has in no way diminished the pervasiveness or intensity of people's desire to live and work in their own culture. Indeed, Walker Connor goes so far as to suggest that few if any examples exist of recognized national groups in this century having voluntarily assimilated to another culture, even though many have had significant economic incentives and political pressures to do so (Connor 1972: 350–1; 1973: 20).

Why are the bonds of language and culture so strong for most people? Commentators offer a number of reasons. Margalit and Raz argue that membership in a societal culture (what they call a 'pervasive culture') is crucial to people's well-being for two reasons. The first reason is the one I have discussed above – namely, that cultural membership provides meaningful options, in the sense that 'familiarity with a culture determines the boundaries of the imaginable'. Hence if a culture is decaying or discriminated against, 'the options and opportunities open to its members will shrink, become less attractive, and their pursuit less likely to be successful' (Margalit and Raz 1990: 449).

But why cannot the members of a decaying culture simply integrate into another culture? According to Margalit and Raz, this is difficult, not only because it is 'a very slow process indeed', but also because of the role of cultural membership in people's self-identity. Cultural membership has a 'high social profile', in the sense that it affects how others perceive and respond to us, which in turn shapes our self-identity. Moreover, national identity is particularly suited to serving as the 'primary foci of identification', because it is based on belonging, not accomplishment:

> Identification is more secure, less liable to be threatened, if it does not depend on accomplishment. Although accomplishments play their role in people's sense of their own identity, it would seem that at the most fundamental level our sense of our own identity depends on criteria of belonging rather than on those of accomplishment. Secure identification at that level is particularly important to one's well-being.

Hence cultural identity provides an 'anchor for [people's] self-identification and the safety of effortless secure belonging'. But this in turn means that people's self-respect is bound up with the esteem in which their national group is held. If a culture is not generally respected, then the dignity and self-respect of its members will also be threatened (Margalit and Raz 1990: 447–9). Similar arguments about the role of respect for national membership in supporting dignity and self-identity are given by Charles Taylor (1992) and Yael Tamir (1993: 41, 71–3).

Tamir also emphasizes the extent to which cultural membership adds an 'additional meaning' to our actions, which become not only acts of individual accomplishment, but also 'part of a continuous creative effort whereby culture is made and remade'. And she argues that, where institutions are 'informed by a culture [people] find understandable and meaningful', this 'allows a certain degree of transparency that facilitates their participation in public affairs'. This in turn promotes a sense of belonging and relationships of mutual recognition and mutual responsibility (Tamir 1993: 72, 85–6). Other commentators make the related point that the mutual intelligibility which comes from shared national identity promotes relationships of solidarity and trust (Miller 1993b; Barry 1991: 174–5). James Nickel emphasizes the potential harm to valuable intergenerational bonds when parents are unable to pass on their culture to their children and grandchildren (Nickel 1995). Benedict Anderson emphasizes the way national identity enables us to transcend our mortality, by linking us to something whose existence seems to extend back into time immemorial, and forward into the indefinite future (Anderson 1983).

No doubt all of these factors play a role in explaining people's bond to their own culture. I suspect that the causes of this attachment lie deep in the human condition, tied up with the way humans as cultural creatures need to make sense of their world, and that a full explanation would involve aspects of psychology, sociology, linguistics, the philosophy of mind, and even neurology (Laponce 1987).

But whatever the explanation, this bond does seem to be a fact, and, like Rawls, I see no reason to regret it. I should emphasize, again, that I am only dealing with general trends. Some people seem most at home leading a truly cosmopolitan life, moving freely between different societal cultures. Others have difficulty making sense of the cultural meanings within their own culture. But most people, most of the time, have a deep bond to their own culture.

It may seem paradoxical for liberals like Rawls to claim that the bonds to one's culture are 'normally too strong to be given up'. What has happened to the much vaunted liberal freedom of choice? But Rawls's view is in fact common within the liberal tradition, as we saw in Chapter 4. The freedom which liberals demand for individuals is not primarily the freedom to go beyond one's language and history, but rather the freedom to move around within one's societal culture, to distance oneself from particular cultural roles, to choose which features of the culture are most worth developing, and which are without value.

This may sound like a rather 'communitarian' view of the self. I do not think this is an accurate label. One prominent theme in recent communitarian writing is the rejection of the liberal view about the importance of being free to revise one's ends. Communitarians deny that we can 'stand apart' from (some of) our ends. According to Michael Sandel, a leading American communitarian, some of our ends are 'constitutive' ends, in the sense that they define our sense of personal identity (Sandel 1982: 150–65; cf. MacIntyre 1981: ch. 15; Bell 1993: 24–54). It makes no sense, on his view, to say that my ends might not be worthy of my allegiance, for they define who I am. Whereas Rawls claims that individuals 'do not regard themselves as inevitably bound to, or identical with, the pursuit of any particular complex of fundamental interests that they may have at any given moment' (1974: 641), Sandel responds that we are in fact 'identical with' at least some of our final ends. Since these ends are constitutive of people's identity, there is no reason why the state should not reinforce people's allegiance to those ends, and limit their ability to question and revise these ends.

I believe that this communitarian conception of the self is mistaken. It is not easy or enjoyable to revise one's deepest ends, but it is possible, and sometimes a regrettable necessity. New experiences or circumstances may reveal that our earlier beliefs about the good are mistaken. No end is immune from such potential revision. As Dworkin puts it, it is true that 'no one can put everything about himself in question all at once', but it 'hardly follows that for each person there is some one connection or association so fundamental that it cannot be detached for inspection while holding others in place' (Dworkin 1989: 489).

Some people may think of themselves as being incapable of questioning or revising their ends, but in fact 'our conceptions of the good may and often do change over time, usually slowly but sometimes rather suddenly', even for those people who think of themselves as having constitutive ends (Rawls 1985: 242). No matter how confident we are about our ends at a particular moment, new circumstances or experiences may arise, often in unpredictable ways, that cause us to re-evaluate them. There is no way to predict in advance when the need for such a reconsideration will arise. As I noted earlier, a liberal society does not compel people to revise their commitments – and many people will go years without having any reason to question their basic commitments – but it does recognize that the freedom of choice is not a one-shot affair, and that earlier choices sometimes need to be revisited. Since our judgements about the good are fallible in this way, we have an interest, not only in pursuing our existing conception of the good, but also in being able to assess and potentially revise that conception. Our current ends are not always worthy of our continued allegiance, and exposure to other ways of life helps us make informed judgements about what is truly valuable.

The view I am defending is quite different, therefore, from the communitarian one, although both views claim that we have a deep bond to a particular sort of social group. The difference is partly a matter of scope. Communitarians typically talk about our attachment to subnational groups – churches, neighbourhoods, family, unions, etc. – rather than to the larger society which encompasses these subgroups. But this difference in scope reflects an even deeper divergence. Communitarians are looking for groups which are defined by a shared conception of the good. They seek to promote a 'politics of the common good', in which groups can promote a shared conception of the good, even if this limits the ability of individual members to revise their ends. They believe that members have a 'constitutive' bond to the group's values, and so no harm is done by limiting individual rights in order to promote shared values.

As most communitarians admit, this 'politics of the common good' cannot apply at 'the national level. As Sandel puts it, 'the nation proved too vast a scale across which to cultivate the shared self-understandings necessary to community in the . . . constitutive sense' (Sandel 1984: 93; cf. MacIntyre 1981: 221; Miller 1988–9: 60–7). The members of a nation rarely share moral values or traditional ways of life. They share a language and history, but often disagree fundamentally about the ultimate ends in life. A common national identity, therefore, is not a useful basis for communitarian politics, which can only exist at a more local level.

The liberal view I am defending insists that people can stand back and assess moral values and traditional ways of life, and should be given not only

the legal right to do so, but also the social conditions which enhance this capacity (e.g. a liberal education). So I object to communitarian politics at the
subnational level. To inhibit people from questioning their inherited social
roles can condemn them to unsatisfying, even oppressive, lives.[5] And at the
national level, the very fact which makes national identity so inappropriate
for communitarian politics – namely, that it does not rest on shared values –
is precisely what makes it an appropriate basis for liberal politics. The national culture provides a meaningful context of choice for people, without
limiting their ability to question and revise particular values or beliefs.

Put another way, the liberal ideal is a society of free and equal individuals.
But what is the relevant 'society'? For most people it seems to be their nation.
The sort of freedom and equality they most value, and can make most use
of, is freedom and equality within their own societal culture. And they
are willing to forgo a wider freedom and equality to ensure the continued
existence of their nation.

For example, few people favour a system of open borders, where people
could freely cross borders and settle, work, and vote in whatever country
they desired. Such a system would dramatically increase the domain within
which people would be treated as free and equal citizens. Yet open borders
would also make it more likely that people's own national community would
be overrun by settlers from other cultures, and that they would be unable
to ensure their survival as a distinct national culture. So we have a choice
between, on the one hand, increased mobility and an expanded domain
within which people are free and equal individuals, and, on the other hand,
decreased mobility but a greater assurance that people can continue to be
free and equal members of their own national culture. Most people in liberal
democracies clearly favour the latter. They would rather be free and equal
within their own nation, even if this means they have less freedom to work
and vote elsewhere, than be free and equal citizens of the world, if this
means they are less likely to be able to live and work in their own language
and culture.

And most theorists in the liberal tradition have implicitly agreed with
this. Few major liberal theorists have endorsed open borders, or even seriously considered it. They have generally accepted – indeed, simply taken
for granted – that the sort of freedom and equality which matters most to
people is freedom and equality within one's societal culture. Like Rawls,
they assume that 'people are born and are expected to lead a complete life'
within the same 'society and culture', and that this defines the scope within
which people must be free and equal (Rawls 1993b: 277).[6]

In short, liberal theorists have generally, if implicitly, accepted that cultures or nations are basic units of liberal political theory. In this sense, as
Yael Tamir puts it, 'most liberals are liberal nationalists' (1993: 139) – that
is, liberal goals are achieved in and through a liberalized societal culture or
nation.

NOTES

1. I am trying to respond here to the cogent questions raised by Binder 1993: 253–5; Buchanan 1991: 54–5; Waldron 1992; Tomasi 1995; Nickel 1995; Lenihan 1991; Margalit and Halbertal 1994, amongst others.

2. For a discussion of these costs, and the extent to which they vary between children and adults, see Nickel 1995.

3. It is worth remembering that, while many immigrants flourish in their new country, there is a selection factor at work. That is, those people who choose to uproot themselves are likely to be the people who have the weakest psychological bond to the old culture, and the strongest desire and determination to succeed elsewhere. We cannot assume a priori that they represent the norm in terms of cultural adaptability. As John Edwards notes, the ability to communicate does not only involve pragmatic language skills, but also the 'inexpressible' knowledge of historical and cultural associations tied up with the language, and this may be difficult or impossible for immigrants to acquire fully: 'the symbolic value of language, the historical and cultural associations which it accumulates, and the 'natural semantics of remembering' all add to the basic message a rich underpinning of shared connotations . . . the ability to read between the lines, as it were, depends upon a cultural continuity in which the language is embedded, and which is not open to all. Only those who grow up within the community can, perhaps, participate fully in this expanded communicative interaction' (Edwards 1985: 17).

4. The only significant difference, Dion notes, concerns openness to immigration, a difference that is understandable in the light of francophone fears as a minority.

5. The danger of oppression reflects the fact that many traditional roles and practices were defined historically on the basis of sexist, racist, classist, and homophobic assumptions. Some social roles are so compromised by their unjust origins that they should be rejected entirely, not just gradually reformed (Phillips 1993b). In some places, Sandel qualifies his idea of constitutive ends in a way that suggests that people can, after all, stand back and assess even their most deeply held ends. But once these qualifications are added in, it is no longer clear how Sandel's conception of the person differs from the liberal one he claims to be criticizing (see Kymlicka 1989: chs. 2–4; 1990: ch. 5). In his more recent work, Rawls has attempted to accommodate the communitarian view, and defend liberalism without insisting on the rational revisability of our ends. I do not think his new defence works.

6. Of course, once that national existence is not threatened, then people will favour increased mobility, since being able to move and work in other cultures is a valuable option for some people under some circumstances. For liberal defenders of open borders – all of whom see themselves as criticizing the orthodox liberal view – see Ackerman 1980: 89–95; Carens 1987; Hudson 1986; King 1983; Bader 1995.

PART II
POLITICAL LEGITIMACY

INTRODUCTION

It is now widely accepted that for political organisations at all levels to claim legitimacy they must claim to be democratic. Although this idea is both historically quite recent and culturally quite specific, there is no doubting that democratic ideals have come to form the mainstay of discussions surrounding political legitimacy. We need only consider how rarely we come across a defence of political organisations that grounds the legitimacy of its institutions on the idea of being undemocratic to see that this is the case. However, it is equally obvious that claiming legitimacy by recourse to democratic ideals takes many different and often competing forms. As the first section of this part reveals, even where theorists broadly agree that democratic legitimacy is best served by deliberative procedures there is still no agreement around what exactly this requires in terms of justification or what this would entail in terms of political practices and institutions. Moreover, if we take refuge in the idea that at the very least democratic legitimacy requires the representation of the people at all levels of political life this itself merely deflects the argument onto an equally contested terrain, as the essay and readings in the second section of this part make clear. One way of tackling these general problems of political legitimacy is to focus on problems that test the limits of the democratic ideal: namely, to what extent can and should democratic institutions tolerate beliefs, lifestyles and political practices that may, arguably, be undemocratic in themselves, and to what extent does the political legitimacy of democratic ideals rest upon a shared democratic culture in an age of deep and irreducible multiculturalism. In addressing these and related questions directly, the third and fourth sections of this part show that the everyday idea that 'democracy equals legitimacy' is not as straightforward as it may at first appear. In large measure, this is due to the fact that once we scratch the surface of the concepts 'toleration' and 'multiculturalism' we find arguments about the rule of law, civil society, human nature, community and difference (to name a few) just beneath. The idea that democracy is the almost unquestioned source of political legitimacy in the contemporary political world, therefore, is not the end of the story but the beginning of a long and winding road through the whole landscape of political concepts.

1

DEMOCRACY

Stephen Elstub

INTRODUCTION

In 1998 James Bohman trumpeted '*the coming of age of deliberative democracy*' and certainly over the last fifteen years, deliberative democracy has become an increasingly dominant strand of democratic theory. It has begun to dominate the literature from enthusiasts and critics and has developed into a mature and complex theory with a diversity of strands and tendencies, gaining popularity and credence as a critique of existing democracy, as a normative force and as an ideal to be approximated. The principal aim of the chapter is to highlight the diversity brought about by an ever-increasing number of strands that are becoming ever more disparate (Saward 2000a: 5). These strands and tendencies are not entirely exclusive, as key features are shared and many crossovers can be identified, making deliberative theory deep and complex but also muddled. This chapter will clearly set out the lines of conflict and agreement.

A secondary aim is to demonstrate the relevance of deliberative theory to key problems faced by democratic theory in general. The theory itself retains many classical elements of democracy as in many respects it reinvents a participatory model of democracy derived from Athenian democracy (Dryzek 2000: 2). Inspiration is taken from some of the most influential democratic theorists over the ages such as Aristotle, John Stuart Mill, Jean-Jacques Rousseau, John Dewey and Hannah Arendt. Therefore, as well as being one of the most provocative and contentious contemporary democratic theories, it provides a great insight into many of the classic, perennial and contemporary issues most pertinent in democratic theory.

Both aims will be achieved by considering six broad questions essential to gaining an understanding of deliberative democracy. These are:

1. What is deliberative democracy?
2. What is so good about deliberative democracy?
3. What is the nature of public reason?
4. Is deliberative democracy a model of democracy?
5. Can deliberative democracy enhance political equality?
6. Can deliberative democracy be institutionalised?

DEFINING DELIBERATIVE DEMOCRACY

Although democracy essentially means 'rule by the people', it has always been a contested concept and has been interpreted in many different ways through its long history. In essence, the theory of deliberative democracy rests upon a statement on the 'true' meaning of democracy in the modern age and, in particular, provides a critique of the dominant conception of democracy found in modern liberal democracies.

As its title suggests there are two key elements, 'democracy' and 'deliberation'. The democratic part is collective decision-making through the participation of all relevant actors. The deliberative strand is the making of the decisions through the give and take of rational arguments (Elster 1998: 8). The ideal of deliberative democracy is best represented in Jürgen Habermas's counterfactual set of procedures termed 'the ideal speech situation' (ISS). Here communication is undistorted, as all participants are free and equal with no power discrepancies and unconstrained from subjection, self-delusion and strategic activity. All views are aired in an unlimited discourse, creating open participation aimed at rational consensus (Habermas 1990b: 56–8), where the 'unforced force of the better argument' is decisive (Habermas 1996a).

The deliberative strand can be described as 'a dialogical process of exchanging reasons for the purpose of resolving problematic situations that cannot be settled without interpersonal co-ordination and co-operation' (Bohman 1996: 27). Through deliberative interaction and communication and therefore the consideration of those with differing preferences, existing preferences can be transformed and new ones formed. Jon Elster sums up preference transformation as the defining mark of deliberative democracy: 'The transformation of preferences through rational deliberation is the ostensible goal of arguing' (Elster 1998: 6). Therefore in order for deliberation to have taken place, communication between participants must induce 'reflection upon preferences in non-coercive fashion'. This deliberation is democratic if these reflective preferences influence collective decisions and all have had an opportunity to participate equally (Dryzek 2000: 2).

However, people will not only adapt preferences because of good reasons, as in the ISS, but also due to other factors such as the provider of the information and the manner in which it is provided.

Nevertheless, deliberative theorists believe that preferences will adapt to reason and conceive preferences as being exogenous, formed during the political process rather than prior to it. In contrast, many other democrats and social-choice theorists share the prevalent liberal conception that perceives preferences as endogenous and unchanging. They think deliberative theorists confuse evidence of changing preferences with a change in the available 'choice set' on a particular decision (Miller 1993a: 90; Dryzek 2000: 32). Whether preferences are exogenous or endogenous is essentially an empirical question. The results from deliberative opinion polls in the USA, UK, Australia and Denmark indicate that preferences will change when citizens participate in democratic deliberation (Issues Deliberation Australia 1999; Fishkin and Luskin 2000: 23; Andersen and Hansen 2004). This is certainly not conclusive empirical evidence, but the increasing volume of results from deliberative opinion polls and citizen juries does indicate that preferences are exogenous and counter-empirical evidence must be provided to suggest differently. This broad conception of the two components of democratic deliberation is then accepted by most within the tradition; however, there are still some key disputes that need to be addressed.

JUSTIFICATIONS OF DELIBERATIVE DEMOCRACY

One of the most significant divides within deliberative democracy derives from alternative justifications. There have always been various justifications of democracy, which advocate 'basic political values' and then illuminate how democracy promotes these values (Christiano 1996: 15), and the deliberative theory is no different. Three prominent justifications of deliberative democracy will be outlined in turn: the prudential justification, the epistemic justification and the fair procedure justification. These justifications are often cited to justify democracy in general, but the deliberative theorists make the case that not any model of democracy will suffice because only deliberative democracy can best promote these 'basic political values'.

1. The prudential justification

According to this justification, deliberative democracy is good because it enables 'each participant to gain an equally clear and reflective understanding of his ideas and interests' (at least in comparison to purely aggregative models of democracy, where decisions are reached without debate because citizens just choose to vote for an outcome). Deliberative democracy can therefore help to overcome inequalities between citizens with respect to information and rationality (Festenstein 2002: 103).

No participant can predict what all participants' opinions would be or know all the information relevant to a decision (Benhabib 1996: 71). Through debate participants' preferences will be revised in light of perspectives and information of which they were previously unaware and that would not be present in purely aggregative mechanisms (Manin 1987: 349). They also have the opportunity to question the information and arguments that have been put forth by partisan sources, and form and enter into debate with their own information and arguments in a manner that is persuasive to others, which will further help them gain a clearer understanding of their own beliefs and preferences. The information provided in the discussion, from the various participants, may also have some direct bearing on the outcomes of the various choices, which could, would or should have an effect on what decision the collective makes.

However, it seems impossible for all relevant and available information to be perfectly disseminated to all citizens in modern complex societies (although in the ISS this would be the case) because democratic deliberation can only ever increase access to available information. Due to the exigency of time, decisions cannot be put on hold until all information has been disseminated. We therefore face the problem of where the trade-off between gathering information and making the decision should be made and perhaps deliberation must proceed with the understanding that in the future, information may come to light that could change the participants' preferences.

2. The epistemic justification

In this justification, deliberative democracy is good because it is the best method of producing good decisions. If another model of democracy, or even an undemocratic method, were more reliable, deliberative democracy would be unnecessary (Estlund 1997: 183). However, the argument is that deliberative democracy is the most reliable method because by generating public reason it can lead to decisions that are true, well justified or commensurate with justice or the common good (Bohman 1998: 403; Festenstein 2002: 99). One of the key problems with this justification is how we know whether deliberative democracy does produce decisions that promote the common good. If we could test that it does then that would mean there is another method for identifying the common good. Moreover, it is also reliant upon there being a 'real truth' about the common good (Festenstein 2002: 99–100). Finally, if there is continuing disagreement after a period of deliberation, the minority will still deny the correctness of the decision and therefore not feel obligated by it (Estlund 1997: 175) and there is no incentive to compromise one's position: 'Participants may insist that the public good was quite satisfactorily expressed in their own original proposals, with supporting reasons, or by some other view which emerged' (Festenstein 2002: 100).

3. The fair procedure justification

This justification is opposed to the epistemic one, claiming there is no external good by which to judge decisions. Rather, the resulting decisions in deliberative democracy will be 'just' because they are derived from the fair procedures in which all have been able to participate equally, regardless of what the actual decision is (Cohen 1989b). It is evident that all get to participate equally in a vote, so the proceduralists must make the further claim that public reason increases the fairness of the procedure by encouraging participants to consider the preferences of others and improves 'the quality of preferences, opinions and reasons'. This then takes the proceduralists towards either the prudentialist or epistemic approach and is also a peculiar use of the term 'fair' because fairness is usually equated with impartiality (Festenstein 2002: 102–3). This justification also fails to account for why the decisions that result from the ideal procedures of deliberative democracy are 'correct' and based upon 'good' or 'compelling' reasons (Estlund 1997: 197). Without good reasons, why should the decision that has been produced by deliberatively democratic procedures be selected over any of the other available options? It would be just as fair to select an option randomly by a coin toss or through a vote (Estlund 1997: 178; Festenstein 2002: 103).

THE NATURE OF PUBLIC REASON

Reasons are the currency of deliberative democracy, and public reason has always played a central but contested role in debates about democracy. A survey of the current debates on the nature and role of public reason in deliberative democracy illuminates the key areas of contestation on the concept. These are central to many models of democracy as well as further demonstrating the various tendencies that are developing in deliberative democracy itself. Three main questions will be considered: Can public reason be produced privately or only collectively? Do the reasons offered need to be compelling to all to be public? Is a consensus likely and desirable?

1. Collective or private deliberation?

Democratic deliberation is generally considered to be a joint, collective activity yet following in the Rawlsian tradition, both Robert Goodin and Adolf Gundersen envisage democratic deliberation as being desirable and possible outside of collective debate. John Rawls and his followers favour individual deliberation, which is structurally different as it contains no dialogue, no give and take of reasons and no influence between actors (Rawls 1993b: 227).

Goodin suggests deliberative democracy can be a solo affair, provided others are made 'imaginatively present' through individuals conducting 'a wide ranging debate within their heads'. Nevertheless, he accepts collective deliberation will still be necessary as we can never know the views of others;

so some will be misportrayed, others completely ignored and few put as persuasively as they would be by the agent themselves (2003: 63–4).

Gundersen advocates 'dyadic' deliberation in his 'Socratic model'. Groups could still assemble to make collective decisions, but communication between them would always be dyadic with 'serial one-to-one encounters' (Gundersen 2000: 98). According to Gundersen, the first advantage of dyadic deliberation over collective deliberation is that it is easier to institutionalise (2000: 98). This may be the case, but unless it can generate the same or preferable normative consequences, it only stands if deliberative democracy is impossible to institutionalise otherwise collective deliberation should be pursued. However, Gundersen does claim dyadic deliberation is normatively superior to the collective alternative. He suggests that the relationship between participants is more interactive and therefore 'allows each partner to more easily ascertain the other's knowledge and interests', making clarification much easier because in a group it would mean the monopolisation of debate between two people (Gundersen 2000: 98–100). This seems uncertain because there may be more than one misunderstanding, sharing similarities with others. A debate about clarification could therefore take place among more than two participants and aid the understanding of many participants. Furthermore, Gundersen suggests that dyadic communication will mean greater equality between participants than collective deliberation because power in dyadic relationships is easier to challenge verbally and exit is also easier (2000: 101). This claim may be true in some cases, but certainly not in all. There are certain dyadic relationships where it is harder to challenge power verbally and exit is even harder than in collective debate; it seems to depend upon context. For example, a dyadic relationship may be dominated by one of the participants if the other holds them in high esteem or with excessive respect, for whatever reason. This of course can occur in collective deliberation, but others would be present and would hopefully challenge the 'esteemed figure' with reasons. Two people may find it very hard to respect deliberative procedures because of the disrespect they feel towards each other, but these feelings may be calmed by the presence of other participants debating. The main problem is that dyadic deliberation cannot generate public reason in the same manner as collective deliberation.

Here we see the quasi-Marxist element in the theory of deliberative democracy. Elster suggests that pure aggregation of preferences (and the argument could be applied to private deliberation) confuses the type of behaviour that is apt in the market place and the forum. In the market the consumer can be sovereign because the different choices will only affect the consumer. This is not the case when making collective political decisions, as many of the citizens' preferences may be defective (Elster 1997: 10) and need to be justified to the rest of the polity because the agents are not just deciding for themselves (Brennan and Lomasky 1993: 33–4). If private, this deliberation does not open people up to the arguments of others, or force people to defend their choice.

The differences between collective and private deliberative theorists derive from different views on the nature of public reason. To be 'public' (for both groups) the reasons offered must be understandable and acceptable to all citizens or at least potentially so (Bohman 1996: 26). However, the private deliberationists see reason as 'singular', meaning that all will reason in the same way, negating the need for others to be present (Rawls 1993b: 227; for a critique see Benhabib 1996: 75 and Dryzek 2000: 15). Therefore, individual citizens must consciously adopt public reason, rather than it being generated by the presence of others (Rawls 1997: 15; for a critique see Dryzek 2000: 15). In contrast, for the collective deliberationists, it is the very presence of other citizens that will encourage people to think 'publicly', the idea being that selfish reasons of the type 'I agree with this because it will really benefit me, but disadvantage others' will be unconvincing to others. Collective deliberation will therefore encourage people to focus on public values if their arguments are to persuade people of the validity of their ideas (Miller 1993a: 82; Benhabib 1996: 72; Elster 1997: 12). Included in the process of collective deliberation will be those who would be disadvantaged from these selfish preferences, and so could not possibly justify their prejudices to these people.

2. Universal or specific reasons?

Collective deliberation, then, seems to have greater normative potential than private deliberation. However, it still does not guarantee the generation of public reason as defined. Rather than offering reasons that are convincing to all, people may offer reasons that are aimed at a majority, or the largest minority. (This is of course dependent upon there being an established majority that is apparent to the participants and as preferences will change during deliberatively democratic debate, this majority may change during the process.) One suggested solution is that deliberative democracy should lead to a result 'that enjoys the widest possible support', not just majority support (Miller 2000a: 152). Perhaps finding reasons that all can accept is too stringent a demand, given the fact of pluralism.

Furthermore, it cannot be expected that the same reasons will convince all citizens of a certain decision. Psychological research has indicated that reflective preference transformation will be limited because people are unresponsive to reasons that do not support their preconceptions of an issue. This might explain why different people will look at the same piece of evidence and use it to support their own distinct interests (Femia 1996: 378–81). Therefore 'the force of an argument is always relative' (Manin 1987: 353; Dahl 1994: 31) and if rational arguments are to persuade an agent of a new belief, they must start by appealing to their present beliefs (Christiano 1997: 260). Consequently, participants in debate will offer different reasons to persuade different citizens of the need for the same outcome and therefore will not be public in the way envisioned by some deliberative theorists (Gaus 1997).

3. The possibility of consensus

Given that deliberative democracy has the potential to generate public reason with participants trying to find reasons that are convincing to all, Joshua Cohen in 'Deliberation and Democratic Legitimacy' and Habermas believe that a consensus would eventually be achieved (Cohen 1989: 23; Habermas 1996a: 17–19). They suggest that public reason would mean people taking on board a common interest over their private or selfish interests, as arguments must be based on the reasons that a proposal will be good for all and will encourage people to identify with each other and the collective as a whole (Cohen 1989b).

However, a key democratic requirement of the ideal of deliberative democracy is that all should be included in the debate. More participants often leads to more opinions, making agreement harder to achieve, especially if some of these are previously unheard (Knight and Johnson 1994: 289). Debate can also increase disagreement as well as reduce it. A collective could easily have a general agreement on some issue, but a debate could generate a greater diversity of opinions on an issue as it is explored more extensively and deeply (Mansbridge 1980: 65; Knight and Johnson 1994: 286; Christiano 1997: 249; Fearon 1998: 57; Budge 2000: 203; Weale 2000: 2). It is further suggested that there is a 'plurality of ultimate values'. People believe in totally different ideas of 'the good life' and are therefore too different, making agreement on ultimate values impossible. In modern cosmopolitan societies there are people from very different cultures who are unlikely to reach a consensus (Christiano 1997: 249; Weale 2000: 2). It seems unlikely that consensus will be achieved, which Cohen and Habermas do accept (Habermas 1996a: 304–5, 1996b: 18; Cohen 1998: 197), but both still maintain that consensus should still remain the 'ideal guiding discussion' (Miller 1993a: 81; Bohman 1996: 35–6).

The agonistic branch of deliberative democracy is not concerned by differences persisting, but rather praises differences as an essential resource for democratic deliberation, without which the deliberative process would be redundant (Young 1996: 127). Agonistics reject the idea that consensus on the common good is the sole aim of deliberation; they fear that the 'common good' might not be common at all, but simply a perpetuation of inequality and that consensus might be achieved through acquiescence to power rather than being rationally motivated (Mansbridge 1980: 32; Gambetta 1998: 21; Gould 1988: 18; Young 1996: 126). It is suggested that dominant social and economic groups are at an advantage because they can put forward their preferences and opinions as 'authoritative knowledge' and their interests as neutral and in the process devalue those with alternative beliefs, preferences and interests (Young 1997: 399).

It seems, then, that consensus is not possible and perhaps not desirable. If this is the case, it is apparent that in order for decisions to be made deliberation can only ever support the aggregation of preferences and not replace them altogether (Johnson 1998: 177; Przeworski 1998: 142; Dryzek 2000: 38). This means that the deliberative ideal of democracy loses some of its critical edge against aggregative models of democracy, which further raises the question of whether deliberative democracy can be considered a model of democracy.

THE DELIBERATIVE MODEL OF DEMOCRACY

For some, if deliberative democracy cannot reach a consensus and voting is still required to make a decision, this is evidence that it is not distinct and separate from aggregative models (Saward 2000b: 67–8; see also Squires 2002: 133–4).[1] Whether this argument is accepted depends upon how one defines a 'model of democracy'. C. B. Macpherson suggests that a 'model' should explain structural relations and have a normative element, which offers a 'model of man' and an 'ethically justificatory theory' (1977: 2–6). With regard to explaining structural relations, public reason is absent in a purely aggregative model and consequently a deliberative model would produce differing structural relations and requires different forms of participation due to the differences between public and private deliberation outlined above. With respect to having a distinctive explanatory or normative approach, a purely aggregative model views the source of legitimacy as citizens' predetermined preferences, while a deliberative model sees the formation of these preferences as the source of legitimacy, which therefore leads to differing normative and empirical claims.

Furthermore, deliberation and aggregation are elements not present in all conceptions of democracy; Habermas (1996b) has suggested in the past that collective deliberation could lead to consensus and William Riker (1982: 5) and Jean-Jacques Rousseau (1968) have perceived democratic arrangements purely dependent on voting without any collective deliberation. Consequently, a purely aggregative model of democracy is not a mythical construct set up as a straw man by deliberative democrats. It is true that liberal democracies do not presently approximate the aggregative model of democracy, as collective deliberation does occur in certain circumstances, through the media for example. Nevertheless, this does not mean the aggregative model does not exist as a theoretical construct. Neither does it rule out the deliberative model being a model, because, as Macpherson realised, new models develop as a critique of previous models, and are suggested as a 'corrective' or 'replacement'. However, this critique only need to be upon part of the preceding model and can therefore embody 'substantial elements of an earlier' model (Macpherson 1977: 8). Therefore, it seems that despite some form of deliberation and voting existing in many conceptions of democracy, it can still be useful, meaningful and enlightening to highlight the empirical and normative differences between these models in relation to democratic forms and structural relations.

POLITICAL EQUALITY IN DELIBERATIVE DEMOCRACY

The normative claims made by deliberative democrats have been challenged by those concerned with the ability of deliberative democracy to achieve political equality, because it relies upon forms of communication that privilege those already dominant, resulting in their gaining unequal influence in the deliberative settings that is not derived from the 'force of the better argument' and therefore reinforces rather than reduces political inequality. Specifically, the capabilities required to participate effectively in democratic deliberation are not neutral. For example, the language required, the formality of the debate and the rationalism will favour dominant social groups such as white middle-class men (Young 1996: 123–5), who are also likely to speak more in discussion and gain undue influence not based upon the quality of their reasons (Sanders 1997: 365–6). 'Insidious prejudices' are also highlighted as a reason why the arguments of minority social groups will not be 'heard'; these prejudices will go unnoticed and therefore will not be countered by reasons offered in deliberation (Sanders 1997: 353).

Instead of deliberative democracy, Iris Marion Young in 'Communication and the Other' (1996) advocates 'communicative democracy', which she suggests will differ from deliberative democracy by favouring greeting, rhetoric and story-telling over rational argument. She argues that this will make communication more compatible with pluralism because these three aspects are more amenable to the particularity of participants. 'Greeting' deals with how participants provide recognition amongst one another and is said to be important as it creates the right atmosphere for deliberation and can indicate a mutual respect. 'Rhetoric' is the use of cultural symbols and values, which can provoke and motivate participants, playing a key role in getting issues on the agenda. 'Story-telling' or 'testimony' is the use of narratives personal or otherwise and claimed to be essential, as people need to share their personal experiences to highlight and demonstrate their specific position.

Many deliberative democrats have accepted that greeting, rhetoric and story-telling could and should play a part in deliberation, but have further responded by highlighting the fact that these communicative aspects are as hierarchical as the rational deliberation criticised. Just as some people are better at forming, expressing and understanding rational argument than others, so some people will have more talent for greeting, rhetoric and story-telling. Moreover, the people who have talents for these things may be those from the same dominant social groups who are talented arguers

(Benhabib 1996: 82; Gutmann and Thompson 1996: 137; Dryzek 2000: 67; Miller 2000a: 156–7).

INSTITUTIONALISING DELIBERATIVE DEMOCRACY

One of the most pertinent critiques levelled against deliberative democracy, and most forms of direct or participatory democracy, is that it is an irrelevant, utopian theory and a counterfactual ideal because it is unachievable in modern complex societies (Zolo 1992; Benhabib 1996: 84; Femia 1996; Miller 2000: 143). The first obstacle of complexity is that modern societies are very plural, making deliberative democracy unlikely, as it decreases the chance of reaching consensus on a common good, due to 'intractable conflicts'.[2] The second aspect is that modern societies are too big and involve too many people to make democratic deliberation possible with its reliance on discussion (Bohman 1996: 2). To have all citizens deliberate together seems to be an empirical impossibility.[3] These factors are intensified by the third aspect of complexity, the need for technical or professional expertise, because modern decisions are also thought to require high demands of expertise and present trends of increasing division of labour and new technologies have meant that citizens are incapable of participating directly in making decisions (Bohman 1996: 151–2; Femia 1996: 362). The fourth and final aspect of complexity is the inequality of deliberative skills in society. A deliberative democracy could therefore effectively lead to rule by elites (Bohman 1996: 3). These are significant obstacles for the institutionalisation of deliberative democracy:

> The facts of complexity seem to present deliberative democracy with a Weberian dilemma: either decision-making institutions gain effectiveness at the cost of democratic deliberation or they retain democracy at the cost of effective decision-making. In either case, citizenship, deliberation, and decision-making fail to be linked together (Bohman 1996: 178).

Nevertheless, many deliberative theorists believe that these problems can be overcome, provided there is an appropriate institutional design, and a myriad of mechanisms have been advocated, again illustrating the diversity of deliberative democracy. These include constitutional issues, political parties, citizen juries, deliberative opinion polls and civil society. For James Bohman it is these considerations of feasibility and institutionalisation now present in deliberative democracy that demonstrates that it has matured and '"come of age" as a practical ideal' (1998: 422).

1. Constitutional issues

Many deliberative theorists believe that deliberative democracy should only be employed when forming the constitution, suggesting this would lead to a constitution that all could accept (Rawls 1993b: 137). However, this would mean that deliberative democracy would not be employed for specific decisions, which is a huge step away from the deliberative ideal. Others see the constitution as a useful tool to ensure decisions are made deliberatively. In the context of the USA, Joseph Bessette argues that the American Constitution ensures Congress's decisions are commensurate with public reasons (Bessette 1994). This means decisions are made by elites and therefore excludes many from participating in deliberation and 'ties deliberation to a needlessly thin conception of democracy' (Dryzek 2000: 3), thereby failing to approximate the deliberative ideal closely.

2. Political parties

Political parties, the fulcrum of modern democracy, have been seen as the appropriate location because they are essential to setting the agenda for debate. Realistic democratic deliberation requires a reduction of possibilities to be discussed and parties do this effectively by raising well-defined issues for debate (Manin 1987: 357; Budge 2000: 198). They also focus on the common good, therefore escaping the narrow, local, sectional and issue-specific interests that deliberative democracy is attempting to eliminate (Cohen 1989b: 31). This requires the democratisation of political parties around the norms of deliberation (Manin 1987: 357), something that has long been considered impossible due to the inevitability of hierarchy (Michels 1959). There is also the problem that in general elections, parties would be granted power by citizens who may not have good reasons to support their vote, as it would be based on pre-political preferences that had not 'run the gauntlet' of 'genuine' democratic deliberation (Barber 1984: 136; Dryzek 1990: 37; Bohman 1996: 187–8).

3. Representation by lot

A rejuvenation of the Athenian method of representation by lot is the focus for those advocating deliberative opinion polls and citizen juries. They can both be seen as mechanisms to strike a balance between the competing choice of rule by deliberative elites or non-deliberative masses. A random sample of the population is selected to achieve a 'deliberative microcosm' of the people, with each citizen having an equal chance of being selected. The sample then discusses a key issue for several days, as well as cross-examining 'experts' (Fishkin and Luskin 2000: 18–20). In citizen juries the number assembled is between ten and twenty while in deliberative opinion polls it is a more representative several hundred. The concern with citizen juries is a lack of a genuinely representative sample, meaning that another jury with a different sample could produce an entirely different decision (Fishkin and Luskin 2000: 20–21). For deliberative opinion polls the problems are ensuring small minorities are not excluded (Smith 2000: 31) and mediating debate between much bigger groups. A significant problem for both institutional mechanisms is that the preferences of the rest of the population will still be pre-deliberative as they have not participated in the debate and the likelihood is that they will not accept the resulting decisions. This is perhaps partially overcome through extensive and varied media coverage of the meetings (Fishkin and Luskin 2000: 21; Smith 2000: 33); however, they have still been excluded from putting forward their own arguments and 'their representatives' are not open to recourse. The organisers or facilitators also have excessive control, which could lead to manipulation of the deliberative process, as they get to set the agenda by selecting the issues for debate and by selecting the experts to provide information (Smith 2000: 33). Finally, in citizen juries the result is recommendations for decisions and the deliberative opinion poll is, exactly as the title suggests, an aggregation of post-deliberative preferences with no collective decision reached.

4. Civil society

The final method of institutionalisation to be considered is probably the most radical, and envisions citizens participating in collective deliberation through membership of voluntary associations and social movements in civil society. These organisations communicate between each other, forming public spheres, 'the space in which citizens deliberate about their common affairs, and hence an institutionalised arena of discursive interaction' (Fraser 1992: 110). This deliberation can potentially influence the opinions of other organisations and the state, and help set the agenda for legislation. However, communication in the public sphere can often deviate considerably from the deliberative ideal due to inequalities of resources between voluntary associations such as money and number and type of members (Habermas 1996a: 363–4; Warren 2001: 212), which can mean complete marginalisation for some associations (Fraser 1992: 120). Moreover, decisions are still being made separately from where the deliberation is occurring: 'Unless a direct link can be established and maintained between informal deliberation and formal decision-making the decisions made cannot realistically benefit from the legitimacy generated by the deliberation alone' (Squires 2002: 142).

To overcome this problem Habermas advocates 'two tracks' of deliberative decision-making, the first in the informal arenas of the public sphere and the second in formal institutions (Habermas 1996a: chapter 8). Parliament would still remain the central focus for decision-making, but would make decisions in accordance with the norms of democratic deliberation and be supported by decentred deliberation in the public sphere. The problem remains that participants in the public sphere will have influence in deliberation but no power to decide, which would still be the privilege of elites located at the centre (Bohman 1996: 179).

Following the recent rejuvenation of associational democracy (Hirst 1994; Cohen and Rogers 1995), decentralisation of powers to voluntary associations to fulfil various functions has been advocated (Perczynski 2000; Warren 2001; Elstub 2004). The associations can then make their own decisions, but this requires them to be internally deliberatively democratic. Currently they are hierarchical, with little participation from their members in their decisions. This decentralisation also requires citizens to devote a lot of time to politics, which they may not be inclined to do, and can exclude citizens affected by the decisions who are not members of the association.

CONCLUSION

Starting from a broad agreement that democracy requires participation in debate because preferences are exogenous and must be justified to others, the theory of deliberative democracy becomes riddled with dispute about nearly all its other elements. It is divided over the appropriate justification from the prudentialists, epistemics and proceduralists, which all have some difficulties. Despite disagreement persisting it was suggested that deliberation should be collective rather than dyadic or solo if the full benefits of public reason are to be enjoyed. There is further discord over whether public reasons should be universal, appealing to all, but it was concluded that inevitably reasons would be context and agent specific. Likewise consensus was accepted by most to be unachievable, especially in plural societies, but agonistics further rejected its desirability. Further dissension came from communicative democrats, who contested the content of deliberation itself. They appreciated that a sole focus on reason could disadvantage certain participants, but failed to recognise the same failings in their own recommendations. Finally, there are extensive disagreements over whether deliberative democracy can be institutionalised, and a variety of methods were considered, each with its own advantages and disadvantages and some much closer to the ideal of deliberative democracy than others.

That deliberative democracy has come to dominate discussions on democracy is perhaps because deliberative democracy has developed this breadth and depth and because it addresses recurring questions that have confronted democracy over time, such as its meaning, most appropriate justification and most suitable institutional design. It is possibly greater attention to this last aspect that has increased the theory's credibility and this still remains its most significant challenge. This though is still just one of the many problems facing the theory of deliberative democracy, and disagreement within the theory will persist, but long may the debate continue.

QUESTIONS FOR DISCUSSION

- Which of the three justifications considered provides the best grounding for a theory of deliberative democracy?
- Is the theory of deliberative democracy too utopian or can it be institutionalised in a meaningful way?

- What type of representation would be most compatible with the norms of deliberative democracy?
- Would deliberative democracy reduce or increase political equality?

NOTES

1. Michael Saward has further suggested that deliberative democrats have 'overdrawn' the distinction between deliberative and aggregative models of democracy, because citizens can deliberate in private prior to voting (Saward 2000b: 68). Hopefully the discussion above has demonstrated the vital differences between private and collective deliberation.
2. This does not affect the agonistic strand of deliberative democracy, as it does not aim to achieve consensus.
3. As discussed earlier, Gundersen (2000: 98) favours a dyadic approach to democratic deliberation, and one of the reasons for this is that it is more realistic than collective deliberation because it is easier to institutionalise owing to the problems of size. However, it was argued earlier that Gundersen's dyadic model misconceives the ideal of democratic deliberation due to its interpretation of public reason and consequently lacks normative value.

JOSHUA COHEN
EXTRACTS FROM 'DELIBERATION
AND DEMOCRATIC LEGITIMACY'

I

[···]

When properly conducted, [···] democratic politics involves *public deliberation focused on the common good*, requires some form of *manifest equality* among citizens, and *shapes the identity and interests* of citizens in ways that contribute to the formation of a public conception of common good. How does the ideal of a fair system of social co-operation provide a way to account for the attractiveness and importance of these three features of the deliberative democratic ideal? Rawls suggests a formal and an informal line of argument. The formal argument is that parties in the original position would choose the principle of participation[1] with the proviso that the political liberties have their fair value. The three conditions are important because they must be satisfied if constitutional arrangements are to ensure participation rights, guarantee a fair value to those rights, and plausibly produce legislation that encourages a fair distribution according to the difference principle.

Rawls also suggests an informal argument for the ordering of political institutions, and I shall focus on this informal argument here:

> Justice as fairness begins with the idea that where common principles are necessary and to everyone's advantage, they are to be worked out from the viewpoint of a suitably defined initial situation of equality in

Joshua Cohen (1989), 'Deliberation and Democratic Legitimacy', in Alan Hamlin and Philip Pettit (eds), *The Good Polity: Normative Analysis of the State*, Oxford: Blackwell.

which each person is fairly represented. The principle of participation transfers this notion from the original position to the constitution ... [thus] preserv[ing] the equal representation of the original position to the degree that this is feasible. (Rawls 1971: 221–2)[2]

Or, as he puts it elsewhere: 'The idea [of the fair value of political liberty] is to incorporate into the basic structure of society an effective political procedure which *mirrors* in that structure the fair representation of persons achieved by the original position' (1982: 45; emphasis added). The suggestion is that, since we accept the intuitive ideal of a fair system of co-operation, we should want our political institutions themselves to conform, in so far as it is feasible, to the requirement that terms of association be worked out under fair conditions. And so we arrive directly at the requirement of equal liberties with fair value, rather than arriving at it indirectly, through a hypothetical choice of that requirement under fair conditions. In this informal argument, the original position serves as an *abstract model* of what fair conditions are, and of what we should strive to mirror in our political institutions, rather than as an initial-choice situation in which regulative principles for those institutions are selected.

I think that Rawls is right in wanting to accommodate the three conditions. What I find less plausible is that the three conditions are natural consequences of the ideal of fairness. Taking the notion of fairness as fundamental, and aiming (as in the informal argument) to model political arrangements on the original position, it is not clear why, for example, political debate ought to be focused on the common good, or why the manifest equality of citizens is an important feature of a democratic association. The pluralist conception of democratic politics as a system of bargaining with fair representation for all groups seems an equally good mirror of the ideal of fairness.

The response to this objection is clear enough: the connection between the ideal of fairness and the three features of democratic politics depends on psychological and sociological assumptions. Those features do not follow directly from the ideal of a fair system of co-operation, or from that ideal as it is modelled in the original position. Rather, we arrive at them when we consider what is required to preserve fair arrangements and to achieve fair outcomes. For example, public political debate should be conducted in terms of considerations of the common good because we cannot expect outcomes that advance the common good unless people are looking for them. Even an ideal pluralist scheme, with equal bargaining power and no barriers to entry, cannot reasonably be expected to advance the common good as defined by the difference principle (Rawls 1971: 360).

But this is, I think, too indirect and instrumental an argument for the three conditions. Like utilitarian defences of liberty, it rests on a series of highly speculative sociological and psychological judgements. I want to suggest that the reason why the three are attractive is not that an order with, for example, no explicit deliberation about the common good and no manifest equality would be unfair (though of course it might be). Instead it is that they comprise elements of an independent and expressly political ideal that is focused in the first instance[3] on the appropriate conduct of public affairs – on, that is, the appropriate ways of arriving at collective decisions. And to understand that ideal we ought not to proceed by seeking to 'mirror' ideal fairness in the fairness of political arrangements, but instead to proceed by seeking to mirror a system of ideal deliberation in social and political institutions. I want now to turn to this alternative.

II[4]

The notion of a deliberative democracy is rooted in the intuitive ideal of a democratic association in which the justification of the terms and conditions of association proceeds through public argument and reasoning among equal citizens. Citizens in such an order share a commitment to the resolution of problems of collective choice through public reasoning, and regard their basic institutions as legitimate in so far as they establish the framework for free public deliberation. To elaborate this ideal, I begin with a more explicit account of the ideal itself, presenting what I shall call the 'formal conception' of deliberative democracy. Proceeding from this formal conception, I pursue a more substantive account of deliberative democracy by presenting an account of an *ideal deliberative procedure* that captures the notion of justification through public argument and reasoning among equal citizens, and serves in turn as a model for deliberative institutions.

The formal conception of a deliberative democracy has five main features:

D1 A deliberative democracy is an ongoing and independent association, whose members expect it to continue into the indefinite future.

D2 The members of the association share (and it is common knowledge that they share) the view that the appropriate terms of association provide a framework for or are the results of their deliberation. They share, that is, a commitment to co-ordinating their activities within institutions that make deliberation possible and according to norms that they arrive at through their deliberation. For them, free deliberation among equals is the basis of legitimacy.

D3 A deliberative democracy is a pluralistic association. The members have diverse preferences, convictions and ideals concerning the conduct of their own lives. While sharing a commitment to the deliberative resolution of problems of collective choice (D2), they also have divergent aims, and do not think that some particular set of preferences, convictions or ideals is mandatory.

D4 Because the members of a democratic association regard deliberative procedures as the source of *legitimacy*, it is important to them that the terms of their association not merely *be* the results of their deliberation, but also be *manifest* to them as such.[5] They prefer institutions in which the connections between deliberation and outcomes are evident to ones in which the connections are less clear.

D5 The members recognize one another as having deliberative capacities, i.e. the capacities required for entering into a public exchange of reasons and for acting on the result of such public reasoning.

A theory of deliberative democracy aims to give substance to this formal ideal by characterizing the conditions that should obtain if the social order is to be manifestly regulated by deliberative forms of collective choice. I propose to sketch a view of this sort by considering an ideal scheme of deliberation, which I shall call the 'ideal deliberative procedure'. The aim in sketching this procedure is to give an explicit statement of the conditions for deliberative decision-making that are suited to the formal conception, and thereby to highlight the properties that democratic institutions should embody, so far as possible. I should emphasize that the ideal deliberative procedure is meant to provide a model for institutions to mirror – in the first instance for the institutions in which collective choices are made and social outcomes publicly justified – and not to characterize an initial situation in which the terms of association themselves are chosen.[6]

Turning then to the ideal procedure, there are three general aspects of deliberation. There is a need to decide on an agenda, to propose alternative solutions to the problems on the agenda, supporting those solutions with reasons, and to conclude by settling on an alternative. A democratic conception can be represented in terms of the requirements that it sets on such a procedure. In particular, outcomes are democratically legitimate if and only if they could be the object of a free and reasoned agreement among equals. The ideal deliberative procedure is a procedure that captures this principle.[7]

I1 Ideal deliberation is *free* in that it satisfies two conditions. First, the participants regard themselves as bound only by the results of their deliberation and by the preconditions for that deliberation. Their consideration of proposals is not constrained by the authority of prior norms or requirements. Second, the participants suppose that they can act from the results, taking the fact that a certain decision is arrived at through their deliberation as a sufficient reason for complying with it.

I2 Deliberation is *reasoned* in that the parties to it are required to state their reasons for advancing proposals, supporting them or criticizing them. They give reasons with the expectation that those reasons (and not, for example, their power) will settle the fate of their proposal. In ideal deliberation, as Habermas puts it, 'no force except that of the better argument is exercised' (1975: 108). Reasons are offered with the aim of bringing others to accept the proposal, given their disparate ends (D3) and their commitment (D2) to settling the conditions of their association through free deliberation among equals. Proposals may be rejected because they are not defended with acceptable reasons, even if they could be so defended. The deliberative conception emphasizes that collective choices should be *made in a deliberative way*, and not only that those choices should have a desirable fit with the preferences of citizens.

I3 In ideal deliberation parties are both formally and substantively *equal*. They are formally equal in that the rules regulating the procedure do not single out individuals. Everyone with the deliberative capacities has equal standing at each stage of the deliberative process. Each can put issues on the agenda, propose solutions, and offer reasons in support of or in criticism of proposals. And each has an equal voice in the decision. The participants are substantively equal in that the existing distribution of power and resources does not shape their chances to contribute to deliberation, nor does that distribution play an authoritative role in their deliberation. The participants in the deliberative procedure do not regard themselves as bound by the existing system of rights, except in so far as that system establishes the framework of free deliberation among equals. Instead they regard that system as a potential object of their deliberative judgement.

I4 Finally, ideal deliberation aims to arrive at a rationally motivated *consensus* – to find reasons that are persuasive to all who are committed to acting on the results of a free and reasoned assessment of alternatives by equals. Even under ideal conditions there is no promise that consensual reasons will be forthcoming. If they are not, then deliberation concludes with voting, subject to some form of majority rule.[8] The fact that it may so conclude does not, however, eliminate the distinction between deliberative forms of collective choice and forms that aggregate non-deliberative preferences. The institutional consequences are likely to be different in the two cases, and the results of voting among those who are committed to finding reasons that are persuasive to all are likely to differ from the results of an aggregation that proceeds in the absence of this commitment.

Drawing on this characterization of ideal deliberation, can we say anything more substantive about a deliberative democracy? What are the implications of a commitment to deliberative decisions for the terms of social association? In the remarks that follow I shall indicate the ways that this commitment carries with it a commitment to advance the common good and to respect individual autonomy.

Common good and autonomy

Consider first the notion of the common good. Since the aim of ideal deliberation is to secure agreement among all who are committed to free deliberation among equals, and the condition of pluralism obtains (D3), the focus of deliberation is on ways of advancing the aims of each party to it. While no one is indifferent to his/her own good, everyone also seeks to arrive at decisions that are acceptable to all who share the commitment to deliberation (D2). (As we shall see just below, taking that commitment seriously is likely to require a willingness to revise one's understanding of one's own preferences and convictions.) Thus the characterization of an ideal deliberative procedure links the formal notion of deliberative democracy with the more substantive ideal of a democratic association in which public debate is focused on the common good of the members.

Of course, talk about the common good is one thing; sincere efforts to advance it are another. While public deliberation may be organized around appeals to the common good, is there any reason to think that even ideal deliberation would not consist in efforts to disguise personal or class advantage as the common advantage? There are two responses to this question. The first is that in my account of the formal idea of a deliberative democracy, I stipulated (D2) that the members of the association are committed to resolving their differences through deliberation, and thus to providing reasons that they sincerely expect to be persuasive to others who share that commitment. In short, this stipulation rules out the problem. Presumably, however, the objection is best understood as directed against the plausibility of realizing a deliberative procedure that conforms to the ideal, and thus is not answerable through stipulation.

The second response, then, rests on a claim about the effects of deliberation on the motivations of deliberators.[9] A consequence of the reasonableness of the deliberative procedure (I2) together with the condition of pluralism (D3) is that the mere fact of having a preference, conviction or ideal does not by itself provide a reason in support of a proposal. While I may take my preferences as a sufficient reason for advancing a proposal, deliberation under conditions of pluralism requires that I find reasons that make the proposal acceptable to others who cannot be expected to regard my preferences as sufficient reasons for agreeing. The motivational thesis is that the need to advance reasons that persuade others will help to shape the motivations that people bring to the deliberative procedure in two ways. First, the practice of presenting reasons will contribute to the formation of a commitment to the deiberative resolution of political questions (D2). Given that commitment, the likelihood of a sincere representation of preferences and convictions should increase, while the likelihood of their strategic misrepresentation declines. Second, it will shape the content of preferences and convictions as well. Assuming a commitment to deliberative justification, the discovery that I can offer no persuasive reasons on behalf of a proposal of mine may transform the preferences that motivate the proposal. Aims that I recognize to be inconsistent with the requirements of deliberative agreement may tend to lose their force, at least when I expect others to be proceeding in reasonable ways and expect the outcome of deliberation to regulate subsequent action.

Consider, for example, the desire to be wealthier come what may. I cannot appeal to this desire itself in defending policies. The motivational claim is the need to find an independent justification that does not appeal to this desire and will tend to shape it into, for example, a desire to have a level of wealth that is consistent with a level that others (i.e. equal citizens) find acceptable. I am of course assuming that the deliberation is known to be regulative, and that the wealth cannot be protected through wholly non-deliberative means.

Deliberation, then, focuses debate on the common good. And the relevant conceptions of the common good are not comprised simply of interests and preferences that are antecedent to deliberation. Instead, the interests, aims and ideals that comprise the common good are those that survive deliberation, interests that, on public reflection, we think it legitimate to appeal to in making claims on social resources. [...]

The ideal deliberative scheme also indicates the importance of autonomy in a deliberative democracy. In particular, it is responsive to two main threats to autonomy. As a general matter, actions fail to be autonomous if the preferences on which an agent acts are, roughly, given by the circumstances, and not determined by the agent. There are two paradigm cases of 'external' determination. The first is what Elster (1982) has called 'adaptive preferences'.[10] These are preferences that shift with changes in the circumstances of the agent without any deliberate contribution by the agent to that shift. This is true, for example, of the political preferences of instinctive centrists who move to the median position in the political distribution, wherever it happens to be. The second I shall call 'accommodationist preferences'. While they are deliberately formed, accommodationist preferences represent psychological adjustments to conditions of subordination in which individuals are not recognized as having the capacity for self-government. Consider Stoic slaves, who deliberately shape their desires to match their powers, with a view to minimizing frustration. Since the existing relations of power make slavery the only possibility, they cultivate desires to be slaves, and then act on those desires. While their motives are deliberately formed, and they act on their desires, the Stoic slaves do not act autonomously when they seek to be good slaves. The absence of alternatives and consequent denial of scope for the deliberative capacities that defines the condition of slaves supports the conclusion that their desires result from their circumstances, even though those circumstances shape the desires of the Stoic slaves through their deliberation.

There are then at least two dimensions of autonomy. The phenomenon of adaptive preferences underlines the importance of conditions that permit and encourage the deliberative formation of preferences; the phenomenon of accommodationist preferences indicates the need for favourable conditions for the exercise of the deliberative capacities. Both concerns are met when institutions for collective decision-making are modelled on the ideal deliberative procedure. Relations of power and subordination are neutralized (I1, I3, I4), and each is recognized as having the deliberative capacities (D5), thus addressing the problem of accommodationist preferences. Further, the requirement of reasonableness discourages adaptive preferences (I2). While preferences are 'formed' by the deliberative procedure, this type of preference formation is consistent with autonomy, since preferences that are shaped by public deliberation are not simply given by external circumstances. Instead they are the result of 'the power of reason as applied through public discussion'.[11]

Beginning, then, from the formal ideal of a deliberative democracy, we arrive at the more substantive ideal of an association that is regulated by deliberation aimed at the common good and that respects the autonomy of the members. And so, in seeking to embody the ideal deliberative procedure in institutions, we seek, *inter alia*, to design institutions that focus political debate on the common good, that shape the identity and interests of citizens in ways that contribute to an attachment to the common good, and that provide the favourable conditions for the exercise of deliberative powers that are required for autonomy.

NOTES

I have had countless discussions of the subject matter of this paper with Joel Rogers, and wish to thank him for his unfailingly sound and generous advice. For our joint treatment of the issues that I discuss here, see Cohen and Rogers (1983: ch. 6). The main differences between the treatment of issues here and the treatment in the book lies in the explicit account of the ideal deliberative procedure, the fuller treatment of the notions of autonomy and the common good, and the account of the connection of those notions with the ideal procedure. An earlier draft of this paper was presented to the Pacific Division Meetings of the American Philosophical Association. I would like to thank Loren Lomasky and the editors of this collection for helpful comments on that draft.

1. The principle of participation states that 'all citizens are to have an equal right to take part in, and to determine the outcome of, the constitutional process that establishes the laws with which they are to comply' (Rawls 1971: 221).
2. I assume that the principle of participation should be understood here to include the requirement of the fair value of political liberty.
3. The reasons for the phrase 'in the first instance' are clarified below.
4. Since writing the first draft of this section of the paper, I have read Elster (1986) and Manin (1987), which both present parallel conceptions. This is especially so with Elster's treatment of the psychology of public deliberation (pp. 112–13). I am

indebted to Alan Hamlin for bringing the Elster article to my attention. The overlap is explained by the fact that Elster, Manin and I all draw on Habermas. See Habermas (1975, 1979, 1984). I have also found the discussion of the contractualist account of motivation in Scanlon (1982) very helpful.

5. For philosophical discussions of the importance of manifestness or publicity, see Kant (1983: 135–9); Rawls (1971: 133 and section 29); Williams (1985: 101–2, 200).

6. The distinction between the ideal procedure and an initial-choice situation will be important in the later discussion of motivation formation and institutions.

7. There are of course norms and requirements on individuals that do not have deliberative justification. The conception of deliberative democracy is, in Rawls's term, a 'political conception', and not a comprehensive moral theory. On the distinction between political and comprehensive theories, see Rawls (1987: 1–25).

8. For criticism of the reliance on an assumption of unanimity in deliberative views, see Manin (1987: 359–61).

9. Note the parallel with Elster (1986) indicated in note 4. See also the discussion in Habermas (1975: 108), about 'needs that can be communicatively shared', and Habermas (1979: ch. 2).

10. For an interesting discussion of autonomous preferences and political processes, see Sunstein (1986: 1145–58; 1984: 1699–700).

11. Whitney *vs*. California, 274 US 357 (1927).

IRIS MARION YOUNG
EXTRACTS FROM 'COMMUNICATION AND THE OTHER: BEYOND DELIBERATIVE DEMOCRACY'

EXCLUSIONARY IMPLICATIONS OF THE DELIBERATIVE MODEL

A primary virtue of a deliberative model of democracy [...] is that it promotes a conception of reason over power in politics. Policies ought to be adopted not because the most powerful interests win but because the citizens or their representatives together determine their rightness after hearing and criticizing reasons. While there are some elitist tendencies in traditional republicanism, most contemporary deliberative theorists believe that a deliberative democracy is potentially more inclusive and egalitarian than an interest-based democracy.[1] Whereas an interest-based democracy does not preclude money and numbers from influencing decisions, for example, deliberative theorists usually assert that democracy requires an equal voice for all citizens to press their claims, regardless of social position or power.

Joshua Cohen gives a clear picture of the conditions of an ideal of deliberative democracy.[2] His formulation is close to Habermas's ideal of discourse that aims to reach understanding, which John Dryzek relies on as a basis for his conception of discursive democracy.[3] In the ideal of deliberative democracy, participants come to a political problem with an open mind about its solution; they are not bound by the authority of prior norms or requirements. The process of political discussion consists in reasoned argument. Participants put forward proposals and criticize them, and each assents to

Iris Marion Young (1996), 'Communication and the Other: Beyond Deliberative Democracy', in Seyla Benhabib (ed.), *Democracy and Difference: Contesting the Boundaries of the Political*, Princeton: Princeton University Press.

a conclusion only because of the 'force of the better argument'. For such assent to be rational, participants must be free and equal. Each must have the equal opportunity to make proposals and criticize, and their speaking situation must be free from domination. No one can be in a position to threaten or coerce others to accept or reject certain proposals. The goal of deliberation is to arrive at consensus; even when this is not possible and participants resort to voting, their result is a collective judgment rather than the aggregate of private preferences.

Deliberative theorists tend to assume that bracketing political and economic power is sufficient to make speakers equal. This assumption fails to notice that the social power that can prevent people from being equal speakers derives not only from economic dependence or political domination but also from an internalized sense of the right one has to speak or not to speak, and from the devaluation of some people's style of speech and the elevation of others. The deliberative ideal tends to assume that when we eliminate the influence of economic and political power, people's ways of speaking and understanding will be the same; but this will be true only if we also eliminate their cultural differences and different social positions. The model of deliberative democracy, that is, tends to assume that deliberation is both culturally neutral and universal. A theory of communicative democracy that attends to social difference, to the way that power sometimes enters speech itself, recognizes the cultural specificity of deliberative practices, and proposes a more inclusive model of communication.

The deliberative model of communication derives from specific institutional contexts of the modern West – scientific debate, modern parliaments, and courts (each with progenitors in ancient Greek and Roman philosophy and politics, and in the medieval academy). These were some of the aspiring institutions of the bourgeois revolution that succeeded in becoming ruling institutions. Their institutional forms, rules, and rhetorical and cultural styles have defined the meaning of reason itself in the modern world. As ruling institutions, however, they have been elitist and exclusive, and these exclusions mark their very conceptions of reason and deliberation, both in the institutions and in the rhetorical styles they represent. Since their Enlightenment beginnings they have been male-dominated institutions, and in class- and race-differentiated societies they have been white- and upper class-dominated. Despite the claim of deliberative forms of orderly meetings to express pure universal reason, the norms of deliberation are culturally specific and often operate as forms of power that silence or devalue the speech of some people.

Parliamentary debates or arguments in court are not simply free and open public forums in which all people actually have the right to express claims and give reasons according to their own understanding. Instead of defining discussion as the open reciprocal recognition of the point of view of everyone, these institutions style deliberation as agonistic. Deliberation is competition. Parties to dispute aim to win the argument, not to achieve mutual understanding. Consenting because of the 'force of the better argument' means being unable to think of further counterargument, that is, to concede defeat.[4] The agonistic norms of deliberation reveal ways that power reenters this arena, even though deliberative theorists may claim to have bracketed it.

Restricting practices of democratic discussion to moves in a contest where some win and others lose privileges those who like contests and know the rules of the game. Speech that is assertive and confrontational is here more valued than speech that is tentative, exploratory, or conciliatory. In most actual situations of discussion, this privileges male speaking styles over female. A growing literature claims to show that girls and women tend to speak less than boys and men in speaking situations that value assertiveness and argument competition. When women do speak in such situations, moreover, they tend to give information and ask questions rather than state opinions or initiate controversy.[5]

In many formal situations the better-educated white middle-class people, moreover, often act as though they have a right to speak and that their words carry authority, whereas those of other groups often feel intimidated by the argument requirements and the formality and rules of parliamentary procedure, so they do not speak, or speak only a way that those in charge find 'disruptive'. Norms of assertiveness, combativeness, and speaking by the contest rules are powerful silencers or evaluators of speech in many actual speaking situations where culturally differentiated and socially unequal groups live together. The dominant groups, moreover, often fail entirely to notice this devaluation and silencing, while the less privileged often feel put down or frustrated, either losing confidence in themselves or becoming angry.

The norms of deliberation also privilege speech that is formal and general. Speech that proceeds from premise to conclusion in an orderly fashion that clearly lays out its inference structure is better than other speech. It is also better to assert one's position in terms of generalities and principles that apply to particular instances. These norms of 'articulateness', however, must be learned; they are culturally specific, and in actual speaking situations in our society exhibiting such speaking styles is a sign of social privilege. Deliberation thus does not open itself equally to all ways of making claims and giving reasons. In formal situations of discussion and debate, such as classrooms, courtrooms, and city council chambers, many people feel they must apologize for their halting and circuitous speech.

The norms of deliberation, finally, privilege speech that is dispassionate and disembodied. They tend to presuppose an opposition between mind and body, reason and emotion. They tend falsely to identify objectivity with calm and absence of emotional expression. Thus expressions of anger, hurt, and passionate concern discount the claims and reasons they accompany. Similarly, the entrance of the body into speech – in wide gestures, movements of nervousness or body expressions of emotion – are signs of weakness that cancel out one's assertions or reveal one's lack of objectivity and control. Deliberative norms tend to privilege 'literal' language over figurative language such as hyperbole, metaphor, and so on.

Once again, in our society these differences of speech privilege correlate with other differences of social privilege. The speech culture of white middle-class men tends to be more controlled, without significant gesture and expression of emotion. The speech culture of women and racial minorities, on the other, tends to be more excited and embodied, more valuing the expression of emotion, the use of figurative language, modulation in tone of voice, and wide gesture.[6]

I conclude from these considerations that this discussion-based theory of democracy must have a broader idea of the forms and styles of speaking that political discussion involves than deliberative theorists usually imagine. I prefer to call such a broadened theory communicative, rather than deliberative, democracy, to indicate an equal privileging of any forms of communicative interaction where people aim to reach understanding. While argument is a necessary element in such effort to discuss with and persuade one another about political issues, argument is not the only mode of political communication, and argument can be expressed in a plurality of ways, interspersed with or alongside other communicative forms.

DELIBERATIVE MODEL ASSUMES UNITY

Unlike the interest-based conception of democracy, communicative democracy emphasizes that people's ideas about political questions often change when they interact with other people's ideas and experiences. If in a public discussion about collective action or public policy people simply say what they want, without any claims of justice or rightness, they will not be taken seriously. Instead, they must appeal to others by presenting proposals they claim are just or good and that others ought to accept. In this process people's own initial preferences are transformed from subjective desires to objective claims and the content of these preferences must also often change to make them publicly speakable, as claims of entitlement or what is right. People's ideas about the solution to collective problems are also sometimes transformed by listening to and learning about the point of view of others.

Deliberative theorists commonly write about this process of moving from subjective self-regarding preferences to more objective or general opinions about the solution to collective problems as a process of discovering or constructing unity among them. I see two approaches that deliberative theorists take in discussing such unity. Some take unity to be a prior condition of deliberation. Michael Walzer, for example, argues that effective social criticism locates and appeals to a community's prior 'shared understandings'.[7] Sometimes Jürgen Habermas writes as though reaching understanding through discourse about norms depends on restoring a disrupted consensus.[8]

There are at least two problems with this way of constructing the process of discussion. First, in contemporary pluralist societies we cannot assume that there are sufficient shared understandings to appeal to in many situations of conflict and solving collective problems. Second, the assumption of prior unity obviates the need for the self-transcendence, which I cited earlier as an important component of a communicative model of democracy. If discussion succeeds primarily when it appeals to what the discussants all share, then none need revise their opinions or viewpoints in order to take account of perspectives and experiences beyond them. Even if they need the others to see what they all share, each finds in the other only a mirror for him- or herself.

Recognizing such problems, some theorists of discussion-based democracy conceptualize unity not as a starting point but as a goal of political dialogue. On this view, participants transcend their subjective, self-regarding perspective on political issues by putting aside their particular interests and seeking the good of the whole. Participants in a communicative democratic interchange often begin with differences of culture, perspective, interest, but the goal of discussion is to locate or create common interests that all can share. To arrive at the common good it may be necessary to work through differences, but difference itself is something to be transcended, because it is partial and divisive.[9]

The problem with this conception of the unity of democratic discussion is that it may harbor another mechanism of exclusion. Assuming a discussion situation in which participants are differentiated by group-based culture and social position, and where some groups have greater symbolic or material privilege than others, appeals to a 'common good' are likely to perpetuate such privilege. As I argued in the previous section, even communication situations that bracket the direct influence of economic or political inequality nevertheless can privilege certain cultural styles and values. When discussion participants aim at unity, the appeal to a common good in which they are all supposed to leave behind their particular experience and interests, the perspectives of the privileged are likely to dominate the definition of that common good. The less privileged are asked to put aside the expression of their experience, which may require a different idiom, or their claims of entitlement or interest must be put aside for the sake of a common good whose definition is biased against them.[10]

CONSIDERING DIFFERENCE A RESOURCE

There is no reason or structure for differently situated groups to engage in democratic discussion if they do not live together in a polity. In this sense some unity is of course a condition of democratic communication. But the unity of a single polity is a much weaker unity, I suggest, than deliberative theorists usually assume. The unity that motivates politics is the facticity of people being thrown together, finding themselves in geographical proximity and economic interdependence such that activities and pursuits of some affect the ability of others to conduct their activities. A polity consists of people who live together, who are stuck with one another.

If a polity is to be a communicative democracy, even more unity is necessary. Its members must have a commitment to equal respect for one another, in the simple formal sense of willingness to say that all have a right to express their opinions and points of view, and all ought to listen. The members of the polity, furthermore, must agree on procedural rules of fair discussion and decision-making. These three conditions – significant interdependence, formally equal respect, and agreed-on procedures – are all the unity necessary for communicative democracy. They are much thinner conditions than those of shared understandings or the goals of finding common goods. Within the context of this minimal unity that characterizes communicative democracy, a richer understanding of processes of democratic discussion results if we assume that differences of social position and identity perspective function as a resource for public reason rather than as divisions that public reason transcends.

I have already argued that one of the problems with assuming unity as a starting point or goal of deliberative democracy is that such a conception cannot account well for the transformation the communicative process should often produce in the opinions of the participants. If we are all really looking for what we have in common – whether as a prior condition or as a result – then we are not transforming our point of view. We only come to see ourselves mirrored in others. If we assume, on the other hand, that communicative interaction means encountering differences of meaning, social position, or need that I do not share and identify with, then we can better describe how that interaction transforms my preferences. Different social positions encounter one another with the awareness of their difference. This does not mean that we believe we have no similarities; difference is not total otherness. But it means that each position is aware that it does not comprehend the perspective of the others differently located, in the sense that it cannot be assimilated into one's own. There is thus something to be learned from the other perspectives as they communicate their meanings and perspectives, precisely because the perspectives are beyond one another and not reducible to a common good. This process of mutual expression of experience and points of view that transcend the initial understanding of each accounts for a transformation in their opinions.

Communication among perspectives that transcend one another preserves the plurality that Hannah Arendt understood as a condition of publicity. The plural standpoints in the public enable each participant to understand more of what the society means or what the possible consequences of a policy will be by each situating his or her own experience and interest in a wider context of understanding something in other social locations. By 'understand' I mean something somewhat different from what some deliberative theorists mean. Frequently in communicative contexts when people say they have come to an understanding or they understand one another, they think that this implies a mutual identification. People have reached understanding, in this conception, when they have transcended what differentiates and divides them and now have the same meaning or beliefs or principles.

If communicative democracy is better conceived as speaking across differences of culture, social position, and need, which are preserved in the process, however, then understanding one another and reaching understanding does not imply this identification. Understanding another social location can here mean that there has been successful expression of experience and perspective, so that other social positions learn, and part of what they understand is that there remains more behind that experience and perspective that transcends their own subjectivity.[11]

Preserving and listening across such differences of position and perspective causes the transformation in preference that deliberative theorists recommend. This transformation occurs in three ways. 1) Confrontation with different perspective, interests, and cultural meanings teaches me the partiality of my own, reveals to me my own experience as perspectival. 2) Knowledge that I am in a situation of collective problem solving with others who have different perspectives on the problems and different cultures and values from my own, and that they have the right to challenge my claims and arguments, forces me to transform my expressions of self-interest and desire into appeals to justice. Proposals for collective policies need not be expressed as general interest, an interest all can share; they may be claims about an obligation on the part of the public to recognize and provide for some unique needs of uniquely situated persons. Nevertheless the plural public perspectives require such expressed claims to appeal across difference, to presume a lack of understanding to be bridged, thus transforming the experience itself. 3) Expressing, questioning, and challenging differently situated knowledge, finally, adds to the social knowledge of all the participants. While not abandoning their own perspective, through listening across difference each position can come to understand something about the ways proposals and claims affect others differently situated. By internalizing this mediated understanding of plural positions to some extent, participants gain a wider picture of the social processes in which their own partial experience is embedded. This greater social objectivity increases their wisdom for arriving at just solutions to collective problems.

NOTES

1. James Fishkin is something of an exception here. He argues that there is a tradeoff between political equality and participation. Giving every citizen an equal influence over outcomes, he suggests, precludes deliberation, because in a large-scale democracy this means one person/one vote in aggregated elections and referenda. See *Deliberative Democracy* (New Haven: Yale University Press, 1991).

2. Joshua Cohen, 'Deliberation and Democratic Legitimacy', in Alan Hamlin and Philip Pettit, *The Good Polity* (London: Blackwell, 1989), 22–23.

3. Habermas, *A Theory of Communicative Action*, vol. 1: *Reason and the Rationalization of Society* (Boston: Beacon Press, 1981); John Dryzek, *Discursive Democracy* (Cambridge: Cambridge University Press, 1990), chaps. 1 and 2.

4. A passage from Habermas's exposition of the function of moral argument shows this unquestioned acceptance of the model of dialogue as competition: 'What happens in argumentation is that the success orientation of competitors is assimilated into a form of communication in which action oriented toward reaching understanding is continued by other means. In argumentation, proponents and opponents engage in *competition with arguments* in order to convince one another, that is, in order to reach a consensus. This dialectical role structure makes forms of disputation available for a comparative search for truth. Argumentation can exploit the conflict between success-oriented competitors for the purpose of achieving consensus so long as the arguments are not reduced to mere means of influencing one another'. *Moral Consciousness and Communicative Action*, trans. Christian Lenhardt and Shierry Weber Nicholsen (Cambridge, Mass.: MIT Press, 1991), 160.

5. See Lynn Sanders, 'Against Deliberation', a paper presented at a meeting of the American Political Science Association, September 1992; she cites studies that show that in juries men talk considerably more than women and are leaders more often. Jane Mansbridge cites studies that show that female state legislators speak less than their male counterparts and that in public meetings women tend more to give information and ask questions, while men state opinions and engage in confrontation. Mansbridge, 'Feminism and Democratic Community', in John W. Chapman and Ian Shapiro, eds., *Democratic Community*, Nomos no. 35 (New York: New York University Press, 1991).

6. Anthony Cortese argues that the model of moral reasoning presupposed by Kohlberg and Habermas is ethnocentric and culturally biased, and tends to locate Chicano speaking and reasoning styles lower in its scale; see *Ethnic Ethics* (Albany: SUNY Press, 1990). Charles Henry discusses the tendency of African-Americans more than whites to couple emotion and anger with argument, influencing African-American styles of public debate; see *Culture and African American Politics* (Bloomington: Indiana University Press, 1990).

7. Michael Walzer, *Interpretation and Social Criticism* (Cambridge, Mass.: Harvard University Press, 1987).

8. Habermas, *Moral Consciousness*, 67.

9. For one statement of this kind of position, see Benjamin Barber, *Strong Democracy*, (Berkeley and Los Angeles: University of California Press, 1984), 197–212.

10. Compare Lynn Sanders, 'Against Deliberation'; I have developed an argument similar to this at greater length in chap. 4 of *Justice and the Politics of Difference* (Princeton: Princeton University Press, 1990).

11. I have developed more of such a conception of understanding across difference in another article, 'Asymmetrical Reciprocity: On Moral Respect, Wonder and Enlarged Thought'. *Constellations* 3, no. 3 (1997).

2

REPRESENTATION

Christian Brütsch

INTRODUCTION

According to the *Oxford English Dictionary*, the primary political connotation of 'representation' refers to the 'fact of representing or being represented in a legislative or deliberative assembly'.[1] The meaning of these two 'facts' seems obvious: the people elect the members of legislative or deliberative assemblies to represent them, which authorises the representatives to make laws and frame public policies on their behalf. The normative assumption that makes representation desirable is implicit in the way the two facts are linked: since all men are equal, no one in particular has a 'natural' right to govern and to be free, government must be founded on the consent of the governed, and thus represent their will. Because it affirms that representatives act in the name of those they represent, the concept of representation has become a central element in the self-understanding of liberal democracies, in which the people are considered free if they have the right to freely elect those who rule them.

However, this view of representation has considerable deficits. It omits the role representation plays in the constitution of the identity of 'the people'. It forgets that the meaning, the conditions and the limits of representation have been the object of intense political debates and social movements. And it ignores that the role of representation is still contended. Thus, if we want to address the problem of representation, we can't rely on definitions of political representation that reflect the working of representative institutions in liberal democracies. We have to understand the premises on which these institutions are built. These premises emerge in the history of the concept that establishes representation as the foundation of political power, legal obligation and the political unity of a people. They form the basis of the constitution debates that shaped the modern institutions of representative government and defined representation in terms of delegation and accountability. And they re-emerge in the contemporary debates on representation that oscillate between a partial recovery and reinterpretation of representation and its radical reformulation with regard to non-representative practices of political agency.

THE CONCEPTUAL HISTORIES OF REPRESENTATION

Ironically, it is easier to grasp the significance of political representation by looking at the way the concept is used outside political discourse. According to the *OED*, representation also refers to an 'appearance' or to a particular form of 'presence.' This appearance or presence can be an 'image, likeness, or reproduction' of something. It can also be a performance or refer to the faculty that enables us to form 'clear images' in our mind. Paradoxically, all these meanings imply that a representation both conceals and defines what it represents. A representation is an appearance or a presence that reveals something that is not there; it is an image of something we cannot see; a performance of something that does not exist in that form; an idea.

The idea that the presence of a representation implies the absence of the represented, and that the performative character of the representive enables her to define the identity of those she represents, is just as important as the more obvious transfer of authority implied by the idea that the representative simply 'stands for' others. Political representation refers to the people by presupposing their absence. Without representation, 'the people' are a politically undetermined aggregate of men and women with multiple and ultimately unstable identities. Indeed, as Carl Schmitt points out, representation produces 'the people' as a political idea, and because it defines the multitudes in terms of their political unity, representation is neither 'a normative event, nor a method nor a procedure, but something *existential*. To represent means to visualise something that is invisible in something that is publicly present' (1993: 209–10).[2]

The nature of the relationship between the 'public presence' of the representation and the absence of the represented has been at the core of the history of the concept ever since Thomas Hobbes made representation the central element for his new 'science' of politics.[3] Hobbes believed that just like geometry and physics, a true political science had to dissect and reconstruct the complex realities of political experience and explain them on the basis of their elementary building blocks: it had to reconstruct political power on the basis of the individual.[4] To do so, Hobbes had to reverse a long tradition of political thought that accepted government as a natural element within a hierarchic social order to prove that men did not have to give up their equality or surrender their liberty to end the state of war that made their lives 'solitary, poore, nasty, brutish, and short' (1985: 186). Hobbes believed that the outbreak of the civil wars had shown that the claim that all men were equal and free had led many to believe that each man was his own 'Judge of Good and Evil actions', both in private and in public matters. At a time in which all attempts to restore the ancient order had failed, the escalation of the conflicts proved that men were 'disposed to debate with themselves, and dispute the commands of the Common-wealth; and afterwards to obey, or disobey them, as in their private judgements they shall think fit' (Hobbes 1985: 365).

The only way to end the perpetual state of war of all against all was, Hobbes argued, to get each and every man to agree on the need to establish a common power whose orders no one would dispute. This could be done because any man who surrendered his authority over his words and deeds in public, recognising instead the 'words or actions' of those exercising the common power, would simply obey the 'natural laws of reason', according to which each man's primary interest was to preserve his life (Hobbes 1985: 217). The problem was that any man could *only* be expected to surrender his rights 'when a Multitude of men do Agree, and Covenant, every one, with every one, that to whatsoever Man, or Assembly of Men, shall be given by the major part, the Right to Present the Person of then all ... that is to say, to be their Representative' (Hobbes 1985: 228).

To establish civil society, those entering a covenant had to oblige themselves to respect their 'voluntary act' to 'lay down his right to all things; and to be contented with so much liberty against other men, as he would allow other men against himself' (Hobbes 1985: 190–1). To make sure everybody respected these rights, 'every one, as well he that Voted for it, as he that Voted against it', had to 'Authorise all the Actions and Judgements' of the representative 'in the same manner, as if they were his own, to the end, to live peaceably amongst themselves, and be protected against other men' (Hobbes 1985: 228–9). The representation of the rights and the authority of those who entered the covenant thus became the logical foundation of sovereignty. Hobbes had achieved his task: political power and political obligation could both be reconstructed on the basis of the individual will.

New problems arose, though. Because the sovereign represented all his subjects, and because every one of them had to be considered the 'Author of all the Actions, and Judgements of the Soveraigne Instituted; it follows, that whatsoever he doth, can be no injury to any of his Subjects; nor ought he to be by any of them accused of Injustice' (Hobbes 1985: 232). In fact, being the source of civil society, the sovereign was 'not subject to the Civill Lawes. For having power to make, and repeale Lawes, he may, when he pleaseth, free himself from that subjection by repealing those Lawes that trouble him, and making of new' (Hobbes 1985: 313).

The idea that the sovereign could do no wrong and that the members of the commonwealth had no right to dispute the commands of the sovereign they had vested with 'the Right of bearing the Person of them all' irritated and troubled those who feared despotism just as much as the dreaded state of nature (Hobbes 1985: 230). Yet Hobbes's blueprint for the constitution of a common power left them little room for manoeuvre.

John Locke recalled that the power vested in the sovereign was 'only a Fiduciary Power to act for certain ends, [and that] there remains still *in the People a Supream Power* to remove or *alter the Legislative*, when they find the legislative act contrary to the trust reposed in them' (1988: 367). But because, like Hobbes, Locke believed that men could only be truly 'free, equal and independent' and lead a 'comfortable, safe, and peacable living . . . in a secure Enjoyment of their Properties' if they gave up their natural liberty and 'put on the bonds of Civil Society', he also acknowledged that this 'supreme power' was difficult to exercise and that it could 'never take place till the Government be dissolved' (1988: 330–1, 367). However, Locke did find an argument that could enable the members of a commonwealth to legitimately check their representatives: 'Men, by entering into Society and Civil Government, have excluded force, and introduced Laws' – and not simply sovereign commands – 'for the preservation of Property, Peace, and Unity amongst themselves.' The representation of the supreme power of the people was first of all a representation of their legislative power, which by its nature was difficult to use against the people. In practice, Locke argued, the legislative 'cannot assume to its self a power to Rule by extempory Arbitrary Decrees, but *is bound to dispense Justice*, and decide the Rights of the Subject *by promulgated standing Laws, and known Authoris'd Judges*' (1988: 358).

For Locke, the main threat to the people was therefore not the legislative, but the executive – traditionally the king or his ministers. If the executive stopped acting in conformity with the laws, it reintroduced the rule of force, and 'whoever they be, who by force break through [the laws], and by force justifie their violation of them, are truly and properly *Rebels*' culpable of bringing back 'the state of War' (Locke 1988: 415–6). This implied that the authority of the legislative and the authority of the executive rested on different forms of representation. The Crown, the Lords and the Commons were all 'procurators' for the good of society. But whilst the legislative declared, and thereby represented, the supreme will of society, the executive vested in the Crown could only be considered 'as the Image, Phantom, or Representative of the Commonwealth, acted by the will of Society, declared in its Laws; and thus he has no Will, no Power but that of the Law' (Locke 1988: 368).[5]

The distinction between legislative and executive power was further developed when Jean-Jacques Rousseau introduced a series of concepts to distinguish between the representation and the sovereignty of the people to show that their sovereignty could not be represented. Those who enter a social contract and establish a republic 'take collectively the name of a people'; 'in its passive role' the 'public person' they create is called 'state', whereas 'it is the *sovereign*' when it 'plays an active role'. According to Rousseau, this distinction is important because, individually, those who enter civil society can 'call themselves citizens' when they participate in the sovereign authority, but must consider themselves 'subjects' when they 'put themselves under the laws of the state' (1968: 61–2). Thus, the people can only be 'represented' in the laws of the state in which 'the people as a whole makes rules for the people as a whole' without considering anything but itself and in which 'the universality of the will' and the 'universality of the field of legislation' are united (Roussean 1968: 81–2).

What cannot be represented is the active sovereignty of the people in which they can only participate as citizens. Legislators can make laws for their subjects, but if they do so, their citizenship is but a word, the people are not (yet) sovereign. Once they conquer their sovereignty, only the people assembled can make or alter laws – and they can *only* make laws. For if the people unite to act upon particular matters, and decide, for example, to prosecute individuals or particular groups, they threaten the sovereignty of the general will no less than magistrates who act against or individuals who disobey the law: 'If the sovereign seeks to govern, or if the magistrate seeks to legislate, or if the subjects refuse to obey, then order gives way to chaos... and the state, disintegrating, will lapse either into despotism or into anarchy' (Roussean 1968: 103).

THE CONSTITUTION OF REPRESENTATIVE GOVERNMENTS

Whereas the concept of representation served as a cornerstone for the legitimation of legislative power and the rational constitution of legal order, the political history of representation was shaped by the role representative institutions played in the constitution of a strong government capable of containing and taming the extremes of civil society. In Great Britain, the gradual erosion of the power of the Crown, the conflict between landed and commercial interests, and the rise of an organised working class provoked heated debates about the nature of representation and the organisation of the franchise that continued from the late eighteenth well into the twentieth century.

Even those who trusted the electoral system were struggling to explain how members of Parliament should represent their constituencies. One of the most straightforward – and soon widely replicated – answers came from Edmund Burke at the conclusion of a poll in which the freemen of Bristol elected him to one of their two seats. Burke warned his constituency that it would be 'no easy task' to represent them and that he did not agree with those who believed that the task could be made any simpler if they embraced 'the perilous extremes of servile compliance, or wild popularity' (1996a: 70). He recognised that political power derived from the will of the people, that the tacit consent of the people kept Parliament in power, and that they choose their representatives in the ballot. But he believed that neither the legislative nor the executive could operate in the abstract terms of the will of the people. Indeed, 'if Government were a matter of Will upon any side, yours, without question, ought to be superior. But Government and Legislation are matters of reason and judgement, and not of inclination' (Burke 1996a: 69).

Burke believed that reason and judgement required debates, and that debates were impossible if positions were predetermined. He recognised that 'it ought to be the happiness and glory of a Representative, to live in the strictest union, the closest correspondence, and the most unreserved communication with his constituents'. He recognised that 'their wishes ought to have great weight with him; their opinion high respect; their business unremitted attention', and that the representative should 'ever, and in all cases, . . . prefer their interest to his own'. But none of this limited the responsibility from the representative; 'his unbiassed opinion, his mature judgement, his enlightened conscience, he ought not to sacrifice to you; to any man, or to any sett of men living' (Burke 1996a: 68–9).

The responsibility of the representative, and one of the main reasons why political deliberation required an unbiased opinion, a mature judgement and an enlightened conscience of those who deliberated on the public interests, was to understand and master the complexity of government. In fact, the elected members of Parliament had to represent not just the 'interests' of their constituencies, but also those of a 'great *Empire*, extended by our Virtue and our Fortune to the farthest limits of the East and of the West. All these wide-spread Interests must be considered; must be compared; must be reconciled if possible' (Burke 1996a: 70).

If such reconciliation was sought, even members of parliament that had been elected to represent particular interests would contribute to the 'virtual represention' of the empire. However, Burke was aware that reconciliation was not always possible, and that it was impossible when these widespread interests had no voice of their own – like the two million people living in the American settlements who 'have not had the liberty and privilege of electing and sending any Knights and Burgesses, or others, to represent them in the High Court of Parliament' (1996b: 146).

Illustrating the colonial views, Thomas Jefferson reminded Parliament that their American subjects had been freemen when they got to the settlements, that they had fought and conquered them for themselves, and that 'for themselves alone' they had the 'right to hold' and thus the right to govern (1999: 65). When the colonies eventually declared their independence and transformed the colonial administration into republican governments of 'free and independent states', several states experimented extending the right of representation from property to majority votes. However, the major American contribution to the doctrine of representation emerged in the course of the constitution debates in 1787–8. In the tenth *Federalist* paper,

James Madison argued against conventional wisdom that the extension of the new American republic, considered excessive by many, was no threat, but the condition for true representation and republican government:

> The smaller the society, the fewer probably will be the distinct parties and interests composing it; the fewer the distinct parties and interests, the more frequently will a majority be found of the same party; and the smaller the number of individuals composing a majority, and the smaller the compass within which they are placed, the more easily will they concert and execute their plans of oppression. Extend the sphere, and you take in a greater variety of parties and interests; you make it less probable that a majority of the whole will have a common motive to invade the rights of other citizens; or if such a common motive exists, it will be more difficult for all who feel it to discover their own strength, and to act in unison with each other. (Hamilton et al. 1948: 46–7)

Madison believed that the constitution had to establish a representative system capable of balancing the contrasting interests that invariably derived from different forms of property because 'the protection of different and unequal faculties of acquiring property' was the 'first object of government'. Indeed, the reconciliation of the conflicts that would invariably arise from the 'various and interfacing interests' that reflected the division of labour in a free society was, Madison believed, 'the principal task of modern legislation, and involves the spirit of party and faction in the necessary and ordinary operations of the government' (Hamilton et al. 1948: 42, 62).

CONTEMPORARY APPROACHES

Most contemporary approaches to political agency have abandoned Hobbes's project of founding political power on 'natural laws' of reason.[6] Social scientists usually share Max Weber's view that the idea of a natural law is outdated, and focus their work on the institutions of political power and the governmental process within the conceptual and the constitutional frameworks that were forged in the nineteenth century (Duso, 1999: 388). Yet the history and the logic of the concept continue to determine the meaning and the significance of representation, and consequently, the interpretation of political agency.

Recovering the idea that representation legitimates legislation, but not the power to govern, libertarians have demanded strict limitation of the scope of public and particularly social policy. They follow Friedrich Hayek, according to whom in an ideal 'constitution of liberty' representative institutions should not be 'shaped by the needs of government', but by the needs of legislation. To interfere as little as possible with markets which Hayek believed to be the most efficient means to structure society, representatives should establish 'general rules of conduct' rather than intervening with 'measures of government concerning particular matters' (Hayek 1979: 22). Since legislation is embedded in a constitutional framework, even these general rules of conduct would not represent the direct authority of the people, but the authority of the constitution.

The idea that the rights and the acts of the representatives derive from the constitution, and not from the direct authority of the voters, reflects Hayek's belief that the right of the people to be governed by consent refers 'not so much to the recurrent election of representatives as to the fact that the people, organised as a constitution-making body, has the exclusive right to determine the powers of the representative legislature' (1960: 178). Although the different branches of government are accountable to the people, the legitimation of government ultimately derives from the constitution, because only the constitution, and neither the legislative nor the executive, 'represents' the will of the people.

How does the shift from representation to accountability affect political power? And what moves the governmental process if it is not driven by the idea that it ought to represent the general will of the people?

According to Joseph Schumpeter, to answer that question it is necessary to be aware of two things. First, it is necessary to understand that 'the will of the people is the product and not the motive power of the political process'. Because political power attempts to reproduce itself, 'the ways in which issues and the popular will on any issue are being manufactured is exactly analogous to the ways of commercial advertising' (Schumpeter 1987: 263). Second, it is necessary to understand the limits of collective action, that 'to different individuals and groups the common good is bound to mean different things' and therefore that there is 'no such thing as a uniquely determined common good that all people could agree on or be made to agree on by the force of rational argument'. Since usually there is no consensus concerning the best ways to achieve certain ends, this is also true for 'universal' goods or values – such as liberty, peace or prosperity – that people might actually agree on (Schumpeter 1987: 251).

The aim of the competition for political leadership is no longer the representation of the people as a political community, but the delegation of its powers to a particular party within the sate (Schumpeter 1987: 269). The question that arises at this point is not only whether those competing for political leadership should represent the aggregate or the general will of the individuals that compose a polity, but also whether it makes sense to delegate collective action to representatives. The question whether delegation makes sense for the individual voter has been re-examined by Geoffrey Brennan and Alan Hamlin (1999), who discuss the role representation plays in a public choice perspective.

Although the standard assumptions about self-interested agency suggest that outcomes of a direct democracy are preferable to outcomes produced by representative institutions, Brennan and Hamlin defend the principle of representation because the 'rational ignorance' of voters in 'direct democracies' impairs (potential) 'losses' of information, which can be avoided if their actions are delegated to competent and virtuous representatives. Like Schumpeter, who believed that citizens have a 'reduced sense of reality' and therefore lacked 'effective volition' in political matters (1987: 261–2), Brennan and Hamlin argue that 'the typical voter cannot bring to policy issues the attention that a minister or president could bring to these issues as a matter of course' (1999: 112). And like Burke, they argue that the primary task of representation is not so much to identify the interests of their constituents as to assess the 'delicate trade-offs and compromises between opposing interests and values' (1999: 113).

Critics of representative government argue that political agency ought to be thought of in terms of citizenship and participation, rather than leadership and representation, if only because the outputs produced by the competition for the leadership in representative institutions is far less desirable than most theories suggest. According to Paul Hirst, it no longer makes sense to vest governments with the authority to frame and implement public policies because 'conventional representative democracy has become little more than a plebiscite that chooses and legitimates the rulers of a big governmental machine that is out of control, in that it is largely unaccountable and cannot tackle major social problems' (1993: 116). The failure of the modern state to sustain full employment has undermined its ability to effectively govern the division of labour. To tackle social problems, marginalised and disadvantaged members of a political community have had to be given the means to bypass the traditional competition for leadership and to participate directly in political processes that concern them.

Some radical critics of representation demand that the 'thin' liberal democracies be altogether abandoned in favour of 'strong' participatory democracies. According to Benjamin Barber, one of the main weaknesses of liberal democracies is that 'under a representative government the voter is free only on the day he casts his ballot'. Even if voters were to decide on a broad range of issues, they still would either approve or sanction decisions that were not their own. Paradoxically, Barber argues, 'to exercise the franchise is unhappily also to renounce it. The representative principle steals from individuals the ultimate responsibility for their values, beliefs, and actions' (1984: 145).

But not all radical critiques of representative government go that far. Because the 'general codes of conduct' that would still be needed to make participatory democracies work would continue to affect different members of a community in different ways, Iris Marion Young argues in favour of representative institutions capable of framing and implementing such public policies as are necessary to protect the particular needs of marginalised groups or minorities. However, she suggests that such policies can only work if representation reflects not only the interests and opinions but also the perspectives of such groups. Because, as Anne Phillips points out, from a feminist perspective the struggle for quotas to balance 'the extraordinary under-representation of women in the world's political assemblies'(1993a: 96) is not so much about the fact 'that women know what they want and have been unable to make themselves heard', as about the more pervasive problem of 'having to "discover" that women were oppressed' and of having to articulate their needs (1993a: 102).

In this perspective, representation is neither an expression of the aggregate interests of abstract individuals, nor an expression of the constituted interests of a group. In fact, it is both, but primarily, representation is a mirror that enables particular groups within a political community to understand and articulate their identity and their particular needs. If representation reflects the position, and thus the perspective, of those who claim their right to be represented, it assumes a performative dimension that constitutes neither the general will nor the political unity of a people, but the (political) subjectivity of marginalised members of society. Representation does not return as a foundation of the political control over the subjects, but as a constituent moment in the recognition, determination and organisation of political agency within a political community.

QUESTIONS FOR DISCUSSION

1. Should politics be left to politicians? Discuss how the struggle for leadership in representative systems could affect the democrative process.
2. Can representation and direct partipation be reconciled? Discuss different ways of thinking about the relationship between representatives and those they represent.
3. Can multicultural societies be represented? Discuss the different roles represention could play in multicultural societies.
4. Should equality prevail over particular needs and interests? Discuss the trade-off between representation and direct participation from an egalitarian point of view.

NOTES

1. 'representation *n.*' *Oxford English Dictionary* (Simpson and Weiner 1989). <http://dictionary.oed.com>
2. On the philosophical dimension of the problem of representation, see also Duso (1988).
3. On the conceptual history of representation, see Hofmann (1974).
4. On Hobbes's role in the framing of a new science of politics, see Strauss (1965).
5. See also: Podelech (1984: 519).
6. The most prominent exception probably being Strauss (1953).

PAUL HIRST
EXTRACTS FROM 'ASSOCIATIONAL DEMOCRACY'

Ideas can be compared to animal species: having lost out to the dominant doctrines and surviving in marginal niches, they may enjoy a new period of evolutionary advantage as selection pressures shift and their hitherto powerful competitors totter toward extinction. This may be the case with associationalism. [. . .] Associationalism may be loosely defined as a normative theory of society the central claim of which is that human welfare and liberty are both best served when as many of the affairs of society as possible are managed by voluntary and democratically self-governing associations.

[. . .]

NEW TIMES FOR OLD IDEAS
[. . .]

Associationalism began in the nineteenth century as a critique of a purely competitive market society and of the concentrated and centralized state power that was necessary to protect that realm of private transactions from foes without and preserve it from social strife within. In this task it was in competition with and was challenged by state socialism and reformist social engineering, and it was defeated by them.

[. . .]

Paul Hirst (1993), 'Associational Democracy', in David Held (ed.), *Prospects for Democracy: North, South, East, West*, Cambridge: Polity Press.

Associationalism failed not because it was inherently impractical and utopian, but because as a political movement it could not compete in given political conditions with collectivism and centralism. The great wars of this century stimulated both of these tendencies as the major states mobilized all social resources to pursue industrialized conflict. In doing so, they decisively reinforced the commitment of the European labour movements to statism. It is possible that in the west centralizing pressures are now lessening steadily. Western states no longer face major military competitors. Class war has for long been a vanished threat. With the lessening of the scope for national macroeconomic management by centralized agencies and the decline of hierarchical and centralized Fordist production organization, so too have the economic imperatives for large-scale concentrated administration lessened markedly.[1]

The main threats to western societies are no longer external and organized but internal and diffuse. They are none the less real for that, but centralized bureaucratic structures cope so badly with these more amorphous threats of crime and drug addiction, for example, that this can hardly provide them with a convincing *raison d'être*. The real problems stem from the failure to sustain full employment and from the side-effects of collectivist welfare. In the US, in Britain, even in Germany we face the growing reality of a two-thirds versus one-third society. The notion of an 'underclass' is both graphic and yet absurd, since its members will not accept their 'place' at the bottom. A differentiated society cannot work if elementary freedoms of movement and association for all are to be preserved.

[...]

Only by resourcing associations that help the poor to organize themselves and then funding the projects for transformation of ghettos and slums can the state help to reverse this corrosive process of social decline.

[...]

Top-down management in welfare institutions is the creature of and the reflection of centralized state power. It is the enemy of all real welfare, of all real education, of all real healing. Each activity depends on the willingness of those who provide such services to act without strict reference to time and money. Each activity only survives as well as it does in the British welfare sector because there are still many such people who have not learned the calculus of utilitarian self-interest and who insist on keeping remote bureaucracies alive by acting on the principles of service and mutual aid.

[...]

Conventional representative democracy has become little more than a plebiscite that chooses and legitimates the rulers of a big governmental machine that is out of control, in that it is largely unaccountable and cannot tackle major social problems. The crisis of citizen participation and of effective accountability of government to society is all too obvious. Democracy needs to be renewed. It needs to be more inclusive, to give voice not only to those who are excluded by poverty and discrimination but to many other citizens as well who see politics as a professional spoils system beyond their control and concern. [. . .] The way is open for the advocacy of a programme of reform that would supplement and extend rather than destroy representative democracy. That supplement would involve a growth in the scope of governance through associations.[2] Associational institutions are in keeping with the fundamental principles of western liberalism; they are libertarian and consistent with fundamental human rights. Associational governance would lessen the tasks of central government to such an extent that greater accountability of both the public power and of the devolved associational agencies would be possible. The main political objective of modern associationalism is to decentralize and devolve as much of the affairs of society as possible to publicly funded but voluntary and self-governing associations.

Such associations are widely regarded in modern democratic theory as the social foundation for plural political interests, as the cement of the 'civil society' that sustains the liberal state. Associationalism, however, treats such self-governing voluntary bodies not as 'secondary associations' but as the *primary* means of organizing social life. In this doctrine, a self-governing civil society becomes primary, and the state becomes a secondary (if vitally necessary) public power that ensures peace between associations, protects the rights of individuals and provides the mechanisms of public finance whereby a substantial part of the activities of associations are funded. The activities of the state, central and local, are thus greatly reduced in scope. Large areas of governance of social affairs come to depend either on associations directly or on processes of coordination and collaboration between associations. In this way what the state does becomes more readily accountable. [. . .] Representative democracy thus becomes viable, providing oversight of a government which is a guardian rather than a service provider. As the state ceases to be both provider of services and the guarantor of the standard of those services, it can begin to perform the latter role adequately. It thus inspects and oversees associations, and ensures their compliance with democratic norms in their internal governance and their conformity to commonly agreed community standards of service provision. Associationalism is thus eventually capable of accomplishing that reduction of the extent of the state's service provision activity that conservative anti-collectivists have sought and failed to achieve by means of privatization and the market. Unlike their efforts, associationalism attains this without a reduction in either the scope of social governance or the extent of publicly funded welfare, for neither of these domains is abandoned to unregulated market mechanisms. The scope of public provision is not reduced, but the form in which it is provided ceases to be directly administered by the state.

[…]

THE POLITICS OF DECENTRALIZATION

[…]

Associationalism hands over great powers and responsibilities to groups. But most associations will not be exclusive groups that enclose the whole of their members' social lives. A self-governing association cannot stand against all the world – if it did it would be a *de facto* 'sovereign' state. Associational law, as we shall see, would limit certain acts as *ultra vires* […]. Thus the purposes and powers of most associations, and certainly the organizations they create for public welfare, would be limited, in the former case by their own choice in the main, and in the latter by law. The members of most associations would also be members of others too. Moreover, for many purposes associations or their organizations would need to coordinate and collaborate with others in like spheres of activity – if only to build coalitions of mutual convenience when funds were distributed or common standards set. Associations might thus gradually create a network of formal and informal relations, which would enable society to enjoy both diversity in social governance and a substantial measure of coordination.[3]

As far as individual citizens are concerned, associational institutions might actually reduce the negative sources of identification with groups and dispose them to regard neighbouring groups in a more tolerant light. Greater democratic governance through voluntary associations means greater control over his or her affairs by the citizen. The possibility of diverse standards of social governance on the part of associations representing groups at least ensures that among those with whom one has chosen to live certain values will prevail. The combination of a reduction in powerlessness in the control of one's own affairs and the removal of the fear of being at the mercy of hostile moral legislators might well promote more widespread feelings of security on the part of citizens and a consequent lessening of hostility toward others. Fear of others' moral politics can be acute where the state is both centralized and claims a plenitude of power in the recognition and regulation of groups and their actions. In such a state moral minorities compete to control or influence power and then compel others to live in a certain way: the state is then either for or against gay rights, either militantly anti-clerical or the upholder of a compulsory religion.

Associationalism is an explicitly normative theory. It starts from the premise that voluntary self-governing associations are the best way of organizing human affairs that combines liberty with social obligation. But it is not merely a doctrine that makes judgements based on values; from this basic value premise, associationalist thinkers have developed powerful theoretical and practical criticisms of the centralized 'sovereign' state, of bureaucratic collectivism and of the individualism of unregulated markets. They have also developed practical models of how to organize the economy and welfare on associationalist lines.

For this reason associationalism is the political theory best able to give effective expression to the feelings of unease that many have about contemporary social organization, but in a more coherent form than moral unease or protest. For example, associationalism provides a rationale for the decentralization of administration and a practical means of accomplishing it.

[...]

John Neville Figgis argued that not only is good government decentralizing, but that the most effective form of government is the self-government of associations freely formed of citizens. The state should leave such associations to their own evolution by the decisions of their own democratic bodies. He argued that the claim of 'sovereignty' – integral to the existence of centralized and concentrated state power – must deny this right to associations and treat all freedom of action of an agency as a concession sanctioned by representatives of the sovereign and revokable by legislation. Whether such 'sovereign' power is democratically legitimated or not, it still has the potential for both tyranny and inefficiency. Indeed, being able to point to the support of a mass electorate made oppression easier.

[...]

Noberto Bobbio in *The Future of Democracy* remarks that democracy has stopped short of 'the two great blocks of descending and hierarchical power in every complex society, big business and public administration. And as long as these blocks hold out against the pressures exerted from below, the democratic transformation of society cannot be said to be complete'.[4] The key test of democracy now is not '"who votes" but "where" they can vote'.[5] But the issue is not where in the literal sense, but in what *kind* of institution and for what *kind* of authority.

The problem is that such hierarchical and large-scale organizations cannot easily be democratized. Voting will change them much less than might be supposed. Indeed, it will legitimate their governing elites if hierarchy persists. Moreover, who is the constituency to vote in such organizations? Critics of industrial democracy have argued that the very idea of self-government here acts against the accountability of such institutions to society – it empowers the employees or providers of a service with a measure of control over its delivery. This was the Fabian critique of administrative and industrial syndicalism, for example – that it enabled the producers to govern themselves at the expense of the consumer.

If such large hierarchical organizations are not readily democratizable by the mere voting of their members, then the present situation remains highly unsatisfactory; for large firms and bureaucracies are not well stewarded by existing 'democratic' mechanisms. The firm as a republic of shareholders is a fiction; the management of firms is only notionally elected by and accountable to the shareholders (it is 'answerable' to the stock market and to major institutional investors, but that is another matter, and the economic consequences are far from satisfactory). Large welfare bureaucracies are only nominally accountable to ministers or councillors; for most practical purposes senior officials make detailed policy and junior ones have a large measure of administrative discretion with regard to clients. The concentration of economic power in large corporations and the concentration of social welfare and social control in large bureaucracies acts against that dispersal of social power and influence that liberal democratic theorists have seen as essential to the preservation of liberty. The sphere of civil society and secondary associations shrinks in the face of bodies that are in effect compulsory (one has to seek work, and large bureaucracies amount to a significant share of the labour force; the unemployed are subject to welfare tutelage) and which are not open to the *social* or *political* influence of the average citizen.[6] As a worker the citizen cannot of right make company policy; at best he or she can only disrupt the service the firm supplies by industrial action to modify that policy. As recipient of state benefits or services the citizen has no political rights or mutual ties in the capacity of claimant.

[. . .]

ROADS TO ECONOMIC DEMOCRACY

The only answer to these problems is a long-term one: to restore the scope of civil society by converting both companies and state welfare service agencies into self-governing associations. This will be a long haul, and in the interim the most realistic policies are those which boost the cooperative economy and the voluntary sector in welfare. The need for the democratization of companies is widely perceived. The most accomplished of modern political theorists, Robert A. Dahl, in his *A Preface to Economic Democracy* argues strongly for the development of a worker-owned cooperative sector as a way of checking the unhealthy concentration of corporate control over the economy that has grown up in the US in this century.[7] Democracy requires the diffusion of ownership. Revisionist socialists have espoused market socialism, an explicit model of an economy that marries cooperation and neo-classical economics.[8] The economic units are to be worker cooperatives and they are linked one with another and with consumers through market transactions.

The problem with views like the latter is that they treat the economy as if it were reducible to its component parts, to enterprises. Get ownership and control within the enterprise into the right balance, add to it an effective competition and anti-monopoly policy to prevent firms getting too big, and then the distribution of rewards will be fair and markets will also operate as efficient allocative mechanisms. Market economies, however, depend for their substantive outcomes on non-market social factors that the firm cannot easily create within itself.[9] Those factors are, for example, the achieving of an effective balance between cooperation and competition among firms that ensures an adequate supply of necessary 'public goods' to firms (suitably trained labour, market information and so on), and the creation of a structure of publicly regulated financial institutions that provide a range of sources of investment finance at suitable rates and terms for the sustained development of the economy.

[...]

The great advantage of associationalism is that it provides principles and concepts for assessing the range of institutions that make a balance between cooperation and competition possible, and for establishing which are most consistent with extended democratic governance in civil society. It does this is in three ways. First, by insisting on the devolution of governmental functions to the lowest level at which they can be efficiently performed, it provides a *political* rationale for the tendencies toward local and regional economic regulation. Secondly, by emphasizing the principles both of organizing social activities through voluntary organizations and of voluntary cooperation between them, it provides political rationales for economic governance through open, inclusive bodies like trade associations, and for firms to cooperate in developing the industrial 'public sphere' of a region or locality. Thirdly, by emphasizing the principle of mutuality, it encourages enterprises and other agencies to develop ongoing relationships and offer one another help in a range of ways (from the informal, such as the established customs of firms sharing work and information, to the formal, such as industrial credit unions).

[...]

There is a great deal of evidence from studies of existing regional economies and industrial districts that such mutualist and associational economic relationships are possible, that they are not inimical to productive efficiency (quite the contrary), and that not all production and distribution need be conducted on a large scale in order to match national and international competitors.[10]

NOTES

1. See P. Hirst and J. Zeitlin, 'Flexible specialisation vs. post-Fordism: theory, evidence and policy implications', *Economy and Society*, 20:1 (1991), 1–50, and M. Piore and C. Sabel, *The Second Industrial Divide* (New York, Basic Books, 1984).
2. Arguments for democratic renewal are numerous. Examples of arguments to make interest group representation more inclusive through institutional reform are P. Schmitter, 'Corporative democracy: oxymoronic, just plain moronic? or a promising way out of the present impasse?', unpublished ms (1988), and J. Cohen and J. Rogers, 'Secondary associations in democratic governance', *Politics and Society*, November (1992).
3. See W. Streek and P. Schmitter, 'Community, market, state and associations', *European University Institute Working Paper No. 94*, Florence (1984).
4. N. Bobbio, *The Future of Democracy* (Cambridge, Polity Press, 1987), p. 57.
5. Bobbio, *The Future of Democracy*, p. 56.
6. See H. Belloc, *The Servile State* (originally published 1913; reprinted Indianapolis, Liberty Classics, 1977).
7. New Haven, CT, Yale University Press, 1985.
8. See J. Le Grand and S. Estin (eds), *Market Socialism* (Oxford, Oxford University Press, 1989), especially ch. 2.
9. On the balance between cooperation and competition and the failure of the market to secure this, see Piore and Sabel, *The Second Industrial Divide*, also P. Hirst and J. Zeitlin, 'Flexible specialisation and the competitive failure of UK manufacturing'. *The Political Quarterly*, 60:2 (1989), 164–78, and C. Sabel, 'Studied trust: building new forms of cooperation in a volatile economy', *Paper No. 11*, Conference on Industrial Districts and Local Economic Regeneration, ILO, Geneva (1990).
10. For studies of two modern industrial districts, both of which have proved strongly competitive in the 1980s, see: for Baden-Württemberg, C. Sabel et al, 'Regional prosperities compared: Massachusetts and Baden-Württemberg in the 1980s', *Economy and Society*, 18:4 (1989), pp. 374–404, and Hubert Schmitz, 'Industrial districts: model and reality in Baden-Württemberg', *Paper No. 5*, Conference on Industrial Districts and Local Economic Regeneration, ILO, Geneva (1990); and, for Emilia-Romagna and Italy generally, S. Brusco, 'The Emilian model: productive decentralisation and social integration', *Cambridge Journal of Economics*, 6:2 (1982), pp. 167–84, and C. Trigilia, 'Italian industrial districts: neither myth nor interlude', *Paper No. 8*, Conference on Industrial Districts and Local Economic Regeneration, ILO, Geneva (1990).

IRIS MARION YOUNG
EXTRACTS FROM *INCLUSION AND DEMOCRACY*

REPRESENTATION AND SOCIAL PERSPECTIVE

[. . .]

Participation and representation

Radical democrats frequently distrust institutions of political representation. They often present representation as violating the values of democracy themselves. Representation, they suggest, 'alienates political will at the cost of genuine self-government', 'impairs the community's ability to function as a regulating instrument of justice', and 'precludes the evolution of a participating public in which the idea of justice might take root'.[1]

Without question a strong democracy should have institutions of direct democracy such as referendum as part of its procedural repertoire. As society is more deeply democratic, moreover, the more it has state-sponsored and civic fora for policy discussion at least some of which ought procedurally to influence authoritative decisions. The anti-representation position, however, refuses to face complex realities of democratic process, and wrongly opposes representation to participation.

Representation is necessary because the web of modern social life often ties the action of some people and institutions in one place to consequences in many other places and institutions. No person can be present at all the decisions or in all the decision-making bodies whose actions affect her life, because they are so many and so dispersed. Though her aspirations are

---

Iris Marion Young (2000), *Inclusion and Democracy*, Oxford: Oxford University Press.

often disappointed, she hopes that others will think about situations like hers and represent them to the issue forum.[2]

One might object that this argument presupposes a large-scale society and polity which a preference for direct democracy rejects. A democracy without representation must consist of small, decentralized, self-sufficient units. Robert Dahl gives a compelling set of arguments, however, that even this vision of decentralized direct democracy cannot avoid representation. The equal participation of everyone in political deliberation, he argues, can occur only in small committees. Even in assemblies of a few hundred people most people will be more passive participants who listen to a few people speak for a few positions, then think and vote. Beyond the small committee, that is, features of time and interaction produce *de facto* representation. But such *de facto* representation is arbitrary; in fact direct democracies often cede political power to arrogant loudmouths whom no one chose to represent them. Thus even in relatively small units of political decision-making like neighbourhoods or workplaces, political equality may best be served by institutions of formal representation, because the rules concerning who is authorized to speak for whom are public and there are some norms of accountability. Dahl also argues, I think plausibly, that in the normal course of social life small decentralized political units are likely to grow larger by means of either conquest or coalition. As soon as scale returns, then, representation also returns.[3]

Critics of representative democracy might object that this enhanced participation, to the degree that it exists, comes at the expense of citizen participation in the deliberative process. Citizens vote for their representatives, and then there is no further need for them. The institutions and culture of some representative democracies do indeed discourage citizens from participating in political discussion and decision-making. One can argue, however, that if they do, so they are not properly representative, because under such circumstances representatives have only a very weak relation to their constituents. Under normative ideals of communicative democracy, representative institutions do not stand opposed to citizen participation, but require such participation to function well.[4]

Representation as relationship

The claim that authentic democracy is not compatible with representation implicitly relies on the logic of identity [. . .], or what Jacques Derrida calls a metaphysics of presence.[5] It imagines an ideal democratic decision-making situation as one in which the citizens are *co-present*. Like at a town meeting, in this image of authentic democracy citizens meet in one place and make their decisions on one occasion.

[. . .]

On this image of democracy, representatives could only properly express the 'will of the people' if they are *present* for their constituents, and act as they would act. On this image, the representative *substitutes* for the constituents, stands for them in a relation of identity. Critics of representation rightly note that it is not possible for one person to be present in place of many, to speak and act as they would if they were present. It is impossible to find the essential attributes of constituents, the single common good that transcends the diversity of their interests, experiences, and opinions. The objection that some people make to the notion of specific representation for marginalized gender or ethnic groups in fact can be extended to all representation. Political representatives usually have a large constituency that is diverse in its interests, backgrounds, experiences, and beliefs. It is perhaps even more difficult to imagine a shared will for the residents of a metropolitan legislative district than for members of an ethnic group.

If we accept the argument that representation is necessary, but we also accept an image of democratic decision-making as requiring a co-presence of citizens, and that representation is legitimate only if in someway the representative is identical with the constituency, then we have a paradox: representation is necessary but impossible. There is a way out of this paradox, which involves conceptualizing representation outside a logic of identity. Taking seriously the decentred nature of large-scale mass democracy entails discarding images of the co-presence of citizens or that representatives must be present for citizens, and instead conceiving democratic discussion and decision-making as mediated through and dispersed over space and time. Rather than a relation of identity or substitution, political representation should be thought of as a process involving a mediated relation of constituents to one another and to a representative.

I rely on the Derridian concept of *différance* to formulate another account of representation. Where the metaphysics of presence generates polarities because it aims to reduce the many to one identity, thinking of entities in terms of *différance* leaves them in their plurality without requiring their collection into a common identity. [. . .] Conceptualizing representation in terms of *différance* means acknowledging and affirming that there is a difference, a separation, between the representative and the constituents. Of course, no person can stand for and speak as a plurality of other persons. The representative function of *speaking for* should not be confused with an identifying requirement that the representative *speak as* the constituents would, to try to be present for them in their absence. It is no criticism of the representative that he or she is separate and distinct from the constituents. At the same time, however, conceiving representation under the idea of *différance* means describing a relationship between constituents and the representative, and among constituents, where the temporality of past and anticipated future leave their traces in the actions of each.

Conceiving representation as a differentiated relationship among plural actors dissolves the paradox of how one person can stand for the experience and opinions of many. There is no single will of the people that can be represented. Because the constituency is internally differentiated, the representative does not stand for or refer to an essential opinion or interest shared by all the constituents which she should describe and advocate.[6]

Rather than construe the normative meaning of representation as properly standing for the constituents, we should evaluate the process of representation according to the character of the relationship between the representative and the constituents. The representative will inevitably be separate from the constituents, but should also be *connected* to them in determinate ways. Constituents should also be connected to one another. Representation systems sometimes fail to be sufficiently democratic not because the representatives fail to stand for the will of the constituents, but because they have lost connection with them. In modern mass democracies it is indeed easy to sever relations between representatives and constituents, and difficult to maintain them.

Anticipating authorization and accountability

[. . .]

Thinking of representation in terms of *différance* rather than identity means taking its temporality seriously. Representation is a process that takes place over time, and has distinct moments or aspects, related to but different from one another. Representation consists in a mediated relationship, both among members of a constituency, between the constituency and the representative, and between representatives in a decision-making body. As a deferring relationship between constituents and their agents, representation moves between moments of authorization and accountability. Representation is a cycle of anticipation and recollection between constituents and representative, in which discourse and action at each moment ought to bear *traces* of the others.

[. . .]

Conceptualized as difference, representation necessarily involves distinction and separation between representatives and constituents. Representation is a differentiated relationship between constituents and representative where disconnection is always a possibility, and connection maintained over time through anticipation and recollection in moments of authorization and accountability. A representative process is worse, then, to the extent that the separation tends towards severance, and better to the extent that it establishes and renews connection between constituents and representative, and among members of the constituency.

[Hanna] Pitkin agrees that authorization is an important sign of representation. One who represents others in an official institutionalized sense must be authorized to speak for and perhaps bind them. Elections are the most common and obvious means of authorizing representations, but other forms of delegate selection to discussion and decision-making bodies sometimes obtain. The delegate model of the representative's responsibility is one interpretation of authorization. On this interpretation, a constituency is an already formed cohesive group with a single will that can be conveyed to the representative as a mandate. [...] In fact, however, in most situations the specific constituency exists at best potentially; the representative institutions and the process of authorization themselves call its members into action.[7] Anticipating the moment when representatives will claim to act at their behest and on their behalf, individuals in the defined constituency go looking for each other. They organize and discuss the issues that are important to them, and call on candidates to respond to their interests. While there is usually a moment when they authorize representatives, in doing so the constituency rarely brings itself to affirm a common will. The constituency is usually too large, or the varying activities of its members are too dispersed, or its definition and borders too vague, to expect a time when the constituency at one moment arrives at a collective will. Instead, in a well-functioning process a public sphere of discussion sets an issue agenda and the main terms of dispute or struggle. For parliamentary processes to be effective as representative, and not merely as a stage on which élites perform according to their own script, the democratic process of the authorization of representatives should be both participatory and inclusively deliberative.

[...]

In the process of calling representatives to account for what they have decided, citizens continue to form themselves into a constituency, and they engage anew in debate and struggle over the wisdom and implications of policy decisions. Such renewed opinion formation may bear the traces of the process of authorization, but it also has new elements, because previously the constituents did not know just how issues would be formulated in the representative body, and what expression, appeals, and arguments would be offered there. The responsibility of the representative is not simply to tell citizens how she has enacted a mandate they authorized or served their interests, but as much to persuade them of the rightness of her judgement.[8]

In most actually existing democracies, the moment of accountability is weaker than the moment of authorization. For many systems of representation, the only form of being held to account is re-authorization by means of re-election. The cycle that returns to authorization is indeed important for motivating accountability. Strong communicative democracy, however, also requires some processes and procedures where constituents call representatives to account over and above re-authorizing them. As with authorization, accountability should occur both through official institutions and in the public life of independent civic association. [...] The major normative problem of representation is the threat of disconnection between the one representative and the many he or she represents. When representatives become too separated, constituents lose the sense that they have influence over policy-making, become disaffected, and withdraw their participation. Establishing and maintaining legitimate and inclusive processes of representation calls up responsibilities for both officials and citizens. Citizens must be willing and able to mobilize one another actively to participate in processes of both authorizing and holding to account. Representatives should listen to these public discussions and diverse claims, stay connected to constituents, and be able to convey reasons for their actions and judgements in terms that recollect their discussions. Such mobilization, listening, and connectedness can be either facilitated or impeded by the design of representative institutions.

[...]

Modes of representation

[...]

Since the representative is necessarily different from the constituents, a democracy is better or worse according to how well those differentiated positions are connected. Democracy can also be strengthened by pluralizing the modes and sites of representation. Systems of political representation cannot make individuals present in their individuality, but rather should represent *aspects* of a person's life experience, identity, beliefs, or activity where she or he has affinity with others. Potentially there are many such aspects or affinity groups. I propose to distinguish here three general modes through which a person can be represented: according to interest, opinion, and perspective.

[...]

Interest. I define interest as what affects or is important to the life prospects of individuals, or the goals of organizations. An agent, whether individual or collective, has an interest in whatever is necessary or desirable in order to realize the ends the agent has set. These include both material resources and the ability to exercise capacities – e.g. for cultural expression, political influence, economic decision-making power, and so on. I define interest here as self-referring, and as different from ideas, principles, and values. The latter may help define the ends a person sets for herself, where the interest defines the means for achieving those ends.

Interests frequently conflict, not only between agents, but also in the action of a single agent. Where agents need resources to accomplish a variety of ends, they are likely to find some of the resources they need to be relatively scarce. Sometimes the means one agent needs to pursue a certain end implies directly impeding another agent's ability to get what he needs to pursue his ends. It is important to note, however, that interests do not necessarily conflict. The pursuit of ends in society and the setting of political frameworks to facilitate that pursuit need not necessarily be structured as a zero-sum relationship among agents.

[...]

Opinions. I define opinions as the principles, values, and priorities held by a person as these bear on and condition his or her judgement about what policies should be pursued and ends sought. This is the primary sphere of what Anne Phillips refers to as the 'politics of ideas',[9] on which much contemporary discussion of pluralism focuses. Rawls's recent discussion of the principles and problems of political liberalism, for example, concentrates on the fact of plural ideas and belief systems in modern societies, how these legitimately influence political life, and how people with differing beliefs and opinions can maintain a working polity.[10] By opinion, I mean any judgement or belief about how things are or ought to be, and the political judgements that follow from these judgements or beliefs. [...] Opinions are certainly contestable, and often some can be shown to be more well founded than others. A communicative democracy, however, requires the free expression and challenging of opinions, and a wide representation of opinions in discussions leading to policy decisions.

Political parties are the most common vehicle for the representation of opinions. Parties often put forward programmes that less express the interests of a particular constituency, and more organize the political issues of the day according to principles, values, and priorities the party claims generally to stand for. Smaller or more specialized associations, however, can and often do form to represent opinions in public life and influence public policy. Traditionally interest group theory has treated such associations as another kind of interest group, and for most purposes this is a harmless conflation. I think it important to distinguish, however, in general between kinds of political association motivated by an instrumentalist interest, on the one hand, and kinds of association motivated by commitment to beliefs and values, on the other. Whereas the former sort of motivation is selfish, even if selfish for a group, the latter often takes itself to be impartial or even altruistic *Perspective*.

[…]

Because of their social locations, people are attuned to particular kinds of social meanings and relationships to which others are less attuned. Sometimes others are not positioned to be aware of them at all. From their social locations people have differentiated knowledge of social events and their consequences. Because their social locations arise partly from the constructions that others have of them, as well as constructions which they have of others in different locations, people in different locations may interpret the meaning of actions, events, rules, and structures differently. Structural social positions thus produce particular location-relative experience and a specific knowledge of social processes and consequences. Each differentiated group position has a particular experience or point of view on social processes precisely because each is part of and has helped produce the patterned processes. Especially in so far as people are situated on different sides of relations of structural inequality, they understand those relations and their consequences differently.

[…]

While different, these social perspectives may not be incompatible. Each social perspective is particular and partial with respect to the whole social field, and from each perspective some aspects of the reality of social processes are more visible than others.

[…]

[Thus] the idea of perspective is meant to capture that sensibility of group-positioned experience without specifying unified content to what the perceptive sees. The social positioning produced by relation to other structural positions and by the social processes that issue in unintended consequences only provide a back-ground and perspective in terms of which particular social events and issues are interpreted; they do not make the interpretation. So we can well find different persons with a similar social perspective giving different interpretations of an issue. Perspective is an approach to looking at social events, which conditions but does not determine what one sees.

[…]

Interests, opinions, and perspectives, then, are three important aspects of persons that can be represented. I do not claim that these three aspects exhaust the ways people can be represented. There may well be other possible modes of representation, but I find these three particularly salient in the way we talk about representation in contemporary politics, and in answering the conceptual and practical problems posed for group representation. None of these aspects reduce to the identity of either a person or a group, but each is an aspect of the person. None of these aspects of persons, moreover, is reducible to the others. They are logically independent in the sense that from a general social perspective one can immediately infer a set of neither interests nor opinions.

NOTES

1. Benjamin Barber, *Strong Democracy* (Berkeley: University of California Press, 1984), 145–6. Compare Paul Hirst, *Representative Democracy and its Limits* (Oxford: Polity Press, (1990); John Dryzek, *Discursive Democracy* (Cambridge: Cambridge University Press, (1990), 42–3.
2. Linda Alcoff argues that the position that a person can and should speak only for herself is an abrogation of responsibility. It ignores the fact that people's lives are affected by the congruence of many distant actions, and that the participation of people in institutions here in turn affects others. See 'The Problem of Speaking for Others', *Cultural Critique*, 20 (Winter 1991), 5–32.
3. Robert Dahl, *Democracy and its Critics* (New Haven: Yale University Press, 1989), ch. 16.
4. See David Plotke, 'Representation is Democracy', *Constellations*, 4/1 (Apr. 1997), 19–34. See also Philip Green, *Retrieving Democracy* (Totowa, NJ: Rowman & Allenheld, 1985), ch. 9.
5. Jacques Derrida, *On Grammatology* (Baltimore: Johns Hopkins University Press, 1973).
6. Derrida himself points towards a theorizing of political representation under the idea of *différance*. See 'Sending: On Representation', trans. Peter Dews and Mary Dews, *Social Research*, 49 (Summer 1982), 294–326.
7. Melissa Williams discusses this fact of the mutual constitution of constituency and representative. See *Voice, Trust and Memory: Marginalized Groups and the Failure of Liberal Representation* (Princeton: Princeton University Press, 1998), 203–5.
8. See Amy Gutmann and Dennis Thompson, *Democracy and Disagreement* (Cambridge, Mass.: Harvard University Press, 1996), ch. 4. Accountability, including the accountability of representatives to constituents, is one of the three procedural principles of deliberative democracy for Gutmann and Thompson. They somewhat emphasize the representative's giving his or her reasons for doing as he or she did, it seems to me, at the expense of articulation of the reasons they have for disagreeing.
9. Anne Phillips, *The Politics of Presence* (Oxford: Oxford University Press, 1995).
10. John Rawls, *Political Liberalism* (New York: Columbia University Press, 1993). With the term 'opinion', however, I do not necessarily intend something so all-encompassing and fundamental as what Rawls calls 'comprehensive doctrine', partly because I doubt that most people in modern societies hold or have most or all of their moral and political judgements guided by a single comprehensive doctrine. See Iris Marion Young, 'Rawls's *Political Liberalism*', *Journal of Political Philosophy*, 3/2 (June 1995), 181–90.

3

TOLERATION

Phillip Cole

Introduction

Toleration is the practice of tolerance as opposed to intolerance. Tolerance can be practised by individuals or by communities and each of these levels needs separate treatment because the practice of toleration takes a different form in each. My primary concern here will be with toleration at the level of political communities, and with liberal political communities in particular. Liberal theory can, to an extent, claim ownership over the tradition of toleration, as it has been at the centre of liberal thought about the nature of political communities. To use the analogy of the liberal garden, the tree of toleration is said to flourish there. That is not to say that it is never to be found in other kinds of garden, but the claim is that the liberal garden is especially conducive to its growth and well-being. For that reason I am going to discuss toleration within the context of liberal thinking rather than any other political theory. But my approach will not be to offer a history of the tradition of liberal thinking about toleration, or even to describe how it is regarded today within that context. Instead, I want to problematise the idea of toleration, to show that it is a deeply puzzling and complex notion, and to show that liberal thought itself gives rise to some of these puzzles and complexities. The liberal garden, I will suggest, is a harsher environment than the liberal gardening 'handbook' has suggested.

Toleration and individuals

First, however, I do want to say something about the practice of toleration at the level of the individual, because some of these puzzles and complexities begin to emerge here. At the level of the individual agent we can understand tolerance as a virtue and intolerance as a vice. This is not to say that tolerance here can be best understood in the context of a theory of virtue ethics – it is a central value of liberal individualist thought and it is in that context that it has its best-known expressions. What is at stake is the individual's boundary between the tolerable and the intolerable. An individual will have a boundary between things (ideas, practices, images, other people – the list is potentially open) which they find unobjectionable and those they find objectionable. They may attach a positive value to those things they find unobjectionable, or they may simply be indifferent to them. But they attach a negative value to those things they find objectionable. However, we can't simply identify a person's boundary of toleration with this distinction between the unobjectionable and the objectionable, because in order to tolerate something one must already find it objectionable – otherwise what is there to tolerate? And so the individual's boundary of toleration lies between those things they find objectionable but are prepared to tolerate, and those things they are not prepared to tolerate. The tolerant person is, therefore, not the person who finds very little objectionable – indifference is not an expression of the virtue of tolerance. Rather, the tolerant person is one who is prepared to tolerate much that they find objectionable. Equally, the intolerant person is not someone who finds a great deal objectionable, but the person who is not prepared to tolerate much, if anything, that they object to. And so alongside the tolerant and intolerant characters we might place two other characters, the indifferent person and the prejudiced person. Although it may appear paradoxical, what follows is that the indifferent person can be intolerant, and the prejudiced person can be tolerant. The indifferent person emerges as intolerant even if there is very little they object to, if they are not prepared to tolerate anything that they do object to. The prejudiced person emerges as tolerant if they are prepared to override their prejudices in most cases. Also, not only can the indifferent person be intolerant, but their indifference in itself may make them an unattractive character. Their indifference may arise because they lack convictions and principles. The tolerant person has convictions and principles but is prepared to set them aside under certain circumstances. On the other hand, it is important to remember that in particular situations indifference may be preferable to tolerance. If one is on the receiving end of a prejudice, there is, of course, an important difference between being discriminated against because of that prejudice and being tolerated and so free from discrimination; but there is still something importantly disturbing in knowing that one is being merely tolerated – one might legitimately hold that others ought to be indifferent towards one's ideas, practices, identity, rather than tolerant of them; they are wrong to object to them at all. Indifference can, therefore, itself be a virtue. And while we can conclude that tolerance is a virtue, we cannot say that the tolerant person is an obviously attractive character – the prejudices they hold which they are setting aside may be such that we would judge them to be an unattractive character. The tolerant racist may be preferable to the intolerant racist, and in exercising that tolerance they are practising an important virtue – but these are still prejudices they ought not to hold, and which make them a deeply unattractive character from a liberal point of view.

Also, if we understand tolerance as simply the setting aside of principles or convictions (or prejudices), it doesn't follow that tolerance is always even a virtue. For tolerance to be a moral virtue, we have to be able to describe the boundary between the tolerable and the intolerable so that it has a recognisable moral dimension. To meet this, the boundary has to be *principled* – the setting aside of principles and convictions has to have an ethical basis. We need to know that the tolerant person's convictions are being set aside, not because of moral cowardice or opportunism or self-interested bargaining, but because of moral principles. And so the exercise of tolerance need not always be virtuous – either that or we refuse to call the setting aside of convictions and principles on any other basis the exercise of tolerance at all, and insist that it is only when this setting aside is principled that tolerance is being genuinely practised. There is still a puzzle here, of course, because what is happening is that one's ethical convictions and principles are being set aside on an ethically principled basis, and how can this be made coherent? There seem to be three possibilities. First, we see the exercise of tolerance as a good in itself, in that it improves our moral character, and this overrides our moral objections to other practices or ideas, etc. This is something like the rationale for tolerance we find in Stoicism. Second, we see the exercise of individual autonomy as good for people, and so it is better to allow them to explore different avenues and pathways which we may consider objectionable, rather than intervening to prevent them from doing so. This is one rationale for tolerance we find within liberal individualism. Third, while we have moral principles and convictions, we hold an epistemological scepticism about their basis, so that we are not in a position to know that the opposing principles and convictions held by others are mistaken, and it would therefore be unethical to impose our own principles and convictions upon them. Again, this is a rationale for tolerance we find within liberal individualism. In each case, then, our ethical convictions and principles are being set aside on a principled basis: because we have a duty to develop our own character; or because the principle of individual autonomy is overriding; or because it would be morally wrong to impose our convictions on others when we are not in a position to know they are true or right.

TOLERATION AND COMMUNITIES

The practice of toleration takes a different shape at the level of the community, because here the crucial boundary is between the 'public' and the 'private'. A community that practises tolerance is one that allows that a wide range of issues are a matter for individual choice rather than collective decision – they are private, not public, matters. These are matters that are characteristically to do with individual 'lifestyle' choices, and in a liberal democratic community there is a list of such issues which are taken to be unproblematically private: the list would include what clothes to wear, what food to eat, what music one listens to or creates, what literature one reads or writes, choice of work or career, whether or not to marry one's partner, how many children one has as a family. The only matters appropriate for collective decision-making are those which have an effect on collective life, on the community itself.

While this makes sense at first sight, it is a touch too simplistic, because it will be impossible to make a clear distinction between matters that have no effect on collective life at all and those that do – potentially anything one does has an impact on collective life. However, these issues are still judged to be private in that the effect they have is benign, or, if it is damaging, the damage is negligible and so should be tolerated.

There are societies which take a very different view, and which are prepared to take a collective decision on what work people should do, what literature they should read or write, whether or not they marry their partners, how many children they should have as a family, what clothing they should wear and so on. These societies, from a liberal point of view, are paradigmatically intolerant communities – there is very little private space for individual choice. Religious states, such as Islamic republics, would be examples where some of these issues are decided at the collective level and which therefore emerge as intolerant from a liberal point of view. Communist states, where they do exist or have existed, have also counted many of these as collective matters, and so would also emerge as intolerant from a liberal point of view. But what we have to remember is that the line between the private and the public in a liberal community is drawn in terms of the impact issues have on the collective life of the community, and this means the location of the public/private boundary is never fixed – it is always possible that circumstances arise under which one of the issues I have listed as unproblematically private from a liberal point of view could genuinely have a significant impact on collective life, or, more likely, it is always possible to interpret them in this way. And so while I included whether or not to marry one's partner on the liberal list, this is in fact a controversial issue in the majority of liberal states when it comes to same-sex relationships. Same-sex relations are seldom given equal legal status, if any at all, in liberal communities. What this means is that both liberal communities and, for example, Islamic republics determine the location of the private/public divide in the same way. Although they would draw that line in, for the most part, very different places, the reasoning is largely the same in both cases. Where liberal communities and Islamic republics differ is over which issues genuinely do have a significantly damaging impact on the collective. For the most part the two approaches are far from incommensurable.

Where they become incommensurable is where a liberal community is genuinely secular, and we then have a fundamental difference between a secular state and a religious state, in that they will indeed have radically different approaches to religious toleration, or on other issues where the religious state applies principles derived directly from authoritative religious texts rather than positive law. A secular state obviously has no authority to impose religious views or religiously inspired policies upon the community, while a religious state obviously has that authority. However, in practice we cannot make too much of this distinction, because we can question the extent to which actual liberal states are genuinely secular. In the United States of America, for example, issues of tolerance are often focused around the predominance of the Christian faith and the teachings of authoritative Christian texts. The problems surrounding the legal status of same-sex relations are, for example, often only problems given a particular religious framework. A genuinely secular state and a religious state would, then, take radically incommensurable approaches to many issues of toleration (but not all – both will be concerned to minimise damage to the community), but this distinction is of little use in practice. And so while the space for private decision is genuinely wider in liberal states than in other kinds of state, this space has no particularly strong protection, and the rulers of a liberal state are in a position to decide that an issue that was taken to be private is in fact of public concern. Even where the private space is defined in a constitution, constitutions can always be amended. We may claim that any such revision of the private/public boundary in a liberal state has an added layer of protection in that it has to be democratically approved by the community, but again in practice this is questionable, and even where democratic approval is required for such a revision, experience shows that it is not difficult to secure. I will say more about this constitutional weakness below.

Another set of problems for liberal theory concerning toleration is the gap between liberal individualism as a moral theory and liberal political theory. From the point of view of liberal individualism, the only concern is whether actions harm others in unacceptable ways and, where paternalism is permitted, harm the agent in unacceptable ways. However, from the point of view of liberal political theory, another issue is whether actions harm liberal political institutions and liberal political culture in unacceptable ways. There is therefore a tension between the value of individual freedom and autonomy that we find at the level of liberal individualism, and the value of liberal political institutions and culture. Of course, liberal institutions and culture are valuable because they foster individual freedom and autonomy (and other liberal values), but the fact remains that the maintenance of these institutions and this culture may require constraints on individual freedom and autonomy which would be unjustifiable from a purely liberal individualist perspective. From the moral point of view, these are choices which should clearly be left to individual conscience, but from the political point of view, these are choices which have such profound implications for the political institutions and culture that they have to be taken at the collective level. There is a set of issues which have been notoriously problematic for liberal polities for precisely this reason – religious identity, sexuality and artistic expression. From the moral point of view of liberal individualism these are all clearly matters of individual lifestyle – the community cannot decide what religion one should practise, one's sexual identity, or what has artistic merit. However, liberal political practice has been much less sure about this, and all three areas have been subjected to collective decision-making in highly controversial circumstances.

Why have these three issues posed particular problems for liberal states? On the face of it, each expresses a different kind of problem for a community. The problem of religion concerns cohesiveness – to what extent can religious diversity be tolerated without undermining that cohesiveness? This takes us into broader areas of tension between cultural diversity and community identity, and for liberal theorists who take this direction the problem is defined as one of respect for liberal political culture and institutions – diverse identities are problematic to the extent that they undermine respect for these. Religious identity has been particularly problematic because of the intensity of religious beliefs – it is, it seems from experience, more likely to pose problems than other forms of diversity. The relevant questions here must be: what kinds of religious or other cultural identity genuinely threaten to undermine liberal political culture and institutions, and so damage the political community as a whole; and to what extent is a liberal community entitled to override individual freedom and autonomy for the sake of cohesiveness? The latter question is important because communal cohesiveness is not a specifically liberal value, and so where non-liberal values clash with core liberal values, such as individual freedom and autonomy, there is a reasonable assumption that, if this is a genuinely liberal community, the non-liberal value should give way. Therefore in a genuine liberal polity there must be a strong presumption in favour of cultural diversity, and some degree of divisive diversity has to be tolerated. A community that ruled out *any* kind of cultural difference because it caused *any* degree of communal divisiveness would be intolerant. And so there may be some forms of cultural difference which are objectionable on the grounds that they genuinely cause communal divisiveness, but they must nevertheless be tolerated. Here, the clash between liberal individualist morality and liberal politics is settled in favour of the individualist morality and the values of freedom and autonomy. The point is, however, that there are going to be limits to toleration where the clash is settled in favour of liberal politics, and liberal political institutions and culture take priority over individual freedom and autonomy. Some judgement therefore has to be made to distinguish between those divisive cultural differences that are to be tolerated and those that are intolerable. How to make that judgement is an extremely complex problem, but it will have something to do with the extent to which liberal political institutions and culture can recover from the damage caused by the divisiveness – we can assume that they are sufficiently robust to withstand some degree of cultural divisiveness, but there have to be limits beyond which they disintegrate and cannot be retrieved. Where those limits lie can only be a matter of political judgement, not philosophical argument.

The problem of sexuality raises a different set of questions for a liberal community, that of the morality of individual conduct. As I pointed out above, same-sex relations have caused tensions in liberal democratic states, and although there seem to be growing levels of acceptance, we can still ask whether this is an expression of growing indifference or increased levels of tolerance. This matters in this case as it could be argued (and I for one would argue it) that sexuality ought to be a matter of indifference not tolerance – this is one case where indifference is morally preferable to tolerance, because what has to be set aside to practise tolerance is an indefensible prejudice rather than any reasoned conviction. However, there is also evidence that same-sex relations are still highly controversial, as there is still a great deal of legal discrimination against such couples, and as I write this the federal government of the United States is considering steps to abolish any legal recognition of same-sex partnerships that individual states may have taken. While the objections in the United States are clearly coming from a Christian perspective, this does raise the issue of whether a liberal community is obliged to tolerate practices it considers to be immoral. Are there issues on which the liberal polity has the right to take a moral stance? Again there are two questions a community that understood itself to be liberal would have to ask of itself. First, does a liberal community have the right to take a moral stance at all? Should it outlaw *any* practices or ideas on grounds of immorality? Second, if it does have that right, to what extent is it still obliged to tolerate practices or ideas it considers to be immoral? Again, a community that banned *any* practice it considered to be immoral to *any* degree would be intolerant. A theory of toleration based on moral scepticism would give a negative answer to the first question. A theory based on a morality of freedom and autonomy could well give a positive answer to it, but be very cautious in the extent to which it sought to outlaw immoral practices. The limits of tolerance would revolve around the notion of harm and the extent to which individuals should be left free to cause harm to themselves or to others. Even if we take a Millian stance and are only concerned with harm to others, the question is still: how much harm to others is tolerable? Consent helps to an extent, but not a great extent – consensual harm is still regarded as highly problematic in law, and consent is most often not a defence. Also, not all non-consensual harm is necessarily ruled out – there is no consensus on the morality of corporal punishment within educational establishments or within the family. When it comes to consensual harm, sports such as boxing are more or less accepted although they are subject to some controversy; and sadomasochistic practices are also more or less accepted – in that they are regarded as a private matter – but again they are subject to some controversy. I will say more about sadomasochism below.

The problem of artistic expression raises a third issue for liberal communities, that of the regulation of offence. To what extent do members of a liberal community – which values individual freedom and autonomy – have the right not to be offended by artistic expression? Forms of pornography are mostly regulated under a version of the harm principle, appealing to a tendency to deprave and corrupt, but the concern here is with artistic expressions that cause offence to a large proportion of the community where there is no question of them being merely pornographic. The publication of Salman Rushdie's *The Satanic Verses* in the United Kingdom is one example where freedom of artistic expression was defended by the establishment despite widespread offence to a significant group within the community who regarded it as blasphemous. On the other hand, the law of blasphemy still stands as far as the Church of England is concerned, and the British Board of Film Classification did refuse a certificate to a video entitled *Visions of Ecstasy* on the grounds that it was blasphemous, a judgement which was upheld by the European Court of Human Rights in 1996 after the video's director appealed against this decision. There is certainly no consistency when it comes to the offence of blasphemy in the United Kingdom, and no great consistency to be found in the regulation of artistic expression that causes other kinds of offence. A tolerant society would allow a certain degree of offence to be caused by artistic expression, but how much is to be tolerated is a deeply complex and unclear question.

So there are three problem areas, of communal divisiveness, immorality, and offence, which in practice constitute the borders of toleration for liberal states. There might be a temptation to subsume the latter two problems under the first, and argue that issues of morality and artistic expression only become problems for a liberal community if they also cause unacceptable levels of communal divisiveness. But it is not clear that this is right – questions of immorality and offence are, on the face of it, genuinely distinct questions for a liberal community, such that even if they did not threaten any degree of communal divisiveness, they could still be causes for concern. And so the liberal community that wishes to practice toleration faces three difficult questions. First, are there certain practices, ideas, identities and so on that are too divisive to be tolerated? Are there some that are too immoral to be tolerated? And are there some that are too offensive to be tolerated? These are all ongoing questions for liberal communities, and it is important to remember that liberal communities need not practise toleration at all – intolerance is always a liberal option: this would rule out *any* degree of communal divisiveness, *any* degree of immorality, *any* degree of offence; or of course a liberal community could focus on any one of these areas and single it out for intolerance. What is emerging, then, is that tolerance is not a necessary feature of liberal communities, and that where these communities feel under threat, they have the capacity to resort to intolerance, and in practice there are few safeguards to protect areas of life now considered to be private from becoming public.

This leads me to two final thoughts. First, in identifying the boundary between the tolerable and the intolerable, it is the intolerable that needs to be explored and defined – it is only when we come to an understanding of what cannot be tolerated that we can ever know where we stand. Second, toleration is a political practice of certain kinds of state, but it is seldom a practice enshrined in legal constitutions – rather, it is a tradition. In communities with no such tradition, it is difficult to see how it can be introduced and nurtured. In communities where toleration is a tradition, it is vulnerable to erosion when communities mobilise around prejudices or states seek to exploit such prejudices in the pursuit of power. One thought is that if toleration is a valuable political practice, it needs to be embodied in constitutional law in such a way that it is not easily overridden. Although liberal states would no doubt claim to be owners of the political tradition of tolerance, an examination of the extent to which it is constitutionally protected would, I think, show how vulnerable it is to political opportunism and irrational prejudice. But although it seems obvious that toleration ought to be embodied in constitutional law, it is difficult to see how this can be done in a way that is not self-contradictory. A case-study that concerns the problem of sadomasochistic practices will illustrate this final problem.

THE 'SPANNER' CASE

In the United Kingdom in what became known as the 'Spanner' case a group of 16 men were arrested and charged with, amongst other things, assault causing actual bodily harm. They had been engaged in consensual sadomasochistic practices, which included beatings, genital abrasions and lacerations. None of the injuries, however, required medical attention. When the case was heard in 1990, the men's defence was based on the fact that they had all consented to these activities, but the presiding judge ruled that the activities fell outside the exceptions of the law of assault, as consent is no defence to assault occasioning actual bodily harm. The judge decreed that bodily harm applied or received during sexual activity was lawful if the pain it caused was 'just momentary' or 'so slight that it can be discounted'. Bodily marks, too, must not be of a lasting nature. Any injury, pain or mark that was more than trifling or momentary, ruled the judge, was illegal. Those charged changed their plea to guilty. They received prison sentences of up to four and a half years, and appeals to the Court of Appeal, the House of Lords, and the European Court of Human Rights all failed, although the Court of Appeal did reduce the sentences. At the House of Lords appeal, one of the judges stated: 'Society is entitled and bound to protect itself against a cult of violence. Pleasure derived from the infliction of cruelty is an evil thing. Cruelty is uncivilised' (all quotes referring to this case come from the following website: www.sexuality.org/l/bdsm/laskey.html).

The appeal to the European Court was based on the argument that the conviction breached Article 8 of the European Convention on Human Rights, which holds that all persons have the right to privacy, and interference by public authorities in the private sphere is ruled out, except in certain conditions when interference is necessary in a democratic society. Assuming that the prosecution and conviction did amount to an interference with private lives, the European Court had to decide whether this interference met these conditions. The court held that a state is unquestionably entitled to regulate activities which involve the infliction of physical harm, and that the 'Spanner' case fell under this heading, and concluded that 'the prosecution and conviction of the applicants were necessary in a democratic society for the protection of health'. Importantly, the court judged that it did not have to determine 'whether the interference with the applicants' right to respect for private life could also be justified on the ground of the protection of morals. This finding, however, should not be understood as calling into question the prerogative of the State on moral grounds to seek to deter acts of the kind in question.' There had been, therefore, no breach of the European Convention. However, one judge on the panel dissented in that he took a more severe view, and argued that the activities in question could not be regarded as private at all, wherever they took place. He said: 'The protection of private life means the protection of a person's intimacy and dignity, not the protection of his baseness or the promotion of criminal immoralism.' Sadomasochistic activities could, he argued, be made a specific criminal offence without any breach of the European Convention on the right to privacy.

What the 'Spanner' case reveals, then, is that the European Court of Human Rights considers that sadomasochistic practices are potentially a concern for the state, and can be legally regulated by the state on grounds of the protection of health and, potentially, on grounds of morality (it is extremely significant that the court, while deciding it did not have to rule on the question of morality, explicitly refused to rule out the legitimacy of prosecution on grounds of immorality in this case). It also illustrates the problem I raised above about how best to embody toleration as a practice within a constitution. This is shown in the way Article 8 of the European Convention is expressed. The first part of the article clearly states that 'everyone has the right to respect for his private and family life, his home and correspondence'. But the second part of the article then outlines a list of issues which can legitimately lead the democratic state to override the right to privacy: 'in the interests of national security, public safety or the economic well-being of the country, for the prevention of disorder or crime, for the protection of health or morals, or for the protection of the rights and freedoms of others'. Also, importantly, there is a 'margin of appreciation' in which the judgement of whether interference is necessary lies with the national authority. And so on the one hand we have a principle of toleration embodied in a European convention with which member states must comply. But on the other hand, the list of concerns which justify intolerance is both lengthy and vague, so that the concern must be that Article 8 in effect defines the whole area of the private space of individual life as open to state interference. Whereas before it could be taken that there was a tradition of toleration which ruled out this kind of interference, that tradition is undermined by embodying the limits of toleration in a legal document.

CONCLUSION

If this is right, then it is by no means clear that the practice of toleration would be best protected by being embodied within constitutional law – it might be best left as a traditional practice which public authorities can be expected to respect. It might be replied that what is needed is a better way of constituting the practice of toleration rather than no constitution at all, but it is hard to see how this could be done. In the end the practice of toleration in liberal thought is caught in a contradictory relationship between liberal individualist morality and liberal political theory, with the former prioritising individual freedom and autonomy and the latter seeking to establish and maintain a liberal political culture and liberal political institutions. And so in practice any constitutional settlement on the limits of toleration is, most likely, going to be drawn up in ways that favour the liberal state over the liberal individual, the public over the private. Even though liberal thought may well, with a degree of justification, claim ownership of the tradition of toleration, what cannot be claimed is that this ownership has been particularly benign or beneficial to the tradition. To return to the analogy of the liberal garden, the tree of toleration, while it has not yet been chopped down, has always been rather severely pruned, and at times dangerously neglected.

THE READINGS

I have selected three readings, two of which are by contemporary writers. This means setting aside the 'classic' texts by John Locke and John Stuart Mill, for example, as there is some value in seeing where liberal political theorists believe we stand on toleration, rather than where we have come from. The first reading is by Michael Walzer, from his book *Spheres of Justice*, one of the key texts in political theory of the twentieth century, forcing liberal theorists to address the nature of community within which the liberal individual pursues their projects. The second is by Susan Mendus, who has written extensively on toleration. This piece was written in response to the crisis of liberal conscience surrounding Salman Rushdie's novel *The Satanic*

Verses and the response to it by the Muslim community in Britain and elsewhere. The third piece is by a 'classic' author, Voltaire, an extract from the entry on toleration in his *Philosophical Dictionary*. The entire entry in the *Dictionary* is, of course, important to read, but here I have used just two sentences from it which seem, to me, to best capture the spirit of toleration.

QUESTIONS FOR DISCUSSION

- To what extent is tolerance a central value in liberal political theory?
- Should works of art which cause offence to members of a community be banned?
- Does multiculturalism raise specific problems of toleration for a liberal community?
- Does the value of tolerance rest upon the centrality of liberty in liberal thought? Or does its importance have another source?

MICHAEL WALZER
EXTRACTS FROM *SPHERES OF JUSTICE*

Divine grace

Grace is the gift presumably of a gracious God. He gives it to whomever He pleases, to those who deserve it (as if recognized by a jury of angels) onto those whom He makes deserving, for reasons known only to Himself. But we know nothing about these gifts. Insofar as men and women come to believe themselves saved, or are believed by others to be saved, they are the recipients of a social good, its distribution mediated by an ecclesiastical organization or a religious doctrine. This isn't a good available in all, perhaps not in most, cultures and societies. But it has been so important in the history of the West that I must take it up here. Grace has often been a disputed good, not because it is necessarily scarce and my having it diminishes your chances of getting it, but for two different reasons: first, its availability is sometimes thought to depend upon specific public arrangements; second, its possession by some people (and not others) is sometimes thought to carry with it certain political prerogatives. Both these beliefs are commonly denied today; but at various times in the past, it has taken some courage to deny them and then to resist their coercive implementation.

What makes the two denials so easy today is the generally held view that the pursuit of grace (and certainly its distribution by an omnipotent God) is necessarily free. The extreme version of this is the Protestant account of the relation between the individual and his God – the possessive pronoun is

Michael Walzer (1983), *Spheres of Justice*, Oxford: Blackwell.

important – as an entirely private affair. 'Each one stands for himself where the divine promise is concerned,' Luther wrote. 'His own faith is required. Each must respond for himself.'[1] But even if we imagine grace to depend upon the social practice of communion, it is still thought that communion must be free, a matter of individual choice. Here is perhaps the clearest example in our own culture of an autonomous sphere. Grace cannot be purchased or inherited; nor can it be coerced. It cannot be had by passing an exam or by holding an office. It is not, though it once was, a matter of communal provision.

This autonomy didn't come easily. Of course, there were always political rulers in the West who argued that religion was a sphere apart – and then that priests should not interfere in politics. But even such rulers often found it useful to control, if they could, the machinery through which communion and the assurance of salvation were distributed. And other rulers, more pious perhaps (themselves the recipients of grace), or pliable in the hands of interfering priests, insisted that it was their duty to organize the political realm so as to make God's gift available, perhaps even equally available, to all their subjects, His children. Since these rulers were mortal men and women, they could do no more; since they bore the secular sword, they could do whatever they did with considerable effect, regulating the teaching of religious doctrine and the administration of the sacraments, requiring church attendance, and so on. I don't want to deny that it was their duty to do these things (though I would hope to draw the line well this side of burning heretics). Whether it was their duty depends upon the understandings of grace and political power that they shared with their subjects – not, it should be stressed, upon their private understandings.

From the beginning, however, political coercion and Christian doctrine sat uneasily together. Grace might be attained through good works freely chosen, or it might come only with faith, but it never seemed something with which princes had much to do. Hence princes who interfered in the worship of their subjects were often called tyrants – at least by those who suffered the interference. Protestants of various sorts, defending religious toleration in the sixteenth and seventeenth centuries, were able to draw upon latent but deep conceptions of what worship, good works, faith, and salvation really meant. When Locke, in his *Letter Concerning Toleration*, insisted that 'no man can, if he would, conform his faith to the dictates of another,' he was merely echoing Augustine's statement, quoted in turn by Luther, that 'No one can or ought to be constrained to believe.'[2]

Christian doctrine was shaped by that original distributive rule, 'Render unto Caesar the things which are Caesar's; and unto God the things that are God's' (Matthew 22:21). Often overridden by imperial or crusading enthusiasms, the rule was regularly reasserted whenever God's servants or Caesar's found it useful. And, in one form or another, it survived to serve the purposes of the early modern opponents of religious persecution.

Two 'renderings', two jurisdictions, two distributive spheres: in the one, the magistrate presides, 'procuring, preserving, and advancing', as Locke argued, the civil interests of his subjects;[3] in the other, God Himself presides, His power invisible, leaving His seekers and worshipers to advance their spiritual interests as best they can, and assure themselves or one another of divine favor. They can organize for that purpose in any way they please and submit themselves if they please to bishops, priests, presbyters, ministers, and so on. But the authority of all such officials is confined to the church, as the authority of magistrates is confined to the commonwealth, 'because the church . . . is a thing absolutely separate and distinct from the commonwealth. The boundaries on both sides are fixed and immoveable. He jumbles heaven and earth together . . . who mixes these two societies.'[4]

The wall between church and state

Within a century after it was written, Locke's *Letter* found legal expression in the first amendment to the United States Constitution: 'Congress shall make no law respecting an establishment of religion, or prohibiting the free exercise thereof.' This simple sentence bars any attempt at communal provision in the sphere of grace. The state is excluded from any concern with curing souls. The citizens cannot be taxed or coerced – not for the cure of their own souls and not for the cure of anyone else's either. State officials cannot even regulate entrepreneurial activity in the sphere of grace; they must watch without comment the steady proliferation of sects offering salvation on the cheap or, perhaps more excitingly, at an enormous expense of money and spirit. Consumers cannot be protected from fraud, for the First Amendment bars the state from recognizing fraud (nor is fraud easy to recognize in the sphere of grace where, as it is said, the most unlikely people may well be doing God's work).

All this is called religious liberty, but it is also religious egalitarianism. The First Amendment is a rule of complex equality. It does not distribute grace equally; indeed, it does not distribute it at all. Nevertheless, the wall that it raises has profound distributive effects. It makes, on the religious side, for the priesthood of all believers; that is, it leaves all believers in charge of their own salvation. They can acknowledge whatever ecclesiastical hierarchies they like, but the acknowledgment is theirs to give or refuse; it is not legally imposed or legally binding. And the wall makes, on the political side, for the equality of believers and non-believers, saints and worldlings, the saved and the damned: all are equally citizens; they possess the same set of constitutional rights. Politics is not dominant over grace nor grace over politics.

I want to stress the second of these negative propositions. Americans are very sensitive to the first. The willingness to tolerate (religious) conscientious objection has its origin in that sensitivity, and it certainly suggests a significant forbearance by the political authorities. People who believe that the safety of their immortal souls depends upon avoiding any sort of participation in warfare are exempt from the draft. Though the state cannot guarantee immortality, it at least refrains from taking it away. The state does not nourish souls; nor does it kill them. But the second negation rules out a kind of dominance that no one talks about today, in the West at least; and so we may well have forgotten its historical significance. For Locke, in the seventeenth century, it was still critically important to deny the claim that 'dominion is founded in grace'.[5] The claim had only recently been put forward, and with considerable vehemence, in the course of the Puritan Revolution. Indeed, Cromwell's first parliament, 'the parliament of saints', was an attempt to give it political effect; and Cromwell opened the first session by asserting precisely what Locke wanted to deny: 'God manifests this to be the day of the power of Christ; having, through so much blood and so much trial as hath been put upon these nations, made this to be one of the great issues thereof: to have His people called to the supreme authority.'[6]

The puritan commonwealth

Cromwell acknowledged the inequality of this 'call'. Only the saints were invited to share in the exercise of power. And it would make no sense to submit the saints to a democratic election or even – what would have been more likely in seventeenth-century England – to an election by male property owners. In neither case would 'His people's' have won a majority of the votes. Cromwell hoped for a day when elections would be possible, that is, for a day when the people themselves, all of them, would be God's elect. 'I would that all were fit to be called.' But 'who knows how soon God may fit the people for such a thing?'[7] Meanwhile, it was necessary to look for the outward signs of inner light. Hence members of Parliament were chosen by a search committee, not an electorate, and England was ruled by the monopolists of grace.

Locke's argument, and the argument embedded in the United States Constitution, is that the saints are free to maintain their monopoly and to rule any society (church or sect) that they themselves establish. Grace is no doubt a great privilege, but there is no way to give it out to those who disbelieve in its existence, or who adopt a view of it radically different from that of the saints, or who hold the same view but with less fervor; nor is there any way to force upon the saints a more egalitarian understanding of their special gift. In any case, the monopoly of the saints is harmless enough so long as it doesn't reach to political power. They have no claim to rule the state, which they did not establish, and for whose necessary work divine assurance is no qualification. The purpose of the constitutional wall is the containment, not the redistribution, of grace.

Yet the state might be differently conceived, not as a secular but as a religious realm; civil interests might be understood as God's interests, too. The wall between church and state is, after all, a human construction; it might be torn down or, as in Islam, never raised in the first place. Then the rule of the saints would look rather different: who else – if not His people – should rule in a realm for which God Himself has legislated? It may be the case, moreover, that only the saints can establish the everyday social arrangements that make the good life, and then the eternal life, available to the rest of the population. For these arrangements, perhaps, have to be read out of Scripture, and it is the inner light that illuminates the Word. The argument has real force, given a sufficiently widespread commitment to the underlying religious doctrine. But if enough people are committed to the rule of the saints, then the saints should have no difficulty winning elections.

In any case, the force of the argument declines as soon as the commitment falters. The New England Puritans offer a nice example of this. Their whole educational system was bent to the task of religious conversion. Its chief end was to reproduce in the second generation the 'experience of grace' that the founders had known. At first, there was no doubt at all that this was possible. 'God has so cast the line of election,' Increase Mather wrote, 'that for the most part it runs through the loins of godly parents.'[8] Teachers had little to do but enliven the latent spirit. But the gift of spiritual liveliness is not so easily passed on, not through the loins and not through the schools: neither nature nor nurture, apparently, can guarantee the inheritance. In the eyes of its elders – in its own eyes, too – the second generation of American Puritans, like many other second generations, turned out to be deficient in grace. Hence the compromise of the Half-Way Covenant of 1662, which permitted the children of the saints, even if they had no experience of grace, to maintain some loose connection with the church for the sake of the grandchildren. But this was only to postpone the obvious difficulty. Consider, writes a modern scholar, 'the irony of a situation in which a chosen people cannot find enough chosen people to prolong its existence'.[9] Secularism sneaks into the Puritan commonwealth in the form of religious discouragement. For membership in the commonwealth is indeed transmitted through the loins of godly *and ungodly* parents. And so the commonwealth soon included not only saints and worldlings – the first group ruling the second – but also worldlings who were the sons and daughters of the saints and saints who were the sons and daughters of the worldlings. The dominion of grace could not survive this entirely predictable and entirely unexpected outcome.

Alternatively, secularism sneaks into the Puritan commonwealth in the form of religious dissent: when the saints disagree about the everyday arrangements necessary for eternal life, or when they deny one another's saintliness. It is always possible, of course, to repress the dissent, to exile the dissenters, or even, as in the Europe of the Inquisition, to torture and kill them for the sake of their own (and everyone else's) salvation. But there are difficulties here, too, common, I think, to all the religions that preach salvation, and which I have already identified with regard to Christianity. The idea of grace seems deeply resistant to coercive distributions. Locke's assertion that 'men cannot be forced to be saved,'[10] may represent the claim of a dissenter or even a skeptic, but it builds on an understanding of salvation shared by many believers. If that is so, then religious disagreement and dissent set limits on the use of force – limits that eventually take the form of a radical separation: the wall between church and state. And then efforts to breach the wall, to impose the arrangements or coerce the behavior that supposedly makes for salvation, are properly called tyrannical.

NOTES

1. Martin Luther, *The Pagan Servitude of the Church*, in *Martin Luther: Selections from His Writings*, ed. John Dillenberger (Garden City, N. Y., 1961), p. 283.
2. John Locke, *A Letter Concerning Toleration*, intro. Patrick Romanell (Indianapolis, 1950), p. 18; Luther, *Secular Authority*, in *Selections* [1], p. 385.
3. Locke, *Letter* [2], p. 17.
4. Ibid., p. 27.
5. Ibid.
6. Oliver Cromwell, *Oliver Cromwell's Letters and Speeches*, ed. Thomas Carlyle (London, 1893), p. 354 (speech to the parliament of saints, 4 July 1653).
7. Ibid., p. 355.
8. Increase Mather, *Pray for the Rising Generation* (1618), quoted by Edmund S. Morgan, *The Puritan Family* (New York, 1966), p. 183; see the discussion in J. R. Pole, *The Pursuit of Equality in American History* (Berkeley, 1978), chap. 3.
9. Alan Simpson, *Puritanism in Old and New England* (Chicago, 1961), p. 35.
10. Locke, *Letter* [2], p. 35.

SUSAN MENDUS
'THE TIGERS OF WRATH AND THE HORSES OF INSTRUCTION'[1]

Reading through the vast and still burgeoning literature on the Rushdie affair, it is surprisingly difficult to establish precisely what the debate is about: in part it is about how to read novels; in part it is about the nature of Islamic fundamentalism; in part it is about the preservation of cultural identity in a multicultural society. Most pervasively, however, it is a debate about the values which inform modern liberal societies – a debate in which liberal culture, with its emphasis on rationality, choice and the sovereignty of the individual, is pitted against cultures which emphasise sanctity, tradition, and group identity.

Fay Weldon asks:

> Who is there left of us brave enough to state what we believe? That, say, the Bible is a superior revelatory work to the Koran – or at any rate reveals a kinder, more interesting, less vengeful, less cruel God, one worth studying, worshipping? ... One you can interpret? All you can do with the Koran is learn it by heart.[2]

The emphasis here is on rationality – on the need to submit texts to scrutiny and interpretation. And religions and cultures are deemed superior in so far as they do admit of interpretation – of 'thoughts, perceptions, and increasing understanding'. Similarly, the role of choice is prominent in the debate. On

Susan Mendus (1993), 'The Tigers of Wrath and the Horses of Instruction', in John Horton (ed.), *Liberalism, Multiculturalism and Toleration*, Basingstoke: Macmillan.

9 March 1989 a meeting of women called by Southall Black Sisters and Southall women's section of the Labour Party issued a statement which declared:

> We will not be dictated to by fundamentalists. Our lives will not be defined by community leaders.
>
> We will take up our right to determine our own destinies, not limited by religion, culture, or nationality.[3]

Here the emphasis is on the control of one's own destiny, and the desire, even the right, of the individual to shake off the shackles of cultural heritage.

Finally, the debate has been informed by a distinction between societies in which the individual is sovereign and societies or cultures which give greater emphasis to group identity (often an identity which is forged through identity of belief). Michael Ignatieff writes;

> In theocratic States like Iran, the law guarantees the inviolability of certain sacred doctrines. In free societies, the law does not protect doctrines as such; it protects individuals – through the law of libel, or the law against incitement to racial hatred.[4]

In so far as the law declines to protect doctrines as such, it also declines to protect the 'social glue' which binds groups together and makes them a coherent whole. For better or worse, it supports the sovereignty of the individual against the identity of the group.

Here then are three themes which lie at the heart of the Rushdie debate: rationality versus sanctity, choice versus tradition, and the sovereignty of the individual versus the identity of the group. In much of the literature the tensions inherent in these distinctions have been presented as battles between the forces of light and darkness; between the rationality and tolerance of liberalism, and the bigotry of fundamentalism; between the horses of instruction and the tigers of wrath.

Two responses to this state of affairs suggest themselves: firstly it might be argued that Western liberal democracies do not, after all, have a monopoly on rationality. This is a line of argument favoured by Shabbir Akhtar, who has urged the necessity for 'a reasonable, intellectually adequate defence of "the virtues of fundamentalism"'. There has, he says 'been an unargued assumption on the part of the press, and indeed of academic writing, that fundamentalism has no intellectual basis. People should be allowed to defend the better side of fundamentalism'.[5] In other words, he claims that fundamentalism has been misrepresented as unthinking and anti-intellectual, when it is not so: the apparent struggle between the tigers of wrath and the horses of instruction is in fact illusory, for fundamentalism is also a rational doctrine, and one which admits of interpretation. A second strategy is that which provides a defence of tradition, sanctity and group identity against the dominant values of liberalism. This defence concedes that there is a battle, but asserts that it is a battle in which the tigers of wrath may yet turn out to be wiser than the horses of instruction.

In what follows I shall suggest that the two strategies are in fact quite similar: attempts to defend fundamentalism as rational may involve appeal to precisely the same kinds of consideration as attempts to invoke values of tradition or group identity. In part, therefore, my argument will be an argument for contextualisation. It will echo Alasdair MacIntyre's theme – 'progress in rationality is achieved only from a point of view'.[6] To the extent that it does this, it is a defence which aligns itself with opponents of the Enlightenment; with anti-Kantians; with the philosophical tigers of wrath.

At the same time, however, my account will invoke rather than reject some basic Kantian tenets – notably Kant's commitment to emotional love as the prerequisite of morality, where morality is nevertheless a rational enterprise. I shall argue that the tigers of wrath must not be completely uninstructed and that arguments for contextualisation, and claims that 'progress in rationality is achieved only from a point of view', need not lead us either to a vicious relativism or to maudlin and ineffective nostalgia for times past.

The terms in which the Rushdie debate have been conducted, and which are exemplified by the earlier quotations, point to a dilemma for modern liberals in multicultural societies: either we say that 'our' values (liberal values) are better, more rational than any others, and refuse to countenance any curtailment of the free speech which those other values dictate; or (with MacIntyre) we spurn rationality, embrace relativism, yearn for a return to lost days, and render ourselves impotent against those who would undermine our commitment to values such as toleration and free speech. The former is a kind of cultural arrogance; the latter, a kind of cultural apathy and, at the limit, cultural suicide. If the tigers of wrath triumph, then we must conclude that really we stand for nothing defensible, and we stand alone. If the horses of instruction triumph, then we must conclude that we do stand for something – we stand for our own values, but again we stand alone. Either way we seem isolated and unable to communicate effectively with others. But in a modern, multicultural society, isolation and separatism are our problems, so they can hardly be our solutions.

This essay aims to marry the tigers of wrath with the horses of instruction: it suggests that although progress in rationality really is achieved only from a point of view, we can still hope to find ways of living one with another. Since its aim is ambitious, it will almost certainly fail, but I hope that it will throw up some interesting ideas en route.

HOW RATIONAL ARE THE HORSES OF INSTRUCTION?

My first question, then, is 'How rational are the horses of instruction?' Put less cryptically, it is the question; 'How much of a defence will appeal to rationality provide for liberal commitment to free speech?' At the beginning I quoted Fay Weldon. Ms Weldon's assertion hints at important and familiar claims about the justification of free speech in liberal societies. It implies the possibility of intellectual progress, and a justification of free speech in terms of its tendency to facilitate such progress. Her distinction between studying and interpreting on the one hand, and 'learning by heart' on the other, is reminiscent of John Stuart Mill's distinction between a faith which allows itself to be put to the test in the free market place of ideas, and a creed which 'remains outside the mind, encrusting and petrifying it against all other influences addressed to the higher parts of our nature'.[7] In both these cases the distinction drawn is between those who submit their beliefs to scrutiny and those who engage in unthinking compliance and acceptance. And the clear judgement is not only that the latter are inferior to the former, but that the latter are inferior precisely because they reject rationality – 'the higher parts of our nature' in Mill's terms, or 'thoughts, perceptions and increasing understanding' in Weldon's. The defence of free speech is thus linked to a belief in the possibility of progress and improvement: free speech is necessary in order to move from a state of benighted acceptance to a state of critical awareness.

Connectedly, both writers imply that societies are superior in so far as they free individuals from passive conformity into a world of rational and individual decision-making. The reason for this is not simply that such rational decision-making will herald progress, it is also that human beings are essentially rational creatures – fulfilled to the extent that they employ their rationality in critical assessment of the socialisation to which they have been submitted. Thus Mill speaks frequently and scathingly of the 'numbing conformity' of nineteenth-century Victorian Britain, and draws unfavourable comparisons between that society and his ideal society of vibrant individuals, all of whom are thinking for themselves and critically evaluating the mores of their social and cultural world. Similarly, Fay Weldon extols the virtues of assessment, evaluation and interpretation. In both cases, the rational is contrasted with 'received opinion', and human beings are seen as beautiful and rational butterflies struggling to escape from the suffocating cocoon of custom, tradition and habit. Again, the debate is one between the forces of light and the forces of darkness; between the horses of instruction and the tigers of wrath. Finally, the quotation points to a defence of free speech in terms of its tendency to deliver truth. Fay Weldon's reference to the superior revelatory powers of the Bible echoes Mill's claim that freedom of thought and discussion is the surest path to truth.

There are therefore three lines of thought implicit in the Weldon claim, and familiar in liberal thinking generally: firstly, that free speech is necessary for progress; secondly that free speech is necessary for human fulfilment; and thirdly that free speech is necessary for the attainment of truth. All three make reference to rationality: progress consists in increased understanding;

human fulfilment consists in the employment of rational faculties, which are the essential faculties of human beings; and truth is something discovered via rational argument. In this section I shall consider whether these appeals to rationality can deliver an adequate defence of an extensive free speech principle. And I begin, briefly, with the claim that free speech is important because of its tendency to deliver truth.

Much has been written about the inadequacies of Mill's defence of free speech in terms of truth: his belief that truth will triumph in the market place of ideas appears naively optimistic and also neglectful of other values, such as racial harmony and sexual equality. We have no guarantee whatever that free discussion will issue in truth, but often we do have reason to believe that free discussion will exacerbate racial tensions, will undermine the self-respect of disadvantaged groups, or will debase the values of some cultures. Faced with these threats, it is not obvious that truth either is or should be the paramount consideration. Additionally, of course, the areas in which free speech is most problematic – areas of moral, political and religious debate – are precisely the ones where the concept of truth is extremely controversial. As Eric Barendt has put it:

> The argument for a free speech principle from truth is said [by Mill] to be particularly applicable to types of expression which can only rarely, if ever, establish truths with the same degree of assurance that obtains in mathematics or the natural sciences.[8]

So in the first place, it requires argument to show that free speech should be valued more highly than civil order or racial harmony, and in the second place, it is far from clear that the cases in which free speech is most problematic are cases in which truth is at issue. I shall not dwell on these points, as I do not believe that they are the central ones in the Rushdie debate. I shall simply add one further consideration, which is that historically, defences of free speech in terms of truth have supported policies of intolerance as well as policies of toleration: where the pursuit of truth is what justifies free speech, then the attainment of truth is what justifies repression – at least in the eyes of would-be persecutors. For this reason, if no other, defences of free speech in terms of truth strike me as dangerously two-edged.

But if free speech is not to be pursued in the name of truth, then its justification must lie elsewhere. This introduces the second argument referred to earlier – the claim that free speech is a necessary condition of human fulfilment. On this account, free expression of opinion is guaranteed because of what human beings essentially are: rational creatures. When we peel away the layers of habit produced by socialisation, we will reveal the essential nature of human beings – their capacity for rationality, independent of time and circumstance. Free speech is therefore required because human beings are rational creatures capable of assessing arguments and employing judgement about them.

This argument is connected with the argument from progress, since both emphasise fixedness and similarity. Just as the argument from human nature supposes a core 'self' which is essentially rational, and distinct from the self produced by socialisation, so the argument from progress supposes a set of fixed problems whose solution we approach by the application of rationality. We make progress in understanding the world via rational investigation, and simultaneously we develop our own true nature by employing our rational faculties. Thus Mill speaks not only of 'higher' parts of our nature (meaning intellectual parts), but also of the importance of freedom in the interests of 'progress' or 'the growth of civilization'. On this view, Muslim fundamentalists are seen as defending a quite arbitrary stopping-place on the route of progress. Their views are backward, primitive and, most importantly, they are views which deny the essential nature of human beings as rational creatures.

Two lines of criticism are pertinent here: the first (associated with the writings of Quentin Skinner) questions whether there are 'perennial problems' in social and political philosophy. What the study of the history of ideas reveals, according to Skinner, is not the essential sameness, but rather 'the essential variety of viable moral assumptions and political commitments'.[9] These different assumptions will generate different moral and political questions, and different conclusions as to what counts as rational. By assuming that there are perennial problems and that the history of political thought is evolutionary, we are led to the erroneous conclusion that our own concerns are the same as those of other times, and that we have arrived at a superior set of answers to one, timeless set of problems in political philosophy.

Secondly, and connectedly, such an account of moral and political philosophy covertly assumes that our own moral and political system is an improvement on those which have gone before – that we stand at the apex of an evolutionary process, which can be judged by fixed and value-free criteria of rationality. But as one writer has put it,

> a common criterion of reasonableness is not necessary in order to explain [differences of moral belief]. To call one set of beliefs irrational often obscures what disagreement amounts to in this context; that the disagreement is itself an expression or a product of a moral judgement.[10]

Thus the questions which are central to us may vary depending on the moral and political assumptions we make, and these moral assumptions can in turn determine what counts as rational, rather than being subject to an overarching and value-free judgement of rationality.

Blasphemy itself is an instructive example here: in the liberal tradition, and in English law, blasphemy is objectionable because of the offence which it causes to individuals (in the case of English law, to Christian believers). Where the blasphemy laws are invoked, therefore, they are invoked in an attempt to protect believers, not in an attempt to protect beliefs. This is the force of Ignatieff's distinction: 'In theocratic states like Iran, the law guarantees the inviolability of certain sacred doctrines. In free societies, the law does not protect doctrines as such, it protects individuals.'[11]

But it requires argument to show that 'free' societies are thereby more rational or better. In a culture in which religious beliefs are central, it is far from clear that it is rational to allow them to be interpreted in the way in which the English blasphemy law is interpreted. Shabbir Akhtar writes:

> The fact the post-Enlightenment Christians tolerate blasphemy is a matter for shame, not for pride. It is true, of course, that God can defend himself, but a believer must vindicate the reputation of God and his spokesmen against the militant calumnies of evil.[12]

In English law, which emphasises individuals, the wrong that is done by blasphemy is the wrong of offending individuals. In the eyes of Muslim (and many Christian) believers, however, the wrong that is done by blasphemy is a wrong against God. Similarly, where blasphemy is tolerated the result is not simply that individual believers are distressed: it is that God is mocked. Where we begin with the belief that the individual is most important, we will find it rational to conclude that blasphemous acts are damaging to the extent that they damage individuals, and conversely that censorship is damaging to the extent that it restricts or suppresses individual development. By contrast, where we begin with the belief that God is most important, we will find it rational to conclude that blasphemy is wrong because it scorns God, and conversely that censorship is a necessary means of affording protection to that which is sacred. Put differently, the basic question for liberals is 'How can we justify individual free speech?'; whereas the basic question for Muslims is 'How can we vindicate the reputation of God?' It is not obvious that the former is more rational than the latter. It is clear only that there are more or less rational strategies to pursue once the basic question has been identified.

I said earlier that discussions of the Rushdie affair tend to be cast in terms of an opposition between the forces of light and the forces of darkness; or between the horses of instruction and the tigers of wrath. Fay Weldon's claim that the God of the Bible is a better God than the God of the Qur'an rests on the belief that the former, unlike the latter, admits of rational investigation and interpretation. It assumes both that the God of the Bible is superior to the God of the Qur'an, and that interpretation of the Bible is superior to mere belief in the Qur'an. These assumptions generate not only characteristically liberal views about the importance of free speech but also, and most importantly, specific views about the wrong which is done by intolerance. For example, they allow that free speech may be restricted in cases where it is likely to cause profound offence or civil unrest. By contrast, if we do not assume an evolutionary view of morality, then the wrong of intolerance will also be understood differently: it will be the wrong of spurning a whole way of life or system of belief. It follows that not only is the justification of toleration drawn differently in the different cases, but also that what counts as intolerance is understood differently. By beginning with the question 'What justifies free speech?' we place the burden of proof on those who would restrict speech. By beginning with the question 'How should we vindicate the reputation of God?' we place the burden of proof on those who would mock God. And again, it is not clear that the former starting point is any more rational than the latter.

These lines of thought may appear to imply that 'to understand all is to forgive all'. In the Rushdie case they may seem to lead to something like the following conclusion: there is, in the end, no way of rationally resolving moral disagreement. Moral beliefs are not determined by interests, but are themselves what determine interests. We therefore have no means of assessing the different moral claims made by members of different groups. In other words, the Bible is not, after all, superior to the Qur'an. Our local prejudices deliver a judgement in favour of the Bible; the local prejudices of Muslim fundamentalists deliver a judgement in favour of the Qur'an. And that is all that can be said about the matter.

But this extreme relativist conclusion is hardly helpful in a multicultural society where differing values must coexist in some kind of harmony, however uneasy. Nor is it, I think, the correct conclusion to draw. The considerations adduced above are simply intended to cast doubt on the claim that free speech may be justified by reference to the concept of truth on the one hand, or the concept of rationality on the other. To reject those assumptions is not thereby to claim that there is no such thing as truth. It is only to claim that questions of truth are not always the most important questions. Similarly, the claim that rationality must be understood within a context, need not be taken to imply that literally anything goes. It implies only that, in deciding what goes, we should take account of the fact that moral judgements influence our beliefs about what is rational, just as much as beliefs about what is rational influence our moral judgements.

I shall return to these points later and say a little more about their implications for the Rushdie affair. For the moment, all I am concerned to indicate is that questions of truth or of rationality will not take us all the way in defences of free speech: the horses of instruction have an understanding of rationality which will not necessarily commend itself to the tigers of wrath.

HOW WISE ARE THE TIGERS OF WRATH?

In his recent book, *Contingency, Irony and Solidarity*, Richard Rorty makes reference to two kinds of writer in social and political philosophy:

> the one tells us that we need not speak only the language of the tribe, that we may find our own words, that we may have a responsibility to ourselves to find them. The other tells us that that responsibility is not the only one we have. Both are right, but there is no way to make both speak a single language.[13]

In the previous section I expressed scepticism about the claim that we may find our own language distinct from the language of the tribe, and suggested that the language we speak and the values we hold may be in large part a function of 'the tribe'. But this claim appears both unhelpful and false when we turn back to the second quotation I used at the beginning of the paper – the demand by Southall Black Sisters. Their statement takes the form of a declaration that they will find their own language distinct from the language of the tribe – that they, at least, will not be determined by socialisation. The claim harks back to Mill's assertion that the ideal for human beings is precisely to 'determine what part of recorded experience is properly applicable to their own circumstances and character'. My earlier criticism of this stance was not so much an attempt to deny that that can happen, as a scepticism about whether, when it does happen, the end result is a more rational state of affairs. It was a worry about whether the Bible may be recommended *tout court* as a better (more rational, more civilised) alternative than the Qur'an. By contrast, the demand made by the Southall Black Sisters is simply that this is their chosen or preferred alternative – not that it is thereby better or more rational. Moreover, they demand this as their right. Unlike Mill, they do not insist upon it as the duty of everyone, nor do their claims contain any commitment to rationality or to progress. My argument in the previous section was intended to cast doubt on the claim that free speech is justified by reference to rationality, to truth or to progress independent of prior moral beliefs. But the Southall declaration insists on the importance, not of truth or of progress, but of individual autonomy. Where the argument from rationality is sometimes used to imply that there is a truth which is the same for all, or a standard of rationality which may be applied to all, this argument allows that different people might choose different ways of life.

Nevertheless, the Southall declaration raises pressing questions about the balance to be struck between different moralities in multicultural societies, and about the role of choice in morality. Specifically, it raises the question of whether free speech should be defended, not because it leads to truth, nor because it leads to progress, but because it enables people to choose the moral and religious beliefs which best suit them – it enables them to develop their autonomy, where the availability of choices is a necessary condition of individual autonomy.

In this section I shall discuss two arguments which are relevant to the autonomy question, but which appear to lead to incompatible conclusions. The first is Bernard Williams's claim that, *pace* the Southall declaration, moral values are not chosen. The second is Joseph Raz's claim that in a multicultural society such as ours, members of minority groups must be encouraged to choose the values of the dominant group. If free speech and toleration are to be justified by reference to the importance of individual autonomy, then we need to know whether values are indeed possible objects of choice. Williams thinks not. He says:

> There are points of resemblance between moral and factual convictions; and I suspect it to be true of moral, as it certainly is of factual convictions, that we cannot take very seriously a profession of them if we are given to understand that a speaker has just decided to adopt them ... We see a man's genuine convictions as coming from somewhere deeper in him than that.[14]

Williams's target here is an aspect of Kantian rationalism: in the Kantian tradition it is often claimed that people should be encouraged to 'decide' upon their moral beliefs, meaning that the beliefs they hold ought to be the result of rational enquiry: they ought to be the consequence of active deliberation, not the consequence of prejudice, tradition or brute emotion. Again, socialisation is understood as something which masks an individual's true nature. But Williams's suggestion implies that there is a sense in which socialisation does not mask an individual's true nature; it *is* an individual's true nature; 'by what is only an apparent paradox, what we see as coming from deeper in him, he – that is the deciding "he" – may see as coming from outside him'.[15] The desire not to be constrained by a social context, by 'prejudice' or tradition, should not lead us to suppose that we should aspire to a choice made completely independent of those things. Put differently, we should not believe that choice within a context is but a pale shadow of what we aspire to – choice unrestricted by any context and dictated by pure rationality alone.

It is this point which Joseph Raz gestures towards in his apparently conflicting claim that 'for those who live in an autonomy supporting environment there is no choice but to be autonomous' and that therefore members of minority groups must be brought 'humanely and decently' to valuing autonomy.[16] At first glance it appears that while Williams is insisting upon the lack of choice in moral matters (on the passivity of moral life), Raz is insisting on the necessity of choice. In fact, however, the difference between the two is less acute than it appears: Raz's claim is intended to emphasise the importance of social circumstances as determinants of flourishing: for people who live in a Western liberal democracy, where liberal values dominate, it is futile to attempt to flourish in any other way than by accepting at least some liberal values. Such acceptance will not, as Williams points out, be a matter of simple decision-taking, nor will it be the result of rational consideration and judgement. The defence of the need for choice in such a society is simply that choice is already a central value of the society. If people expect to flourish, then they must come to terms with that fact.

Several consequences spring from this argument: the first is that it implies an understanding of moral change as something distinct from moral progress. Whereas the argument from rationality pitted light against darkness, this argument simply reflects on differences, and also acknowledges that in the move from one set of moral values to another there may be not merely difference but loss. The second consequence is that it does not assume a concept of rationality distinct from social circumstances: quite the reverse, for the importance of social circumstances is precisely what forces the need for moral change.

But if moral values are not the objects of decision or choice, and if there is genuine loss in the move from one set of values to another, then the focus of attention must shift away from our original question. 'What justifies free speech?' We need to do less by way of defending our own values, and more by way of understanding the values of other groups. We need, in other words, to understand precisely what will be lost when values are replaced, and precisely what wrong is done by attempting to compel changes in value. Equally, however, we must be aware that change is needed, and is needed precisely because the values of the tribe are so important. The recognition that socialisation goes all the way down should not lead us to believe that nothing can be done to change moral values. On the contrary, it impresses upon us the importance of seeing that something is done.

THE LION AND THE LAMB

What conclusions are to be drawn from these discussions of rationality, choice and the sovereignty of the individual? In the liberal tradition, defences of the toleration of free speech tend to be couched in terms of truth, of rationality, and of individual choice. However, the claim that the *telos* of toleration is truth carries little force in cases where what is at issue is the toleration of moral or religious beliefs. The focus of attention thus shifts to the concepts of rationality and choice. In the former case it was argued that rationality requires reference to prior moral beliefs: there is no rational vantage point devoid of moral belief – no 'view from nowhere'. Additionally, it was suggested that moral and religious beliefs do not admit of choice or decision, but are to some extent 'given' by social circumstance.

These points, however, need to be set against the demands of the Southall declaration – the demand by members of minority groups that they be allowed to shape their own destiny and decide upon the forms their lives will take: 'We will not be dictated to by fundamentalists. Our lives will not be defined by community leaders.' It is tempting to interpret this demand as a proof that liberal standards are better, more rational than any other, since they are the standards which people will choose when once they are released from the constraints of fundamentalist socialisation. But equally it may be interpreted as the only appropriate response to the requirements of a different kind of socialisation – the socialisation inherent in a Western liberal democracy. In other words, the Southall declaration is not a refutation, but a confirmation of the belief that the individual is subject to the group – in this case to the influences of the dominant culture, as well as to the influences of the minority culture.

If this is correct, then it suggests an alternative account of the value of toleration – one which does not appeal to truth, to progress, or to individualist conceptions of rationality and choice, but which emphasises the individual's need to locate himself within a group. On this account, the wrong which is done by intolerance is not the denial of rational decision-making, or of choice, but the wrong of exclusion.

Richard Rorty has recently argued for the possibility of a certain kind of 'liberal utopia'. He says:

> In my utopia, human solidarity would be seen not as a fact to be recognized by clearing away prejudice, or burrowing down to previously hidden depths but, rather, as a goal to be achieved. It is to be achieved not by inquiry but by imagination, the imaginative ability to see strange people as fellow sufferers. Solidarity is not discovered by reflection but created. It is created by increasing our sensitivity to the particular details of the pain and humiliation of other, unfamiliar sorts of people.[17]

Rorty's argument shifts the focus of debate in three distinct but connected ways, all of which are hinted at in the earlier discussion: by emphasising solidarity, he urges a move from individual to social considerations; by emphasising imagination he urges a move from reason to emotion; and by emphasising humiliation he urges a move from the rights of the tolerators to the wrongs suffered by the oppressed. However, Rorty's reference to the wrong of humiliation strikes me as insufficiently strong.

Earlier I argued that defences of free speech in terms of rationality and choice are defective because the moral beliefs which we hold, and which define what we are, are not primarily objects of choice, nor are they the deliverances of an abstract rationality. It follows from this that there is a strong sense in which what we are is given rather than chosen. This is most obviously the case where what we are is a matter of ethnic identity, or of gender. But it is also true in the areas of moral and religious belief, which are equally incapable of being given up simply by act of will or on the basis of 'rational' argument. Moreover, beliefs of this sort define what we are, in the sense of specifying where we belong. If they are undermined or despised, we ourselves are also undermined and despised. But that is not, it seems to me, simply a case of individual humiliation. I shall conclude with a short example, which may help to explain what I mean.

It is often argued (and successfully) that racist or sexist literature should be restricted or banned. The reasons given for this are various: sometimes it is claimed that such literature is profoundly offensive (to blacks or women); sometimes that it is disruptive of the good order and harmony of society; sometimes that it serves to undermine the autonomy of the members of the groups in question. All these arguments are fundamentally individualist. They acknowledge that the standing of the group as a whole is threatened by the literature in question, but their primary focus is the state of mind of the individual who happens to belong to that group. (It is individual women whose autonomy is jeopardised by the proliferation of pornographic material, and it is therefore in the interests of individual women, or in deference to their feelings, that such literature should be restricted.) The question of whether material should be restricted thus becomes a matter of balancing the autonomy of the pornographer against the autonomy of women; or the rights of the pornographer against the feelings of (some) women. If the free speech argument wins, then it is not simply the case that the women in question are humiliated, in the sense of being offended, distressed or upset. Nor is it necessarily the case that the autonomy of any particular woman is threatened (though often it is). Rather, it is the case that what one essentially is scorned. If socialisation goes all the way down, then the toleration of pornography may be interpreted as a statement of the worthlessness of women. The situation is only exacerbated if that toleration is justified by appeal to rationality, since it then reinforces the judgement of worthlessness.

Where we take 'what one essentially is' as referring to membership of groups, then the situation is made yet more complex: the Southall women may be Muslims, whose identity is determined by their membership of the Muslim community. They are also women, whose identity is determined by their gender. They inhabit a Western pluralist society, and their identity is formed by that membership too. When what we are is defined by reference to groups, and when the groups themselves contain inconsistent values, then the demands of solidarity become increasingly painful. That pain cannot be eased by constant appeal to rationality and choice, for both these concepts operate only against backgrounds which are given and understood. Equally, however, it cannot be eased by categorising people in terms which refer only to their group membership. The humiliation which is felt by fundamentalist

Muslims is the humiliation inherent in the rejection of a whole way of life –
the rejection of what one essentially is.

Free speech, I suggest, is important in so far as it increases the possibility
of mutual understanding. The wrong which is standardly done by the denial
of free speech must therefore be understood in these terms too, and these
terms will both justify and set limits to toleration in liberal societies. But
mutual understanding, like self-knowledge, is something which must be
created, not discovered. To defend free speech by reference to rationality is
to suppose that there is a truth which will emerge in the free market place of
ideas. Against this I have suggested that often there is no such truth, and that
even if there were, we should be wary of supposing that it will always emerge
in that way. Similarly, to defend free speech by reference to rationality is
to ignore the extent to which rationality is itself context-dependent. And
to defend free speech by reference to autonomy or individual choice is to
ignore the sense in which we are not self-made, but self-made only within
certain limits: the limits provided by our membership of often diverse and
inconsistent groups.

What is needed therefore is a commitment to freedom of speech as one of
the conditions for obtaining a better understanding of different groups. In
Kant's terms, we must understand speech not simply as expression, but as
communication. The justification of free speech will then be that it enhances
rather than thwarts the possibilities of communication between different
people. Additionally, however, the conditions of communication, and of
morality generally, include our capacity for emotional love – our ability to
recognise the needs of others and their similarities to us. Where free speech
is employed in such a way as to destroy the possibility of communication,
and of mutual understanding, then its *raison d'être* is destroyed. It is in this
way that we come to ask whether the tigers of wrath are wiser than the
horses of instruction, when the question we should be asking is 'How can
the lion lie down with the lamb?'

NOTES

1. The title is taken from William Blake's *Proverbs of Hell*, in which Blake tells us that
   'the tigers of wrath are wiser than the horses of instruction'. Blake's claim here is
   part of his general onslaught against Reason, and reflects his belief that Reason may
   not be the most reliable way of discovering Truth. I am grateful to Professor Jacques
   Berthoud and Professor David Moody for helping me to understand Blake's text.
2. Fay Weldon, *Sacred Cows* (London: Chatto & Windus, 1989), p. 33.
3. As quoted in Lisa Appignanesi and Sara Maitland (eds), *The Rushdie File* (London:
   Fourth Estate, 1989), pp. 241–2.
4. As quoted in Appignanesi and Maitland, op. cit., p. 251.
5. As quoted in Appignanesi and Maitland, op. cit., p. 229.
6. See Alasdair MacIntyre, *Whose Justice? Which Rationality?* (London: Duckworth,
   1988).
7. John Stuart Mill, *On Liberty*, 1859, chapter 2, 'Of the Liberty of Thought and
   Discussion'.
8. Eric Barendt, *Freedom of Speech* (Oxford: Clarendon Press, 1985), p. 11.

9. Quentin Skinner, 'A reply to my Critics', in James Tully (ed.), *Meaning and Context: Quentin Skinner and His Critics* (Oxford and Cambridge: Polity, 1988), pp. 231–88.

10. D. Z. Phillips, 'Allegiance and Change in Morality', in *Through a Darkening Glass* (Oxford: Blackwell, 1982), p. 25.

11. Michael Ignatieff, in Appignanesi and Maitland, op. cit., p. 251.

12. Shabbir Akhtar, in Appignanesi and Maitland, op. cit., p. 240.

13. Richard Rorty, *Contingency, Irony, and Solidarity* (Cambridge: Cambridge University Press, 1989), p. xiv.

14. Bernard Williams, 'Morality and the Emotions', in *Problems of the Self* (Cambridge: Cambridge University Press, 1973), p. 227.

15. Ibid.

16. Joseph Raz, *The Morality of Freedom* (Oxford: Claredon Press, 1986), p. 391.

17. Richard Rorty, op. cit., p. xvi.

VOLTAIRE
EXTRACT FROM
PHILOSOPHICAL DICTIONARY

What is toleration? It is the prerogative of humanity. We are all steeped in weaknesses and error: let us forgive one another's follies, it is the first law of nature.

Voltaire ([1764] 1971), *Philosophical Dictionary*, tr. and ed. T. Bestermann, Harmondsworth: Penguin.

4

MULTICULTURALISM

Paul Graham

Introduction

The term 'multiculturalism' has gained wide currency in both academic and popular debate, and its employment is not restricted to political theory or political science: there are multicultural perspectives not only in other social sciences, but also in the humanities, and even in the natural sciences. For this reason it is important to demarcate the debate within political theory. If we say that what makes politics possible is, on the one side, conflict, and on the other, the possibility of co-operation, then multiculturalism is concerned with the possibility of political co-operation in the face of cultural conflict: can a given set of political institutions or principles be defended from a diverse range of cultural perspectives? If not, can we conceive of alternative institutions which would be defensible? And it is important to recognise that political theory isn't concerned merely with what political principles should be operative in society, but also with how those principles are *justified*. Therefore, the legitimacy of political principles turns not on what is empirically accepted, but on the *reasons* which could be given for accepting them. Following John Rawls, we assume a 'closed society', not in the sense that people cannot leave it, but rather that the possibility of emigration cannot be taken as evidence that those who 'choose' not to emigrate have 'tacitly consented' to the existing political order. Further, we assume that political principles will be enforced by an entity which, as Max Weber defined it, 'claims to command a monopoly on the legitimate use of coercion in a particular territory'. Given the assumption of a closed society, whose members are subject to coercive authority, we can refine what is at issue in the multiculturalism debate: multiculturalism implies a diversity of 'cultures' within a territory, but since each person is obliged to obey the state, we need to determine how that obligation can be rendered compatible with claims emerging from each person's culture.

Expressed in this way the multiculturalism debate appears merely to be an extension of arguments over political obligation, which have characterised western political thought since at least the seventeenth century. And indeed, despite the relatively recent emergence of multiculturalism as a topic in political theory, the debate over cultural diversity must be located in wider and older debates about the relationship between the individual and the state, debates dominated by liberal thought. Liberalism and multiculturalism stand in a close but complex relationship to each other. Liberals accept that we live in a pluralistic society – there is no single good way to live your life, or if there is, there is no means of persuading others that you have found it – and diversity of culture is one expression of that pluralism. But the compatibility of liberalism and multiculturalism turns upon the conceptualisation of pluralism. If by 'pluralism' we mean an irreconcilable difference over the good then allegiance to the state might simply be understood as a willingness not to impose upon others our conception of the good, and the justification for such 'toleration' of 'difference' is nothing more than social peace. If, however, we see pluralism as a natural outcome of the exercise of human freedom then the justification for tolerance of other conceptions of the good is grounded in something which is itself a good, namely, personal autonomy. Once personal autonomy takes on the status of a political value, the question arises as to whether the political order depends upon the existence and sustenance of particular cultural forms to the exclusion of others.

CULTURE

The question of whether a liberal political order can be culturally inclusive must depend, at least in part, not only on how we conceptualise pluralism, but also on how we define 'culture'. Whilst the term 'multiculturalism' suggests a multiplicity of cultures within a 'social system', it might also imply a particular attitude towards culture: one which values diversity. A difficulty which runs through the multiculturalism debate in political theory is the failure to explain what is meant by culture. Will Kymlicka, for example, in the opening lines of his book *Multicultural Citizenship*, makes the following claim:

> Most countries are culturally diverse. According to recent estimates, the world's 184 independent states contain over 600 living language groups, and 5,000 ethnic groups. In very few countries can the citizens be said to share the same language, or belong to the same ethnonational group (1995: 1).

In a few short sentences it is implied that 'culture' equates to a language group, an ethnic group and an ethnonational group. Kymlicka goes on to define the kind of culture with which he is concerned as an 'intergenerational community, more or less institutionally complete, occupying a given state territory, sharing a distinct language and history' (1995: 18) and further suggests that a culture provides 'meaningful ways of life across the full range of human activities' (1995: 76). The problem is that there is a proliferation of concepts with which culture is equated, but this simply shifts the strain of definition onto these other, equally problematic, concepts. Furthermore, the defence of culture is rendered circular by defining it in terms of a legally recognised entity, when legal recognition is precisely what is at issue. Other political theorists, such as James Tully, do make explicit their reliance on a particular theory of culture – in Tully's case Clifford Geertz's semiotic theory – but they fail to discuss fully the implications of such commitments. And in popular discussion 'culture' is frequently run together with race, ethnicity and religion; whilst there are important connections between these concepts they are not synonyms. The structure of a religion is quite different to the structure of, say, a linguistic community, and each generates distinct political claims.

If we want to find a serious discussion of culture we have to turn to anthropologists, for whom arguably 'culture' is the central, defining concept of their discipline. Edward Tylor's definition of culture as 'that complex whole which includes knowledge, belief, art, morals, law, custom, and any other capabilities and habits acquired by man as a member of society' (1871: 1), whilst very broad, does capture the notion of culture as something artificial, in contrast to 'nature', which is a 'given'. We can then characterise the anthropologists' discussion of culture as an attempt to answer the question: given a shared biological nature and largely similar physical needs, why is there such cultural diversity? From Tylor onwards responses have fallen into two categories: universalist and relativist. These categories contain, of course, a huge variety of different theories. In the universalist camp we find those Marxists who argue that 'forms of consciousness' (culture) are to be explained by underlying material forces, and cultural change is derivative of changes in the relations of production. For such Marxists culture is a secondary phenomenon, and not the true 'subject of history'. But a universalist can hold culture to be basic, maintaining that cultural diversity is explained by different rates of evolution. Nineteenth-century anthropologists, Tylor included, viewed what they termed 'primitive cultures' as of the same type as earlier European cultural forms. This has clear imperialist overtones, and it is no coincidence that anthropology developed on the back of colonisation. Evolutionism could, however, take a liberal form, if one maintained, as John Stuart Mill did, that human beings have innate rational capacities which can only be realised under particular cultural conditions. These Marxist, 'imperialist', and liberal theories are all evolutionary, but universalism need not be evolutionist. One might argue that there are underlying non-cultural needs which are satisfied by diverse cultural forms; such a *functionalist* view explains culture in terms of something non-cultural without a commitment to the evolutionary superiority of one culture over another.

In its early phase anthropology was dominated by universalist theories, but by the late nineteenth and early twentieth centuries it came under sustained attack by relativists, such as Franz Boas, and his students Ruth Benedict and Alfred Kroeber. Benedict, in her book *Patterns of Culture*, quotes Ramon, chief of the Californian Digger Indians, who laments that with colonisation American Indian culture had died; taking Ramon's analogy of a cup, Benedict maintains that his culture could not be preserved by 'tinkering with an addition here, lopping off something there', rather, 'the modelling had been fundamental, it was somehow all of a piece' (1934: 16). A culture, Benedict suggests, is as an integrated pattern of intelligent, albeit sometimes unconscious, behaviour. It involves an apparently arbitrary selection of ways of being which are reinforced over time; the corollary of such selection is the implicit rejection of other ways of being. There are no underlying non-cultural needs, drives or capacities, nor is a particular culture, following Hegel, an instantiation of a process of cultural change. Pattern theory implies that there can be no cultural *diversity* within a society, for culture is integral, and it is perhaps not surprising that those political theorists, such as Tully, who make explicit their theoretical commitments, appeal to an alternative and more recent form of cultural relativism, that advanced by, among others, Geertz and James Fernandez. Culture for Geertz is a complex of signs, whose meaning is dependent upon perspective, not in the sense that an 'outsider' cannot understand the signs, but rather that such understanding – *interpretation* – must make reference to the context – or location in what might be termed 'semiotic space' – of the participants. For Geertz one does not 'have' a culture in the sense that culture is predicated upon a subject, but rather culture is a shorthand for a 'multiplicity of complex conceptual structures, many of them superimposed upon or knotted into one another, which are at once strange, irregular, and inexplicit' (1993: 10).

THE 'STRUGGLE FOR RECOGNITION' AND THE 'POLITICS OF IDENTITY'

At the heart of multiculturalism is the charge that liberals fail to recognise the role that culture plays in the self-worth of individuals, a failure which expresses itself both at the substantive level of political institutions, by, for example, offering inadequate political representation of cultural groups, and at the level of the justification of those institutions, meaning the arguments used to explain and defend political institutions are culturally biased. As Charles Taylor argues, the sense of who we are is constructed in the eyes of others, so that to fail to be recognised by others is to be denied the basis of one's identity: 'Non-recognition or misrecognition can inflict harm, can be a form of oppression, imprisoning someone in a false, distorted, and reduced mode of being' (1994: 25). The politics of recognition is a modern concept, developing out of the collapse of hierarchies in the eighteenth century. Hierarchies were the basis of honour, and honour was linked to distinction, and hence inequality; against honour we have dignity, which Taylor takes to be the basis of a democratic society. At the same time as we shift from honour to dignity, we also experience individualisation: morality is no longer to be understood in terms of mores but is a matter of individual conscience, either in the form of a moral sense, or, following Kant, the capacity of an individual to will the moral law. However, after Kant we get what Taylor terms a 'displacement of the moral accent': the inner voice is no longer primarily concerned to tell us what to do – to connect us to an objective moral order – but has become an end in itself. It is the terminus of identity. We have to be true to our 'inner voice' if we are to be 'full human beings'. The conjunction of inwardness and authenticity – following that inner voice – creates a danger that we lose sight of the fact that one's identity is only possible through other people's recognition of us. Somehow we need to reconcile the inwardness of authenticity with the 'outwardness' of recognition. In the days of 'honour' the two were unproblematic because 'general recognition was built into the socially derived identity by virtue of the very fact that it was based on social categories that everyone took for granted' (Taylor 1994: 34). Inwardly derived, as distinct from externally imposed, identity doesn't enjoy this automatic recognition, but must win it, and that process may fail, such that 'what has come about with the modern age is not the need for recognition but the conditions in which the attempt to be recognized can fail' (Taylor 1994: 35). Recognition is recognition of *difference*, but this is combined with a 'traditional' liberal emphasis on equality:

> The politics of difference often redefines non-discrimination as requiring that we make these distinctions the basis of differential treatment. So members of aboriginal bands will get certain rights and powers not enjoyed by other Canadians . . . and certain minorities will get the right to exclude others in order to preserve their cultural integrity, and so on (Taylor 1994: 39–40).

The conflict between 'traditional' liberalism and identity politics would be less severe were it not for the fact that 'the demand for equal recognition extends beyond an acknowledgement of the equal value of all humans potentially, and comes to include the equal value of what they have made of this potential in fact' (Taylor 1994: 42–3).

What is interesting about Taylor's presentation of multiculturalism is that 'culture' is conceptualised not as an imposition or constraint, but as something we *identify with*, and in the process it becomes our *identity*. The difficulty Taylor implicitly acknowledges is that political debate becomes a matter of 'my identity, right or wrong'. If we recall that the problem is how we legitimate the state from a multiplicity of cultural perspectives, bearing in mind that the state both enables and constrains, the danger with identity politics is that there is no means by which we can, from a standpoint of moral equality, communicate our demands to one another and assess the reasonableness of each demand. Taylor quite rightly argues that 'traditional liberalism', with its 'colour blind' notion of equality, is often the imposition of a hegemonic culture and that 'only the minority or suppressed cultures are being forced to take alien form' (1994: 43). However, this does not advance the argument for a politics of identity. What we need is a source of value in society, and an explanation of the role that values – or 'conceptions of the good' – play in political theory. What Taylor has identified is the way 'culture', as a source of value, has been transformed under conditions of modernity; and the clue to that transformation lies in the notion of hierarchy. If we say that 'value' is a state of betterness, such that to value A over B is to say that A is better than B, in a hierarchical society value is inscribed in culture, not in the sense that self-conscious individuals don't exist, or that culture is a self-conscious being, but rather that value is unproblematic. If in hierarchical societies value is given to individuals by their culture, then it would appear that in post-hierarchical societies the move is the other way: the individual endows his or her culture with value. The difficulty is that the process by which we value, or identify with, 'our' culture is not innocent of metaphysical commitments. It presupposes powers of reason, whereby we reject some aspects of what we have inherited and accept others; that process of rejection and acceptance is itself not straightforward, for there is a dialectic at work, whereby the significance of 'cultural traits', to use Benedict's term, is transformed. For example, the hijab worn by Muslim women may acquire new significance as a sign of liberation in societies saturated with sexualised images of women.

It is interesting that whilst not always explicit, arguments over cultural recognition, and its relationship to fundamental questions of rationality, have been at the heart of criticism of two of the most important political theorists of the late twentieth century: John Rawls and Jürgen Habermas. For Rawls, we reason our way to political principles from a standpoint which models our capacities as 'rational' and 'reasonable' beings, and this takes the form of the 'original position', in which we are denied knowledge of our identities, including, very importantly, our conception(s) of the good (read: culture). For Habermas, everyday communication 'counterfactually presupposes' validity claims which the speaker must redeem if he or she is to act successfully. Although he later abandoned the concept of the 'ideal speech situation', with its similarity to Rawls's original position, Habermas's position, like that of Rawls, entails an abstraction from the individual's cultural context. Both bodies of work have been subject to the same charge, namely, that the capacity to give value to one's life, and by extension to accept as legitimate institutions which fundamentally affect one's life chances, depends upon the capacity to reason from a cultural perspective, and not in abstraction from it. The counter-charge is that multiculturalism, in the form of identity politics, is *fundamentally* illiberal – that is, illiberal not only at an institutional level, but at the level of justification of those institutions. The capacity to reason, whether over our own interests or over moral principles, requires the capacity to compare and categorise alternative ways of being. If culture is understood in relativist terms, which is how it must be understood by defenders of identity politics, then it is resistant to reason. Of course, most people, *on reflection*, value culture, which would suggest that culture is *not* resistant to reason; however, the task for political theorists is to conceptualise the relationship between reason and culture. I want briefly to survey three such attempts.

Three models of multiculturalism: kymlicka, tully, habermas

Will Kymlicka

Will Kymlicka has, in a large number of works, sought to reconcile liberalism and multiculturalism. He argues that culture provides a 'context of choice'. This is problematic, for it is unclear whether culture is instrumentally or intrinsically valuable: does value reside in what we choose or in the fact that we have chosen it? If the ends we choose are of instrumental value then it wouldn't much matter which culture you identified with, although the more compatible with liberal values the better. It is nevertheless clear that for Kymlicka one's culture must have intrinsic value and indeed in an earlier book, *Liberalism, Community, and Culture*, he argued that liberals do not stress the importance of human freedom as if freedom were an end in itself, but rather the ends we pursue are what really matter. The difficulty is, however, that the ends we pursue must be compatible with the exercise of freedom and Kymlicka relies on an empirical observation to support his contention that they are. He cites Quebec as an example of a culture that has 'liberalised':

> Before the Quiet Revolution, the Québécois generally shared a rural, Catholic, conservative, and patriarchal conception of the good. Today, after a period of liberalization, most people have abandoned this traditional way of life, and Québécois society now exhibits all the diversity that any modern society contains . . . to be a Québécois today, therefore, simply means being a participant in the francophone society of Quebec (1995: 87).

In the absence of an adequate theorisation of culture it is not clear whether the example of Quebec can help us to see whether 'cultural membership' enhances or diminishes freedom. After all, the struggle within Quebec is fundamentally over language, and although the freedom of one linguistic community is threatened by the other, the capacity to use language, whether it is French or English, is fundamental to human autonomy. Other dimensions of culture, such as religion, may not contain the same freedom-enhancing potential.

Kymlicka argues that individuals should have rights to cultural membership. Rights are central to a liberal polity, and for the purposes of this discussion we can define a right as an advantage held against another (or others). Kymlicka distinguishes three different types of right: self-government rights, polyethnic rights, and special representation rights. Self-government rights usually entail the devolution of power to a political unit 'substantially controlled by the members of an ethnic minority'. Examples of polyethnic rights would be state funding of 'cultural institutions' and exemptions from certain policies, such as those relating to the slaughter of animals. Special representation rights are intended to ensure the 'fair' representation of minority groups. Each of these types of right, but especially the first two, can take the form of an 'internal restriction' or an 'external protection'; Kymlicka maintains that a study of the empirical evidence would suggest that most campaigns for cultural recognition take the form of a demand for external protections from wider society, rather than restricting the freedom of the members of that culture, and so are compatible with liberalism. The basic problem is that rights are a specific cultural form, and the effects of rights on a culture depends on how one conceptualises culture. If cultures are integral patterns (Benedict, Kroeber) then rights may well upset those patterns. If, on the other hand, we conceive culture(s) as overlapping semiotic relationships (Geertz, Fernandez) then we have a different problem: rights imply a uniform legal system and yet a semiotic theory of culture suggests that interpretation may be relativistic.

James Tully

That last point leads us to consider the work of James Tully. Constitutional uniformity (or modern constitutionialism) is the object of his attack, and modern political thinkers are (largely) its proponents. Modern constitutionialism stresses sovereignty, regularity and uniformity, and this contrasts with the implied rejection of sovereignty and the irregularity and pluralism of 'ancient constitutionialism'. Although there are notable exceptions, Tully maintains that the process of colonisation entailed the confrontation of these two forms of constitutionialism, and that contemporary cultural conflicts in, for example, the Americas have their roots in the imposition of an alien constitutional form on native Americans. This imperial legacy is still with us not simply in political practice, but also in political theory. Writers such as John Rawls, Habermas and Kymlicka, whilst arguing for cultural diversity, do so in the language of modern constitutionialism.

Drawing on Geertz and the later work of Ludwig Wittgenstein, Tully contrasts two models of intercultural communication (he prefers the term 'interculturalism' to multiculturalism). The first requires shared terms of reference, so, for example, we might disagree about what rights people have, but we implicitly assume that rights have certain features. The second is based on 'family resemblances' between cultures: we find common ground not through an implicitly agreed, shared language, but by a piecemeal case-by-case agreement, and the political forms are themselves 'essentially contested'. This suggests that constitutional formation cannot be understood from an abstract standpoint, such as Rawls's original position or Habermas's discursive public sphere. And Europeans have resources within their own culture(s) to engage in such case-by-case communication; English common law is an example of an ancient constitution, and Tully considers it significant that there were cases of interaction between Europeans and native Americans based on recognition of the *affinities* between their legal systems.

Tully's argument, whilst interesting and provocative, has a number of serious weaknesses. First, there is a tension between his espousal of a semiotic theory of culture, which stresses looseness of cultural boundaries, and his talk of 12,000 'diverse cultures, governments and environmental practices' struggling for recognition (Tully 1995: 3) (he provides no source for that figure) and '15,000 cultures who demand recognition' (Tully 1995: 8) (again, no source). To count something you have to identify it, and identification implies 'hard boundaries'. Second, he says very little about how cultural conflicts can be mediated in the contemporary world, despite the underlying purpose of his book being to show the relevance of ancient constitionialism. It's not clear what institutional forms would express cultural diversity, especially for geographically dispersed minorities. Third, and most important, he fails to address the charge that protection of culture can have detrimental consequences for individual freedom. He does maintain that culture is the basis of self-respect, such that to be denied recognition is a serious thing, but he offers only metaphorical observations to support the claim that interculturalism is not a threat to individual freedom.

Jürgen Habermas

Finally, we turn to Jürgen Habermas's argument. His reflections are grounded in a complex theory of rationality and societal modernisation. He argues, along with Max Weber, that the 'taken-for-granted horizon of expectations' – one possible definition of culture – is, under conditions of modernity, dissolved. Social relations are rationalised. However, against Weber, Habermas argues that this process of rationalisation takes two forms: (1) social interaction through communicative action and (2) strategic (instrumental) interaction through the social sub-systems of money and bureaucratic power. The positive, binding qualities of pre-modern societies are regenerated through (1), but threatened by (2). The apparent tension between individual rights and culture can be resolved if we recognise that human autonomy is only possible through the regeneration of cultural forms, and culture must itself become 'reflexive'.

What does Habermas mean by 'communicative action'? If I *promise* to meet you on Thursday, or *request* you stop smoking, or *confess* I find your actions distasteful, or *predict* it will rain, then I am implicitly offering you something, which you can contest. In the first two cases I am making a claim to normative rightness, in the third case I am making a claim to sincerity, and in the final case a claim to truth. You can contest all three such *validity claims*. The success of each speech-act depends upon both parties orienting themselves to principles of reason which are not reducible to individual intentions: in addressing another person I am treating him/her as an end in him/herself. The problem is that these validity claims abstract from everyday life, but to redeem them requires appeal to a stock of culturally specific values.

To inject some 'concretion' into the abstraction of discourse ethics Habermas argues that language is the proof that forms of life can be reinvigorated. Alfred Schutz, in his book *The Structure of the Lifeworld*, is credited with developing the concept of the 'lifeworld'. He defined it as that area of human interaction which is, and must be, 'taken-for-granted': it is a horizon beyond which we cannot see. Habermas argues: 'The lifeworld is the intuitively present, in this sense familiar and transparent, and at the same time vast and incalculable web of presuppositions that have to be satisfied if an actual utterance is to be at all meaningful, that is, valid or invalid' (1987b: 131). For Schutz the lifeworld can never be problematic, it can only fall apart and this follows from his definition of the lifeworld as a background resource of taken-for-granted (tacit) knowledge (cf. Benedict and the pattern theory of culture). Habermas takes issue with this – the lifeworld involves social (cultural) reproduction and this means the lifeworld, *contra* Schutz, involves activity and not passivity: the possibility of discourse ethics depends upon the ability to raise – to make explicit – the validity claims implicit in language. This is then connected to a theory of rights.

Habermas argues that there is a tradition in Anglophone legal and political theory of conceiving of the state as grounded in the protection of individual 'private' rights (rights derived from the market contract model). Hobbes is the *locus classicus* of this conception of individual–state relations. If we operate with such a theory then it is inevitable that individual rights will be a threat to cultural reproduction; in effect, increasing reliance on rights would be another example of the system colonising the lifeworld. We are then left with a choice: either we assert the primacy of individual rights at the expense of cultural interaction, or we maintain the authority of the collective over the individual. Private rights entail the assertion of personal autonomy, but they ignore the other half of the concept of autonomy – public autonomy:

> From a normative point of view, the integrity of the individual legal person cannot be guaranteed without protecting the intersubjectively shared experiences and life contexts in which the person has been socialized and has formed his or her identity. The identity of the individual is interwoven with collective identities and can be stabilized only in a cultural network that cannot be appropriated as private property any more than the mother tongue itself can be (Habermas 1994: 129).

The difficulty with many arguments for multiculturalism is that this inadequately analysed thing called 'culture' is frozen, such that those individuals who 'bear' that culture are not recognised as autonomous human beings. This applies especially to women from ethnic minority groups, as Yasmin Ali outlines in her essay 'Muslim Women and the Politics of Ethnicity in Northern England' (1992). What Habermas attempts to do – and space does not permit an adequate critique of his argument – is to suggest a way in which culture and autonomy are not only compatible but mutually entangled.

QUESTIONS FOR DISCUSSION
- Does the development of a political theory of multiculturalism require the selection of a particular anthropological theory of culture?
- What reforms should be made to political institutions so that they reflect cultural difference?
- Is culture best protected through individual rights or group rights?
- Is it possible to be a feminist and a multiculturalist?

JAMES TULLY
EXTRACTS FROM *STRANGE MULTIPLICITY: CONSTITUTIONALISM IN AN AGE OF DIVERSITY*

The historical formation of common
constitutionalism: the rediscovery of cultural
diversity, part i
The hidden constitutions of contemporary societies

[...]

The recognition and accommodation of cultural diversity in the broader
language of contemporary constitutionalism discloses what might be called
the 'hidden constitutions of contemporary societies'. [...] As contemporary
societies begin to enter a post-imperial age, a vast undergrowth of cultural
diversity and its partial recognition in constitutions has begun to come to
light as the shadow of the imperial epoch begins to recede.

[...]

In one of the most famous passages of the *Philosophical investigations*,
Wittgenstein, thinking of his two homes, Vienna and Cambridge, compares
language to an ancient city:[1]

> Our language can be seen as an ancient city: a maze of little streets and
> squares, of old and new houses, and of houses with additions from

---

James Tully (1995), *Strange Multiplicity: Constitutionalism in an Age of Diversity*, Cambridge:
Cambridge University Press.

various periods; and this surrounded by a multitude of new boroughs with straight and regular streets and uniform houses.

[...]

The ancient city, with its multiplicity of old, new and overlapping additions is now surrounded by 'a multitude of new boroughs with straight and regular streets and uniform houses'. Constitutional uniformity is not the 'soul' of the city, as Pufendorf and other modern theorists suggested it should be. Neither Kant's nor Paine's republican constitution determines every aspect of the whole.

[...]

Understanding constitutionalism: Wittgenstein and Hale
Wittgenstein introduces the analogy between language and an ancient city to illustrate the understanding of language one comes to acquire by working through all the examples carefully assembled in the *Philosophical investigations*. Since this concept of understanding will enable us to understand the language of constitutionalism, let me review his main points. Language, like a city, has grown up in a variety of forms through long use and practice, interacting and overlapping in many ways in the endless diversity and strife of human activities.

[...]

Consequently, the grammar of words is too multiform to be represented in a theory or comprehensive rule that stipulates the essential conditions for the correct application of words in every instance, just as there is no such comprehensive view of the constitution of a city. 'We do not *command a clear view* of the use of our words', not because the definitive theory has yet to arrive, but because language 'is lacking in this sort of perspicuity'. [...] Language is aspectival: 'a labyrinth of paths. You approach from *one* side and know your way about; you approach the same place from another side and no longer know your way about'.[2]

[...]

The image of an ancient city graphically illustrates the way that the craving for generality overlooks and generates a contemptuous attitude towards the irreducible multiplicity of concrete usage that defeats its aspiration.

[...]

Understanding a general term is nothing more than the practical activity of being able to use it in various circumstances: 'there is a way of grasping a rule which is *not* an *interpretation*, but which is exhibited in what we call "obeying the rule" and "going against it" in actual cases'. Such a grasp is not the possession of a theory, but the manifestation of a repertoire of practical, normative abilities, acquired through long use and practice, to use the term and go against customary use in actual cases.

[...]

Some theorists, such as Peter Winch, have gone on to infer that people using general terms in the everyday activities of life are still following rules. The rules are said to be 'implicit' or background 'understandings' embedded in practice and shared by all members of a culture or community. The role of the theorist is then to make explicit the implicit rules embodied in practice in a culture or community. We have seen Rawls take this turn in his recent work. [...] In so doing, these theorists of practice have uncritically retained the older assumption of cultures and communities as homogeneous wholes and insouciantly carried on with a contemptuous attitude towards particular cases. They have neglected Wittgenstein's [...] argument that the 'grasp' exhibited in 'obeying' or 'going against' a rule in actual cases cannot be accounted for in terms of following general rules implicit in practice because the multiplicity of uses is too various, tangled, contested and creative to be governed by rules.

[...]

Like many practical activities that are mastered by examples more than by rules, understanding a general concept consists in being able to give reasons why it should or should not be used in any particular case by describing examples with similar or related aspects, drawing analogies or disanalogies of various kinds, finding precedents and drawing attention to intermediate cases so that one can pass easily from familiar cases to the unfamiliar and see the relation between them.

[...]

The final aspect of Wittgenstein's [argument] I wish to draw to your attention is that his examples of understanding a general term by assembling examples always take place in dialogue with others who see things differently.

[...]

This is the point of his dictum that you approach from one side and know your way about; you approach the same place from another side and no longer know your way about. To understand a general term, and so know your way around its maze of uses, it is always necessary to enter into a dialogue with interlocutors from other regions of the city.

[. . .]

Wittgenstein's philosophy is an alternative worldview to the one that informs modern constitutionalism. First, contrary to the imperial concept of understanding in modern constitutionalism [. . .], it provides a way of understanding others that does not entail comprehending what they say within one's own language of redescription, for this is now seen for what it is: one heuristic description of examples among others; one interlocution among others in the dialogue of humankind. Second, it furnishes a philosophical account of the way in which exchanges of views in intercultural dialogues nurture the attitude of 'diversity awareness' by enabling the interlocutors to regard cases differently and change their way of looking at things.

Finally, it is a view of how understanding occurs in the real world of overlapping, interacting and negotiated cultural diversity in which we speak, act and associate together.

[. . .]

Examples of the three conventions: the aboriginal and common-law system and the conventions of mutual recognition and consent

The following examples of the recognition and accommodation of cultural diversity illustrate the multiplicity of uses of the concepts of contemporary constitutionalism and disclose the hidden constitutions of contemporary societies. They also bring to light the three conventions of common constitutionalism: mutual recognition, continuity and consent. Constitutional 'conventions' in this common-law sense are norms that come into being and come to be accepted as authoritative in the course of constitutional practice, including criticism and contestation of that practice. They gradually gain their authority by acts in conformity with them and by appeals to them by both sides, as warrants of justification, when they are transgressed. These three conventions form the sturdy fibres of Ariadne's thread through the labyrinth of conflicting claims to cultural recognition which currently block the way to a peaceful twenty-first century. If they guide constitutional negotiations, the negotiations and resulting constitutions will be just with respect to cultural recognition.

The first and most spectacular example is the mutual recognition and accommodation of the Aboriginal peoples of America and the British Crown as equal, self-governing nations. This form of mutual recognition was worked out in the early modern period in a common association of 'treaty constitutionalism'.

[. . .]

The problem of mutual recognition is classically formulated by John Marshall, the first Chief Justice of the Supreme Court of the United States, in his final and definitive judgement on US – Aboriginal relations in *Worcester v. the State of Georgia* of 1832.

[. . .]

If the Aboriginal peoples of America are recognised as 'independent nations', as Marshall argues, [. . .] the situation is a continent of over five hundred sovereign Aboriginal nations governing themselves by their own institutions and authoritative traditions of interpretation for roughly twenty thousand years before Europeans arrive in the seventeenth century. The Europeans refuse to become immigrants of the existing Aboriginal nations, as the US and Canadian governments would certainly insist today in an analogous situation, and demand instead that their nationhood be recognised and accommodated so they may govern themselves by their own laws and traditions.

The question is how can the people in this diverse form reach agreement on a constitutional association just to both parties. The answer was worked out through hundreds of treaty negotiations between agents of the Crown and the Aboriginal nations from the 1630s to 1832. In *Worcester*, Marshall reviewed the history of treaty making and presented a synopsis of the customary system of treaty constitutionalism that evolved over the previous two centuries. He took as a major precedent the Royal Proclamation of 7 October 1763, in which the Crown set out its understanding of the relations between British North America and the Aboriginal nations. The Proclamation, in turn, was based on a review of treaties since 1664, Royal Commissions on Indian Affairs since 1665, Royal Instructions to colonial administrators since 1670, the Board of Trade's recognition of Aboriginal sovereignty in 1696 (when Locke was a member) and in the case of the Mohegan nation versus Connecticut of 1705 (which John Bulkley attacked with Locke's arguments), and the advice of the Superintendent of Indian Affairs in North America, Sir William Johnson (Joseph Brant's step father).

[. . .]

The first convention of constitutional negotiations is to agree on a form of mutual recognition. In this case, it involves the mutual recognition of both parties as independent and self-governing nations. The initial reason Crown negotiators recognised the Aboriginal peoples as nations is that they did not redescribe the Aboriginal peoples in the forms of recognition constructed by the armchair European theorists. Instead, they simply listened to how the Aboriginal negotiators presented themselves in countless meetings.

[…]

The second reason why Crown negotiators applied the term 'nation' and 'republic' to the Aboriginal peoples is that the forms of Aboriginal political organisation they observed, while not identical, were similar in a number of respects to European nations. They did not apply criteria that only seventeenth-century European nations met and conclude that Aboriginal peoples were savages at the lowest stage of development. As the terms of Marshall's description neatly illustrate, they were able to see the cross-cultural family resemblances between Aboriginal and European forms of political association. Whereas long use and occupation of a territory gave them jurisdiction, as the 1665 Royal Commission had ruled, the ability to govern themselves in accord with their own laws and ways for a long time and to have their independence recognised by other similarly organised peoples gave them nationhood.

[…]

The negotiators were quite aware that the Aboriginal peoples did not have European-style states, representative institutions, formalised legal systems, prisons and independent executives. They observed the conciliar and con-federal forms of government, consensus decision making, rule by authority rather than coercion, and customary law. Yet this did not cause them to situate the Aboriginal peoples in a lower stage of development. Quite the contrary. They were constantly instructed by the Privy Council to study and respect their constitutions and forms of government, ensure that they 'not be molested or disturbed' and punish the 'great frauds and abuses' committed against them by the settlers.[…]

The reasons why the Aboriginal nations reciprocally recognised the Europeans as nations are similar. The Aboriginal peoples who encountered Europeans in the first two centuries had long traditions of recognising each other as nations and entering into various forms of treaty alliances and confederations. This is especially true of the *Haudenosaunee* confederacy, whose constitution, the Great Law of Peace (*Gayaneshakgowa*), dates from the 1450s. It is none the less true of the Cherokee, Shawnee, Delaware, Mohegan, Pequot, Ottawa, Huron, Mi'kmaq and many others. […]

Although both parties are recognised as nations, the Aboriginal nations are prior or 'First Nations', as they are called in Canada, since they were in North America when the Europeans arrived. Once this form of mutual recognition was worked out, the only just way that the Crown could acquire land and establish its sovereignty in North America was to gain the consent of the Aboriginal nations.

[. . .]

The form of consent should always be tailored to the form of mutual recognition of the people involved. In this case, Marshall concludes, this is the form of 'mutual consent' the Crown established in the treaty system and the United States inherited after the war of independence. In this system, the Crown negotiated, and continues to negotiate, with the First Nations to purchase territory from them, to gain their recognition of Crown government in America, and to work out various relations of protection and co-operation over time. In one of the most generous acts of recognition and accommodation in history, the Aboriginal nations in turn negotiated, and continue to negotiate, to cede land and settle boundaries, recognise the legitimacy of Crown governments and work out relations of protection and co-operation. However, they consent to this on the condition that the Crown governments and their successors always respect the equal and prior sovereignty of the Aboriginal nations on the territories they reserve to themselves.

[. . .]

The aboriginal and common-law system and the convention of continuity

The continuity of both parties' independent nationhood illustrates the third and final constitutional convention. The mutually recognised cultural identities of the parties continue through the constitutional negotiations and associations agreed to unless they explicitly consent to amend them.

[. . .]

The decision by the Crown and its representatives to recognise and continue the cultures of the Aboriginal nations appears as one of the most enlightened acts of the eighteenth century. The contrary tendency to discontinue and extinguish their cultural ways, justified in the imperial language of modern constitutionalism, appears regressive – the application of the doctrine of the Norman conquest. Yet the axis of this reversal of vision is not the postmodern deconstruction of constitutionalism, but the ancient convention of continuity.

[...]

The aboriginal and common-law system of constitutional dialogue

[...]

Over the last three hundred years, elaborate genres of presentation, speaking in French, English and Aboriginal languages, exchanging narratives, stories and arguments, translating back and forth, breaking off and starting again, striking new treaties and redressing violations of old ones have been developed to ensure that each speaker speaks in her or his cultural voice and listens to the others in theirs.

[...]

The three schools of modern constitutionalism disregard the hidden diversity of actual constitutional dialogue not only by laying down simplistic concepts of popular sovereignty and constitutional association as premises, but also by their corresponding concepts of constitutional dialogue. In recent work (still written in monological form), two concepts of dialogue predominate: the participants aim to reach agreement either on universal principles or on norms implicit in practice and, in both cases, to fashion a constitutional association accordingly. Both concepts are, for example, present in the work of Jürgen Habermas.

The presupposition of shared, implicit norms is manifestly false in this case, as well as in any case of a culturally diverse society. Also, the aim of negotiations over cultural recognition is not to reach agreement on universal principles and institutions, but to bring negotiators to recognise their differences and similarities, so that they can reach agreement on a form of association that accommodates their differences in appropriate institutions and their similarities in shared institutions.

[...]

Writers such as Seyla Benhabib are critical of the monological theories of dialogue and argue that a democratic constitutional discussion in a culturally diverse society will involve a multiplicity of speech genres. Nevertheless, she goes on optimistically to suggest that we will always be able to put ourselves in the shoes of others and understand things from their point of view, 'either by actually listening to all involved or by representing to ourselves imaginatively the many perspectives of those involved'. In her path-breaking paper, 'Communication and the other', Iris Young deepens our understanding of the value of speaking in and listening to a variety of speech modes in such a discussion. 'Free and open communnication enables different groups each to learn of their own partiality by learning something about other perspectives on their collective problems and on themselves.' However, she is sceptical of Benhabib's claim that the participants could reach full reciprocity and symmetry of understanding. There remains 'much about the others that they do not understand'.[3]

This seems to be an unduly pessimistic view of the possibility of understanding among culturally diverse human beings. It is certainly true that we cannot understand culturally different others simply 'by representing to ourselves imaginatively the many perspectives of those involved', any more than I can master tennis by imagining various exchanges. Understanding comes, if it comes at all, only by engaging in the volley of practical dialogue. We need the dialogue itself to become aware of all the aspects of our association that ought to be recognised and accommodated in the constitution. It is also true that the diversity awareness one comes to acquire in dialogue does not consist in being able to replace the other person and speak for him or her. Much remains opaque. However, there is no reason to believe that the participants in the dialogue could not come to 'understand' each other.

The reason it is possible to understand one another in intercultural conversations is because this is what we do all the time in culturally diverse societies to some extent. The everyday mastery of the criss-crossing, overlapping and contested uses of terms is not different in kind (but of course in degree) from the understanding demanded by constitutional dialogue. If one thinks of understanding in the way I presented it in the previous section, the connection becomes clear. The dialogue in such constitutional negotiations usually consists in the back and forth exchange of speech acts of the form, 'let me see if I understand what you said', 'let me rephrase what you said and see if you agree', 'is what you said analogous to this example in my culture', or 'I am sorry, let me try another intermediate example that is closer', or 'can you acknowledge this analogy?' 'Now I think I see what you are saying – let me put it this way for I now see that it complements my view.' The participants are gradually able to see the association from the points of view of each other and cobble together an acceptable intercultural language capable of accommodating the truth in each of their limited and complementary views and of setting aside the incompatible ones.

[. . .]

Young may take a sceptical stance towards reciprocal intercultural understanding because she believes that, if it is possible, then dialogue might be reduced to a mere stepping stone to a monological and universal overview of the ensemble. This concern is suggested by her conclusion that only the 'preservation of difference and the recognition of asymmetry – the non-reciprocity – of social positions can preserve publicity and the need for continued communication'. But this path out of the world of cultural diversity is closed, not by the inability to understand one another, but by the constitution of the phenomenon we are trying to understand. It is lacking in this sort of perspicuity as a result of the three features of cultural diversity. Understanding it consists in being able to move about within the dialogue, passing from one neighbourhood to the next, exchanging stories and noticing our similarities and differences *en passant*, not by transcending the human condition.

NOTES

1. Ludwig Wittgenstein, *Philosophical Investigations*, trans. G. E. M. Anscombe, Oxford: Basil Blackwell, 1967, section 18.
2. Ibid., sections 122, 203.
3. Seyla Benhabib, *Situating the Self: Gender, Community, and Postmodernism in Contemporary Ethics*, New York: Routledge, 1992, p. 54.

JÜRGEN HABERMAS
EXTRACTS FROM 'STRUGGLES FOR RECOGNITION IN THE DEMOCRATIC CONSTITUTIONAL STATE'

[...]

In the political arena those who encounter one another are collective actors contending about collective goals and the distribution of collective goods. Only in the courtroom and in legal discourse are rights asserted and defended as actionable individual rights that can be sued for. Existing law also has to be interpreted in new ways in different contexts in view of new needs and new interests. This struggle over the interpretation and satisfaction of historically unredeemed claims is a struggle for legitimate rights in which collective actors are once again involved, combatting a lack of respect for their dignity. [...] Can these phenomena be reconciled with a theory of rights that is individualistically designed?

[...]

Does not the recognition of cultural forms of life and traditions that have been marginalized, whether in the context of a majority culture or in a Eurocentric global society, require guarantees of status and survival – in other words, some kind of collective rights that shatter the outmoded self-understanding of the democratic constitutional state, which is tailored to individual rights and in that sense is 'liberal'?

Jürgen Habermas (1994), 'Struggles for Recognition in the Democratic Constitutional State', in Charles Taylor, *Multiculturalism: Examining the Politics of Recognition* (ed. Amy Gutmann), Princeton: Princeton University Press.

[...] Charles Taylor gives us a complex answer to this question, an answer that advances the discussion significantly. [...] He distinguishes two readings of the democratic constitutional state, for which Michael Walzer provides the terms Liberalism 1 and Liberalism 2. These designations suggest that the second reading, which Taylor favors, merely corrects an inappropriate understanding of liberal principles. On closer examination, however, Taylor's reading attacks the principles themselves and calls into question the individualistic core of the modern conception of freedom.

TAYLOR'S 'POLITICS OF RECOGNITION'

[...]

Taylor proceeds on the assumption that the protection of collective identities comes into competition with the right to equal individual [*subjektive*] liberties – Kant's one original human right – so that in the case of conflict a decision must be made about which takes precedence over the other. The argument runs as follows: Because the second claim requires consideration of precisely those particularities from which the first claim seems to abstract, the principle of equal rights has to be put into effect in two kinds of politics that run counter to one another – a politics of consideration of cultural differences on the one hand and a politics of universalization of individual rights on the other. The one is supposed to compensate for the price the other exacts with its equalizing universalism. Taylor spells out this opposition – an opposition that is falsely construed, as I will try to show – using the concepts of the good and the just, drawn from moral theory. Liberals like Rawls and Dworkin call for an ethically neutral legal order that is supposed to assure everyone equal opportunity to pursue his or her own conception of the good. In contrast, communitarians like Taylor and Walzer dispute the ethical neutrality of the law and thus can expect the constitutional state, if need be, actively to advance specific conceptions of the good life.

[...]

Taylor understands Liberalism 1 as a theory according to which all legal consociates are guaranteed equal individual freedoms of choice and action in the form of basic rights. In cases of conflict the courts decide who has which rights; thus the principle of equal respect for each person holds only in the form of a legally protected autonomy that every person can use to realize his or her personal life project. This interpretation of the system of rights is paternalistic in that it ignores half of the concept of autonomy. It does not take into consideration that those to whom the law is addressed can acquire autonomy (in the Kantian sense) only to the extent that they can understand themselves to be the authors of the laws to which they are subject as private legal persons. Liberalism 1 fails to recognize that private and public autonomy are equiprimordial. It is not a matter of public autonomy supplementing and remaining external to private autonomy, but rather of an internal, that is, conceptually necessary connection between them. For in the final analysis, private legal persons cannot even attain the enjoyment of equal individual liberties unless they themselves, by jointly exercising their autonomy as citizens, arrive at a clear understanding about what interests and criteria are justified and in what respects equal things will be treated equally and unequal things unequally in any particular case.

[. . .]

The color-blindness of the selective reading vanishes once we assume that we ascribe to the bearers of individual rights an identity that is conceived intersubjectively. Persons, and legal persons as well, become individualized only through a process of socialization. A correctly understood theory of rights requires a politics of recognition that protects the integrity of the individual in the life contexts in which his or her identity is formed. This does not require an alternative model that would correct the individualistic design of the system of rights through other normative perspectives. All that is required is the consistent actualization of the system of rights.

[. . .]

Struggles for recognition: the phenomena and the levels of their analysis

Feminism, multiculturalism, nationalism, and the struggle against the Eurocentric heritage of colonialism are related phenomena that should not be confused with one another. They are related in that women, ethnic and cultural minorities, and nations and cultures defend themselves against oppression, marginalization, and disrespect and thereby struggle for the recognition of collective identities, whether in the context of a majority culture or within the community of peoples. We are concerned here with liberation movements whose collective political goals are defined primarily in cultural terms, even though social and economic inequalities as well as political dependencies are also always involved.

[. . .]

Liberation movements in multicultural societies are not a uniform phenomenon. They present different challenges depending on whether it is a question of endogenous minorities becoming aware of their identity or new minorities arising through immigration, and depending on whether the nations faced with the challenge have always understood themselves to be countries open to immigration on the basis of their history and political culture or whether the national self-understanding needs first to be adjusted to accommodate the integration of alien cultures. The challenge becomes all the greater, the more profound are the religious, racial, or ethnic differences or the historical-cultural disjunctions to be bridged. The challenge becomes all the more painful, the more the tendencies to self-assertion take on a fundamentalist and separatist character, whether because experiences of impotence lead the minority struggling for recognition to take a regressive position or because the minority in question has to use mass mobilization to awaken consciousness in order to articulate a newly constructed identity.

[...]

THE PERMEATION OF THE CONSTITUTIONAL STATE BY ETHICS

From the point of view of legal theory, the primary question that multiculturalism raises is the question of the ethical neutrality of law and politics. By 'ethical' I mean all questions that relate to conceptions of the good life, or a life that is not misspent. Ethical questions cannot be evaluated from the 'moral point of view' of whether something is 'equally good for everyone'; rather, impartial judgment of such questions is based on strong evaluations and determined by the self-understanding and perspectival life-projects of particular groups, that is, by what is from their point of view 'good for us', all things considered. [...]

The neutrality of the law – and of the democratic process of enacting laws – is sometimes understood to mean that political questions of an ethical nature must be kept off the agenda and out of the discussion by 'gag rules' because they are not susceptible of impartial legal regulation. On this view, in the sense of Liberalism 1, the state is not to be permitted to pursue any collective goals beyond guaranteeing the personal freedom and the welfare and security of its citizens. The alternative model (in the sense of Liberalism 2), in contrast, expects the state to guarantee these fundamental rights in general but beyond that also to intervene on behalf of the survival and advancement of a 'particular nation, culture, religion, or of a (limited) set of nations, cultures and religions', in Michael Walzer's formulation. Walzer regards this model too as fundamental; it leaves room, however, for citizens to choose to give priority to individual rights under certain circumstances. Walzer shares Taylor's premise that conflicts between these two fundamental normative orientations are quite possible and that in such cases only Liberalism 2 permits collective goals and identities to be given precedence. Now, the theory of rights does in fact assert the absolute precedence of rights over collective goods, so that arguments about goals, as Dworkin shows, can only 'trump' claims based on individual rights if these goals can in turn be justified in the light of other rights that take precedence.[1] But that alone is not sufficient to support the communitarian view, which Taylor and Walzer share, that the system of rights is blind to claims to the protection of cultural forms of life and collective identities and is thus 'levelling' and in need of revision.

[...]

To the extent to which the shaping of citizens' political opinion and will is oriented to the idea of actualizing rights, it cannot, as the communitarians suggest, be equated with a process by which citizens reach agreement about their ethical-political self-understanding.[2] But the process of actualizing rights is indeed embedded in contexts that require such discourses as an important component of politics – discussions about a shared conception of the good and a desired form of life that is acknowledged to be authentic. In such discussions the participants clarify the way they want to understand themselves as citizens of a specific republic, as inhabitants of a specific region, as heirs to a specific culture, which traditions they want to perpetuate and which they want to discontinue, how they want to deal with their history, with one another, with nature, and so on. And of course the choice of an official language or a decision about the curriculum of public schools affects the nation's ethical self-understanding. Because ethical-political decisions are an unavoidable part of politics, and because their legal regulation expresses the collective identity of a nation of citizens, they can spark cultural battles in which disrespected minorities struggle against an insensitive majority culture. What sets off the battles is not the ethical neutrality of the legal order but rather the fact that every legal community and every democratic process for actualizing basic rights is inevitably permeated by ethics. We see evidence of this, for instance, in the institutional guarantees enjoyed by Christian churches in countries like Germany – despite freedom of religion – or in the recently challenged constitutional guarantee of status accorded the family in distinction to other marriage-like arrangements.

[...]

EQUAL RIGHTS TO COEXISTENCE VERSUS THE PRESERVATION OF SPECIES

Federalization is a possible solution only when members of different ethnic groups and cultural lifeworlds live in more or less separate geographical areas. In multicultural societies like the United States this is not the case. Nor will it be the case in countries like Germany, where the ethnic composition is changing under the pressure of global waves of migration. Even if

Quebec became culturally autonomous, it would find itself in the same situation, having merely traded an English majority culture for a French one. If a well-functioning public sphere with open communication structures that permit and promote discussions oriented to self-understanding can develop in such multicultural societies against the background of a liberal culture and on the basis of voluntary associations, then the democratic process of actualizing equal individual rights will also extend to guaranteeing different ethnic groups and their cultural forms of life equal rights to coexistence. This does not require special justification or an alternative principle. For from a normative point of view, the integrity of the individual legal person cannot be guaranteed without protecting the intersubjectively shared experiences and life contexts in which the person has been socialized and has formed his or her identity. The identity of the individual is interwoven with collective identities and can be stabilized only in a cultural network that cannot be appropriated as private property any more than the mother tongue itself can be. Hence the individual remains the bearer of 'rights to cultural membership', in Will Kymlicka's phrase.[3] But as the dialectic of legal and actual equality plays itself out, this gives rise to extensive guarantees of status, rights to self-administration, infrastructural benefits, subsidies, and so on. In arguing for their support, endangered indigenous cultures can advance special moral reasons arising from the history of a country that has been appropriated by the majority culture. Similar arguments in favor of 'reverse discrimination' can be advanced for the long-suppressed and disavowed cultures of former slaves.

These and similar obligations arise from legal claims and not from a general assessment of the value of the culture in question. Taylor's politics of recognition would not have much to stand on if it were dependent on the 'presumption of equal, value' of cultures and their contributions to world civilization. The right to equal respect, which everyone can demand in the life contexts in which his or her identity is formed as well as elsewhere, has nothing to do with the presumed excellence of his or her culture of origin, that is, with generally valued accomplishments.

[...]

The ecological perspective on species conservation cannot be transferred to cultures. Cultural heritages and the forms of life articulated in them normally reproduce themselves by convincing those whose personality structures they shape, that is, by motivating them to appropriate productively and continue the traditions. The constitutional state can make this hermeneutic achievement of the cultural reproduction of life-worlds possible, but it cannot guarantee it. For to guarantee survival would necessarily rob the members of the very freedom to say yes or no that is necessary if they are to appropriate and preserve their cultural heritage. When a culture has become reflexive, the only traditions and forms of life that can sustain themselves are those that bind their members while at the same time subjecting themselves to critical examination and leaving later generations the option of learning from other traditions or converting and setting out for other shores. This is true even of relatively closed sects like the Pennsylvania Amish.[4] Even if we considered it a meaningful goal to protect cultures as though they were endangered species, the conditions necessary for them to be able to reproduce successfully would be incompatible with the goal of 'maintain[ing] and cherish[ing] distinctness, not just now but forever' (Taylor).

[...]

In the modern era rigid forms of life succumb to entropy. Fundamentalist movements can be understood as an ironic attempt to give one's own lifeworld ultrastability by restorative means. The irony lies in the way traditionalism misunderstands itself. In fact, it emerges from the vortex of social modernization and it apes a substance that has already disintegrated. As a reaction to the overwhelming push for modernization, it is itself a thoroughly modern movement of renewal. [...]

As the Rushdie case reminded us, a fundamentalism that leads to a practice of intolerance is incompatible with the democratic constitutional state. Such a practice is based on religious or historico-philosophical interpretations of the world that claim exclusiveness for a privileged way of life. Such conceptions lack an awareness of the fallibility of their claims, as well as a respect for the 'burdens of reason' (Rawls). Of course, religious convictions and global interpretations of the world are not obliged to subscribe to the kind of fallibilism that currently accompanies hypothetical knowledge in the experimental sciences. But fundamentalist worldviews are dogmatic in that they leave no room for reflection on their relationship with the other worldviews with which they share the same universe of discourse and against whose competing validity claims they can advance their positions only on the basis of reasons. They leave no room for 'reasonable disagreement'.[5]

In contrast, the subjectivized 'gods and demons' of the modern world are distinguished by a reflexive attitude that does more than allow for a modus vivendi – something that can be legally enforced given religious freedom. In a spirit of tolerance à la Lessing, the non-fundamentalist worldviews that Rawls characterizes as 'not unreasonable comprehensive doctrines'[6] allow for a civilized debate among convictions, in which one party can recognize the other parties as co-combatants in the search for authentic truths without sacrificing its own claims to validity. In multicultural societies the national constitution can tolerate only forms of life articulated within the medium of such non-fundamentalist traditions, because coexistence with equal rights for these forms of life requires the mutual recognition of the different cultural memberships: all persons must also be recognized as members of ethical communities integrated around different conceptions of the good. Hence the ethical integration of groups and subcultures with their own collective idenies must be uncoupled from the abstract political integration that includes all citizens equally.

[...]

IMMIGRATION, CITIZENSHIP AND NATIONAL IDENTITY

[...]

The ethical substance of a political integration that unites all the citizens of the nation must remain 'neutral' with respect to the differences among the ethical-cultural communities within the nation, which are integrated around their own conceptions of the good. The uncoupling of these two levels of integration notwithstanding, a nation of citizens can sustain the institutions of freedom only by developing a certain measure of loyalty to their own state, a loyalty that cannot be legally enforced.

It is this ethical-political self-understanding on the part of the nation that is affected by immigration; for the influx of immigrants alters the composition of the population in ethical-cultural respects as well. Thus the question arises whether the desire for immigration runs up against limits in the right of a political community to maintain its political-cultural form of life intact. Assuming that the autonomously developed state order is indeed shaped by ethics, does the right to self-determination not include the right of a nation to affirm its identity vis-à-vis immigrants who could give a different cast to this historically developed political-cultural form of life?

From the perspective of the recipient society, the problem of immigration raises the question of legitimate conditions of entry. Ignoring the intermediate stages, we can focus on the act of naturalization, with which every state controls the expansion of the political community defined by the rights of citizenship. Under what conditions can the state deny citizenship to those who can advance their claim to naturalization? Aside from the usual provisos (as against criminals), the most relevant question in our context is in what respect a democratic constitutional state can demand that immigrants assimilate in order to maintain the integrity of its citizens' way of life. Philosophically, we can distinguish two levels of assimilation:

1. assent to the principles of the constitution within the scope of interpretation determined by the ethical-political self-understanding of the citizens and the political culture of the country; in other words, assimilation to the way in which the autonomy of the citizens is institutionalized in the recipient society and the way the 'public use of reason' is practiced there;

2. the further level of a willingness to become acculturated, that is, not only to conform externally but to become habituated to the way of life, the practices, and customs of the local culture. This means an assimilation that penetrates to the level of ethical-cultural integration and thereby has a deeper impact on the collective identity of the immigrants' culture of origin than the political socialization required under (1) above.

The results of the immigration policy practiced in the United States support a liberal interpretation that exemplifies the first of these alternatives. An example of the second is the Prussian policy on immigration from Poland under Bismarck, which despite variations was oriented primarily to Germanization.

A democratic constitutional state that is serious about uncoupling these two levels of integration can require of immigrants only the political socialization described in (1) above (and practically speaking can expect to see it only in the second generation). This enables it to preserve the identity of the political community, which nothing, including immigration, can be permitted to encroach upon, since that identity is founded on the constitutional principles anchored in the political culture and not on the basic ethical orientations of the cultural form of life predominant in that country. Accordingly, all that needs to be expected of immigrants is the willingness to enter into the political culture of their new homeland, without having to give up the cultural form of life of their origins by doing so. The right to democratic self-determination does indeed include the right of citizens to insist on the inclusive character of their own political culture; it safeguards the society from the danger of segmentation – from the exclusion of alien subcultures and from a separatist disintegration into unrelated subcultures.

NOTES

1. Ronald Dworkin, *Taking Rights Seriously* (Cambridge, Mass: Harvard University Press, 1977).
2. Ronald Beiner, *Political Judgment* (Chicago: University of Chicago Press, 1984), p. 138.
3. Will Kymlika, *Liberalism, Community and Culture* (Oxford: University Press, 1991).
4. Cf. the Supreme Court decision in *Wisconsin v. Yoder*, 406 U.S. 205 (1972).
5. Jürgen Habermas, *Justification and Application: Remarks on Discourse Ethics* (Cambridge, Mass.: MIT Press, 1993).
6. John Rawls, 'The Idea of an Overlapping Consensus', *Oxford Journal of Legal Studies* 7 (1987): 1–25.

PART III
GOVERNING THE POLITICAL

INTRODUCTION

What counts as 'the political' in contemporary political theory is constantly under discussion and debate. In recent times, feminists have challenged the idea that the political is a public domain to be differentiated from the private realm of family life, sexual relations and gender identity. Similarly, a variety of different approaches with their lineage in structuralism, phenomenology and hermeneutics – such as poststructuralism, deconstruction, discourse theory and communitarianism – have questioned the traditional categories of political thought to the point where it seems that everything is, or at least could be, political. For all the undoubted insights of these approaches, and the many other approaches that have stretched our understanding of the political, one legacy of these interventions has been a relative neglect of political concepts that once formed the very core of political thought. In this section, the essays and selected readings on the state, the rule of law and civil society provide a contemporary perspective on how best to reinvigorate these core concepts without assuming a limited or truncated conception of 'the political'. What emerges are compelling accounts of how our understanding of political life is shaped and reshaped by the organisations, frameworks and associations that govern our collective lives. In this context, moreover, we are reminded of the centrality of power to political life and also of the vastly different ways in which the idea of power has been conceptualised. Indeed, while poststructuralist approaches to power were pivotal in expanding the realm of politics beyond the complex relations of state/law/civil society, as the essay in this section makes clear, they are also now at the forefront of attempts to provide open and inclusive, yet nonetheless definitive, accounts of what we mean by 'the political'. As such, the importance of power to our grasp of 'the political' cannot be underestimated: on the one hand, it compels us to think beyond our normal categories of politics; on the other hand, it reminds us that thinking through the intricate workings of power in social and political life inevitably takes us back to questions regarding the nature of the state, the rule of law and civil society. In this way, the essays and selected readings in this section serve to create a debate about the constitution of 'the political' that can be viewed as pivotal to the essays in all the other sections. Of particular interest, however, may be the overlaps to be found between the discussions of the state and those of the nation and the body politic; the rule of law and the essays in Part I; civil society and the debates surrounding globalisation; power and the essays and readings on discourse and difference. From these fruitful connections the whole text will open up and the question of how we ought to conceive of the governance of our political lives will be put centre stage again.

I

THE STATE

John McGovern

Introduction

Charles Tilly has suggested that we 'define states as coercion-wielding organizations that are distinct from households and kinship groups and exercise clear priority in some respects over all other organizations within substantial territories'. This definition includes 'city-states, empires, theocracies, and many other forms of government' (Tilly 1992: 1). What is distinctive about the *modern* state, however, in contrast to the other types which Tilly mentions, is its separation from society as a differentiated, specialized form of rule, an 'office' distinct, both from those who happen to occupy it, the rulers, and from those over whom rule is exercised, the ruled. Autonomy, in that sense, should be regarded as the ideal towards which some of those forms of public authority which we call 'states' have striven. Not all 'states' have achieved it. There have been states which have not attempted to embody this ideal. Wherever communism has been the prevalent political ideology, the state has not been 'modern', because the communist state does not so much rule an independently existing social sphere as absorb 'civil society' (Keane 1988: 2–3). The reverse is the case for nations, most notably Britain and America, in which the effect of a certain tradition of liberalism has been to strengthen the claims of 'society' to such an extent as to diminish the power of the state to act autonomously as a distinct 'person' (Dyson 1980: 20 n. 4, 51–2).

Even in those states where the attempt to establish state autonomy has been most successful, the achievement has never been complete. It was clear to Gottfried Leibniz in the 1670s that the states then emerging throughout

Europe were engaged in a political and military struggle to establish themselves in place of a multiplicity of traditional authorities and jurisdictions, and that not even France, the most 'statist' of all the early modern European polities, possessed a state as unified, centralized and sovereign as the ideal proposed (Leibniz 1988: 111–21). A matter of great contemporary concern is the problem of 'failed states', characterized by civil war, foreign occupation, economic instability and political disorder. These are nations in which the state barely exists or has failed to achieve autonomy. The threat posed to the autonomy of the contemporary liberal-democratic state by economic globalisation is a commonplace of current political journalism, but the fact that the autonomy of the liberal-democratic state is inherently incomplete should not be overlooked. The reason for this is that the authority of the liberal-democratic state depends on its being able to satisfy simultaneously two apparently incommensurable requirements. It must permit different interest groups to form and it must mediate between them when, inevitably, their differences lead to conflict.

Though there are late modern liberals who suggest that something called 'civil society' spontaneously generates 'the conditions of liberty' (Gellner 1996: 80), Pierre Bourdieu was right to stress that the state is constantly engaged in a struggle to impose its authority, the idea of the state, upon society (Bourdieu and Wacquant 1992: 111–13). The idea of the modern state arose in response to certain historical conditions (Hall 1985, ch. 5). European states began to emerge during the medieval period from within societies which shared a common Catholic culture but which were otherwise highly pluralistic and in which political power was decentralised. An already existing 'civil society' in which a market economy was developing required government, however, to provide military protection and to promote trade. A condition for the emergence of modern European states was the presence of pre-existent autonomous societies. The Renaissance and the Reformation gave cultural expression to the spirit of self-assertion and moral individualism which such societies fostered. The type of state which was conditioned by and, in turn, conditioned these autonomous, pluralistic and individualistic societies was one characterised by 'despotic weakness' (it could not rule arbitrarily) but 'infrastructural strength' (it penetrated 'civil society' by means of fiscal management, territorial administration and judicial regimentation) (Mann 1986). A relationship was established between state and society, at once antagonistic and mutually beneficial, which has proved to be remarkably persistent. If modern states continue to struggle to maintain their authority in the face of resistance from society, it is the underlying cause of this resistance, the presence of a pluralistic 'civil society', which called into being the concept of the modern state in the first place.

No doubt differences in attitudes towards the state are partly determined by national traditions. The tradition of French statism has no exact equivalent in anglophone nations, and the often virulent reaction against it is an equally distinctive feature of French intellectual life. Nevertheless, when Bourdieu suggested that we should look for the state, not simply 'out there', as a set of observable institutions, but also, more importantly, within us, as well as stressing the extent to which the state penetrates 'society', he made clear the essentially ideal nature of the state wherever it appears (Bourdieu 1996: xviii). It is an ambivalent ideal. Perhaps only a consistent anarchist, if there is such a thing, looks forward to the abolition of the state. Generally, the 'actually existing' state is seen as a qualified good or a necessary evil. Though Bourdieu often described the state as a force engaged in a struggle to dominate society, he also recognised that society required its protection (Bourdieu 1998: 1–8). Like many liberals, he regarded criticizing existing states as almost a duty, but such criticism, short of anarchism, is only intelligible in the light of belief in the possibility that the ideal of the state might be more adequately embodied. For most contemporary socialists, there *is* a 'good state', often reckoned as one more 'universal' than existing states in two senses, being both internationalist or 'cosmopolitan' and more directly democratic (Bourdieu 1998: 9, 60–9; Held 1995a).

The state is criticised by liberals, socialists, and 'the right', both 'far' and 'new', and though there are different visions of what would count as the good state, the occasion for such criticism is the same. It is that the authority of the state is not, or is not adequately, grounded in an independent principle. What criticism of the state reveals is that, according to the ideal embodied within actually existing states, the state is the source of its own authority. As we shall see, on the account given by the thinker whom many regard as the author of the concept of the modern state, Thomas Hobbes, this is as it should be, because there is no independent principle in terms of which the authority of the state could be justified. Bourdieu's sociology of politics may be seen as a rigorous exposure of the groundlessness of the authority claimed by modern states. But what, for a thinker like Bourdieu, is the principle which would justify the state? Since the eighteenth century, two principles, above all, have been widely considered to give independent grounds for the authority of the state, *consent* and *reason*. These principles are, so to speak, society's response to the self-justifying authority of the state. However, as we shall see, it is not clear that the ideal of the state can be accounted for in these terms.

Despite the fact that now, as ever, empirical political reality resists the complete imposition upon it of the idea of the state, it remains the case that there are polities, 'modern states', whose self-interpretation, and, to that extent, government, is premised on the value of an autonomous political sphere. The modern state is not to be defined simply by pointing towards the existence of visible institutions, such as parliaments, executives, bureaucracies, militaries, police forces and judiciaries. It must be seen as the concept which provides a way of understanding such institutions, an idea which, to the extent that it has been embodied, has been responsible for giving form to such institutions. Quentin Skinner has emphasized that 'autonomy' has been the distinctive feature of the modern concept of the state ever since it emerged during the Renaissance. What first arose then was the ideal of a 'distinct form of "civil" or "political" authority which is wholly autonomous, which exists to regulate the public affairs of an independent community, and which brooks no rivals as a source of coercive power within its own *civitas* or *respublica*' (Skinner 1989: 107).

In this chapter I want to look at some of the ways in which the concept of the modern state has been understood since the early modern period, and, in particular, at some of the ways in which it has been understood in relation to democracy. The belief that the state should be democratic has become virtually an article of faith. However, even socialists now recognise that to substitute participatory, direct democracy for representative government in a modern society is neither possible nor desirable (Held 1996: 153–4, 313; Keane 1989: xi). The functions which are required for the governance of a modern society are, evidently, compatible with 'representative democracy', but the question of how genuinely democratic 'representative democracy' is remains an open one. It might be that, to the extent that modern states are states, their relation to democracy is a necessarily uneasy one, and that, whilst there may be a democratic society, the idea of a democratic state is at odds with the very concept of the state. 'Liberal democracy' co-exists with and, indeed, depends upon the state without, it would seem, being able adequately to justify this relationship. Michel Foucault took the view that liberalism was not so much 'a coherent doctrine' as 'a form of critical reflection on governmental practice' (Foucault 1997: 77). Stephen Holmes, pointing to the fact that 'liberal states have, from the very beginning, proved breathtakingly powerful', has disputed the view that liberalism should be identified with 'a crusade to restrict state power' (Holmes 1995: 18). Holmes is surely right to draw attention to the enormous power enjoyed by the 'liberal-democratic' state. However, the political ideology which has provided for liberal-democratic states a certain self-understanding, and the libertarian 'critical reflection' to which Foucault refers, are really very different. The liberties prized by the former are limited by the political, military, economic and cultural imperatives which certain states obey. They are simply the privileges enjoyed by some of the inhabitants of a handful of nations. The 'critique' of the state recommended by authors such as Foucault and Bourdieu is directed towards a universal 'emancipation' from the existing state.

THE STATE AND AUTONOMY

A feature of late medieval Italian political literature which was to be especially important for the development of the concept of the state was the way in which it elaborated a usage of the term *stato* which distinguished between a current regime and the institutions of government which exist independently of any particular ruler (Skinner 1989: 101). Instead of the 'state' being thought of as the private possession of a ruler, the classical republicans spoke of the 'state' as an independent structure of laws and institutions which rulers are trusted to administer on behalf of the community. It is within this classical republican tradition that 'we first encounter the familiar understanding of the state as a monopolist of legitimate force' (Skinner 1989: 107). However, the current revival of interest in republicanism evident in the writings of historians like Skinner should not blind us to the part played by Christian theology in the development of the modern concept of the state. There is no equivalent in ancient Greek or classical Latin for the term 'state' as it is used in modern political discourse. *Respublica* referred to the concrete political community whereas a 'state' is not the community as a whole but, rather, a distinct structure of relations within a community which provides for their governance. This autonomy of 'the political' only became possible when people came to understand themselves as being represented in terms other than those provided for them by the concrete political community (O'Donovan 1996: 231–2).

St Augustine's doctrine of the 'two cities', by counter-posing the kingdom of God to the earthly city, gave powerful and lasting expression to just this possibility. According to Augustinian political theology, Christians are subject to the power of the state. It is the supreme earthly authority and, as such, enjoys autonomous political power. However, as an earthly authority, it too is subject to a higher, divine authority. The supreme power over worldly affairs granted to the state is conceived of by Augustine as primarily judicial in nature. The principal function of the state is to order social relations by upholding 'the rule of law'. In Augustine's view, the state's power to coerce and to represent society must be restricted to the minimum necessary for it to order society. In this Christian understanding there is the essence of the idea of a 'minimal' and 'constitutional' state, a state the power of which is limited, not because there are limits inherent in the nature of political authority as such, but because secular authority is conceived of as a concession gifted to rulers by God. The state is autonomous with respect to rulers and ruled but it is not freed from divine authority. Indeed, the condition for its worldly autonomy is that it remains subject to the rule of the Creator. It was when it came to be seen as subject to permissive divine authority that the state came to be to understood, not as identical with the community as a whole, but as a differentiated, organisational structure arising within, whilst also ruling, the community. This concern to establish an authentic but limited political sphere lay behind Augustine's repudiation of the notion of an *imperium Christianum*. Any identification of the City of God with an earthly city would lead to the idolatrous sacralisation of merely human arrangements (Markus, 1988).

It is particularly important to recognise the formative influence exercised by Christianity over the development of the modern concept of the state because it helps us to understand a problem which arose as soon as the concept had been articulated. Upon what does the authority of the state rest? A determination, common to early modern theorists of the sovereign state, to rule out the notion that the state's authority derived from 'the people' led Hobbes, most notably, to conclude that the state derived its authority from no source other than itself. In the heated religious atmosphere of Hobbes's time, 'the people' were understood to be *God's people*. Perhaps the single most powerful motive behind Hobbes's political theory was his resolve to undermine the claims of such sacralised politics. Nevertheless, whilst it is true that it is difficult to see how the power of the state to coerce subjects or citizens may be accounted for as a consequence of either consent or consensus, it is equally hard to accept that there is no independent ground whatsoever for political authority. Christianity made it possible for Hobbes and the other early modern theorists of state sovereignty to regard the state as independent of the concrete political community. However, the condition for that independence of the 'political' was that the authority of the state was justified and limited, because it had been permitted, by a radically independent, divine authority. When its dependence upon divine authority was no longer acknowledged, and Hobbes was already well on the way towards such a recognition, the problem of the 'secular' state's legitimacy was to become an acute one. It remains a problem, not only in the 'west', where popular cynicism prevails, but also in Islamic nations, where the question of the authority of the state takes a more intense form. The existence of a separate and autonomous political sphere would seem to be incompatible with Islamic tradition, according to which government is understood to be essentially lacking in authority, and either to be tolerated without being seen as legitimate, or abolished and theocracy established in its place (Ruthven 2000: 171–3).

THE STATE AS 'PERSON'

The modern idea of the state discloses an organisational structure which is 'distinct' in two senses. Its authority is separate, not merely from the power which happens to be enjoyed by rulers who are its transitory instruments, but also from the community over which it rules. The tradition of classical republicanism enjoined a separation of the authority of the state from the privilege to administer its power granted to a ruler but it did not regard the state as autonomous of the community. On the contrary, it was just in order to place 'the people' in the position of sovereign that the state was understood to be independent of rulers. Since the publication of John Pocock's influential reinterpretation of classical republicanism (Pocock 1975), the attempt to revive that tradition is a noteworthy feature of contemporary anglophone political theory (Brennan and Pettit 2003; Honohan 2002; Maynor 2003; Pettit 1997; Viroli 2002).

It was, however, 'statist' thinkers such as Jean Bodin, Francisco de Suarez, Samuel Pufendorf and Hobbes who, recognising the value of strong, unified government, provided a description of the state as an entity distinct not only from rulers, but also from 'society', the ruled. Though the tradition which commenced with these thinkers eventually came to view the state as secular, the influence of Augustinian Christianity is evident in its insistence that the state must be independent of 'society'. Secularised Augustinian moral theology also lies behind the profoundly pessimistic view of the human condition which, as Carl Schmitt observed, is a common feature of this tradition (Schmitt, 1996: 64–5). These men were responsible for articulating what may be called 'the modern state concept', according to which the state was to be conceived of as an autonomous being with a life of its own, as a *person*. Thus, Hobbes, who is often regarded as the most systematic expositor, if not the inventor, of the modern state concept (Van Creveld 1999: 178–80), referred to the sovereign, in whom the power of the state was embodied, as 'an artificial person' (Hobbes 1968: 218). Some contemporary anglophone philosophers influenced by the republican tradition have rediscovered the idea that the state may be described as a 'person'. Robert Goodin, for instance, refers to it as a 'moral agent' since, like the individual person who is normally held to be the paradigm of moral agency, it too embodies purposefulness and deliberation, even though, as Alan Hamlin and Philip Pettit observe, 'the property of being a state would not appear to be definable in individualistic terms' (Goodin 1989: 129; Hamlin and Pettit 1989: 6). To view the state as possessing 'personality' in some sense seems to be entailed by the concept of it as something neither identified with the will of the ruler nor with the sectional interests of the population but as acting independently of both. However, it is not clear that characterising the 'personality' of the state as *moral* is consistent with this concept.

Hobbes was careful to attribute to the 'person' of the state not a 'moral' but a *legal* character. In *Leviathan*, he claimed that a 'commonwealth' (the term used to translate *respublica*) is constituted when a 'multitude' of men transfer their natural right of self-government to 'one Man' or to 'one Assembly' who will 'reduce all their Wills...unto one Will'. This, Hobbes stated, amounts to saying that the 'multitude' undertakes 'to appoint one man, or Assembly of men, to beare their Person' (1968: 227). The notion of 'personality' implied in this claim was one which Hobbes had derived from Roman Law, where the term *persona* referred to a set of rights or to the bearer of those rights, whether an individual or a thing (Green 1927: 61). Because the concept of a 'right' presupposes the existence of a bearer of that right, 'person' may be used to refer to either. Hence, Hobbes called the commonwealth created by the social contract a 'person', referring to the transferred natural rights of the multitude, and he also says of the sovereign who now 'bears' that 'person', because he now bears those rights, that he or it too is 'one person' (1968: 220). This legal conception of the person which is 'the essence of the Commonwealth' (Hobbes 1968: 228) permitted Hobbes to elaborate a concept of the state which was intended to undermine a rival theory, according to which the state is not a 'person' at all but must withdraw before the agency of another 'person', 'the people'.

It should also be distinguished from another different view of the 'personality' of the state, according to which that is construed as a 'moral' character. Moral persons are responsible for the actions which they perform because those actions are 'their own'. To understand the state as a moral person is to ascribe ownership of the actions performed in the name of the state by office-holders to the state regarded as an independently existing agent. This implies that the state is not, as Hobbes believed, an 'artificial' person, but a *real* or, as he called it, 'natural' one (Hobbes 1968, ch. xvi). There is a long tradition in continental Europe of understanding the concept of the state as disclosing a 'real' moral person, and this understanding has sustained political systems in which a higher degree of authority has been ascribed to the state than government in 'stateless societies' such as Britain and America has ever enjoyed (Dyson 1980: 12–15). French *dirigisme* is a notable instance of the effects of this tradition. However, whereas the dilemma facing 'stateless' modern societies is that the state is not sufficiently strong in relation to society, continental *étatisme* tends towards the domination of society by the state. It might be argued that the tradition of conceiving of the state as a moral person is ultimately inconsistent with an understanding of it as existing independently of both rulers and ruled, to the extent that the state tends to be identified with the realm of officialdom and, as Bourdieu has called it, a new 'nobility' emerges, 'the state nobility' (Bourdieu 1996).

THE STATE AND 'THE PEOPLE'

Hobbes carefully designed his concept of the state in such a way as to rule out the notion that 'the people' are autonomous *vis-à-vis* the sovereign or, in other words, that what we would now call 'society' exists, as a single entity, independently of its politically organised form, the state. He did this in order to make the strongest possible case against the claim that the limits to the power of the state should be decided by 'the people', since if 'the people' does not exist in the relevant sense then any claim to popular sovereignty is ruled out, not merely on political grounds, but philosophically. As we have seen, this notion was central to the tradition of classical republicanism. In different, less urbane, often sectarian, forms, it had also been put to polemical use in Hobbes's time during the English Civil War, by those who claimed that 'the people' enjoyed a natural right to limit the power of the sovereign. Indeed, in *Behemoth*, Hobbes proposed that it was just the mischevious manipulation of the notion of 'the people' , especially the belief that 'society' has the right to judge which laws are just and that the dictates of private conscience justify resistance to civil authority, that had caused the English Civil War (Hobbes 1990). For the same reasons, in the historically comparable circumstances of Weimar Germany, Schmitt followed Hobbes in re-asserting the primacy of the state as 'the ultimate authority' (Schmitt 1996: 20). What both Hobbes and, just as contentiously, Schmitt argued was that the ideal of state autonomy is a necessary condition for producing the political good, social order, which causes us to value the state in the first place. But, for statists like Hobbes and Schmitt, because democracy, certainly in its more 'direct' forms, threatens social order, to view the state as autonomous, as we must if we truly value the good of social order which only it can provide, is to view it as autonomous of 'the people'.

In Hobbes's 'state of nature', there is no sense in speaking of 'the people'. What exists before the constitution of the state is, rather, a 'multitude', a plurality of particular, individual and potentially conflicting wills (Hobbes 1968: 220). The singularity of will attributed to 'the people' by those who subscribe to the doctrine of popular sovereignty could become a feature of the 'multitude' only in 'civil society', that is, in the state. For Hobbes, 'society' is constituted by the state. Hobbes's account of the relationship between state and society gives theoretical expression to the real historical conditions under which the modern European state emerged, as an autonomous organisational structure set over against a plurality of autonomous social groups and capable of ordering them only by penetrating them, by presenting itself within the realm of social relations as a special type of social relation, distinct from the others in being directed towards uniting and ordering them. The unity of the multitude – 'the essence of the Commonwealth' – resides in nothing other than the fact that they have, as Michael Oakeshott put it, 'not a common will (for there can be no such thing), but a common object of will' (1946: lvi). Hobbes reveals the essentially non-democratic character of the ideally autonomous modern state by showing how it must introduce itself as 'a common object of will' in the place of 'a common will'.

Hobbes's denial of the existence of a common will underlies Oakeshott's own conception of the state as 'civil association', which he distinguishes from 'enterprise association'. Civil association refers to relationships based not on needs, wants or purposes, but on generally acknowledged rules. The political order sustaining such non-instrumental rules, which, as a body, compose the law, is the 'civil state', in which the presence of the rule of law permits *individuals* to determine for themselves which course of action they will pursue, provided only that it is consistent with the law. An enterprise state, in contrast, imposes a common substantive purpose upon individuals (Oakeshott 1975, part III). The *dirigiste* state dedicated to economic planning and the provision of universal welfare entitlements is an instance of Oakeshott's 'enterprise state'. The understanding of the modern state as at once authoritarian and minimal, however, should be seen as Hobbes's contribution to political thought, according to Oakeshott. Though not a liberal,

Oakeshott once remarked, Hobbes 'had in him more of the philosophy of liberalism than most of its professed defenders' (Oakeshott 1946: lxvii).

THE STATE AND MARXISM

The belief that something variously described as 'the people', 'society', 'the nation', 'the community' or even 'humanity' exists independently of politically organised society has not lost its power to inspire, and today, when there are demands to limit the powers of the state in the name of 'democracy', almost invariably the reason given is that the rights of the allegedly sovereign 'people' are said to have been impaired. There are many 'society-centred' conceptions of the state present within contemporary political science, amongst which Marxism is particularly prominent (Dunleavy and O'Leary 1987, ch. 5; Schwarzmantel 1994, ch. 5). Although there is a bewildering variety of Marxist and neo-Marxist theories of the state (Jessop 1990), all have in common the presupposition that behind the state lies something *social*, whether the 'bourgeois class' or some or other structural feature of the capitalist economic system. Because of the implausibility of the view taken by Karl Marx and Friedrich Engels in *The Communist Manifesto*, that the state is 'but a committee for managing the common affairs of the whole bourgeoisie', which, because of its merely epiphenomenal nature, was bound to 'wither away' (Marx 1977: 223), Marxists such as Nicos Poulantzas have been compelled to find within Marx's writings evidence of a theory of the 'relative' autonomy of the state (Poulantzas 1978: 134–9).

Nevertheless, the word 'relative' has been sorely overworked by Marxist theoreticians in order to square a circle. It is difficult to see how any genuine Marxist can avoid assigning priority, both 'in theory' and 'in practice', to the 'social' over the 'political'. When Marxists claim that the state is 'relatively' autonomous, that amounts to the claim that it is *apparently* independent of socio-economic forces, whilst the 'reality' is that it is determined by or derives from them (Hall 1986: 6–11; Mann 1986: 109–10). The modern state is always the 'capitalist state' for the Marxist. It is debatable, then, whether Marxism can produce a theory of the modern *state* at all, since it commences from an *a priori* denial of the ideal of political autonomy which is the essence of the modern state concept (Bobbio 1987, ch. 2). The Marxist concept of 'society' has the inherently polemical, anti-statist purpose of justifying 'direct' democracy based on the sovereignty of 'the people' (Held 1996, ch. 4).

The opinion that, on the contrary, the Marxist doctrine of the state is itself 'statist' has been a commonly held one ever since the nineteenth-century anarchists first expressed it (Marshall 1993: 24–8). However, the communist dictatorships inspired by Marxist dogma were not 'modern' states and, therefore, not 'statist' in the sense of that term used here. Marx himself dreamed of a society freed from the state, which he believed to be an essentially illegitimate instrument of oppression. When Vladimir Lenin and others seized the opportunity to translate this vision into reality, their not obviously unfaithful interpretation of Marx's proposal, that a temporary 'dictatorship of the proletariat' would be necessary to force freedom upon 'the people', entailed the creation of states capable of exercising seemingly limitless coercive power. The Marxist state attempted to incorporate, or eliminate, 'society' on behalf of 'the people'. 'The people' were regarded as a moral agent or 'person' furnished with a single will. If, as a result of the 'false consciousness' from which they suffer, individual men and women failed to recognise this, the Marxist state would recognise it for them. The state, in turn, was identified with the will of a ruling elite recruited from the Communist Party. It is not only Marxists who would use the state as a means towards the 'emancipation' of 'the people'. Fascism identifies state, party and 'the people'. Liberal imperialists, from the nineteenth century until the present day, have also seized upon the state as an instrument by means of which populations may be coerced in the name of 'freedom', 'democracy', 'civilisation' or, as Schmitt observed, the 'cosmopolitan' ideal of 'humanity' (Schmitt 1996: 54). Those who resist 'the will of the people' may be regarded as enemies of humanity, whether they are the bourgeoisie, 'alien' ethnic groups or 'terrorists'. As Hobbes knew, 'the people' is an essentially religious symbol, and the attempt to use it as an independent principle, by means of which actually existing states may be judged, and the good state justified, is to institute a limitless, because sacred, authority.

THE STATE AND PLURALISM

In normative political terms, because of its association with liberalism, contemporary pluralist theory of the state would appear to be opposed to Marxism. However, it is no less 'society centred'. According to the 'classical' pluralist account which dominated American political science during the 1950s and 1960s (Dahl 1956, 1971; Lindblom 1965), the modern state is identified with the 'liberal-democratic' state which, in turn, is conceived of as a 'polyarchy' or political system in which power is essentially fragmented. In a 'polyarchy', the principal agents in political life are not states but neither are they individuals nor social classes. Rather, such pluralists claim that a variety of more or less coherent groups and associations compete with one another in applying 'pressure' to government in order to secure their private interests. The role of the state, on this account, is to 'process' demands laid upon it by these 'social' agents in such a way as to create equilibrium by delivering policies which coincide with the prevalent public consensus. On this view, the state is conceived of as independent of society, in that its role is to act as a neutral power-broker, but it is not understood in the terms of autonomy proposed by the modern state concept. Because power is viewed as dispersed throughout society, no single agent, including the state, is regarded as being in a position to dominate 'the political process'. For this reason, it has been said that such pluralism does not compose a theory of the state but, rather, a theory of *society* (Dunleavy and O'Leary 1987: 41–2). Similarly, Schmitt claimed that liberalism generally was incapable of generating a properly *political* theory (1996: 61). Like Marxism, and despite the positivist claim that this is a purely 'empirical' theory, pluralism is premised on an *a priori* rejection of the ideal of the modern state and simply assumes, in advance, that the 'social' is prior to the 'political'.

It is no accident that contemporary pluralist political theory originated in America, the most 'stateless' of all modern societies, where John Locke's individualistic form of liberalism 'takes on a natural, "matter-of-fact" quality as a common code or way of life' (Dyson 1980: 20). 'Classical' American pluralism, even amongst its original authors, gave way to 'neo-pluralism' during the 1970s, when the growth of bureaucracy and widespread state intervention forced upon American political scientists a recognition of state autonomy. However, the understanding of such governmental activity as evidence of a 'distorted liberal state' (Nordlinger 1981: 157) indicates that neo-pluralism remains normatively, if less emprically, 'society centred'. In the 'state debate' which took place within sociology during the 1980s, the battleline was drawn between such 'society-centred' approaches and new 'state-centred' empirical theories which were understood to emphasize state autonomy (Evans *et al.* 1985). But it is worth noting that the author who sparked the debate, Theda Skocpol, regards her work as a fusion of the two approaches (Skocpol 1979: 13–14, 304 n. 4). This is typical of other contemporary sociological theorists of the state (Hall 1986: 10; Mann 1986: 111). In general, anglophone social science tends to reflect its *provenance*. Its exponents are inclined to account for the state in terms of 'society' not simply for scientific reasons but also because their liberal political culture has always contained strongly anti-statist elements.

THE AUTHORITY OF THE STATE

Hobbes's scepticism entailed the belief that the only wills that exist are individual wills. There is no scope for the concept of a 'common' or, in Jean-Jacques Rousseau's formulation, 'general' will in Hobbes's thought. The object at which all individual wills must aim, of course, is that there should be a sovereign power, and that aim is only achieved, if it is achieved, by being given effect in the single will of the sovereign, who, provided with the authority to act on behalf of all individual wills, 'is enabled to form the wills of them all' (Hobbes 1968: 227). On this basis, Hobbes proposed a non-voluntarist theory of political obligation. The effect of the social contract is to render individuals 'a reall Unitie of them all, in one and the same Person' and, as Hobbes added, 'this is more than Consent' (Hobbes 1968: 227). After the passage into 'civil society', the question 'should I obey the state?' has no meaning because it presupposes that political obligation is something which I happen to have but might not. Just to ask the question seriously, and not in a merely speculative way, is to return oneself to the state of nature. It is precisely the purpose of 'civil society' to lay me under a general political obligation to the state. As Oakeshott has observed, a genuine authority just is 'something which we cannot go behind, something from which there is no possibility of appeal, something irresponsible, inescapable and complete in itself' (1993: 85).

On the non-voluntarist view of obligation, the authority of the state is not grounded in reason as an independent principle because, if the grounds for my obeying the law are that I have a reason to do so, then, on just the same grounds, I may permissibly disobey the law, in which case the state is not the public authority it must be if it is to stand apart from both rulers and ruled, furnished with the power to govern both. This does not mean that acknowledging the state as the supreme authority is not reasonable. It was Hobbes's argument that a reasonable individual will conclude that a general political obligation is necessary and, ultimately, the grounds for vesting authority in the state for Hobbes, as Oakeshott has said, 'resides solely in the completeness of the satisfaction which the state affords to the needs of concrete persons' (1993: 87). For Hobbes, as for Oakeshott, there is no, or no knowable, independent source for the authority of the state. The state, Hobbes's 'Leviathan', is a 'Mortall God' (Hobbes 1968: 227).

It hardly needs to be said that Hobbes's account of the authority of the state is at odds with the self-image of contemporary liberal democracies. The popular justification for political authority in such states is invariably based on a voluntarist theory according to which, as Locke put it in the *Second Treatise*, 'men being . . . by nature all free, equal, and independent, no one can be put out of this estate, and subjected to the political power of another, without his own consent' (1963: 374). However, the requirement that all individuals must express actual consent to each and every law for the state to be regarded as possessing authority over them is absurd, since the point of political authority is to remove the unsatisfiable need for unanimity in making decisions about matters which affect all of the members of a society (Finnis 1979: 248). For this reason, voluntarist theories tend to regard consent as essential, not to political decision-making, but to the constitution of the authority which takes such decisions. However, this view also faces serious difficulties (Simmons 1979: 57–100). Essentially, if the reason why the state has authority over me is because I have consented to its foundation, since I may always withdraw my consent, the state never possessed authority over me in the first place, and nor would any other, differently constituted state to which I may prefer to give my consent instead. The concept of consent does not help us to explain why it is that we should put ourselves under binding obligations.

Nor does the concept of 'fairness'. John Rawls argued that, if I accept the benefits of a fair or equitable scheme, then I am obliged to keep to the terms of that scheme and not take a 'free ride' (Rawls 1964). But it is not at all clear that receiving certain benefits from the state *for that reason* puts me under binding obligations to it. For Rawls, coercive power may be used by a liberal-democratic state if and only if the exercise of that power coincides with the 'reasonable' views of its citizens (Rawls 1993b). This too is a voluntarist theory but one which is based not on consent, but on *consensus*. A 'reasonable' principle, on Rawls's account, is one which proposes fair terms of co-operation with other equally 'reasonable' persons. The most obvious of the difficulties with this account is that it requires the existence of a consensus about what will count as 'fair' and 'reasonable' which may not exist and, even where it does, must be less than universal (Waldron 1999). How will the question of what is to count as 'fair' and 'reasonable' be settled? More to the point, *who* will decide? There is no use in saying, like Rawls, that 'reasonable' persons should decide what will count as 'reasonable' policy unless there already exists a universal consensus about what counts as 'reasonable'. If there were a universal consensus about what counted as 'reasonable' in substantive, and not merely procedural, terms then it would make sense to say, with Rawls, that 'reasonable' persons should decide. But if that were the case there would be no need for political authority. It is precisely because there is no such consensus that an authority is required to make the decision. Such an authority must also be furnished with the power to enforce decisions. Schmitt defined the sovereign as the one who makes such a decision (Schmitt 1985: 5). This Hobbesian view of sovereignty is consistent with the belief that the essence of 'the political' lies in the distinction between 'friend' and 'enemy', that the authority of the state derives from its capacity to enforce such a distinction, and that, tragically, political authority is fully revealed by war (Schmitt 1996: 29–30). If there is no universal consensus about what passes as 'reasonable' in a given society, what counts as 'reasonable' will be the result of a decision which stipulates who are 'friends' of 'reason' and who are its 'enemies'. Late modern liberalism would appear to depend upon the presence of an authority the existence of which it is incapable of accounting for.

Ronald Dworkin may be seen as attempting to supply the account of authority which is missing from Rawls's work, when he argues that political association, like more intimate forms of association such as the family and friendship, 'is itself pregnant of obligation' (1986: 206). He also argues that political obligation is general, in the sense that, having accepted the authority of the state, an individual may not then permissibly choose which of its laws to obey (1986: 198). Dworkin's reason for positing a general political obligation is that we may impute to citizens certain beliefs which amount to the conviction that the state has authority over them when it is a certain type of 'community', one in which each member sees herself as bound by common principles to all of the others, a 'community of principle'. Given that there will be disagreement about which principles should be common and how such abstractions should be interpreted, Dworkin gives to judges the role of deciding. Belief in the authoritative principles is imputed to citizens by the judiciary (Dworkin 1986: 201). The judiciary is vested with the autonomous power of the state. Moreover, amongst the four basic conditions which Dworkin claims must be satisfied for a state to be a 'community of principle', two stipulate equal treatment of all citizens. It is not clear from Dworkin's account why a regard for the principle of equality rather than, say, the principle of liberty, must be regarded as constitutive of the authority of the state. A more democratic understanding of the state would lay greater stress on the legislative process, its inherent tendency towards disagreement about political principle and the liberty of 'the people' to change the law. It would appear that, when there is a *rapprochement* between the state and late modern liberalism, democracy is marginalised. When judicial proceedings settled the outcome of the US Presidential election in 2000, few regarded this as supporting the greatest democracy on earth.

Dworkin fails to give a coherent account of the authority of the state. There is a significant difference between his account and Hobbes's. As Leslie Green remarks, Hobbes explained the nature of political authority by showing that it endows those who rule 'with the power to create binding, content-independent reasons for others to act' (Green 1988: 42). That is, on Hobbes's analysis, it is 'not the nature of the action commanded but the *fact* that one is commanded to do it which is intended to be taken as a reason' (Green 1988: 41). The principles composing Dworkin's 'community of principle' are not 'content independent' in this sense, since they are considered binding *because* they embody a certain egalitarian content. Nor is it clear how Dworkin might account for a duty of obedience to the state if it is seen as a 'community' like the family or a group of friends. It might be said that I owe a duty of respect to friends but not *obedience*. As for the family, although a duty of obedience may be ascribed to children, the state lays adults under such a duty. The reason why Hobbes insisted that commands issued by political authority (it may be otherwise for different types of authority) must be content independent and binding was that this was the only analysis of political authority consistent with his vision of the state as a power standing apart from both rulers and ruled, capable of extracting obedience from both.

THE STATE AND REPRESENTATIVE GOVERNMENT

It is not too much to say that the modern state concept is essentially authoritarian. However, it is not clear that in being non-democratic the state which embodies this ideal therefore ceases to serve the interests of society. Schmitt's criticism of liberal democracy from a statist point of view is now attracting a great deal of attention amongst liberal and left-wing intellectuals (Agamben 1998; Dyzenhaus 1998; Kennedy 1985; Mouffe 1993; Piccone and Ulmen 1987). But Hobbes had already made it clear that, if there are limits to the power of the sovereign, they are not discovered in 'the will of the people'. This need not imply, however, that statism does not promote the interests of individual men and women. Hobbes's argument was that there is more to fear from 'the people' than from the state. 'The people' is a false construction which, once acted upon, can lead only to a 'war of all against all' because the reality misrecognised by the notion of 'the people' is the *multitude*, a plurality of intrinsically different, individual wills. The real effect of any politics which would remove sovereignty from the state and allocate it to 'the people' will be to restore the predatory state of nature, in which it will be precisely 'the common people' who suffer most as the powerful flourish: 'The power of the mighty hath no foundation but in the opinion and belief of the people' (Hobbes 1990: 16). It is the fact that the power of the state may be used to do justice, redistribute wealth, provide welfare, educate its citizens and prevent the civil strife which is characteristic of societies where state power is weak that has caused even neo-Marxists such as Claus Offe to acknowledge that, however 'relative', the autonomous power of the state may promote the common good (Offe 1996: 67).

In the last century, the anti-statist doctrine of popular sovereignty has been made use of by assorted ideologues, nationalists and religious fanatics, from the Bolshevik revolution to the anti-colonialist movements of the twentieth century, from the fascism of the 1930s to the numerous religious fundamentalisms which began to appear from the late 1940s. As Hobbes knew, it is not clear that people flourish under the politics of 'the people'. In so-called 'Western' nations, lip-service is paid to the sovereignty of 'the people' on all sides. But the politics of 'the West' is the politics of *representative* 'democracy', and the extent to which modern states, however well governed, have ever been truly democratic remains in doubt. James Madison, one of the first to articulate what he called 'the scheme of representation', stated candidly that representative government is both different from and superior to democracy (Madison et al. 1987: 126–8). Representative government he called 'republican', thus redefining a word which had, traditionally, populist implications. And what, above all, was to distinguish the American republic from any democracy was *'the total exclusion of the people in their collective capacity'* from any part in government. A non-democratic, federal state in which not the people but an *elite* governed was, Madison insisted, in the interests of the American people because it would provide for good government (Madison et al. 1987: 373).

Theorists of 'democratic elitism', like the Founding Fathers of the American republic, view the prospect of a genuinely democratic modern state, in which there is widespread participation and popular self-government, as illusory (Dunleavy and O'Leary 1987, ch. 4; Held 1996, ch. 5; Schwarzmantel 1994, ch. 4). Not only thinkers associated with fascism, such as Vilfredo Pareto, but liberals such as Max Weber and Joseph Schumpeter, and socialists such as Pierre Bourdieu, have cast doubt on the democratic pretensions of representative, liberal democracy. Various schemes, involving 'participation' (Pateman 1986), 'association' (Hirst 1994) and 'deliberation' (Fishkin 1991), have been put forward as substitutes for or supplements to representative democracy. Such 'models of democracy' might lead to a re-configuration of the pattern of state action, but it is difficult to see how they could be substituted for the autonomous activity of a supreme public authority. To 'participate' in or 'deliberate' about 'the decision-making process' is one thing: to decide is another. If citizens must be 'active' but choose to remain 'passive', are they to be compelled to 'participate'? If so, by whom? Whose 'deliberation', ultimately, counts in the balance? 'Association' is valued precisely because it is voluntary. It is not clear what is to be gained from viewing the essentially non-voluntary character of the relationship between state and citizens as if it was something other than it is. Supporters of 'associative democracy' accept that a state possessed of minimal power is necessary (Hirst 1994: 39) They tend to avoid noticing the painful fact that this power must extend to defining and policing the very terms of political association, where that is more than a merely marginal activity of no great public significance. A serious difficulty facing democratic theorists is that the state, which they claim is not or is insufficiently democratic, has pre-empted them in securing the good at which democracy also aims, the welfare of 'the people'. The criticism that the state does not provide enough welfare may be more or less justified, but it should not be used to conceal the fact that it is only because of the state that welfare is provided at all.

QUESTIONS FOR DISCUSSION

- Is the idea of the modern state compatible with democracy?
- In what sense are liberal-democratic states 'liberal'?
- What gives to the state its authority over citizens?
- Does the modern state have a future? If not, what, if anything, will replace it?

MICHAEL OAKESHOTT
EXTRACTS FROM *RATIONALISM*
IN POLITICS AND OTHER ESSAYS

TALKING POLITICS

[...]

Two

A modern state, as it emerged from a medieval realm, a patrimonial estate, a military protectorate, or a collection of colonial settlements, had three distinct features that it has never lost: an office of authority, an apparatus of power, and a mode of association. Each was in the making, not out of nothing but out of current beliefs and by the imposition of an allegedly more desirable shape upon what happened to be there. And this making and remaking has gone on ever since. In the history of some states there have been short pauses when one or another of these features seemed to acquire a temporarily acceptable shape, but nowhere has the shape of any of them become unquestionably fixed. Politics, the consideration of the shapes of these features in terms of their desirability, which one optimistic *Federalist* writer thought might be done once and for all, has been a continuous and unremitting engagement.

First, the office of authority. A state is an association of human beings constituted in the only manner in which such an association may be constituted; namely, in the acknowledgment of the authority of its rules and arrangements. And here, where these rules and arrangements are eligible to be changed and none is immune from amendment, this acknowledgment is

Michael Oakeshott (1991), *Rationalism in Politics and Other Essays*, rev. ed., Indianapolis: Liberty Fund.

the recognition of the authority of the office in whose custody they lie and of the procedures by which they may be changed and come to be prescribed. And by the acknowledgment of authority I do not mean approval of what is prescribed or the recognition of power to enforce prescriptions; I mean the recognition of an antecedent right to prescribe. This recognition is given in virtue of the shape or constitution of the office and not at all in virtue of the quality of its enactments or of their outcomes. When on the eve of the battle of Agincourt the soldier Bates said in conversation with his fellows, 'We know enough, if we know we are the King's subjects', he, briefly, acknowledged the authority of a King-shaped office of rule and recognized an obligation that perhaps he might not always adequately discharge but that he could not deny without declaring himself quit of the realm. We may think we are more sophisticated than this man of long ago, but we are not; we merely have different beliefs about what is authoritative and are more muddled about them.

[...]

Three

The second feature of a state is the apparatus of governing annexed to the office of rule. The consideration here is not authority but power.

The word 'power' in a political vocabulary stands, properly, for a human relationship. It means the ability to procure with certainty a wished-for response in the substantive conduct of another. And, since it is a relationship of human beings, and thus depends upon both the ability and the disposition of the respondent to make the wished-for response, this certainty can never be absolute and power can never be irresistible.

The considerations in terms of which the wished-for response is sought are the beliefs of the respondent about the consequences to himself of compliance or noncompliance to the demand. Thus, there is a relationship of power between one who makes a demand threatening the respondent with some harmful consequence if he does not comply, and a respondent who fears the threatened consequence both because of his aversion from it and because he believes there are the resources and the intention to implement the threat; or between one whose demand is joined with the promise of a satisfaction, and a respondent who is so far unwilling to forgo it that he regards it as an otherwise unobtainable necessity and who believes there are the resources and the intention to provide it. And since fear of injury or want elevated into need are the conditions of a power relationship, he who neither fears anything nor needs anything cannot be drawn into it.

Power, then, is categorically distinguished from authority. To have power does not, itself, endow a man or an office with authority; to be acknowledged to have authority does not, itself, endow a man or an office with power; and to recognize the power behind a demand, although it may be a good reason for complying with what is demanded, cannot be a reason for acknowledging an obligation to do so. Thus, a well-informed blackmailer and his fearful subject may be said to stand to one another in a transitory relationship of power.

In a modern state there is a carefully assembled, durable apparatus of power annexed to the office of authority. Its ingredients do not themselves entail a relationship of power. They are the procedures, inventions, devices, machines, and contrivances of all sorts which in modern times have greatly increased our information about what is going on and the certainty with which it may be controlled – which, for the most part, is at the disposal of anyone who can afford to use it for the satisfaction of his wants. They compose an apparatus of power when they are mobilized and deployed to exact, under threat of injury or disadvantage, specific performances from assignable agents.

But where, as in a modern state, such an apparatus is annexed to an office of authority, both its ingredients and its employment are subject to conditions. The only legitimate use of this apparatus is to enforce subscription to the rules and arrangements to which the associates are already obligated to subscribe; and the threatened disadvantageous consequences are penalties and not merely injuries. In short, what turns a person into a subject of this apparatus of power is not merely his fears or needs but his failure to fulfil an obligation. And in a state this apparatus is the only power that the associates may legally invoke for the protection of themselves or be required to submit to. What it adds to an association constituted in the acknowledgment of the authority of an office of rule is the assurance, or at least the expectation, that obligations cannot be breached with impunity.

[...]

Four

The third feature of a modern state is its character as an association of human beings. Here, the consideration is neither authority nor power but the relationship of the associates to one another and the engagements of the office of rule.

For two or more persons to compose an association is for them to be related to one another in terms of some recognized conditions of association that they may make for themselves or accept ready-made. These conditions may be displayed in somewhat vague customs of conduct, they may be spelled out in a rule-book, or they may be declared in an acknowledged common purpose. Thus, associates are never whole persons. They are *personae*; that is, persons in their relation to one another in terms of some specified conditions: brothers, partners in business, colleagues, playmates, comrades, friends, and so on. No one such relationship can exhaust the associational potentialities of any man; there can be no unconditional human relationship (that is, persons related but not by particular conditions); and there is no *ensemble* in which all relationships coalesce in the sense that our common use of the word 'society' suggests. If the word 'social' is used to denote a relationship, it must be some particular relationship distinguished from all others. To investigate the character of a state as an association is, then, to consider the mode of association it constitutes and the *persona* that these particular conditions of relationship impose upon the associates.

Now, the conditions that constitute a state as an association are the actual obligations prescribed by its office of authority. Consequently, an inquiry into the character of such an association is an inquiry, not into the beliefs that give authority to this office, but into the obligations it uses its authority to prescribe, and into the *persona* that these obligations actually impose upon those who are subject to its rule. In other words, it is an inquiry into the engagements of government; and, if the word 'citizen' may stand for the *persona* concerned, it is an investigation of this *persona* and not of any other that other relationships may generate.

This, then, is the third great theme of political reflection in regard to a modern state, distinguished and continuously explored since the sixteenth century. And since a modern state has never ceased to be recognized as an association in the making, attention has always been directed to the sort of association it might be made to become no less than to what it may be perceived to be. But the exploration of this theme has been sadly hindered by confusion.

First, it is usually conducted in terms of the vocabularies of authority or of power; but in this connection these words are meaningless. To say, for example, that the conditions of association are or should be 'democratic' is absurd. The word 'democracy' denotes, not the engagements of a government, but a belief in which an office of rule is recognized to have authority; there are no 'democratic' rules of relationships. And the obligations in terms of which 'citizens' are associated cannot be characterized by the power to enforce them. Secondly, this inquiry has been almost obliterated by drivel about something called 'society', a fanciful total of unspecified relationships which only a simpleton would think of identifying with a state.

Nevertheless, over the years two tolerably distinct (and many very indistinct) doctrines have emerged about the character of a state as an association of human beings – both, of course, concerned not only with what a state may be perceived to be but also with what it might be made to become.

In the first of these doctrines a state is presented to us as an association of human beings related to one another in terms of their joint pursuit of some recognized substantive purpose. The associates are obligated to engage in this common enterprise, the custodian of which is the office of authority. What is here attributed to a state, or is said to be what a state may or should be made to become, is a well-known mode of association: that in which a Many becomes One in virtue of a common substantive engagement. Let me briefly sketch its general character before considering it in relation to a state.

The central feature is the uniting purpose in terms of which the associates are related to one another. This purpose must be known to the associates and it must be a substantive condition of things to be procured or an interest in such a condition of things to be promoted. But, since pursuing such a purpose necessarily means responding to emergent situations by choosing to do *this* rather than *that* in the hope of procuring a wished-for outcome favourable to the achievement of the purpose, those who are associated in this manner are related to one another not only in recognizing their joint purpose but in making such choices (or acknowledging them as their own choices) and in performing such actions. It is association in terms of substantive conduct instrumental to the purpose concerned. If such an association has rules for the conduct of the associates, then these also are instrumental rules whose desirability lies in their propensity to promote, or at least not to hinder, the pursuit of the purpose. The government of such an association is a managerial engagement and the *persona* it imposes upon the associates is that of servants of the purpose.

This is a familiar mode of association; it is hardly surprising that a state should have invoked this understanding of itself and that inquiry concerned with a state as an association should have been directed to the specification of the purpose of interest attributable to it.

[...]

In the other, somewhat older, doctrine the mode of association attributed to a state is relationship in terms of non-instrumental rules of conduct, called 'the law'. And by calling these rules 'non-instrumental' I mean that they are not rules that specify a practice or routine purporting to promote the achievement of a substantive purpose. They are more like (although they are not exactly like) the rules of a game which are directions, not about how to win but about how to play, or the rules of public debate, which do not tell a speaker what to say and are wholly indifferent to any particular conclusion. These non-instrumental rules specify and prescribe, not choices to be made or actions to be performed, but conditions to be subscribed to in choosing and acting. Like all other rules they exist in advance of conduct, but they are incapable of initiating action or utterance. Association here is not in terms of the projected or the actual outcome of what is done, but in terms of formal conditions to be subscribed to in doing. If the word 'civility', or indeed the word 'justice', were taken to stand for the general character of these conditions of conduct, then a state thus understood would be recognized as a 'civil association' or association in terms of 'just' conduct. And since the injunction to act 'civilly' or 'justly' is not an injunction to perform any substantive action whatever, a state, in this understanding of it, is a moral and not a purposive association.

Persons thus associated may be otherwise assumed to be agents seeking the satisfaction of their various wants and related to some others in all or any of the ways in which human beings may be related; but in *persona civica* they exist and are related solely in respect to their obligations to observe the conditions prescribed in these non-instrumental rules of conduct. They have no common substantive purpose, but they have a common concern.

This, then, is a distinct mode of association – relationship in terms of obligations to subscribe to non-instrumental rules of conduct that are indifferent to the success or to the failure of the substantive enterprises being pursued. The engagements of the office of rule in such an association and the apparatus of power annexed to it will reflect this mode of association. They will be neither managerial nor conciliatory of interests. Ruling here has no ingredient of 'lordship', and rules can perform their office only because they have no substantive interest of their own and are indifferent to the substantive interests of their subjects. They are custodians of the rules that constitute this mode of association. And politics in such a state, concerned with deliberating, from the standpoint of their desirability, the civil obligations imposed upon the conduct of the associates, cannot be concerned with who gets what, when and how, because these rules are not awards of advantage or disadvantage. It cannot be the consideration of the propensity of these rules to promote or hinder the achievement of a common substantive purpose; there is none.

A rule of civil association is desirable in respect to the accuracy with which it reflects, or does not affront, the moral imagination of the associates when it is directed to what they have learned to distinguish as a relationship not of moral perfection but of civility or justice. There are, in this matter, no absolute standards; this moral imagination, concerned with civil obligations, is all there is. Nevertheless, this political engagement to deliberate the rules that spell out an acceptable image of civility is the most difficult of all human engagements simply because it has no place for the consideration of what is most readily considered, namely, interests.

Now, this mode of association attributed to a state, or said to be what a state should be made to become, is grossly misunderstood and misdescribed both by those who think it is a desirable mode of association for a state and those who do not. For the most part, we know it now only in the parodies it has evoked.

The use of the word 'democracy' to describe it is an elementary mistake; this word properly denotes neither a mode of association nor the engagements of a government but its constitutional shape. But the description of civil association as relationship in terms of the enjoyment of 'rights' is as profoundly misleading as it is common, even where 'rights' are not confused with allocations of substantive satisfactions.

The rules of civil association specify and prescribe, as exactly as may be, the obligations to be subscribed to in doing and speaking. What they remove from the scene is not choice of what to do or to say but a notional unconditional choice. The associates are related in the recognition of their obligation to observe these conditions. And it cannot be otherwise. Nevertheless, this sort of association is often said to be relationship not in terms of obligations but in the enjoyment of 'rights'. But what can these 'rights' be? They cannot be the fanciful unconditionals ('liberty' or 'the pursuit of happiness') because it is precisely this unconditionality of conduct that the obligation to subscribe to conditions removes. They cannot denote the postulate of human agency (choice); this can neither be assured nor taken away by rules of conduct and without it rules of conduct are meaningless. Nor can they be exemptions from obligations, although this is often what they are made to appear. These 'rights' are in fact the totally unspecifiable obverse of civil obligations – the right to 'privacy', to a fair trial, or the newly announced 'basic right to reproduce' – that become determinate and lose their deceptive appearance of being unconditionals only when they are specified in a collection of exactly described obligations. The language of rights is the language of pretended unconditionals and misdescribes the terms of civil association.

Further, it is commonly said that, in contrast to that of a purposive association, the government of a civil association is notably 'inactive', indisposed to 'intervene' in the conduct of its subjects, or permitted to do so only to a 'limited' extent. Such an association is called a 'minimal' state. But to distinguish between these two modes of association in terms of different amounts of 'interference' by their governments is a total misrepresentation, making the distinction appear to be one of degree and not of mode, and distracting our attention from the political choice they offer us. Wherever our preference lies, it is unscrupulous or foolish to describe the first merely as a more thoroughly organized version of the second, and the second as only a diminished or 'moderate' version of the first.

[...]

But it is the third theme – the mode of association attributed to a state– that has now captured most of our attention. It is not a new theme – they were discussing it in the sixteenth century – but it is now our central concern. And how sadly confused is our handling of it. It is ill-distinguished from the other themes; often we do not get even to the point of recognizing that it concerns the particular relationship that human beings may have as members of a state. The modes of association that may be and have been attributed to a state are ill-specified and ill-distinguished from one another – or worse, they are mistaken for points on what is called the spectrum of political belief in this matter. The words in which we struggle to express this particular alignment of political belief are sadly inadequate. It is not a contrast between dictatorship and democracy (these are authority-words), or between Left and Right (these merely represent an insignificant squabble about the common purpose to be imposed upon a state already assumed to be a purposive association). The words Liberal and Conservative are already so overloaded with meanings that they must fail to be explicit here. And those who understand it in terms of Communism and Capitalism, collectivism and free enterprise, centralism and pluralism, merely add to the confusion by suggesting a substantive purpose for civil association. This alignment of political belief is not between those who value purposive association and those who do not, or between those who have a compassionate regard for their fellow men and those who have none; it concerns only the character of a *state* as an association of human beings.

We who (if I may presume) are disposed to elect for a state as a civil association have, perhaps, a harder task than our opponents, who are well served by the confusion into which political discourse has fallen. They have a ready response from those who are not averse from the warm embrace of even a compulsory *solidarité commune*, who are not dismayed when they find themselves bound to ends they have not chosen for themselves, particularly when (as part of the bargain) they are allocated a so-called 'social income' of unknown value. And perhaps we should not be so eager as we often are to disturb them. But the cooler virtues of civil association have much to recommend them, especially to those disposed to choose their own destinations even if they do not reach them. After all, this least burdensome of all human relationships in terms of obligations to subscribe to non-instrumental rules of conduct is the only kind of association that excludes no other and that mitigates conflict without imposing uniformity. And it is particularly appropriate to a state because it is the only morally tolerable form of compulsory association.

But if we are to make better known this most notable human invention, we must stop hiding behind such irrelevant expressions as 'democracy' and 'capitalism', and such ambiguous expressions as 'conservative' and 'moderate'; we must get to know, not only our opponents, but ourselves more exactly than we do at present; we must defend our position with reasons appropriate to it; and we must refuse to entangle ourselves with equivocal alliances.

There was once, so Schopenhauer tells us, a colony of porcupines. They were wont to huddle together on a cold winter's day and, thus wrapped in communal warmth, escape being frozen. But, plagued with the pricks of each other's quills, they drew apart. And every time the desire for warmth brought them together again, the same calamity overtook them. Thus they remained, distracted between two misfortunes, able neither to tolerate nor to do without one another, until they discovered that when they stood at a certain distance from one another they could both delight in one another's individuality and enjoy one another's company. They did not attribute any metaphysical significance to this distance, nor did they imagine it to be an independent source of happiness, like finding a friend. They recognized it to be a relationship in terms not of substantive enjoyments but of contingent considerabilities that they must determine for themselves. Unknown to themselves, they had invented civil association.

'Talking Politics' was originally given as an address in New York City under the auspices of *National Review* and first appeared in *National Review* on December 5, 1975. It is new to this edition of *Rationalism in Politics*. Reprinted by permission. © 1975 by *National Review*, Inc., 150 East 35th Street, New York, New York 10016.

CARL SCHMITT
EXTRACTS FROM *THE CONCEPT OF THE POLITICAL*

In memory of my friend, August Schaetz of Munich, who
fell on August 28, 1917, in the assault on Moncelul

I

The concept of the state presupposes the concept of the political.

According to modern linguistic usage, the state is the political status of an organized people in an enclosed territorial unit. This is nothing more than a general paraphrase, not a definition of the state. Since we are concerned here with the nature of the political, such a definition is unwarranted. It may be left open what the state is in its essence – a machine or an organism, a person or an institution, a society or a community, an enterprise or a beehive, or perhaps even a basic procedural order. These definitions and images anticipate too much meaning, interpretation, illustration, and construction, and therefore cannot constitute any appropriate point of departure for a simple and elementary statement.

In its literal sense and in its historical appearance the state is a specific entity of a people.[a] Vis-à-vis the many conceivable kinds of entities, it is

---

[a] Schmitt has in mind the modern national sovereign state and not the political entities of the medieval or ancient periods. For Schmitt's identification with the epoch of the modern state see George Schwab, *The Challenge of the Exception: An Introduction to the political Ideas of Carl Schmitt between 1921 and 1936* 2d ed. (New York: Greenwood Press, 1989), pp. 27, 54; also, George Schwab, 'Enemy oder Foe: Der Konflikt der modernen Politik', tr. J. Zeumer, *Epirrhosis: Festgabe für Carl Schmitt*, ed. H. Barion, E.-W. Böckenförde, E. Forsthoff, W. Weber (Berlin: Duncker & Humblot, 1968), II, 665–6.

Carl Schmitt (1996), *The Concept of the Political*, tr. George D. Schwab, Chicago: University of Chicago Press.

in the decisive case the ultimate authority. More need not be said at this moment. All characteristics of this image of entity and people receive their meaning from the further distinctive trait of the political and become incomprehensible when the nature of the political is misunderstood.

One seldom finds a clear definition of the political. The word is most frequently used negatively, in contrast to various other ideas, for example in such antitheses as politics and economy, politics and morality, politics and law; and within law there is again politics and civil law,[1] and so forth. By means of such negative, often also polemical confrontations, it is usually possible, depending upon the context and concrete situation, to characterize something with clarity. But this is still not a specific definition. In one way or another 'political' is generally juxtaposed to 'state' or at least is brought into relation with it.[2] The state thus appears as something political, the political as something pertaining to the state – obviously an unsatisfactory circle.

Many such descriptions of the political appear in professional juridic literature. Insofar as these are not politically polemical, they are of practical and technical interest and are to be understood as legal or administrative decisions in particular cases. These then receive their meaning by the presupposition of a stable state within whose framework they operate. Thus there exists, for example, a jurisprudence and literature pertaining to the concept of the political club or the political meeting in the law of associations. Furthermore, French administrative law practice has attempted to construct a concept of the political motive (*mobile politique*) with whose aid political acts of government (*actes de gouvernement*) could be distinguished from nonpolitical administrative acts and thereby removed from the control of administrative courts.[3]

Such accommodating definitions serve the needs of legal practice. Basically, they provide a practical way of delimiting legal competences of cases within a state in its legal procedures. They do not in the least aim at a general definition of the political. Such definitions of the political suffice, therefore, for as long as the state and the public institutions can be assumed as something self-evident and concrete. Also, the general definitions of the political which contain nothing more than additional references to the state are understandable and to that extent also intellectually justifiable for as long as the state is truly a clear and unequivocal eminent entity confronting nonpolitical groups and affairs – in other words, for as long as the state possesses the monopoly on politics. That was the case where the state had either (as in the eighteenth century) not recognized society as an antithetical force or, at least (as in Germany in the nineteenth century and into the twentieth), stood above society as a stable and distinct force.

The equation state = politics becomes erroneous and deceptive at exactly the moment when state and society penetrate each other. What had been up to that point affairs of state become thereby social matters, and, vice versa, what had been purely social matters become affairs of state – as must necessarily occur in a democratically organized unit. Heretofore ostensibly neutral domains – religion, culture, education, the economy – then cease to be neutral in the sense that they do not pertain to state and to politics. As a polemical concept against such neutralizations and depoliticalizations of important domains appears the total state, which potentially embraces every domain. This results in the identity of state and society. In such a state, therefore, everything is at least potentially political, and in referring to the state it is no longer possible to assert for it a specifically political characteristic.

The development can be traced from the absolute state of the eighteenth century via the neutral (noninterventionist) state of the nineteenth to the total state of the twentieth.[4] Democracy must do away with all the typical distinctions and depoliticalizations characteristic of the liberal nineteenth century, also with those corresponding to the nineteenth-century antitheses and divisions pertaining to the state–society (= political against social) contrast, namely the following, among numerous other thoroughly polemical and thereby again political antitheses:

religious   as antithesis of political
cultural   as antithesis of political
economic   as antithesis of political
legal   as antithesis of political
scientific   as antithesis of political

The more profound thinkers of the nineteenth century soon recognized this. In Jacob Burckhardt's *Weltgeschichtliche Betrachtungen* (of the period around 1870) the following sentences are found on 'democracy, i.e., a doctrine nourished by a thousand springs, and varying greatly with the social status of its adherents. Only in one respect was it consistent, namely, in the insatiability of its demand for state control of the individual. Thus it blurs the boundaries between state and society and looks to the state for the things that society will most likely refuse to do, while maintaining a permanent condition of argument and change and ultimately vindicating the right to work and subsistence for certain castes.'

[...]

2

[...]

The specific political distinction to which political actions and motives can be reduced is that between friend and enemy.[b] This provides a definition in the sense of a criterion and not as an exhaustive definition or one indicative of substantial content.[c] Insofar as it is not derived from other criteria, the antithesis of friend and enemy corresponds to the relatively independent criteria of other antitheses: good and evil in the moral sphere, beautiful and ugly in the aesthetic sphere, and so on. In any event it is independent, not in the sense of a distinct new domain, but in that it can neither be based on any one antithesis or any combination of other antitheses, nor can it be traced to these. If the antithesis of good and evil is not simply identical with that of beautiful and ugly, profitable and unprofitable, and cannot be directly reduced to the others, then the antithesis of friend and enemy must even less be confused with or mistaken for the others. The distinction of friend and enemy denotes the utmost degree of intensity of a union or separation, of an association or dissociation. It can exist theoretically and practically, without having simultaneously to draw upon all those moral, aesthetic, economic, or other distinctions. The political enemy need not be morally evil or aesthetically ugly; he need not appear as an economic competitor, and it may even be advantageous to engage with him in business transactions. But he is, nevertheless, the other, the stranger; and it is sufficient for his nature that he is, in a specially intense way, existentially something different and alien, so that in the extreme case conflicts with him are possible. These can neither be decided by a previously determined general norm nor by the judgment of a disinterested and therefore neutral third party.

Only the actual participants can correctly recognize, understand, and judge the concrete situation and settle the extreme case of conflict. Each participant is in a position to judge whether the adversary intends to negate his opponent's way of life and therefore must be repulsed or fought in order to preserve one's own form of existence. Emotionally the enemy is easily treated as being evil and ugly, because every distinction, most of all the political, as the strongest and most intense of the distinctions and categorizations, draws upon other distinctions for support. This does not alter the autonomy of such distinctions. Consequently, the reverse is also true: the morally evil, aesthetically ugly or economically damaging need not necessarily be the enemy; the morally good, aesthetically beautiful, and economically profitable need not necessarily become the friend in the specifically political sense of the word. Thereby the inherently objective nature and autonomy of the political becomes evident by virtue of its being able to treat,

---

[b] Since Schmitt identified himself with the epoch of the national sovereign state with its *jus publicum Europaeum*, he used the term *Feind* in the enemy and not the foe sense.

[c] Of the numerous discussions of Schmitt's friend–enemy criterion, particular attention is called to Hans Morgenthau's *La Notion du 'politique' et la théorie des différends internationaux* (Paris: Sirey, 1933), pp. 35–7, 44–64. The critique contained therein and Schmitt's influence on him is often implied in Morgenthau's subsequent writings.

distinguish, and comprehend the friend–enemy antithesis independently of other antitheses.

3

The friend and enemy concepts are to be understood in their concrete and existential sense, not as metaphors or symbols, not mixed and weakened by economic, moral, and other conceptions, least of all in a private-individualistic sense as a psychological expression of private emotions and tendencies. They are neither normative nor pure spiritual antitheses. Liberalism in one of its typical dilemmas [...] of intellect and economics has attempted to transform the enemy from the viewpoint of economics into a competitor and from the intellectual point into a debating adversary. In the domain of economics there are no enemies, only competitors, and in a thoroughly moral and ethical world perhaps only debating adversaries. It is irrelevant here whether one rejects, accepts, or perhaps finds it an atavistic remnant of barbaric times that nations continue to group themselves according to friend and enemy, or hopes that the antithesis will one day vanish from the world, or whether it is perhaps sound pedagogic reasoning to imagine that enemies no longer exist at all. The concern here is neither with abstractions nor with normative ideals, but with inherent reality and the real possibility of such a distinction. One may or may not share these hopes and pedagogic ideals. But, rationally speaking, it cannot be denied that nations continue to group themselves according to the friend and enemy antithesis, that the distinction still remains actual today, and that this is an ever present possibility for every people existing in the political sphere.

The enemy is not merely any competitor or just any partner of a conflict in general. He is also not the private adversary whom one hates. An enemy exists only when, at least potentially, one fighting collectivity of people confronts a similar collectivity. The enemy is solely the public enemy, because everything that has a relationship to such a collectivity of men, particularly to a whole nation, becomes public by virtue of such a relationship. The enemy is *hostis*, not *inimicus* in the broader sense; πολέμιος, not ἐχθρός.[5] As German and other languages do not distinguish between the private and political enemy, many misconceptions and falsifications are possible. The often quoted 'Love your enemies' (Matt. 5:44; Luke 6:27) reads 'diligite inimicos vestros,' ἀγαπᾶτε τοὺς ἐχθροὺς ὑμῶν, and not *diligite hostes vestros*. No mention is made of the political enemy. Never in the thousand-year struggle between Christians and Moslems did it occur to a Christian to surrender rather than defend Europe out of love toward the Saracens or Turks. The enemy in the political sense need not be hated personally, and in the private sphere only does it make sense to love one's enemy, i.e., one's adversary. The Bible quotation touches the political antithesis even less than it intends to dissolve, for example, the antithesis of good and evil or beautiful and ugly. It certainly does not mean that one should love and support the enemies of one's own people.

The political is the most intense and extreme antagonism, and every concrete antagonism becomes that much more political the closer it approaches the most extreme point, that of the friend–enemy grouping. In its entirety the state as an organized political entity decides for itself the friend–enemy distinction. Furthermore, next to the primary political decisions and under the protection of the decision taken, numerous secondary concepts of the political emanate. As to the equation of politics and state discussed under Section 1, it has the effect, for example, of contrasting a political attitude of a state with party politics so that one can speak of a state's domestic religious, educational, communal, social policy, and so on. Notwithstanding, the state encompasses and relativizes all these antitheses. However an antithesis and antagonism remain here within the state's domain which have relevance for the concept of the political.[6] Finally even more banal forms of politics appear, forms which assume parasite- and caricature-like configurations. What remains here from the original friend–enemy grouping is only some sort of antagonistic moment, which manifests itself in all sorts of tactics and practices, competitions and intrigues; and the most peculiar dealings and manipulations are called politics. But the fact that the substance of the political is contained in the context of a concrete antagonism is still expressed in everyday language, even where the awareness of the extreme case has been entirely lost.

This becomes evident in daily speech and can be exemplified by two obvious phenomena. First, all political concepts, images, and terms have a polemical meaning. They are focused on a specific conflict and are bound to a concrete situation; the result (which manifests itself in war or revolution) is a friend–enemy grouping, and they turn into empty and ghostlike abstractions when this situation disappears. Words such as state, republic,[7] society, class, as well as sovereignty, constitutional state, absolutism, dictatorship, economic planning, neutral or total state, and so on, are incomprehensible if one does not know exactly who is to be affected, combated, refuted, or negated by such a term.

[…]

4

[…]

That the state is an entity and in fact the decisive entity rests upon its political character. A pluralist theory is either the theory of state which arrives at the unity of state by a federalism of social associations or a theory of the dissolution or rebuttal of the state. If, in fact, it challenges the entity and places the political association on an equal level with the others, for example, religious or economic associations, it must, above all, answer the question as to the specific content of the political. Although in his numerous books Laski speaks of state, politics, sovereignty, and government, one does not find in these a specific definition of the political. The state simply transforms itself into an association which competes with other associations; it becomes a society among some other societies which exist within or outside the state. That is the pluralism of this theory of state. Its entire ingenuity is directed against earlier exaggerations of the state, against its majesty and its personality, against its claim to possess the monopoly of the highest unity, while it remains unclear what, according to this pluralist theory of state, the political entity should be. At times it appears in its old liberal form, as a mere servant of the essentially economically determined society, at times pluralistically as a distinct type of society, that is, as one association among other associations, at times as the product of a federalism of social associations or an umbrella association of a conglomeration of associations. Above all, it has to be explained why human beings should have to form a governmental association in addition to the religious, cultural, economic, and other associations, and what would be its specific political meaning. No clear chain of thought is discernible here. What appears finally is an all-embracing, monistically global, and by no means pluralist concept, namely Cole's 'society' and Laski's 'humanity'.

The pluralist theory of state is in itself pluralistic, that is, it has no center but draws its thoughts from rather different intellectual circles (religion, economics, liberalism, socialism, etc.). It ignores the central concept of every theory of state, the political, and does not even mention the possibility that the pluralism of associations could lead to a federally constructed political entity. It totally revolves in a liberal individualism. The result is nothing else than a revocable service for individuals and their free associations. One association is played off against another and all questions and conflicts are decided by individuals. In reality there exists no political society or association but only one political entity – one political community. The ever present possibility of a friend-and-enemy grouping suffices to forge a decisive entity which transcends the mere societal-associational groupings. The political entity is something specifically different, and vis-à-vis, other associations, something decisive.[8] Were this entity to disappear, even if only potentially, then the political itself would disappear. Only as long as the essence of the political is not comprehended or not taken into consideration is it possible to place a political association pluralistically on the same level with religious, cultural, economic, or other associations and permit it to compete with these. As we shall attempt to show below (Section 6), the concept of the political yields pluralistic consequences, but not in the sense that, within one and the same political entity, instead of the decisive friend-and-enemy grouping, a pluralism could take its place without destroying the entity and the political itself.

5

A people which exists in the sphere of the political cannot in case of need renounce the right to determine by itself the friend-and-enemy distinction. It can solemnly declare that it condemns war as a means of solving international disputes and can renounce it as a means of national policy, as was done in the so-called Kellogg Pact of 1928.[9] In so doing it has neither repudiated war as an instrument of international politics (and a war as an instrument of international politics can be worse than a war as an instrument of a national policy only) nor condemned nor outlawed war altogether. Such a declaration is subject, first of all, to specific reservations which are explicitly or implicitly self-understood as, for example, the reservation regarding the autonomous existence of the state and its self-defense, the reservation regarding existing treaties, the right of a continuing free and independent existence, and so on. Second, these reservations are, according to their logical structure, no mere exceptions to the norm, but altogether give the norm its concrete content. They are not peripheral but essential exceptions; they give the treaty its real content. in dubious cases. Third, as long as a sovereign state exists, this state decides for itself, by virtue of its independence, whether or not such a reservation (self-defense, enemy aggression, violation of existing treaties including the Kellogg Pact, and so on) is or is not given in the concrete case. Fourth, war cannot altogether be outlawed, but only specific individuals, peoples, states, classes, religions, etc., which, by being outlawed, are declared to be the enemy. The solemn declaration of outlawing war does not abolish the friend–enemy distinction, but, on the contrary, opens new possibilities by giving an international *hostis* declaration new content and new vigor.

Were this distinction to vanish then political life would vanish altogether. A people which exists in the political sphere cannot, despite entreating declarations to the contrary, escape from making this fateful distinction. If a part of the population declares that it no longer recognizes enemies, then, depending on the circumstance, it joins their side and aids them. Such a declaration does not abolish the reality of the friend-and-enemy distinction. Quite another question concerns citizens of a state who declare that they personally have no enemies. A private person has no political enemies. Such a declaration can at most say that he would like to place himself outside the political community to which he belongs and continue to live as a private individual only.[10] Furthermore, it would be a mistake to believe that a nation could eliminate the distinction of friend and enemy by declaring its friendship for the entire world or by voluntarily disarming itself. The world will not thereby become depoliticalized, and it will not be transplanted into a condition of pure morality, pure justice, or pure economics. If a people is afraid of the trials and risks implied by existing in the sphere of politics, then another people will appear which will assume these trials by protecting it against foreign enemies and thereby taking over political rule. The protector then decides who the enemy is by virtue of the eternal relation of protection and obedience.

On this principle rests the feudal order and the relation of lord and vassal, leader and led, patron and clients. This relation is clearly and explicitly seen here. No form of order, no reasonable legitimacy or legality can exist without protection and obedience. The *protego ergo obligo* is the *cogito ergo sum* of the state. A political theory which does not systematically become aware of this sentence remains an inadequate fragment. Hobbes designated this (at the end of his English edition of 1651, p. 396) as the true purpose of his *Leviathan*, to instill in man once again 'the mutual relation between Protection and Obedience'; human nature as well as divine right demands its inviolable observation.

Hobbes himself had experienced this truth in the terrible times of civil war, because then all legitimate and normative illusions with which men like to deceive themselves regarding political realities in periods of untroubled security vanish. If within the state there are organized parties capable of according their members more protection than the state, then the latter becomes at best an annex of such parties, and the individual citizen knows whom he has to obey. As has been shown (under Section 4 above), a pluralistic theory of state can justify this. The fundamental correctness of the protection-obedience axiom comes to the fore even more clearly in foreign policy and interstate relations: the simplest expression of this axiom is found in the protectorate under international law, the federal state, the confederation of states dominated by one of them, and the various kinds of treaties offering protection and guarantees.

It would be ludicrous to believe that a defenseless people has nothing but friends, and it would be a deranged calculation to suppose that the enemy could perhaps be touched by the absence of a resistance. No one thinks it possible that the world could, for example, be transformed into a condition of pure morality by the renunciation of every aesthetic or economic productivity. Even less can a people hope to bring about a purely moral or purely economic condition of humanity by evading every political decision. If a people no longer possesses the energy or the will to maintain itself in the sphere of politics, the latter will not thereby vanish from the world. Only a weak people will disappear.

6

The political entity presupposes the real existence of an enemy and therefore coexistence with another political entity. As long as a state exists, there will thus always be in the world more than just one state. A world state which embraces the entire globe and all of humanity cannot exist. The political world is a pluriverse, not a universe. In this sense every theory of state is pluralistic, even though in a different way from the domestic theory of pluralism discussed in Section 4. The political entity cannot by its very nature be universal in the sense of embracing all of humanity and the entire world. If the different states, religions, classes, and other human groupings on earth should be so unified that a conflict among them is impossible and even inconceivable and if civil war should forever be foreclosed in a realm which embraces the globe, then the distinction of friend and enemy would also cease. What remains is neither politics nor state, but culture, civilization, economics, morality, law, art, entertainment, etc. If and when this condition will appear, I do not know. At the moment, this is not the case. And it is self-deluding to believe that the termination of a modern war would lead to world peace – thus setting forth the idyllic goal of complete and final depoliticalization – simply because a war between the great powers today may easily turn into a world war.

Humanity as such cannot wage war because it has no enemy, at least not on this planet. The concept of humanity excludes the concept of the enemy, because the enemy does not cease to be a human being – and hence there is no specific differentiation in that concept. That wars are waged in the name of humanity is not a contradiction of this simple truth; quite the contrary, it has an especially intensive political meaning. When a state fights its political enemy in the name of humanity, it is not a war for the sake of humanity, but a war wherein a particular state seeks to usurp a universal concept against its military opponent. At the expense of its opponent, it tries to identify itself with humanity in the same way as one can misuse peace, justice, progress, and civilization in order to claim these as one's own and to deny the same to the enemy.

The concept of humanity is an especially useful ideological instrument of imperialist expansion, and in its ethical-humanitarian form it is a specific vehicle of economic imperialism, Here one is reminded of a somewhat modified expression of Proudhon's: whoever invokes humanity wants to cheat. To confiscate the word humanity, to invoke and monopolize such a term probably has certain incalculable effects, such as denying the enemy the quality of being human and declaring him to be an outlaw of humanity; and a war can thereby be driven to the most extreme inhumanity.[11]

But besides this highly political utilization of the nonpolitical term humanity, there are no wars of humanity as such. Humanity is not a political concept, and no political entity or society and no status corresponds to it. The eighteenth-century humanitarian concept of humanity was a polemical denial of the then existing aristocraticfeudal system and the privileges accompanying it. Humanity according to natural law and liberal-individualistic doctrines is a universal, i.e., all-embracing, social ideal, a system of relations between individuals. This materializes only when the real possibility of war is precluded and every friend and enemy grouping becomes impossible. In this universal society there would no longer be nations in the form of political entities, no class struggles, and no enemy groupings.

[...]

I have pointed out several times[12] that the antagonism between the so-called authoritarian and anarchist theories can be traced to these formulas. A part of the theories and postulates which presuppose man to be good is liberal. Without being actually anarchist they are polemically directed against the intervention of the state. Ingenuous anarchism reveals that the belief in the natural goodness of man is closely tied to the radical denial of state and government. One follows from the other, and both foment each other. For the liberals, on the other hand, the goodness of man signifies nothing more than an argument with whose aid the state is made to serve society. This means that society determines its own order and that state and government are subordinate and must be distrustingly controlled and bound to precise limits. The classical formulation by Thomas Paine says: society is the result of our reasonably regulated needs, government is the result of our wickedness.[13] The radicalism vis-à-vis state and government grows in proportion to the radical belief in the goodness of man's nature. Bourgeois liberalism was never radical in a political sense. Yet it remains self-evident that liberalism's negation of state and the political, its neutralizations, depoliticalizations, and declarations of freedom have likewise a certain political meaning, and in a concrete situation these are polemically directed against a specific state and its political power. But this is neither a political theory nor a political idea. Although liberalism has not radically denied the state, it has, on the other hand, neither advanced a positive theory of state nor on its own discovered how to reform the state, but has attempted only to tie the political to the ethical and to subjugate it to economics. It has produced a doctrine of the separation and balance of powers, i.e., a system of checks and controls of state and government. This cannot be characterized as either a theory of state or a basic political principle.

NOTES

1. The antithesis of law and politics is easily confused by the antithesis of civil and public law. According to J. K. Bluntschli in *Allgemeines Staatsrecht*, 4th ed. (Munich: J. G. Cotta, 1868), I, 219: 'Property is a civil law and not a political concept.' The political significance of this antithesis came particularly to the fore in 1925 and 1926, during the debates regarding the expropriation of the fortunes of the princes who had formerly ruled in Germany. The following sentence from the speech by deputy Dietrich (Reichstag session, December 2, 1925, *Berichte*, 4717) is cited as an example: 'We are of the opinion that the issues here do not at all pertain to civil law questions but are purely political ones....'
2. Also in those definitions of the political which utilize the concept of power as the decisive factor, this power appears mostly as state power, for example, in Max Weber's 'Politik als Beruf', *Gesammelte politische Schriften*, 3rd ed., ed. Johannes

Winckelmann (Tübingen: J. C. B. Mohr [Paul Siebeck], 1971), pp. 505, 506: 'aspiring to participate in or of influencing the distribution of power, be it between states, be it internally between groups of people which the state encompasses', or 'leadership or the influencing of a political association, hence today, of a state'; or his 'Parliament und Regierung im neugeordneten Deutschland,' *ibid.*, p. 347: 'The essence of politics is...combat, the winning of allies and of voluntary followers.' H. Triepel, *Staatsrecht und Politik* (Berlin: W. de Gruyter & Co., 1927), pp. 16–17, says: 'Until recent decades politics was still plainly associated with the study of the state....In this vein Weitz characterizes politics as the learned discussion of the state with respect to the historical development of states on the whole as well as of their current conditions and needs.' Triepel then justly criticizes the ostensibly nonpolitical, purely juristic approach of the Gerber-Laband school and the attempt at its continuation in the postwar period (Kelsen). Nevertheless, Triepel had not yet recognized the pure political meaning of this pretense of an apolitical purity, because he subscribes to the equation politics = state. As will still be seen below, designating the adversary as political and oneself as nonpolitical (i.e., scientific, just, objective, neutral, etc.) is in actuality a typical and unusually intensive way of pursuing politics.

3. ...For the criterion of the political furnished here (friend–enemy orientation), I draw upon the particularly interesting definition of the specifically political *acte de gouvernement* which Dufour...(*Traité de droit administratif appliqué*, V, 128) has advanced: 'Defining an act of government is the purpose to which the author addresses himself. Such an act aims at defending society itself or as embodied in the government against its internal or external enemies, overt or covert, present or future....'

4. See Carl Schmitt, *Der Hüter der Verfassung* (Tübingen: J. C. B. Mohr [Paul Siebeck], 1931; Berlin: Duncker & Humblot, 1969), pp. 78–9.

5. In his *Republic* (Bk. V, Ch. XVI, 470) Plato strongly emphasizes the contrast between the public enemy (πολέμιος) and the private one (ἐχθρός), but in connection with the other antithesis of war (πόλεμος) and insurrection, upheaval, rebellion, civil war (στάσις). Real war for Plato is a war between Hellenes and Barbarians only (those who are 'by nature enemies'), whereas conflicts among Hellenes are for him discords (στάσεις). The thought expressed here is that a people cannot wage war against itself and a civil war is only a self-laceration and it does not signify that perhaps a new state or even a new people is being created. Cited mostly for the *hostis* concept is Pomponius in the *Digest* 50, 16, 118. The most clear-cut definition with additional supporting material is in Forcellini's *Lexicon totius latinitatis* (1965 ed.), II, 684: 'A public enemy (*hostis*) is one with whom we are at war publicly....In this respect he differs from a private enemy. He is a person with whom we have private quarrels. They may also be distinguished as follows: a private enemy is a person who hates us, whereas a public enemy is a person who fights against us.'

Stasis also means the exact opposite, i.e., peace and order. The dialectic inherent in the term is pointed out by Carl Schmitt in *Politische Theologie II: Die Legende von der Erledigung jeder Politischen Theologie* (Berlin: Duncker & Humblot, 1970), pp. 117–18.

6. A social policy existed ever since a politically noteworthy class put forth its social demands; welfare care, which in early times was administered to the poor and distressed, had not been considered a sociopolitical problem and was also not called such. Likewise a church policy existed only where a church constituted a politically significant counterforce.

7. Machiavelli, for example, calls all nonmonarchical states republics, and his definition is still accepted today. Richard Thoma defines democracy as a nonprivileged state; hence all nondemocracies are classified as privileged states.

8. 'We can say that on the day of mobilization the hitherto existing society was transformed into a community.' E. Lederer, 'Zur Soziologie des Weltkriegs,' *Archiv für Sozialwissenschaft und Sozialpolitik*, 39 (1915), p. 349.

9. ...The Kellogg Pact text of August 27, 1928, contains most important reservations – England's national honor, self-defense, the League Covenant and Locarno, welfare and territorial integrity of territories such as Egypt, Palestine, and so forth; for France: self-defense, League Covenant, Locarno and neutrality treaties, above all the observance of the Kellogg Pact; for Poland: self-defense, observance of the Kellogg Pact, the League Covenant....The general juristic problem of reservations has so far received no systematic treatment, not even there where explicit treatments mention the sanctity of treaties and the sentence *pacta sunt servanda*. To fill this gap a noteworthy beginning is to be found in Carl Bilfinger, 'Betrachtungen über politisches Recht', *Zeitschrift für ausländisches öflentliches Recht und Völkerrecht*, I (1929), 57–76. [...] On the fact that the Kellogg Pact does not outlaw war, but sanctions it, see E. M. Borchard, 'The Kellogg Treaties Sanction War', *ibid.*, pp. 126–31, and Arthur Wegner, *Einführung in die Rechtswissenschaft* (Berlin: Walter de Gruyter, 1931), pp. 109–11.

   On the Kellogg Pact see also Carl Schmitt, *Der Nomos der Erde im Völkerrecht des Jus Publicum Europaeum* (Cologne: Greven Verlag, 1950; Berlin: Duncker & Humblot, 1974), pp. 255, 272.

10. In this case it is a matter for the political community somehow to regulate this kind of nonpublic, politically disinterested existence (by privileges for aliens, internment, exterritoriality, permits of residence and concessions, laws for metics, or in some other way).

11. [...] Pufendorf (*De jure naturae et gentium*, VIII, 6, #5) quotes approvingly Bacon's comment that specific peoples are 'proscribed by nature itself,' e.g., the Indians, because they eat human flesh. And in fact the Indians of North America were then exterminated. As civilization progresses and morality rises, even less harmless things than devouring human flesh could perhaps qualify as deserving to be outlawed in such a manner. Maybe one day it will be enough if a people were unable to pay its debts.

12. *Politische Theologie*, pp. 50 ff.; *Die Diktatur: Von den Anfängen des modernen Souveränitätsgedankens bis zum proletarischen Klassenkampf* (Munich: Duncker & Humblot, 1921, 1928; Berlin, 1964), pp. 9, 109, 112 ff., 123, 148.

13. See *Die Diktatur*, p. 114. The formulation by Babeuf in the *Tribun du Peuple*: any institution which does not presuppose the people to be good and the officials corruptible...(is reprehensible) is not liberal but meant in the sense of the democratic identity of ruler and ruled.

2

RULE OF LAW

Sylvie Delacroix

Introduction

From a rhetorical perspective, the 'rule of law' is one of these concepts whose evocative power directly depends on its enigmatic character. Despite its currency in contemporary political debates, its lack of precise meaning makes it apt to various and often incompatible uses. Far from being the politicians' privilege, this concept is at the root of ground-breaking legal cases which significantly shaped today's democracies. Yet its vague and controversial meaning has raised alarm among some contemporary critical thinkers, who see the rule of law as a conservative ideology standing in the way of social and political justice. On a literal – and limited – understanding, the rule of law indeed requires a 'law of rules'(Scalia 1989: 1175), and in some cases justice can only be achieved by departing from the rules.

'The rule of law, it is argued, is preferable to that of any individual' (Aristotle 1986: 88). Aristotle's famous phrase is quoted as an introduction to most accounts of the rule of law, and yet this sentence is likely to sound rather peculiar to many contemporary readers. In the Middle Ages, Aristotle's phrase was associated with the widely shared feeling that the world was indeed ruled by a Supreme Law that flowed either from God or from some understanding of Nature. Existing independently of the will of any individual, these 'natural laws' (as instantiations of the Supreme Law) bound all members of society, kings and subjects alike.[1] Since the sixteenth century, that understanding of law has been seriously challenged, notably by Michel de Montaigne, who, questioning the existence of natural laws, writes: 'Laws are often made by fools, and even more often by men who fail in equity because they hate equality: but always by men, vain authorities who can resolve nothing'(1991: 1216). According to Montaigne, what makes men's authority so vain is precisely the impossibility of relying on some superior, natural law that could rescue the law-makers from their foolishness and short-sightedness. Today, there is no reason to think that our legislators and legal decision-makers have gained greater wisdom. And yet, few people believe in the existence of 'natural' laws existing prior to or independently of any human choice.[2] So how are we to understand 'the rule of law', which Aristotle deems preferable to that of any individual, if the only law we know originates from individuals anyway?

Aristotle may actually be pointing towards an answer when he states:

> There may indeed be cases which the law seems unable to determine, but such cases a man could not determine either. But the law trains officers for this express purpose, and appoints them to determine matters which are left undecided by it, to the best of their judgment. Further, it permits them to make any amendment of the existing laws which experience suggests. Therefore he who bids the law rule may be deemed to bid God and Reason alone rule, but he who bids man rule adds an element of the beast; for desire is a wild beast, and passion perverts the minds of rulers, even when they are the best of men. The law is reason unaffected by desire. (1996: 88)

If the rule of law is the rule of Reason over fallible, desire-led individuals, one may endeavour to translate the demands of Reason into specific, formal constraints over law-making and law-adjudicating practices. The inventory of a certain number of requirements specifically aimed at controlling and hindering the potential excesses of arbitrariness on the part of legal decision-makers would then ensure that a society is ruled by law and not by the caprices of the politically powerful.

JOSEPH RAZ

The most famous contemporary exponent of this 'formal' understanding of the rule of law is undoubtedly Joseph Raz. In 'The Rule of Law and Its Virtue', Raz identifies what he deems to be the 'basic intuition' underlying the doctrine of the rule of law: 'the law must be capable of guiding the behaviour of its subjects'. That basic intuition, in his sense, logically implies a set of eight requirements or 'principles' that are particularly important. One of the most fundamental of these principles is that (1) *all laws should be prospective, open and clear*.[3] A law cannot possibly rule over the conduct of people if it did not exist at the time of the action, or if it is excessively ambiguous or obscure. The rest of the principles continue as follows. (2) *Laws should be relatively stable*, so as to allow people to reliably plan their actions in accordance with the law. (3) *The making of particular laws should be guided by open, stable, clear and general rules.* Here the idea is to take into account the fact that law cannot consist exclusively of general rules applicable to everybody. In order to ensure that particular orders or regulations do not arise out of purely preferential or discriminatory considerations, these orders should be made within a general and stable framework. (4), (5) and (7) *The courts should be independent, easily accessible, and respect the principles of natural justice* (i.e. open and fair hearing, unbiased judges etc.). (6) *The courts should make sure that the administration and Parliament respect principles 1, 2 and 3.* (8) *The discretion of crime-preventing agencies (i.e. police, prosecuting authorities) should not be allowed to pervert the law*: they should not have the power to decide arbitrarily whether to prosecute or not, or whether to allocate resources to detect certain crimes and not others.

All these requirements will sound very familiar to most readers and seem to provide an uncontroversial picture of the characteristics commonly associated with a system governed by law and not by the arbitrary rulings of some individual. One issue has nevertheless triggered a debate that still takes centre stage today: even if one added a large number of extra safeguards, like ensuring that the legal profession as a whole (and not only the judges) is independent, it seems that the most evil legal systems could easily be deemed to comply with this formal conception of the rule of law. Fascist Italy was highly concerned to maintain and abide by a strict legality, and some Italian apologists went as far as claiming that the fascist regime maintained the rule of law to a higher degree than ever before! From this perspective, it is hard to see why 'the rule of law is preferable to that of any individual'. Conceived as a set of formal safeguards aimed at regulating the power of legal decision-makers, the rule of law seems to boil down to a mere varnish that would only be of real concern to those regimes seeking to ease their own conscience. Such a disappointing conclusion may only come from expecting *too much*[4] from the 'rule of law' though. Raz would indeed emphasise that conformity to the eight formal requirements he put forward only makes the law a good instrument for achieving certain goals. These goals may be purely evil.[5] 'But that does not show that it [the rule of law] is not a virtue, just as the fact that a sharp knife can be used to harm does not show that being sharp is not a good-making characteristic for knives' (Raz 1979: 225). On this view, law is an instrument in the hands of the powerful, and the rule of law is a quality of that instrument, which it can possess to various degrees, reflecting its capacity to promote whatever goal it is meant to serve.

LON FULLER

Some people will argue that there is an important piece missing in that argument. The analogy Raz draws between a knife and the law actually helps us to understand the problem with the formality of his instrumental approach. Try to define a knife independently of its purpose. You may try to describe its parts, its general aspect etc., but it will be very difficult to convey what a knife is like until you mention that its purpose is to cut things. The same problem applies to law. You may describe law as an organised set of rules made and enforced by some people who hold authority. This description could fit a set of managerial rules within a multinational company as well as school regulations. Even if you added a complex description of how these rules are enforced and applied, you still would not necessarily point to a legal system. That is because, just like a knife, you cannot define law independently of its purpose. This argument lies at the core of Lon Fuller's account of the rule of law. Like Raz, Fuller enumerates a set of formal precepts (which are slightly different from Raz's[6]) that are meant to encapsulate the rule of law. Unlike Raz, Fuller claims that these precepts actually tell us something specific about what law is for (hence law is not a tool that can serve just any purpose). When you say that a knife is sharp, it suggests that a knife's purpose is to cut things. Likewise, when you describe the fact that a legal system complies to a certain degree to Fuller's eight precepts (i.e. most of its rules are prospective, general etc.), it tells you something about what law aspires to. According to Fuller, the creation of a social order based on the observance of clear and declared rules (which the eight precepts of the rule of law are meant to guarantee) aspires to promote and encourage 'purposeful and creative activity', free from the erratic constraints of unbridled arbitrariness.[7] This teleological interpretation of the rule of law gives it a very different twist from its formal counterpart, as it presents the rule of law as a *moral aspiration* rather than just a recipe for efficient rule-making. But what about the apparent facility of evil regimes to comply with the rule of law?[8] Does that not undermine the rule of law's characterisation as a moral aspiration? There are at least two different strategies available to those seeking to maintain that this characterisation remains valid whether or not evil regimes can comply with the rule of law.

RONALD DWORKIN

The first strategy consists in putting forward a more robust conception of the rule of law, including some substantive requirements, which an evil regime by definition will not meet. Along this line, Ronald Dworkin would probably argue that Raz asks *too little* of the concept of the rule of law. In 'Political Judges and the Rule of Law', Dworkin contrasts what he calls 'the rule-book conception' of the rule of law to the 'rights conception'. While the 'rule-book conception' is very much like Raz's account, in that its point is to emphasise that the state's power should be exercised according to certain rules that are to be clearly set out in advance, the 'rights conception' both assumes and demands more. It assumes more in that it presupposes the existence of another form of law that pre-exists the positive, enacted law of a particular regime. According to the rights conception, individuals indeed have moral and political rights that are 'distinct and prior' (Dworkin 1985: 13) to those given by positive enactment. In other words, there is a moral law that confers some inalienable rights to individuals, and the aim of positive law, if it wants to comply with the rule of law, is to make sure that these rights are respected. The 'rights conception' thus also demands more in that it submits positive law to a duty to achieve a certain *result* (the preservation and fostering of certain moral and political rights), and not only to a duty to comply with a certain *form*.

Now you may want to know what exactly these moral and political rights are. Indeed any person advocating a 'rights conception' of the rule of law needs to be able to enumerate the moral and political rights it relies on. But most of the time they would rather not. That's because any enumeration of such rights would by definition prove to depend on a certain understanding of what constitutes a 'good' life, and in a pluralist society that understanding is bound to be challenged by competing views, thus questioning the necessity of the rights in question. Dworkin avoids that problem thanks to a particularly demanding – and challenging – theory of adjudication. In his view, the responsibility for maintaining the rule of law falls mainly with the judges. Beyond their duty to scrutinise the formal qualities of laws (their generality, accessibility etc.), the courts are also entrusted with a duty to assert the moral principles *underlying* the law. On this view, the law consists not only of rules but also of a certain number of principles that are embedded in the community's sociolegal practices (these principles themselves give rise to the moral and political rights mentioned above). The role of the judge is to find out what these underlying principles are by constructing an overall theory of law that fits and justifies the current legal rules and practices.[9] Dworkin illustrates this point by reference to a particularly evocative case: in *Riggs v. Palmer*, a murderer claimed that he was entitled to inherit under the will of his victim. That will was perfectly valid, and inheritance laws did not contain any exception relating to such a case. The court nevertheless decided against the murderer's inheriting from his victim, holding that the application of the relevant legal rules was subject to general principles of law. Among these was the principle that no man should profit from his own wrong. This general principle was found to justify a wide range of established legal rules (for example, a prostitute cannot sue for her earnings, a gambler cannot sue for his winnings), and was hence deemed to be an integral part of the law, applicable to the case in question.

Dworkin's 'robust' conception of the rule of law, whereby the arbitrariness of legal decision-makers is controlled not only by rules, but also by general principles translating some moral or political concerns, is not without problems. The main difficulty is related to the diversity of moral and political concerns which define and constitute a pluralist society. Dworkin's entrusting the courts with the task of articulating the community's moral and political commitments may save him the trouble of having to enumerate the moral and political 'rights'[10] which the rule of law is supposed to protect. Conceived as an ongoing process, the courts' articulation of the community's moral and political values is meant to reflect changing attitudes towards the law, whose justification evolves with time. What his theory seems to underestimate, however, is the fact that the judges may have as varied interpretations of what is to count as a legal system's moral and political principles as there are various moral and political positions among the population. The construction of an overall theory of law may be informed by the existing legal rules and practices, but ultimately it depends on what the judge holds to be the valid and important moral commitments underlying the law.[11] If the 'rule of law' becomes the rule of whatever the judge deems morally important, it seems to turn into exactly what it was supposed to avoid: the rule of individuals. So is there no way one may defend the moral significance of the rule of law without denaturing it into exactly what it was supposed to prevent?

LAW, MORALITY AND TELEOLOGY

Remember that the rule of law's moral significance was raised in answer to a model describing the rule of law as the quality of an instrument – law – that can serve just about any goal. By contrast, Fuller emphasises that the effort to comply with the eight precepts constitutive of the rule of law typically arises out of a concern to promote the moral ideal of liberty. Indeed, when the law consists of intelligible and followable rules,

> citizens will enjoy certain areas of optional conduct. These areas of conduct will receive some protection from interference (probably in the form of general prohibitions on trespass and assault) and their existence will be independent of the will of any person, being dependent solely upon the content of the law. (Simmonds, forthcoming a)

According to Fuller, severing the idea of the rule of law from the moral aspiration it embodies can only result in a sterile concept. Its excessive formality may be deemed rather unhelpful by the judges, who can read its eight precepts in the light of whatever moral view they happen to hold, thus inviting precisely the kind of arbitrariness the rule of law is supposed to avoid.

By contrast, a definition of the rule of law that emphasises its teleological element – that is, the ideal it seeks to promote – may provide more of a guideline to judges, and may suggest an answer to our initial question, 'does the apparent facility of evil regimes to comply with the rule of law undermine its characterisation as a moral aspiration?'. Dworkin's theory has been analysed as one way of answering that question negatively. Another possible strategy consists in relying on a teleological definition of the rule of law. That definition would allow us to highlight that an evil regime cannot ever be deemed to comply with the rule of law, as by definition it will never have tried to promote any moral ideal whatsoever. The idea, in other words, consists in considering the fact that the rule of law typically seeks to promote a moral ideal as an intrinsic and necessary part of its definition. Hence, observance of the formal precepts of the rule of law does not in itself suffice to conclude that a legal system complies with the rule of law. One also has to establish that the legal system's compliance with the rule of law's precepts is actually aimed at promoting a moral ideal, and more specifically the ideal of liberty (as 'not being under the power of another'). One can anticipate quite a few objections here.

The first and obvious objection amounts to highlighting the apparent circularity of this 'teleological strategy'. If some legal systems comply with the rule of law's precepts without ever trying to promote a moral ideal, this may show that our teleological definition was misguided form the start, as it proves that the rule of law need not be connected to any moral aspiration.[12] This argument can be defeated in two ways. One may dismiss the premise on which it rests as 'straightforwardly false', and assert that legal systems that are not committed to promoting the ideal of liberty will have no reason to only use violence when authorised by a pre-existing law, which is one of the rule of law's main requirements.[13] Alternatively, one may emphasise that a teleological definition of the rule of law does not rely on a *necessary* connection between the rule of law and the moral ideal it is deemed to serve. One may indeed argue that the rule of law's precepts *make most sense* when interpreted as pointing towards a moral ideal. The claim that some legal systems may comply with its requirements without ever intending to promote any moral ideal does not endanger or diminish the significance of a teleological definition of the rule of law, nor does it prove its moral neutrality.

The second objection one may raise consists in questioning the necessity of the specific moral aspiration – liberty – that the rule of law is deemed to embody. If we go back to Aristotle's idea – 'The rule of law, it is argued, is preferable to that of any individual' – one may emphasise that this ideal can be translated in many ways, some of which may give more importance to alternative moral values, such as equality, for instance.[14] Some societies may indeed build a legal system principally out of a concern to ensure equality among citizens, and freedom from arbitrary punishment may only be deemed secondary. Fuller's construction of the rule of law in terms of eight precepts embodying the ideal of liberty flows from an interpretation of law as promoting a society favouring unhindered creativity and purposefulness. Now, reflection upon various legal practices and institutions may yield an altogether different interpretation, seeing law as essentially promoting a sense of community and equality, for instance. That model is favoured by Dworkin, whose markedly different theory reflects a distinctive understanding of law and its role in society.

CONCLUSION

Deciding between these different models and arguing for one particular conception of the rule of law cannot be isolated from a wider reflection about the values law is meant to serve. What do we want law for? This question is readily forgotten by most lawyers, used to considering law as a *given* that is meant to be applied by the judges and that regulates interaction between citizens. The current focus upon the formal requirements entailed by the rule of law (and the amount of discretion it may or may not entrust the judges with) has probably contributed to the rule of law being discredited as a 'rhetorical device' supplementing the politician's empty talk or the judge's lack of inspiration. Relocating our reflection about the rule of law within a wider discussion about the values law is meant to preserve should enable politicians and judges alike to renew a debate that is vital to the fostering of a true democratic culture.

QUESTIONS FOR DISCUSSION

- Must the rule of law embody a moral purpose?
- To what extent, if any, should the rule of law shape our understanding of what is meant by 'human flourishing'?
- Are rights at the core of the rule of law?
- What is the relationship between multiculturalism and the rule of law?

NOTES

1. 'The king must not be under man but under God and under the law, because law makes the king' (Bracton 1968: 33).
2. Among the people who do believe in the existence of such natural laws, some, such as John Finnis, present them as flowing from a certain conception of human flourishing, while others, following a realist perspective, maintain that they flow from some 'intrinsically normative entities' that are part of the fabric of the world.
3. The numbers refer to Raz's own numbering.
4. Or too little, see below.
5. 'A non-democratic legal system, based on the denial of human rights, on extensive poverty, on racial segregation, sexual inequalities, and religious persecution may, in principle, conform to the requirements of the rule of law better than any of the legal systems of the more enlightened Western democracies' (Raz 1979: 211).
6. According to Fuller, law-making must observe some practical precepts if it is to be able to fulfil its purpose: there must be rules, these rules must be prospective, published, intelligible, relatively stable, not contradictory; compliance with these rules must be possible, and there must be some congruence between the rules as declared and as applied by officials (Fuller 1969: 33–94).
7. Note that this interpretation of the rule of law as promoting liberty may be challenged, and one may endeavour to replace 'liberty' with 'equality' and so on (see below).
8. Some people argue that the rule of law does not partake of any moral significance because it can be complied with for purely prudential reasons. For a discussion of this argument, see below.

9. For a particularly clear and helpful discussion of Dworkin's theory, see Simmonds (2002: 181ff.).
10. Dworkin himself acknowledges that the 'rights vocabulary' is more akin to the American model than to the English one: 'Americans are still fascinated by the idea of individual rights, which is the zodiac sign under which their country was born' (Dworkin 1985: 31). Ultimately, the moral and political rights Dworkin is referring to can be deemed to flow from some fundamental moral and political principles, and that is why I have not elaborated further on this distinction between 'rights' and 'principles', which could in another context lead to interesting developments.
11. Dworkin does acknowledge that 'law would founder if the various interpretive theories in play in court and classroom diverged too much in any one generation' (Dworkin 1988: 88). But that danger is allegedly avoided by various 'unifying and socialising factors', such as the 'conservatism of legal education', the 'general intellectual environment' etc.
12. This is basically the kind of argument (although stated in different terms) which Matthew Kramer puts forward in Kramer (2004).
13. For a full development of this strategy, which is used by Nigel Simmonds to defeat Kramer's argument, see Simmonds (2004).
14. Among these alternative values, the value of justice may come to mind. For Fuller, justice is undeniably important, but it comes *after* liberty: 'Since justice depends crucially on choices actually made by individuals, no pattern of allocation can be regarded as just unless individuals have been free to make decisions for themselves' (Winston 2001: 585).

RONALD DWORKIN
EXTRACTS FROM 'POLITICAL JUDGES AND THE RULE OF LAW'

Two questions and two ideals

This essay is about two questions, and the connections between them. The first is a practical question about how judges do and should decide hard cases. Do judges in the United States and Great Britain make political decisions? Should their decisions be political? Of course the decisions that judges make *must* be political in one sense. In many cases a judge's decision will be approved by one political group and disliked by others, because these cases have consequences for political controversies. In the United States, for example, the Supreme Court must decide important constitutional issues that are also political issues, like the issue whether accused criminals have procedural rights that make law enforcement more difficult. In Britain the courts must decide cases that demand an interpretation of labor legislation, like cases about the legality of secondary picketing, when the Trades Union Congress favors one interpretation and the Confederation of British Industry another. I want to ask, however, whether judges should decide cases on political *grounds*, so that the decision is not only the decision that certain political groups would wish, but is taken on the ground that certain principles of political morality are right. A judge who decides on political grounds is not deciding on grounds of party politics. He does not decide in favor of the interpretation sought by the unions because he is (or was) a member of the Labour

Ronald Dworkin (1978), 'Political Judges and the Rule of Law', *Proceedings of the British Academy*, 64.

party, for example. But the political principles in which he believes, like, for example, the belief that equality is an important political aim, may be more characteristic of some political parties than others.

There is a conventional answer to my question, at least in Britain. Judges should not reach their decisions on political grounds. That is the view of almost all judges and barristers and solicitors and academic lawyers. Some academic lawyers, however, who count themselves critics of British judicial practice, say that British judges actually do make political decisions, in spite of the established view that they should not. J. A. G. Griffiths of the London School of Economics, for example, in a polemical book called *The Politics of the Judiciary*, argued that several recent decisions of the House of Lords were political decisions, even though that court was at pains to make it appear that the decisions were reached on technical legal rather than political grounds.[1] It will be helpful briefly to describe some of these decisions.

In *Charter*[2] and *Dockers*[3] the House of Lords interpreted the Race Relations Act so that political clubs, like the West Ham Conservative Club, were not obliged by the Act not to discriminate against coloured people. In *Tameside* the House overruled a Labour minister's order reversing a local Conservative council's decision not to change its school system to the comprehensive plan favored by the Labour government.[4] In the notorious *Shaw's Case*, the House of Lords sustained the conviction of the publisher of a directory of prostitutes.[5] It held that he was guilty of what it called the common law crime of 'conspiracy to corrupt public morals', even though it conceded that no statute declared such a conspiracy to be a crime. In an older case, *Liversidge v. Anderson*, the House upheld the decision of a minister who, in the Second World War, ordered someone detained without trial.[6] Griffiths believes that in each of these cases (and in a great many other cases he discusses) the House acted out of a particular political attitude, which is defensive of established values or social structures and opposed to reform. He does not say that the judges who took these decisions were aware that, contrary to the official view of their function, they were enforcing a political position. But he believes that that was nevertheless what they were doing.

So there are those who think that British judges do make political decisions. But that is not to say that they should. Griffiths thinks it inevitable, as understand him, that the judiciary will play a political role in a capitalist or semi-capitalist state. But he does not count this as a virtue of capitalism; on the contrary, he treats the political role of judges as deplorable. It may be that some few judges and academics – including perhaps Lord Justice Denning – do think that judges ought to be more political than the conventional view recommends. But that remains very much an eccentric – some would say dangerous – minority view.

Professional opinion about the political role of judges is more divided in the United States. A great party of academic lawyers and law students, and even some of the judges in the prestigious courts, hold that judicial decisions are inescapably and rightly political. They have in mind not only the grand constitutional decisions of the Supreme Court but also the more ordinary civil decisions of state courts developing the common law of contracts and tort and commercial law. They think that judges do and should act like legislators, though only within what they call the 'interstices' of decisions already made by the legislature. That is not a unanimous view even among sophisticated American lawyers, nor is it a view that the public at large has fully accepted. On the contrary, politicians sometimes campaign for office promising to curb judges who have wrongly seized political power. But a much greater part of the public accepts political jurisprudence now than did, say, twenty-five years ago.

My own view is that the vocabulary of this debate about judicial politics is too crude, and that both the official British view and the 'progressive' American view are mistaken. The debate neglects an important distinction between two kinds of political arguments on which judges might rely in reaching their decisions. This is the distinction (which I have tried to explain and defend elsewhere) between arguments of political principle that appeal to the political rights of individual citizens, and arguments of political policy that claim that a particular decision will work to promote some conception of the general welfare or public interest.[7] The correct view, I believe, is that judges do and should rest their judgments on controversial cases on arguments of political principle, but not in arguments of political policy. My view is therefore more restrictive than the progressive American view but less restrictive than the official British one.

The second question I put in this essay is, at least at first sight, less practical. What is the rule of law? Lawyers (and almost everyone else) think that there is a distinct and important political ideal called the rule of law. But they disagree about what that ideal is. There are, in fact, two very different conceptions of the rule of law, each of which has its partisans. The first I shall call the 'rule-book' conception. It insists that, so far as is possible, the power of the state should never be exercised against individual citizens except in accordance with rules explicitly set out in a public rule book available to all. The government as well as ordinary citizens must play by these public rules until they are changed, in accordance with further rules about how they are to be changed, which are also set out in the rule book. The rule-book conception is, in one sense, very narrow, because it does not stipulate anything about the content of the rules that may be put in the rule book. It insists only that whatever rules are put in the book must be followed until changed. Those who have this conception of the rule of law do care about the content of the rules in the rule book, but they say that this is a matter of substantive justice, and that substantive justice is an independent ideal, in no sense part of the ideal of the rule of law.

I shall call the second conception of the rule of law the 'rights' conception. It is in several ways more ambitious than the rule-book conception.

It assumes that citizens have moral rights and duties with respect to one another, and political rights against the state as a whole. It insists that these moral and political rights be recognized in positive law, so that they may be enforced *upon the demand of individual citizens* through courts or other judicial institutions of the familiar type, so far as this is practicable. The rule of law on this conception is the ideal of rule by an accurate public conception of individual rights. It does not distinguish, as the rule-book conception does, between the rule of law and substantive justice; on the contrary it requires, as part of the ideal of law, that the rules in the rule book capture and enforce moral rights.

That is a complex ideal. The rule-book conception of the rule of law has only one dimension along which a political community might fall short. It might use its police power over individual citizens otherwise than as the rule book specifies. But the rights conception has at least three dimensions of failure. A state might fail in the *scope* of the individual rights it purports to enforce. It might decline to enforce rights against itself, for example, though it concedes citizens have such rights. It might fail in the *accuracy* of the rights it recognizes: it might provide for rights against the state, but through official mistake fail to recognize important rights. Or it might fail in the *fairness* of its enforcement of rights: it might adopt rules that put the poor or some disfavored race at a disadvantage in securing the rights the state acknowledges they have.

The rights conception is therefore more complex than the rule-book conception. There are other important contrasts between the two conceptions; some of these can be identified by considering the different places they occupy in a general theory of justice. Though the two conceptions compete as deals of the legal process (because, as we shall see, they recommend different theories of adjudication), they are nevertheless compatible as more general, ideals for a just society. Any political community is better, all else equal, if its courts take no action other than is specified in rules published in advance, and also better, all else equal, if its legal institutions enforce whatever rights individual citizens have. Even as general political ideals, however the two conceptions differ in the following way. Some high degree of compliance with the rule-book conception seems necessary to a just society. Any government that acts contrary to its own rule book very often – at least in matters important to particular citizens – cannot be just, no matter how wise or fair its institutions otherwise are. But compliance with the rule book is plainly not sufficient for justice; full compliance will achieve very great injustice if the rules are unjust. The opposite holds for the rights conception. A society that achieves a high rating on each of the dimensions of the rights conception is almost certainly a just society, even though it may be mismanaged or lack other qualities of a desirable society. But it is widely thought, at least, that the rights conception is not necessary to a just society, because it is not necessary, in order that the rights of citizens be protected, that citizens be able to demand adjudication and enforcement of these rights as individuals. A government of wise and just officers will protect rights (so the argument runs) on its own initiative, without procedure whereby by citizens can dispute, as individuals, what these rights are. Indeed, the rights conception of the rule of law, which insists on the importance of that opportunity, is often dismissed as legalistic, as encouraging a mean and selfish concern with individual property and title.

The two conceptions also differ in what might be called their philosophical neutrality. The rights conception seems more vulnerable to philosophical objections. It supposes that citizens have moral rights – that is, rights other than and prior to those given by positive enactment – so that a society can sensibly be criticized on the ground that its enactments do not recognize the rights people have. But many philosophers doubt that people have any rights that are not bestowed on them by enactments or other official decisions; or even that the idea of such rights makes sense. They doubt particularly that it is sensible to say that people have moral rights when (as the rights conception must concede is often the case) it is controversial within the community what moral rights they have. The rights conception must suppose, that is, that a state may fail along the dimension of accuracy even when it is controversial whether it has failed; but that is just what philosophers doubt makes sense. The rights conception therefore seems open to the objection that it presupposes a philosophical point of view that it itself controversial, and which will therefore not be accepted by all members of the community.

The last contrast I shall mention will join the two issues of this essay. For the two conceptions of the rule of law offer very different advice on the question of whether judges should make political decisions in hard cases – that is, cases in which no explicit rule in the rule book firmly decides the case either way. Though the two conceptions, as general political ideals, may both have a place in a full political theory, it makes a great difference which is taken to be the ideal of *law* because it is that ideal which governs our attitudes about adjudication. The rule-book conception has both negative and positive advice about hard case. It argues, positively, that judges should decide hard cases by trying to discover what is 'really' in the rule book, in one or another sense of that claim. It argues, negatively, that judges should never decide such cases on the ground of their own political judgment, because a political decision is not a decision about what is, in any sense, in the rule book, but rather a decision about what ought to be there. The rule-book conception supports the conventional British view about political judges.

I must now pause to explain the idea this positive advice uses: the idea that it makes sense to ask, in a hard case, about what is 'really' in the rule book. In a modern legal system hard cases typically arise, not because there is nothing in the rule book that bears on the dispute, but because the rules that are in the book speak in an uncertain voice. *Charter*, for example, was a hard case because it was unclear whether the rule Parliament put in the rule book – the rule that organizations that serve 'a section of the public' must not discriminate – forbade a political club to deny membership to blacks. It is, in that sense, 'unclear' what the rule book really, properly understood, provides. A lawyer who speaks this way treats the rule book as an attempt at communication and supposes that an unclear rule can be better understood by applying techniques that we use to improve our understanding of other sorts of communication.

Different generations of rule-book lawyers – and different lawyers within each generation – advocate different techniques for this purpose. Some prefer semantic questions. They argue in the following way. 'The legislature uses words when it enacts a rule, and the meaning of these words fix what rules it has enacted. So any theory about the meaning of the phrase "a section of the public" is a theory that makes the Race Relations Act more precise. The rule-book conception therefore directs judges to try to form semantic theories. They should ask, for example, what the phrase "a section of the public" would be taken to mean in a similar context in ordinary discourse. Or what the most natural meaning of some component of the phrase, like the word "public", is. Or what similar phrases were taken to mean in other statutes. It is understood that different judges will give different answers to these semantic questions; no one answer will be so plainly right that everyone will agree. Nevertheless each judge will be trying, in good faith, to follow the rule-book ideal of the rule of law, because he will be trying, in good faith, to discover what the words in the rule book really mean.'

These semantic questions are very popular in Britain. A different set of questions – group-psychological questions – are now more popular in the United States. Those who favor group-psychological questions rather than semantic questions take decisions rather than words to be the heart of the matter. 'Why are the particular rules that a legislature enacts (rather than, for example, the rules that law professors prefer) the rules that form the rule book for law? Because legislators have been given authority by the community as a whole to *decide* what rules shall govern. The words they choose are formally the best evidence of what they have decided, because it is asumed that legislators use words in their standard meanings to report their decisions. But if, for some reason, the words used do not uniquely report a particular decision, then it is necessary to turn to whatever other evidence of what they intended to do we can find. Did the legislators – or some important group of them – suppose that their Race Relations Act would apply to political clubs so as to forbid racial discrimination there? If so, then the Act represents that decision, and it is that decision that is embedded in the rule book properly understood. But if they supposed that the Act would not apply to political clubs, then the rule book, properly understood, contains that decision instead.'

Once again there is no assumption that all reasonable lawyers will agree about what the legislators intended. On the contrary, defenders of the rule-book model know that even skilled lawyers will disagree over inferences of legislative intention drawn from the same evidence. They insist that the question of intention is nevertheless the right question to ask, because each judge who asks it is at least doing his best to follow the rule-book model and therefore (on this conception) to serve the rule of law.

The semantic and psychological questions these different groups propose are historical rather than political. A third (and more sophisticated) set of historical questions has recently gained in popularity. 'Suppose a hard case cannot be decided on semantic grounds. Perhaps the phrase "a section of the public" might just as properly be used to include as to exclude associations like political clubs. Suppose it cannot be decided by asking what the legislators who enacted that statute intended to accomplish. Perhaps very few legislators had even thought of the question whether political clubs should be included. We must then ask a question different from either the semantic or the psychological question, which is this. What would the legislature have decided if, contrary to fact, it *had* decided whether or not political clubs were to be included?' Lawyers who want to answer this counterfactual question might consider, for example, other decisions the same legislators reached in other areas of law. Or they might consider more broadly the pattern of legislation about race relations or freedom of association in recent years. They might use such evidence to argue, for example, that if Parliament had for some reason been forced to debate a clause explicitly extending the acts to political clubs, it would have approved that clause.

It is even more obvious in the case of this counterfactual historical question than in the case of the semantic or psychological question that reasonable lawyers will disagree about the conclusions to be drawn from the same evidence. But once again the rule-book conception deems it better that they try to answer this question, even though they disagree, than that they ask the different and political question, about which they will surely disagree, of what Parliament *should* have done. For the counterfactual question, like the semantic and psychological questions but unlike the political question, is supported by a theory that also supports and explains the rule-book conception itself. We follow the rule book, on this theory, because we assign to a political institution the responsibility and the power to decide how the police power of the state shall be used. If, on some occasion, that institution has in fact not decided that question (because it did not realize that a decision was necessary) but would have decided one way rather than the other if it had, then it is more in keeping with the rationale of the rule book that the power be used that way than the contrary way. If neither of the two decisions that a court might reach is actually recorded in the rule book, it is fairer, on this argument, to take the decision that would have been in the rule book but for a historical accident.

This argument for the counterfactual question concedes that the rule that is to be applied is not in the actual rule book. In this respect the counter factual question is different from the semantic and psychological questions' each of which can more plausibly be said to reveal what is in the actual rule book 'properly understood'. But the three sorts of questions have a more fundamental unity. Each aims at developing what might be called a 'rectified' rule book in which the collection of sentences is improved so as more faithfully to record the will of the various institutions whose decisions put those sentences into the rule book. The questions are all, in themselves, politically neutral questions, because they seek to bring to the surface a historical fact – the will of responsible lawmakers – rather than to impose a distinct and contemporary political judgment upon that will. It is perfectly true – and conceded, as I said, by the rule-book model – that any particular judge's answer to these political neutral questions may well be different from another judge's answer. It is the virtue of the different historical questions, not the certainty or predictability of the answer, that recommends these questions to the rule-book model. That conception of the rule of law opposes political questions, like the question of what the legislators should have done, not because these questions admit of different answers, but because they are simply the wrong questions to ask.

The rights conception, on the other hand, will insist that at least one kind of political question is precisely the question that judges faced with hard cases must ask. For the ultimate question *it* asks in a hard case is the question of whether the plaintiff has the moral right to receive, in court, what he or she or it demands. The rule book is *relevant* to that ultimate question. In a democracy, people have at least a strong *prima facie* moral right that courts enforce the rights that a representative legislature has enacted. That is why some cases are easy cases on the rights model as well as on the rule-book model. If it is clear what the legislature has granted them, then it is also clear what they have a moral right to receive in court. (That statement must be qualified in a democracy whose constitution limits legislative power. It must also be qualified (though it is a complex question how it must be qualified) in a democracy whose laws are fundamentally unjust.)

But though the rights model concedes that the rule book is in this way a source of moral rights in court, it denies that the rule book is the exclusive source of such rights. If, therefore, some case arises as to which the rule book is silent, or if the words in the rule book are subject to competing interpretations, then it is right to ask which of the two possible decisions in the case best fits the background moral rights of the parties. For the ideal of adjudication, under the rights model, is that, so far as is practicable, the moral rights that citizens actually have should be available to them in court.

So a decision that takes background rights into account will be superior, from the point of view of that ideal, to a decision that instead speculates on, for example, what the legislation would have done if it had done anything.

It is important to notice, however, that the rule book continues to exert an influence on the question of what rights the parties have, under the rights model, even when background moral rights also exert an influence. A judge who follows the rights conception of the rule of law will try, in a hard case, to frame some principle that strikes him as capturing, at the appropriate level of abstraction, the moral rights of the parties that are pertinent to the issues raised by the case. But he cannot apply such a principle unless it is, as a principle, consistent with the rule book, in the following sense. The principle must not conflict with other principles that must be presupposed in order to justify the rule he is enforcing, or any considerable part of the other rules. Suppose a judge himself approves what might be called a radical Christian principle: that each citizen is morally entitled that those who have more wealth than he does make available to him the surplus. He might wish to apply that principle to hard cases in tort or contract so as to refuse damages against a poor defendant, on the ground that the richer plaintiff's right to damages must be set off against the defendant's right to charity. But he cannot do so, because (for better or for worse) that principle is inconsistent with the vast bulk of the rules in the rule book. No adequate justification of what is in the rule book could be given, that is, without presupposing that the radical Christian principle has been rejected. The rights conception supposes that the rule book represents the community's efforts to capture moral rights and requires that any principle rejected in those efforts has no role in adjudication.

So a judge following the rights conception must not decide a hard case by appealing to any principle that is in that way incompatible with the rule book of his jurisdiction. But he must still decide many cases on political grounds, because in these cases contrary moral principles directly in point are each compatible with the rule book. Two judges will decide such a hard case differently because they hold different views about the background moral rights of citizens. Suppose a case applying a commercial statute requires a choice between a moral principle enforcing *caveat emptor* and a competing principle stressing the moral rights of contractual partners against each other, as members of a cooperative enterprise. It may well be – at a given stage of development of commercial law – that neither answer is in the sense described plainly incompatible with the British rule book taken as a whole. Each judge deciding that issue of principle decides as he does, not because all alternatives are excluded by what is already in the rule book, but because he believes his principle to be correct, or at least closer to correct than other principles that are also not excluded. So his decision is a political decision in the sense described. It is precisely that sort of political decision that the rule-book conception steadily condemns.

The two topics of this essay are in that way joined. The practical question, which asks whether judges should make political decisions in hard cases, is joined to the theoretical question of which of two conceptions of the rule of law is superior. The connection is threatening to the rights conception, because many people are convinced that it is wrong for judges to make political decisions and they will be anxious to reject any theory about the ideals of law that recommends them.

NOTES

1. J. A. G. Griffiths, *The Politics of the Judiciary* (Manchester: Manchester University Press, 1977; paperback ed., New York: Fontana Books, 1977).
2. Charter v. Race Relations Board (1973), A.C. 868.
3. Dockers' Labour Club v. Race Relations Board (1975), A.C. 259.
4. Secretary of State for Education and Science v. Tameside Metropolitan Borough Council (1976), 3 W.L.R. 641.
5. Shaw v. D.P.P. (1961), 2 W.L.R. 897.
6. Liversidge v. Anderson (1942), A.C. 206.
7. *Taking Rights Seriously* (Cambridge, Mass.: Harvard University Press, 1977; London: Duckworth, 1978).

LON FULLER
EXTRACTS FROM *THE MORALITY OF LAW*

This chapter will begin with a fairly lengthy allegory. It concerns the un-happy reign of a monarch who bore the convenient, but not very imaginative and not even very regal sounding name of Rex.

Eight ways to fail to make law

Rex came to the throne filled with the zeal of a reformer. He considered that the greatest failure of his predecessors had been in the field of law. For generations the legal system had known nothing like a basic reform. Procedures of trial were cumbersome, the rules of law spoke in the archaic tongue of another age, justice was expensive, the judges were slovenly and sometimes corrupt. Rex was resolved to remedy all this and to make his name in history as a great lawgiver. It was his unhappy fate to fail in this ambition. Indeed, he failed spectacularly, since not only did he not succeed in introducing the needed reforms, but he never even succeeded in creating any law at all, good or bad.

His first official act was, however, dramatic and propitous. Since he needed a clean slate on which to write, he announced to his subjects the immediate repeal of all existing law, of whatever kind. He then set about drafting a new code. Unfortunately, trained as a lonely prince, his education had been very defective. In particular he found himself incapable of making

Lon L. Fuller (1969), *The Morality of Law*, rev. ed., New Haven and London: Yale University Press.

even the simplest generalizations. Though not lacking in confidence when it came to deciding specific controversies, the effort to give articulate reasons for any conclusion strained his capacities to the breaking point.

Becoming aware of his limitations, Rex gave up the project of a code and announced to his subjects that henceforth he would act as a judge in any disputes that might arise among them. In this way under the stimulus of a variety of cases he hoped that his latent powers of generalization might develop and, proceeding case by case, he would gradually work out a system of rules that could be incorporated in a code. Unfortunately the defects in his education were more deep-seated than he had supposed. The venture failed completely. After he had handed down literally hundreds of decisions neither he nor his subjects could detect in those decisions any pattern whatsoever. Such tentatives toward generalization as were to be found in his opinions only compounded the confusion, for they gave false leads to his subjects and threw his own meager powers of judgment off balance in the decision of later cases.

After this fiasco Rex realized it was necessary to take a fresh start. His first move was to subscribe to a course of lessons in generalization. With his intellectual powers thus fortified, he resumed the project of a code and, after many hours of solitary labor, succeeded in preparing a fairly lengthy document. He was still not confident, however, that he had fully overcome his previous defects. Accordingly, he announced to his subjects that he had written out a code and would henceforth be governed by it in deciding cases, but that for an indefinite future the contents of the code would remain an official state secret, known only to him and his scrivener. To Rex's surprise this sensible plan was deeply resented by his subjects. They declared it was very unpleasant to have one's case decided by rules when there was no way of knowing what those rules were.

Stunned by this rejection Rex undertook an earnest inventory of his personal strengths and weaknesses. He decided that life had taught him one clear lesson, namely, that it is easier to decide things with the aid of hindsight than it is to attempt to foresee and control the future. Not only did hindsight make it easier to decide cases, but – and this was of supreme importance to Rex – it made it easier to give reasons. Deciding to capitalize on this insight, Rex hit on the following plan. At the beginning of each calendar year he would decide all the controversies that had arisen among his subjects during the preceding year. He would accompany his decisions with a full statement of reasons. Naturally, the reasons thus given would be understood as not controlling decisions in future years, for that would be to defeat the whole purpose of the new arrangment, which was to gain the advantages of hindsight. Rex confidently announced the new plan to his subjects, observing that he was going to publish the full text of his judgments with the rules applied by him, thus meeting the chief objection to the old plan. Rex's subjects received this announcement in silence, then quietly explained through their leaders that when they said they needed to know the rules, they meant they needed to know them *in advance* so they could act on them. Rex muttered something to the effect that they might have made that point a little clearer, but said he would see what could be done.

Rex now realized that there was no escape from a published code declaring the rules to be applied in future disputes. Continuing his lessons in generalization, Rex worked diligently on a revised code, and finally announced that it would shortly be published. This announcement was received with universal gratification. The dismay of Rex's subjects was all the more intense, therefore, when his code became available and it was discovered that it was truly a masterpiece of obscurity. Legal experts who studied it declared that there was not a single sentence in it that could be understood either by an ordinary citizen or by a trained lawyer. Indignation became general and soon a picket appeared before the royal palace carrying a sign that read, 'How can anybody follow a rule that nobody can understand?'

The code was quickly withdrawn. Recognizing for the first time that he needed assistance, Rex put a staff of experts to work on a revision. He instructed them to leave the substance untouched, but to clarify the expression throughout. The resulting code was a model of clarify, but as it was studied it became apparent that its new clarity had merely brought to light that it was honeycombed with contradictions. It was reliably reported that there was not a single provision in the code that was not nullified by another provision inconsistent with it. A picket again appeared before the royal residence carrying a sign that read, 'This time the king made himself clear – in both directions.'

Once again the code was withdrawn for revision. By now, however, Rex had lost his patience with his subjects and the negative attitude they seemed to adopt toward everything he tried to do for them. He decided to teach them a lesson and put an end to their carping. He instructed his experts to purge the code of contradictions, but at the same time to stiffen drastically every requirement contained in it and to add a long list of new crimes. Thus, where before the citizen summoned to the throne was given ten days in which to report, in the revision the time was cut to ten seconds. It was made a crime, punishable by ten years' imprisonment, to cough, sneeze, hiccough, faint or fall down in the presence of the king. It was made treason not to understand, believe in, and correctly profess the doctrine of evolutionary, democratic redemption.

When the new code was published a near revolution resulted. Leading citizens declared their intention to flout its provisions. Someone discovered in an ancient author a passage that seemed apt: 'To command what cannot be done is not to make law; it is to unmake law, for a command that cannot be obeyed serves no end but confusion, fear and chaos,' Soon this passage was being quoted in a hundred petitions to the king.

The code was again withdrawn and a staff of experts charged with the task of revision. Rex's instructions to the experts were that whenever they encountered a rule requiring an impossibility, it should be revised to make compliance possible. It turned out that to accomplish this result every provision in the code had to be substantially rewritten. The final result was, however, a triumph of draftsmanship. It was clear, consistent with itself, and demanded nothing of the subject that did no lie easily within his powers. It was printed and distributed free of charge on every street corner.

However, before the effective date for the new code had arrived, it was discovered that so much time had been spent in successive revisions of Rex's original draft, that the substance of the code had been seriously overtaken by events. Ever since Rex assumed the throne there had been a suspension of ordinary legal processes and this had brought about important economic and institutional changes within the country. Accommodation to these altered conditions required many changes of substance in the law. Accordingly as soon as the new code became legally effective, it was subjected to a daily stream of amendments. Again popular discontent mounted; an anonymous pamphlet appeared on the streets carrying scurrilous cartoons of the king and a leading article with the title: 'A law that changes every day is worse than no law at all.'

Within a short time this source of discontent began to cure itself as the pace of amendment gradually slackened. Before this had occurred to any noticeable degree, however, Rex announced an important decision. Reflecting on the misadventures of his reign, he concluded that much of the trouble lay in bad advice he had received from experts. He accordingly declared he was reassuming the judicial power in his own person. In this way he could directly control the application of the new code and insure his country against another crisis. He began to spend practically all of his time hearing and deciding cases arising under the new code.

As the king proceeded with this task, it seemed to bring to a belated blossoming his long dormant powers of generalization. His opinions began, indeed, to reveal a confident and almost exuberant virtuosity as he deftly distinguished his own previous decisions, exposed the principles on which he acted, and laid down guide lines for the disposition of future controversies. For Rex's subjects a new day seemed about to dawn when they could finally conform their conduct to a coherent body of rules.

This hope was, however, soon shattered. As the bound volumes of Rex's judgments became available and were subjected to closer study, his subjects were appalled to discover that there existed no discernible relation between those judgments and the code they purported to apply. Insofar as it found expression in the actual disposition of controversies, the new code might just as well not have existed at all. Yet in virtually every one of his decisions Rex declared and redeclared the code to be the basic law of his kingdom.

Leading citizens began to hold private meetings to discuss what measures, short of open revolt, could be taken to get the king away from the bench and back on the throne. While these discussions were going on Rex suddenly died, old before his time and deeply disillusioned with his subjects.

The first act of his successor, Rex II, was to announce that he was taking the powers of government away from the lawyers and placing them in the hands of psychiatrists and experts in public relations. This way, he explained, people could be made happy without rules.

The consequences of failure

Rex's bungling career as legislator and judge illustrates that the attempt to create and maintain a system of legal rules may miscarry in at least eight ways; there are in this enterprise, if you will, eight distinct routes to disaster. The first and most obvious lies in a failure to achieve rules at all, so that every issue must be decided on an ad hoc basis. The other routes are: (2) a failure to publicize, or at least to make available to the affected party, the rules he is expected to observe; (3) the abuse of retroactive legislation, which not only cannot itself guide action, but undercuts the integrity of rules prospective in effect, since it puts them under the threat of retrospective change; (4) a failure to make rules understandable; (5) the enactment of contradictory rules or (6) rules that require conduct beyond the powers of the affected party; (7) introducing such frequent changes in the rules that the subject cannot orient his action by them; and, finally, (8) a failure of congruence between the rules as announced and their actual administration.

A total failure in any one of these eight directions does not simply result in a bad system of law; it results in something that is not properly called a legal system at all, except perhaps in the Pickwickian sense in which a void contract can still be said to be one kind of contract. Certainly there can be no rational ground for asserting that a man can have a moral obligation to obey a legal rule that does not exist, or is kept secret from him, or that came into existence only after he had acted, or was unintelligible, or was contradicted by another rule of the same system, or commanded the impossible, or changed every minute. It may not be impossible for a man to obey a rule that is disregarded by those charged with its administration, but at some point obedience becomes futile – as futile, in fact, as casting a vote that will never be counted. As the sociologist Simmel has observed, there is a kind of reciprocity between government and the citizen with respect to the observance of rules.[1] Government says to the citizen in effect, 'These are the rules we expect you to follow. If you follow them, you have our assurance that they are the rules that will be applied to your conduct.' When this bond of reciprocity is finally and completely ruptured by government, nothing is left on which to ground the citizen's duty to observe the rules.

The citizen's predicament becomes more difficult when, though there is no total failure in any direction, there is a general and drastic deterioration in legality, such as occurred in Germany under Hitler.[2] A situation begins to develop, for example, in which though some laws are published, others, including the most important, are not. Though most laws are prospective in effect, so free a use is made of retrospective legislation that no law is immune to change ex post facto if it suits the convenience of those in power. For the trial of criminal cases concerned with loyalty to the regime, special military tribunals are established and these tribunals disregard, whenever it suits their convenience, the rules that are supposed to control their decisions. Increasingly the principal object of government seems to be, not that of giving the citizen rules by which to shape his conduct, but to frighten him into impotence. As such a situation develops, the problem faced by the citizen is not so simple as that of a voter who knows with certainty that his ballot will not be counted. It is more like that of the voter who knows that the odds are against his ballot being counted at all, and that if it is counted, there is a good chance that it will be counted for the side against which he actually voted. A citizen in this predicament has to decide for himself whether to stay with the system and cast his ballot as a kind of symbolic act expressing the hope of a better day. So it was with the German citizen under Hitler faced with deciding whether he had an obligation to obey such portions of the laws as the Nazi terror had left intact.

In situations like these there can be no simple principle by which to test the citizen's obligation of fidelity to law, any more than there can be such a principle for testing his right to engage in a general revolution. One thing is, however, clear. A mere respect for constituted authority must not be confused with fidelity to law. Rex's subjects, for example, remained faithful to him as king throughout his long and inept reign. They were not faithful to his law, for he never made any.

The aspiration toward perfection in legality

So far we have been concerned to trace out eight routes to failure in the enterprise of creating law. Corresponding to these are eight kinds of legal excellence toward which a system of rules may strive. What appear at the lowest level as indispensable conditions for the existence of law at all, become, as we ascend the scale of achievement, increasingly demanding challenges to human capacity. At the height of the ascent we are tempted to imagine a utopia of legality in which all rules are perfectly clear, consistent with one another, known to every citizen, and never retroactive. In this utopia the rules remain constant through time, demand only what is possible, and are scrupulously observed by courts, police, and everyone else charged with their administration. For reasons that I shall advance shortly, this utopia, in which all eight of the principles of legality are realized to perfection, is not actually a useful target for guiding the impulse toward legality; the goal of perfection is much more complex. Nevertheless it does suggest eight distinct standards by which excellence in legality may be tested.

In expounding in my first chapter the distinction between the morality of duty and that of aspiration, I spoke of an imaginary scale that starts at the bottom with the most obvious and essential moral duties and ascends upward to the highest achievements open to man. I also spoke of an invisible pointer as marking the dividing line where the pressure of duty leaves off and the challenge of excellence begins. The inner morality of law, it should now be clear, presents all of these aspects. It too embraces a morality of duty and a morality of aspiration. It too confronts us with the problem of knowing where to draw the boundary below which men will be condemned for failure, but can expect no praise for success, and above which they will be admired for success and at worst pitied for the lack of it.

In applying the analysis of the first chapter to our present subject, it becomes essential to consider certain distinctive qualities of the inner morality of law. In what may be called the basic morality of social life, duties that run toward other persons generally (as contrasted with those running toward specific individuals) normally require only forbearances, or as we say, are negative in nature: do not kill, do not injure, do not deceive, do not defame, and the like. Such duties lend themselves with a minimum of difficulty to formalized definition. That is to say, whether we are concerned with legal or moral duties, we are able to develop standards which designate with some precision – though it is never complete – the kind of conduct that is to be avoided.

The demands of the inner morality of the law, however, though they concern a relationship with persons generally, demand more than forbearances; they are, as we loosely say, affirmative in nature: make the law known, make it coherent and clear, see that your decisions as an official are guided by it, etc. To meet these demands human energies must be directed toward specific kinds of achievement and not merely warned away from harmful acts.

Because of the affirmative and creative quality of its demands, the inner morality of law lends itself badly to realization through duties, whether they be moral or legal. No matter how desirable a direction of human effort may appear to be, if we assert there is a duty to pursue it, we shall confront the responsibility of defining at what point that duty has been violated. It is easy to assert that the legislator has a moral duty to make his laws clear and understandable. But this remains at best an exhortation unless we are prepared to define the degree of clarity he must attain in order to discharge his duty. The notion of subjecting clarity to quantitative measure presents obvious difficulties. We may content ourselves, of course, by saying that the legislator has at least a moral duty to try to be clear. But this only postpones the difficulty, for in some situations nothing can be more baffling than to attempt to measure how vigorously a man intended to do that which he has failed to do. In the morality of law, in any event, good intentions are of little avail, as King Rex amply demonstrated. All of this adds up to the conclusion that the inner morality of law is condemned to remain largely a morality of aspiration and not of duty. Its primary appeal must be to a sense of trusteeship and to the pride of the craftsman.

To these observations there is one important exception. This relates to the desideratum of making the laws known, or at least making them available to those affected by them. Here we have a demand that lends itself with unusual readiness to formalization. A written constitution may prescribe that no statute shall become law until it has been given a specified form of publication. If the courts have power to effectuate this provision, we may speak of a legal requirement for the making of law. But a moral duty with respect to publication is also readily imaginable. A custom, for example, might define what kind of promulgation of laws is expected, at the same time leaving unclear what consequences attend a departure from the accepted mode of publication. A formalization of the desideratum of publicity has obvious advantages over uncanalized efforts, even when they are intelligently and conscientiously pursued. A formalized standard of promulgation not only tells the lawmaker where to publish his laws; it also lets the subject – or a lawyer representing his interests – know where to go to learn what the law is.

One might suppose that the principle condemning retroactive laws could also be very readily formalized in a simple rule that no such law should ever be passed, or should be valid if enacted. Such a rule would, however, disserve the cause of legality. Curiously, one of the most obvious seeming demands of legality – that a rule passed today should govern what happens tomorrow, not what happened yesterday – turns out to present some of the most difficult problems of the whole internal morality of law.

With respect to the demands of legality other than promulgation, then, the most we can expect of constitutions and courts is that they save us from the abyss; they cannot be expected to lay out very many compulsory steps toward truly significant accomplishment.

Legality and economic calculation

In my first chapter I attempted to demonstrate how, as we leave the morality of duty and ascend toward the highest levels of a morality of aspiration, the principle of marginal utility plays an increasing role in our decisions. On the level of duty, anything like economic calculation is out of place. In a morality of aspiration, it is not only in place, but becomes an integral part of the moral decision itself – increasingly so as we reach toward the highest levels of achievement.

It is not difficult to show that something like an economic calculation may become necessary when a conflict arises between the internal and external moralities of law. From the standpoint of the internal morality of law, for example, it is desirable that laws remain stable through time. But it is obvious that changes in circumstances, or changes in men's consciences, may demand changes in the substantive aims of law, and sometimes disturbingly frequent changes. Here we are often condemned to steer a wavering middle course between too frequent change and no change at all, sustained by the conviction, not that the course chosen is the only right one, but that we must in all events keep clear of the shoals of disaster that lie on either side.

It is much less obvious, I suspect, that antinomies may arise within the internal morality of law itself. Yet it is easy to demonstrate that the various desiderata which go to make up that morality may at times come into opposition with one another. Thus, it is simultaneously desirable that laws should remain stable through time and that they should be such as impose no insurmountable barriers to obedience. Yet rapid changes in circumstances, such as those attending an inflation, may render obedience to a particular law, which was once quite easy, increasingly difficult, to the point of approaching impossibility. Here again it may become necessary to pursue a middle course which involves some impairment of both desiderata.

During a visit to Poland in May of 1961 I had a conversation with a former Minister of Justice that is relevant here. She told how in the early days of the communist regime an earnest and sustained effort was made to draft the laws so clearly that they would be intelligible to the worker and peasant. It was soon discovered, however, that this kind of clarity could be attained only at the cost of those systematic elements in a legal system that shape its rules into a coherent whole and render them capable of consistent application by the courts. It was discovered, in other words, that making the laws readily understandable to the citizen carried a hidden cost in that it rendered their application by the courts more capricious and less predictable. Some retreat to a more balanced view therefore became unavoidable.

These examples and illustrations could be multiplied. Enough has been said, I believe, to show that the utopia of legality cannot be viewed as a situation in which each desideratum of the law's special morality is realized to perfection. This is no special quality – and certainly no peculiar defect – of the internal morality of law. In every human pursuit we shall always encounter the problem of balance at some point as we traverse the long road that leads from the abyss of total failure to the heights of human excellence.

NOTES

1. *The Sociology of Georg Simmel* (1950), trans. Wolff, §4, 'Interaction in the Idea of "Law"', pp. 186–9. Simmel's discussion is worthy of study by those concerned with defining the conditions under which the ideal of 'the rule of law' can be realized.

2. I have discussed some of the features of this deterioration in my article, 'Positivism and Fidelity to Law', 71 *Harvard Law Review* 630, 648–57 (1958). This article makes no attempt at a comprehensive survey of all the postwar judicial decisions in Germany concerned with events occurring during the Hitler regime. Some of the later decisions rested the nullity of judgments rendered by the courts under Hitler not on the ground that the statutes applied were void, but on the ground that the Nazi judges misinterpreted the statutes of their own government. See Pappe, 'On the Validity of Judicial Decisions in the Nazi Era', 23 *Modern Law Review* 260–74

(1960). Dr. Pappe makes more of this distinction than seems to me appropriate. After all, the meaning of a statute depends in part on accepted modes of interpretation. Can it be said that the postwar German courts gave full effect to Nazi laws when they interpreted them by their own standards instead of the quite different standards current during the Nazi regime? Moreover, with statutes of the kind involved, filled as they were with vague phrases and unrestricted delegations of power, it seems a little out of place to strain over questions of their proper interpretation.

3

CIVIL SOCIETY

Birgit Schippers

Introduction

Striking workers in Gdansk and civil rights campaigners in East Berlin; anti-globalisation marches in Seattle and anti-war protests in London; Zapatistas in Mexico and the mothers of the disappeared in Argentina: these are but a few examples which point to the need for understanding the political importance of civil society. Recent years have indeed seen a strong interest in civil society, resulting in a burgeoning literature on the topic (Cohen and Arato 1994; Keane 1998; Rosenblum and Post 2002; Baker 2002a). This renewed attention, although theoretical in nature, is a response to the transformation processes in Eastern Europe and South America, the discontent with democratic politics in the West and current debates on globalisation. Central to this revival are attempts to clarify civil society's relationship with the state, with citizenship and with democracy. Moreover, this renewed interest confirms civil society as a core concept of political thought which has engaged ancient, modern and contemporary political thinkers alike.

In this essay, I explore three related aspects which highlight the contemporary relevance of civil society. These are the link between civil society, active citizenship and democracy; the relationship between the state and civil society; and finally, the location of the political. I begin my discussion with an overview of the development of civil society in modern political thought, before outlining some of the discussions in contemporary political thought. I conclude by highlighting more recent deployments of the term 'civil society' in the context of globalisation.

CIVIL SOCIETY AND MODERN POLITICAL THOUGHT

The origins of the concept of civil society go back to ancient Greek and Roman political thought. Aristotle's *polis*, as well as Cicero's *societas civilis*, articulates the idea of a civil society, understood as a political community where citizens are actively engaged in the running of their affairs. This ancient equation between civil society and political community or the state persists well into the modern era. However, it is usually with the beginnings of modern political thought, with its emphasis on individualism, rights and contractualism, and with the establishment of a capitalist-bourgeois society that the concept of civil society receives a systematic treatment. It is important to bear in mind that the selection of thinkers mentioned in this section does not do justice to the breadth of writings on civil society that we find in modern political thought. In fact, the engagement with this idea was so widespread that almost every modern political thinker was occupied, to some extent, with this notion.

As mentioned above, both ancient and early modern political thought equate civil society with political society. The distinctive contribution of modern political thought towards the concept of civil society is its association with contract theory. According to contract theory, civil society, still understood as political society or the state, stands in contrast to natural society, and it emerges out of a social contract agreed upon by previously dispersed individuals. For Thomas Hobbes (1588–1679), for example, the social contract and the setting up of civil society emerge out of a necessity explained by his account of the state of nature. According to Hobbes, the state of nature is characterised by anarchy and disorder, a war of every man against every man. It is only with the Leviathan, a Hobbesian metaphor for civil or political society, that order and peace can be guaranteed. While this peace comes at the price of man's submission to the Leviathan, it protects the individual from arbitrary treatment at the hands of others. John Locke (1632–1704), another contract theorist, is equally concerned with the themes of safety and security. Like Hobbes, he distinguishes civil society, understood as the body politic which administers law, from the state of nature and he claims that 'those who are united into one body, and have a common established law and judicature to appeal to, with authority to decide controversies between them, and punish offenders, are in civil society one with another' (1993: 158). Moreover, 'wherever therefore any number of men are so united into one society, as to quit every one of his executive power of the law of nature, and to resign it to the public, there and there only is a political, or civil society' (Locke 1993: 159). For Jean-Jacques Rousseau (1712–78), civil society is equally synonymous with political society, and it is in civil society that civil liberties as well as the right to property are guaranteed and upheld. Thus, it is fair to claim that despite substantial differences, Hobbes, Locke and Rousseau see civil society as coterminous with the state, defined as a political community which upholds and guarantees the rights established with the transition from the state of nature into a civil community.

An important shift which paves the way towards a contemporary understanding of civil society occurs with the writings of the German philosopher Georg Wilhelm Friedrich Hegel (1770–1831). Hegel is often credited with providing *the* account of civil society, but, as we have seen above, his account is in fact only one amongst many. For Hegel, civil society is part of a triad which also comprises the family and the state. Crucially, civil and political society, or the state, become two distinct spheres. Civil society is now a realm of private associations, defined by contractual relationships between individuals which facilitate the pursuit of selfish interests. Hegel's philosophy in general and his account of civil society in particular have been enormously influential, shaping subsequent accounts of civil society. His influence is most obvious in the Marxist treatment of civil society, and it is Karl Marx (1818–83) himself who transforms Hegel's understanding of civil society.

Playing on the dual meaning of 'civil society' within the German language, which signifies civic as well as bourgeois society, Marx, in his essay 'On the Jewish Question' (2000), declares that civil society is, in effect, bourgeois. It is within civil society that the idea of the contract, an arrangement between two free individuals, is maintained. The idea of the free contract, according to Marx, disguises the fundamental inequality that exists between the capitalist, who owns the means of production, and the proletarian, who is forced to sell his labour since he is without the means of production. Marx deploys the notion of civil society in his radical critique of capitalism. However, his emphasis on the contractual aspect of civil society neglects the important civic dimension of this concept, a lack which is rectified in the works of another Marxist thinker, Antonio Gramsci (1891–1937).

Unlike Marx, Gramsci (1971) explicitly includes the political or civic aspect of civil society and he explores the political function which civil society fulfils. Civil society, according to Gramsci, is positioned between the realm of the (capitalist) economy and the state, or political society. Deploying a series of military metaphors, Gramsci contends that a rich and developed civil society can shield the state from a frontal revolutionary attack. The institutions of civil society, such as cultural organisations, schools, the churches and so on, provide a cohesive function which tie citizens into the state. Referring to the political conditions during the 1920s and 1930s in Europe, Gramsci claims that such a civil society exists in the West, and that the protective shield of associational life prevents a successful socialist attack on the Western liberal state. Unlike Western systems, which possessed such a developed civil society, pre-revolutionary Russia lacked a well-developed civil society, hence tsarist Russia was fully exposed to the revolutionary campaigns of the Bolsheviks.

What makes Gramsci's reworking of civil society so important for contemporary understandings is his recognition that civil society fulfils a political function, and it is with Gramsci that the political is no longer confined to the state, but finds a place in the realm of civil society. This reconceptualisation of the link between civil society and the political recognises the importance of civil society as an arena for political struggle and for transformative politics, captured for example by the struggles of the women's movement. Gramsci's ideas have been influential for contemporary reworkings of civil society, and his influence can be found in particular in the works of Louis Althusser, whose work on the role of ideological state apparatuses develops Gramsci's account of the political function of civil society. Michel Foucault's work on governmentality (1991a), although by no means a Marxist account of either state or civil society, also resembles Gramsci's claim of the political function of civil society. The ideas of Gramsci, as indeed of Althusser and Foucault, have also influenced the works of two other contemporary thinkers, Ernesto Laclau and Chantal Mouffe. I shall turn to a discussion of their ideas in the next section.

CIVIL SOCIETY AND CONTEMPORARY POLITICAL THOUGHT

With the exception of Gramsci, it is fair to claim that the engagement with civil society, which, as we have seen, is so prominent in modern political thought, suffers a setback in the mid-nineteenth century. Indeed, John Keane, an influential scholar of civil society, defines the 1850s as the beginning of a 'century of neglect' (1988: 1) which has only recently been overcome. This revival of civil society, as I have already indicated, owes much to the transformation processes in Eastern Europe and South America, developments which have been covered extensively in the literature (cf. Baker 2000a; Kaviraj and Khilnani 2001; Laxer and Halperin 2003). It is crucial to stress, though, that the renewed interest in civil society also reflects discontent with late capitalist states and their democratic deficit. This discontent with the inability of modern systems of representation to accommodate views outside the mainstream and to facilitate forms of active citizenship has led to the hope that civil society may invigorate democratic politics and counter the stifling grip of the late modern, bureaucratic capitalist state.

This emphasis on the democratising potential of civil society is shared by normative theorists, poststructuralists and theorists of radical democracy alike. It is a central thesis of two contemporary theoreticians of civil society, Jean Cohen and Andrew Arato (1994). Cohen and Arato present possibly the most detailed treatment of civil society in contemporary political thought. They define civil society as a layer consisting of voluntary organisations and non-state actors which lies outside the realm of the state on the one hand and the capitalist economy on the other (1994: 2). This layer of associational life is accorded an important role, namely the reinvigoration and expansion of democratic participation. The importance of associational life, independent of the state, is also stressed by Charles Taylor. Referring to the transformation processes in Eastern Europe, he conceptualises civil society as 'a web of autonomous associations, independent of the state, which [binds] citizens together in matters of common concern, and [which] by their mere existence or action could have an effect on public policy' (1997: 66). Importantly, Taylor emphasises that civil society can only flourish in a liberal political environment, a claim shared by Jürgen Habermas, who contends that 'a robust civil society can develop only in the context of a liberal political culture' (1997: 371). This claim, however, points to an important aspect: that civil society is not unproblematically independent or autonomous with respect to the state. In fact, we can see from the works of Cohen and Arato, Taylor and Habermas alike that the relationship between civil society and the state is intertwined. This claim is given empirical as well as theoretical credence. For example, social movements are considered amongst the privileged agents of civil society. Through their political practice, they deepen the prospects for active participation and they strive towards more extensive forms of democratic citizenship. Social-movement politics, however, is not confined to the realm of civil society, but finds its way into the established political system. As articulated by Taylor, it may have an effect on policy. Over the last thirty-five years, the politics of the women's movement, for example, has had a profound impact upon policy, such as equality legislation, the establishment of an Equal Opportunities Commission, and changes in policy in the realm of reproductive rights. Likewise, the ecology movement has made 'green issues' part of the political agenda and the policy process. By setting up green parties, it has also entered into the realm of the formal institutions of the state. These parties contest elections and in some cases even participate in government.

Habermas in particular stresses the importance of translating associational politics into institutional politics, if it is to become effective. While sympathetic towards a politics emerging from within civil society, he concludes that the impetus coming from within civil society must be transformed into what he calls the 'institutionalised procedures of democratic opinion and will formation':

> Public influence is transformed into communicative power only after it passes through the filters of the institutionalised procedures of democratic opinion- and will-formation and enters through parliamentary debates into legitimate law-making.... Not influence per se, but influence transformed into communicative power legitimates political decisions. The popular sovereignty set communicatively aflow cannot make itself felt solely in the influence of informal public discourses – not even when these discourses arise from autonomous

public spheres. To generate political power, their influence must have an effect on the democratically regulated deliberations of democratically elected assemblies and assume an authorized form in formal decisions. (1997: 371–2)

Thus, despite the general recognition of the democratic and participatory potential of civil society, many theorists of civil society remain sceptical as to its efficacy. This scepticism towards civil society is reflected in the selected excerpts, and although all of the chosen theorists recognise the importance of civil society for a democratic polity, they are also, in different ways, hesitant as to the prospect that civil society can promise a fair, just and equal society. The two approaches presented in the excerpts, post-Marxism and communicative democracy, share a concern with the extension of democratic participation and the restriction of influence of a bureaucratic state, as well as with issues of social justice and equality. They affirm the importance of a politics of civil society, which they see as a potential guarantor of democratic involvement and an arena for citizenship. They are also, however, for various reasons, sceptical regarding the democratic potential of civil society.

The emphasis on the democratic impetus of civil society is a central motif of Laclau and Mouffe's account. Laclau and Mouffe are concerned with three issues: the extension and deepening of the democratic struggle beyond a liberal-democratic framework; the dividing line between the state and civil society; and the location of the political. They engage in a project they call 'post-Marxism', an attempt to rework and develop the Marxist project while avoiding what they consider the dual pitfalls of Marxist classism and essentialism. According to Laclau and Mouffe, class should no longer be considered the primary category of social analysis and political action, and they propose to extend the field of analysis to previously marginalised categories such as gender or race. This recognition of the importance of identity as a category of analysis and political practice, however, should not be based upon the assumption that identity is fixed or given. Rather, building upon the poststructuralist critique of the unified subject, they insist on the discursive production of all identity.

Developing their critique of Marxist classism and essentialism, Laclau and Mouffe also target the alleged 'statism' and 'economism' of Marxism. In their view, one of the weaknesses of Marxist theory and practice was its focus on the state and its pre-occupation with economic issues. Against such a state-centred focus and developing the work of Gramsci, they propose to extend the field of democratic struggles to civil society. They assert that 'it is not in the abandonment of the democratic terrain but, on the contrary, in the extension of the field of democratic struggles to the whole of civil society and the state, that the possibility resides for a hegemonic strategy of the Left' (1985: 176). Unlike the work of Habermas, which is woven into the fabric of liberal democracy, Laclau and Mouffe suggest a model of democracy which does not just deepen but goes beyond liberal democracy, and they offer an understanding of civil society which aims to work towards a model of radical and plural democracy, based upon alliances and hegemonic projects.

Like other theorists of civil society, Laclau and Mouffe envisage social movements as important agents of these struggles. However, they do not claim that social movements are privileged agents of political change. Moreover, they do not wish to substitute civil societal struggles with struggles within the state apparatus. For them, civil society is not the privileged terrain of political struggle. Indeed, while they propose to extend the terrain of struggle to civil society in order to further their project of radical democracy, they are aware of the limitations of civil society. Crucially, Laclau and Mouffe stress that civil society generates and displays forms of oppression which can only be regulated and indeed overcome by the state. Referring to the struggles of the women's movement, they contend that 'the state is an important means for effecting an advance, frequently against civil society, in legislation which combats sexism' (1985: 180). Central to their argument is the claim that the line between state and civil society in the struggle for radical democracy cannot be determined in advance. This also precludes any predictions regarding the role that either state or civil society may play. Civil society is but one terrain of the struggle for radical democracy; besides, it can uphold and maintain relationships of subordination. In such a case, it may be necessary to invoke the state in order to rectify forms of subordination.

Whilst Laclau and Mouffe contend that the role of civil society in the advancement of transformative politics cannot be decided in advance and indeed depends upon concrete historical circumstances, Carole Pateman (1989) proffers a much stronger critique of civil society. It is her central thesis that civil society does not adequately facilitate feminist struggles, and that women are only selectively included into this realm. Pateman's work belongs to a tradition of feminist scholarship which emerged over the last three decades and which has been instrumental in formulating a critique of the core concepts of political thought, highlighting in particular the exclusionary assumptions of the canon of political thought. It is safe to say that Pateman has been at the forefront of articulating this critique. She returns to the writings of the contract theorists, such as Hobbes, Locke and Rousseau. In her reading of these classics of modern political thought, Pateman pinpoints the blind spots of these classics, based upon the split between the public and private realms and the exclusion or merely partial inclusion of women. Her target is contract theory, which presumes a disembodied subject and excludes those associated with the body: women. According to Pateman, political theory is thoroughly patriarchal (1989: 34). It is this patriarchal nature of political theory which constitutes the concepts of political discourse in opposition to an alleged female nature. Moreover, civil society emerges out of a fraternal social contract which is contingent upon the patriarchal domination of men over women. Following Pateman, 'the "original" creation of civil society through the social contract is a patriarchal construction which is also a separation of the sexes' (1989: 34). She contends that civil society is constituted as a fraternal pact, effectively establishing a patriarchal-masculine order.

Crucially, Pateman argues that the public–private distinction which is central to modern contract theory undergoes a shift: initially, the realm of the civil is part of the public sphere. However, following the transformations in the concept of civil society, from an association with political society or the state towards its separation from the state, Pateman outlines how civil society, together with the realm of the family, becomes part of the private sphere. Women, however, do not gain much from this transformation, as their inclusion into the sphere of politics remains selective. And even though contemporary citizenship includes women, they are only included as men: 'women in civil society must disavow our bodies and act as part of the brotherhood – but since we are never regarded as other than women, we must simultaneously continue to affirm the patriarchal conception of femininity, or patriarchal subjection' (Pateman 1989: 52).

Iris Marion Young, who could be described as a friendly critic of the idea of civil society, is nevertheless sceptical as to the potential of civil society. Unlike Pateman, she is not so concerned with the origins of the concept or with the exclusionary processes of civil society. Rather, she wonders whether civil society can provide the kind of justice necessary for non-oppressive political relations. Like other thinkers on civil society, Young endorses the democratic and democratising potential of civil society. However, she is sceptical as to the potential for justice which may emerge from civil society. According to Young, only state institutions can adequately protect citizens from injustice and promote justice and self-development. The potential for self-development requires resorting to the state. Young's emphasis lies with the human potential for self-development. This includes mechanisms for redistribution, in accordance with principles of justice. She fears that the power of the market, and of a profit-driven market economy, may undermine liberty and the potential for self-development of individual citizens. According to Young, it is the 'endemic consequences of profit- and market-oriented economic processes' which need to be corrected by the state.

Like Laclau and Mouffe, Young emphasises how civil society enhances democracy and social solidarity. However, she is particularly concerned with the limits of civil society. In fact, she emphasises the importance of the state and state institutions if we want to undermine oppression and promote social justice. Whilst the critics of the state, including libertarians, communitarians and post-Marxists, emphasise the potential for self-determination which civil society facilitates, Young contends that self-determination must be balanced against the equally important value of self-development. Too much reliance on civil society, including the market forces of civil society, can in fact undermine self-development and hinder the development of the most vulnerable and marginalised groups in society. It is the state, over and potentially against civil society, which guarantees self-development by intervening, directing and regulating economic activity. This regulation of market forces, according to Young, cannot be achieved by civil society (2000: 186), since civil society lacks the required powers of co-ordination and may even exacerbate existing inequalities. Thus it is necessary to rely on public policy to promote social justice. Nevertheless, Young acknowledges that state activity alone cannot sufficiently guarantee a good life. Public policy must be coupled with the critical accountability which emerges in and from within civil society.

TOWARDS A GLOBAL CIVIL SOCIETY

Given Young's concern with the unfettered forces of the market, she insists that the state is necessary to provide the kind of regulation which civil society cannot deliver. Her decisive endorsement of the role of the state stands in contrast to Laclau and Mouffe's emphasis on the undecidability of the location of the political. However, it would be wrong to accuse Young of a naïve favouring of the state over and against civil society. Whilst she could be criticised for an optimistic assessment of the state's capacity or indeed willingness to interfere in the market, she also acknowledges that civic accountability is required in order to regulate the state. In fact, this civil societal control over the state seems ever more pressing in an age of globalisation, where multinational corporations impact upon the lives of people across national boundaries, and where many states are exposed to the movements of global capital and the decisions made by international financial institutions, such as the International Monetary Fund, which lack democratic accountability. Young acknowledges this and thus insists on the need for a global civil society which can organise people across the globe.

Young's concern with the global dimension of civil society is reflected in the growing literature on the topic (cf. Colás 2002; Baker 2002b; Kaldor 2003; Keane 2003). What, though, is meant by global civil society? How does it constitute itself? If, as we have seen, civil society sets itself up in relation to the state, is it possible to talk about a global civil society in the absence of a global state? Despite the absence of a consensus on the nature and capacity of a global civil society, most debates highlight three related aspects: the challenge to economic globalisation; the exercise of global citizenship; and its link with issues of global justice and peace. Let us take a closer look at these three dimensions of global civil society, beginning with the challenge posed to the processes and implications of economic globalisation.

Globalisation, the general interconnectedness of different parts of the globe, is undoubtedly one of the buzzwords of recent debates. Given the omnipresence of globalisation, it has not failed to make an impact upon discussions of civil society. Although the term 'globalisation' captures a variety of phenomena, it is the focus on economic globalisation which has attracted particular attention. A contested development, it has been endorsed as a contribution to wealth and prosperity on the one hand, and condemned as the source of the widening gap between rich and poor, the origin of a new colonialism and of ecological destruction on the other. Economic globalisation, the integration of different regions of the world into a global market, and the operation of multinational businesses, unrestrained from government control, national laws and regulations, as well as the policies of those international organisations which support neo-liberal policies on a global level, such as the IMF, have led to widespread protests which united disparate groups: indigenous peoples from Central and South America, ecologists and development agencies from the northern hemisphere, women's organisations, human rights groups and so on. The political practices deployed by these groups, such as loosely co-ordinated activities, independent of state institutions and transcending national boundaries and confines, effectively constitute what we might call a global civil society.

The resistance to economic globalisation can also be considered as an act of global citizenship, against the power of multinational corporations and unaccountable international organisations. Referring to well-publicised campaigns, such as the protests against the free trade policy of the international governmental regime, the 'Battle of Seattle' in 1999, and protests in Washington in 2000 and Genoa in 2001, Naomi Klein, a well-known figure in the anti-globalisation movement, contends that 'world leaders can't have lunch together these days without somebody organizing a counter-summit – gatherings that bring together everyone from sweatshop workers trying to unionize the zones to teachers fighting the corporate takeover of education' (2001: 443). This link between global associational activities in a global civil society and global citizenship, the exercise of political agency above and beyond the level of the state, is not confined to the protest against economic globalisation. In fact, the activities of international non-governmental organisations (INGOs) such as Amnesty International or Greenpeace could all be subsumed under the label 'global citizenship in a global civil society'. These associational activities across boundaries also highlight the distinctive nature of global civil society: whereas civil society on a national level is contingent upon the existence of the state, global civil society thrives in the absence of a global state. Moreover, it may provide global politics with the kind of democratic impetus which intergovernmental activities, or those actions confined to the system of international organisations, such as the

United Nations, lack, as it allows for active participation not just across national boundaries, but also in a variety of organisational forms.

However, the relationship between associations on the one hand, and intergovernmental institutions and states on the other, should not be seen as a dichotomy, and nowhere is this clearer than in the realm of global justice and security. To take one example: attempts to establish an international criminal court to provide a judicial response to crimes which are not prosecuted nationally are only possible because of a concerted effort from human rights campaigners, international organisations and individual states, thus effectively establishing a system of global governance. To take a further example: repeated attempts to develop an effective and enforceable system of human rights which shall serve as an enforceable standard of acceptable political behaviour and as a deterrent against human rights abuses could also be seen as the outcome of global civil society.

These concerted efforts of INGOs, intergovernmental organisations and individual states are also said to contribute to international security and peace. According to Mary Kaldor, global civil society 'has to be understood in the context of an emerging framework of global governance that includes international organizations as well as states, and in which states are transformed from unilateralist war-making states to multilateralist law-making states' (2003: 13). Providing a legal framework which guides the actions of state and non-state actors will contribute, according to Kaldor, to a more accountable international arena. Moreover, 'the role of global civil society in a system of global governance is not a substitute for democracy at a national level, but rather should be viewed as a supplement in an era when classical democracy is weakened in the context of globalization' (2003: 13).

Not all commentators are so optimistic. In fact, some contend that the most effective resistance to globalisation occurs nationally (Laxer and Halperin 2003). Still, the idea of a global civil society is undoubtedly an important development in the history of the concept.

CONCLUSION

In this essay, I have argued that civil society is a concept to be reckoned with if we take seriously the challenge of democratic participation and active citizenship. As I have outlined, it is in particular recent developments relating to discussions of globalisation, including the global distribution of wealth, the ecological protection of the planet, global justice and peace, which have sparked the renewed interest in civil society. However, civil society is not easy to pin down, and its relationship with the state, and indeed its democratising impulse, remain contested. It is fair to predict that these issues will continue to engage students of civil society for years to come. Despite a lack of clarity, civil society engages politics, and by broadening the concept of the political from the realm of state institutions to wider aspects of society it has deserved its place amongst the concepts of contemporary political thought.

QUESTIONS FOR DISCUSSION

- Does civil society facilitate democratic politics?
- Is civil society a gendered concept?
- How would you characterise the relationship between civil society and the state?
- Is it possible to talk about global civil society in the absence of a global state?

IRIS MARION YOUNG
EXTRACTS FROM *INCLUSION AND DEMOCRACY*

[···]

The limits of civil society

The rediscovery of civil society [···] is an important development in both contemporary political theory and practice. Especially when we understand civil society as a third sector outside of and anchoring both state and economy, the theory of civil society reveals powerful means of enhancing democracy and social solidarity. These functions have been relatively neglected by political theorists concentrating on state and economy. Renewed interest in civil society, however, coincides with new expressions of scepticism about state institutions. Anti-state sentiment in many parts of the world has helped to create conditions for dismantling state enterprises, regulatory and planning functions, and welfare services. Coincidentally, some political analysts regard civil society more highly than the state as a means for citizens to pursue social justice and well-being.

In this section I challenge this tendency to regard civil society as an alternative site for the performance of public-spirited, caring, and equalizing functions that have long been associated with governments. While civil society can promote democracy, social justice, and well-being in ways I have outlined, there are limits to what citizens can accomplish through institutions of civil society alone. Some argue that the fragmentation and plurality

Iris Marion Young (2000), *Inclusion and Democracy*, Oxford: Oxford University Press.

of civil society can undermine the trust and solidarity necessary for self-determining democracy,[1] and I think that there is merit to this argument. Here I will be more concerned with limits to the ability of civil society to address issues of justice as self-development. Especially because profit- and market-oriented economic activities inhibit the self-development of many people, citizens must rely on state institutions to take positive action to undermine oppression and promote justice. While state power must always be subject to vigilant scrutiny by citizens alert to dangers of corruption and domination, democratic state institutions nevertheless have unique and important virtues for promoting social justice.

I assume that no critics of state institutions today deny that states are important for policing, adjudicating conflict, and enforcing basic liberties. Nevertheless, many consider state institutions as necessary evils which ought to be kept to a minimum and are not to be trusted. We should not look to states, on this view, to take more expansive and substantial action to further the well-being of persons and groups. While it is always good to reduce suffering or injustice, solve social problems, and promote well-being, we should not depend on states to do it. Critics of the state have at least three kinds of argument for the claim that citizens should reject reliance on state institutions to solve social problems and promote justice as the equal opportunity for everyone to develop and exercise capacities: libertarian, communitarian, and post-Marxist. I will reconstruct each of these arguments, and then respond to them together.

The libertarian argument is familiar. Maximizing the liberty of individuals and organizations to pursue their own ends is the primary principle of justice. Coercive state institutions are justified only in order to enforce liberty, that is, to prevent some agents from interfering with others' legitimate exercise of their liberty. Although a society may contain many social and economic problems, many conflicts, injustices, and harmful inequalities, these are more properly addressed by voluntary co-operation in settings of private enterprise and civil society than by means of state regulation. It is wrong to use state institutions to try to produce substantive social outcomes in the way of resources use, income distribution, or the allocation of social positions. Aiming to do so, moreover, is likely to produce irrational or inefficient consequences. Minimizing the reach of state institutions is thus the social ideal.[2]

The communitarian argument differs from the libertarian in its positive concern for substantive values of caring, solidarity, and civic virtue. While communitarians endorse the value of liberty, protection of liberty is but one among several principles that ought to guide moral and political life, and may be overridden for the sake of promoting values of community. Communitarian morality, moreover, aims at fostering and nurturing substantive ends of mutual aid and shared cultural symbols and practices. As grounds for preferring institutions of civil society to state institutions to realize the ends of mutual aid, caring, and social justice, some communitarians suggest the following. State bureaucratic institutions that provide social services, re-distribute income, regulate economic activity, and so on, break down and distort local communities because they universalize and formalize these ac-tivities and curtail local autonomy. Government regulatory, redistributive, welfare, and social service bureaucracies, moreover, transform citizens into passive followers of orders and clients of services. State efforts to promote citizen well-being, furthermore, allow individuals and communities to shirk their personal and particular responsibilities to contribute to the well-being of community members. State actions break up the civic sources of mutual aid and solidarity. Government programmes to achieve substantive ends of equality or self-development generate an 'entitlement' mentality according to which citizens clamour for particular benefits to serve their interests with-out being willing to make social contributions, thus ultimately overloading and weakening the state. Good citizens are independent and autonomous, rather than dependent on others, at the same time that they manifest a com-mitment to promote the well-being of others and of the institutions and values of the community. Thus, rather than create and sustain bureaucratic state institutions to promote the well-being of citizens, public policy should devote itself to supporting civic education to instil in citizens a sense of obligation to others and the skills to organize civic institutions of solidarity and mutual aid.[3]

I call 'post-Marxist' those writers and activists in the socialist tradition who continue to be critical of capitalist economic processes and who argue for radical democracy, but who also criticize some aspects of historic Marx-ism. Post-Marxists express several reasons for turning to civil society as the arena for pursuing democracy and social justice, and for taking a distance from the state.

Most socialists traditionally understood their political project to consist in using state institutions to control the means of production and direct them to meeting needs and developing capacities. Some post-Marxists question this state socialist project because it assumes that the state can be a single agent outside society directing its operations as a whole, when the state should be understood as part of society. Even if it holds democratic ide-als, moreover, state socialism collapses the distinction between state and economy which helps the lifeworld of civil society to maintain its freedom and autonomy from coercive regulation.[4] The radical anti-capitalist pursuit of justice is better thought of as a project of democratizing both the state, corporate economy, and civil society than bringing all the production and distribution of goods under democratic state direction.

While most post-Marxists support existing social insurance and welfare programmes, they also raise critical questions about capitalist welfare states. Interventionist and redistributive policies in the context of capitalism can be sustained under conditions of rapid growth and relative insulation from foreign competition. Without these conditions, the fiscal and managerial tensions of supporting large welfare states become manifest, and states retreat from economic regulation and welfare provision.[5] Activities to meet needs and provide social services that come under the bureaucratic rationality of the state, moreover, disorganize the democratic communicative potential of family and community, replacing them with normalizing, dominating, and pacifying regulatory regimes to which clients must submit or do without help.[6]

Like traditional Marxists, finally, some post-Marxists argue that in capitalist societies states do not neutrally represent all social sectors, but rather respond most to the imperatives of capital accumulation. States that try to control investment and service provision in ways that conflict with the interests of big economic actors are faced with capital flight and disinvestment. When states are thus dominated by economic power, social change movements of environmentalists or economic egalitarians are bound to be co-opted if they try to work within the state. Movements for social justice should thus limit their activity to pressuring state and economy from outside in civil society, and to enlarging the activity of democratic associations and economic co-operatives in the independent sector.[7]

Each of these arguments gives primary value to self-determination. The libertarian position above all values individual self-determination defined as the negative liberty of persons and enterprises. Both communitarians and neo-Marxists hold that libertarians do not recognize how the power of large organizations often seriously inhibits an individual's self-determination, and how the interdependence of modern social life transforms the meaning of self-determination. Because individual well-being depends on communicative and associative relations with others, and because social and economic processes generate collective problems, individuals can determine the conditions of their action primarily as participants in democratic decisions about community affairs. In my view, all three of these arguments tend to forget that social justice involves not only self-determination but also self-development.

[···] Self-development means being able actively to engage in the world and grow. Just social institutions provide conditions for all persons to learn and use satisfying and expansive skills in socially recognized settings, and enable them to play and communicate with others or express their feelings and perspective on social life in contexts where others can listen. Self-development in this sense certainly entails meeting people's basic needs for food, shelter, health care, and so on. It also entails the use of resources for education and training. Self-development does not depend simply on a certain distribution of material goods. Using satisfying skills and having one's particular cultural modes of expression and ways of life recognized also depend on the organization of the division of labour and the structures of communication and co-operation. While self-development is thus not reducible to the distribution of resources, market- and profit-oriented economic processes particularly impinge on the ability of many to develop and exercise capacities. Because this is so, pursuit of justice as self-development cannot rely on the communicative and organizational activities of civil society alone, but requires positive state intervention to regulate and direct economic activity.

Before making that argument, I should make clear that I agree with the post-Marxist critique of state socialism for its totalizing tendencies. State power threatens freedom and self-determination, and should be limited by markets and independent economic enterprise, on the one hand, and strong independent networks of civic and politcal associations, on the other. Confining state institutions to enforcing agreements, adjudicating disputes, and protecting private liberties, however, cedes too much scope for economically based oppression. Social justice requires the mutual limitation of state, economy, and civil society.

Profit- and market-oriented economic processes impede the ability of many people in most societies to develope and exercise capacities, due to at least the following factors. Business cycles, along with technological and organizational changes aimed at reducing labour costs, regularly throw people out of work. Commodity markets increasingly favour big producers over the small farmer or craftsperson. Vast numbers of people are thereby economically marginalized, without meaningful work and means of subsistence. Many unemployed people are so worried about survival that they have little time and energy for volunteer contributions to their communities, and many employed people also lack the time. Many currently employed people live at the edge of economic insecurity. This would not count as remediable injustice if their society lacked resources for remediation. Both locally and globally, however, there are such vast inequalities of wealth, comfort, and privilege that structural change could enable more people to develop and exercise capacities. Rationalization of production or service delivery to minimize costs per unit by mechanization often subdivides the work process so thoroughly that performing it does not require learning and using satisfying skills even when the work requires significant concentration. Market-driven investment and pricing decisions encourage the proliferation of gadgets and cheap entertainment at the same time that they fail to provide housing, health care, and quality education and training affordable to everyone. Markets produce numbers of harmful or socially costly consequences as 'externalities' difficult to charge to particular responsible parties, such as pollution, congestion, needs to travel greater distances, despoliation of city and countryside, and other damages to the collective quality of life.

If promoting social justice means that societies should, as much as possible, aim to make conditions for self-development available for everyone, then these endemic consequences of profit- and market-oriented economic processes ought to be corrected. The most direct and rational response entails, on the one hand, socially directed investment decisions to meet needs, provide education and training, and create and maintain quality infrastructure, parks, pleasant and well-lighted streets, and other such public spaces; and, on the other hand, the organization of the necessary, useful, and creative work of the society so that everyone able to make social contributions has the opportunity to do so.

The associations of civil society certainly can respond to the failures of firms and markets to enable the development exercise of capacities. Civil society alone, however, cannot do the major work of directing investment towards meeting needs and developing skills and usefully employing its members. Ensuring investment in needs, infrastructure, and education and training enough to support self-development for everyone and the organization of the work of society so that everyone who is able does meaningful work requires much society-wide decision-making and co-ordinated action. Precisely the virtues of civil society, however – voluntary association, decentralization, freedom to start new and unusual things – mitigate against such co-ordination. Indeed, the activities of civil society may exacerbate problems of inequality, marginalization, and inhibition of the development of capabilities. For persons and groups with greater material and organizational resources are liable to maintain and even enlarge their social advantages through their associational activity. Especially to the extent that their associational life is private as distinct from civicly oriented, their associational activities often reinforce unequal opportunities for developing capabilities. Associations of civil society, moreover, cannot mobilize the amount of resources necessary to support conditions for the self-development of everyone.

State institutions in principle are the most important means of regulating and directing economic life for the sake of the self-development of everyone. Only state institutions have the kind of power that can limit the power of large private enterprises and facilitate the use of that private power for the collective well-being. Well-organized states accomplish large-scale collective goals by facilitating social co-ordination among individuals and groups. To manage such co-ordination states must be centralized and regulative: they must gather useful information, monitor implementation and compliance, and rely on coercion in case of non-compliance. Only state institutions can facilitate the co-ordination required for a society to ensure investment in needs, skills development, infrastructure, and quality environment for everyone, and to organize many useful occupations so that those not self-employed or working for private enterprise have options for meaningful work. Democratically legitimized states are not necessary evils; potentially and sometimes actually, they exhibit uniquely important virtues to support social justice in ways no other social processes do.[8]

The claim that citizens ought to promote justice as self-development as well as self-determination, and that state institutions are the most important means of doing so, raises many questions about how this should be done. Reasonable people disagree about what values and priorities come under the umbrella of social justice. They disagree as well about what policies are most efficient and effective for promoting the well-being of citizens, and require the fewest trade-offs with other values. Addressing all these debates would require much more than I can accomplish here. The point of this argument is not to advocate particular policy solutions to problems of poverty, segregation, or economic domination. It is rather only to argue that democratic citizens should look to law and public policy to address these and related problems, and should consider state institutions and their actions major sites of democratic struggle, not merely for the sake of resisting corruption and the abuse of power, but also for taking action to foster social changes to promote greater justice.

Libertarians, of course, object that the use of the state to promote particular social outcomes wrongly interferes with the liberty of individuals, organizations, and firms. I have assumed that social justice requires that everyone has an equal opportunity to develop and exercise capacities. I have argued that such opportunities are by no means guaranteed by the workings of private enterprise and civil society, and further that profit- and market-oriented economic activity contributes to the inhibition of the capacities of many. As Robert Goodin argues, the libertarian claim that each should be allowed to attend to his or her own business without interference does not apply where discharging a moral obligation is the business of nobody in particular.[9] Under such circumstances, the state is the means by which the collective discharges its obligations, and it is permissible for the democratic state to compel everyone to contribute to those moral priorities.

From both communitarians and post-Marxists might come the dependency-domination objection. If states co-ordinate investment and the division of labour in ways to ensure that everyone can develop and exercise capacities, they do so at the cost of making citizens dependent on state action and submitting them to bureaucratic rules. Society-wide co-ordination of action through the state does generate formal regulation and bureaucracy which can have pacifying and dominating effects. The proper response to such dangers is not to reject state action to achieve objectives best achieved by governments, but rather to couple that action with the flexibility and critical accountability of civil society. [· · ·]

One of the post-Marxist arguments for restricting the pursuit of social justice to activities in civil society may work most directly against the image of the virtuous state I have offered. Don't I assume that the state is a neutral instrument citizens can use to co-ordinate their collective lives towards particular ends? Isn't it rather the case that the very economic powers I argue ought to be regulated for the sake of ensuring self-development and well-being themselves manipulate states for the sake of their own interests? There is considerable truth in this claim, especially in these days of globalization, when economic powers larger and more powerful than states hamper the ability of most states to fashion policies that will promote the self-development of their citizens. Multinational corporations, trade agreements, financial institutions such as the International Monetary Fund exercise significant power to influence the policies of many states in ways that often make ordinary working and poor people worse off. To the extent that this is a global reality it should be recognized, but not accepted as either necessary or good.

At this point, however, we return to the role of civil society, as the lived world where social and systemic problems are felt, and the world of communicative organizing that by protest and persuasion shifts public opinion and the forces that influence state policies. Both social movement activists such as Zapatistas and scholars of international relations appeal to expanded activities of an international civil society as a means for citizens to respond to the economic powers that transcend states. People organized across borders can expose the power of transnational economic actors and work to develop and strengthen democratic international regulation and co-operation. Both within and across societies, strengthening the associative life of civil society for the sake of promoting self-determination and self-development for everyone remains a crucial project. This chapter has discussed how civil society performs unique functions of social solidarity, identity support, and criticism of state and economic actors. To perform these functions associations must remain independent enough of state institutions both to provide alternative spaces for public action and to critcize state action.

NOTES

1. See Margaret Levi, 'Social and Unsocial Capital: A Review Essay of Robert Putnam's *Making Democracy Work*', *Politics and Society*, 24/1 (March 1996), 45–55, and Nancy L. Rosenblum, *Membership and Morals* (Princeton: Princeton University Press, 1998.

2. I derive this argument primarily from Milton Friedman, *Capitalism and Freedom* (Chicago: University of Chicago Press, 1962). For the idea that it is wrong for state institutions to aim to produce distributive patterns, however, I am thinking of Robert Nozick's argument in *Anarchy, State and Utopia* (Cambridge, Mass.: Harvard University Press, 1974).

3. This argument is my own reconstruction, which I derive from contemporary public policy rhetoric in the United States and from the writings of Amitai Etzioni and William Galston. See Etzioni, *The Spirit of Community* (New York: Crown, 1993) and William Galston, *Liberal Purposes* (Cambridge: Cambridge University Press, 1991). Neither Etzioni nor Galston, however, would likely endorse the complete anti-state formulation I have attributed to the communitarian position here. Certain versions of African American community-based self-help discourse might also be said to fall within this general communitarian position.

4. See Jean L. Cohen and Andrew Arato, *Civil Society and Political Theory* (Cambridge, Mass.: MIT Press, 1992), 418, 466, 481.

5. Ibid. 462–8; see also Claus Offe, *Contradictions of the Welfare State* (Cambridge, Mass.: MIT Press, 1984); and Iris Marion Young, *Justice and the Politics of Difference* (Princeton: Princeton University Press, 1990), ch. 2.

6. This process is part of what Habermas refers to as the 'colonization of the lifeworld'. See *The Theory of Communicative Action*, ii; see also Nancy Fraser, 'Struggle over Needs', in *Unruly Practices* (Minneapolis: University of Minnesota Press, 1989).

7. John Dryzek, 'Political Inclusion and the Dynamics of Democratization', *American Political Science Review*, 90/1 (Summer 1996), 475–87; *Democracy in Capitalist Times* (Oxford: Oxford University Press, 1996).

8. Robert Goodin, 'The State as a Moral Agent', in *Utilitarianism as a Public Philosophy* (Cambridge: Cambridge University Press, 1995).

ERNESTO LACLAU AND CHANTAL MOUFFE EXTRACTS FROM *HEGEMONY AND SOCIALIST STRATEGY: TOWARDS A RADICAL DEMOCRATIC POLITICS*

Hegemony and radical democracy
The democratic revolution
[···]

The struggle against subordination cannot be the result of the situation of subordination itself. Although we can affirm, with Foucault, that wherever there is power there is resistance, it must also be recognized that the forms of resistance may be extremely varied. Only in certain cases do these forms of resistance take on a political character and become struggles directed towards putting an end to relations of subordination as such. If throughout the centuries there have been multiple forms of resistance by women against male domination, it is only under certain conditions and specific forms that a feminist movement which demands equality (equality before the law in the first place, and subsequently in other areas) has been able to emerge. Clearly, when we speak here of the 'political' character of these struggles, we do not do so in the restricted sense of demands which are situated at the level of parties and of the State. What we are referring to is a type of action whose objective is the transformation of a social relation which constructs a subject in a relationship of subordination. Certain contemporary feminist practices, for example, tend to transform the relationship between masculinity and femininity without passing in any way through parties or the State. Of course, we are not seeking to deny that certain practices require

Ernesto Laclau and Chantal Mouffe (1985), *Hegemony and Socialist Strategy: Towards a Radical Democratic Politics*, London and New York: Verso.

the intervention of the political in its restricted sense. What we wish to point out is that politics as a practice of creation, reproduction and transformation of social relations cannot be located at a determinate level of the social, as the problem of the political is the problem of the institution of the social, that is, of the definition and articulation of social relations in a field criss-crossed with antagonisms.

Our central problem is to identify the discursive conditions for the emergence of a collective action, directed towards struggling against inequalities and challenging relations of subordination. We might also say that our task is to identify the conditions in which a relation of subordination becomes a relation of oppression, and thereby constitutes itself into the site of an antagonism. We enter here onto a terrain constituted by numerous terminological shifts which have ended by establishing a synonymity between 'subordination', 'oppression', and 'domination'. The base which makes this synonymity possible is, as is evident, the anthropological assumption of a 'human nature' and of a unified subject: if we can determine *a priori* the essence of a subject, every relation of subordination which denies it automatically becomes a relation of oppression. But if we reject this essentialist perspective, we need to differentiate 'subordination' from 'oppression' and explain the precise conditions in which subordination becomes oppressive. We shall understand by a *relation of subordination* that in which an agent is subjected to the decisions of another – an employee with respect to an employer, for example, or in certain forms of family organization the woman with respect to the man, and so on. We shall call *relations of oppression*, in contrast, those relations of subordination which have transformed themselves into sites of antagonisms. Finally, we shall call *relations of domination* the set of those relations of subordination which are considered as illegitimate from the perspective, or in the judgement, of a social agent external to them, and which, as a consequence, may or may not coincide with the relations of oppression actually existing in a determinate social formation. The problem is, therefore, to explain how relations of oppression are constituted out of relations of subordination. It is clear why relations of subordination, considered in themselves, cannot be antagonistic relations: a relation of subordination establishes, simply, a set of differential positions between social agents, and we already know that a system of differences which constructs each social identity as *positivity* not only cannot be antagonistic, but would bring about the ideal conditions for the elimination of all antagonisms – we would be faced with a sutured social space, from which every equivalence would be excluded. It is only to the extent that the positive differential character of the subordinated subject position is subverted that the antagonism can emerge. 'Serf', 'slave', and so on, do not designate in themselves antagonistic positions; it is only in the terms of a different discursive formation, such as 'the rights inherent to every human being', that the differential positivity of these categories can be subverted and the subordination constructed as oppression. This means that there is no relation of oppression without the presence of a discursive 'exterior' from which the discourse of subordination can be interrupted.[1] The logic of equivalence in this sense displaces the effects of some discourses towards others. If, as was the case with women until the seventeenth century, the ensemble of discourses which constructed them as subjects fixed them purely and simply in a subordinated position, feminism as a movement of struggle against women's subordination could not emerge. Our thesis is that it is only from the moment when the democratic discourse becomes available to articulate the different forms of resistance to subordination that the conditions will exist to make possible the struggle against different types of inequality. In the case of women we may cite as an example the role played in England by Mary Wollstonecraft, whose book *Vindication of the Rights of Women*, published in 1792, determined the birth of feminism through the use made in it of the democratic discourse, which was thus displaced from the field of political equality between citizens to the field of equality between the sexes.

[···]

Radical democracy: alternative for a new left
[···]

It is clear [···] that a left alternative can *only* consist of the construction of a different system of equivalents, which establishes social division on a new basis. In the face of the project for the reconstruction of a hierarchic society, the alternative of the Left should consist of locating itself fully in the field of the democratic revolution and expanding the chains of equivalents between the different struggles against oppression. *The task of the Left therefore cannot be to renounce liberal-democratic ideology, but on the contrary, to deepen and expand it in the direction of a radical and plural democracy.* We shall explain the dimensions of this task in the following pages, but the very fact that it is possible arises out of the fact that the *meaning* of liberal discourse on individual rights is not definitively fixed; and just as this unfixity permits their articulation with elements of conservative discourse, it also permits different forms of articulation and redefinition which accentuate the democratic moment. That is to say, as with any other social element, the elements making up the liberal discourse never appear as crystallized, and may be the field of hegemonic struggle. It is not in the abandonment of the democratic terrain but, on the contrary, in the extension of the field of democratic struggles to the whole of civil society and the state, that the possibility resides for a hegemonic strategy of the Left.

[···]

In recent years much has been talked about the need to deepen the line of separation between state and civil society. It is not difficult to realize, however, that this proposal does not furnish the Left with any theory of the surface of emergence of antagonisms which can be generalized beyond a limited number of situations. It would appear to imply that every form of domination is incarnated in the state. But it is clear that civil society is also the seat of numerous relations of oppression, and, in consequence, of antagonisms and democratic struggles. With a greater or lesser clarity in their results, theories such as Althusser's analysis of 'ideological state apparatuses' sought to create a conceptual framework with which to think these phenomena of displacement in the field of domination. In the case of the feminist struggle, the state is an important means for effecting an advance, frequently *against* civil society, in legislation which combats sexism. In numerous underdeveloped countries the expansion of the functions of the central state is a means of establishing a frontier in the struggle against extreme forms of exploitation by landowning oligarchies. Furthermore, the state is not a homogeneous medium, separated from civil society by a ditch, but an uneven set of branches and functions, only relatively integrated by the hegemonic practices which take place within it. Above all, it should not be forgotten that the state can be the seat of numerous democratic antagonisms, to the extent that a set of functions within it – professional or technical, for example – can enter into relations of antagonism with centres of power, within the state itself, which seek to restrict and deform them. None of this means to say, of course, that in certain cases the division between state and civil society *cannot* constitute the fundamental political line of demarcation: this is what happens when the state has been transformed into a bureaucratic excrescence imposed by force upon the rest of society, as in Eastern Europe, or in the Nicaragua of the Somozas, which was a dictatorship sustained by a military apparatus. At any event, it is clearly impossible to identify either the state or civil society *a priori* as *the* surface of emergence of democratic antagonisms. The same can be said when it is a question of determining the positive or negative character, from the point of view of the politics of the Left, of certain organizational forms. Let us consider, for example, the 'party' form. The party as a political institution can, in certain circumstances, be an instance of bureaucratic crystallization which acts as a brake upon mass movements; but in others it can be the organizer of dispersed and politically virgin masses, and can thus serve as an instrument for the expansion and deepening of democratic struggles. The important point is that in as much as the field of 'society in general' has disappeared as a valid framework of political analysis, there has also disappeared the possibility of establishing a *general* theory of politics on the basis of topographic categories – that is to say, of categories which fix in a permanent manner the meaning of certain contents as differences which can be located within a relational complex.

The conclusion to be drawn from this analysis is that it is impossible to specify *a priori* surfaces of emergence of antagonisms, as there is no surface which is not constantly subverted by the over-determining effects of others, and because there is, in consequence, a constant displacement of the social logics characteristic of certain spheres towards other spheres. This is, among other things, the 'demonstration effect' that we have seen in operation in the case of the democratic revolution. A democratic struggle can autonomize a certain space within which it develops, and produce effects of equivalence with other struggles in a different political space. It is to this plurality of the social that the project for a radical democracy is linked, and the possibility of it emanates directly from the decentred character of the social agents, from the discursive plurality which constitutes them as subjects, and from the displacements which take place within that plurality. The original forms of democratic thought were linked to a *positive* and *unified* conception of human nature, and, to that extent, they tended to constitute a single space within which that nature would have to manifest the effects of its radical liberty and equality: it was thus that there was constituted a public space linked to the idea of citizenship. The public/private distinction constituted the separation between a space in which differences were erased through the universal equivalence of citizens, and a plurality of private spaces in which the full force of those differences was maintained. It is at this point that the over-determination of effects linked to the democratic revolution begins to displace the line of demarcation between the public and the private and to *politicize* social relations; that is, to multiply the spaces in which the new logics of equivalence dissolve the differential positivity of the social: this is the long process which stretches from the workers' struggles of the nineteenth century to the struggle of women, diverse racial and sexual minorities, and diverse marginal groups, and the new anti-institutional struggles in the present century. Thus what has been exploded is the idea and the reality itself of a unique space of constitution of the political. What we are witnessing is a politicization far more radical than any we have known in the past, because it tends to dissolve the distinction between the public and the private, not in terms of the encroachment on the private by a unified public space, but in terms of a proliferation of radically new and different political spaces. We are confronted with the emergence of a *plurality of subjects*, whose forms of constitution and diversity it is only possible to think if we relinquish *the* category of 'subject' as a unified and unifying essence.

[···]

Radical democracy: alternative for a new left

The discourse of radical democracy is no longer the discourse of the universal; the epistemological niche from which 'universal' classes and subjects spoke has been eradicated, and it has been replaced by a polyphony of voices, each of which constructs its own irreducible discursive identity. This point is decisive: there is no radical and plural democracy without renouncing the discourse of the universal and its implicit assumption of a privileged point of access to 'the truth', which can be reached only by a limited number of subjects. In political terms this means that just as there are no surfaces which are privileged *a priori* for the emergence of antagonisms, nor are there discursive regions which the programme of a radical democracy should exclude *a priori* as possible spheres of struggle. Juridical institutions, the educational system, labour relations, the discourses of the resistance of marginal populations construct original and irreducible forms of social protest, and thereby contribute all the discursive complexity and richness on which the programme of a radical democracy should be founded. The classic discourse of socialism was of a very different type: it was a discourse of the universal, which transformed certain social categories into depositories of political and epistemological privileges; it was an a priori discourse concerning differential levels of effectiveness within the social – and as such it reduced the field of the discursive surfaces on which it considered that it was possible and legitimate to operate; it was, finally, a discourse concerning the privileged points from which historical changes were set in motion – the Revolution, the General Strike, or 'evolution' as a unifying category of the cumulative and irreversible character of partial advances. Every project for radical democracy necessarily includes, as we have said, the socialist dimension – that is to say, the abolition of capitalist relations of production; but it rejects the idea that from this abolition there necessarily follows the elimination of the other inequalities. In consequence, the de-centring and autonomy of the different discourses and struggles, the multiplication of antagonisms and the construction of a plurality of spaces within which they can affirm themselves and develop, are the conditions *sine qua non* of the possibility that the different components of the classic ideal of socialism – which should, no doubt, be extended and reformulated – can be achieved. And as we have argued abundantly in these pages, this plurality of spaces does not deny, but rather requires, the overdetermination of its effects at certain levels and the consequent hegemonic articulation between them.

NOTE

1. On the concept of 'interruption' see D. Siverman and B. Torode, *The Material Word* London 1980, chapter one.

4

POWER

Mark Anthony Wenman

INTRODUCTION

In 1974 Steven Lukes published *Power: A Radical View* and William Connolly published *The Terms of Political Discourse*. In each of these books 'power' is described as an 'essentially contested concept' (Connolly 1993a: 10, 4; Lukes 1974: 26). According to W. B. Gallie, who first elaborated this notion in 1956, it is 'impossible to fix a general principle for deciding' the proper use of an essentially contested concept (Gallie 1956: 177). Connolly applied this view to a variety of concepts 'commonly employed in political thought' (1993a: 4). He disputed the idea – characteristic of behaviouralism – that political discourse forms a technical language of 'neutral, descriptive concept[s], definable in operational terms' (1993a: 4). For example, Robert Dahl has argued that an 'analysis of power may be neutral as to values' (1968b: 406). Whereas, from Connolly's perspective, power is a 'concept bounded by normative considerations', its application necessarily involves 'endless disputes' about proper use and meaning within a 'context of partly shared assumptions' (Connolly 1993a: 6, 97). As he put it, to question the meaning of 'power' is 'not a prelude to politics but a dimension of politics' (Connolly 1993a: 3).

In this essay, my objective is to introduce and engage (but not to resolve) some pre-eminent issues in the ongoing debate about the meaning of 'power'. The paper assesses the impact on this debate of the work of the 'poststructuralists': Michel Foucault, Claude Lefort, and Ernesto Laclau.[1] I recognise that by proceeding down this pathway, as Connolly says, I am already engaged in a political exercise. I seek to implicate the reader in my convictions about the most important contemporary contributions to this dispute. I make no claims to comprehensiveness in this short essay: intelligent contemporary contributions have no doubt also been made by feminists, Marxists, Jürgen Habermas and Anthony Giddens. None of these are examined here in any detail. After an initial consideration of the notion of 'power over', the exposition of the concept of power in this paper hinges around two juxtapositions. First I evaluate the combined insights of post-structuralism, in respect of the interpretations of 'power' in mainstream political science. Second, I bring out the tensions within the post-structuralist approaches, with Foucault's conception of power as a productive 'network' of strategies and techniques on one side, and Lefort's understanding of power as an 'empty space' on the other. Laclau's analysis complements Lefort's; he theorises 'hegemony' as the strategic force that attempts to fill the empty space of power.

The enquiry into the meaning of 'power' presupposes the association of this concept with a range of strategic terms: persuasion, manipulation, domination, coercion, force, violence, and so on; also with a collection of agency terms: cause, capacity, freedom, will, end, interest, and so on; with a chain of legitimacy terms: authority, responsibility, sovereignty, and so on; and with all those political terms that derive from the Greek *kratos* (strength) or *arche* (rule) and which denote alternative forms of rule or order: monarchy, oligarchy, democracy, patriarchy, hierarchy, and so on. In my account of the insights of poststructuralism *vis-à-vis* the conceptions of power in political science, I am concerned with the relationship between power and agency. The discussion of the differences within the poststructuralist perspectives focuses on the notion of 'sovereign' power. I conclude with a consideration of the impact of poststructuralism for the relationship between power and freedom.

A PARADIGM OF 'POWER OVER'

It was an additional feature of Gallie's theory that, despite endless disputes about their meaning, essentially contested concepts are typically derived 'from an original exemplar whose authority is acknowledged by all the contestant users of the concept' (Gallie 1956: 180). In the discussion of the concept 'power', it would not be implausible to single out Thomas Hobbes as the original exemplar. In *Leviathan* Hobbes defined the 'Power of a man' as 'his present means, to obtain some future apparent Good' (1985: 150). Power, in other words, is a *capacity* that an agent possesses and may exercise in order to achieve his ends. This conception is often described in the literature as 'power to'. However, Hobbes also recognised that the salient point in the study of politics is the power *relationship*, that is, between conflicting agents. In *The Elements of Law* he said, 'Because the power of one man resisteth and hindereth the effects of the power of another: power simply is no more, but the excess of the power of one above that of another' (1969: 34). This is the notion of 'power over' (coercion or domination), which has had a crucial impact on modern theorising about power. Theorists have disagreed about whether the agents of power should be understood as individuals, groups or social classes. They have dissented about whether the agents' ends should be conceived in terms of the realisation of his/her 'will', or his/her 'policy preferences', or his/her 'objective interests'. However, most agree that the analysis of power centres on the notion of the predominant capacity of an agent to pursue (and perhaps to realise) his/her ends in conflict with opposing ends, and over and above subordinate powers. This is evident in two renowned definitions of power. Max Weber defined power as 'the probability that one actor within a social relationship will be in a position to carry out his will despite resistances' (1968: 53). Dahl's 'intuitive idea of power' is that 'A has power over B to the extent that he can get B to do something that B would not otherwise do' (Dahl, cited in Lukes 1986: 2).

There are detractors from this paradigm of power over. The best known are Hannah Arendt (who defined power as the 'human ability not just to act, but to act in concert') and Talcott Parsons (who defined power as a 'mechanism operating to bring about changes...in the process of social interaction') (Arendt 1970: 44; Parsons 1967: 299). In their different ways, these theories emphasise a correlation between power and authority, by locating the basis of the exercise of power in consent. Despite important points of divergence, these assumptions also underpin Habermas's and Giddens's respective theories of power.[2] Lukes argued that by treating power as a simple capacity, the 'conflictual aspect of power... disappears altogether' from Arendt's and Parsons's theories (1974: 31). He said that these perspectives are out of line with the 'concerns' that have 'centrally preoccupied students of power' (1974: 31). Later, I will show that the poststructuralists repudiate certain assumptions implicit in the Hobbesean paradigm, but they do not discard the notion of 'power over'. Foucault says that when 'we speak of the...mechanisms of power...we [necessarily] suppose that certain persons exercise power over others' (1983: 217).

THE CONCEPTIONS OF POWER IN MAINSTREAM POLITICAL SCIENCE

According to Dahl, it is the 'assumption of practically every political theorist for several thousand years, that it is possible to speak...of different amounts of power' (Dahl 1968b: 407–8). In the same way, he says, that 'wealth may be distributed in different patterns, so too [may] the distribution of power' (Dahl 1968b: 408). Furthermore, as he sees it, political analysts agree 'that differences between political systems...can...be interpreted as differences in the way power is distributed' (Dahl 1968b: 405). This notion certainly underpinned the debate between the pluralists and the elite theorists that took place in American political science during the late 1950s and early 1960s. In fact the idea can be traced to Aristotle, who distinguished between alternative 'constitutions' on the basis of distinctions in the location of power and authority. He contrasted 'monarchy', 'aristocracy' and 'polity' in terms of the rule respectively of the one, the few, or the many (1981: 190). In twentieth-century political science, the various attempts to determine the distributions of power in contemporary societies have also engendered a dispute about the strategic exercise of power that is retold by Lukes in terms of three 'dimensions of power'.

In *The Power Elite* (1956) C. Wright Mills argued that at the national level, a single 'power elite' rules modern America. The elite is comprised of those 'men' who occupy the 'strategic command posts' of a distinct 'power system' that 'enters into . . . every cranny of the social structure' (Mills 1956: 4, 7). These command posts are situated at the 'summits' of the great 'hierarchies of state, corporation and army', which together form an encompassing 'triangle of power' (Mills 1956: 5, 8). Mills identified the powerful as 'those who are able to realise their will, even if others resist it' (1956: 288). The decisions of the elite 'mightily affect the everyday worlds of ordinary men and women', and they must be held to account (Mills 1956: 3). Similarly, in his study of the local 'community power structure' of Atlanta, Georgia, Floyd Hunter concluded that the city was ruled by a small 'clique' at 'the top' of a rigid 'power hierarchy' (1953: 113). In 'A Critique of the Ruling Elite Model', Dahl argued that elite theory is a 'polemical doctrine' rather than a 'scientific theory' (1968a: 269). He insisted that no hypothesis about the distribution of power in contemporary society could be established 'without basing' it upon conclusions drawn from the empirical observation of the strategic exercise of power, that is, from a 'careful examination' of the outcome of a 'series of concrete [governmental] decisions' (1968a: 272). His *Who Governs?* (1961) was guided by this empiricist agenda, and represents a study of the local decision-making process in New Haven, Connecticut. Dahl examined different 'issue areas' in which 'important public decisions are made' in order to see 'what processes of influence are at work', to see which groups are able to realise their interests, understood as policy preferences (1961: 64, 103). Dahl reached pluralist conclusions about the distribution of power in New Haven. Pluralism is not exactly an equal distribution of power, but an approximate balance of power, where any 'legitimate' group will make itself heard at some point in the decision-making process.

Dahl's approach represents what Lukes called the 'one dimensional view' of the exercise of power (Lukes 1974: 15). This was challenged by Peter Bachrach and Morton Baratz, who argued that there are 'two faces of power', only 'one of which' the pluralists see (1962: 947–8). As they put it, 'of course power is exercised when A participates in the making of decisions that affect B' (Bachrach and Baratz 1962: 948). However, 'power is also exercised when A devotes his energies' to 'confining the scope of decision making' to issues which are 'innocuous to A' (Bachrach and Baratz 1962: 948). In other words, an exposition of power 'cannot be made in the absence of an analysis of the "mobilisation of bias" in the community' that prevents 'potentially dangerous issues being raised' (Bachrach and Baratz 1962: 950, 952). Bachrach and Baratz proposed the examination of strategies of 'non decision-making', by investigating the emergence of 'sub-political grievances' (Lukes, 1974: 20). Lukes emphasised the similarities between these approaches: they both assume that 'observable conflict is necessary' to the exercise of power (1974: 20, 23). Whereas, from his perspective, the most 'insidious use of power is to prevent conflict from arising in the first place' (Lukes 1974: 23). Lukes described the 'radical' third dimension of power as the 'power to prevent people' from 'having grievances by shaping their perceptions, cognitions and preferences in such a way that they accept their role in the existing order of things' (1974: 24). As he sees it, 'individuals', 'groups', and 'collectivities' exercise power when they 'work against' the 'real interests' of other groups and individuals, by manipulating their 'very wants' and preventing genuine 'choice' (Lukes 1974: 34, 39). Lukes cited Antonio Gramsci to make the case for the significance of the third dimension of power. According to Gramsci, a 'subordinate group' is subject to the exercise of 'hegemony' precisely when it adopts a 'conception of the world' that 'is not its own' but 'is borrowed from another group' (Gramsci, cited in Lukes 1974: 47). As I will explain below, Laclau reworks this notion of 'hegemony' from a poststructuralist perspective. However, first I will demonstrate the ways in which the poststructuralist approaches detract from the basic premises underlying the conceptions of power developed in political science.

A POSTSTRUCTURALIST CRITIQUE OF THE THREE DIMENSIONS OF POWER

Lukes says that, 'despite their differences', the three views of power 'can be seen as alternative' *dimensions* of one 'underlying concept of power' (1974: 27). They all presume that 'A exercises power over B when A affects B in a manner contrary to B's interests' (Lukes 1974: 27). In other words, they are all in keeping with the paradigm of 'power over'. If we examine this underlying conception, we see that these theories all assume that 'power' is some 'thing' that the agent of power possesses, as Dahl says, in the form of a piece of wealth. This possession may only be temporary and in relation to the outcome of a specific governmental decision (as in pluralist theory), or more permanent, and understood as a consequence of the agents' occupation of the strategic command posts of the power system (as in elite theory). Nonetheless, as Lukes says, political scientists are typically concerned with identifying which 'people *have* power and how much power they *have*' (Lukes 1986: 8). This does not mean that these are actually theories of 'power to'. As Bachrach and Baratz put it, power is not a 'simple property . . . which can belong to a person or group considered in itself' (Bachrach and Baratz 1963: 632–3). However, their theory does suppose that the power relationship '*endows* A with power over B' (Bachrach and Baratz 1963: 634). In fact, in all three theories, what the agent of power enjoys is the possession of the 'excess' of power (that is, the excess capacity to achieve his/her ends) over subordinate powers, which is the essence of the power relationship according to Hobbes. The poststructuralist theories of 'power over' break with these paradigmatic assumptions in at least two significant ways. First, they put forward a *radically relational* concept of power, in which the power relationship (as opposed to the identities of the agents who comprise that relationship) is primary. Second, these theories reject the idea that the agent of power ever fully possesses 'it', even in the form of a temporary endowment.

In the theories of power developed in political science, the power relationship is conceptualised as a relationship between discernible agents (A and B), which are understood to possess pregiven identities that manifest themselves as fully determinable ends, interests, policy preferences and so on. As Laclau puts it, in this type of theory 'it is because A is . . . fully A, that its relation with B' can produce an effect of power (Laclau and Mouffe 1985: 125). Whereas, from his perspective, the power relationship does not arise between agents understood as 'full totalities'; instead the agents' identities are politically constructed in the 'act of power and identity as such *is* power' (Laclau 1990: 31). Foucault says virtually the same thing about the primacy of the power relationship. He says, 'The individual is not a pre-given entity which is seized on by the exercise of power. The individual, with his identity and characteristics, is the product of a relation of power' (1980: 74). These approaches should not to be confused with structuralist conceptions of power. For example, in Nicos Poulantzas's structural Marxist theory power is conceived of straightforwardly as an *effect* of structural determination. In Poulantzas's theory agents are simply 'bearers of objective interests' determined at the level of the relations of production (Poulantzas 1969: 70). By way of contrast, in Laclau's *post*structuralist theory the agent of power is never located at a 'homogenous point' in an underlying structure, but always more or less precariously 'sutured' within 'a field of relational semi-identities' (Laclau 1990: 24, 32). Foucault and Laclau both draw attention to the 'incomplete, open and politically negotiable character' of the identity of every agent of power (Laclau and Mouffe 1985: 104). From Laclau's viewpoint, the power relationship signifies the 'impossibility' of the agent's coherent identity (Laclau and Mouffe 1985: 125). He says that, in so far as I find myself in a relationship of power, 'I cannot be a full presence for myself. But nor is the force that antagonises me such a presence' (Laclau and Mouffe 1985: 125). Similarly, Foucault maintains that 'anyone who exercises power' finds him/herself situated 'in a field of complex relations where he occupies a transient [and unstable] point' (1988a: 88).

Because of this precariousness there is an essential non-coincidence – or 'dislocation' (Laclau) – between the site of agency and the full acquisition of power. From these poststructuralist perspectives, the exercise of power can never be referred back to an organising instance – the individual, a group, the ruling class etc. – that fully commandeers 'it'. As Foucault puts it, power is 'never localised here or there, never in anybody's hands, never appropriated as a commodity or as a piece of wealth' (Foucault 1980: 98). Power 'serves' but is never 'in the service of' any 'interest taken as primary' (Foucault 1980: 142). Consequently, he says, we 'should refrain from posing the ... unanswerable question: "who then has power?"' (Foucault 1980: 97).[3] These are important points of coincidence between the poststructuralist perspectives. There is not the scope here to explore all of the implications of Foucault's and Laclau's interventions *vis-à-vis* the conceptions of power in mainstream political science. However, we can say that the poststructuralist approach implies a much broader conception of 'the political' than is traditionally understood in political science. The radically relational concept of power is essentially *incommensurate* with the conventional paradigm of 'power over', where politics is understood as a relationship between agents with pre-constituted identities and in which (the commodity) 'power' is fully appropriated by the dominant agent, who then exercises it over subordinates. From the poststructuralist viewpoint, power and politics extend to the asymmetrical (but intrinsically unstable) practices of identity formation, and therefore potentially to all areas of social life. I will now examine more carefully the significance of the poststructuralist intervention, by surveying the differences between Foucault's, Lefort's and Laclau's approaches. The discussion focuses on their respective engagements with the notion of 'sovereign' power.

FOUCAULT: THE DIVERSE 'MICROPHYSICS' OF POWER

Foucault formulated his conception of power from the middle of the 1970s, the time of *Discipline and Punish* (1977). The most detailed exposition is set out in *The History of Sexuality, volume 1* (1979), from which the section reproduced here is taken. Whatever their thoughts on the value of Foucault's approach, few would deny that his contribution represents one of the most innovative interventions in this field in the late twentieth century.[4] Yet, ironically, Foucault claimed that 'power as such does not exist' (1983: 217). Indeed, he 'suspect[s] that an extremely complex configuration of realities is allowed to escape' when we use the term 'power' as 'an all embracing and reifying term' (1983: 217). In his various writings, Foucault analysed 'power relations and not power itself', that is, power relations 'in the diversity of their logical sequence' and their effects (1983: 219). He surveyed and described power relations in their distinct modalities, strategies, tactics, practices and techniques. This is in order to uncover the 'different modes by which, in our culture, human beings are made subjects' (Foucault 1983: 208). These multifarious techniques of power correspond in their common divergence from a particular modality of power that Foucault referred to variously as the 'juridical conception' of power, or the 'uniform edifice of sovereignty' (Foucault 1980: 96).

According to Foucault, in 'western societies since medieval times it has been royal power that has provided the essential focus around' which political 'thought has been elaborated' (Foucault 1980: 94). He says that political theory 'has never ceased to be obsessed with the person of the sovereign', with the 'domination of the king in his central position' (Foucault 1980: 96, 121). The democratisation of sovereignty since the eighteenth century – 'through the constitution of a public right articulated upon collective sovereignty' – has not altered the fact that the 'representation of power has remained under the spell of monarchy' (Foucault 1980: 105; Foucault 1979: 88).[5] As James Tully puts it, the idea of sovereignty – of the singular location and the homogenous effect of power – 'dominates conservative, liberal and Marxist social theory' and 'is woven into modern political . . . institutions . . . from absolute monarchies to direct democracies' (Tully 1998b: 18). Similarly, Laclau has argued that this idea remains implicit in the theories of power developed in political science. He says there is 'no difference, from this point of view, between holistic and pluralist conceptions of power' (Laclau and Zac 1994: 17). The pluralists' notion of approximate equilibrium (in which forces cancel each other out) is simply the obverse of the idea that 'power is located' at single point within society, from where its effects would . . . spread over . . . the social structure as a whole' (Laclau and Zac, 1994: 17). Foucault portrays the notion of sovereign power as inadequate for understanding the diverse modalities of power at work in modern societies. As he put it, 'we need to cut off the king's head: in political theory that still needs to be done' (Foucault 1980: 121).

Foucault's 'genealogies' uncover the contingency of the techniques of power that have become 'part of our most familiar landscape', which 'we don't perceive . . . any more', but which at one time 'scandalised people' (Foucault 1980: 148; Martin 1988: 11). His studies are historically sensitive and rich in descriptive content. Put schematically – that is, in a very un-Foucauldian fashion – some of these modalities of power are as follows:

- 'Governmentality': 'concerned with . . . the question of how to introduce economy . . . into the management of the state', and which Foucault traced to a series of sixteenth- and seventeenth-century texts on the 'art of government' (Foucault 1991a: 92). These discourses have engendered a now familiar feature of modern politics:

the 'permanent intervention of the state in [the] social processes' (Foucault 1988b: 159).

- 'Biopolitics': takes as its object 'individuals' understood as 'working, trading, living, beings', in contrast with traditional sovereign power, which is exercised essentially over territory and only as a consequence of this over the 'subjects who inhabit it' (Foucault 1988b: 160; Foucault 1991a: 93). The emergence of 'biopower' is traced to the early modern concern with the 'problems of population', with 'demography, public health, hygiene, housing conditions' and so on (Foucault 1991a: 99).

- 'Pastoral power': originated in the institutions of the Christian Church and especially its practice of confession. The 'ultimate aim' of traditional pastoral power was 'to assure individual salvation in the next world', which required individuals to 'reveal their innermost secrets', so that the pastorate could obtain 'a knowledge of the conscience and an ability to direct it' (Foucault 1983: 213–14). In modern society pastoral power has 'spread out into the whole social body', been transformed into a set of 'worldly' aims (health, wellbeing, security and so on), and has inaugurated a 'series of [particular] powers: those of family, medicine, psychiatry, [and] education' (Foucault 1983: 214).

- 'Disciplinary power': tied up with the 'question of the normal and the abnormal' (sane/mad, healthy/sick, upright/criminal) that generates the 'rituals of exclusion' characteristic of modern societies (Foucault 1977: 198, 216). The 'spread of disciplinary procedures' emerges in the eighteenth century in a variety of institutions (prisons, hospitals, factories, schools and the military). Here, individual subjects are constituted through a 'tightly-knit grid of material coercions', a complex of asymmetrical 'micro-powers', and through uninterrupted 'systems of surveillance' (Foucault 1977: 212, 222; Foucault 1980: 104, 155). The agents of disciplinary power – penal reformers, social workers, doctors, teachers, (PhD supervisors) – 'produce bodies that [are] both docile and capable'; they are 'technicians of behaviour, engineers of conduct, orthopaedists of individuality' (Foucault 1977: 294).

Despite his emphasis on surveying these specific modalities of power, there are a number of places in Foucault's work where he puts forward what can only be described as a set of general 'hypotheses' about the basic nature of power.[6] For example, he says, power 'needs to be considered as a productive network which runs through the whole social body, much more than as a negative instance whose function is repression' (1980: 119). Power 'traverses and produces things, it induces pleasure, forms knowledge, produces discourse' (Foucault 1980: 119). Power is 'technical' and 'strategic' in its operations rather than 'juridical'; one should 'try to locate power at the extreme points of its exercise, where it is always less legal in character' (Foucault 1980: 97, 121). Power is 'most intimately related to our bodies and to our everyday behaviour', and there are no 'relations of power without resistances' (Foucault 1980: 80, 142). Indeed, the purpose of Foucault's genealogies seems to be to provoke opportunities for the transgression of particular techniques of power, by demonstrating their arbitrary and contingent make-up. Perhaps most importantly, Foucault insists that power 'is not homogenous'; the 'polymorphous techniques of subjugation' at work in our societies are only ever 'partially susceptible of integration into overall strategies' (Foucault 1980: 96, 142). His analyses establish a 'theoretical horizon which . . . has nothing in common' with 'relations of sovereignty' (Foucault 1980: 104, 106). From his perspective the exclusive concern with 'sovereignty' in modern political theory has 'allowed a system of right to be superimposed upon the mechanisms of discipline', at the cost of concealing their 'actual procedures' (Foucault 1980: 105). These comments are significant, because, as we will now see, Lefort and Laclau develop poststructuralist theories of power that effectively rework the traditional problematic of sovereignty.

Lefort and laclau: filling the empty space of power

Lefort's analysis of power is probably not as well known as Foucault's. The piece reproduced here is taken from his *Democracy and Political Theory* (1988).[7] Lefort's exposition centres on his particular rendition of 'modern democracy'. He rejects the idea that modern democracy can be comprehended in a procedural sense, whereby it is 'reduced to a system of institutions' (1988: 14). Instead, modern democracy must be understood as a historically specific form of society – a distinct 'regime' – characterised by the principal fact that 'the locus of power becomes an empty space' (Lefort 1988: 2, 16–17). In order to grasp the significance of this 'revolutionary and unprecedented feature' of modern politics, Lefort contrasts modern democracy with the pre-modern European system of the 'Ancien Régime' (1988: 17). Under the monarchical system of the *Ancien Régime* sovereign 'power was embodied in the person of the prince', he was 'the guarantor and representative of the unity of the kingdom' (Lefort 1988: 17). The sovereign was perceived as a Christ-like figure: simultaneously human and divine, who – as intermediary with the divine – provided legitimacy to the power of the kingdom. As Lefort puts it, being 'at once subject to the law and placed above laws', the prince 'condensed within his body, which was at once mortal and immortal, the principle [of legitimate power] that generated the order of the kingdom' (Lefort 1988: 17). This is the original theory of sovereignty that Foucault suggests we need to fully dispense with, in order to grasp the diverse microphysics of biopower operative in modern societies. Whereas, from Lefort's perspective, there is no need to 'cut off the king's head'. This is because the European regicides of the seventeenth and eighteenth centuries have already instituted a fundamental 'mutation in the symbolic order', where the 'locus of power becomes an empty space', that is, the (virtual) space of a decapitated head (Lefort 1988: 16–17).

Lefort's analysis of the modern 'democratic revolution' emphasises the singular importance of the withdrawal of the theological foundations of the social order. Under conditions of modern democracy 'the people' are the source of sovereign authority, but the identity of 'the people' is essentially indeterminable and 'division' is therefore 'in a general way, constitutive of the very unity of society' (Lefort 1988: 18). In marked contrast with the uncontested and divinely sanctioned authority of the prince, under conditions of modern democracy no 'group can be consubstantial with' the (empty) place of sovereign power, and legitimate power *as such* 'cannot be represented' (Lefort 1988: 17). Only the 'mechanisms of the exercise of power are visible, or only the men, the mere mortals, who hold political authority' at any given time (Lefort 1988: 17). Nevertheless, from Lefort's perspective, the (ghost-like) presence of sovereign authority – which remains present as an 'empty space' – is the very condition of the modern 'democratic adventure' with its perpetual reversals of power (Lefort 1988: 16, 19). In the piece reproduced here, Lefort also refers to the phenomenon of totalitarianism, which he understands as a distinct form of power that can only manifest itself under conditions of modern democracy. In contrast to the traditional authority of the prince, who was a 'mediator between mortals and gods', modern totalitarian 'power is accountable to no one' (Lefort 1988: 13, 17). According to Lefort, totalitarianism (which is exemplified in the experience of Stalinism and Nazism) follows from the 'fantasy of the People-as-One', from the attempt to overcome the indeterminacy constitutive of modern democracy, from the quest for a 'social body which is welded to its head' (Lefort 1988: 20).

Laclau endorses Lefort's account of modern democracy, and of the corresponding threat of totalitarianism. He says that the perpetuity of 'democracy presupposes that the place of power remains empty' (2001: 7). However, Laclau adds that 'in order to have democracy we need particular forces that occupy the empty place of power but do not identify with it' (2001: 7). He theorises 'hegemony' as the strategic force that attempts to fill the empty space of power. This theory was initially set out in *Hegemony and Socialist Strategy* (1985, with Chantal Mouffe), and is further elaborated in Laclau's subsequent writings.[8] Once the democratic revolution has ensured the withdrawal of the omnipotent power of God, traditionally embodied in the sovereign person of the prince, Laclau rejects the idea that we can think in terms of 'the total diffusion of power within the social' (Laclau and Mouffe 1985: 142). As he sees it, Foucault's approach 'blinds' political analysis to the 'partial concentrations of power' – or what he calls 'nodal points' – 'existing in every concrete social formation' (Laclau and Mouffe 1985: 142). Laclau theorises these 'nodal points' in terms of a 'non-dialectical mediation' of 'organisation and its lack' (Laclau and Zac, 1994: 12). Without some attempt to fill the empty space of sovereign power (without some attempt to construct what Laclau calls a 'society effect', that is, the full authority of a universal 'order'), he says society would rapidly degenerate into chaos. The threat of generalised disorder – that Laclau refers to variously in Gramscian terms (as an 'organic crisis') or in terms taken from Lacanian psychoanalytic theory (as a 'constitutive lack') – generates a series of particularistic struggles to complete the necessary (but impossible) task of filling the empty space of power.

Laclau describes 'hegemony' as a type of power relationship whereby 'a particularity assumes the representation of an (impossible) universality entirely incommensurate with it' (2001: 5). This is, we might say, the theory of the 'man who would be king', of the strategic agent who would im*person*ate the body of divinely ordained authority. Laclau takes the formal features of his theory from Antonio Gramsci. Gramsci described the operation of hegemony as the construction of a 'collective will', whereby a 'fundamental class' (or in Laclau's poststructuralist theory any social agent) is able to present its 'own corporate interests' as the 'motor force of a universal expansion' (Forgacs 1988: 205, 240). In the exercise of hegemony, says Gramsci, the 'dominant group become[s] the interests of other subordinate groups' (Forgacs 1988: 205). This clearly resonates with Steven Lukes's conception of the 'third face of power', a notion which is equally significant in Laclau's theory. That is, with the crucial exception that Laclau does not envisage the exercise of hegemony in terms of the realisation of what Lukes called the 'real interests' of the dominant group through the misdirection of the 'real interests' of the subordinate groups. From Laclau's poststructuralist perspective, the 'hegemonic act' does not 'realise' a set of interests 'preceding it' (Laclau 1990: 29). On the contrary, the exercise of hegemony is always an act of 'radical construction' (Laclau 1990: 29). Hegemony is 'politically constructed only through the equivalence of a plurality of demands', whereby one of those demands stands in strategically for all the rest, and in relation to an external force that is presumed to antagonise them all (Laclau 2000: 55). Furthermore, from Laclau's perspective, hegemony is never realised. Because of the radical 'asymmetry between the universality of the task and the particularity of the social agent capable of taking it up', modern democracy is characterised by endless strategic displacements of the – essentially 'vain' – attempt to fill the empty space of power (Laclau 2001: 6–7). In other words, Laclau depicts modern democracy in terms of an iron law of (impossible) *mon*archy, that is, in terms of a permanent yet unattainable struggle to incarnate the universal fullness of sovereign authority.

The difference between Foucault's and Laclau's approaches is confirmed in their respective comments on Hobbes's account of sovereign power. *Leviathan* represented a decisive shift in the direction of the democratisation of sovereign authority, that is, with its location of the foundations of sovereignty in an act of contract. In Hobbes's theory, the individuals in a highly unstable 'state of nature' agree to hand over their 'natural powers' to the protection of a single sovereign authority – the 'leviathan' – who is 'able to over-awe them all' (Hobbes 1985: 185). Foucault described his approach as entirely heterogeneous with the problematic of *Leviathan* (1980: 106). He says that for Hobbes, sovereignty is 'precisely the spirit of the Leviathan', which resides in the 'heart' and the 'head' of this 'fabricated man' (1980: 98). He continues: 'Well, rather than worry about the problem of the central spirit, I believe that we must attempt to study the myriad of bodies which are constituted as peripheral subjects as a result of the effects of power' (1980: 98). Laclau's comments are very different. He notes that for Hobbes the 'covenant which surrenders total power to the Leviathan is an essentially non-political act in that it totally excludes the interaction between antagonistic wills' (2000: 54). However, he says, 'if we have a situation in which the ruler is less than omnipotent, and the state of nature less than totally unstructured', then the 'individual wills' in the state of nature 'will be forced to engage in a succession of partial covenants' (Laclau and Zac 1994: 22, 23). In this case, 'power, not being absolute, cannot ensure the conditions of its own legitimacy' (Laclau and Zac 1994: 23). Therefore 'the claim of a sector to rule [to become the 'central spirit'] will depend on its ability to present its own particular aims as the ones which are compatible with the actual functioning of the community' (Laclau 2000: 54). This is, he says, 'precisely, what is intrinsic to the hegemonic operation' (2000: 54).

CONCLUSION: POWER AND FREEDOM

In the second half of this essay, my intention has been to illustrate the divergence between the poststructuralist approaches. I do not propose to decide between these alternatives here. However, it is important to emphasise this difference for the benefit of students and analysts of power, as well as those who find themselves caught up in relations of power, and who may want to develop strategies of transgression or resistance. Despite their congruity *vis-à-vis* the theories of power in mainstream political science, these approaches ultimately appear opposed in their most fundamental respects, in their understanding of the location and the principal characteristics of the exercise of power. Foucault likened the study of power to physics: it is, he said, always a question of force in relation with force. The gap that separates his problematic from Laclau's seems to be as great as the rift in contemporary theoretical physics that distinguishes quantum mechanics from the general theory of relativity. On the one hand, we have a meticulous survey of the diverse microphysics of disciplinary biopower effective in modern institutions: prisons, schools, factories and so on. On the other hand, we have a general formulation of democracy in terms of the hegemonic struggle to fill the empty space of sovereign power.[9] However, by way of a conclusion, I want to once more note a point of affinity between the poststructuralist approaches, by focusing on the question of the relationship between power and freedom.

According to Laclau, 'classical' conceptions of 'human emancipation' often present power and freedom as antonyms; a free society 'would be one from which power relations would have been abolished' (Laclau 1996b: 52). This is evident, for example, in Marxist conceptions of the post-revolutionary society, in terms of the 'end of politics' and the 'withering away' of the state. Foucault and Laclau both reject this idea. As Foucault put it, a 'society without power relations' is 'an abstraction' (Foucault 1983: 223). If 'power is the prerequisite of any identity', says Laclau, then the 'radical disappearance of power would amount to the disintegration of the social fabric' (1990: 33). However, Foucault adds that to 'say that one is never "outside" power does not mean that one is trapped and condemned to defeat', because there are no *particular* 'relationship[s] of power without the means of possible escape or flight' (1980: 141–2; 1983: 225). The subordinate subject in a relationship of power is always partially free, that is, in the sense that he or she is 'faced with a field of possibilities in which . . . several reactions . . . may be realised' (Foucault 1983: 221). Without the 'possibility of recalcitrance, power would be equivalent to . . . physical determination' (Foucault 1983: 221). Foucault and Laclau both draw attention to the 'complicated interplay' of power and freedom (Foucault 1983: 221). Laclau says this relationship 'is one of permanent renegotiations and displacement of their mutual frontiers, while the two terms of the equation always remain' (1996b: 52). They construe what Foucault calls the 'agonistic' games of power/freedom in distinct ways. Towards the end of his life Foucault became increasingly interested in the 'ethical work of the self on the self', whereby the individual negotiates his/her 'relation to the rules' that govern his/her conduct (1986: 27; 1988a: 91).[10] Whereas for Laclau the important point is always the collective transformation of the social order through the construction of a new hegemonic project. Despite this difference, Foucault would have agreed with Laclau when he says that emancipation always entails 'the construction of a new power' and 'not its radical elimination' (2001: 8).

QUESTIONS FOR DISCUSSION

- Is power something that can be possessed and/or quantified, in the sense which is implicit in the following statements: 'the bourgeoisie *has* power over the proletariat' or 'the Prime Minister *has more* power and influence than any other Cabinet minister'?

- Is power best understood as something which is concentrated, for example in 'the state', or is it better understood as something which is diffuse, and perhaps disseminated through a network of strategies and throughout all of the institutions in civil society, the family, the workplace, schools, prisons and so on?
- If power is both concentrated and diffuse, can these alternative modalities of power be brought together in a single comprehensive theory, for example a theory of the 'hegemonic power' of a given group, class or some other social agent?
- If theorists such as Foucault and Laclau are correct to say that there is no 'outside' of power, then what implications does this have for the traditional normative discourses of political theory, the discussions about 'justice' and 'human rights' and so on?

NOTES

1. I use the term 'poststructuralism' here in a loose and non-technical sense to en-compass all those who draw upon the variety of perspectives (including Lacanian psychoanalysis) which have emerged in French social theory in relation to struc-turalism.
2. Habermas presents his theory as a 'more realistic version' of Arendt's notion of the 'communicative production of power' (Habermas 1977: 22). See also Giddens (1984).
3. Despite the differences indicated above, the poststructuralist conception of power is prefigured to some degree in the work of Arendt. Arendt maintained that the word 'power' 'like its Greek equivalent *dynamis*, [or] the Latin *potentia* . . . indicates its "potential" character'; power, she said, is 'never fully materialised' (Arendt 1958: 200).
4. There is a mass of secondary literature on Foucault. I do not propose to engage with any of it here, for want of space. For a critique of his conception of power from a feminist perspective see Hartsock (1990). For other notable critiques see Fraser (1989, ch. one) and Habermas (1987a: 266–93). For theorists who effectively en-dorse Foucault's approach, whilst raising minor points of disagreement, see Deleuze and Guattari (1988: 531) and Hart and Negri (2001: 22–41).
5. Once again, parallels can be drawn with Arendt. She maintained that modern con-ceptions of power 'derive from the old notion of absolute power that accompanied the rise of the sovereign European nation-state' (1970: 38).
6. In addition to the piece reproduced here, see for example Foucault (1980: 142).
7. This is one of two of Lefort's books that have been translated into English. See also Lefort (1986).
8. The question of the nature of power (and particularly of hegemonic power) runs throughout Laclau's writings, and he addresses this question explicitly in various passages. See especially Laclau (1996: 52, 2000: 54 and 2001: 3–14) and Laclau and Zac (1994: 17–23). See also the selections from Laclau's work reproduced in other parts of this volume. Laclau's theory is complex and multifaceted. I do not presume to give a complete account of his position here. For a more detailed exposition and critical analysis see Wenman (2003b).
9. For an original attempt to uncover the 'hidden point of intersection' between these two models of power see Agamben (1998). According to Giorgio Agamben, the various processes of subjectification at work in modern institutions 'refer back to a common centre', which is the 'activity of sovereign power' (Agamben 1998: 5–6). Indeed, as he sees it, the biopolitical 'inclusion of bare life in the political realm

constitutes the original – if concealed – nucleus of sovereign power' (Agamben 1998: 5–6). This is not a position to which Foucault subscribed. From his perspective, sovereignty and the heterogeneous disciplines of biopower 'cannot possibly be reduced to each other' (Foucault 1980: 106).

10. This aspect of Foucault's work in particular has been taken up by a number of prominent theorists in the English-speaking world. See for example Connolly (1993b) and Tully (1999). For a critical overview of these 'agonistic' theories see Wenman (2003a).

MICHEL FOUCAULT
EXTRACTS FROM *THE HISTORY OF SEXUALITY, VOLUME 1: AN INTRODUCTION*

THE DEPLOYMENT OF SEXUALITY

Objective

[...]

Why is this juridical notion of power, involving as it does the neglect of everything that makes for its productive effectiveness, its strategic resourcefulness, its positivity, so readily accepted? In a society such as ours, where the devices of power are so numerous, its rituals so visible, and its instruments ultimately so reliable, in this society that has been more imaginative, probably, than any other in creating devious and supple mechanisms of power, what explains this tendency not to recognize the latter except in the negative and emaciated form of prohibition? Why are the deployments of power reduced simply to the procedure of the law of interdiction?

Let me offer a general and tactical reason that seems self-evident: power is tolerable only on condition that it mask a substantial part of itself. Its success is proportional to its ability to hide its own mechanisms. Would power be accepted if it were entirely cynical? For it, secrecy is not in the nature of an abuse; it is indispensable to its operation. Not only because power imposes secrecy on those whom it dominates, but because it is perhaps just as indispensable to the latter: would they accept it if they did not see it as a

Michel Foucault (1979), *The History of Sexuality, vol. 1: An Introduction*, London: Allen Lane.

mere limit placed on their desire, leaving a measure of freedom – however slight – intact? Power as a pure limit set on freedom is, at least in our society, the general form of its acceptability.

There is, perhaps, a historical reason for this. The great institutions of power that developed in the Middle Ages – monarchy, the state with its apparatus – rose up on the basis of a multiplicity of prior powers, and to a certain extent in opposition to them: dense, entangled, conflicting powers, powers tied to the direct or indirect dominion over the land, to the possession of arms, to serfdom, to bonds of suzerainty and vassalage. If these institutions were able to implant themselves, if, by profiting from a whole series of tactical alliances, they were able to gain acceptance, this was because they presented themselves as agencies of regulation, arbitration, and demarcation, as a way of introducing order in the midst of these powers, of establishing a principle that would temper them and distribute them according to boundaries and a fixed hierarchy. Faced with a myriad of clashing forces, these great forms of power functioned as a principle of right that transcended all the heterogeneous claims, manifesting the triple distinction of forming a unitary regime, of identifying its will with the law, and of acting through mechanisms of interdiction and sanction. The slogan of this regime, *pax et justitia*, in keeping with the function it laid claim to, established peace as the prohibition of feudal or private wars, and justice as a way of suspending the private settling of lawsuits. Doubtless there was more to this development of great monarchic institutions than a pure and simple juridical edifice. But such was the language of power, the representation it gave of itself, and the entire theory of public law that was constructed in the Middle Ages, or reconstructed from Roman law, bears witness to the fact. Law was not simply a weapon skillfully wielded by monarchs; it was the monarchic system's mode of manifestation and the form of its acceptability. In Western societies since the Middle Ages, the exercise of power has always been formulated in terms of law.

A tradition dating back to the eighteenth or nineteenth century has accustomed us to place absolute monarchic power on the side of the unlawful: arbitrariness, abuse, caprice, willfulness, privileges and exceptions, the traditional continuance of accomplished facts. But this is to overlook a fundamental historical trait of Western monarchies: they were constructed as systems of law, they expressed themselves through theories of law, and they made their mechanisms of power work in the form of law. The old reproach that Boulainvilliers directed at the French monarchy – that it used the law and jurists to do away with rights and to bring down the aristocracy – was basically warranted by the facts. Through the development of the monarchy and its institutions this juridico-political dimension was established. It is by no means adequate to describe the manner in which power was and is exercised, but it is the code according to which power presents itself and prescribes that we conceive of it. The history of the monarchy went hand in hand with the covering up of the facts and procedures of power by juridico-political discourse.

Yet, despite the efforts that were made to disengage the juridical sphere from the monarchic institution and to free the political from the juridical, the representation of power remained caught within this system. Consider the two following examples. Criticism of the eighteenth-century monarchic institution in France was not directed against the juridico-monarchic sphere as such, but was made on behalf of a pure and rigorous juridical system to which all the mechanisms of power could conform, with no excesses or irregularities, as opposed to a monarchy which, notwithstanding its own assertions, continuously overstepped the legal framework and set itself above the laws. Political criticism availed itself, therefore, of all the juridical thinking that had accompanied the development of the monarchy, in order to condemn the latter; but it did not challenge the principle which held that law had to be the very form of power, and that power always had to be exercised in the form of law. Another type of criticism of political institutions appeared in the nineteenth century, a much more radical criticism in that it was concerned to show not only that real power escaped the rules of jurisprudence, but that the legal system itself was merely a way of exerting violence, of appropriating that violence for the benefit of the few, and of exploiting the dissymmetries and injustices of domination under cover of general law. But this critique of law is still carried out on the assumption that, ideally and by nature, power must be exercised in accordance with a fundamental lawfulness.

At bottom, despite the differences in epochs and objectives, the representation of power has remained under the spell of monarchy. In political thought and analysis, we still have not cut off the head of the king. Hence the importance that the theory of power gives to the problem of right and violence, law and illegality, freedom and will, and especially the state and sovereignty (even if the latter is questioned insofar as it is personified in a collective being and no longer a sovereign individual). To conceive of power on the basis of these problems is to conceive of it in terms of a historical form that is characteristic of our societies: the juridical monarchy. Characteristic yet transitory. For while many of its forms have persisted to the present, it has gradually been penetrated by quite new mechanisms of power that are probably irreducible to the representation of law. As we shall see, these power mechanisms are, at least in part, those that, beginning in the eighteenth century, took charge of men's existence, men as living bodies. And if it is true that the juridical system was useful for representing, albeit in a nonexhaustive way, a power that was centered primarily around deduction (*prélèvement*) and death, it is utterly incongruous with the new methods of power whose operation is not ensured by right but by technique, not by law but by normalization, not by punishment but by control, methods that are employed on all levels and in forms that go beyond the state and its apparatus. We have been engaged for centuries in a type of society in which the juridical is increasingly incapable of coding power, of serving as its system of representation. Our historical gradient carries us further and further away from a reign of law that had already begun to recede into the past at a time when the French Revolution and the accompanying age of constitutions and codes seemed to destine it for a future that was at hand.

[...]

Method

Hence the objective is to analyze a certain form of knowledge regarding sex, not in terms of repression or law, but in terms of power. But the word *power* is apt to lead to a number of misunderstandings – misunderstandings with respect to its nature, its form, and its unity. By power, I do not mean 'Power' as a group of institutions and mechanisms that ensure the subservience of the citizens of a given state. By power, I do not mean, either, a mode of subjugation which, in contrast to violence, has the form of the rule. Finally, I do not have in mind a general system of domination exerted by one group over another, a system whose effects, through successive derivations, pervade the entire social body. The analysis, made in terms of power, must not assume that the sovereignty of the state, the form of the law, or the over-all unity of a domination are given at the outset; rather, these are only the terminal forms power takes. It seems to me that power must be understood in the first instance as the multiplicity of force relations immanent in the sphere in which they operate and which constitute their own organization; as the process which, through ceaseless struggles and confrontations, transforms, strengthens, or reverses them; as the support which these force relations find in one another, thus forming a chain or a system, or on the contrary, the disjunctions and contradictions which isolate them from one another; and lastly, as the strategies in which they take effect, whose general design or institutional crystallization is embodied in the state apparatus, in the formulation of the law, in the various social hegemonies. Power's condition of possibility, or in any case the viewpoint which permits one to understand its exercise, even in its more 'peripheral' effects, and which also makes it possible to use its mechanisms as a grid of intelligibility of the social order, must not be sought in the primary existence of a central point, in a unique source of sovereignty from which secondary and descendent forms would emanate; it is the moving substrate of force relations which, by virtue of their inequality, constantly engender states of power, but the latter are always local and unstable. The omnipresence of power: not because it has the privilege of consolidating everything under its invincible unity, but because it is produced from one moment to the next, at every point, or rather in every relation from one point to another. Power is everywhere; not because it embraces everything, but because it comes from everywhere. And 'Power', insofar as it is permanent, repetitious, inert, and self-reproducing, is simply the over-all effect that emerges from all these mobilities, the concatenation that rests on each of them and seeks in turn to arrest their movement. One needs to be nominalistic, no doubt: power is not an institution, and not a structure; neither is it a certain strength we are endowed with; it is the name that one attributes to a complex strategical situation in a particular society.

Should we turn the expression around, then, and say that politics is war pursued by other means? If we still wish to maintain a separation between war and politics, perhaps we should postulate rather that this multiplicity of force relations can be coded – in part but never totally – either in the form of 'war', or in the form of 'politics'; this would imply two different strategies (but the one always liable to switch into the other) for integrating these unbalanced, heterogeneous, unstable, and tense force relations.

Continuing this line of discussion, we can advance a certain number of propositions:

- Power is not something that is acquired, seized, or shared, something that one holds on to or allows to slip away; power is exercised from innumerable points, in the interplay of nonegalitarian and mobile relations.

- Relations of power are not in a position of exteriority with respect to other types of relationships (economic processes, knowledge relationships, sexual relations), but are immanent in the latter; they are the immediate effects of the divisions, inequalities, and disequilibriums which occur in the latter, and conversely they are the internal conditions of these differentiations; relations of power are not in superstructural positions, with merely a role of prohibition or accompaniment; they have a directly productive role, wherever they come into play.

- Power comes from below; that is, there is no binary and all-encompassing opposition between rulers and ruled at the root of power relations, and serving as a general matrix – no such duality extending from the top down and reacting on more and more limited groups to the very depths of the social body. One must suppose rather that the manifold relationships of force that take shape and come into play in the machinery of production, in families, limited groups, and institutions, are the basis for wide-ranging effects of cleavage that run through the social body as a whole. These then form a general line of force that traverses the local oppositions and links them together; to be sure, they also bring about redistributions, realignments, homogenizations, serial arrangements, and convergences of the force relations. Major dominations are the hegemonic effects that are sustained by all these confrontations.

- Power relations are both intentional and nonsubjective. If in fact they are intelligible, this is not because they are the effect of another instance that 'explains' them, but rather because they are imbued, through and through, with calculation: there is no power that is exercised without a series of aims and objectives. But this does not mean that it results from the choice or decision of an individual subject; let us not look for the headquarters that presides over its rationality; neither the caste which governs, nor the groups which control the state apparatus, nor those who make the most important economic decisions direct the entire network of power that functions in a society (and makes *it* function); the rationality of power is characterized by tactics that are often quite explicit at the restricted level where they are inscribed (the local cynicism of power), tactics which, becoming connected to one another, attracting and propagating one another, but finding their base of support and their condition elsewhere, end by forming comprehensive systems: the logic is perfectly clear, the aims decipherable, and yet it is often the case that no one is there to have invented them, and few who can be said to have formulated them: an implicit characteristic of the great anonymous, almost unspoken strategies which coordinate the loquacious tactics whose 'inventors' or decisionmakers are often without hypocrisy.

- Where there is power, there is resistance, and yet, or rather consequently, this resistance is never in a position of exteriority in relation to power. Should it be said that one is always 'inside' power, there is no 'escaping' it, there is no absolute outside where it is concerned, because one is subject to the law in any case? Or that, history being the ruse of reason, power is the ruse of history, always emerging the winner? This would be to misunderstand the strictly relational character of power relationships. Their existence depends on a multiplicity of points of resistance: these play the role of adversary, target, support, or handle in power relations. These points of resistance are present everywhere in the power network. Hence there is no single locus of great Refusal, no soul of revolt, source of all rebellions, or pure law of the revolutionary. Instead there is a plurality of resistances, each of them a special case: resistances that are possible, necessary, improbable; others that are spontaneous, savage, solitary, concerted, rampant, or violent; still others that are quick to compromise, interested, or sacrificial; by definition, they can only exist in the strategic field of power relations. But this does not mean that they are only a reaction or rebound, forming with respect to the basic domination an underside that is in the end always passive, doomed to perpetual defeat. Resistances do not derive from a few heterogeneous principles; but neither are they a lure or a promise that is of necessity betrayed. They are the odd term in relations of power;

they are inscribed in the latter as an irreducible opposite. Hence they too are distributed in irregular fashion: the points, knots, or focuses of resistance are spread over time and space at varying densities, at times mobilizing groups or individuals in a definitive way, inflaming certain points of the body, certain moments in life, certain types of behavior. Are there no great radical ruptures, massive binary divisions, then? Occasionally, yes. But more often one is dealing with mobile and transitory points of resistance, producing cleavages in a society that shift about, fracturing unities and effecting regroupings, furrowing across individuals themselves, cutting them up and remolding them, marking off irreducible regions in them, in their bodies and minds. Just as the network of power relations ends by forming a dense web that passes through apparatuses and institutions, without being exactly localized in them, so too the swarm of points of resistance traverses social stratifications and individual unities. And it is doubtless the strategic codification of these points of resistance that makes a revolution possible, somewhat similar to the way in which the state relies on the institutional integration of power relationships.

It is in this sphere of force relations that we must try to analyze the mechanisms of power. In this way we will escape from the system of Law-and-Sovereign which has captivated political thought for such a long time. And if it is true that Machiavelli was among the few – and this no doubt was the scandal of his 'cynicism' – who conceived the power of the Prince in terms of force relationships, perhaps we need to go one step further, do without the persona of the Prince, and decipher power mechanisms on the basis of a strategy that is immanent in force relationships.

CLAUDE LEFORT
EXTRACTS FROM *DEMOCRACY*
AND POLITICAL THEORY

THE QUESTION OF DEMOCRACY

[…]

I would like now to draw attention to what reinterpreting the political means in our times.

The rise of totalitarianism, both in its fascist variant (which has for the moment been destroyed, though we have no grounds to think that it might not reappear in the future) and in its communist variant (which is going from strength to strength) obliges us to re-examine democracy. The widespread view to the contrary notwithstanding, totalitarianism does not result from a transformation of the mode of production. In the case of German or Italian fascisms, the point does not have to be stressed, as they adapted themselves to the maintenance of capitalist structures, whatever changes they may have undergone as a result of increased state intervention into the economy. But it is important at least to recall that the Soviet regime acquired its distinctive features before the era of the socialization of the means of production and of collectivization. Modern totalitarianism arises from a political mutation, from a mutation of a symbolic order, and the change in the status of power is its clearest expression. What in fact happens is that a party arises, claiming to be by its very nature different from traditional parties, to represent the aspirations of the whole people, and to possess a legitimacy which places it above the law. It takes power by destroying

Claude Lefort (1988), *Democracy and Political Theory*, Cambridge: Polity Press.

all opposition; the new power is accountable to no one and is beyond all legal control. But for our purposes, the course of events is of little import; we are concerned with the most characteristic features of the new form of society. A condensation takes place between the sphere of power, the sphere of law and the sphere of knowledge. Knowledge of the ultimate goals of society and of the norms which regulate social practices becomes the property of power, and at the same time power itself claims to be the organ of a discourse which articulates the real as such. Power is embodied in a group and, at its highest level, in a single individual, and it merges with a knowledge which is also embodied, in such a way that nothing can split it apart. The theory – or if not the theory, the spirit of the movement, as in Nazism – may well turn everything to account as circumstances demand, but it can never be challenged by experience. State and civil society are assumed to have merged; this is brought about through the agency of the ubiquitous party which permeates everything with the dominant ideology and hands down power's orders, as circumstances demand, and through the formation of a multiplicity of microbodies (organizations of all kinds in which an artificial socialization and relations of power conforming to the general model are reproduced). A logic of identification is set in motion, and is governed by the representation of power as embodiment. The proletariat and the people are one; the party and the proletariat are one; the politbureau and, ultimately, the *egocrat*, and the party are one. Whilst there develops a representation of a homogeneous and self-transparent society, of a People-as-One, social division, in all its modes, is denied, and at the same time all signs of differences of opinion, belief or mores are condemned. We can use the term despotism to characterize this regime, but only if we specify that it is modern and differs from all the forms that precede it. Power makes no reference to anything beyond the social; it rules as though nothing existed outside the social, as though it had no limits (these are the limits established by the idea of a law or a truth that is valid in itself); it relates to a society beyond which there is nothing, which is assumed to be a society fulfilling its destiny as a society produced by the people who live in it. The distinctively modern feature of totalitarianism is that it combines a radically artificialist ideal with a radically organicist ideal. The image of the body comes to be combined with the image of the machine. Society appears to be a community all of whose members are strictly interdependent; at the same time it is assumed to be constructing itself day by day, to be striving towards a goal – the creation of the new man – and to be living in a state of permanent mobilization.

We can ignore other features, which I have described at length elsewhere, such as the phenomenon of the production–elimination of the enemy (the enemy within being defined as an agent of the enemy without, as a parasite on the body, or as an interference with the workings of the machine). Nor am I trying here to reveal the contradictions totalitarianism comes up against. Even this brief outline allows us to re-examine democracy. When seen against the background of totalitarianism, it acquires a new depth and cannot be reduced to a system of institutions. In its turn, democracy too is seen to be a form of society; and our task is to understand what constitutes its uniqueness, and what it is about it that leads to its overthrow and to the advent of totalitarianism.

[...]

Democracy thus proves to be the historical society *par excellence*, a society which, in its very form, welcomes and preserves indeterminancy and which provides a remarkable contrast with totalitarianism which, because it is constructed under the slogan of creating a new man, claims to understand the law of its organization and development, and which, in the modern world, secretly designates itself as *a society without history*.

We will, however, remain within the limits of a description if we simply extend Tocqueville's analyses, as they themselves urge us to identify those features which point to the formation of a new despotism. The indeterminacy we were discussing does not pertain to the order of empirical facts, to the order of economic or social facts which, like the gradual extension of equality of condition, can be seen to be born of other facts. Just as the birth of totalitarianism defies all explanations which attempt to reduce that event to the level of empirical history, so the birth of democracy signals a mutation of the symbolic order, as is most clearly attested to by the new position of power.

I have tried on several occasions to draw attention to this mutation. Here, it will be enough to stress certain of its aspects. The singularity of democracy only becomes fully apparent if we recall the nature of the monarchical system of the Ancien Regime. This is not in fact a matter of recovering from a loss of memory but, rather, of recentering our investigations on something that we failed to recognize because we lost all sense of the political. It is in effect within the framework of the monarchy, or that of a particular type of monarchy which, originally developed in a theologico-political matrix, gave the prince sovereign power within the boundaries of a territory and made him both a secular agency and a representative of God, that the features of state and society were first outlined, and that the first separation of state and civil society occurred. Far from being reducible to a superstructural institution whose function can be derived from the nature of a mode of production, the monarchy was the agency which, by levelling and unifying the social field and, simultaneously, by inscribing itself in that field, made possible the development of commodity relations and rationalized activities in a manner that paved the way for the rise of capitalism.

Under the monarchy, power was embodied in the person of the prince. This does not mean that he held unlimited power. The regime was not despotic. The prince was a mediator between mortals and gods or, as political activity became secularized and laicized, between mortals and the transcendental agencies represented by a sovereign Justice and a sovereign Reason. Being at once subject to the law and placed above laws, he condensed within his body, which was at once mortal and immortal, the principle that generated the order of the kingdom. His power pointed towards an unconditional, other-worldly pole, while at the same time he was, in his own person, the guarantor and representative of the unity of the kingdom. The kingdom itself was represented as a body, as a substantial unity, in such a way that the hierarchy of its members, the distinction between ranks and orders appeared to rest upon an unconditional basis.

Power was embodied in the prince, and it therefore gave society a body. And because of this, a latent but effective knowledge of what *one* meant to the *other* existed throughout the social. This model reveals the revolutionary and unprecedented feature of democracy. The locus of power becomes *an empty place*. There is no need to dwell on the details of the institutional apparatus. The important point is that this apparatus prevents governments from appropriating power for their own ends, from incorporating it into themselves. The exercise of power is subject to the procedures of periodical redistributions. It represents the outcome of a controlled contest with permanent rules. This phenomenon implies an institutionalization of conflict. The locus of power is an empty place, it cannot be occupied – it is such that no individual and no group can be consubstantial with it – and it cannot be represented. Only the mechanisms of the exercise of power are visible, or only the men, the mere mortals, who hold political authority. We would be wrong to conclude that power now resides *in* society on the grounds that it emanates from popular suffrage; it remains the agency by virtue of which society apprehends itself in its unity and relates to itself in time and space. But this agency is no longer referred to an unconditional pole; and in that sense, it marks a division between the *inside* and the *outside* of the social, institutes relations beween those dimensions, and is tacitly recognized as being purely symbolic.

Such a transformation implies a series of other transformations, and they cannot be regarded merely as effects, as cause and effect relations have no pertinence in the order of the symbolic. On the one hand, the phenomenon of disincorporation, which we mentioned earlier, is accompanied by the disentangling of the sphere of power, the sphere of law and the sphere of knowledge. Once power ceases to manifest the principle which generates and organizes a social body, once it ceases to condense within it virtues deriving from transcendent reason and justice, law and knowledge assert themselves as separate from and irreducible to power. And just as the figure of power in its materiality and its substantiality disappears, just as the exercise of power proves to be bound up with the temporality of its reproduction and to be subordinated to the conflict of collective wills, so the autonomy of law is bound up with the impossibility of establishing its essence. The dimension of the development of right unfolds in its entirety, and it is always dependent upon a debate as to its foundations, and as to the legitimacy of what has been established and of what ought to be established. Similarly, recognition of the autonomy of knowledge goes hand in hand with a continual reshaping of the processes of acquiring knowledge and with an investigation into the foundations of truth. As power, law and knowledge become disentangled, a new relation to the real is established; to be more accurate, this relation is guaranteed within the limits of networks of socialization and of specific domains of activity. Economic, technical, scientific, pedagogic and medical facts, for example, tend to be asserted, to be defined under the aegis of knowledge and in accordance with norms that are specific to them. A dialectic which externalizes every sphere of activity is at work throughout the social. The young Marx saw this only too well, but he mistakenly reduced it to a dialectic of alienation. The fact that it operates within the density of class relations, which are relations of domination and exploitation, should not make us forget that it stems from a new symbolic constitution of the social. The relation established between the competition mobilized by the exercise of power and conflict in society is no less remarkable. The erection of a political stage on which competition can take place shows that division is, in a general way, constitutive of the very unity of society. Or to put it another way, the legitimation of purely political conflict contains within it the principle of a legitimation of social conflict in all its forms. If we bear in mind the monarchical model of the Ancien Regime, the meaning of the transformation can be summarized as follows: democratic society is instituted as a society without a body, as a society which undermines the representation of an organic totality. I am not suggesting that it therefore has no unity or no definite identity: on the contrary, the disappearance of natural determination, which was once linked to the person of the prince or to the existence of a nobility, leads to the emergence of a purely social society in which the people, the nation and the state take on the status of universal entities, and in which any individual or group can be accorded the same status. But neither the state, the people nor the nation represent substantial entities. Their representation is itself, in its dependence upon a political discourse and upon a sociological and historical elaboration, always bound up with ideological debate.

Nothing, moreover, makes the paradox of democracy more palpable than the institution of universal suffrage. It is at the very moment when popular sovereignty is assumed to manifest itself, when the people is assumed to actualize itself by expressing its will, that social interdependence breaks down and that the citizen is abstracted from all the networks in which his social life develops and becomes a mere statistic. Number replaces substance. It is also significant that in the nineteenth century this institution was for a long time resisted not only by conservatives and bourgeois liberals, but also by socialists – and this resistance cannot simply be imputed to the defence of class interests. It was provoked by the idea of a society which had now to accept that which cannot be represented.

In this brief sketch of democracy, I have been forced to ignore a major aspect of the empirical development of those societies which are organized in accordance with its principles – a development which justified socialist-inspired criticisms. I am certainly not forgetting that democratic institutions have constantly been used to restrict means of access to power, knowledge and the enjoyment of rights to a minority. Nor am I forgetting – and this would merit a lengthy analysis – that, as Tocqueville foresaw, the emergence of an anonymous power facilitated the expansion of state power (and, more generally, the power of bureaucracies). I have, on the other hand, chosen to concentrate upon a range of phenomena which are, it seems to me, usually misunderstood. In my view, the important point is that democracy is instituted and sustained by the *dissolution of the markers of certainty*. It inaugurates a history in which people experience a fundamental indeterminancy as to the basis of power, law and knowledge, and as to the basis of relations between *self* and *other*, at every level of social life (at every level where division, and especially the division between those who held power and those who were subject to them, could once be articulated as a result of a belief in the nature of things or in a supernatural principle). It is this which leads me to take the view that, without the actors being aware of it, a process of questioning is implicit in social practice, that no one has the answer to the questions that arise, and that the work of ideology, which is always dedicated to the task of restoring certainty, cannot put an end to this practice. And that in turn leads me to at least identify, if not to explain, the conditions for the formation of totalitarianism. There is always a possibility that the logic of democracy will be disrupted in a society in which the foundations of the political order and the social order vanish, in which that which has been established never bears the seal of full legitimacy, in which differences of rank no longer go unchallenged, in which right proves to depend upon the discourse which articulates it, and in which the exercise of power depends upon conflict. When individuals are increasingly insecure as a result of an economic crisis or of the ravages of war, when conflict between classes and groups is exacerbated and can no longer be symbolically resolved within the political sphere, when power appears to have sunk to the level of reality and to be no more than an instrument for the promotion of the interests and appetites of vulgar ambition and when, in a word, it appears *in* society, and when at the same time society appears to be fragmented, then we see the development of the fantasy of the People-as-One, the beginnings of a quest for a substantial identity, for a social body which is welded to its head, for an embodying power, for a state free from division.

It is sometimes said that democracy itself already makes room for totalitarian institutions, modes of organization and modes of representation. Whilst this is certainly true, it is also still true to say that a change in the economy of power is required if the totalitarian form of society is to arise.

PART IV
POLITICAL IDENTITIES

INTRODUCTION

As we think about politics we cannot but think about the nature of human beings and the nature of the various contexts in which we find ourselves. The concepts discussed in this part take the reader on a journey from one of the most timeless questions in political theory, 'what can we say about human nature and what does this imply about our understanding of politics?', to one of the most recent, 'are our political identities now irrevocably global and what does this mean for politics if they are?'. Along the way, we find discussion of two of the most important facets of our identity as political actors: our ties to the communities and the nations that we belong to. In the ordering of the part, there is an implicit assumption that this journey takes us from features of our identity that are the most intimate and irremovable to those that are, in some sense, distant from us and contingent to our identity. However, it is important to be aware of the deeply contestable nature of this implicit assumption and to ask throughout one's reading of the section if it can be upheld or not and what alternative renderings of the relationship between these concepts could be given. In doing so, I would suggest, one may well be drawn back to the discussions of power and liberty for instance and forward to the discussions of ideology and discourse, where fundamental problems and issues are raised surrounding our sense of ourselves as political actors possessed of political identities.

I

HUMAN NATURE

Christopher J. Berry

John Major, when he was the British Prime Minister, is reported as saying, 'I cannot legislate to change human nature.' There is no reason to think this was a studied remark; it is far more likely that he was simply voicing a cliché. The locutions 'you can't change human nature' or 'it's only human nature to . . .' have a prominent place in the everyday repertoire of explanations and justifications. The view that individuals have of human nature – we are selfish, we are sociable, we are competitive, we are co-operative, we are inherently flawed in some respect, we are capable of improvement (and so on) – shapes or underpins their view of xenophobia, the feasibility of socialism, the efficacy of punishment, the ineliminability of nepotism, the value or rationality of religion (and so on).

These more-or-less random examples illustrate two characteristics of the way the concept of human nature operates. First, invocations of 'human nature' appear to be ubiquitous so that virtually any aspect of human activity can be traced back to or related to human nature; indeed, it is tantamount to a tautology that this should be so. However, the second characteristic is that this ubiquity seems unaffected by the absence of any agreement as to what human nature actually is. The concept of human nature is contentious and this is a politically salient feature. It appears to be the very stuff of politics that it should thrive on differing identifications of human nature; witness the frequent talk of the socialist, the liberal, the conservative, the anarchist (and so on) view of 'man'.

We seem to have a paradox. There is a convergent recognition that human nature is a basic, underlying idea but there is divergence when it comes to identifying that basis. The contents of this book bear this out. The concepts of justice, liberty, equality and rights; the principles of legitimacy and toleration; the practices of multiculturalism; the rule of law; the institutions of the state or civil society; the debates over identity and the very idea of the political; all, without distortion, can be seen to imply a view of human nature *and* they all exhibit, again without distortion, the presence of fundamental disagreement. The aim of this chapter is to render this combination of ubiquity and contentiousness less paradoxical.

I

It is a necessary feature of an issue, if it is to be 'political', that it is disputable and practical – we do not dispute politically the geological and chemical processes that result in the formation of oil, we do dispute politically the ownership of that mineral or the extent to which economies should rely on its exploitation. Where does the difference between these lie? An initial answer might be that chemistry deals with the world as it is, while politics deals with the world as it might be. There is a difference between governments deciding whether or not to invest tax revenues into developing sources of renewable energy and the molecular structure of carbon. The former is an option (a question of choice), the latter is fixed (a matter of 'fact'). From the discussion so far, 'human nature' might seem to be a 'non-factual' topic. That, however, is too simple and explaining why will throw considerable light on the paradox as well as serving to identify the dominant features of the current debate.

If we return to John Major's pronouncement, we can see that 'human nature' is there regarded as beyond, or outside the feasible remit of, politics; it looks like 'it' is partaking of the fixity of carbon molecules. The established scientific facts are, indeed, that humans (like all other entities in our universe) are made of carbon. However, this is not the key point. There is a difference between statements that refer to human beings (such as their biochemical composition) and statements about human nature. The former do not have any purchase on how humans are believed to act, the latter do. This difference can be highlighted by the status of the fact that humans possess forty-six chromosomes. Some theorists regard this as on a par with the carbon base, others regard it as a crucial truth about human nature. The issue is not about the presence or the number of chromosomes, on which both sides agree, but whether those facts are relevant. That is, the dispute does not turn on the established view that humans are products of natural and sexual selection but, rather, whether this has decisive explanatory power. The dispute(s) over the neo-Darwinian account of human nature are now the major focus of the debate on the relation between human nature and politics. It is for that reason that I have chosen extracts from the work of Clifford Geertz (1972) and Roger Masters (1989).

II

Implied within invocations of human nature are three interrelated claims (cf. Berry 1986). Firstly, it is not neutral. To invoke human nature is to claim that something follows that is relevant to politics. What a notion of human nature does is establish what can count as a premise to a political conclusion. In other words, it is a presupposition that defines the field (or conceptual space) within which politics operates. For example, E. O.Wilson (1978: 208), one of the pioneers of sociobiology, declared that its findings made anarchism impossible. This is obviously not a neutral statement. What Wilson's conception of human nature is effectively doing here is 'staking out' or demarcating the field; he is pre-empting the conceptual space. Any account of politics, such as anarchism, that is incompatible with this demarcation can be dismissed as unrealistic. Yet anarchism too has its theory of human nature and it operates in the same presuppositional way. According to an anarchist, like the late eighteenth-century philosopher William Godwin, humans are perfectly capable of living together without the necessity of coercive institutions. For Godwin 'the science of the human mind' reveals that all possess reason and this is sufficient for regulating their actions and is capable of indefinite improvement (Godwin 1976: 135, 128). From this perspective it is Wilson's prescription that is faulty since, in effect, (as Godwin puts it) it unrealistically makes man a vegetable governed by sensations of heat and cold, dryness and moisture. Not only does this case illustrate the contentiousness of 'human nature', it also brings out how this is basic. It is because the contention operates at the level of presupposition that there is no neutral ground to which adjudication can be devolved. This absence of neutrality explains why 'human nature' looms so large in ideological argument.

The work of Donald Symons (1979) will illustrate the point. Symons presents what is a standard 'scientific' argument about the different reproductive strategies of males and females. Based on their relative investments in reproduction (cheap and plentiful sperm, costly and few eggs), males seek as many mates as possible while avoiding parental commitments where paternity is not guaranteed, whereas females seek a mate with as good a set of genes as possible and nurturing support. This is held to provide an explanation for sexual double standards. It is 'natural' for males, and 'unnatural' (that is, contrary to human nature) for females, to seek multiple partners. From the male point of view female promiscuity is more damaging than that of males. If a male has been 'entrapped' into nurturing offspring then he wants to be sure that his investment in terms of time, resources and responsibility is to the benefit of his, and not another male's, genes (hence such practices as chastity and claustration as well as infibulation). But to a critic that whole argument is suspect; it serves to pass this difference off as 'human nature' – a neutral scientific fact – when, in practice, it serves male interests to the detriment of females. This possesses all the hallmarks of an ideological argument (something Symons vehemently denies). The particular interests of males (a woman's place, and sexual activity, is in 'the home' while men are less constrained) are presented as general truths, as 'how the world is'.

The second and third claims amount to specifications of what is implicitly invoked by a theory of human nature. To invoke human nature is to invoke a belief that humans possess some common attributes. These are not optional extras but what belong to all humans (and significantly so). They are universals in the sense that whenever and wherever humans are encountered these attributes will also be found (such as genetic heritability for Wilson, or rationality for Godwin). This is not a claim that humans are identical in all respects. Indeed much of the purpose behind identifying what is universal stems from the recognition that there are differences. The essential claim is, rather, that these differences do not destroy universality but overlay it. Obviously there are difficulties when it comes to distinguishing between the universal and the local and these are the central concern in the Geertz extract.

The third claim elaborates upon an implication of this universalism. To claim human nature is universal is to claim it is invariant. This lack of variation means that human nature is a fixed item (or a 'given'). We can illustrate this claim 'in operation' by means of another eighteenth-century philosopher, David Hume, in his *Treatise of Human Nature* (2002). Hume declared that the human nature in all times and places possesses constant principles and operations. Among these principles are that humans are governed by self-interest and that they are more prompted to act by immediate rather than long-term interest. However, on Hume's account of it, social order depends on the dominance of the latter, which he summarises as the principles of justice. This means that order is always under threat from the natural preference humans have to act unjustly, to pursue what is immediately advantageous to them (and their 'immediate' family). This threat needs to be met. Since human nature, precisely because it is human nature, cannot be changed then all that can be altered is the social circumstances. These are changed by the introduction of government, which has the task of enforcing the observance of justice throughout society. Human nature is thus the given, political organisation the human response. This example reinforces the other two claims: it is universally true (all that changes for Hume is the relative institutional complexity of the governance) and it is not neutral (because self-interest is given, justice has to be enforced; anarchism is not a realistic option).

III

Hume was deliberately attempting to establish the foundations of a 'science of Man' and in this endeavour he was a fully signed-up member of the Enlightenment, as Geertz characterises it (see the following extract). The work of Roger Masters is in that tradition.

The common ground in all contemporary sciences of man is the acceptance of Charles Darwin's theory of evolution as amended by the inclusion of Mendelian genetics to constitute what is usually termed neo-Darwinism. In summary, all organisms possess a genetic code and gene frequency is constant from generation to generation. However, this constancy is subject to alteration due to drift, recombination and random mutation. If an alteration results in the organism producing more viable offspring than those without it, and the alteration is inherited, so that those offspring in their turn have more viable offspring, then this gives those organisms an 'advantage'. This is natural selection for reproductive fitness in a given environment. These principles cover all organisms and so must apply to humans; there is a fundamental continuity between them and other animals (primates, in particular, as their closest relatives). Work in human sociobiology or evolutionary psychology (like that of Wilson or Symons, and see representatively Barkow et al. (1992) and Betzig (1997)) proceeds on that basis. Not all of these tackle the issue of politics directly but those that do are chiefly concerned to make a case for what Arnhart (1995) calls 'the new Darwinian naturalism in political theory'.

Perhaps the most thoughtful and worked-out version is provided by Masters. At the beginning of the extract, Masters partially defines politics in terms of behaviour shared with other mammals such as bonding, dominance and submission. While this is only a partial definition, because Masters also refers to legal and customary regulations as distinctively human, other writers have made much of this shared behaviour. Willhoite (1976), for example, maintains that dominance hierarchies exist in all human societies because they were adaptive in primate evolution and Frans De Waal has written a book entitled *Chimpanzee Politics*. De Waal interprets chimpanzee behaviour as Machiavellian because it is based on opportunistic and manipulative power-seeking, and he quotes Harold Lasswell's definition of politics as 'who gets what, when and how' and declares that 'there can be no doubt that chimpanzees engage in it' (1989: 214). The clear implication here is that if chimpanzees practise politics then, given the genetic proximity between chimpanzees and humans, politics is a natural ingredient in the repertoire of human behaviour.

There are a number of difficulties with this. De Waal appears to ignore the other part of Masters's definition. More generally it falls foul of what Williams has labelled the 'representation problem' (1995: 102). The crux of this problem is how a 'behavioural tendency' (like, say, dominance hierarchies or pecking order) is 'represented' in humans with their linguistic and conceptually constituted 'cultures'. As we will see this looms large in the issues raised by Geertz but here Williams seems to share some ground with Masters when he identifies human communities as embodying 'norms'. However, where Williams would differ from Masters is in rejecting the latter's dualism, that is, his treatment of political behaviour as both common with primates and different because of language. For Williams, where there is 'culture' then this affects everything. In humans, on Williams's reading, and here he shares some of Geertz's territory, culture is constitutive, humans are conventional creatures; hence his declaration that 'the study of human nature *is* in good part the study of human conventions' (1995: 103– Williams's emphasis).

In the extract Masters identifies political science as lying at the intersection between the social and natural sciences. He is of the view that the study of politics has suffered from its isolation from the rapid developments in biology. Once the perspective of the life sciences is adopted then both practical and theoretical issues can be clarified. An example of the latter is the long-standing debate over whether the state is natural (as Aristotle argued) or not (as the social-contract theorists, such as Thomas Hobbes and Jean-Jacques Rousseau, argued). Masters's discussion of this point is worth elaborating as a 'case-study' in order to reveal how the perspective he represents on the relation between politics and human nature operates. He argues that 'humans survived and flourished for millennia in face to face social groups or tribes'. They did not need states; indeed, natural selection seems in other mammals to prevent the emergence of large-scale co-operative organisations. This means that the presence of such organisations among humans is a 'biological problem'. For Masters, what should now exercise political theory is how this was overcome; how a centralised state originated.

What are the governing assumptions in this type of argument? One of the key building blocks in evolutionary psychology is that, as Wilson put it, 'human nature is a hodge-podge of genetic adaptations to an environment largely vanished, the world of the Ice Age hunter-gatherer' (1978: 196). This view stands in opposition to what has been called the 'Standard Social Science Model' (Tooby and Cosmides 1992), which is purported to hold that evolved (or biological or innate) aspects of human behaviour are negligible because they have been superseded by the capacity for culture, which has led to flexibility (Tooby and Cosmides 1992: 32; they cite Geertz as adhering to this model). The basic objection to this model is that a psychological 'architecture' consisting merely of general-purpose or content-free processes could not solve the problems confronting humans. Rather, the mind has evolved a number of distinct mechanisms or modules (this is often characterised as the 'Swiss-army knife' model). Many such modules have been identified, including language acquisition, mate preferences, sexual jealousy, mother–infant communication and cheat detection. These exist because they are specialised adaptations constructed by natural selection 'to mesh with the detailed structural regularities common to our ancestral environments' (Tooby and Cosmides 1992: 89). It is *this* environment that is decisive and it is in virtue of this that 'human nature is everywhere the same' (Tooby and Cosmides 1992: 38); there is a 'single human metaculture' (Tooby and Cosmides 1992: 91).

Two basic related problems with this view of human nature as an Ice Age adaptation exist. The first problem concerns its lack of explanatory power. For example, it is claimed that tensions in step-relations are cross-culturally ubiquitous and, more particularly, that step-fathers maltreat their step-children more than their 'own' offspring (Daly & Wilson 1992: 307), the reason for this being that their genes are not involved in the former and humans (like all evolved organisms) act so as to maximise the presence of their genes in the next generation. However, although this behaviour can be construed as adaptational, it is the case that in the majority of cases step-parents prove to be as loving and supportive of their step-children as of their own but that, too, can be construed as adaptational (see Miller 2000: 193–4). It is this difference that needs to be explained. If the *contrary* behaviours of step-parental maltreatment and step-parental love of children are *both* adaptations to the environment then, because one cause cannot be responsible for two contradictory effects, no explanation has been given.

The second problem is the lack of evidence. It is clear that much weight is placed on the Ice Age hunter-gatherers but we are in no position to know about their behaviour. Because of the prior acceptance of universalism, what is held to be true of humans (this has to mean *all* humans) today is presumed to have been adaptational then. But this is now circular. You can't invoke 'then' to explain 'now' if your knowledge of 'then' is derived from 'now'. Evolutionary theorists attempt to break the circle in (broadly) two ways. They refer to contemporary hunter-gatherer societies, though it is admitted that few of these exist and the same cases recur, with the bush-folk of the Kalahari and the Yanomano of the Amazon basin being perhaps the most frequently cited (see Musonda 1991 for a survey and assessment). However, this mistakenly presumes that humans who live in industrial societies somehow are less revealing of human nature than hunter-gatherers. The second way, perhaps, deflects this point because experiments can be conducted to test predicted inferences, for example, that sex differences in spatial ability map on to males as hunters and females as forgers (see Silverman and Eals 1992). But this still seems to beg the question of universalism and is only as strong as its inferential assumptions about Ice Age role differentiation.

As we would expect, this 'scientific' view of 'human nature' is contentious. It also exhibits another trait of 'human nature' theorising; its non-neutral prescriptive nature (recall Wilson's view of anarchism, a view that is echoed by F. H. Willhoite). This prescriptive element is present in Masters. It comes in a weak and a strong form. The weak form is apparent in his methodological claim as to what theorists should now do. The biological perspective has identified the problems that 'need' answering. The implication is that other pursuits are less worthwhile if progress is to be made. Others are more forthright. Glendon Schubert (1976: 174), for example, thinks biological theory will 'jack political philosophy off its classical presumptions', since the only way to make progress is from recognising the evolutionary roots of political behaviour. The strong form is expressed by Masters in another passage in his book. There he writes that a 'new naturalism' based non-reductively on evolutionary biology 'provides objective criteria for preferring a constitutional regime in which citizens are subject to the law and play a legitimate role in political life'(1989: xiv, cf. 183, 227).

However, the 'objectivity' to which Masters here appeals seems problematic. For example, his 'constitutionalism' appears to smuggle in some teleology or purpose that has no justification. In other words, it seems exceedingly suspect to assume that a set of human arrangements that has only recently and locally come into existence fits 'human nature' better than any other set that has existed throughout recognisable human history. 'Politics' has taken a variety of forms but even if these forms are connected to certain facts about humans as evolved animals they do not (so to speak) constitute preshaped 'holes' into which only some particular 'pegs' will fit. On the same grounds and for the same reasons despotism seems just as 'natural' as constitutionalism (cf. Somit and Peterson 1997, for an argument about the exceptionalism of democracy from the evolutionary perspective).

IV

Nobody denies that humans have 'culture'; what is disputed is what that means. If the notion of a universal metaculture is at one end of a spectrum then Geertz is perhaps at the other. This should not be misunderstood. There is no suggestion that Geertz dismisses neo-Darwinism; indeed, he argues that human evolution occurred within a 'cultural setting'. As he puts it in the extract, humans are 'unfinished animals' who complete themselves through culture. Culture is not properly considered as an add-on to biological evolution but, rather, is an intrinsic ingredient; humans are 'cultural artifacts' (a more recent version of this has been articulated by Shore 2000). The inference Geertz draws from this is that 'we all begin with the natural equipment to live a thousand kinds of life but end in the end having lived only one'.

Geertz is an anthropologist and this inference is at the root of one his major field-studies, Bali. According to Geertz the Balinese possess an interacting system of symbolic structures (the crux of 'culture') which defines, for example, what they mean by a 'person', but this is interwoven with conceptions of time (calendars do not measure the rate of time passing but identify the kind of time) and a highly formalised, ceremonial form of daily life. Geertz allows that this interdependency is a general phenomenon but, crucially, holds that this cannot be comprehended by any universalist scheme. It misses the point to claim that Balinese conduct is comparable with conduct A from culture Z and with conduct B from culture Y and all instances of the general (metacultural) rule R.

This Geertzian approach has clear political implications. Perhaps the most significant of these is whether the specificity on which this approach insists precludes the viability of what the United Nations calls the *Universal Declaration of Human Rights*. The idea of human, or natural, rights was historically developed to establish universal grounds of political legitimacy or a set of criteria to assess a regime independently of its own principles of justification. If a government infringed these rights it forfeited the right to obedience from its subjects. The source of these rights has always been linked to human nature or 'the natural condition of mankind'. While originally couched in theological terms (by, for example, one its major exponents, John Locke (1965), or the American Declaration of Independence), the focus has increasingly been more secular and reposed on some conception of human nature (see Donnelly 1982, for example). If, however, there are only men and women (say, Balinese or Britons or Brazilians) and no Man then the ability to criticise particular regimes seems blunted. For example, it is not usually held to be a defence of clitoridectomy or slavery or stoning adulteresses to death that it is the culturally 'done thing' in their part of the world.

Nor is the language of rights the only way that the universality of human nature is used politically. Jeremy Bentham (1748–1832), for example, was a fervent critic of 'rights' (as he notoriously put it, natural and imprescriptible rights were 'nonsense on stilts' (Parekh 1973: 269)). Nonetheless he saw all humans as under the governance of 'two sovereign masters, pain and pleasure' (Parekh 1973: 66) and these rule regardless of location. Bentham wrote, in 1802, an essay entitled *of the Influence of Time and Place in matters of Legislation* (1859), where he argued that since the definition of any good law was that it reduced mischief (the sum of pain), and all humans avoid pain, then the same criterion of good law will apply, wherever and whenever. This means, he further maintained, that all laws can be reformed and there was no inherent obstacle in transferring laws from one society to another (Bentham's follower James Mill (1773–1836) wrote a history of India (1975) which was able to argue on these grounds that British rule was a great improvement).

This is not to claim either in the utilitarian Benthamite or Lockean rights case that the cogency of their argument is beyond question. Indeed, in so far as they rely on human nature that cannot be the case. What, however, their arguments do suggest is that the recourse to universalist principles, and seemingly thereby a conception of human nature, is politically powerful.

V

It does not follow, however, that just because 'appeals to human nature' are contentious and not definitive that 'human nature' therefore does not exist. It is difficult to know what that claim might mean. Arguments that human nature is non-existent are saying, in effect, that it is a just function of a (temporally specific) discourse (cf. for example Foucault 1970; Rorty 1982). When this is not an all-encompassing dismissal of any realism (as applicable to rainbows as it is to human nature), it often amounts to the claim that this function is ideological. 'Human nature' serves to declare 'off limits' a particular course of action but the consequence of this is to endorse the status quo; it turns a question of choice into a matter of fact. There is no necessity here though. There are plenty of examples of radical critics also employing the notion. For example, Marx's argument that capitalism is alienating makes little sense without a conception of an unalienated human life, manifesting a non-distorted human nature (Marx 1975; cf. Geras 1983). Similarly, while some proponents of the 'scientific' evolutionary approach think this underwrites a reduction in state activity (cf. Ridley 1996, ch. 12), others think it underwrites increased planning and control to confront 'ecological imperatives' (Corning 1977).

What this suggests, in conclusion, is that its very contentiousness is indicative that there is 'something' worth contending. It is hard to see why this disputation persists if nothing hinges on it. The reason it does seem a prize worth having is because, as a presupposition of any political 'position', a conception of human nature claims for itself a special authority as it seeks to make ostensibly rival accounts play on its territory (just as these accounts seek to do for their own conception). As long as there is politics the debate about human nature is not going to go away.

QUESTIONS FOR DISCUSSION

- Can there ever be an agreed view of human nature?
- Do you agree that to have a political agenda or political philosophy implies having a concept of human nature?
- Does each community have its own concept of human nature or does the concept necessarily apply universally?
- Is the concept of human nature inevitably ideological?

CLIFFORD GEERTZ
EXTRACTS FROM 'THE IMPACT OF
THE CONCEPT OF CULTURE ON THE
CONCEPT OF MAN'

[···]

The rise of a scientific concept of culture amounted to, or at least was connected with, the overthrow of the view of human nature dominant in the Enlightenment – a view that, whatever else may be said for or against it, was both clear and simple – and its replacement by a view not only more complicated but enormously less clear. The attempt to clarify it, to reconstruct an intelligible account of what man is, has underlain scientific thinking about culture ever since. Having sought complexity and, on a scale grander than they ever imagined, found it, anthropologists became entangled in a tortous effort to order it. And the end is not yet in sight.

The Enlightenment view of man was, of course, that he was wholly of a piece with nature and shared in the general uniformity of composition which natural science, under Bacon's urging and Newton's guidance, had discovered there. There is, in brief, a human nature as regularly organized, as thoroughly invariant, and as marvelously simple as Newton's universe. Perhaps some of its laws are different, but there *are* laws; perhaps some of its immutability is obscured by the trappings of local fashion, but it *is* immutable.

[···]

The great, vast variety of differences among men, in beliefs and values, in customs and institutions, both over time and from place to place, is

Clifford Geertz (1965), 'The Impact of the Concept of Culture on the Concept of Man', in John R. Platt (ed.), *New Views of the Nature of Man*, Chicago: Chicago University Press.

essentially without significance in defining his nature. It consists of mere accretions, distortions even, overlaying and obscuring what is truly human – the constant, the general, the universal – in man.

[···]

This circumstance makes the drawing of a line between what is natural, universal, and constant in man and what is conventional, local, and variable extraordinarily difficult. In fact, it suggests that to draw such a line is to falsify the human situation, or at least to misrender it seriously.

Consider Balinese trance. The Balinese fall into extreme dissociated states in which they perform all sorts of spectacular activities – biting off the heads of living chickens, stabbing themselves with daggers, throwing themselves wildly about, speaking with tongues, performing miraculous feats of equilibration, mimicking sexual intercourse, eating feces, and so on – rather more easily and much more suddenly than most of us fall asleep. Trance states are a crucial part of every ceremony. In some, fifty or sixty people may fall, one after the other ('like a string of firecrackers going off', as one observer puts it), emerging anywhere from five minutes to several hours later, totally unaware of what they have been doing and convinced, despite the amnesia, that they have had the most extraordinary and deeply satisfying experience a man can have. What does one learn about human nature from this sort of thing and from the thousand similarly peculiar things anthropologists discover, investigate, and describe? That the Balinese are peculiar sorts of beings, South Sea Martians? That they are just the same as we at base, but with some peculiar, but really incidental, customs we do not happen to have gone in for? That they are innately gifted or even instinctively driven in certain directions rather than others? Or that human nature does not exist and men are pure and simply what their culture makes them?

It is among such interpretations as these, all unsatisfactory, that anthropology has attempted to find its way to a more viable concept of man, one in which culture, and the variability of culture, would be taken into account rather than written off as caprice and prejudice and yet, at the same time, one in which the governing principle of the field, 'the basic unity of mankind', would not be turned into an empty phrase. To take the giant step away from the uniformitarian view of human nature is, so far as the study of man is concerned, to leave the Garden. To entertain the idea that the diversity of custom across time and over space is not a mere matter of garb and appearance, of stage settings and comedic masques, is to entertain also the idea that humanity is as various in its essence as it is in its expression. And with that reflection some well-fastened philosophical moorings are loosed and an uneasy drifting into perilous waters begins.

Perilous, because if one discards the notion that Man, with a capital 'M', is to be looked for 'behind', 'under', or 'beyond' his customs and replaces it with the notion that he, uncapitalized, is to be looked for 'in' them, one is in some danger of losing sight of him altogether.

[···]

In attempting to launch such an integration from the anthropological side and to reach, thereby, an exacter image of man, I want to propose two ideas. The first of these is that culture is best seen not as complexes of concrete behavior patterns – customs, usages, traditions, habit clusters – as has, by and large, been the case up to now, but as a set of control mechanisms – plans, recipes, rules, instructions (what computer engineers call 'programs') – for the governing of behavior. The second is that man is precisely the animal most desperately dependent upon such extragenetic, outside-the-skin control mechanisms, such cultural programs, for ordering his behavior.

Neither of these ideas is entirely new, but a number of recent developments, both within anthropology and in other sciences (cybernetics, information theory, neurology, molecular genetics) have made them susceptible of more precise statement as well as lending them a degree of empirical support they did not previously have. And out of such reformulations of the concept of culture and of the role of culture in human life comes, in turn, a definition of man stressing not so much the empirical commonalities in his behavior, from place to place and time to time, but rather the mechanisms by whose agency the breadth and indeterminateness of his inherent capacities are reduced to the narrowness and specificity of his actual accomplishments. One of the most significant facts about us may finally be that we all begin with the natural equipment to live a thousand kinds of life but end in the end having lived only one.

The 'control mechanism' view of culture begins with the assumption that human thought is basically both social and public – that its natural habitat is the house yard, the market place, and the town square. Thinking consists not of 'happenings in the head' (though happenings there and elsewhere are necessary for it to occur) but of a traffic in what have been called, by G. H. Mead and others, significant symbols – words for the most part but also gestures, drawings, musical sounds, mechanical devices like clocks, or natural objects like jewels – anything, in fact that is disengaged from its mere actuality and used to impose meaning upon experience. From the point of view of any particular individual, such symbols are largely given. He finds them already current in the community when he is born, and they remain, with some additions, subtractions, and partial alterations he may or may not have had a hand in, in circulation there after he dies. While he lives he uses them, or some of them, sometimes deliberately and with care, most often spontaneously and with ease, but always with the same end in view: to put a construction upon the events through which he lives, to orient himself within 'the ongoing course of experienced things', to adopt a vivid phrase of John Dewey's.

Man is so in need of such symbolic sources of illumination to find his bearings in the world because the non-symbolic sort that are constitutionally ingrained in his body cast so diffused a light. The behavior patterns of lower animals are, at least to a much greater extent, given to them with their physical structure; genetic sources of information order their actions within much narrower ranges of variation, the narrower and more thorough-going the lower the animal. For man, what are innately given are extremely general response capacities, which although they make possible far greater plasticity, complexity, and on the scattered occasions when everything works as it should, effectiveness of behavior, leave it much less precisely regulated. This, then, is the second face of our argument: undirected by culture patterns – organized systems of significant symbols – man's behavior would be virtually ungovernable, a mere chaos of pointless acts and exploding emotions, his experience virtually shapeless. Culture, the accumulated totality of such patterns, is not just an ornament of human existence but – the principal basis of its specificity – an essential condition for it.

[···]

We are, in sum, incomplete or unfinished animals who complete or finish ourselves through culture – and not through culture in general but through highly particular forms of it: Dobuan and Javanese, Hopi and Italian, upper-class and lower-class, academic and commercial. Man's great capacity for learning, his plasticity, has often been remarked, but what is even more critical is his extreme dependence upon a certain sort of learning: the attainment of concepts, the apprehension and application of specific systems of symbolic meaning. Beavers build dams, birds build nests, bees locate food, baboons organize social groups, and mice mate on the basis of forms of learning that rest predominantly on the instructions encoded in their genes and evoked by appropriate patterns of external stimuli: physical keys inserted into organic locks. But men build dams or shelters, locate food, organize their social groups, or find sexual partners under the guidance of instructions encoded in flow charts and blueprints, hunting lore, moral systems, and aesthetic judgments: conceptual structures molding formless talents.

We live, as one writer has neatly put it, in an 'information gap'. Between what our body tells us and what we have to know in order to function, there is a vacuum we must fill ourselves, and we fill it with information (or misinformation) provided by our culture. The boundary between what is innately controlled and what is culturally controlled in human behavior is an ill-defined and wavering one. Some things are, for all intents and purposes, entirely controlled intrinsically: we need no more cultural guidance to learn how to breathe than a fish needs to learn how to swim. Others are almost certainly largely cultural: we do not attempt to explain on a genetic basis why some men put their trust in centralized planning and others in the free market, though it might be an amusing exercise. Almost all complex human behavior is, of course, the vector outcome of the two. Our capacity to speak is surely innate; our capacity to speak English is surely cultural. Smiling at pleasing stimuli and frowning at unpleasing ones are surely in some degree genetically determined (even apes screw up their faces at noxious odors); but sardonic smiling and burlesque frowning are equally surely predominantly cultural, as is perhaps demonstrated by the Balinese definition of a madman as someone who, like an American, smiles when there is nothing to laugh at. Between the basic ground plans for our life that our genes lay down – the capacity to speak or to smile – and the precise behavior we in fact execute – speaking English in a certain tone of voice, smiling enigmatically in a delicate social situation – lies a complex set of significant symbols under whose direction we transform the first into the second, the ground plans into the activity.

Our ideas, our values, our acts, even our emotions, are, like our nervous system itself, cultural products – products manufactured, indeed, out of tendencies, capacities, and dispositions with which we were born, but manufactured none the less. Chartres is made of stone and glass. But it is not just stone and glass; it is a cathedral, and not only a cathedral, but a particular cathedral built at a particular time by certain members of a particular society. To understand what it means, to perceive it for what it is, you need to know rather more than the generic properties of stone and glass and rather more than what is common to all cathedrals. You need to understand also – and, in my opinion, most critically – the specific concepts of the relations between God, man, and architecture that, having governed its creation, it consequently embodies. It is no different with men: they, too, every last one of them, are cultural artifacts.

Whatever differences they may show, the approaches to the definition of human nature adopted by the Enlightenment and by classical anthropology have one thing in common: they are both basically typological. They endeavor to construct an image of man as a model, an archetype, a Platonic idea or an Aristotelian form, with respect to which actual men – you, me, Churchill, Hitler, and the Bornean headhunter – are but reflections, distortions, approximations. In the Enlightenment case, the elements of this essential type were to be uncovered by stripping the trappings of culture away from actual men and seeing what then was left – natural man. In classical anthropology, it was to be uncovered by factoring out the commonalities in culture and seeing what then appeared – consensual man. In either case, the result is the same as tends to emerge in all typological approaches to scientific problems generally: the differences among individuals and among groups of individuals are rendered secondary. Individuality comes to be seen as eccentricity, distinctiveness as accidental deviation from the only legitimate object of study for the true scientist: the underlying, unchanging, normative type. In such an approach, however elaborately formulated and resourcefully defended, living detail is drowned in dead stereotype: we are in quest of a metaphysical entity, Man with a capital 'M', in the interests of which we sacrifice the empirical entity we in fact encounter, man with a small 'm'.

The sacrifice is, however, as unnecessary as it is unavailing. There is no opposition between general theoretical understanding and circumstantial understanding, between synoptic vision and a fine eye for detail. It is, in fact, by its power to draw general propositions out of particular phenomena that a scientific theory – indeed, science itself – is to be judged. If we want to discover what man amounts to, we can only find it in what men are: and what men are, above all other things, is various. It is in understanding that variousness – its range, its nature, its basis, and its implications – that we shall come to construct a concept of human nature that, more than a statistical shadow and less than a primitivist dream, has both substance and truth.

It is here, to come round finally to my title, that the concept of culture has its impact on the concept of man. When seen as a set of symbolic devices for controlling behavior, extrasomatic sources of information, culture provides the link between what men are intrinsically capable of becoming and what they actually, one by one, in fact become. Becoming human is becoming individual, and we become individual under the guidance of cultural patterns, historically created systems of meaning in terms of which we give form, order, point, and direction to our lives. And the cultural patterns involved are not general but specific – not just 'marriage' but a particular set of notions about what men and women are like, how spouses should treat one another, or who should properly marry whom; not just 'religion' but belief in the wheel of karma, the observance of a month of fasting, or the practice of cattle sacrifice. Man is to be defined neither by his innate capacities alone, as the Enlightenment sought to do, nor by his actual behaviors alone, as much of contemporary social science seeks to do, but rather by the link between them, by the way in which the first is transformed into the second, his generic potentialities focused into his specific performances. It is in man's *career*, in its characteristic course, that we can discern, however dimly, his nature, and though culture is but one element in determining that course, it is hardly the least important. As culture shaped us as a single species – and is no doubt still shaping us – so too it shapes us as separate individuals. This, neither an unchanging subcultural self nor an established cross-cultural consensus, is what we really have in common.

ROGER MASTERS
EXTRACTS FROM *THE NATURE*
OF POLITICS

A BIOLOGICAL DEFINITION OF POLITICS

A distinctive characteristic of *Homo sapiens*, related to the evolutionary emergence of the large brain, language, and cultural diversification, is the sheer complexity of the factors contributing to human behavior. Morin (1973) has spoken of 'hypercomplexity', arguing that the wide range of human adaptability necessarily implies an equally high risk of irrationality, insanity, and conflict; he speaks of our species as the 'crisis animal' and suggests that its appropriate scientific designation should be '*Homo sapiens/demens*'.

Such an understanding of human nature provides added rationale for the Aristotelian concept of the *zoon politikon*, the political animal. From a biological perspective, conflicts between the behavioral programs encoded in genes, in language, or in individual learning must be regulated, though not necessarily resolved, if the species is to survive. Just as a computer can be rendered inoperable by certain contradictory programs, an organism can be seriously disturbed, if not destroyed, when genetic and learned behavioral programs are in radical contradiction. This occurs, for example, when primates deprived of normal maternal care and social experience fail to learn behaviors congruent with innate propensities, leading to severe abnormalities similar to human psychoses and, in extreme cases, inability to copulate or rear young (Harlow and Harlow 1963; Harlow 1971).

Roger D. Masters (1989), *The Nature of Politics,* New Haven and London: Yale University Press.

Given the complex information which must be integrated by the human central nervous system, it should hardly be surprising that discontinuities between genetic, cultural, and individually learned behavioral programs constantly produce deviance and social conflict. The biological function of politics thus arises from the insufficiency of other modes of regulating social interaction. Laws, whether customary or written, do not suffice in all situations; as common experience has long indicated, they are all too easily broken. The political process, by which laws are changed, enforced, and challenged, would seem to be an inevitable counterpart of the 'hypercomplexity' represented in figure 4.4 [not included in this selection].

In the common usage of the term, politics is a form of rivalry to determine which humans are permitted to transmit 'authoritative' messages or commands to the rest of the society (Easton 1965a, 1965b). In this sense, high status and political office are in themselves symbolic messages; just as dominance in animal societies is communicated by gestures or personal recognition, humans represent social and political status by verbal and nonverbal symbols that organize social interactions (Maclay and Knipe 1972).

In a secondary sense, however, politics is also rivalry concerning the content of authoritative messages in a human population (Edelman 1964). While this is obvious when political conflict concerns the substance of laws or customs, behavior can be said to have a political element even when it is not openly directed to legal or institutional change. For example, novels or popular songs can convey crucial political messages, particularly in regimes where other channels of communication are closed to significant sectors of the population (Holland 1968; Green and Walzer 1969).

One can therefore define politics more precisely as behavior that simultaneously partakes of the attributes of bonding, dominance, and submission (which the human primate shares with many other mammals) and those of legal or customary regulation of social life (characteristic of human groups endowed with language). Politics is not merely what ethologists have called agonic or agonistic behavior (Altmann 1967): competitive rivalry for dominance exists in sports, on school playgrounds, and in business without thereby deserving the name politics. Nor is all behavior governed by legal norms automatically political: as cultural anthropology teaches us, legal or customary rules govern childhood, marriage, and the entire range of human social life.

Political behavior, properly so called, comprises actions in which the rivalry for and perpetuation of social dominance and loyalty impinges on the legal or customary rules governing a group. As such, political science has a peculiar status, for it lies at the intersection of ethology and anthropology – or, more broadly, at the point where the social and natural sciences meet. Indeed, this definition of politics may help explain why political theorists, at least before the middle of the nineteenth century, were almost always concerned with the definition of human nature and the relationship between nature and society.

While the biological approach suggested here is generally compatible with much recent work in political science, it permits the inclusion of dimensions that are frequently ignored. There is no reason to limit the analysis of biological variables in politics to the remark that human nature is 'essentially uniform' or that 'biological traits' are part of the 'environment' of the political system (Deutsch 1963: 12, 29; Easton 1965a: 72). On each of the three levels of analysis distinguished above (the species, societies, and the individual), a biological definition of politics points to phenomena that have not traditionally been studied by political scientists.

For example, our species has not been 'liberated' from natural constraints merely because of the tremendous extension of human technology (Meadows et al. 1972), and the possibility of 'Limits to Growth' poses specifically political problems (Ophuls 1973, 1977; Sprout and Sprout 1971). Can one find, in biological evolution, criteria that would permit a better understanding of these new issues, if not guidelines for policy (Caldwell 1964; Corning 1971)? In the study of modern societies, much has been said of the decline in power of legislatures and the rising influence of individual leaders. To what extent is this development – and the related increase in the phenomenon of charismatic leadership – linked to rapid social and cultural change? Can charisma be more fully understood in the context of ethological studies of dominance and submission (Hummel 1973; Larsen 1973; Sullivan and Masters 1988)? Do increased population densities, which produce behavioral disturbances in other species, rigidify dominance hierarchies and increase the frequency of pathological or aggressive behaviors (Bouthoul 1970; Galle et al. 1972)?

Although the political behavior of individuals, whether leaders or followers, has traditionally been interpreted in terms of attitudes and interests, recent events often seem irrational according to these criteria. Biological research shows the role of physiological variables in dominance behavior (Corning and Corning 1972; McGuire and Raleigh 1986; Madson 1985a, 1985b). Are there natural factors that help to explain the different political behaviors of males and females (Tiger 1969; Dearden 1974; Watts 1984; Schubert 1985)? Are the physiological correlates of drug use relevant to political departicipation among the poor or powerless (Stauffer 1971)?

Even if the above questions were irrelevant to political analysis, they concern issues on which policymakers will necessarily make decisions of biological as well as political importance. What are the political implications of biomedical technologies that could drastically modify the human gene pool (Taylor 1968; Blank 1981; Rifkin 1983)? Proposals for Zero Population Growth, genetic or drug screening, and mapping of the human genome have manifold political consequences (Attah 1973; Hemphill 1973). Should psychosurgical or psychopharmacological technologies be used as an alternative to the penal system, regulating deviant behavior without formal legal processes (Somit 1968; Corover 1973)? Should leaders be treated with drugs in order to limit their aggressive behaviors, thereby diminishing the risk of global warfare (Clark 1971)?

These issues, and many others like them, cannot be understood without reference to the biological sciences. Although it has been traditional to distinguish nature and culture, the resulting dichotomy between the natural and social sciences is contradicted not only by scientific findings, but by the dilemmas facing contemporary governments. Lest political science continue its isolation from the rapid developments in contemporary biology, it is important to treat political behavior as a biological phenomenon on both causal and functional levels.

In suggesting a biological definition of politics, human behavior is not thereby reduced to animal instinct or evolutionary necessity. Each of the three levels of systems distinguished in figure 4.4 is open; naive reductionism, whether in the form of 'pop sociobiology' (Kitcher 1985) or 'behaviorism' (Skinner 1965), is as outmoded as nineteenth-century Social Darwinism or eighteenth-century materialism. Complex living systems can be better understood as a reflection of structures encoding information and evolving in ways that are not always determinate and predictable (Anderson 1972; Gal-Or 1972; Morin 1973; Gleick 1987). Traditional philosophic debates about the nature of man have been inconclusive because the term *man* confuses heterogeneous levels of analysis and not, as is sometimes claimed, because our species lacks a nature.

EVOLUTIONARY BIOLOGY AND POLITICAL THEORY

In addition to improving our understanding of practical matters, the perspective of the life sciences can clarify many issues in the tradition of political thought. Three specific questions have already been mentioned. First, the debate between materialists and idealists. Second, the so-called quarrel of the ancients and the moderns; and finally, the relationship between human nature and politics. On each of these topics, evolutionary biology leads to a reformulation and clarification of questions that have long seemed insoluble.

Materialism and idealism

The relationship between phenotype and genotype, which serves as one of the foundations of the neo-Darwinian theory of evolution, suggests a way of reconsidering the traditional debates between materialists and idealists. No species can survive unless its phenotypic representatives are sufficiently viable, in the environments where they live, to produce offspring; natural selection operates on the visible organism, not directly on the gene pool. Because the physical requisites of life are essential factors in organic evolution, biology at first appears to favor materialism, particularly as an alternative to the traditional theological account of creation. But this appearance is deceptive.

For those who no longer explain life as an act of God's creative will and divine plan, the relationship between genotype and phenotype shows the need for a more complex view than simple materialism. In individual life history, genes functioning as a set of instruction have a priority over the physical structures they produce; at the level of species, the gene pool represents phylogenetically evolved structures and adaptations to the environment that are transmitted from one generation to another. The development and life of the phenotype is directed by genetic information, which serves as a code or plan for the formation of organisms that fit the species' nature.

Biologists who reject the traditional concept of teleology associated with divine creation nonetheless admit a category of events that can be understood only in terms of what Aristotle called 'formal' and 'final causes', although to avoid misunderstanding some speak of 'teleonomic' processes rather than teleological ones (Pittendrigh 1958; Mayr 1974; Masters 1978). Others use the term 'ultimate causation' to describe the long-term effects of natural selection, as distinct from the 'proximate causation' operating on the individual phenotype (Barash 1977: 37–9).

There does not seem to be a way to reduce biology to a single set of material causes, on the model of the seventeenth-century physics used by Hobbes and Locke. Nor can it be said that the physical and social environment necessarily causes species to have a particular characteristic, as Engels and some materialists in the Marxist tradition concluded: while adaptation to the environment is one of the factors in evolution, other characteristics of population genetics are due to genetic drift, sampling, and genomic structure – attributes of the informational system for transmitting genetic information, rather than of the material environment per se. Treating the gene pool as a constituent element of living forms is hardly mysticism, but it limits the scope of the mechanistic causation emphasized by traditional materialists.

Evolutionary biology points to the irreducible importance of processes at different systemic levels, much along the lines of Aristotle's conceptualization of four types of causality. Efficient causes are those actually producing or triggering the motions of living things; they include the sources of energy in the physical environment as well as stimuli impinging on each organism. Material causation is broader, since it includes those attributes of an organism that are necessary requisites of behavior as well as physical constraints that influence species over time and space (even without immediate physical effects on an individual). The central nervous system of each species, for example, is a material cause determining which environmental events can be perceived as stimuli; the ecological setting functions as a material cause of natural selection, favoring some genotypes over others. While both efficient and material causation concern the phenotypical or visible systems in nature, there is surely a meaningful difference between the causes whose presence or absence triggers or drives a specific event, and material factors that are necessary conditions without being an efficient cause of the phenomenon observed.

Other causal processes operate on the level of the genetic material and its mode of influencing the phenotype. Formal causation could be identified with the way an organism's basic shape and behavior are preprogrammed in the genome. A dog does not look like a cat or an elephant. In ontogeny, genes provide instructions for cellular differentiation and growth until the organism corresponds to the fundamental shape or Form (sometimes called 'bauplan') of the species. Activity can also have a form. In the behavior of individuals, the characteristics of displays or environmental cues that function as releasing mechanisms are often inherited or at least influenced by the species' evolutionary past (Lorenz 1970–71). At this level, causation can be called formal because it concerns the genetic information controlling the material processes of growth, development, and behavior.

Final causation, perhaps the most difficult of the Aristotelian categories, represents the tendency of living forms to seek behavioral and functional responses consistent with the species' strategy of adaptation. Whereas formal causes concern the information coded in the genome, final causes concern the reasons we discover to explain why such information evolved. At the most general level, of course, the final cause is always the same, namely, relative advantage in the transmission of genes from generation to generation; for this reason, critics have often attacked discussions of biological adaptation as 'just so stories', incapable of empirical verification (Lewontin et al. 1984). In extreme cases, the concept of final cause can be misused absurdly to imply that whatever exists is the production of evolution and natural selection, as in the classic 'the nose evolved to hold up eyeglasses'. Because there is a very real risk of converting the principle of natural selection into a justification for the status quo, analysis of final causation – which is to say, of adaptation to the environment – requires special care. To be convincing, such explanations need to show that the phenotypic traits claimed as adaptations actually have the presumed effects on reproductive success. This task is difficult. Not only should adaptive forms enhance the organism's contribution to the gene pool, but, given time for selection to operate, they should not occur in ecological settings where the presumed functional benefits would not arise (Barash 1977; Kitcher 1985).

Lest this formulation seem too abstract, consider its relevance to a human behavior such as greeting an old friend. Humans exhibit a natural (in the sense of species-typical) set of displays and gestures whenever two old friends see each other after an absence; in addition, each culture has verbal and nonverbal symbols of its own that are customary in this situation. The efficient cause of these displays is the circumstance of a meeting between acquaintances or friends after an absence. The material causes are more complex, since they include the features of the central nervous system that make possible individual facial recognition as well as those implicated in the production of the nonverbal and verbal greeting behavior. Other elements of the central nervous system are, however, equally important material causes of greeting behavior: if the motor cortex associated with the movement of facial muscles has been damaged, for example, some of the nonverbal displays associated with greeting will not be produced normally.

In contrast to these efficient and material causes of greeting behavior are the formal and final causes associated with the informational systems making communication possible. The form of a nonverbal greeting display, like the form of a verbal utterance of greeting, can be specified in abstract terms. The smile, defined as a pattern of the mouth, is a signal with communicative properties; similarly; the cultural forms used in greeting are defined at the level of the social system, determining which behavioral response is appropriate ('Bonjour, Monsieur' is more likely to be an appropriate greeting in France than in the United States – but can also occur if I meet a French acquaintance in New York).

The final causes of greeting displays are concerned with the adaptive functions that presumably explain their evolution. In many reptilian species, the behavioral repertoire does not include such social displays; clearly a greeting response will not be distinguished from other behaviors if an animal never encounters situations in which its survival will be enhanced by cooperative interaction with other members of its own species (MacLean 1983). Like formal causes, final causes are not directly visible, but they are essential in order to provide a complete evolutionary explanation of phenotypic traits and especially of social behavior (Roe and Simpson 1958; Lorenz 1967).

The phenomena traditionally stressed by materialist philosophers have been either efficient or material causes; idealists have tended to argue that formal or final causes have priority. It would seem that neither is correct to dismiss the other completely. Materialists and idealists were focusing on distinct but equally real problems. Neither the simplistic materialism that denies the independent role of ideas in human history nor the naive idealism that rejects material causation as a matter of principle is scientifically adequate. Among political philosophers, Aristotle exemplifies a theorist whose dialectical understanding encompasses both material and nonmaterial causal processes: his position thus seems more fully consistent with evolutionary biology than either that of Hegelians for whom the priority of the Idea is total, or of Marxists who take a mechanistic view of materialism.

The quarrel of the ancients and the moderns

Because the quarrel of the ancients and the moderns can be understood as a theoretical disagreement about the nature and direction of human history, it can be illuminated by evolutionary biology. There are, of course, other differences between ancient and modern philosophy. As Rousseau argues in his *First Discourse*, for example, the moderns replace the classic notion of 'civic virtue' with a concern for 'money and business' or utility; Hobbes, one of the foremost exponents of the modern view, denies there is a *'finus ultimus*, utmost aim, or *summum bonum*, highest good, such as is spoken of in the books of the ancient philosophers' (Hobbes *Leviathan* 1.11).

The theoretical controversy between the ancients and the moderns also concerns the relevance of a study of nature to political and social standards of right and wrong. Beginning with Machiavelli, and more fully developed in the tradition from Hobbes and Locke to Bentham, Mill, and contemporary social science, one strand of modernity has openly replaced the notion of virtue with a descriptive science of human behavior devoted to utility. In this view, nature at most establishes the individual's rights or claims, but not duties or obligations. Another strand of modern thought, represented most notably by Hegel and Marx, stressed the process of history; for these thinkers, standards of right and wrong are produced by culture and history rather than by individual choice and agreement. In neither case do the characteristic modern thinkers judge political life in terms of standards of excellence or virtue derived from human nature. Even the exceptional case of Rousseau seems to reinforce this difference between the ancients and moderns: though seeking to challenge his contemporaries in the name of ancient virtue (*First Discourse*), Rousseau derives natural standards of human behavior from the rights of the individual in a prepolitical state of nature (*Second Discourse*) and distinguishes sharply between humanly created political right and this natural condition (*Social Contract*).

The changed attitude toward standards of virtue that characterizes modern thought was intimately related to the belief that humans could conquer natural necessity and radically improve the human condition. This change can be associated with Machiavelli, who insists not only that he is opening a 'new route' in philosophy (*Discourses on Titus Livy* 1, Introduction), but also that this novel teaching will help humans to control 'fortune' or necessity (*The Prince*, chap. 25). As a result, the modern perspective shifts from virtue to utility as the means of achieving material political progress (Strauss 1953). If science makes possible a transformation of the human condition, clearly the useful is prior to the natural.

The issue dividing the ancients and moderns can therefore be restated in terms of the divergent concepts of human history that have predominated in the two epochs (Masters 1977). For the ancient philosophers, humans could at best observe and understand nature: scientific or philosophic knowledge was not expected to conquer natural necessity, overcome the political conflict between the rich and the poor, or produce a regime capable of lasting indefinitely (Plato *Republic* 8.546a; Aristotle *Politics* 7.9.1329a; 7.10.1329b; 7.13.1332a; Thucydides *History of the Peloponnesian War* 1.1–23). Following Machiavelli and especially Bacon, who was the first to speak explicitly of science 'conquering nature' for 'the relief of man's estate', the moderns imagined a scientific knowledge of nature capable of controlling necessity and emancipating political life from prior limitations. This view of historical progress is evident in Hobbes's claim that his theory made possible a commonwealth capable, at least in principle, of becoming 'eternal' (*Leviathan* 1.11–16), as well as in Marx's assertion that humans could, and in time would, complete the 'conquest' of nature and open an era of unparalleled 'freedom' (*Economic and Philosophic Manuscripts of 1844*; *German Ideology*).

Evolutionary biology speaks directly to the extent to which humans, through scientific knowledge of nature, can hope to achieve progress. The so-called modern project is hardly an absurd concept: modern genetics, as well as physics, chemistry, and the other natural sciences, has indeed achieved control over vast ranges of necessity by means of a more exact understanding of nature. At the same time, neo-Darwinian theory teaches that there is no inherent direction to natural change, and that all living species are subject to extinction just as individual organisms are subject to death. Each side in the quarrel of the ancients and the moderns touched upon a very profound element of truth, which may help explain the difficulty of resolving the debate.

As with many philosophical controversies, the issue seems insoluble until it is realized that each position deals with different phenomena. The pagan philosophers of ancient Greece did not live in communities that believed in the beneficent creation of the world as the willful action of an omnipotent monotheistic God; hence they could accept natural change without challenging religious dogma. According to Socrates in Plato's *Republic*, for example, the Muses themselves tell us that 'for everything that has come into being there is decay' (*Republic* 8.546a). Even when Aristotle emphasizes the relatively unchanging character of nature as contrasted to the variability of human convention, he points out that natural things are subject to change (*Nicomachean Ethics* 5.7). Today one would have to agree: the solar system and all heavenly bodies, as well as all living things on earth, are characterized by change throughout a life cycle of birth, maturity, decay, and death. If the sun will one day burn itself out, not to mention the possibility that the entire universe may ultimately reach a state of perfect entropy, it is hard to understand what is meant by a definitive or 'eternal' conquest of nature by means of human science (Hawking 1988).

The ancient view of the limits of progress could be said to focus on the overall pattern of evolutionary processes, and therewith on the question of human emancipation from the ultimate constraint of death that confronts all visible beings. Contemporary evolutionary theory concurs with the ancient view that there is no inherent directionality in the evolution or change in nature; human knowledge cannot conquer all natural necessities. Although human science may, to use Hobbes's analogy, make possible the creation of 'artificial' forms of life (be they machines, animal chimeras, or

human social systems) that can rival God's creation of animals for historical success (*Leviathan*, Author's Introduction), neither human artifacts nor
other living beings can overcome all natural sources of change and decay.

The most famous exponents of the modern view do not respond effectively to this view of evolution: even those optimists who think of transcending the natural resource limitations of the earth through the colonization
of space have to confront the ultimate death of stars like the sun, as well
as the possibility of a collapse of the entire cosmos. Current models of the
origin of the universe seem to approximate the cosmology of ancients like
Empedocles more than that of moderns like Newton or Descartes; while
only a few of the ancients, like Lucretius, seem to have understood something like biological evolution, the pagan philosophers' understanding of
human history is remarkably consistent with modern evolutionary thought
(Masters 1978, 1983).

The moderns could, however, be dealing with a different and much more
limited phenomenon. Thinkers from Machiavelli, Bacon, and Hobbes to
Hegel, Marx, and Engels, whatever their many differences, agree that human science can transform the day-to-day living conditions of the mass of
mankind. For these moderns, this transformation would alter political and
social life. It is hard to consider the effects of technology without agreeing
to some degree. The impact of natural selection must have been substantially reduced to make possible the extraordinary growth in the total human
population that has occurred over the last three centuries. Science and technology have probably modified daily life to a greater extent since 1900
than in the preceding two or three millennia: changes in science and technology have eradicated most epidemic diseases, expanded food supplies in
both quantity and reliability, and produced human microenvironments that
insulate human activity from temperature and weather.

At this level, the modern judgment has clearly been confirmed. Although
the ancients were correct in thinking that the entire historical or evolutionary process could not be overcome eternally, they were wrong to assume
that science and technology are incapable of controlling natural necessities in a way that can transform human society and politics over the short
run. The optimism of modern political philosophers can therefore explain
the immense political triumph of Western civilization in the nineteenth and
twentieth centuries without being interpreted as an expectation of a total
perfection of human existence; when moderns like Marx speak as if history
will lead to the definitive establishment of unlimited plenty and happiness,
one can suspect Victorian overoptimism rather than serious philosophic
contemplation of human nature.

As this reflection suggests, reconsideration of traditional philosophic debates in the light of contemporary evolutionary biology can be very fruitful.
Past philosophers were at a vast disadvantage when compared to our generation: on the one hand, we dispose of a theoretical understanding of the

mechanisms of evolution that is more precise and complete than at any prior epoch; on the other, the data used to verify and deepen this theory – including fossil evidence, radioactive dating, and even comparison of the genetics and biochemistry of different species – are superior to those available even fifty years ago. Precisely for this reason, the theory of the evolutionary process and the findings concerning the emergence of the hominids have a central role in deepening our understanding of the human condition.

Human nature and the state

Although the demonstration that human nature is intrinsically political appears to resolve the theoretical dispute about natural sociability, this issue points to the new insights made possible by the study of evolution. Many political philosophers have held that nature 'dissociates' men (Hobbes *Leviathan* 1.13) or 'little prepared their sociability' (Rousseau *Second Discourse*, Pt. 1). For such theorists, whose views can be traced to the Sophists in ancient Greece, political society is the result of an agreement or social contract among naturally selfish individuals for whom the gains of cooperation in a state are greater than the costs of continued competition in the 'state of nature'.

In this philosophical tradition, the state is unnatural because individual humans are naturally competitive or asocial. Paradoxically, contemporary research shows that although the premises of the social contract tradition in political theory are inadequate, its conclusion is sound. The existence of centralized states and governments is indeed a biological puzzle, even though empirical evidence from the study of human evolution, ethology, and cultural anthropology confirms the social and political nature of our species.

The premises of social contract theories can no longer be sustained. No living primate species studied by ethologists is totally asocial; as Köhler said, 'it is hardly an exaggeration to say that a chimpanzee kept in solitude is not a real chimpanzee at all' (1959: 251). Although fossils of early hominids include little evidence of behavior as such, there are many indications of social life; by the Paleolithic epoch, our ancestors engaged in burial rituals, art, and complex toolmaking techniques – all of which imply some degree of social cooperation. As far as specialists are concerned, there is no question that *Homo sapiens* has always been a social animal; debate centers, rather, on the kind of group that was characteristic at various periods of hominid evolution (Portmann 1961; Reynolds 1966; Fox 1967; Spuhler 1959; DeVore and Washburn 1967; Washburn and Howell 1960; Morin 1973; Thompson 1976; Isaac 1978; G. Schubert 1986).

This is not to say that the theories of Hobbes, Rousseau, and other social contract theorists were absurd; the issue they posed was very real, although it can now be stated more accurately in terms of human evolution instead of human nature. Hobbes was quite right to point to self-interest and competition as decisive problems undermining cooperation within the centralized state, just as Rousseau had good reason to challenge the presumption that inherited wealth, social class, and political institutions were part of the natural condition of mankind. Civil societies with governments and bureaucracies are neither ubiquitous nor easily explained from the perspective of evolutionary theory. Humans survived and flourished for millennia in face-to-face social groups or tribes that did not need the institution of a state; anthropological research has shown that politics exists in 'stateless societies' and other primitive political systems without centralized bureaucracies (Fortes and Evans-Pritchard 1940; Lévi-Strauss 1967; Masters 1964; Harris 1977; Gruter and Masters 1986). The natural status of the state is therefore not established by asserting that humans are naturally social and political.

In the tradition of thinkers like Aristotle, Aquinas, and Marx, for whom humans are naturally social, history or evolution led to the formation of political systems with organized governments. Even from this perspective, however, a definition of human nature is not adequate to explain the emergence of civilized societies and governments. Since natural selection seems to prevent large-scale cooperative organizations like the centralized state among other mammals, the specific pattern of historical or evolutionary change leading to large-scale social systems remains a biological problem. In Book 1 of the *Politics*, Aristotle contents himself with a description of the rise of the city-state, or *polis*, without fully explaining how different human social systems came into being or why the state arose where it did. Marx argues that the division of labor gave rise to property, social class distinctions, and ultimately political authority; he does not give an account of the difference between humans and other animals that goes beyond the assertion that humans produce 'freely' whereas other animals are limited by instinct or necessity (*Economic and Philosophic Manuscripts of 1844*; *German Ideology*).

Social contract theory, while misplaced as a description of human nature at the individual or group level, thus points to a problem not resolved by those thinkers for whom humans are naturally sociable: the origin of the state must be shown to have adaptive benefits for competing individuals who did not need to cooperate with strangers or support governments in order to survive and reproduce. Psychological hedonists like Antiphon the Sophist and Hobbes therefore seem to have transposed to the individual a cost–benefit calculus like that reflecting the selective pressures against indiscriminate altruism in other species (Dawkins 1976; Campbell 1972).

For most traditional political theorists, explanations of political institutions are based on definitions of human nature that do not consider the evolutionary process in a way that is entirely consistent with contemporary biological theory. In accounting for social behavior, as for any phenotypical trait, the environment is as much a factor as the genotype (or nature) of an organism. Whatever one might say about this principle in general, it surely must be relevant to the emergence of the centralized state, since hominids have lived for so much of their evolutionary history in face-to-face groups of such a different scale and character.

From a biological perspective, the traditional concern of political theorists should be rephrased. Instead of seeking to deduce the existence of the state from human nature, we need to discover the environmental circumstances that could have led human political behavior to take a form so radically different from other mammalian social structures. More specifically, we need to find out why the natural selection against extending social cooperation to large impersonal groups was overcome. Why do people obey governments whose decisions often benefit genetic competitors, individuals or groups who are neither related to the law-abiding citizen nor guaranteed to reciprocate? In short, the problem facing political theory is not the origin of politics and society; rather, it is the foundation of civilization and the centralized state.

2

COMMUNITY

Adrian Little

INTRODUCTION

Community is one of the most contested concepts in contemporary political and social theory. It has attracted support and criticism from across the ideological spectrum and inspired the rise of new political movements. As a result its precise meaning is unclear. Indeed, it has been argued that such is the opacity surrounding the idea of community that its utility for political analysis is somewhat limited. In the light of this situation, it is important to revisit the concept of community and analyse the reasons why different thinkers and ideologues have used the concept in the ways they have. In so doing we can clarify the multiplicity of ways in which community emerges in contemporary politics.

Whilst there is a long tradition of theorising community in sociological and political theory, its importance to contemporary debates resurfaced as a result of the critical backlash to the publication of John Rawls's *A Theory of Justice* in 1971. As a consequence of this much of the ensuing debate was constructed around the idea of there being two identifiable camps: liberals and communitarians. As we shall see, however, such a homogenised categorisation of the theorists involved was not sustainable. For example, the communitarian camp was supposedly populated by thinkers as diverse as Michael Sandel, Alasdair MacIntyre, Charles Taylor and Michael Walzer.[1] Clearly some of these thinkers shared much more in common with liberals than others and the term 'communitarian' was rarely used in their own writings. So it is evident that the label 'communitarian' was controversial and misleading in itself. Moreover, the idea that it sat in clear opposition to something equally homogenous called 'liberalism' was also misleading. This caveat aside, it is worth noting that this debate did ignite Anglo-American political philosophy in the 1970s and 1980s, although it has waned a little in the intervening years.

Whilst this 'philosophical' branch of communitarianism remained within the parameters of the academy, a new 'political' communitarian movement was to emerge during the 1990s.[2] Where the former had steered clear of firm political commitment, the new movement, with Amitai Etzioni as its figurehead, began to apply some of the philosophical principles to the practical political issues of the day. Etzioni has written a wide variety of popular and academic commentaries on social and moral issues and debates, ranging from parenting to crime and gun control. His work has been deeply influential on political parties and movements, especially those established around the idea of 'Third Way' politics. However, in this manifestation, 'community' has become linked to a rather conservative brand of politics – one that is often regarded as morally authoritarian (Hughes and Little 1999, Little 2002b). Whilst Etzioni and his supporters would reject this charge, many critics see this form of political communitarianism as incapable of providing a theoretical foundation for the organisation of complex, diverse societies.

In this chapter the links between philosophical and political forms of communitarianism are analysed along with the ways in which community can be used to reinforce different ideological positions. In so doing it should become clear that community can be a problematic concept in political theory. At the same time it is equally clear that people do give meaning to community in everyday life, be that at the level of the local community, other small associations, the national community or even the international community. This necessitates a clarification of the concept to see whether it can help us to make sense of the myriad ways in which it appears in popular and academic discourses. The contention in this chapter is that the most useful way to understand community is in the sense of smaller associations and that we should be careful not to elide the idea of community with a whole society or the nation as some communitarians do. For political communitarians, community tends to be used in such a way as to shore up society through the establishment of some kind of moral consensus. However, a more critical understanding could theorise community as a reflection of the diverse range of associations in complex societies; crucially this chapter contends that this takes us towards community as a sphere of conflict and disagreement rather than the consensus that communitarians yearn for.

COMMUNITARIANISM AND THE CRITIQUE OF RAWLS

The group of theorists who came to be regarded as the central figures in communitarianism found fault with several aspects of Rawls's theory of justice. The major bone of contention was Rawlsian individualism, which was accused of atomism by Taylor and criticised for its model of the unencumbered self by Sandel. Moreover, communitarians have also been critical of the constructivist methodology employed by Rawls to establish his contractarian thesis. In order to understand the communitarian critique, it is important to provide a brief synopsis of Rawls's argument. Rawls contended that justice required that people were treated fairly despite the fact that brute luck had endowed each individual with different skills and attributes. In order to ascertain what a fair and just distribution of goods would be, Rawls imagined an 'original position' where individuals would be behind a 'veil of ignorance'. Thus, in the original position, individuals would have no knowledge of who they were and whether the attributes they possessed would be valued or not when the veil of ignorance was lifted. Rawls argued that, placed in the original position and requiring a social contract to bind people together, individuals would choose a basically equal distribution of goods. This thesis is based on the assumption that people in the original position would not risk penury but instead elect for the safety of fairness. On the basis of this theory Rawls then makes a case for justice as fairness as the most appropriate contractual form for liberalism and democracy.

The metaphor of the original position attracted considerable criticism from communitarian thinkers, most notably Sandel. As is seen from the extract here, he objected to the individualist methodology employed by Rawls and the way that the self was constructed as if unencumbered by the social structures and other phenomena around it. Sandel also challenged the commonplace liberal view that the 'right is prior to the good'. By this he means the liberal tendency, at least in the work of thinkers such as Rawls, to see justice in terms of the establishment of correct procedures to adjudicate between the competing claims that individuals put forward. For communitarians, this is a problematic approach because these procedures are supposedly constructed in such a way as to be neutral in judging between opposing viewpoints. Whereas, for the liberal, it is possible to build such impartial procedures, communitarians such as Sandel argue that rules and institutions will always reflect particular ideas and/or the historical context in which they are established. As such it is a liberal pretence to argue for neutral institutions when, in fact, such bodies are not achievable. Thus, what liberals see as neutral are actually the institutions of liberalism. The procedural argument is one that shores up liberal societies because the procedures established reflect the *modus vivendi* of liberal democracy. Communitarians such as Sandel argue instead that democratic institutions should reflect the common good of the people of any given polity. This stands in stark contradiction to the procedural form of liberalism inspired by Immanuel Kant, which says that 'what makes the just society just is not the *telos* or purpose or end at which it aims, but precisely its refusal to choose in advance among competing purposes and ends' (Sandel, see extract).

In what sense then do communitarians differ methodologically from liberals when it comes to the relationship between the individual and community? Sandel argues that liberals such as Rawls see an unencumbered self where the individual is 'understood as prior to and independent of purposes and ends' (Sandel, see extract). The problem here is that in order to place the right before the good we need to be able to think of individuals as being capable of free rational choice. However, Sandel contends that not all communities are voluntary associations that are joined electively. Instead, he suggests that there are always constitutive communities or communities of fate which have a bearing on how individuals are. If this is the case, then individuals can never be wholly unencumbered and, for Sandel, this undermines the whole case for proceduralism, which tries to put the right prior to the good. If we are at least partly constituted by the environment we find ourselves in, then we can never be completely free, rational choosers of particular procedures. The procedures we favour will tend to reflect our individual conceptions of the good, which may be more or less altruistic.

Sandel recognises that the model of the unencumbered self is alluring as a philosophical device, but it has little value in terms of practical application because of the impossibility of shedding the characteristics which make us who we are. This fundamentally undermines Rawls's thesis because his difference principle requires that we share assets amongst a certain group of people who we see as part of the same society or nation. But, if the self is unencumbered, individuals are consequently unable to know about the group of people they belong to. For Sandel, what 'the difference principle requires, but cannot provide, is some way of identifying those among whom the assets I bear are properly regarded as common, some way of seeing ourselves as mutually indebted and morally engaged to begin with' (Sandel, see extract). In other words, individuals have moral convictions as a result of the various communities they belong to and these generate feelings of obligation and visions of the good which may generate the kind of redistributive programme that Rawls supports. That programme cannot emerge from unencumbered selves; instead it relies upon situated selves with allegiances, attachments and commitments.

For Sandel, this leaves us with a number of problems in contemporary liberal democracies. He notes how the idea of a national political community has given way since the middle of the twentieth century, to be replaced by the procedural republic. By this he means that the increased diversity and complexity in modern societies has undermined bonds and allegiances of political community. Instead we face a procedural republic that is defined in terms of 'an individual's guarantee against what the majority might will. I am free in so far as I am the bearer of rights, where rights are trumps' (Sandel, see extract). Thus Sandel sees the procedural republic as a polity that is governed by discourses of individual rights and which attaches great importance to the judicial system and bureaucracy to maintain social order. This rights-driven polity stands in stark contrast to a political community held together by common interest and a shared allegiance to that community. For Sandel, this inevitably centralises power as rights are universalised by nation-states instead of being allowed to be interpreted in more particularistic ways by local communities. Ultimately, he contends that this undermines democracy because power gravitates towards institutions such as the judiciary which are insulated from democratic pressures, unlike political parties for example. In short, then, Sandel sees the procedural republic as a polity driven by a culture of rights in which democratic organisation is increasingly replaced by bureaucracy.

Sandel argues that the dangerous implications of the development of the procedural republic are increasingly evident in, for example, the challenge to the legitimacy of the welfare state and the growing lack of trust in and attachment to politics and public life. As we become more engrossed in and enslaved to the idea of ourselves as free individuals with certain inviolable rights, we increasingly question the demands that are still made of us as members of a political community. These demands, such as paying taxes to fund welfare, sit uncomfortably with discourses that tell us that our individual rights are paramount. After all, if these rights are trumps then there is no reason that we should be forced to pay those taxes to fund the welfare state. However, what this points to is the fact that alongside the development of the procedural republic, there have remained elements of political communities to which many of us feel we do owe degrees of allegiance. What we need to point to, then, is the tension between the rights-driven discourse of the free individual and the practical reality that we live within political communities (of many kinds) in which individual rights are not always paramount. The point to remember, then, is that contemporary politics is likely to continue to reflect the tension between liberal discourses of individual rights and the practical realities of the political communities which actually exist in liberal democracies.

Whilst the work of Sandel provided an archetypal communitarian rebuttal of liberal ideas, others such as Taylor have also objected to the individualism of Rawls whilst simultaneously challenging the manner in which the liberal–communitarian dichotomy has been constructed. Indeed, for Taylor, the debate that has been construed as one of liberals against communitarians is at cross-purposes, not least in homogenising both of these categories. Not only do many liberals and communitarians share many ideas but many within each of the two categories disagree with one another in key aspects of their thought. For Taylor's purposes, we need to differentiate separate levels of the debate – those that deal with ontological issues on the one hand and those that focus on advocacy issues on the other. Although he takes exception to the atomistic ontological stance that Rawls adopts, Taylor's main concern is with the way in which this feeds into the advocacy of procedural liberalism as the most appropriate form of political organisation in diverse societies.

Taylor attempts to construct an alternative model that is built upon the civic humanist republican tradition. His thesis is built around two key ideas: firstly, that citizens act together to respond to abuses of power that contravene the principles of liberal democracy, and, secondly, that people react as they do not out of self-interest but 'a species of patriotic identification' (Taylor 2003: 204). This sense of patriotism is, Taylor argues, derived from an allegiance to particular ideals that have developed as a result of a common historical background. To use his own example, Americans reacted as they did to Watergate precisely because it contravened the American way of life that had been imbued in people through their shared history. Although Taylor recognises the potentially harmful aspects of patriotism (racism, exclusion and so on), he still sees it as a fundamental feature of modern liberal democracies.

Importantly, Taylor sees in this an element of procedural liberalism – after all, the reaction to Watergate came about because rules and procedures were broken. So he contends that one can still be a procedural liberal without subscribing to the ontological atomism of Rawls. Nonetheless, where the problem emerges for procedural liberalism is in the protection of historically endowed institutions. Procedural liberals require the state to be neutral between competing conceptions of the good but, for Taylor, the historic nature of the state and its contemporary preservation cannot maintain such neutrality. The preservation of a common history in the present cannot take place within the theoretical confines of procedural liberalism. It is indeed difficult to imagine a patriotic liberal regime that meets the requirements of neutrality that proceduralists endorse.

This is the reason why Taylor returns to the republican tradition and, in particular, its traditional focus on participatory self-rule. To this extent he contends that a 'free society requires a patriotism ... But it must be one whose core values incorporate freedom. Historically republican patriotism has incorporated self-rule in its definition of freedom. Indeed ... this has been at the core of this definition' (Taylor 2003: 208). This vision runs contrary to the model of rights-based citizenship, whereby active individuals act in pursuit of their own rights within the courts of the procedural republic. For Taylor, this is not participation in the republican sense for it is not about 'us' governing but pursuing self-interest.

The republican model, on the other hand, 'defines participation in self-rule as of the essence of freedom' (Taylor 2003: 208). Thus, for Taylor, a republican perspective implies that, at least some of the time, we do not have an adversarial relationship with government but instead governing is sometimes what we ourselves do through our participation in politics. The point is, then, that the republican model provides greater scope for patriotism where we value the historical institutions of the political community and participate in their reproduction. This stands in stark contrast to procedural liberalism, where we view these institutions either as functional bodies that ensure our rights or else as a range of bodies which may threaten our freedom. The procedural republic promises a litigious culture where the judiciary plays a pre-eminent role whereas republicanism invites us to take pride in and participate in the political community and its institutions.

The outstanding question, then, is where these 'communitarian' objections to procedural liberalism take us politically. In other words, what are the implications of these theories when it comes to the advocacy of particular political institutions and arrangements? This is a question that has not always been addressed by communitarian philosophers (indeed, many presumably would not see it as their task). Nonetheless it is a key question for our purposes because the practical political issues engendered by the term 'community' have been increasingly blurred by the multiplicity of usages of the word in contemporary politics. Following Sandel's arguments we can sense a longing for different types of community at the small, local and sub-state level. The key implication of this model is that the empowerment of the local would generate different services and provisions in different localities depending on the needs or wants of that community. Obviously this gives rise to potential inequalities between different communities that liberal universalism tries to obviate, but the communitarian would argue that there are inequalities anyway despite the efforts of universal state welfare, as different communities require divergent things. For the likes of Sandel, it seems, the best scenario would be one where the state initiates universal laws but leaves open the possibility that some of those laws may be interpreted in different ways by empowered local communities.

Taylor's argument, on the other hand, is less concerned with the sub-state or local community. Instead he focuses on the political community writ large in the institutions of the state. Here the vagaries of different localities are overridden by a national political community that cherishes the kind of universalism promoted by the liberal state but sees the participation of citizens in their political community as paramount in guaranteeing freedom. Of course, this republican model demands patriotism and allegiance to the political community. Questions must be asked about the viability of such a model as the foundation of contemporary multicultural societies. Even if patriotism of this kind was somehow achievable, we need to ask why people would invest such significance in the national political community instead of the smaller (or indeed larger) associations of which they are a part. For example, why should I value my membership of a polity over and above my associations as a member of a gendered community or sexual community or religious community? For many, it will be the smaller communities of which they are a part which form the major backdrop to their existence and identity. Certainly the political community may be important but it is asking a lot for us to have to regard it as paramount over other meaningful associations in our lives.

This tension between different levels of community pervades the communitarian literature. When politicians argue for the values of community, they can be talking about wildly varying types of association. This tension has been evident in much contemporary writing on community, not least in the work of the most notable 'political communitarian' in popular debate, Amitai Etzioni.

THE GROWTH OF POLITICAL COMMUNITARIANISM

Just as the liberal–communitarian debate appeared to be waning with the emergence of theories of deliberative democracy and multiculturalism, the advancement of community within the realm of politics became more notable. In part this was a response to the aggressive individualism of the Thatcher/Reagan years, but it was also due to the development of communitarianism as a political movement. Much of the credit or responsibility for this advancement of community must be attributed to Etzioni, who has published widely on communitarian politics in recent years (for a representative sample see Etzioni 1993, 1995, 1997, 2000, 2001). This can be regarded as a backlash against the hegemony of individualism and an attempt to reassert a new moral politics to underpin the rootedness of individuals within communal groups. In this guise the communitarian credo highlighted the importance of bonds of community to the re-establishment of a strong moral fabric for wider society. However, in recent years it has also been evident that political communitarianism has become intrinsically bound up with 'Third Way' politics and discourses of community and re-moralisation are commonplace in the utterances of politicians such as Tony Blair (Hughes and Little 1999; Little 2002b).

Etzioni's project focuses on both the localised community and the wider political community but there is sometimes a blurring of the two which obfuscates the communitarian agenda. The common link between political communitarianism and 'Third Way' theory lies in the fact that both want to shift the political agenda away from the question of the state versus the market. Indeed, these two perspectives see both state and markets as central to their political vision although it must be said that this is an argument embraced to a greater or lesser extent by all influential political ideologies today. Etzioni contends that state and market alone are insufficient to maintain social cohesion and that modern societies also need to shore up bonds of community which emanate from 'the things people do for one another as members of families and neighbourhoods, as friends and co-workers' (Etzioni, see extract). Thus, he argues that certain aspects of contemporary societies should not be commodified and left to the whims of markets or dealt with centrally by the bureaucratic state. Instead communities have a central role to play in enabling society to function through mutuality and co-operation. Here the argument suggests that rather than expecting the state to provide services, we should take responsibility for meeting the needs of our communities. This has a fundamental impact on social policy, where communitarians suggest a role for community in areas from neighbourhood policing and crime prevention to health promotion to caring for the environment.

Certainly there is a role for communities in these areas but there is a real danger that Etzioni overstates the case and neglects the continuing importance of the state as the guarantor of basic rights. He overlooks the different perceptions of what is good that will pervade all communities and indeed the ways in which the prevailing view within communities may be damaging or contrary to human rights. Moreover, the potentially authoritarian dimension of Etzioni's thought shines through when we ask questions of what we should do when our own moral convictions are at odds with those of the majority in a community. Ultimately, it seems, we return to majoritarianism, which, as noted above, can be extremely damaging. Questions also remain as to how we foster these burdens of responsibility. Here Etzioni blithely nominates a key group and notes the psychological benefits that would accrue to them: 'The largest and fastest-growing group that can do more are senior citizens, who live longer and healthier lives and would benefit psychologically from doing more for one another and their communities' (Etzioni, see extract). Leaving aside the fact that senior citizens already tend to do more community work than younger citizens, it sticks in the craw to see them singled out in this way. Why not try to reduce working hours to enable everyone to participate more? Etzioni shies away from this kind of argument as it would involve too much intervention in the economy. This demonstrates the way in which the model of community employed in the 'Third Way' fails to deal with the ways in which markets might have detrimental effects on the sphere of communities.

The rather conservative bent of communitarian politics is also evident in Etzioni's warnings about multiculturalism as a danger to Britain. He rejects the claims of those who want to promote recognition of greater diversity as potentially leading to a dilution of Britishness but simultaneously indicates awareness of the dangers of patriotism. Where then does that leave us? For Etzioni, communitarianism has the answer:

> It can see Britain as a community of communities. The nation can welcome, indeed feel enriched by, people of divergent background and heritage, and happily tolerate differences of habit and subculture. At the same time, it can expect all citizens to buy into a significant set of shared values and mores. (Etzioni, see extract)

Herein lies the rub. The glib assertion that everyone can just get along with each other shows how political communitarianism asserts its ability to resolve the fundamental conflicts that permeate complex, diverse societies. Etzioni fails to comprehend the ways in which the demands and practices of some communities may come into conflict with the perspective of the wider political community. In asserting the idea of 'the community of communities' he elides two very different understandings of the meaning of 'community'. This elision underestimates the tensions and conflicts that may appear between groups and between particular communities and wider society. The problem with Etzioni's vision of political communitarianism and the 'Third Way' is that its depiction of harmony and consensus is unpersuasive in a world permeated by conflict and division. Many of these tensions emanate from communities and therefore we should not neglect the potentially divisive implications of strengthening communities in contemporary politics.

CONCLUSION: TOWARDS A RADICAL POLITICS OF COMMUNITY?

It is clear that the concept of community is central to many contemporary political discourses but also that it is deployed in a multiplicity of different ways to suit varying political objectives. There remains a schism between the idea of community that has been articulated in political philosophy and the use of the term in normative political communitarianism. However, there still appear to be problematic elements in both of these manifestations of community. In so far as they demonstrate the methodological limitations of Rawlsian individualism, the arguments of theorists such as Sandel and Taylor make a valuable contribution to contemporary thinking about community, but it is in drawing out the political implications of a communitarian philosophy that we encounter greater difficulties.

The two dominant approaches to this task outlined here have been in the political communitarianism of Etzioni and the republican theory of Taylor. The former constructs a harmonious model of community, where an overarching community at the level of society plays host to a mosaic of smaller communities with different moral and cultural values. For Etzioni, because these differences are primarily expressed in the private sphere, a wider political community can be developed which provides a public domain in which the common good of all can articulated. However, this view has been challenged on the grounds that it is established upon a romantic nostalgia for an imagined community of the past that too often lapses into a moral authoritarianism when it comes to policy prescriptions for contemporary times (Hughes and Little 1999). Moreover, this perspective plays fast and loose with the rationalities of markets and the state and underplays the potentially damaging impact they can have on the sphere of community.

In Taylor's republican model even less attention is focused on the meaning of community at sub-state level. According to this view, a communitarian polity would be one in which the populace of a given society has a (benign) patriotic attachment to it and the political institutions of the society would enable people to participate in processes of governance. The contention here has been that, despite the intuitive attractions of such a model, it is difficult to reconcile this view with the realities of diverse, multicultural societies. The republican communitarian model put forward by Taylor is driven by a consensual impetus which seeks to establish a solidaristic foundation for different groups of people to coalesce around a common participatory democratic system. The problem with this view is the way in which it misunderstands the fundamental disagreements that emerge from the value pluralism of diverse societies. If the values held by different groups are understood to be incommensurable (Gray 2000, Crowder 2002, Little 2004), then the construction of this kind of republican polity is a difficult task to achieve.

An alternative argument is for a more radical democratic understanding of community.[3] According to this perspective societies comprise a multiplicity of communities and associations of varying sizes. These communities should not be elided with the idea of a nation-state or a society-level community. Instead communities must be understood pluralistically and the existence of a wide range of moral viewpoints makes the articulation of a consensual whole impossible. However, this does not mean that we should reject communitarian politics and retreat into Rawlsian procedural liberalism. Instead it gives us opportunities to redevelop our understanding of democratic politics so as to recognise that it is often constituted by political disagreement and conflict. Community can play a significant role in this understanding of democracy as the sphere in which groups and associations are able to articulate political differences beyond the domain of the state and without the influence of market rationality.[4] That is to say, community is a useful concept to operationalise if we want to broaden political engagement and seek greater representation for ideas which are often marginalised from the mainstream. This potentially radical understanding of community actually builds upon the issue of political disagreement and views such dissensus as a sign of a healthier polity than those theories which seek to establish community as a sphere of consensus.

QUESTIONS FOR DISCUSSION

- How do communitarian theories of justice differ from those of liberalism?
- In what ways has communitarian political philosophy been translated into a coherent communitarian politics?
- How relevant are theories of political community in an era of globalisation?
- What political space is occupied by community with regard to debates about the relationship between the state and civil society?

NOTES

1. See, for example, MacIntyre (1981), Sandel (1982), Walzer (1983) and Taylor (1990).
2. The distinction is made by Elizabeth Frazer (1999).
3. The argument here is influenced by the work of Chantal Mouffe (2000).
4. This is not to say that community can ever be insulated from the rationalities of markets and the state but that it is valuable to try and protect communal associations from being overpowered by the logics of markets or the state. For more detail on this kind of argument, see Little (2002c).

MICHAEL SANDEL
EXTRACT FROM 'THE PROCEDURAL REPUBLIC AND THE UNENCUMBERED SELF'

THE RIGHT AND THE GOOD

We might begin by considering a certain moral and political vision. It is a liberal vision, and like most liberal visions gives pride of place to justice, fairness and individual rights. Its core thesis is this: a just society seeks not to promote any particular ends, but enables its citizens to pursue their own ends, consistent with a similar liberty for all; it therefore must govern by principles that do not presuppose any particular conception of the good. What justifies these regulative principles above all is not that they maximize the general welfare, or cultivate virtue, or otherwise promote the good, but rather that they conform to the concept of right, a moral category given prior to the good, and independent of it.

This liberalism says, in other words, that what makes the just society just is not the *telos* or purpose or end at which it aims, but precisely its refusal to choose in advance among competing purposes and ends. In its constitution and its laws, the just society seeks to provide a framework within which its citizens can pursue their own values and ends, consistent with a similar liberty for others.

The ideal I've described might be summed up in the claim that the right is prior to the good, and in two senses: the priority of the right means, first, that individual rights cannot be sacrificed for the sake of the general good (in this it opposes utilitarianism), and, second, that the principles of justice

Michael Sandel (1984), 'The Procedural Republic and the Unencumbered Self', *Political Theory*, 12.

that specify these rights cannot be premised on any particular vision of the good life. (In this it opposes teleological conceptions in general.)

This is the liberalism of much contemporary moral and political philosophy, most fully elaborated by Rawls, and indebted to Kant for its philosophical foundations.[1] But I am concerned here less with the lineage of this vision than with what seem to me three striking facts about it.

First, it has a deep and powerful philosophical appeal. Second, despite its philosophical force, the claim for the priority of the right over the good ultimately fails. And, third, despite its philosophical failure, this liberal vision is the one by which we live. For us in the late-twentieth-century America, it is our vision, the theory most thoroughly embodied in the practices and institutions most central to our public life. And seeing how it goes wrong as philosophy may help us to diagnose our present political condition. So, first, its philosophical power; second, its philosophical failure; and, third, however briefly, its uneasy embodiment in the world.

But before taking up these three claims, it is worth pointing out a central theme that connects them. And that is a certain conception of the person, of what it is to be a moral agent. Like all political theories, the liberal theory I have described is something more than a set of regulative principles. It is also a view about the way the world is, and the way we move within it. At the heart of this ethic lies a vision of the person that both inspires and undoes it. As I will try to argue now, what makes this ethic so compelling, but also, finally, vulnerable, are the promise and the failure of the unencumbered self.

[···]

FROM TRANSCENDENTAL SUBJECT TO THE UNENCUMBERED SELF

The original position tries to provide what Kant's transcendental argument cannot – a foundation for the right that is prior to the good, but still situated in the world. Sparing all but essentials, the original position works like this: it invites us to imagine the principles we would choose to govern our society if we were to choose them in advance, before we knew the particular persons we would be – whether rich or poor, strong or weak, lucky or unlucky – before we knew even our interests or aims or conceptions of the good. These principles – the ones we would choose in that imaginary situation – are the principles of justice. What is more, if it works, they are principles that do not presuppose any particular ends.

What they do presuppose is a certain picture of the person, of the way we must be if we are beings for whom justice is the first virtue. This is the picture of the unencumbered self, a self understood as prior to and independent of purposes and ends.

Now the unencumbered self describes first of all the way we stand towards the things we have, or want, or seek. It means there is always a distinction between the values I *have* and the person I *am*. To identify any characteristics as *my* aims, ambitions, desires, and so on, is always to imply some subject 'me' standing behind them, at a certain distance, and the shape of this 'me' must be given prior to any of the aims or attributes I bear. One consequence of this distance is to put the self *itself* beyond the reach of its experience, to secure its identity once and for all. Or to put it another way, it rules out the possibility of what we might call *constitutive* ends. No role or commitment could define me so completely that I could not understand myself without it. No project could be so essential that turning away from it would call into question the person I am.

For the unencumbered self, what matters above all, what is most essential to our personhood, are not the ends we choose but our capacity to choose them. The original position sums up this central claim about us. 'It is not our aims that primarily reveal our nature,' writes Rawls, 'but rather the principles that we would acknowledge to govern the background conditions under which these aims are to be formed . . . We should therefore reverse the relation between the right and the good proposed by teleological doctrines and view the right as prior.'[2]

Only if the self is prior to its ends can the right be prior to the good. Only if my identity is never tied to the aims and interests I may have at any moment can I think of myself as a free and independent agent, capable of choice.

This notion of independence carries consequences for the kind of community of which we are capable. Understood as unencumbered selves, we are of course free to join in voluntary associations with others, and so we are capable of community in the co-operative sense. What is denied to the unencumbered self is the possibility of membership in any community bound by moral ties antecedent to choice; he cannot belong to any community where the self *itself* could be at stake. Such a community – call it constitutive as against merely co-operative – would engage the identity as well as the interests of the participants, and so implicate its members in a citizenship more thoroughgoing than the unencumbered self can know.

For justice to be primary, then, we must be creatures of a certain kind, related to human circumstance in a certain way. We must stand to our circumstance always at a certain distance, whether as transcendental subject in the case of Kant, or as unencumbered selves in the case of Rawls. Only in this way can we view ourselves as subjects as well as objects of experience, as agents and not just instruments of the purposes we pursue.

The unencumbered self and the ethic it inspires, taken together, hold out a liberating vision. Freed from the dictates of nature and the sanction of social roles, the human subject is installed as sovereign, cast as the author of the only moral meanings there are. As participants in pure practical reason, or as parties to the original position, we are free to construct principles of justice unconstrained by an order of value antecedently given. And as actual, individual selves, we are free to choose our purposes and ends unbound by such an order, or by custom or tradition or inherited status. So long as they are not unjust, our conceptions of the good carry weight, whatever they are, simply in virtue of our having chosen them. We are, in Rawls's words, 'self-originating sources of valid claims'.[3]

This is an exhilarating promise, and the liberalism it animates is perhaps the fullest expression of the Enlightenment's quest for the self-defining subject. But is it true? Can we make sense of our moral and political life by the light of the self-image it requires? I do not think we can, and I will try to show why not by arguing first within the liberal project, then beyond it.

JUSTICE AND COMMUNITY

We have focused so far on the foundations of the liberal vision, on the way it derives the principles it defends. Let us turn briefly now to the substance of those principles, using Rawls as our example. Sparing all but essentials once again, Rawls's two principles of justice are these: first, equal basic liberties for all, and, second, only those social and economic inequalities that benefit the least-advantaged members of society (the difference principle).

[···]

What the difference principle requires, but cannot provide, is some way of identifying those *among* whom the assets I bear are properly regarded as common, some way of seeing ourselves as mutually indebted and morally engaged to begin with. But as we have seen, the constitutive aims and attachments that would save and situate the difference principle are precisely the ones denied to the liberal self; the moral encumbrances and antecedent obligations they imply would undercut the priority of right.

What, then, of those encumbrances? The point so far is that we cannot be persons for whom justice is primary, and also be persons for whom the difference principle is a principle of justice. But which must give way? Can we view ourselves as independent selves, independent in the sense that our identity is never tied to our aims and attachments?[4]

I do not think we can, at least not without cost to those loyalties and convictions whose moral force consists partly in the fact that living by them is inseparable from understanding ourselves as the particular persons we are – as members of this family or community or nation or people, as bearers of that history, as citizens of this republic. Allegiances such as these are more than values I happen to have, and to hold, at a certain distance. They go beyond the obligations I voluntarily incur and the 'natural duties' I owe to human beings as such. They allow that to some I owe more than justice requires or even permits, not by reason of agreements I have made but instead in virtue of those more or less enduring attachments and commitments that, taken together, partly define the person I am.

To imagine a person incapable of constitutive attachments such as these is not to conceive an ideally free and rational agent, but to imagine a person wholly without character, without moral depth. For to have character is to know that I move in a history I neither summon nor command, which carries consequences none the less for my choices and conduct. It draws me closer to some and more distant from others; it makes some aims more appropriate, others less so. As a self-interpreting being, I am able to reflect on my history and in this sense to distance myself from it, but the distance is always precarious and provisional, the point of reflection never finally secured outside the history itself. But the liberal ethic puts the self beyond the reach of its experience, beyond deliberation and reflection. Denied the expansive self-understandings that could shape a common life, the liberal self is left to lurch between detachment on the one hand, and entanglement on the other. Such is the fate of the unencumbered self, and its liberating promise.

THE PROCEDURAL REPUBLIC

But before my case can be complete, I need to consider one powerful reply. While it comes from a liberal direction, its spirit is more practical than philosophical. It says, in short, that I am asking too much. It is one thing to seek constitutive attachments in our private lives; among families and friends, and certain tightly knit groups, there may be found a common good that makes justice and rights less pressing. But with public life – at least today, and probably always – it is different. So long as the nation-state is the primary form of political association, talk of constitutive community too easily suggests a darker politics rather than a brighter one; amid echoes of the moral majority, the priority of right, for all its philosophical faults, still seems the safer hope.

This is a challenging rejoinder, and no account of political community in the twentieth century can fail to take it seriously. It is challenging not least because it calls into question the status of political philosophy and its relation to the world. For if my argument is correct, if the liberal vision we have considered is not morally self-sufficient but parasitic on a notion of community it officially rejects, then we should expect to find that the political practice that embodies this vision is not practically self-sufficient either – that it must draw on a sense of community it cannot supply and may even undermine. But is that so far from the circumstance we face today? Could it be that through the original position darkly, on the far side of the veil of ignorance, we may glimpse an intimation of our predicament, a refracted vision of ourselves?

How does the liberal vision – and its failure – help us make sense of our public life and its predicament?

[· · ·]

What matters for our purpose is that, in the twentieth century, liberalism made its peace with concentrated power. But it was understood at the start that the terms of this peace required a strong sense of national community, morally and politically to underwrite the extended involvements of a modern industrial order. If a virtuous republic of small-scale, democratic communities was no longer a possibility, a national republic seemed democracy's next best hope. This was still, in principle at least, a politics of the common good. It looked to the nation, not as a neutral framework for the play of competing interests, but rather as a formative community, concerned to shape a common life suited to the scale of modern social and economic forms.

But this project failed. By the mid- or late twentieth century the national republic had run its course. Except for extraordinary moments, such as war, the nation proved too vast a scale across which to cultivate the shared self-understandings necessary to community in the formative, or constitutive sense. And so the gradual shift, in our practices and institutions, from a public philosophy of common purposes to one of fair procedures, from a politics of good to a politics of right, from the national republic to the procedural republic.

OUR PRESENT PREDICAMENT

A full account of this transition would take a detailed look at the changing shape of political institutions, constitutional interpretation, and the terms of political discourse in the broadest sense. But I suspect we would find in the practice of the procedural republic two broad tendencies foreshadowed by its philosophy: first, a tendency to crowd out democratic possibilities; second, a tendency to undercut the kind of community on which it none the less depends.

Where liberty in the early republic was understood as a function of democratic institutions and dispersed power,[5] liberty in the procedural republic is defined, in opposition to democracy, as an individual's guarantee against what the majority might will. I am free in so far as I am the bearer of rights, where rights are trumps.[6] Unlike the liberty of the early republic, the modern version permits – in fact even requires – concentrated power. This has to do with the universalising logic of rights. In so far as I have a right, whether to free speech or a minimum income, its provision cannot be left to the vagaries of local preferences but must be assured at the most comprehensive level of political association. It cannot be one thing in New York and another in Alabama. As rights and entitlements expand, politics is therefore displaced from smaller forms of association and relocated at the most universal form – in our case, the nation. And even as politics flows to the nation, power shifts away from democratic institutions (such as legislatures and political parties) and towards institutions designed to be insulated from democratic pressures, and hence better equipped to dispense and defend individual rights (notably the judiciary and bureaucracy).

These institutional developments may begin to account for the sense of powerlessness that the welfare state fails to address and in some way doubtless deepens. But it seems to me a further clue to our condition recalls even more directly the predicament of the unencumbered self – lurching, as we left it, between detachment on the one hand, the entanglement on the other. For it is a striking feature of the welfare state that it offers a powerful promise of individual rights, and also demands of its citizens a high measure of mutual engagement. But the self-image that attends the rights cannot sustain the engagement.

As bearers of rights, where rights are trumps, we think of ourselves as freely choosing, individual selves, unbound by obligations antecedent to rights, or to the agreements we make. And yet, as citizens of the procedural republic that secures these rights, we find ourselves implicated willy-nilly in a formidable array of dependencies and expectations we did not choose and increasingly reject.

In our public life, we are more entangled, but less attached, than ever before. It is as though the unencumbered self presupposed by the liberal ethic had begun to come true – less liberated than disempowered, entangled in a network of obligations and involvements unassociated with any act of will, and yet unmediated by those common identifications or expansive self-definitions that would make them tolerable. As the scale of social and political organization has become more comprehensive, the terms of our collective identity have become more fragmented, and the forms of political life have outrun the common purpose needed to sustain them.

Something like this, it seems to me, has been unfolding in America for the past half-century or so. I hope I have said at least enough to suggest the shape a fuller story might take. And I hope in any case to have conveyed a certain view about politics and philosophy and the relations between them – that our practices and institutions are themselves embodiments of theory, and to unravel their predicament is, at least in part, to seek after the self-image of the age.

NOTES

1. J. Rawls, *A Theory of Justice* (Oxford, 1971). I. Kant, *Groundwork of the Metaphysics of Morals*, trans H. J. Paton (1785; New York, 1956). Kant, *Critique of Pure Reason*, trans. N. Kemp Smith (1781, 1787; London, 1929). Kant, *Critique of Practical Reason*, trans. L. W. Beck (1788; Indianapolis, 1956). Kant, 'On the Common Saying: "This may be true in theory, but it does not apply in practice",' in H. Reiss (ed.), *Kant's Political Writings* (1793; Cambridge 1970). Other recent versions of the claim for the priority of the right over good can be found in R. Nozick, *Anarchy, State, and Utopia* (New York, 1974); R. Dworkin, *Taking Rights Seriously* (London, 1977); B. Ackerman, *Social Justice in the Liberal State* (New Haven, Conn., 1980).
2. Rawls, *A Theory of Justice*, p. 560.

3. Rawls, 'Kantian Constructivism in Moral Theory: The Dewey Lectures 1980', *Journal of Philosophy,* 77 (1980), 543.
4. The account that follows is a tentative formulation of themes requiring more detailed elaboration and support.
5. See, e.g., L. Tribe, *American Constitutional Law* (Mineola, NY, 1978), 2–3.
6. See R. Dworkin, 'Liberalism', in S. Hampshire (ed.) *Public and Private Morality* (Cambridge, 1978), 136.

AMITAI ETZIONI
'THE THIRD WAY IS A TRIUMPH'

There must be a secret prize for whoever comes up with the most dismissive epitaph for the Third Way. This seems the only possible explanation for the torrent of phrases depicting it as 'vague', 'fuzzy', a 'waffle', 'a masterwork of ambiguity' or as the *Economist* had it: 'Trying to pin down an exact meaning is like wrestling an inflatable man. If you get a grip on one limb, all the hot air rushes to another.'

Yet consider what this much-maligned public philosophy has actually achieved. In the US, the Third Way not only gave us Bill Clinton but also bit George W. Bush so hard in the tail that he may yet disappoint his so-far dominant right wing. Having lost control of the Senate after only four months in office, Bush may be forced to move closer to the centre from which he campaigned rather than from where he has governed so far. In Britain, it has given Labour an unprecedented second full term in power. In Germany, soon after Tony Blair spoon-fed it to the reluctant Gerhard Schroeder, the Third Way (or 'new middle') brought another previously failing left party to power; now, the SPD seems poised for an even stronger second term. Third Way thinking is a major force in the Dutch miracle and it is a road from which Scandinavian parties benefit whenever they can find it. Yes, I know that the Italians veered to the right, but they were never quite centred; previously they were somewhere off in left field.

Better still, the Third Way is not merely a potent recipe for gaining power, it is also a solid public philosophy. True, it has a somewhat blurred

Amitai Etzioni (2001), 'The Third Way is a Triumph', *New Statesman*, 25 June.

margin – and thanks be given that it is far less detailed than a Soviet dogma or a Catholic doctrine. But it has a clear core.

Part of that core is to make opponents who used to hobble each other into productive partners. How quickly we forget the days when the prevailing ideology was that government is the problem, and not even a part of the solution, and that the more we throw people on the tender mercies of the market, the better not just we but they will be. Even Bush no longer dares speak such Thatcher-Reaganisms. Cutting the civil service or closing down the education department, the environment department and public service television – all of which were once conservative targets – are not now even mentioned. On the contrary, Bush has just increased the federal government's budget and its role in education.

On the other side of the coin, the Third Way has banished not only the belief that the market is the source of all evil, but also the simplistic notion that if citizens just pay their taxes the welfare state will do the rest.

The Third Way's central tenet is that both the state and the market are part of the solution; that each has [a] significant and legitimate [role] to play; and that they need to cooperate rather than constantly be at loggerheads. Both Blair and Clinton have been supportive of the free market and have been rewarded with economic success. Far from shutting down or undermining the welfare state, stronger economic growth helped sustain it. We tend to think of the economy as producing widgets and ball bearings, toothpaste and chewing gum. But when its engines are humming, it delivers much more. Hefty economic growth provides hefty additional tax revenues that can be used to finance numerous goodies from more policing to better education. Moreover, the 'extra' growth curtails unemployment, which in turn reduces welfare costs, thus freeing yet more money for public services. But, at the same time, the market should not be allowed to run amok. The role of the state is to keep it in place by, for example, requiring proper notification before a factory is closed.

The second core element of the Third Way is communitarian. It holds that society is like a stool that rests on three legs, two of which (the state and the market) are too long and one too short. The third leg is the things people do for one another as members of families and neighbourhoods, as friends and co-workers. The underlying theory is that we should not commodify all social relations. After the loss of a spouse, a parent or a child, a visit from a family member or friend is far better than a session with a 'grief counsellor'. When people grow old, it is far better for them to help each other and to perform minor chores (which many more can for many more years these days) than rely merely on social workers.

Blair made such concepts of community and responsibility (for oneself and for others) a core element in his first election campaign. In his first years in office, his ministers helped launch or support or extend a considerable number of programmes that have a communitarian ring to them: community policing, neighbourhood watch and anti-crime patrols (of the kind found in Balsall Heath, Birmingham), tenant management associations, and local food buying groups. Gordon Brown, toward the end of his first term, encouraged charitable giving and volunteerism by, for example, scrapping the £250 minimum limit for donations to attract tax relief. Other measures encourage people to make gifts of shares.

These are merely baby steps on this stretch of the Third Way. The US has hundreds of thousands of groups (often, misleadingly, called self-help groups, when the reality is that they are mutual help groups) that provide services far more carefully tailored to the individual than anything a government can provide. They help millions cope with alcoholism, depression, breast cancer, spousal abuse, and much else. These are not goody-two-shoes 'voluntary associations' in which the affluent members of the community set out to bring good deeds to the poor, acts of charity and altruism (such as reading to the blind), although these too have their place and merit. Mutual help groups are much more sustainable and can carry much heavier loads because their members are deeply engrossed and they benefit one another day in and day out. It is hard to see how the health service will ever find its way unless it joins the Third Way, as millions of people take more responsibility for themselves (quit smoking, reduce alcohol abuse, take exercise) and for each other.

More generally, whether it is a matter of child care or protecting the environment, people need to assume responsibility. The largest and fastest-growing group that can do more are senior citizens, who live longer and healthier lives and would benefit psychologically from doing more for one another and their communities. Taking responsibility is a key element of the Third Way, which Blair has often pointed to, here and there introduced, but not quite led the British people truly to embrace, with his top-down government and stress on efficiency.

This is particularly notable when it comes to devolution. Blair devolved, but not far enough. Devolving to regions that have ethnic affinities and cultures of their own is a risky business. While separatist sentiments and voices have temporarily quietened down, their nascent threat is never far behind. This term, Blair should work much more directly with smaller, more local communities. And he should fashion an increasing number of development projects that cut across regional borders, for instance across northeast England and southern Scotland.

Those who charge that there is no place on the Third Way for equality are right. There has never been a country that came close to equality; surely not the USSR. Even the small islands of true socialism in Israel, the kibbutzim, are on their last legs. Yet the Third Way must address the question of social justice. It cannot just wax and wane about 'opportunity' and look the other way as inequality rises to the point that a growing segment of the population leads a life immune from all the travails the rest have to tolerate, from riding the tube to queuing for X-rays.

In a previous article for the NS (15 May 2000), I proposed that everyone should be entitled to a rich basic minimum. Blair's proposal to grant everyone a bond at birth is a step in that direction. This is an approach to social justice that seeks, not to take people's assets away and distribute them equally, which is either an illusion or a recipe for brutality, but to flatten the pyramid mainly by lifting the lower levels, again and again, and to a significant degree.

Even if they work, the poor will always be with us, as long as they have no assets. People who own assets, especially a place of residence, are more likely to 'buy' into a society, to feel that they are part of the community and to be an active member of it. One way to advance home ownership is through schemes that allow those on low incomes to obtain mortgages. This might be achieved by giving poor people, say, £2 for every £1 they set aside to provide them with the seed money for buying a home. Alternatively, 'sweat' equity might be counted as a contribution if, for instance, a potential home owner works on his or her future house.

The greatest challenge to Blair in his second term may well come not from Europe but from multiculturalism, from the dangerous clash between those who want to abolish Britishness to accommodate diversity and those who retain patriotic sentiments. But here the Third Way, and particularly its communitarian elements, provides an answer. It can see Britain as a community of communities. The nation can welcome, indeed feel enriched by, people of divergent background and heritage, and happily tolerate differences of habits and subculture. At the same time, it can expect all citizens to buy into a significant set of shared values and mores.

For instance, there is no reason to object to people who pray in a mosque rather than in a church. But people's freedom to marry whom they like should be one of the shared values, thus ruling out forced marriages. Again, parents may be free, indeed welcome, to teach their children the language of their country of origin. But this should not be at the cost of a full command of English.

So all in all, there are clear signposts on the Third Way. True, Blair has passed only some of them and many are barely in sight. But this road is far better than the first road, which was raw capitalism, or the second road, which was the planned economy.

3

NATION

Alice Ludvig

Introduction: controversies over defining the nation

Searching for criteria to define 'a nation', one will most likely first refer to a group of people living within a territory and, secondly, will try to link them to shared traits such as a common language, religion, historical traditions and common norms and values. This is a form of objective definition; it ascribes cultural factors to the concept of a nation. For instance, Joseph Stalin, the Soviet communist leader, defined the nation thus: 'A nation is an historically constituted, stable community of people, formed on the basis of a common language, territory, economic life and psychological make-up manifested in a common culture' (1954: 307). According to Stalin's definition, the former Soviet Union itself must have been perceived by most communist elites in Moscow as something like a 'multinational' empire, including many such nations under the umbrella of the USSR. However, from the perspective of many of those nations, it must have been seen as an imperial state, oppressing their 'national' aspirations.

This leads us to the second way of defining a nation: a concept oriented to the subjective experience of its members. Ernest Renan made a classic statement in Paris in his famous lecture 'What is a Nation?' in 1882: 'A nation is a soul, a spiritual principle. Two things, which in truth are but one, constitute this soul or spiritual principle. One lies in the past, one in the present. One is the possession in common of a rich legacy of memories; the other is a present-day consent, the desire to live together, the will to perpetuate the value of the heritage that one has received in an individual form' (1996: 52). Thus there are at least two possible views on the nation: one from outside and one from the inside, with the latter having, as Renan suggests, two focuses: one towards the past and the other in the present.

Other scholars have pointed to discrepancies in these concepts. The German sociologist Max Weber held that purely objective criteria, such as language, religion, territory or genealogy, will on one hand always fail to include some nations, but on the other hand subjective criteria may take in too large a number of cases (1964: 675f.). Later, Ernest Gellner stated in *Nations and Nationalism*: 'To put it in the simplest terms: there is a large number of potential nations on earth. Our planet only contains room for a certain number of independent or autonomous political units' (1983: 2). Gellner's work leads us to the political factor in the concept of a nation, not explicitly addressed in either Stalin's definition above or Renan's work. The nation becomes political in the sense that it occupies a common territory, or demands to do so, and, in some cases, it aims to possess sovereign authority over this territory. However, a community characterised by a common language, a shared belief or religion, or common territory, as well as a genealogy, thereby marked off from other communities by some distinctions, can also be described as an 'ethnic community'. Still, without a common public culture and a sovereign political authority it is not a nation (see also Miller 1995: 25); it is a different way of thinking about collective identity from ethnicity and it is misleading to use the language of kinship and descent to characterise nations (Calhoun 1997: 36ff.). Consequently, and in short, a nation is characterised by a common belief in political self-determination on a sovereign territory for a homogeneously imagined group of people, sharing certain features which intend to distinguish them from others.

It is worth stressing that one must be careful not to confuse the term 'nation' with the terms 'country' or 'state'. For instance, World War I gave birth to the League of Nations, World War II to the United Nations. Yet both are conglomerates not of nations but rather of states. Likewise, the term 'nationality' does not refer to membership of a nation, but of a state, also called citizenship. Around the world there are many nations without states, such as the Kurdish people in Central Asia, the Jewish Zionists before 1948, when the state of Israel was founded, or the Palestinian people in the same country. This means that not every nation has its own state, and, importantly, the reverse may also be the case: not many states have, in fact, a singular and homogeneous nation within their territorial boundaries.

One can define with certainty the following: firstly, a nation is *not* a state, and, secondly, a nation is *not* an ethnic community. It is less than a state, because it lacks its institutional preconditions such as a polity, sovereignty and a government. Yet it is more than an ethnic community because an ethnic community is characterised by a collective cultural identity and not a 'political' identity. Still, the borders are blurred and there is by no means a consensus in scholarly debates about defining a nation.

NATIONALISM

Nationalism is the conscious identification and solidarity with a national community. Above we have split up the concept of the nation into a view from inside and a view from outside; in the same manner we can distinguish here between two forms of nationalism: an inclusive and an exclusive notion. Inclusive nationalism aims to include certain groups and wants to evoke integrating and legitimising effects (for example for support of a certain political system). Exclusive nationalism is characterised by strong self-centring attitudes and intends to distinguish itself from other nations. Sometimes this can result in demands for correspondence of ethnic and political borders or, more precisely, the congruency of territory and people. Furthermore, it can be that corresponding national characteristics take on an exaggerated significance. While exclusive nationalism flows to differentiation and demarcation from other ethnic groups and, depending on the case, to radical disapproval of foreign rule, inclusive nationalism primarily aims to arouse feelings of community within a nation.

In reference to nationalism Gellner states that 'nationalism holds that they [nations and states] were destined for each other; that either without the other is incomplete, and constitutes a tragedy' (1983: 6). In short, as a political concept, nationalism is in some way or other always longing for the result that the boundaries of the nation and those of a state should, in so far as possible, coincide. There is at least one serious objection to this normative nationalist principle, formulated here by Gellner:

> On any reasonable calculation, the former number of (potential nations) is probably much, much larger than that of possible viable states. If this argument or calculation is correct, not all nationalisms can be satisfied, at any rate not at the same time. The satisfaction of some spells the frustration of others. This argument is furthered and immeasurably strengthened by the fact that very many of the potential nations of this world live, or until recently have lived, not in compact territorial units but intermixed with each other in complex patterns. It follows that a territorial political unit can only become ethnically homogenous, in such cases if it either kills, or expels, or assimilates all non-nationals (1983: 2).

The emerging question is what takes place first: the demands of a collective community, considering itself 'a nation', for a congruent common territory? Or is it nationalism that arouses these feelings of belonging and taking part in 'a nation' in individual people, succeeding in the claims to sovereignty, secession or simply just patriotism in times of war or crisis? What came first, the nation or the collective sentiment towards it (nationalism)?

Scholars largely approach this from two different viewpoints. On the one hand, the *perennalists* (also called *primordialists*) argue that nations have been around for a very long time, except that they have had different shapes at different moments in history. They assume that there is a continuity in history between pre-modern ethnic communities and the nations of modernity. On the other hand, the *modernists* (or *constructionists*) argue that nations are an entirely modern phenomenon and that they are constructed. The latter are the more recent and are currently prevalent. Of course, there is no sharp line between both approaches. For example, although Anthony Smith emphasises, in *The Ethnic Origin of Nations* (1986), the importance of ethnic cores in nations as an historic congruency and, therefore, argues in a perennialistic way, he also holds that they are a modern phenomenon as well. Thus, in his view the nation is modern; however, it has developed on the basis of ethnic cores or 'ethnic navels' (Smith 1991). Smith stands between both views, which have merged in recent years, as he himself says:

> In the past, one could be sure that modernists were also instrumentalists (and vice-versa), while perennialists were always primordialists of one kind or another (and vice-versa). But this simple dualism has given way to more variegated and complex formulations. Not all modernists embrace a robust instrumentalism; and not all perennialists turn out primordialists. We can even find an instrumentalist who is a perennialist of sorts; though the converse, a thorough-going primordialist who could propound a modernist account of nations and nationalism, is rare. What we can find instead are theorists who embrace a perennialist view of ethnicity (with some primordialist overtones), only to adopt a modernist approach to nations and nationalism (1998: 159).

If, like the perennialists, one regards nations as a natural and historically timeless phenomenon, just like humanity itself, then there will be no reason to explain how and when they have emerged. There is no need to delve too deeply into the primordialist and perennialist view. Today few scholars continue to consider the nation as an unchanging and eternal entity. Yet, if one agrees with the modernists that the nation is constructed, it becomes important to explain how and why nations have developed. Though most of the constructivists locate the origin of nations historically in different times and places, they all locate the emergence of nationalism and the building of the nation-states in some social change leading from the pre-modern world to the modern one. Gellner himself postulates three stages in human history (the hunter-gatherer, the agro-literate and the industrial) and locates it in the turning point from agro-literate to industrial society. Specifically, the connection between power and culture has changed: in the industrial society there is a need for a 'shared culture' to hold power, therefore nationalism is 'invented'. In the reading he proposes four 'false theories of nationalism' as the basis for his chain of reasoning: the false theory of nationalism as naturalism, the theory of nationalism being artificial, the 'wrong address' theory and the theory of the 'Dark Gods' (1983: 129–30). None of these theories are tenable; furthermore, Gellner argues as a constructionist: 'In fact, nations, like states, are a contingency, and not a universal necessity. Neither nations nor states exist at all times in all circumstances; moreover, nations and states are not the same contingency' (1983: 6).

When we declare nations as solemnly existing in the real world within the borders of modern nation-states, they are, historically, a very young phenomenon. They emerged with modernity at the beginning of the eighteenth century. The historian Eric Hobsbawn comes, like Gellner, to the conclusion that nationalism existed *before* nations and that it is nationalism itself that creates the nation:

> Like most serious students, I do not regard the 'nation' as a primary nor as an unchanging social entity. It belongs exclusively to a particular, and historically recent, period. It is a social entity only insofar as it relates to a certain kind of modern territorial state, the 'nation-state', and it is pointless to discuss nation and nationality except insofar as both relate to it. Moreover, with Gellner I would stress the element of artefact, invention and social engineering which enters into the making of nations. 'Nations as a natural, God-given way of classifying men, as an inherent ... political destiny, are a myth; nationalism, which sometimes takes preexisting cultures and turns them into nations, sometimes invents them, and often obliterates preexisting cultures: that is a reality'. In short, for the purposes of analysis nationalism comes before nations. Nations do not make states and nationalisms but the other way round (1990: 9f.).

THE CONSTRUCTION OF THE NATION

If we agree with some of the constructivists' view that the nation as a natural fact is a social construct and a myth used by nationalism for its specific aims, then we still have no explanation for the very real fact that many of the most enduring conflicts in this world turn around the question of whether a particular group is, or should become 'a nation'. At the same time it will appear rather shocking that millions of individuals throughout history have been ready to lose their lives in the name of something that scholars call a 'myth'. Therefore we need to reveal more on how the nation is constructed and how it is effective in the heads of people.

One of the most interesting advocates of a constructionist view is Benedict Anderson. In his work he searches for reasons why people in modern times have so emotionally identified with 'their' nation. In particular, he has emphasised the fact that the nation is an 'imagined' community:

> It is *imagined* because the members of even the smallest nation will never know most of their fellow-members, meet them, or even hear of them, yet in the minds of each lives the image of their communion. [...] In fact, all communities larger than primordial villages of face-to-face contact (and perhaps even these) are imagined (1991: 6f.).

It is, however, certain that any society that goes beyond 'face-to-face' contacts is 'imagined' in this way. Therefore the criterion of 'imagination' cannot be the only one for the nation in particular. Anderson states that, historically, the nation as an imagined community emerges against the background of the dissolution of hegemonic religious regimes in society (secularisation). Nations grew out of and replaced the religious communities and dynastic realms of the Middle Ages. In concrete terms, this change is driven mostly via changes in the arrangements of *language, state, time* and *space*. Owing to the invention of the printing press, firstly it became possible to reach a broader readership and secondly a unified *language* took hold, reducing the importance of regional dialects. Furthermore, the emergence of the *state* and its institutions superseded the pre-modern dynastic empires whose frontiers were blurred and, usually, detached from a common 'national language'. Anderson also links a historic shift in time perception, like the one in language, to the development of the technology of book print in the eighteenth century: novels and newspapers count as the first capitalist mass products. Any general identification with a greater anonymous national collective is only possible via widespread circulation of novels and newspapers. The feeling of community is especially created by the latter, as people read them *at the same time*, and this experience of simultaneousness is Anderson's key to national community. Finally the concept of *space* changed with modernity. Concerning the nation there are three main aspects of space: a geographical (the map), a demographical (the population census) and a representational level (the museum). One necessary precondition for imagining the nation is the idea of a clearly demarcated country, a limited territory:

> 'The nation is imagined as *limited* because even the largest of them encompassing perhaps a billion living human beings, has finite, if elastic boundaries, beyond which lie other nations. No nation imagines itself coterminous with mankind. The most messianic nationalists do not dream of a day when all the members of the human race will

join their nation in the way that it was possible, in certain epochs, for, say, Christians to dream of a wholly Christian planet' (Anderson 1991: 7).

The concept of the nation differentiates itself in particular from the imagination of an ethnic community through the specific idea of a 'perfectly tailored' home territory with sharp edges like a puzzle. By way of the census, it is demonstrated that there is a limit as well to the population that lives within these boundaries. Ultimately, the museum functions as the ideal place where all images of national space, national population and national time perception come together. In the museum certain national symbols are represented, most often linked to a fateful date in history; the national space-time incidents are represented and reproduced.

It is very hard to give enough space here to Anderson's very original work. Since its first publication in 1983, his book has probably been the most cited theoretical work on nationalism. He differs from Smith in that he does not read the emergence of nations as the result of a process of unification of pre-existing ethnic cores. He also rejects Gellner and Hobsbawm for their 'macro-perspective' from above, where the concept of a specific elite invents traditions and creates the sentiment of nationalism predating the historical appearance of nation(-states). Anderson's imagined community contrasts to Gellner's notion of the nation; as a fabricated entity. There are historic pre-conditions for the emergence of the nation; in this idea of the nation as a political community, people and events are emotionally linked, even if they do not stand in connection with each other. At least one question emerges here, namely Anderson's emphasis on the emergence of print capitalism; for at least the first hundred years only a few elite people actually had access to, or were able to read, such material. Anderson gives particular prominence to the ways in which nations are constructed through cultural representation and symbols. Consequently, some scholars accuse him of 'cultural reductionism', disregarding the political dimension (Breuilly 1993). In that sense, for instance, the German and the Italian nation-states were political creations, and the 'cultural' unification took place afterwards.

Certainly, his theory doesn't hold for all nation-building processes. Another counter-argument to his approach is that religion and nationalism are not opposing principles. Religion played a very important part in the rise of national consciousness in many cases, even in the later stages, when the nation had replaced religion as the governing passion. For instance, Liah Greenfeld locates the emergence of the nation in sixteenth-century England, and she argues that '[t]he already growing national consciousness was strengthened manifold when it became confluent with the Protestant Reformation' (1992: 87). According to Greenfeld, it was in times when

religious identity grew more and faith became more significant that nationalism emerged; it developed with the support of religion and not, as
Anderson suggests, with secularisation. We know religious nationalism today for example in the Islamic world, in India, in Europe and in parts of
the former Soviet Union.

The study of nations and nationalism amounts to the study of myths
and manipulations which intermingle with objective and subjective factors
which all further intermingle and intersect. The recent debate that centred
around the question of whether nations are *only* fictional – constructed by
pure will – or if they are *also* based upon real differences and communal-
ities shared between individuals remains open, unless we change our perspective. Then we may regard it rather as a kind of structuring discourse,
an all-encompassing ideology that shapes the way in which we perceive
and constitute the world. This way we are produced and reproduced as
'nationals', as 'citizens' through symbols, passports, TV, bureaucracy and
day-to-day actions. It determines our collective identity in a form of seeing
and interpreting which conditions our daily speech, behaviours, interactions
and attitudes. At this point one may suggest that this is a very broad perspective, yet it has the advantage that additional sub-categories can always
be added.

National identity

Has anyone ever *seen* a nation? For social research on the concept of the
nation and, related to it, nationalism, it is worth stressing again that we
can better deal with it not as a real 'thing', but treat it as one category
that describes a specific historical and socio-cultural configuration. When
reviewing the mass of scholarly literature on the issue, one can also regard it
from a greater distance. There are those who use the notion of nation more
affirmatively and others who use it critically. No doubt, one portion of the
literature has to be seen in itself as a substantial element for nation-building
processes. It is a question of distance from the object:

> For nationalists themselves, the role of the past is clear and unprob-
> lematic. The nation was always there, indeed it is part of the natural
> order, even when it was submerged in the hearts of its members. The
> task of the nationalist is simply to remind his or her compatriots of
> their glorious past, so that they can recreate and relive those glories
> (Smith 1994, 18).

All this does certainly not mean that the object of identification has to
be something real. Neither nations nor ethnic communities are objectively
conceivable groups. However, there are other constructivist scholars who
argue that the nation exists in social reality not because people 'invent' it, as
Gellner theorises, or because they 'think' or 'imagine' it, as Anderson holds.

Instead they emphasise the idea that it is rather something that *happens*. It is because people 'act' and 'behave' it. In this view, the human behaviour of 'practising the nation' has no primordial and universal historically determined character because it happens not only in the social superstructures, but also in the heads and bodies of real people on the micro level. Rogers Brubaker (1996, 1998, 2002) and Craig Calhoun (1997) are amongst the supporters of this line of argumentation. Brubaker, for instance, differentiates between nation, nationhood and nationness:

> We should focus on nation as a category of practice, nationhood as an institutionalised cultural and political form, and nationness as contingent event or happening, and refrain from using the analytically dubious notion of 'nations' as substantial, enduring collectivities. A recent book by Julia Kristeva bears the title 'Nations without Nationalism'; but the analytical task at hand, I submit, is to think about nationalism without nations (1996: 21).

Brubaker warns us against the danger of reifying nations and treats nationalism first and foremost as a structuring discourse. Likewise, national identity is not something static that a person possesses, it is something that happens and has to be produced and reproduced in everyday actions and interactions. Therefore it might be more precise to talk of 'national identification' in order to get hold of identity as a process. Brubaker convincingly argues that nationalist discourse can only be effective if it is reproduced on a daily basis. It is a heterogeneous set of 'nation-oriented' practices, idioms and possibilities that are continuously available or 'endemic' in modern cultural and political life (Brubaker 1996: 10).

What differentiates Brubaker's theory of the concept of the nation from the modernist and constructivist approaches? The latter have made it plausible that the nation is a modern social construction. While their focus of analysis lay on the macroperspective of social reality, Brubaker introduces with his analytical tools 'nationhood' and 'nationness' the meso level: everyday practices and interactions between people. The remaining micro level takes place at the location where nation actually 'happens': in a cognitive process within the individual.

Identification with the Nation in a Globalising World

In *Nations and Nationalism since 1780*, Hobsbawm foresees the end of the peak in the study of nationalism:

> As I have suggested, 'nation' and 'nationalism' are no longer adequate terms to describe, let alone to analyse, the political entities described as such, or even sentiments once described by these words. It is not

impossible that nationalism will decline with the decline of the nation-state, without which being English or Irish or Jewish, or a combination of all these, is only one way in which people describe their identity among the many others which they use for this purpose, as occasion demands. It would be absurd to claim that this day is already near. However, I hope it can at least be envisaged. After all, the very fact that historians are at least beginning to make some progress in the study and analysis of nations and nationalism suggests that, as so often, the phenomenon is past its peak. The owl of Minerva which brings wisdom, says Hegel, flies out at dusk. It is a good sign that it is now circling around nations and nationalism (1990: 192).

Indeed, the 1980s marked a turning point in the study of nationalism: with Anderson's *Imagined Communities* (1983), Gellner's *Nations and Nationalism* (1983), Hobsbawm and Terence Roger's *The Invention of Traditions* (1983) and Smith's *The Ethnic Origins of Nations* (1986) among many others, the theories on nationalism have grown increasingly sophisticated. Still, though many scholars have deconstructed the 'myth of nationalism', the national in its social reality is still prevalent. It has come as a surprise to many that, since the end of the East–West conflict, an increasing upsurge of nationalisms and nationalist conflicts around the world has been taking place. A truly vast array of articles and books over the last fifteen years begin by referring to how nationalism has recently become important. They quote similar examples: Bosnia, Rwanda, Albania, Somalia, Eritrea, Indonesia and so on. This has been called the 'return of the repressed' perspective (Brubaker 1998), which emphasises that there is a new wave of emerging nationalisms following the collapse of the Eastern Bloc.

Brubaker refers to the communist regimes of Eastern Europe and the Soviet Union when he declares that these obviously *did* repress nationalism, but the 'return of the repressed' view mistakes the manner in which they did so because it suggests that these regimes repressed not only nationalism, but nationhood. For Brubaker, nationalism flourishes today in the post-Soviet national struggles *because* of the regimes' policies, as these former policies were not anti-national, they were only anti-national*ist*; the USSR's more than fifty national territories were each defined as the homelands of particular ethnonational groups, and constituted an elementary form of political identity (Brubaker 1998: 286–90).

Ultimately, there is a pervading view on nationalism that manifests itself only under extreme conditions, such as a natural disaster or epidemic which arrives unforeseen and unpredictably. To me it seems as if this view draws an underlying distinction between a 'good' and a 'bad' nationalism within these parameters. In such a distinction lies the danger of a disguised paternalistic Eurocentric view combined with an evolutionary linear notion of history: accordingly, in Europe we find a 'good' harmless form of nationalism (for example enacted in football stadiums). The horrible forms of nationalism are a problem for those marginalised on the periphery. Only when they have completed their nation-building processes and their ethnic and territorial struggles will they have reached the stage of what a 'proper nation' is supposed to look like, including a nation-state's politico-institutional preconditions. However, nationalism has many different forms and continues to be an issue in the Western world as well, as we see, for example, in Quebec, Northern Ireland, the Basque country and Corsica.

Nonetheless, since the end of the 1990s new global tendencies in economic, political and sociocultural relationships have put the future of the nation-state as the primary actor in the international arena increasingly into question. Global tendencies are crystallising in a shift towards the development of 'macroregions' and supranational political units, such as the EU, with increasing independence from the rule of nation-state regimes. For many scholars of nationalism, it has acted as an engine or a vehicle, catapulting mankind from pre-modernity to modernity. This implies that the further the process of change is advanced, the less the need will be for it. Let me modestly suggest the following: the specific form of nationalism which has driven the twentieth century's two world wars, fuelled by the competition (economic and military) between these nation(-states) no longer prevails. It seems as if the world is once again on the threshold of momentous change. Of course, regional identification with nation(-states) is still alive and will continue to play a significant role, but what will happen in the long run to the nation is unclear at this stage.

QUESTIONS FOR DISCUSSION

- Is the nation a useful unit for contemporary political analysis?
- Which came first: nations or nationalism?
- Is Anderson correct to claim that the nation is an imagined community?
- What is the difference between a state and a nation?

BENEDICT ANDERSON
EXTRACTS FROM *IMAGINED*
COMMUNITIES: REFLECTIONS ON THE
ORIGIN AND SPREAD OF NATIONALISM

Concepts and definitions

It seems advisable to consider briefly the concept of 'nation' and offer a workable definition. Theorists of nationalism have often been perplexed, not to say irritated, by these three paradoxes: (1) The objective modernity of nations to the historian's eye vs. their subjective antiquity in the eyes of nationalists. (2) The formal universality of nationality as a socio-cultural concept – in the modern world everyone can, should, will 'have' a nationality, as he or she 'has' a gender – vs. the irremediable particularity of its concrete manifestations, such that, by definition, 'Greek' nationality is sui generis. (3) The 'political' power of nationalisms vs. their philosophical poverty and even incoherence. In other words, unlike most other isms, nationalism has never produced its own grand thinkers: no Hobbeses, Tocquevilles, Marxes, or Webers. This 'emptiness' easily gives rise, among cosmopolitan and polylingual intellectuals, to a certain condescension. Like Gertrude Stein in the face of Oakland, one can rather quickly conclude that there is 'no there there'. It is characteristic that even so sympathetic a student of nationalism as Tom Nairn can nonetheless write that: ' "Nationalism", is the pathology of modern developmental history, as inescapable as "neurosis" in the individual, with much the same essential ambiguity attaching to it, a similar built-in capacity for descent into dementia, rooted in the dilemmas of helplessness thrust upon most of the world (the equivalent of infantilism for societies) and largely incurable'.[1]

Benedict Anderson (1991), *Imagined Communities: Reflections on the Origin and Spread of Nationalism*, rev. ed., London: Verso.

Part of the difficulty is that one tends unconsciously to hypostasize the existence of Nationalism-with-a-big-N (rather as one might Age-with-a-capital-A) and then to classify 'it' as *an* ideology. (Note that if everyone has an age, Age is merely an analytical expression.) It would, I think, make things easier if one treated it as if it belonged with 'kinship' and 'religion', rather than with 'liberalism' or 'fascism'.

In an anthropological spirit, then, I propose the following definition of the nation: it is an imagined political community – and imagined as both inherently limited and sovereign.

It is *imagined* because the members of even the smallest nation will never know most of their fellow-members, meet them, or even hear of them, yet in the minds of each lives the image of their communion.[2] Renan referred to this imagining in his suavely back-handed way when he wrote that 'Or l'essence d'une nation est que tous les individus aient beaucoup de choses en commun, et aussi que tous aient oublié bien des choses'.[3] With a certain ferocity Gellner makes a comparable point when he rules that 'Nationalism is not the awakening of nations to self-consciousness: it *invents* nations where they do not exist'.[4] The drawback to this formulation, however, is that Gellner is so anxious to show that nationalism masquerades under false pretences that he assimilates 'invention' to 'fabrication' and 'falsity', rather than to 'imagining' and 'creation'. In this way he implies that 'true' communities exist which can be advantageously juxtaposed to nations. In fact, all communities larger than primordial villages of face-to-face contact (and perhaps even these) are imagined. Communities are to be distinguished, not by their falsity/genuineness, but by the style in which they are imagined. Javanese villagers have always known that they are connected to people they have never seen, but these ties were once imagined particularistically – as indefinitely stretchable nets of kinship and clientship. Until quite recently, the Javanese language had no word meaning the abstraction 'society'. We may today think of the French aristocracy of the *ancien régime* as a class; but surely it was imagined this way only very late.[5] To the question 'Who is the Comte de X?' the normal answer would have been, not 'a member of the aristocracy', but 'the lord of X', 'the uncle of the Baronne de Y', or 'a client of the Duc de Z'.

The nation is imagined as *limited* because even the largest of them, encompassing perhaps a billion living human beings, has finite, if elastic, boundaries, beyond which lie other nations. No nation imagines itself coterminous with mankind. The most messianic nationalists do not dream of a day when all the members of the human race will join their nation in the way that it was possible, in certain epochs, for, say, Christians to dream of a wholly Christian planet.

It is imagined as *sovereign* because the concept was born in an age in which Enlightenment and Revolution were destroying the legitimacy of the divinely-ordained, hierarchical dynastic realm. Coming to maturity at a stage of human history when even the most devout adherents of any universal religion were inescapably confronted with the living *pluralism* of such religions, and the allomorphism between each faith's ontological claims and territorial stretch, nations dream of being free, and, if under God, directly so. The gage and emblem of this freedom is the sovereign state.

Finally, it is imagined as a *community*, because, regardless of the actual inequality and exploitation that may prevail in each, the nation is always conceived as a deep, horizontal comradeship. Ultimately it is this fraternity that makes it possible, over the past two centuries for so many millions of people, not so much to kill, as willingly to die for such limited imaginings.

These deaths bring us abruptly face to face with the central problem posed by nationalism: what makes the shrunken imaginings of recent history (scarcely more than two centuries) generate such colossal sacrifices? I believe that the beginnings of an answer lie in the cultural roots of nationalism.

NOTES

1. *The Break-up of Britain*, p. 359.
2. Cf. Seton-Watson, *Nations and States*, p. 5: 'All that I can find to say is that a nation exists when a significant number of people in a community consider themselves to form a nation, or behave as if they formed one'. We may translate 'consider themselves' as 'imagine themselves'.
3. Ernest Renan, 'Qu'est-ce qu'une nation?' in *Oeuvres Complètes*, 1, p. 892. He adds: 'tout citoyen français doit avoir oublié la Saint-Barthélemy, les massacres du Midi au XIIIe siècle. Il n'y a pas en France dix familles qui puissent fournir la preuve d'une origine franque . . .'
4. Ernest Gellner, *Thought and Change*, p. 169. Emphasis added.
5. Hobsbawm, for example, 'fixes' it by saying that in 1789 it numbered about 400,000 in a population of 23,000,000. (See his *The Age of Revolution*, p. 78). But would this statistical picture of the noblesse have been imaginable under the *ancien régime*?

ROGERS BRUBAKER
AND FREDERICK COOPER
EXTRACTS FROM
'BEYOND "IDENTITY"'

'The worst thing one can do with words', wrote George Orwell a half a century ago, 'is to surrender to them'. If language is to be 'an instrument for expressing and not for concealing or preventing thought', he continued, one must 'let the meaning choose the word, and not the other way about'.[1] The argument of this article is that the social sciences and humanities have surrendered to the word 'identity'; that this has both intellectual and political costs; and that we can do better. 'Identity', we argue, tends to mean too much (when understood in a strong sense), too little (when understood in a weak sense), or nothing at all (because of its sheer ambiguity). We take stock of the conceptual and theoretical work 'identity' is supposed to do and suggest that this work might be done better by other terms, less ambiguous, and unencumbered by the reifying connotations of 'identity'.

We argue that the prevailing constructivist stance on identity – the attempt to 'soften' the term, to acquit it of the charge of 'essentialism' by stipulating that identities are constructed, fluid, and multiple – leaves us without a rationale for talking about 'identities' at all and ill-equipped to examine the 'hard' dynamics and essentialist claims of contemporary identity politics. 'Soft' constructivism allows putative 'identities' to proliferate. But as they proliferate, the term loses its analytical purchase. If identity is everywhere, it is nowhere. If it is fluid, how can we understand the ways in which self-understandings may harden, congeal, and crystallize? If it is constructed, how can we understand the sometimes coercive force of external identifications? If it is multiple, how do we understand the terrible

Rogers Brubaker and Frederick Cooper (2000), 'Beyond "Identity"', *Theory and Society*, 29(1).

singularity that is often striven for – and sometimes realized – by politicians seeking to transform mere categories into unitary and exclusive groups? How can we understand the power and pathos of identity politics?

'Identity' is a key term in the vernacular idiom of contemporary politics, and social analysis must take account of this fact. But this does not require us to use 'identity' as a category of analysis or to conceptualize 'identities' as something that all people have, seek, construct, and negotiate. Conceptualizing all affinities and affiliations, all forms of belonging, all experiences of commonality, connectedness, and cohesion, all self-understandings and self-identifications in the idiom of 'identity' saddles us with a blunt, flat, undifferentiated vocabulary.

We do not aim here to contribute to the ongoing debate on identity politics.[2] We focus instead on identity as an analytical category. This is not a 'merely semantic' or terminological issue. The use and abuse of 'identity', we suggest, affects not only the language of social analysis but also – inseparably – its substance. Social analysis – including the analysis of identity politics – requires relatively unambiguous analytical categories. Whatever its suggestiveness, whatever its indispensability in certain practical contexts, 'identity' is too ambiguous, too torn between 'hard' and 'soft' meanings, essentialist connotations and constructivist qualifiers, to serve well the demands of social analysis.

[. . .]

'STRONG' AND 'WEAK' UNDERSTANDINGS OF 'IDENTITY'

We suggested at the outset that 'identity' tends to mean either too much or too little. This point can now be elaborated. Our inventory of the uses of 'identity' has revealed not only great heterogeneity but a strong antithesis between positions that highlight fundamental or abiding sameness and stances that expressly reject notions of basic sameness. The former can be called strong or hard conceptions of identity, the latter weak or soft conceptions.

Strong conceptions of 'identity' preserve the common-sense meaning of the term – the emphasis on sameness over time or across persons. And they accord well with the way the term is used in most forms of identity politics. But precisely because they adopt for analytical purposes a category of everyday experience and political practice, they entail a series of deeply problematic assumptions:

1. Identity is something all people have, or ought to have, or are searching for.
2. Identity is something all groups (at least groups of a certain kind – e.g., ethnic, racial, or national) have, or ought to have.

3. Identity is something people (and groups) can have without being aware of it. In this perspective, identity is something to be *discovered*, and something about which one can be *mistaken*. The strong conception of identity thus replicates the Marxian epistemology of class.

4. Strong notions of collective identity imply strong notions of group boundedness and homogeneity. They imply high degrees of groupness, an 'identity' or sameness among group members, a sharp distinctiveness from nonmembers, a clear boundary between inside and outside.[3]

Given the powerful challenges from many quarters to substantialist understandings of groups and essentialist understandings of identity, one might think we have sketched a 'straw man' here. Yet in fact strong conceptions of 'identity' continue to inform important strands of the literature on gender, race, ethnicity, and nationalism.[4]

Weak understandings of 'identity', by contrast, break consciously with the everyday meaning of the term. It is such weak or 'soft' conceptions that have been heavily favored in theoretical discussions of 'identity' in recent years, as theorists have become increasingly aware of and uncomfortable with the strong or 'hard' implications of everyday meanings of 'identity'. Yet this new theoretical 'common sense' has problems of its own. We sketch three of these.

The first is what we call 'clichéd constructivism'. Weak or soft conceptions of identity are routinely packaged with standard qualifiers indicating that identity is multiple, unstable, in flux, contingent, fragmented, constructed, negotiated, and so on. These qualifiers have become so familiar – indeed obligatory – in recent years that one reads (and writes) them virtually automatically. They risk becoming mere place-holders, gestures signaling a stance rather than words conveying a meaning.

Second, it is not clear why weak conceptions of 'identity' are conceptions *of identity*. The everyday sense of 'identity' strongly suggests at least some self-sameness over time, some persistence, something that remains identical, the same, while other things are changing. What is the point in using the term 'identity' if this core meaning is expressly repudiated?

Third, and most important, weak conceptions of identity may be *too* weak to do useful theoretical work. In their concern to cleanse the term of its theoretically disreputable 'hard' connotations, in their insistence that identities are multiple, malleable, fluid, and so on, soft identitarians leave us with a term so infinitely elastic as to be incapable of performing serious analytical work.

We are not claiming that the strong and weak versions sketched here jointly exhaust the possible meanings and uses of 'identity'. Nor are we claiming that sophisticated constructivist theorists have not done interesting and important work using 'soft' understandings of identity. We argue, however, that what is interesting and important in this work often does not depend on the use of 'identity' as an analytical category. Consider three examples.

Margaret Somers, criticizing scholarly discussions of identity for focusing on categorical commonality rather than on historically variable relational embeddedness, proposes to 'reconfigur[e] the study of identity formation through the concept of narrative', to 'incorporate into the core conception of identity the categorically destabilizing dimensions of *time, space,* and *relationality'*. Somers makes a compelling case for the importance of narrative to social life and social analysis, and argues persuasively for situating social narratives in historically specific relational settings. She focuses on the ontological dimension of narratives, on the way in which narratives not only represent but, in an important sense, constitute social actors and the social world in which they act. What remains unclear from her account is why – and in what sense – it is *identities* that are constituted through narratives and formed in particular relational settings. Social life is indeed pervasively 'storied'; but it is not clear why this 'storiedness' should be axiomatically linked to identity. People everywhere and always tell stories about themselves and others, and locate themselves within culturally available repertoires of stories. But in what sense does it follow that such 'narrative *location* endows social actors with identities – however multiple, ambiguous, ephemeral, or conflicting they may be?' What does this soft, flexible notion of identity add to the argument about narrativity? The major analytical work in Somers's article is done by the concept of narrativity, supplemented by that of relational setting; the work done by the concept of identity is much less clear.[5]

Introducing a collection on *Citizenship, Identity, and Social History,* Charles Tilly characterizes identity as a 'blurred but indispensable' concept and defines it as 'an actor's experience of a category, tie, role, network, group or organization, coupled with a public representation of that experience; the public representation often takes the form of a shared story, a narrative'. But what is the relationship between this encompassing, open-ended definition and the work Tilly wants the concept to do? What is gained, analytically, by labeling *any* experience and public representaion of *any* tie, role, network, etc. as an *identity*? When it comes to examples, Tilly rounds up the usual suspects: race, gender, class, job, religious affiliation, national origin. But it is not clear what analytical leverage on these phenomena can be provided by the exceptionally capacious, flexible concept of identity he proposes. Highlighting 'identity' in the title of the volume signals an openness to the cultural turn in the social history and historical sociology of citizenship; beyond this, it is not clear what work the concept does. Justly well-known for fashioning sharply focused, 'hard-working' concepts, Tilly here faces the difficulty that confronts most social scientists writing about identity today: that of devising a concept 'soft' and flexible enough to satisfy the requirements of relational, constructivist social theory, yet robust enough to have purchase on the phenomena that cry out for explanation, some of which are quite 'hard'.[6]

Craig Calhoun uses the Chinese student movement of 1989 as a vehicle for a subtle and illuminating discussion of the concepts of identity, interest, and collective action. Calhoun explains students' readiness to 'knowingly risk death' in Tiananmen Square on the night of June 3, 1989 in terms of an honor-bound identity or sense of self, forged in the course of the movement itself, to which students became increasingly and, in the end, irrevocably committed. His account of the shifts in the students' lived sense of self during the weeks of their protest – as they were drawn, in and through the dynamics of their struggle, from an originally 'positional', class-based self-understanding as students and intellectuals to a broader, emotionally charged identification with national and even universal ideals – is a compelling one. Here too, however, the crucial analytical work appears to be done by a concept other than identity – in this case, that of honor. Honor, Calhoun observes, is 'imperative in a way interests are not'. But it is also imperative in a way *identity*, in the weak sense, is not. Calhoun subsumes honor under the rubric of identity, and presents his argument as a general one about the 'constitution and transformation of identity'. Yet his fundamental argument in this article, it would seem, is not about identity in general, but about the way in which a compelling sense of honor can, in extraordinary circumstances, lead people to undertake extraordinary actions, lest their core sense of self be radically undermined.[7]

Identity in this exceptionally strong sense – as a sense of self that can imperatively require interest-threatening or even life-threatening action has little to do with identity in the weak or soft sense. Calhoun himself underscores the incommensurability between 'ordinary identity self-conceptions, the way people reconcile interests in everyday life' and the imperative, honor-driven sense of self that can enable or even require people to be 'brave to the point of apparent foolishness'.[8] Calhoun provides a powerful characterization of the latter; but it is not clear what analytical work is done by the former, more general conception of identity.

In his edited volume on *Social Theory and the Politics of Identity*, Calhoun works with this more general understanding of identity. 'Concerns with individual and collective identity', he observes, 'are ubiquitous'. It is certainly true that '[we] know of no people without names, no languages or cultures in which some manner of distinctions between self and other, we and they are not made'.[9] But it is not clear why this implies the ubiquity of identity, unless we dilute 'identity' to the point of designating *all* practices involving naming and self-other distinctions. Calhoun – like Somers and Tilly – goes on to make illuminating arguments on a range of issues concerning claims of commonality and difference in contemporary social movements. Yet while such claims are indeed often framed today is an idiom of 'identity', it is not clear that adopting that idiom for *analytical* purposes is necessary or even helpful.

IN OTHER WORDS

What alternative terms might stand in for 'identity', doing the theoretical work 'identity' is supposed to do without its confusing, contradictory connotations? Given the great range and heterogeneity of the work done by 'identity', it would be fruitless to look for a *single* substitute, for such a term would be as overburdened as 'identity' itself. Our strategy has been rather to unbundle the thick tangle of meanings that have accumulated around the term 'identity', and to parcel out the work to a number of less congested terms. We sketch three clusters of terms here.

Identification and categorization

As a processual, active term, derived from a verb, 'identification' lacks the reifying connotations of 'identity'.[10] It invites us to specify the agents that do the identifying. And it does not presuppose that such identifying (even by powerful agents, such as the state) will necessarily result in the internal sameness, the distinctiveness, the bounded groupness that political entrepreneurs may seek to achieve. Identification – of oneself and of others – is intrinsic to social life; 'identity' in the strong sense is not.

One may be called upon to identify oneself – to characterize oneself, to locate oneself vis-à-vis known others, to situate oneself in a narrative, to place oneself in a category – in any number of different contexts. In modern settings, which multiply interactions with others not personally known, such occasions for identification are particularly abundant. They include innumerable situations of everyday life as well as more formal and official contexts. How one identifies oneself – and how one is identified by others – may vary greatly from context to context; self- and other-identification are fundamentally situational and contextual.

One key distinction is between *relational* and *categorical* modes of identification. One may identify oneself (or another person) by position in a relational web (a web of kinship, for example, or of friendship, patron–client ties, or teacher–student relations). On the other hand, one may identify oneself (or another person) by membership in a class of persons sharing some categorical attribute (such as race, ethnicity, language, nationality, citizenship, gender, sexual orientation, etc.). Craig Calhoun has argued that, while relational modes of identification remain important in many contexts even today, categorical identification has assumed ever greater importance in modern settings.[11]

Another basic distinction is between self-identification and the identification and categorization of oneself by others.[12] Self-identification takes place in dialectical interplay with external identification, and the two need not converge.[13] External identification is itself a varied process. In the ordinary ebb and flow of social life, people identify and categorize others, just as they identify and categorize themselves. But there is another key type of external identification that has no counterpart in the domain of self-identification: the formalized, codified, objectified systems of categorization developed by powerful, authoritative institutions.

The modern state has been one of the most important agents of identification and categorization in this latter sense. In culturalist extensions of the Weberian sociology of the state, notably those influenced by Bourdieu and Foucault, the state monopolizes, or seeks to monopolize, not only legitimate physical force but also legitimate symbolic force, as Bourdieu puts it. This includes the power to name, to identify, to categorize, to state what is what and who is who. There is a burgeoning sociological and historical literature on such subjects. Some scholars have looked at 'identification' quite literally: as the attachment of definitive markers to an individual via passport, fingerprint, photograph, and signature, and the amassing of such identifying documents in state repositories. When, why, and with what limitations such systems have been developed turns out to be no simple problem.[14] Other scholars emphasize the modern state's efforts to inscribe its subjects onto a classificatory grid: to identify and categorize people in relation to gender, religion, property-ownership, ethnicity, literacy, criminality, or sanity. Censuses apportion people across these categories, and institutions – from schools to prisons – sort out individuals in relation to them. To Foucauldians in particular, these individualizing and aggregating modes of identification and classification are at the core of what defines 'governmentality' in a modern state.[15]

The state is thus a powerful 'identifier', not because it can create 'identities' in the strong sense – in general, it cannot – but because it has the material and symbolic resources to impose the categories, classificatory schemes, and modes of social counting and accounting with which bureaucrats, judges, teachers, and doctors must work and to which non-state actors must refer.[16] But the state is not the only 'identifier' that matters. As Charles Tilly has shown, categorization does crucial 'organizational work' in all kinds of social settings, including families, firms, schools, social movements, and bureaucracies of all kinds.[17] Even the most powerful state does not monopolize the production and diffusion of identifications and categories; and those that it does produce may be contested. The literature on social movements – 'old' as well as 'new' – is rich in evidence on how movement leaders challenge official identifications and propose alternative ones.[18] It highlights leaders' efforts to get members of putative constituencies to identify themselves in a certain way, to see themselves – for a certain range of purposes – as 'identical' with one another, to identify emotionally as well as cognitively with one another.[19]

The social movement literature has valuably emphasized the interactive, discursively mediated processes through which collective solidarities and self-understandings develop. Our reservations concern the move from discussing the work of identification – the efforts to build a collective self-understanding – to positing 'identity' as their necessary result. By considering authoritative, institutionalized modes of identification together with alternative modes involved in the practices of everyday life and the projects of social movements, one can emphasize the hard work and long struggles over identification as well as the uncertain outcomes of such struggles. However, if the outcome is always presumed to be an 'identity' – however provisional, fragmented, multiple, contested, and fluid – one loses the capacity to make key distinctions.

'Identification', we noted above, invites specification of the agents that do the identifying. Yet identification does not *require* a specifiable 'identifier'; it can be pervasive and influential without being accomplished by discrete, specified persons or institutions. Identification can be carried more or less anonymously by discourses or public narratives.[20] Although close analysis of such discourses or narratives might well focus on their instantiations in particular discursive or narrative utterances, their force may depend not on any particular instantiation but on their anonymous, unnoticed permeation of our ways of thinking and talking and making sense of the social world.

There is one further meaning of 'identification', briefly alluded to above, that is largely independent of the cognitive, characterizing, classificatory meanings discussed so far. This is the psychodynamic meaning, derived originally from Freud.[21] While the classificatory meanings involve identifying oneself (or someone else) *as* someone who fits a certain description or belongs to a certain category, the psychodynamic meaning involves identifying oneself emotionally *with* another person, category, or collectivity. Here again, 'identification' calls attention to complex (and often ambivalent) *processes*, while the term 'identity', designating a *condition* rather than a *process*, implies too easy a fit between the individual and the social.

Self-understanding and social location

'Identification' and 'categorization' are active, processual terms, derived from verbs, and calling to mind particular acts of identification and categorization performed by particular identifiers and categorizers. But we need other kinds of terms as well to do the varied work done by 'identity'. Recall that one key use of 'identity' is to conceptualize and explain action in a non-instrumental, non-mechanial manner. In this sense, the term suggests ways in which individual and collective action can be governed by particularistic understandings of self and social location rather than by putatively universal, structurally determined interests. 'Self-understanding' is therefore the second term we would propose as an alternative to 'identity'. It is a dispositional term that designates what might be called 'situated subjectivity':

one's sense of who one is, of one's social location, and of how (given the first two) one is prepared to act. As a dispositional term, it belongs to the realm of what Pierre Bourdieu has called *sens pratique*, the practical sense – at once cognitive and emotional – that persons have of themselves and their social world.[22]

The term 'self-understanding', it is important to emphasize, does not imply a distinctively modern or Western understanding of the 'self' as a homogeneous, bounded, unitary entity. A sense of who one is can take many forms. The social processes through which persons understand and locate themselves may in some instances involve the psychoanalyst's couch and in others participation in spirit-possession cults.[23] In some settings, people may understand and experience themselves in terms of a grid of intersecting categories; in others, in terms of a web of connections of differential proximity and intensity. Hence the importance of seeing self-understanding and social locatedness in relation to each other, and of emphasizing that both the bounded self and the bounded group are culturally specific rather than universal forms.

Like the term 'identification', 'self-understanding' lacks the reifying connotations of 'identity'. Yet it is not restricted to situations of flux and instability. Self-understandings may be variable across time and across persons, but they may be stable. Semantically, 'identity' implies sameness across time or persons; hence the awkwardness of continuing to speak of 'identity' while repudiating the implication of sameness. 'Self-understanding', by contrast, has no privileged semantic connection with sameness *or* difference.

Two closely related terms are 'self-representation' and 'self-identification'. Having discussed 'identification' above, we simply observe here that, while the distinction is not sharp, 'self-understandings' may be tacit; even when they are formed, as they ordinarily are, in and through prevailing discourses, they may exist, and inform action, without themselves being discursively articulated. 'Self-representation' and 'self-identification', on the other hand, suggest at least some degree of explicit discursive articulation.

'Self-understanding' cannot, of course, do *all* the work done by 'identity'. We note here three limitations of the term. First, it is a subjective, auto-referential term. As such, it designates *one's own* understanding of who one is. It cannot capture *others'* understandings, even though external categorizations, identifications, and representations may be decisive in determining how one is regarded and treated by others, indeed in shaping one's own understanding of oneself. At the limit, self-understandings may be overridden by overwhelmingly coercive external categorizations.[24]

Second, 'self-understanding' would seem to privilege cognitive awareness. As a result, it would seem not to capture – or at least not to highlight – the affective or cathectic processes suggested by some uses of 'identity'. Yet self-understanding is never purely cognitive; it is always affectively tinged or charged, and the term can certainly accommodate this affective dimension.

However, it is true that the emotional *dynamics* are better captured by the term 'identification' (in its psychodynamic meaning).

Finally, as a term that emphasizes situated subjectivity, 'self-understanding' does not capture the objectivity claimed by strong understandings of identity. Strong, objectivist conceptions of identity permit one to distinguish 'true' identity (characterized as deep, abiding, and objective) from 'mere' self-understanding (superficial, fluctuating, and subjective). If identity is something to be discovered, and something about which one can be mistaken, then one's momentary self-understanding may not correspond to one's abiding, underlying identity. However analytically problematic these notions of depth, constancy, and objectivity may be, they do at least provide a reason for using the language of identity rather than that of self-understanding.

Weak conceptions of identity provide no such reason. It is clear from the constructivist literature why weak understandings of identity are *weak*; but it is not clear why they are conceptions *of identity*. In this literature, it is the various *soft predicates* of identity – constructedness, contingency, instability, multiplicity, fluidity – that are emphasized and elaborated, while what they are predicated *of* – identity itself – is taken for granted and seldom explicated. When identity itself is elucidated, it is often represented as something – a sense of who one is,[25] a self-conception,[26] – that can be captured in a straightforward way by 'self-understanding'. This term lacks the allure, the buzz, the theoretical pretensions of 'identity', but this should count as an asset, not a liability.

Commonality, connectedness, groupness

One particular form of affectively charged self-understanding that is often designated by 'identity' – especially in discussions of race, religion, ethnicity, nationalism, gender, sexuality, social movements, and other phenomena conceptualized as involving *collective* identities – deserves separate mention here. This is the emotionally laden sense of belonging to a distinctive, bounded group, involving both a felt solidarity or oneness with fellow group members and a felt difference from or even antipathy to specified outsiders.

The problem is that 'identity' is used to designate *both* such strongly groupist, exclusive, affectively charged self-understandings *and* much looser, more open self-understandings, involving some sense of affinity or affiliation, commonality or connectedness to particular others, but lacking a sense of overriding oneness vis-à-vis some constitutive 'other'.[27] Both the tightly groupist and the more loosely affiliative forms of self-understanding – as well as the transitional forms between these polar types – are important, but they shape personal experience and condition social and political action in sharply differing ways.

Rather than stirring all self-understandings based on race, religion, ethnicity, and so on into the great conceptual melting pot of 'identity', we would do better to use a more differentiated analytical language. Terms such as commonality, connectedness, and groupness could be usefully employed here in place of the all-purpose 'identity'. This is the third cluster of terms we propose. 'Commonality' denotes the sharing of some common attribute, 'connectedness' the relational ties that link people. Neither commonality nor connectedness alone engenders 'groupness' – the sense of belonging to a distinctive, bounded, solidary group. But commonality and connectedness together may indeed do so. This was the argument Charles Tilly put forward some time ago, building on Harrison White's idea of the 'catnet', a set of persons comprising both a *category*, sharing some common attribute, and a *network*.[28] Tilly's suggestion that groupness is a joint product of the 'catness' and 'netness' – categorical commonality and relational connectedness – is suggestive. But we would propose two emendations.

First, categorical commonality and relational connectedness need to be supplemented by a third element, what Max Weber called a *Zusammengehörigkeitsgefühl*, a feeling of belonging together. Such a feeling may indeed depend in part on the degrees and forms of commonality and connectedness, but it will also depend on other factors such as particular events, their encoding in compelling public narratives, prevailing discursive frames, and so on. Second, relational connectedness, or what Tilly calls 'netness', while crucial in facilitating the sort of collective action Tilly was interested in, is not always necessary for 'groupness'. A strongly bounded sense of groupness may rest on categorical commonality and an associated feeling of belonging together with minimal or no relational connectedness. This is typically the case for large-scale collectivities such as 'nations': when a diffuse self-understanding as a member of a particular nation crystallizes into a strongly bounded sense of groupness, this is likely to depend not on relational connectedness, but rather on a powerfully imagined and strongly felt commonality.[29]

The point is not, as some partisans of network theory have suggested, to turn from commonality to connectedness, from categories to networks, from shared attributes to social relations.[30] Nor is it to celebrate fluidity and hybridity over belonging and solidarity. The point in suggesting this last set of terms is rather to develop an analytical idiom sensitive to the multiple forms and degrees of commonality and connectedness, and to the widely varying ways in which actors (and the cultural idioms, public narratives, and prevailing discourses on which they draw) attribute meaning and significance to them. This will enable us to distinguish instances of strongly binding, vehemently felt groupness from more loosely structured, weakly constraining forms of affinity and affiliation.

NOTES

1. From 'Politics and the English Language,' in George Orwell, *A Collection of Essays* (New York: Harcourt Brace, 1953), 169–170.

2. For a tempered critique of identity politics, see Todd Gitlin, *The Twilight of Common Dreams: Why America Is Wracked by Culture Wars* (New York: Henry Holt, 1995), and for a sophisticated defense, Robin D. G. Kelley, *Yo' Mama's Disfunktional!: Fighting the Culture Wars in Urban America* (Boston: Beacon, 1997). For a suggestion that the high noon of identity politics may have passed, see Ross Posnock, 'Before and After Identity Politics,' *Raritan* 15 (Summer 1995): 95–115; and David A. Hollinger, 'Nationalism, Cosmopolitanism, and the United States,' in Noah Pickus, editor, *Immigration and Citizenship in the Twenty-first Century* (Lanham, MD: Rowman Littlefield, 1998).

3. Avrum Stroll, 'Identity,' *Encyclopedia of Philosophy* (New York: MacMillan, 1967), Vol. IV, p. 121–124. For a contemporary philosophical treatment, see Bartholomaeus Boehm, *Identitaet und Identifikation: Zur Persistenz physikalischer Gegenstaende* (Frankfurth/Main: Peter Lang, 1989). On the history and vicissitudes of 'identity' and cognate terms, see W. J. M. Mackenzie, *Political Identity* (New York: St. Martin's 1978), 19–27, and John D. Ely, 'Community and the Politics of Identity: Toward the Genealogy of a Nation-State Concept,' *Stanford Humanities Review* 5/2 (1997), 76ff.

4. See Philip Gleason, 'Identifying Identity: A Semantic History,' *Journal of American History* 69/4 (March 1983): 910–931. The 1930s *Encyclopedia of the Social Sciences* (New York: Macmillan: 1930–1935) contains no entry on identity, but it does have one on 'identification' – largely focused on fingerprinting and other modes of judicial marking of individuals (Thorstein Sellin, Vol. 7, pp. 573–575). The 1968 *International Encyclopedia of the Social Sciences* (New York: Macmillan), contains an article on 'identification, political' by William Buchanan (Vol. 7, pp. 57–61), which focuses on a 'person's identification with a group' – including class, party, religion – and another on 'identity, psychosocial,' by Erik Erikson (ibid., 61–65), which focuses on the individual's 'role integration in his group.'

5. Gleason, 'Identifying Identity,' 914ff; for the appropriation of Erikson's work in political science, see Mackenzie, *Political Identity*.

6. Gleason, 'Identifying Identity, 915–918.

7. Anselm Strauss, *Mirrors and Masks: The Search for an Identity* (Glencoe, Ill.: Free Press, 1959).

8. Erving Goffman, *Stigma: Notes on the Management of Spoiled Identity* (Englewood Cliffs, N.J.: Prentice-Hall, 1963); Peter Berger and Thomas Luckmann, *The Social Construction of Reality* (Garden City, NY: Doubleday, 1966); Peter Berger, Brigitte Berger, and Hansfried Kellner, *The Homeless Mind: Modernization and Consciousness* (New York: Random House, 1973); Peter Berger, 'Modern Identity: Crisis and Continuity,' in *The Cultural Drama: Modern Identities and Social Ferment*, ed. Wilton S. Dillon (Washington: Smithsonian Institution Press, 1974).

9. As Philip Gleason has pointed out, the popularization of the term began well before the turbulence of the mid- and late 1960s. Gleason attributes this initial popularization to the mid-century prestige and cognitive authority of the social sciences, the wartime and postwar vogue of national character studies, and the postwar critique of mass society, which newly problematized the 'relationship of the individual to society' ('Identifying Identity,' 922ff).

10. On the merits of 'identification', see Stuart Hall, 'Who Needs "Identity?"', in Stuart Hall and Paul Du Gay, editors, *Questions of Cultural Identity* (London: Sage, 1996). Although Hall's is a Foucauldian/post-Freudian understanding of 'identification', drawing on the 'discursive and psychoanalytic repertoire', and quite different from that proposed here, he does usefully warn that identification is 'almost as tricky as, though preferable to, 'identity' itself; and certainly no guarantee against the

conceptual difficulties which have beset the latter' (p. 2). See also Andreas Glaeser, 'Divided in Unity: The Hermeneutics of Self and Other in the Postunification Berlin Police' (Ph.D. Dissertation, Harvard University, 1997), esp. chapter 1.

11. Craig Calhoun, *Nationalism* (Minneapolis: University of Minnesota Press, 1997), 36ff.

12. For an anthropological perspective, usefully extending the Barthian model, see Richard Jenkins, 'Rethinking Ethnicity: Identity, Categorization and Power', *Ethnic and Racial Studies* 17/2 (April 1994): 197–223, and Jenkins, *Social Identity* (London and New York: Routledge, 1996).

13. Peter Berger, 'Modern Identity', 163–164, makes a similar point, though he phrases it in terms of a dialectic – and possible conflict – between subjective and objective identity.

14. Gerard Noiriel, *La tyrannie du national* (Paris: Calmann-Lévy, 1991), 155–180; idem, 'L'identification des citoyens: Naissance de l'état civil republicain', *Genèses* 13 (1993): 3–28; idem, 'Surveiller des déplacements ou identifier les personnes? Contribution à l'histoire du passeport en France de la Ier à la III République', *Genèses* 30 (1998): 77–100; Béatrice Fraenkel, *La signature: genèse d'un signe* (Paris: Gallimard, 1992). A number of scholars, including Jane Caplan, historian at Bryn Mawr College, and John Torpey, sociologist at University of California, Irvine, are currently engaged in projects on passports and other identification documents.

15. Michel Foucault, 'Governmentality', in Graham Burchell et al., editors, *The Foucault Effect: Studies in Governmentality* (Chicago: University of Chicago Press, 1991), 87–104. Similar conceptions have been applied to colonial societies, especially in regard to the way colonizers' schemes for classification and enumeration shape and indeed constitute the social phenomena (such as 'tribe' and 'caste' in India) being classified. See, in particular, Bernard Cohn, *Colonialism and Its Forms of Knowledge: The British in India* (Princeton: Princeton University Press, 1996).

16. On the dilemmas, difficulties, and ironies involved in 'administering identity', in authoritatively determining who belongs to what category in the implementation of race-conscious law, see Christopher A. Ford, 'Administering Identity: The Determination of 'Race' in Race-Conscious Law', *California Law Review* 82 (1994): 1231–1285.

17. Charles Tilly, Durable Inequality (Berkeley: University of California Press, 1998).

18. Melissa Nobles, ' "Responding with Good Sense" ': The Politics of Race and Censuses in Contemporary Brazil', Ph.D. Dissertation, Yale University, 1995.

19. See, for example, A. Melucci, 'The Process of Collective Identity', in Hank Johnston and Bert Klandermanns, editors, *Social Movements and Culture* (London: UCL Press, 1995); Denis-Constant Martin, 'The Choices of Identity', *Social Identities* 1/1 (1995): 5–20.

20. Stuart Hall, 'Introduction: Who Needs "Identity?" '; Margaret Somers, 'The Narrative Constitution of Identity', *Theory and Society* 23 (1994), 605–649.

21. See Hall, 'Introduction', 2ff; and Alan Finlayson, 'Psychology, psychoanalysis and theories of nationalism', *Nations and Nationalism* 4/2 (1998): 157ff.

22. Pierre Bourdieu, *The Logic of Practice*, trans. Richard Nice (Cambridge: Polity Press, 1990).

23. An extensive anthropological literature on African and other societies, for example, describes healing cults, spirit possession cults, witchcraft eradication movements, and other collective phenomena that help to constitute particular forms of self-understanding, particular ways in which individuals situate themselves socially. See studies ranging from classics by Victor Turner, *Schism and Continuity in an African Society: A Study of Ndembu Village Life* (Manchester: Manchester University Press, 1957) and I. M. Lewis, *Ecstatic Religion: An Anthropological Study of Spirit Possession and Shamanism* (Harmondsworth, U.K.: Penguin, 1971) to more recent work by Paul Stoller, *Fusion of the Worlds: An Ethnography of Possession*

among the Songhay of Niger (Chicago: University of Chicago Press, 1989) and Janice Boddy, *Wombs and Alien Spirits: Women, Men and The Zar Cult in Northern Sudan* (Madison: University of Wisconsin Press, 1989).

24. For a poignant example, see Slavenka Drakulic's account of being 'overcome by nationhood' as a result of the war in the former Yugoslavia, in *Balkan Express: Fragments from the Other Side of the War*, trans. Maja Soljan (New York: W. W. Norton, 1993), 50–52.

25. See, for example, Peter Berger, 'Modern Identity: Crisis and Continuity', 162.

26. See, for example, Craig Calhoun, 'The Problem of Identity in Collective Action', in Joan Huber, editor, *Macro-Micro Linkages in Sociology* (Beverly Hills: Sage, 1991), 68, characterizing 'ordinary identity'.

27. For a good example of the latter, see Mary Waters's analysis of the optional, exceptionally unconstraining ethnic 'identities' – or what Herbert Gans has called the 'symbolic ethnicity' – of third- and fourth-generation descendants of European Catholic immigrants to the United States in *Ethnic Options: Choosing Identities in America* (Berkeley: University of California Press, 1990).

28. Charles Tilly, *From Mobilization to Revolution* (Reading, Mass.: Addison-Wesley, 1978), 62ff.

29. On the centrality of categorical commonality to modern nationalism, see Richard Handler, *Nationalism and the Politics of Culture in Quebec* (Madison: University of Wisconsin Press, 1988), and Calhoun, *Nationalism*, chapter 2.

30. See, for example, the discussion of the 'anti-categorical imperative' in Mustafa Emirbayer and Jeff Goodwin, 'Network Analysis, Culture, and the Problem of Agency', *American Journal of Sociology* 99/6 (May 1994): 1414.

4

GLOBALISATION

Debbie Lisle

Introduction

Globalisation is simultaneously one of the easiest and most difficult political concepts to understand. It is *easy* because all of us have an implicit sense of what is meant by globalisation: a McDonald's restaurant in every city; the deployment of UN peacekeepers; a televised World Cup final watched by billions of people; the destruction of the ozone layer; global pandemics such as AIDS; using the internet and e-mail; the plight of millions of refugees; buying a Coke anywhere in the world; the human genome project; participating in anti-war demonstrations; the business strategies of multinational companies such as Sony and Microsoft; and the global recognition of cultural icons such as Madonna, Princess Diana and Nelson Mandela. While it is easy to make such lists about globalisation, it is difficult to make any coherent or analytical sense of these diverse phenomena. How can one term include both Madonna and ozone layer depletion? This is precisely the difficulty with globalisation – we *implicitly* know what it means, but we find it very difficult to be *explicit* about that meaning. In many ways, this confusion arises because globalisation has become a catch-all term for contemporary life – it is used to explain everything from debt levels in Africa to the latest trends in high-street fashion. Often, the imprecise use of 'globalisation' obscures its political importance, and allows us to ignore how the forces of globalisation have produced the most pressing political problems we currently face.

In order to reveal the political importance of globalisation, this essay does five things. Firstly, it presents some of the current definitions and explanations of globalisation in order to establish the foundations of this concept. Secondly, it illustrates how globalisation has transformed our understanding of fundamental categories such as space, time and identity. Thirdly, it introduces the main questions that shape the study and practice of globalisation – keeping in mind that these questions are constantly being fought over in academia, in the public sphere, in pubs and living rooms, and in government circles. Fourthly, it illustrates how those questions are playing out in both the main issue areas of globalisation (economics, politics and culture) as well as more specific areas such as the environment. Lastly, the paper introduces and explains two selected readings that will help illustrate the concept of globalisation and give you a greater understanding of the issues at stake.

DEFINING GLOBALISATION

Given the implicit sense we all have of globalisation, it is no wonder that a concrete definition is hard to come by. While the term 'globalisation' emerged in the 1960s, it was only widely understood as a social and political phenomenon starting in the mid-1980s (Scholte 2001a: 44–5; Waters 1995: 2). It was at this point that a more intense kind of global interconnectedness 'captured the public imagination' such that the term 'globalisation' became widely used (Held and McGrew 2000: 1). This does not mean that relations between people across the globe only started in the 1980s – if that was the case, we could not explain important global historical phenomena such as the Roman Empire, voyages of discovery and the slave trade. However, the widespread acceptance of the term 'globalisation' was a recognition that contemporary global relations were intensifying on a variety of levels in a variety of ways. It was no longer simply trade, diplomacy and war that produced global connections; it was also less obvious things such as tourism, television, sporting events and e-mail.

Despite the popular acceptance of the term, David Held and Anthony McGrew are right to suggest that no single definition of globalisation exists, just as Jan Aarte Scholte is right to worry that globalisation has become a shorthand 'buzzword' for everything under the sun (Held and McGrew 2000; Scholte 2001a). The concerns of these authors signal the three main difficulties in attempting to define globalisation. Firstly, as I have indicated, it is impossible to include such diverse phenomena in a single definition. Secondly, it is impossible to provide an 'objective' definition of a process that affects every person on the planet – including the intellectuals, academics, journalists and politicians who construct definitions. Very simply, nobody can stand outside of globalisation in order to provide a coherent definition for it. Often, these difficulties of defining globalisation make us shy away from what is at stake here, namely, the unequal operation of power across the globe that can cause as much joy as it does misery. And this is the third difficulty in defining globalisation: embedded in each definition of globalisation are *normative* concerns, that is, concerns about how globalisation should work (Held and McGrew 2000: 3–8). We know that globalisation affects every person on the planet; however, any worthwhile study must be explicit about the damages, injustices and inequalities that are caused by the forces of globalisation. For example, there is a huge difference between the benefits received by the shareholders of a major multinational corporation (MNC) and the often violent constraints imposed on refugees, asylum-seekers and migrant workers. The forces of globalisation are affecting both, but the effects of those forces are radically different. It is this lack of universality in the experience of globalisation – the gross inequality of effects – that makes a coherent and objective definition of globalisation impossible.

For these reasons, scholars use 'working definitions' of globalisation in order to highlight the contested nature of the term, and the impossibility of reaching any consensus on the subject. With this in mind, the following working definition simplifies and explains what is generally understood by globalisation: 'the process of increasing interconnectedness between societies such that events in one part of the world more and more have effects on peoples and societies far away' (Baylis and Smith 2001: 7). While this emphasises the 'interconnectedness' of political and social relations across the world, it does not provide an adequate sense of the particular characteristics of globalisation. Held expands on this general definition and suggests that globalisation involves three interlinked processes: stretching, intensification and deepening (Held 2000: 15–16). Political relations are now stretched across the world in such a way that they penetrate the boundaries of the nation-state and local communities. In this sense, our interactions are made up of networks that span the entire globe. The relations that occur within and through these networks have become intensified, that is, we are using them more and more. For example, globalisation is not just about material developments (e.g. the technology of computers), but also about our everyday practices (e.g. the fact that we use computers every day to send billions of e-mails around the world). For Held, globalisation is characterised by a fundamental shift from horizontal relations between nation-states to a deepening of relations between the local and the global. Local sites are penetrated by global products (e.g. exotic foods at your local supermarket) and global sites are penetrated by local traditions (e.g. *British Airways* adorned their aeroplanes with local art from around the world). Whenever we explain globalisation, we need to take account of the increased interconnectedness of the world, how those networks of interconnection have been *stretched* across the globe, how they are being used *intensively* by people, and how they indicate a *deep* relation between local and global sites.

TRANSFORMING SPACE, TIME AND IDENTITY

Globalisation has had a profound effect on the fundamental categories we use to make sense of modern life, namely, space, time and identity. How can we distinguish between 'here' and 'there' when the boundaries between these spaces are collapsing? For example, how can citizens of the UK cling to outdated notions of 'Britishness' when they regularly eat at curry houses, drive Japanese cars, support 'local' football teams made up of international players, and live beside a group of Kurdish asylum-seekers? How can we distinguish between now and then when the time it takes to get anywhere and do anything has become so *speedy*? How can we estimate the tangible assets of a company when billions of dollars can be moved around the globe at the click of a mouse? Most importantly, how can we make sense of our communities, our homes and ourselves when traditional boundaries of identity and loyalty are breaking down? For example, how can a person consider herself *primarily* French when she is sustained and fulfilled by a community of other feminists scattered across the globe, rather than by individuals in her local neighbourhood or town? Re-thinking these three fundamental categories leads many scholars to place globalisation within wider debates about modernity and postmodernity. Do the forces of globalisation indicate a fundamental break with modern life, or are they a continuation of modernity in a different guise (Harvey 1989; Appadurai 1990; Giddens 1990; Jameson 1991; Lash and Urry 1994; King 1995; Albrow 1996; Scott 1997)?

One of the easiest ways to conceptualise globalisation is spatially – it seems common sense to suggest that the world is becoming a smaller place. In fact, some scholars argue that globalisation has led to the end of geography altogether: various technological developments such as speedy air travel and e-mail have reduced the distances between here and there to such an extent that these distances no longer matter. This is not to say that the *actual* space of the globe has changed but, rather, to argue that our understandings of, and interactions with, global space have been transformed. As Held's formulation suggests, this spatial reconfiguration is about the relationships currently being forged between the local and the global (2000: 16). These are no longer opposite ends of a spectrum but, rather, intricately tied to one another in a variety of ways. Think of the cliché that the beating of a butterfly's wings in the Amazon can have an effect on weather patterns across the world, or the bumper sticker that reads 'Think Globally, Act Locally'. These new relationships have prompted many scholars to speak of globalisation in terms of the 'local–global nexus', or to transform the term into 'glocalisation' (Robertson 1995; Wilson and Dissanayake 1996; Cvetkovich and Kellner 1997; Eade 1997).

The biggest difficulty in this reconfiguration of fundamental modern categories is whether space and time are moving closer together or farther apart. David Harvey argues that globalisation and postmodernity are characterised by 'time-space compression', that is, the collapse of separate notions of space and time (1989). Crucially, he points to the development of the mechanical clock, which meant that time was understood as linear (past, present, future) and also universal (everyone on the globe can be positioned at some point on the 24-hour clock). For Harvey, this meant that time effectively *annihilated* space. As Malcolm Waters explains, the resulting 'time-space compression' can be felt through developments in technology:

> If people in Tokyo can experience the same thing at the same time as others in Helsinki, say a business transaction or a media event, then they in effect live in the same place, space has been annihilated by time compression (Waters 1995: 55).

In contrast to Harvey, Anthony Giddens argues that time and space remain separate things in globalisation, and are in fact moving farther apart. Giddens argues that globalisation is characterised by 'time-space distanciation'; that is, when both time and space are 'stretched' across the world, they lose something meaningful in the process. He is especially concerned with how this process leads to 'disembedding' – when social relations are 'lifted out' of their local context and restructured across time and space (1990: 21). Disembedding is a problem for Giddens because it prevents the opportunity for authentic 'face-to-face' encounters.

Neither of these approaches to space and time – either crashing together or exploding apart – can ignore the way that both have been reconfigured by *speed*. As Paul Virilio argues, technological developments such as satellites, telecommunications and computing have fundamentally altered our relationship to, and experience of, space and time (Virilio 1986). We usually understand space and time as fixed, static and linear. However, as life and technology move at increasing speeds, these spatiotemporal understandings evaporate. For Virilio, we are living in an 'instantaneous present' where it is impossible to distinguish between what is real and what is simulated. This last point highlights one of the reasons why globalisation is so contentious: it challenges the status of reality itself. No wonder we feel so disoriented – if our usual anchors of space and time have been transformed, we can no longer locate things according to a fixed grid of here/there, or then/now. However, this feeling of disorientation is not necessarily constraining. In fact, the disorientation of globalisation has given way to an important change in collective consciousness. Think of how surprising it must have been to see the first global satellite images of the earth beamed back from the Apollo space missions in the 1960s. This were the first tangible image of global humanity: it solidified the idea that we are all living in a single place. Those images, coupled with Marshall McLuhan's idea of the 'global village', were the first time that modern technology helped to make the concept of globalisation real for millions of people (McLuhan 1964).

For many scholars, the emergence of a global consciousness is the most persuasive evidence that the current phase of globalisation is qualitatively different from earlier phases. Indeed, this idea is central to Roland

Robertson's famous definition of globalisation as 'a concept that refers both to the compression of the world and the intensification of consciousness of the world as a whole' (1992: 8). For Robertson, global consciousness has profound effects on how individuals see themselves and their attachments to the world. Globalisation redefines the individual as a 'complete person', that is, not subordinate to wider political structures. As globalisation takes hold, individuals are forced to conceive of themselves in wider terms – simultaneously within the competing spheres of local community, nation-state and global order. This leads Robertson to argue that individuals are now conceiving of themselves in terms of a common humanity – the widest grouping within which one can find meaning, community and belonging regardless of class, gender, race, culture etc. Perhaps the easiest way to conceive of this change in consciousness is to think about how each individual has multiple sites within which he/she finds meaning, belonging and community. For example, members of the Jewish diaspora might share their political loyalties between the state of Israel and their chosen homeland; a Greenpeace activist might find a virtual community with other activists from all over the globe; a Muslim from Indonesia might make the journey to Mecca and discover an instant community with other Muslims; a clubber from New York might find other like-minded souls in the night-clubs of Ibiza, Rio, London or Sydney; and a feminist from Manila might be inspired to start her own political movement after reading about the Northern Ireland Woman's Coalition. While our identities and loyalties used to be shaped primarily by the family, the local community and the nation, the emergence of a global consciousness means that we now have multiple identities and loyalties, some of which are articulated through the category of humanity.

GLOBAL QUESTIONS

If things are moving at an unprecedented speed, if space and time have taken on new formulations, if our sense of meaning and belonging cannot be confined to traditional structures such as families and states, it becomes difficult to locate what might be political about all of these transformations. How can we work out the politics of global life – who is getting excluded, exploited, silenced – when the categories and boundaries of modern life are themselves transforming? As Jan Nederveen Pieterse suggests, globalisation can produce complex, hybrid and bewildering novelties:

> How do we come to terms with phenomena such as Thai boxing by Moroccan girls in Amsterdam, Asian rap in London, Irish bagels, Chinese tacos and Mardi Gras Indians in the United States . . . How do we interpret Peter Brook directing the Mahabharata, or Adriane Manouchkine staging a Shakespeare play in Japanese Kabuki style for a Paris audience in the Theatre Soleil? (Pieterse 1995: 53)

In order to politicise globalisation, it is necessary to work out how all these 'novelties' are directed and shaped by wider structures of power. For example, what formations of power prevent refugees from having the same freedom of movement as Western tourists? But this task is a difficult one. Because globalisation introduces phenomena we have never encountered before, it forces us to question the normative and ethical foundations of our explanatory categories. The difficulties of defining globalisation are instructive here. To even discuss globalisation – to explain or understand it – always involves a series of judgements. We cannot discuss globalisation without using value-laden language, without revealing our normative claims about how we think the world should be. With this in mind, there are a series of normative questions that are always implicit in any discussion of globalisation – whether those engaging with the discussion are aware of it or not. Therefore, before we discuss *what* is happening in globalisation, we need to confront the following questions:

- Is globalisation good or bad?
- Is globalisation a new phenomenon, or is it just the newest phase of something that has been going on for a long time (e.g. modernity or capitalism)?
- To what extent is globalisation destroying the nation-state?
- Is globalisation producing one world (making us all the same) or many worlds (emphasising our differences)?
- Is globalisation just another name for Western domination?

It remains to be seen *how* these questions shape our experience and understanding of globalisation. What is not in doubt is that these five questions are always present in any examination of globalisation – whether implicitly or explicitly. It is worth keeping them in mind as we turn to the more specific aspects of globalisation.

GLOBAL ISSUES

The three main areas that scholars have identified as being central to globalisation are economics, culture and political organisation. In addition, there are several political issues, such as the environment, that cross all three spheres. By using these broad categories, it becomes possible to illustrate some of the specific effects of globalisation, as well as indicating how those five normative questions penetrate even the briefest experience of globalisation.

Economics

Economics is often seen as the most important facet of globalisation because all other spheres (e.g. culture, the environment) are dependent on rates of economic growth. For many scholars, the forces of globalisation cannot be divorced from the expansion of capitalism as an economic system (Wallerstein 1979; Jameson 1991). Indeed, it is the eradication of any other possible contender to capitalism (e.g. communism) that signals the completion of globalisation. In explaining the economic shape of globalisation, scholars examine the following areas: *trade* (are tariff barriers being broken down to encourage free trade?), *production* (why do MNCs such as Nike, Microsoft and Shell locate their production centres all over the world?), *investment* (if MNCs are not restricted by national boundaries, where are they investing their money?), *organisational ideology* (is the global economy being governed by an ethos of flexibility?), *financial markets* (how far are markets being decentralised and run from major financial centres such as London, New York and Tokyo?), and *the labour market* (are workers able to move freely outside national boundaries to find work?) (Waters 1995: 65–95; Held and McGrew 2000: 249). Within these areas, many of the normative questions are played out between two radically different approaches – loosely, the 'optimists' and the 'sceptics'. The optimists argue that the expansion of capitalism across the entire world encourages more economic trade, stimulates more economic growth and results in greater profit for all of humanity. This belief holds true for governments and policy-makers arguing for an increase in free trade and a decrease of tariff barriers, and in fact has governed many of the recent meetings of the World Trade Organization and the industrialised nations of the G8. This approach suggests that it is only by letting the market operate freely at a global level that economic growth will occur. The belief here is that any profit will 'trickle down' from the wealthier sections of society to those less well off. The optimists argue that it is economic growth (and *not* more state interference) that will allow us to eradicate global problems such as poverty, debt and inequality. For scholars such as Kenichi Ohmae, the stimulation of economic growth through free trade is a positive force because it reduces the capacity of governments to control financial flows, and it increases the power of MNCs, who have a proven record of increasing economic growth (Ohmae 1996).

While many of these insights on free trade are important, the optimists celebrate the economic benefits of globalisation by ignoring its more serious political questions. Those making efforts to increase free trade and celebrate the market assume that the people amassing the profits from economic growth will easily part with their money in order to eradicate global problems such as poverty, debt and inequality. But the fact that these endemic and structural problems still persist – and have become worse in many cases – reveals major flaws in the optimist viewpoint. An alternative approach, inspired by sceptical thinkers in the Marxist tradition, suggests that the expansion of capitalism has actually entrenched global inequalities that have endured since colonial times. A leading scholar of this approach is Immanuel Wallerstein, who charts the development of capitalism as a world system and illustrates its political effects. He traces the birth of capitalism in sixteenth-century Europe, the division of the world into a core (Europe) and a periphery (the Empire) in order to facilitate economic growth, and the current manifestation of capitalism as a 'world economy' (Wallerstein 1974, 1980, 1989). Wallerstein's main concern is to illustrate how unequal the capitalist system is, and, as such, he sees the current forces of globalisation as simply the latest stage in capitalist expansion. Sceptics like Wallerstein argue that addressing global problems such as poverty, debt and inequality will only occur once the entire system is changed in such a way that (a) economic growth is not pursued at the expense of other social, ethical and cultural considerations, and (b) all of humanity benefits in equal measure. Thus, debates about economic globalisation are shaped by, on the one hand, those who would pursue profit and economic growth, and, on the other hand, those who would pursue a more ethical redistribution of capital and wealth.

Culture

Rather than affording economics a privileged position within globalisation, many scholars choose instead to examine the area of culture. Indeed, scholars such as Robertson are critical when studies of globalisation neglect the cultural dimension (Robertson 1992: 144–5). Not only does the cultural sphere reveal unprecedented global integration, but also, culture is a crucial part of globalisation because this is where people's identities are located. Although culture is a notoriously difficult word to define, we know it is an important marker of a person's identity – it tells us who we are, where we belong, and how to behave. As such, we usually understand culture to be located in a *particular* space (e.g. Japan), produced and experienced by *particular* people (e.g. the Japanese), and structured around *particular* characteristics (e.g. industrious, methodical, respectful). To this end, one might examine the 'fit' between culture and nation, that is, explore a distinct French culture, Indonesian culture, Mexican culture or Swedish culture. The problem with this 'national' approach is that the relationship between culture and nation has never been an exact fit, and, what's more, this relationship is always developing and changing. Culture becomes a political issue when rigid boundaries are constructed around particular cultures, for example, when all 'Japanese' are expected to behave in an 'industrious' fashion. Taking this into account, Benedict Anderson argues that we live in 'imagined communities' where our cultural identities are never completely contained within national boundaries (1983). Think of how religious cultures span many nations – there are Muslims, Christians and Buddhists living all over the world.

But if cultures and identities stretch across national boundaries, is it possible to locate communities that exist at a global level? Some scholars argue that there now exists a distinct global culture that is both a patchwork of many different local cultures and something entirely new. Robertson argues that global culture is 'just as meaningful as the idea of national and local culture', and many scholars examine the new loyalties, networks and allegiances that emerge within this community (Robertson 1992: 114). For the most part, a global culture is identified through the consumption habits of its members, for example, the way fan groups for Britney Spears, Real Madrid football club and the Ferrari motor racing team span countries, continents and classes. Global culture can also be identified in a common lifestyle that can be experienced almost anywhere in the world – one can sip a Starbucks coffee, shop at Gap, purchase Nike trainers and listen to an Eminem CD in any major world city. But there are also many critics of global culture who argue that it is nothing more than a particular Western culture imposing itself on the rest of the world by masquerading as something universal. As such, many critics call this cultural imperialism, and focus on 'the perceived threat of cultural domination posed by the economically powerful Western culture industries through their ownership of the means of production and transmission of cultural goods within the global capitalist market' (Beynon and Dunkerly 2000: 28).

Proponents of global culture promote the idea of diversity: everyone can be a member of the global culture, regardless of their own particular cultural background. They assume that everyone wants to be a part of this new and heterogeneous humanity, because that will give them access to the same opportunities for cultural consumption. Similar to the argument about 'trickle-down' economics, proponents of global culture assume that its diverse membership ensures that it will develop in a benign way that will benefit everyone equally. However, what is masked in the equation of 'global culture = diversity' is that global culture is powerfully underscored by capitalism, inequality and consumerism. We know, for instance, that capitalism requires an international division of labour to sustain itself. There is nothing 'equal' between the workers who produce Nike shoes in South-East Asia for under $1 a day, and the wealthy, middle-class Westerners who purchase Nike trainers for $200. Critics of global culture argue that these inequalities are obscured when people celebrate the diverse but common humanity of global culture. One of the ways those inequalities are hidden is by promoting global culture as the *reciprocal* circulation of 'local' cultural products between global consumers. That is to say, a CD by the Irish boy band *Westlife*, released by the multinational record company BMG, is equal in cultural value to a CD by the Australian aboriginal group *Blekbala Mujik* produced locally on the independent music label CAAMA (Central Australian Aboriginal Media Association). This myth of cultural equivalence ignores how cultural products are attached to capitalism in profoundly unequal ways. For example, the capacity for global production, distribution and publicity of a *Westlife* CD dwarfs the production efforts of local and indigenous groups such as *Blekbala Mujik* – even when these indigenous groups are picked up by major record labels and repackaged as 'world music'. This discrepancy suggests another problem with the capitalist foundation of global culture: it promotes consumerism as an ideal lifestyle. Because global culture is based on the commodification of everything and the endless accumulation of goods and services, the principal identity formation is the consumer rather than the citizen. As Engene Halton explains, you can find out who you are through acts of consumption: 'Buy me, drink me, eat me, dream me, desire me, and you will be yourself' (Halton 1995: 272). While it might be 'liberating' to eat at McDonald's in almost every city around the globe, many scholars suggest that endless consumption is an empty act because consumers disengage from authentic social relations and search for meaning in brand names and lifestyle choices (Featherstone 1991; Ritzer 1996).

While the cultural imperialism thesis is useful in illustrating the massive inequalities underscoring global culture, it can also be very reductionist. That is, it locates every cultural product as *either* hegemonic (e.g. the music of *Westlife* can be heard anywhere in the world), or exploited (e.g. the music of *Blekbala Mujik* is changed irrevocably when it is commodified as 'world music') (Chambers 1986; Tomlinson 1991; Negus 1996). Many scholars have argued that cultural production and consumption are much more complex than simple hegemony and exploitation (Lash and Urry 1994; Howes 1996). Arjun Appadurai explains that because global culture is made up of hybrid cultural formations, it is too simple to characterise global culture as encouraging an inevitable shift towards Western homogeneity (1990). He divides the globalized world into five 'scapes' – ethnoscapes, technoscapes, finanscapes, mediascapes and ideascapes – that highlight the complexity, hybridity and disjuncture of global flows rather than reductionist views of a homogenous global culture. What distinguishes Appadurai's analysis from those who either celebrate or denigrate global culture is that while he pays attention to structures of power, he never portrays them in an overdetermined way that eradicates the possibility of resistance.

Political organisation

While economics and culture pose important questions in terms of equality and the operation of power, one of the most pressing issues of globalisation is how we organize it. If the world is changing beyond all recognition, how can we possibly govern ourselves and create some kind of order out of chaos? Questions of order are not a problem when we understand governance, authority and legitimacy solely in terms of nation-states. Indeed, since the Treaty of Westphalia in 1648, the international system has been based, more or less, on the idea of autonomous nation-states interacting in an anarchical system. Within this tradition, the concept of sovereignty is crucial – sovereignty is what makes states autonomous entities capable of making their own way in an often hostile international system. A state is sovereign when it has established territorial boundaries, when it can control the population within those boundaries through a national government, when it can secure and protect those borders from attack by another sovereign state, and when its sovereignty is recognised as legitimate by other sovereign states. This seems commonsense enough, but the forces of globalisation are eroding sovereignty as the foundation for the world system, and provoking difficult questions about how we might govern ourselves in a globalised world.

This question of governance – of the creation, organisation and maintenance of order – is the primary issue for scholars making sense of how globalisation is affecting the state system (Rosenau 1990; Camilleri and Falk 1992; Mann 1997; McGrew 2000; Scholte 2001b). Many argue that the state itself is in crisis because it cannot effectively address the global political problems we now face. The experience of globalisation suggests that an international system based on sovereign states is at odds with the complex and overlapping relationships that are developing between the local and the global. As Jan Aarte Scholte argues, 'when . . . social relations acquire a host of supraterritorial qualities, and borders are transcended with a deluge of electronic and other flows, crucial preconditions for effective sovereignty no longer prevail' (Scholte 2001b: 22). National governments are now being forced to negotiate their legitimacy and effectiveness with other authorities in a system of 'multilayered governance'. State authority is now affected from below (local, municipal and city authorities), from above (by international authorities such as the UN) and also from across the political spectrum (by non-governmental organisations (NGOs) such as Amnesty International) (McGrew 2000: 163; Scholte 2001b: 23).

If globalisation has resulted in the recognition of a political category called 'humanity', rather than separate categories of 'Polish', 'Argentinean' and 'Nepalese', how is that category to be politically expressed? In answer to this, many scholars have drawn on idealist thinkers in international relations and developed ideas about global governance (Prakash and Hart 2000). The most obvious indicator of these ideas is, of course, the United Nations, which replaced the League of Nations after the Second World War. From the outset, the UN was based on three principles: the sovereign equality of states, that only international problems (and not national ones) will be dealt with by the UN, and that the UN would be concerned primarily with issues of peace and security (Mingst 1999: 246). While these principles might have made sense after the Second World War, all three have changed with the onset of globalisation. Firstly, a rapid increase in the number of states (especially after decolonisation) has meant that within the UN framework, powerful states such as the USA are legally equal to small states such as Madagascar. To get around that pressure of equality, the UN replicates the de facto hierarchy of the international system in its very structure (i.e. the five permanent members of the Security Council). Secondly, as we know with the crisis of the state, the forces of globalisation make it very difficult to delineate what is, and what is not, an international problem. For example, what role does the UN play in the global spread of disease? This is a 'national' problem because national healthcare systems have to respond to epidemics, but it is also an international problem because research and prevention have to be co-ordinated across national boundaries. Thirdly, the UN has widened its remit to cover economic, social, cultural and legal questions as well as the original issues of peace and security. In fact, the 'military' definition of security has now been broadened out to include issues of 'human security' such as feeding starving populations and managing refugee movements.

Aside from the UN as an institution, globalisation has also changed the way we think about global order and authority in general. Many scholars feel that 'official' forms of politics – at local, state and international levels – are unable to address some of the more pressing political problems we face. In short, we need a redefinition of politics outside of these 'official' channels so that global civil society, citizen groups and NGOs – groups that transcend the boundaries of sovereignty – can also be included. To the extent that the network of authorities operating at the international level has supplanted the state, it is perhaps more appropriate to talk about *trans*national politics rather than *inter*national politics. Within a transnational framework, it is possible to locate evidence of agreement between different authorities around certain norms and rules. For this reason, many scholars talk about the development of a global society that focuses on issues facing *all* of humanity, such as promoting human rights, securing democratic freedom, reducing poverty and decreasing violence (Shaw 1994; Held 1996; Linklater 1998). David Held argues that in order for this complex network of global authorities to have any effect, it must be organised around the principles of 'cosmopolitan democracy', that is, democracy that transcends the limits of statehood (1995a). Proponents of global society argue that it has the potential to transform our traditional understandings of sovereignty and citizenship. If people adhere to universal principles such as justice, freedom, equality and democracy, and if those principles are agreed to by all of humanity, then states might not be the most appropriate political structure within which to implement these principles. Having said that, the difficulty with global society is knowing that these 'universal' principles are *not* agreed upon everywhere in the world. As we saw with disagreements over the invasion of Iraq in March 2003, there are competing visions of what might constitute a 'universal' principle worth fighting for.

Global issues

Scholars usually categorise globalisation in terms of economics, culture and political organisation, rather than in terms of sovereignty, because we are facing political problems that, by their very nature, transcend state boundaries. How can we begin to address, let alone solve, current political problems when our framework of understanding is so grounded in the idea of national territories? To get away from the conceptual constraints of sovereignty, many scholars analyse globalisation from the bottom up, that is, from the very material issues that cross sovereign borders and are simultaneously economic, cultural and political. Everyday events and movements *force* us to think differently, because they reveal the complexity of globalisation and the inability of sovereign categories to explain what is happening. Below are five brief examples of material issues that cross sovereign boundaries and force us to think differently about how we automatically contain questions of economics, culture and politics within categories of statehood. It is by no means a complete list, and many more examples of globalisation can be found in this collection. However, the following provide some idea of the way globalisation is transforming the way we think about and categorize the world.

Media and technology
No era of globalisation could ever have happened without the innovations and technologies to make it so. As Marshall McLuhan argued in the 1960s, our present media culture of television, newspapers and the Internet owes a huge debt to the development of the printing press in the fifteenth century (McLuhan 1964). The two big changes since McLuhan's observations are that communication is now instantaneous and global: developments in information technology make it possible to disseminate information instantly to anywhere in the world. In effect, globalisation is unthinkable without the technologies that link us together – computers, aeroplanes, telephones, optic fibres and satellites. Held's argument that relations have intensified within globalisation is nowhere more apparent than in the information and communication sectors. More communication can occur at any given time because that communication is instantaneous: we can say more in twenty four hours than we used to. But we can also say it in different ways because we have different technologies: paper, telephone, e-mail, fax, mobile phones, PDAs (personal digital assistants), websites etc. Economically, computer technology has dramatically changed the speed at which capital transfers take place. More money moves around the stock markets in a 24-hour period. Culturally, satellite technology has penetrated every area of the globe so even the most local site can be opened for consumption. People in rural Morocco can listen to the BBC World Service, and a middle-class family in England can decorate their house with the newest Moroccan designs on offer at *Ikea*. Politically, technology such as e-mail and the Internet are radically changing the character of public participation and citizenship. E-mail lists and websites mobilise groups around specific political issues, and Internet voting is rapidly becoming a thing of the present. All this is to say that the effects of globalisation cannot be divorced from the technologies that deliver globalisation to us. So while we may discuss the

general effects of globalisation, or its effects in different parts of the world, those discussions cannot neglect the role of technology in actually making globalisation possible in the first place.

The environment

It is quite easy to see that pollution, the ozone layer, animal migration, nuclear fallout and climate change do not adhere to national boundaries. By their very nature, environmental issues are transnational, and must be addressed by multiple global actors working at different levels. For example, the international community cannot formulate a policy on deforestation in tropical areas until they consult a variety of local, global and transnational actors (e.g. private logging companies, state governments, UN environmental agencies, environmental activists, scientists and local families). In many ways, this was what the Kyoto Treaty in 2001 attempted to do with regard to climate change. However, one of the problems with Kyoto is that the main contributor to climate change – the USA – refused to sign the treaty. As this example suggests, while environmental issues demand solutions based on a local–global nexus, it is often the authority of sovereign states that directs policy change. By examining the roots and causes of our present environmental decay, the environmental movement has launched a profound and wide-reaching critique of industrialisation and Western consumerism. The way of life in the West is damaging for the environment: we all own cars to navigate our cities; we create masses of garbage every day without a second thought; we eat fast food and processed food; we ignore the damaging effects of air travel in favour of our annual holiday; we prefer our experiences with nature to be mediated by zoos and parks; we export our garbage to third-world nations rather than deal with it ourselves; and we depend on expensive and environmentally damaging energy sources rather than renewable resources. Environmental issues reveal the extremes of globalisation – from the depressing statistics about environmental damage, to the heartening efforts of local groups to co-ordinate globally around particular environmental issues (e.g. saving the rainforests).

Disease, science and biology

If one of the effects of globalisation is that more and more people are travelling, then one of the unintended consequences of that travel is that more people are capable of spreading disease. This was certainly the case with the spread of AIDS in the late 1980s, and more recently with the SARS pandemic in 2003 – an illness that began in a hotel lift in Hong Kong and rapidly spread around the world. While there has been much global medical co-operation in terms of researching cures for these diseases, there are still massive problems to do with the distribution of treatment. For example, African nations argue that despite having the highest concentration of people with AIDS, their debt-ridden status means they cannot afford the prescription drugs required to combat the disease. Is there an ethical imperative for the global community to force multinational pharmaceutical companies to develop and distribute cheaper generic drugs for people in the developing world who are infected with HIV? The reluctance of these companies to do so is evidence of how structural inequalities and the pursuit of economic growth can overshadow even questions of life or death. Similarly, one of the most controversial scientific and medical developments over the past decade has been the Human Genome Project – the effort to map every human gene in the hope of eradicating genetic diseases. Like the treatment of HIV, the Genome Project reveals massive discrepancies between scientific research, the medical community, national governments, pharmaceutical companies, patient advocacy groups, international lawyers and questions of medical ethics. For example, during the consultation process, Western scientists were happy to take medical samples from indigenous groups, but were not willing to consult these groups on how the resulting genetic information would be used. The political question here is how our biological information, that is, the genetic information of every person on the planet, is to be used, by whom, and for what purpose. Many argue that this information should be freely available so that any cures for genetic diseases can be shared with all of humanity. However, those altruistic efforts are constrained by powerful pharmaceutical companies – many commercial genetic companies argue that if they spend the money to research a particular DNA sequence (e.g. for breast cancer), they should be able to patent that sequence and receive profits from it.

Violence, terrorism and intervention
What became clear after the attacks of 9/11 was that violence, terrorism and intervention are *all* transnational activities. Al-Qaeda is a perfect example of a 'cell-like' or 'network' organisation that is both highly flexible in its operations and global in its reach. In order to wage a 'war on terror', the military responses to the events of 9/11 had to be similarly transnational and flexible. The end of the Cold War inaugurated this change in global security so that now 'sanctioned' state violence takes place through multilateral interventions in 'problem' areas rather than through sovereign states fighting one another. These changes have exposed a contradiction enshrined in the UN charter between non-intervention and humanitarian assistance. It is against international law to violate the sovereignty of a particular state (e.g. Iraq's invasion of Kuwait in 1990), but certain interventions can be justified – and indeed, are deemed necessary – if there is a legitimate humanitarian crisis underway (e.g. Somalia in 1993). The problem, as we have seen, is the extent to which the international community agrees on the criteria that must be met if an intervention is to take place (Wheeler 2000). Over and over again we have seen deliberation on this issue at the international level – Iraq, Bosnia, Rwanda, Somalia, and Iraq again. And over and over

again we have seen the tension between national interest (e.g. did the US invade Iraq to protect its oil supply?) and the more humanitarian concerns of global society (e.g. did the 'coalition of the willing' invade Iraq to oust a tyrannical regime who committed gross crimes against humanity?) In short, what we know is that global conflict no longer operates in the same manner as it did during the Cold War. The question is no longer how to establish order in an anarchical system, but rather, how to achieve order in a system of multiple actors where violence is perpetrated transnationally.

Justice and resistance

At the World Trade Organization (WTO) meeting in Seattle in 1999, a popular movement upstaged the official economic negotiations of the main industrial nations. An unprecedented number of groups – trade unions, student groups, socialists, Teamsters, activists, farmers, anarchists – protested on the streets of Seattle against the way globalisation was being directed by large international institutions such as the WTO, the IMF and the World Bank, and large MNCs. Their main argument was that globalisation was *not* bringing the unprecedented economic growth its architects had predicted. Rather, it was entrenching global inequality and fostering cleavages between the 'haves' and the 'have-nots'. At every WTO summit since Seattle in 1999, a coalition of concerned groups and individuals has protested against the official structures and institutions that are directing the forces of globalisation. Initially, this coalition of groups claimed to be anti-globalisation, for they envisioned globalisation in wholly negative terms. But this approach has changed – especially since the events of 9/11. As environmental activist George Monbiot explains, it is no longer appropriate to call this an 'anti-globalisation' movement, but rather to focus on issues of equality and justice (Bygrave 2002). Many journalists and scholars have commented on how this Global Justice Movement (GJM) is different from other social movements and protests because of its flexible and highly mobile character, its lack of identifiable leadership, and its ability to directly influence public debates on globalisation. In many ways, the GJM reveals the changing face of international politics in that popular movements emerging from civil society are starting to have a huge effect on the future operation of globalisation. These popular movements are instantly global and linked with similar movements elsewhere. For example, environmental groups pushing to save the rainforest of Clayoquot Sound in British Columbia in the 1990s became an international movement that linked itself to other groups fighting to save rainforests in places such as Brazil, India and Indonesia (Shaw and Magnusson 2003). This is an example of a movement going global and mobilising a variety of people around a political issue – in this case, an environmental issue. Similar popular movements can be seen around issues such as feminism, where women from around the world link up and mobilise in the fight against patriarchy. What all these social movements suggest is that individuals are capable of resisting some of the more unpalatable effects of globalisation. And the more voices that reveal the inequalities and injustices perpetrated in the name of globalisation, the more the membership of social movements will grow.

SELECTIONS

This chapter has highlighted some of the difficulties, debates and issues about globalisation. Both of the selections below continue to focus on the main issues of globalisation, while at the same time providing more detailed analysis about a specific aspect of golbalization. The first selected reading is the Reith Lecture on globalisation from Professor Anthony Giddens. The BBC holds the Reith Lectures every year in Britain, in honour of its founder, John Reith, who believed strongly that the public should have free access to broadcasting. In 1999, Professor Giddens delivered a series of five lectures across the world – in London, Delhi, Hong Kong and Washington, DC – entitled 'Runaway World'. His opening lecture, delivered in London, is a very general outline of some of the main debates of globalisation. It is important not just for its clarity and simplicity, but also because it transcends the narrow confines of academia and makes efforts to discuss issues of globalisation with the public at large. The second selected reading is from Doreen Massey's book *Space, Place and Gender* (1994) and goes some way to explaining the difficult concept of time–space compression. Massey is a geographer concerned with how our spatial conceptions of globalisation reflect existing power relations of race, gender, sexuality and colonialism. Her work is important because it expresses an enthusiasm for what globalisation can bring, while calling attention to some of its more unsavoury effects. While both of these authors are concerned with the difficulties of framing globalisation, their explanations will help you decide which criteria you want to utilise when making judgements about the forces and effects of globalisation.

QUESTIONS FOR DISCUSSION

- How has your everyday life been affected by the forces of globalisation (e.g. the food you eat, the clothes you wear, the music you listen to, the bank you use, the movies you watch)?
- What are the main differences between your 'worldview' and that of your parents and grandparents? How have these differences been shaped by the forces of globalisation?
- Given that the nation-state is transforming in a context of globalisation, what other forms of political organisation will take its place? What are the main issues these new political communities will have to address, and will they be more successful than the traditional nation-state?
- Is globalisation just, fair and equal? If not, why not?

ANTHONY GIDDENS
'GLOBALISATION'

A friend of mine studies village life in central Africa. A few years ago, she paid her first visit to a remote area where she was to carry out her fieldwork. The evening she got there, she was invited to a local home for an evening's entertainment. She expected to find out about the traditional pastimes of this isolated community. Instead, the evening turned out to be a viewing of *Basic Instinct* on video. The film at that point hadn't even reached the cinemas in London.

Such vignettes reveal something about our world. And what they reveal isn't trivial. It isn't just a matter of people adding modern paraphernalia – videos, TVs, personal computers and so forth – to their traditional ways of life. We live in a world of transformations, affecting almost every aspect of what we do. For better or worse, we are being propelled into a global order that no one fully understands, but which is making its effects felt upon all of us.

Globalisation is the main theme of my lecture tonight, and of the lectures as a whole. The term may not be – it isn't – a particularly attractive or elegant one. But absolutely no one who wants to understand our prospects and possibilities at century's end can ignore it. I travel a lot to speak abroad. I haven't been to a single country recently where globalisation isn't being intensively discussed. In France, the word is *mondialisation*. In Spain and Latin America, it is *globalización*. The Germans say *Globalisierung*.

The global spread of the term is evidence of the very developments to which it refers. Every business guru talks about it. No political speech is

Anthony Giddens (1999), 'Globalisation', *Runaway World: How Globalisation is Reshaping Our Lives*, London: Profile Books.

complete without reference to it. Yet as little as ten years ago the term was hardly used, either in the academic literature or in everyday language. It has come from nowhere to be almost everywhere. Given its sudden popularity, we shouldn't be surprised that the meaning of the notion isn't always clear, or that an intellectual reaction has set in against it. Globalisation has something to do with the thesis that we now all live in one world – but in what ways exactly, and is the idea really valid?

Different thinkers have taken almost completely opposite views about globalisation in debates that have sprung up over the past few years. Some dispute the whole thing. I'll call them the sceptics. According to the sceptics, all the talk about globalisation is only that – just talk. Whatever its benefits, its trials and tribulations, the global economy isn't especially different from that which existed at previous periods. The world carries on much the same as it has done for many years.

Most countries, the sceptics argue, only gain a small amount of their income from external trade. Moreover, a good deal of economic exchange is between regions, rather than being truly worldwide. The countries of the European Union, for example, mostly trade among themselves. The same is true of the other main trading blocs, such as those of the Asia Pacific or North America.

Others, however, take a very different position. I'll label them the radicals. The radicals argue that not only is globalisation very real, but that its consequences can be felt everywhere. The global marketplace, they say, is much more developed than even two or three decades ago, and is indifferent to national borders. Nations have lost most of the sovereignty they once had, and politicians have lost most of their capability to influence events. It isn't surprising that no one respects political leaders any more, or has much interest in what they have to say. The era of the nation-state is over. Nations, as the Japanese business writer Keniche Ohmae puts it, have become mere 'fictions'. Authors like Ohmae see the economic difficulties of last year and this as demonstrating the reality of globalisation, albeit seen from its disruptive side.

The sceptics tend to be on the political left, especially the old left. For if all of this is essentially a myth, governments can still intervene in economic life and the welfare state remain intact. The notion of globalisation, according to the sceptics, is an ideology put about by free-marketeers who wish to dismantle welfare systems and cut back on state expenditures. What has happened is at most a reversion to how the world was a century ago. In the late nineteenth century there was already an open global economy, with a great deal of trade, including trade in currencies.

Well, who is right in this debate? I think it is the radicals. The level of world trade today is much higher than it ever was before, and involves a much wider range of goods and services. But the biggest difference is in the level of finance and capital flows. Geared as it is to electronic money – money that exists only as digits in computers – the current world economy has no parallels in earlier times. In the new global electronic economy, fund managers, banks, corporations, as well as millions of individual investors, can transfer vast amounts of capital from one side of the world to another at the click of a mouse. As they do so, they can destabilise what might have seemed rock-solid economies – as happened in east Asia.

The volume of world financial transactions is usually measured in US dollars. A million dollars is a lot of money for most people. Measured as a stack of thousand dollar notes, it would be eight inches high. A billion dollars – in other words, a million million – would be over 120 miles high, twenty times higher than Mount Everest.

Yet far more than a trillion dollars is now turned over each day on global currency markets, a massive increase from only ten years ago, let alone the more distant past. The value of whatever money we may have in our pockets, or our bank accounts, shifts from moment to moment according to fluctuations in such markets. I would have no hesitation, therefore, in saying that globalisation, as we are experiencing it, is in many respects not only new, but revolutionary.

However, I don't believe either the sceptics or the radicals have properly understood either what it is or its implications for us. Both groups see the phenomenon almost solely in economic terms. This is a mistake. Globalisation is political, technological and cultural, as well as economic. It has been influenced above all by developments in systems of communication, dating back only to the late 1960s.

In the mid-nineteenth century, a Massachusetts portrait painter, Samuel Morse, transmitted the first message, 'What hath God wrought?', by electric telegraph. In so doing, he initiated a new phase in world history. Never before could a message be sent without someone going somewhere to carry it. Yet the advent of satellite communications marks every bit as dramatic a break with the past. The first communications satellite was launched only just over thirty years ago. Now there are more than 200 such satellites above the earth, each carrying a vast range of information. For the first time ever, instantaneous communication is possible from one side of the world to the other. Other types of electronic communication, more and more integrated with satellite transmission, have also accelerated over the past few years. No dedicated transatlantic or transpacific cables existed at all until the late 1950s. The first held less than 100 voice paths. Those of today carry more than a million.

On the first of February 1999, about 150 years after Morse invented his system of dots and dashes, Morse code finally disappeared from the world stage, discontinued as a means of communication for the sea. In its place has come a system using satellite technology, whereby any ship in distress can be pinpointed immediately. Most countries prepared for the transition some while before. The French, for example, stopped using Morse as a distress code in their local waters two years ago, signing off with a Gallic flourish: 'Calling all. This is our last cry before our eternal silence.'

Instantaneous electronic communication isn't just a way in which news or information is conveyed more quickly. Its existence alters the very texture of our lives, rich and poor alike. When the image of Nelson Mandela maybe is more familiar to us than the face of our next-door neighbour, something has changed in the nature of our everyday experience.

Nelson Mandela is a global celebrity, and celebrity itself is largely a product of new communications technology. The reach of media technologies is growing with each wave of innovation. It took forty years for radio in the United States to gain an audience of fifty million. The same number were using personal computers only fifteen years after the PC was introduced. It needed a mere four years after it was made available for fifty million Americans to be regularly using the Internet.

It is wrong to think of globalisation as just concerning the big systems, like the world financial order. Globalisation isn't only about what is 'out there', remote and far away from the individual. It is an 'in here' phenomenon too, influencing intimate and personal aspects of our lives. The debate about family values, for example, that is going on in many countries, might seem far removed from globalising influences. It isn't. Traditional family systems are becoming transformed, or are under strain, in many parts of the world, particularly as women stake claim to greater equality. There has never before been a society, so far as we know from the historical record, in which women have been even approximately equal to men. This is a truly global revolution in everyday life, whose consequences are being felt around the world in spheres from work to politics.

Globalisation thus is a complex set of processes, not a single one. And these operate in a contradictory or oppositional fashion. Most people think of it as simply 'pulling away' power or influence from local communities and nations into the global arena. And indeed this is one of its consequences. Nations do lose some of the economic power they once had. However, it also has an opposite effect. Globalisation not only pulls upwards, it pushes downwards, creating new pressures for local autonomy. The American sociologist Daniel Bell expresses this very well when he says that the nation becomes too small to solve the big problems, but also too large to solve the small ones.

Globalisation is the reason for the revival of local cultural identities in different parts of the world. If one asks, for example, why the Scots want more independence in the UK, or why there is a strong separatist movement in Quebec, the answer is not to be found only in their cultural history. Local nationalisms spring up as a response to globalising tendencies, as the hold of older nation-states weakens.

Globalisation also squeezes sideways. It creates new economic and cultural zones within and across nations. Examples are the Hong Kong region, northern Italy, or Silicon Valley in California. The area around Barcelona in northern Spain extends over into France. Catalonia, where Barcelona is located, is closely integrated into the European Union. It is part of Spain, yet also looks outwards.

The changes are being propelled by a range of factors, some structural, others more specific and historical. Economic influences are certainly among the driving forces, especially the global financial system. Yet they aren't like forces of nature. They have been shaped by technology, and cultural diffusion, as well as by the decisions of governments to liberalise and deregulate their national economies.

The collapse of Soviet communism has added further weight to such developments, since no significant group of countries any longer stands outside. That collapse wasn't just something that happened to occur. Globalisation explains both why and how Soviet communism met its end. The Soviet Union and the East European countries were comparable to the West in terms of growth rates until somewhere around the early 1970s. After that point, they fell rapidly behind. Soviet communism, with its emphasis upon state-run enterprise and heavy industry, could not compete in the global electronic economy. The ideological and cultural control upon which communist political authority was based similarly could not survive in an era of global media.

The Soviet and the East European regimes were unable to prevent the reception of Western radio and TV broadcasts. Television played a direct role in the 1989 revolutions, which have rightly been called the first 'television revolutions'. Street protests taking place in one country were watched by the audiences in others, large numbers of whom then took to the streets themselves.

Globalisation, of course, isn't developing in an even-handed way, and is by no means wholly benign in its consequences. To many living outside Europe and North America, it looks uncomfortably like Westernisation – or, perhaps, Americanisation, since the US is now the sole superpower, with a dominant economic, cultural and military position in the global order. Many of the most visible cultural expressions of globalisation are American – Coca-Cola, McDonald's.

Most of the giant multinational companies are based in the US too. Those that aren't all come from the rich countries, not the poorer areas of the world. A pessimistic view of globalisation would consider it largely an affair of the industrial North, in which the developing societies of the South play little or no active part. It would see it as destroying local cultures, widening world inequalities and worsening the lot of the impoverished. Globalisation, some argue, creates a world of winners and losers, a few on the fast track to prosperity, the majority condemned to a life of misery and despair.

And indeed the statistics are daunting. The share of the poorest fifth of the world's population in global income has dropped from 2.3% to 1.4% over the past ten years. The proportion taken by the richest fifth, on the other hand, has risen from 70% to 85%. In sub-Saharan Africa, twenty countries have lower incomes per head in real terms than they did two decades ago. In many less developed countries, safety and environmental regulations are low or virtually non-existent. Some trans-national companies sell goods there that are controlled or banned in the industrial countries – poor quality medical drugs, destructive pesticides or high tar and nicotine content cigarettes. As one writer put it recently, rather than a global village, this is more like global pillage.

Along with ecological risk, to which it is related, expanding inequality is the most serious problem facing world society. It will not do, however, merely to blame it on the wealthy. It is fundamental to my argument that globalisation today is only partly Westernisation. Of course the Western nations, and more generally the industrial countries, still have far more influence over world affairs than do the poorer states. But globalisation is becoming increasingly decentred – not under the control of any group of nations, and still less of the large corporations. Its effects are felt just as much in the Western countries as elsewhere.

This is true of the global financial system, communications and media, and of changes affecting the nature of government itself. Examples of 'reverse colonisation' are becoming more and more common. Reverse colonisation means that non-Western countries influence developments in the west. Examples abound – such as the Latinising of Los Angeles, the emergence of a globally-oriented high-tech sector in India, or the selling of Brazilian TV programmes to Portugal.

Is globalisation a force promoting the general good? The question can't be answered in a simple way, given the complexity of the phenomenon. People who ask it, and who blame globalisation for deepening world inequalities, usually have in mind economic globalisation, and within that, free trade. Now it is surely obvious that free trade is not an unalloyed benefit. This is especially so as concerns the less developed countries. Opening up a country, or regions within it, to free trade can undermine a local subsistence economy. An area that becomes dependent upon a few products sold on world markets is very vulnerable to shifts in prices as well as to technological change.

Trade always needs a framework of institutions, as do other forms of economic development. Markets cannot be created by purely economic means, and how far a given economy should be exposed to the world marketplace must depend upon a range of criteria. Yet to oppose economic globalisation, and to opt for economic protectionism, would be a misplaced tactic for rich and poor nations alike. Protectionism may be a necessary strategy at some times and in some countries. In my view, for example, Malaysia was correct to introduce controls in 1998, to stem the flood of capital from the country. But more permanent forms of protectionism will not help the development of the poor countries, and among the rich would lead to warring trade blocs.

The debates about globalisation I mentioned at the beginning have concentrated mainly upon its implications for the nation-state. Are nation-states, and hence national political leaders, still powerful, or are they becoming largely irrelevant to the forces shaping the world? Nation-states are indeed still powerful and political leaders have a large role to play in the world. Yet at the same time the nation-state is being reshaped before our eyes. National economic policy can't be as effective as it once was. More importantly, nations have to rethink their identities now the older forms of geopolitics are becoming obsolete. Although this is a contentious point, I would say that, following the dissolving of the cold war, nations no longer have enemies. Who are the enemies of Britain, or France, or Japan? Nations today face risks and dangers rather than enemies, a massive shift in their very nature.

It isn't only of the nation that such comments could be made. Everywhere we look, we see institutions that appear the same as they used to be from the outside, and carry the same names, but inside have become quite different. We continue to talk of the nation, the family, work, tradition, nature, as if they were all the same as in the past. They are not. The outer shell remains, but inside all is different – and this is happening not only in the US, Britain, or France, but almost everywhere. They are what I call shell institutions, and I shall talk about them quite a bit in the lectures to come. They are institutions that have become inadequate to the tasks they are called upon to perform.

As the changes I have described in this lecture gather weight, they are creating something that has never existed before, a global cosmopolitan society. We are the first generation to live in this society, whose contours we can as yet only dimly see. It is shaking up our existing ways of life, no matter where we happen to be. This is not – at least at the moment – a global order driven by collective human will. Instead, it is emerging in an anarchic, haphazard, fashion, carried along by a mixture of economic, technological and cultural imperatives.

It is not settled or secure, but fraught with anxieties, as well as scarred by deep divisions. Many of us feel in the grip of forces over which we have no control. Can we re-impose our will upon them? I believe we can. The powerlessness we experience is not a sign of personal failings, but reflects the incapacities of our institutions. We need to reconstruct those we have, or create new ones, in ways appropriate to the global age.

We should and we can look to achieve greater control over our runaway world. We shan't be able to do so if we shirk the challenges, or pretend that all can go on as before. For globalisation is not incidental to our lives today. It is a shift in our very life circumstances. It is the way we now live.

DOREEN MASSEY
EXTRACTS FROM *SPACE, PLACE AND GENDER*

A GLOBAL SENSE OF PLACE

This is an era – it is often said – when things are speeding up, and spreading out. Capital is going through a new phase of internationalization, especially in its financial parts. More people travel more frequently and for longer distances. Your clothes have probably been made in a range of countries from Latin America to South-East Asia. Dinner consists of food shipped in from all over the world. And if you have a screen in your office, instead of opening a letter which – care of Her Majesty's Post Office – has taken some days to wend its way across the country, you now get interrupted by e-mail.

This view of the current age is one now frequently found in a wide range of books and journals. Much of what is written about space, place and postmodern times emphasizes a new phase in what Marx once called the annihilation of space by time'. The process is argued, or – more usually – asserted, to have gained a new momentum, to have reached a new stage. It is a phenomenon which has been called 'time–space compression'. And the general acceptance that something of the sort is going on is marked by the almost obligatory use in the literature of terms and phrases such as speed-up, global village, overcoming spatial barriers, the disruption of horizons, and so forth.

One of the results of this is an increasing uncertainty about what we mean by 'places' and how we relate to them. How, in the face of all this movement and intermixing, can we retain any sense of a local place and

Doreen Massey (1994), *Space, Place and Gender*, Cambridge: Polity Press.

its particularity? An (idealized) notion of an era when places were (supposedly) inhabited by coherent and homogeneous communities is set against the current fragmentation and disruption. The counterposition is anyway dubious, of course; 'place' and 'community' have only rarely been coterminous. But the occasional longing for such coherence is none the less a sign of the geographical fragmentation, the spatial disruption, of our times. And occasionally, too, it has been part of what has given rise to defensive and reactionary responses – certain forms of nationalism, senti-mentalized recovering of sanitized 'heritages', and outright antagonism to newcomers and 'outsiders'. One of the effects of such responses is that place itself, the seeking after a sense of place, has come to be seen by some as necessarily reactionary.

But is that necessarily so? Can't we rethink our sense of place? Is it not possible for a sense of place to be progressive; not self-enclosing and defensive, but outward-looking? A sense of place which is adequate to this era of time–space compression? To begin with, there are some questions to be asked about time–space compression itself. Who is it that experiences it, and how? Do we all benefit and suffer from it in the same way?

For instance, to what extent does the currently popular characterization of time–space compression represent very much a western, colonizer's, view? The sense of dislocation which some feel at the sight of a once well-known local street now lined with a succession of cultural imports – the pizzeria, the kebab house, the branch of the middle-eastern bank – must have been felt for centuries, though from a very different point of view, by colonized peoples all over the world as they watched the importation, maybe even used, the products of, first, European colonization, maybe British (from new forms of transport to liver salts and custard powder), later US, as they learned to eat wheat instead of rice or corn, to drink Coca-Cola, just as today we try out enchiladas.

Moreover, as well as querying the ethnocentricity of the idea of time–space compression and its current acceleration, we also need to ask about its causes: what is it that determines our degrees of mobility, that influences the sense we have of space and place? Time–space compression refers to movement and communication across space, to the geographical stretching-out of social relations, and to our experience of all this. The usual interpretation is that it results overwhelmingly from the actions of capital, and from its currently increasing internationalization. On this interpretation, then, it is time, space and money which make the world go round, and us go round (or not) the world. It is capitalism and its developments which are argued to determine our understanding and our experience of space.

But surely this is insufficient. Among the many other things which clearly influence that experience, there are, for instance, 'race' and gender. The degree to which we can move between countries, or walk about the streets at night, or venture out of hotels in foreign cities, is not just influenced by 'capital'. Survey after survey has shown how women's mobility, for instance, is restricted – in a thousand different ways, from physical violence to being ogled at or made to feel quite simply 'out of place' – not by 'capital', but by men. Or, to take a more complicated example, Birkett, reviewing books on women adventurers and travellers in the nineteenth and twentieth centuries, suggests that 'it is far, far more demanding for a woman to wander now than ever before'.[1] The reasons she gives for this argument are a complex mix of colonialism, ex-colonialism, racism, changing gender relations and relative wealth. A simple resort to explanation in terms of 'money' or 'capital' alone could not begin to get to grips with the issue. The current speed-up may be strongly determined by economic forces, but it is not the economy alone which determines our experience of space and place. In other words, and put simply, there is a lot more determining how we experience space than what 'capital' gets up to.

What is more, of course, that last example indicated that 'time–space compression' has not been happening for everyone in all spheres of activity. Birkett again, this time writing of the Pacific Ocean:

> Jumbos have enabled Korean computer consultants to fly to Silicon Valley as if popping next door, and Singaporean entrepreneurs to reach Seattle in a day. The borders of the world's greatest ocean have been joined as never before. And Boeing has brought these people together. But what about those they fly over, on their islands five miles below? How has the mighty 747 brought them greater communion with those whose shores are washed by the same water? It hasn't, of course. Air travel might enable businessmen to buzz across the ocean, but the concurrent decline in shipping has only increased the isolation of many island communities ... Pitcairn, like many other Pacific islands, has never felt so far from its neighbours.[2]

In other words, and most broadly, time–space compression needs differentiating socially. This is not just a moral or political point about inequality, although that would be sufficient reason to mention it; it is also a conceptual point.

Imagine for a moment that you are on a satellite, further out and beyond all actual satellites; you can see 'planet earth' from a distance and, unusually for someone with only peaceful intentions, you are equipped with the kind of technology which allows you to see the colours of people's eyes and the numbers on their numberplates. You can see all the movement and tune in to all the communication that is going on. Furthest out are the satellites, then aeroplanes, the long haul between London and Tokyo and the hop from San Salvador to Guatemala City. Some of this is people moving, some of it is physical trade, some is media broadcasting. There are faxes, e-mail, film-distribution networks, financial flows and transactions. Look in closer and there are ships and trains, steam trains slogging laboriously up hills somewhere in Asia. Look in closer still and there are lorries and cars and buses, and on down further, somewhere in sub-Saharan Africa, there's a woman – amongst many women – on foot, who still spends hours a day collecting water.

Now, I want to make one simple point here, and that is about what one might call the *power geometry* of it all; the power geometry of time–space compression. For different social groups, and different individuals, are placed in very distinct ways in relation to these flows and interconnections. This point concerns not merely the issue of who moves and who doesn't, although that is an important element of it; it is also about power in relation *to* the flows and the movement. Different social groups have distinct relationships to this anyway differentiated mobility: some people are more in charge of it than others; some initiate flows and movement, others don't; some are more on the receiving-end of it than others; some are effectively imprisoned by it.

In a sense at the end of all the spectra are those who are both doing the moving and the communicating and who are in some way in a position of control in relation to it – the jet-setters, the ones sending and receiving the faxes and the e-mail, holding the international conference calls, the ones distributing the films, controlling the news, organizing the investments and the international currency transactions. These are the groups who are really in a sense in charge of time–space compression, who can really use it and turn it to advantage, whose power and influence it very definitely increases. On its more prosaic fringes this group probably includes a fair number of western academics and journalists – those, in other words, who write most about it.

But there are also groups who are also doing a lot of physical moving, but who are not 'in charge' of the process in the same way at all. The refugees from El Salvador or Guatemala and the undocumented migrant workers from Michoacán in Mexico, crowding into Tijuana to make a perhaps fatal dash for it across the border into the US to grab a chance of a new life. Here the experience of movement, and indeed of a confusing plurality of cultures, is very different. And there are those from India, Pakistan, Bangladesh, the Caribbean, who come half way round the world only to get held up in an interrogation room at Heathrow.

Or – a different case again – there are those who are simply on the receiving end of time–space compression. The pensioner in a bed-sit in any inner city in this country, eating British working-class-style fish and chips from a Chinese take-away, watching a US film on a Japanese television; and not daring to go out after dark. And anyway the public transport's been cut.

Or – one final example to illustrate a different kind of complexity – there are the people who live in the *favelas* of Rio, who know global football like the back of their hand, and have produced some of its players; who have contributed massively to global music, who gave us the samba and produced the lambada that everyone was dancing to last year in the clubs of Paris and London; and who have never, or hardly ever, been to downtown Rio. At one level they have been tremendous contributors to what we call time–space compression; and at another level they are imprisoned in it.

This is, in other words, a highly complex social differentiation. There are differences in the degree of movement and communication, but also in the degree of control and of initiation. The ways in which people are placed within 'time–space compression' are highly complicated and extremely varied.

But this in turn immediately raises questions of politics. If time–space compression can be imagined in that more socially formed, socially evaluative and differentiated way, then there may be here the possibility of developing a politics of mobility and access. For it does seem that mobility, and control over mobility, both reflects and reinforces power. It is not simply a question of unequal distribution, that some people move more than others, and that some have more control than others. It is that the mobility and control of some groups can actively weaken other people. Differential mobility can weaken the leverage of the already weak. The time–space compression of some groups can undermine the power of others.

This is well established and often noted in the relationship between capital and labour. Capital's ability to roam the world further strengthens it in relation to relatively immobile workers, enables it to play off the plant at Genk against the plant at Dagenham. It also strengthens its hand against struggling local economies the world over as they compete for the favour of some investment. The 747s that fly computer scientists across the Pacific are part of the reason for the greater isolation today of the island of Pitcairn. But also, every time someone uses a car, and thereby increases their personal mobility, they reduce both the social rationale and the financial viability of the public transport system – and thereby also potentially reduce the mobility of those who rely on that system. Every time you drive to that out-of-town shopping centre you contribute to the rising prices, even hasten the demise, of the corner shop. And the 'time–space compression' which is involved in producing and reproducing the daily lives of the comfortably-off in First World societies – not just their own travel but the resources they draw on, from all over the world, to feed their lives – may entail environmental consequences, or hit constraints, which will limit the lives of others before their own. We need to ask, in other words, whether our relative mobility and power over mobility and communication entrenches the spatial imprisonment of other groups.

But this way of thinking about time–space compression also returns us to the question of place and a sense of place. How, in the context of all these socially varied time–space changes do we think about 'places'? In an era when, it is argued, 'local communities' seem to be increasingly broken up, when you can go abroad and find the same shops, the same music as at home, or eat your favourite foreign-holiday food at a restaurant down the road – and when everyone has a different experience of all this – how then do we think about 'locality'?

Many of those who write about time–space compression emphasize the insecurity and unsettling impact of its effects, the feelings of vulnerability which it can produce. Some therefore go on from this to argue that, in the middle of all this flux, people desperately need a bit of peace and quiet – and that a strong sense of place, of locality, can form one kind of refuge from the hubbub. So the search after the 'real' meanings of places, the unearthing of heritages and so forth, is interpreted as being, in part, a response to desire for fixity and for security of identity in the middle of all the movement and change. A 'sense of place', of rootedness, can provide – in this form and on this interpretation – stability and a source of unproblematical identity. In that guise, however, place and the spatially local are then rejected by many progressive people as almost necessarily reactionary. They are interpreted as an evasion; as a retreat from the (actually unavoidable) dynamic and change of 'real life', which is what we must seize if we are to change things for the better. On this reading, place and locality are foci for a form of romanticized escapism from the real business of the world. While 'time' is equated with movement and progress, 'space'/'place' is equated with stasis and reaction.

There are some serious inadequacies in this argument. There is the question of why it is assumed that time–space compression will produce insecurity. There is the need to face up to – rather than simply deny – people's need for attachment of some sort, whether through place or anything else. None the less, it is certainly the case that there is indeed at the moment a recrudescence of some very problematical senses of place, from reactionary nationalisms, to competitive localisms, to introverted obsessions with 'heritage'. We need, therefore, to think through what might be an adequately progressive sense of place, one which would fit in with the current global–local times and the feelings and relations they give rise to, *and* which would be useful in what are, after all, political struggles often inevitably based on place. The question is how to hold on to that notion of geographical difference, of uniqueness, even of rootedness if people want that, without it being reactionary.

There are a number of distinct ways in which the 'reactionary' notion of place described above is problematical. One is the idea that places have single, essential, identities. Another is the idea that identity of place – the sense of place – is constructed out of an introverted, inward-looking history based on delving into the past for internalized origins, translating the name from the Domesday Book. Thus Wright recounts the construction and appropriation of Stoke Newington and its past by the arriving middle class (the Domesday Book registers the place as 'Newtowne'): 'There is land for two ploughs and a half... There are four villanes and thirty seven cottagers with ten acres.' And he contrasts this version with that of other groups – the white working class and the large number of Important minority communities.[3] A particular problem with this conception of place is that it seems to require the drawing of boundaries. Geographers have long been exercised by the problem of defining regions, and this question of 'definition' has almost always been reduced to the issue of drawing lines around a place. I remember some of my most painful times as a geographer have been spent unwillingly struggling to think how one could draw a boundary around somewhere like the 'east midlands'. But that kind of boundary around an area precisely distinguishes between an inside and an outside. It can so easily be yet another way of constructing a counterposition between 'us' and 'them'.

And yet if one considers almost any real place, and certainly one not defined primarily by administrative or political boundaries, these supposed characteristics have little real purchase.

Take, for instance, a walk down Kilburn High Road, my local shopping centre. It is a pretty ordinary place, north-west of the centre of London. Under the railway bridge the newspaper stand sells papers from every county of what my neighbours, many of whom come from there, still often call the Irish Free State. The postboxes down the High Road, and many an empty space on a wall, are adorned with the letters IRA. Other available spaces are plastered this week with posters for a special meeting in remembrance: Ten Years after the Hunger Strike. At the local theatre Eamon Morrissey has a one-man show; the National Club has the Wolfe Tones on, and at the Black Lion there's *Finnegans Wake*. In two shops I notice this week's lottery ticket winners: in one the name is Teresa Gleeson, in the other, Chouman Hassan.

Thread your way through the often almost stationary traffic diagonally across the road from the newsstand and there's a shop which as long as I can remember has displayed saris in the window. Four life-sized models of Indian women, and reams of cloth. On the door a notice announces a forthcoming concert at Wembley Arena: Anand Miland presents Rekha, live, with Aamir Khan, Salman Khan, Jahi Chawla and Raveena Tandon. On another ad, for the end of the month, is written, 'All Hindus are cordially invited'. In another newsagents I chat with the man who keeps it, a Muslim unutterably depressed by events in the Gulf, silently chafing at having to sell the *Sun*. Overhead there is always at least one aeroplane – we seem to be on a flight-path to Heathrow and by the time they're over Kilburn you can see them clearly enough to tell the airline and wonder as you struggle with your shopping where they're coming from. Below, the reason the traffic is snarled up (another odd effect of time–space compression!) is in part because this is one of the main entrances to and escape routes from London, the road to Staples Corner and the beginning of the M1 to 'the North'.

This is just the beginnings of a sketch from immediate impressions but a proper analysis could be done of the links between Kilburn and the world. And so it could for almost any place.

Kilburn is a place for which I have a great affection; I have lived there many years. It certainly has 'a character of its own'. But it is possible to feel all this without subscribing to any of the static and defensive – and in that sense reactionary – notions of 'place' which were referred to above. First, while Kilburn may have a character of its own, it is absolutely not a seamless, coherent identity, a single sense of place which everyone shares. It could hardly be less so. People's, routes through the place, their favourite haunts within it, the connections they make (physically, or by phone or post, or in memory and imagination) between here and the rest of the world vary enormously. If it is now recognized that people have multiple identities then the same point can be made in relation to places. Moreover, such multiple identities can either be a source of richness or a source of conflict, or both.

One of the problems here has been a persistent identification of place with 'community'. Yet this is a misidentification. On the one hand, communities can exist without being in the same place – from networks of friends with like interests, to major religious, ethnic or political communities. On the other hand, the instances of places housing single 'communities' in the sense of coherent social groups are probably – and, I would argue, have for long been – quite rare, Moreover, even where they do exist this in no way implies a single sense of place. For people occupy different positions within any community. We could counterpose to the chaotic mix of Kilburn the relatively stable and homogeneous community (at least in popular imagery) of a small mining village. Homogeneous? Communities' too have internal structures. To take the most obvious example, I'm sure a woman's sense of place in a mining village – the spaces through which she normally moves, the meeting places, the connections outside – are different from a man's. Their 'senses of the place' will be different.

Moreover, not only does 'Kilburn', then, have many identities (or its full identity is a complex mix of all these), it is also, looked at in this way, absolutely *not* introverted. It is (or ought to be) impossible even to begin thinking about Kilburn High Road without bringing into play half the world and a considerable amount of British imperialist history (and this certainly goes for mining villages too). Imagining it this way provokes in you (or at least in me) a really global sense of place.

And finally, in contrasting this way of looking at places with the defensive reactionary view, I certainly could not begin to, nor would I want to, define 'Kilburn' by drawing its enclosing boundaries.

So, at this point in the argument, get back in your mind's eye on a satellite; go right out again and look back at the globe. This time, however, imagine not just all the physical movement, nor even all the often invisible communications, but also and especially all the social relations, all the links between people. Fill it in with all those different experiences of time–space compression. For what is happening is that the geography of social relations is changing. In many cases such relations are increasingly stretched out over space. Economic, political and cultural social relations, each full of power and with internal structures of domination and subordination, stretched out over the planet at every different level, from the household to the local area to the international.

It is from that perspective that it is possible to envisage an alternative interpretation of place. In this interpretation, what gives a place its specificity is not some long internalized history but the fact that it is constructed out of a particular constellation of social relations, meeting and weaving together at a particular locus. If one moves in from the satellite towards the globe, holding all those networks of social relations and movements and communications in one's head, then each 'place' can be seen as a particular, unique, point of their intersection. It is, indeed, a *meeting* place. Instead then, of thinking of places as areas with boundaries around, they can be imagined as articulated moments in networks of social relations and understandings, but where a large proportion of those relations, experiences and understandings are constructed on a far larger scale than what we happen to define for that moment as the place itself, whether that be a street, or a region or even a continent. And this in turn allows a sense of place which is extroverted, which includes a consciousness of its links with the wider world, which integrates in a positive way the global and the local.

This is not a question of making the ritualistic connections to 'the wider system' – the people in the local meeting who bring up international capitalism every time you try to have a discussion about rubbish-collection – the point is that there are real relations with real content – economic, political, cultural – between any local place and the wider world in which it is set. In economic geography the argument has long been accepted that it is not possible to understand the 'inner city', for instance its loss of jobs, the decline of manufacturing employment there, by looking only at the inner city. Any adequate explanation has to set the inner city in its wider geographical context. Perhaps it is appropriate to think how that kind of understanding could be extended to the notion of a sense of place.

These arguments, then, highlight a number of ways in which a progressive concept of place might be developed. First of all, it is absolutely not static. If places can be conceptualized in terms of the social interactions which they tie together, then it is also the case that these interactions themselves are not motionless things, frozen in time. They are processes. One of the great one-liners in Marxist exchanges has for long been, 'Ah, but capital is not a thing, it's a process.' Perhaps this should be said also about places; that places are processes, too.

Second, places do not have to have boundaries in the sense of divisions which frame simple enclosures. 'Boundaries' may of course be necessary, for the purposes of certain types of studies for instance, but they are not necessary for the conceptualization of a place itself. Definition in this sense does not have to be through simple counterposition to the outside; it can come, in part, precisely through the particularity of linkage *to* that 'outside' which is therefore itself part of what constitutes the place. This helps get away from the common association between penetrability and vulnerability. For it is this kind of association which makes invasion by newcomers so threatening.

Third, clearly places do not have single, unique 'identities'; they are full of internal conflicts. Just think, for instance, about London's Docklands, a place which is at the moment quite clearly *defined* by conflict: a conflict over what its past has been (the nature of its 'heritage'), conflict over what should be its present development, conflict over what could be its future.

Fourth, and finally, none of this denies place nor the importance of the uniqueness of place. The specificity of place is continually reproduced, but it is not a specificity which results from some long, internalized history. There are a number of sources of this specificity – the uniqueness of place.[4] There is the fact that the wider social relations in which places are set are themselves geographically differentiated. Globalisation (in the economy, or in culture, or in anything else) does not entail simply homogenization. On the contrary, the globalisation of social relations is yet another source of (the reproduction of) geographical uneven development, and thus of the uniqueness of place. There is the specificity of place which derives from the fact that each place is the focus of a distinct *mixture* of wider and more local social relations. There is the fact that this very mixture together in one place may produce effects which would not have happened otherwise. And finally, all these relations interact with and take a further element of specificity from the accumulated history of a place, with that history itself imagined as the product of layer upon layer of different sets of linkages, both local and to the wider world.

In her portrait of Corsica, *Granite Island*, Dorothy Carrington travels the island seeking out the roots of its character.[5] All the different layers of peoples and cultures are explored; the long and tumultuous relationship with France, with Genoa and Aragon in the thirteenth, fourteenth and fifteenth centuries, back through the much earlier incorporation into the Byzantine Empire, and before that domination by the Vandals, before that being part of the Roman Empire, before that the colonization and settlements of the Carthaginians and the Greeks...until we find...that even the megalith builders had come to Corsica from somewhere else.

It is a sense of place, an understanding of 'its character', which can only be constructed by linking that place to places beyond. A progressive sense of place would recognize that, without being threatened by it. What we need, it seems to me, is a global sense of the local, a global sense of place.

NOTES

1. D. Birkett, *New Statesman & Society*, 13 June 1990, pp. 41–2.
2. D. Birkett, *New Statesman & Society*, 15 March 1991, p. 38.
3. P. Wright, *On Living in an Old Country* (London, Verso, 1985), pp. 227, 231.
4. D. Massey, *Spatial Divisions of Labour: Social Structures and the Geography of Production* (Basingstoke, Macmillan, 1984).
5. D. Carrington, *Granite Island: A Portrait of Corsica* (Harmondsworth, Penguin, 1984).

PART V
STRUCTURING THE POLITICAL

INTRODUCTION

In the General Introduction it was argued that one of the key features of thinking conceptually about political life was thinking about 'the political' itself as a concept. In a variety of different ways all the essays in the book address this feature of political thinking. That said, the concepts in this part all have this feature as an explicit and arguably core aspect of their internal conceptual make-up. What is more, they all address, again in an explicit fashion, the very fine line that exists between thinking conceptually about politics and thinking conceptually about thought itself. The concept of ideology that opens this part is the now classic way of introducing this dimension of political thinking: not only is it a core concept of political life itself, it also expresses an idea of what it means to think (or more accurately, the various conceptions of ideology express various ideas of what it is to think). Similarly, the concept of discourse prioritises a novel and challenging view of 'the political' both by bringing to light the fundamentally linguistic construction of our conceptual tools, including 'the political', and by foregrounding discussion on what it means to think, through its inheritance of semiotic analysis. It is no surprise, therefore, that underpinning both ideology and discourse are some of the most fundamental questions of political and philosophical analysis, questions that are, in this part, brought under the banner of difference. Can we think about 'the political' itself in a way which maintains the identity of 'the political' without sacrificing the myriad differences that make it such a vibrant and vital object of study? In this way, we are brought to the closing essay of the part, which examines some of the different ways in which the political itself has been expressed as a body with an identity and also how the identity of the body as a politicised phenomenon has come to be differentiated as a site of multiple political effects. Taken together, these essays provide a rich insight into the complex geological shifts and irruptions that occur beneath our feet as we traverse the landscape of politics.

I

IDEOLOGY

Robert Porter

INTRODUCTION

The intention in this essay is to explore the notion of ideology. Or, more specifically, to explore the issue of whether it is possible to develop what we will call a *critical conception of ideology*. But what would such a critical conception of ideology look like? In order to try to address this question we will draw on the thought of Jürgen Habermas, Gilles Deleuze and Félix Guattari, and Slavoj Žižek. Each of these thinkers will offer us a way of thinking about ideology in critical terms. In other words, Habermas, Deleuze and Guattari, and Žižek will, albeit in their own idiosyncratic way, provide us with three images or ways of picturing what a critical conception of ideology would look like. Now, although these different pictures or images will vary in tone, texture and effect, they will nonetheless be framed in relation to one common theme that is immediately worthy of our attention. That is to say, we will find in Habermas, Žižek and Deleuze and Guattari a (sometimes implicit, sometimes explicit) belief that a critical, and substantive, distinction can be drawn between ideology or the ideological and what we will call *the real*. In this sense, a core element or aspect of the critical conception of ideology to be garnered from Habermas, Žižek and Deleuze and Guattari is that it entails a belief in the autonomy of the real from the ideological. What this will imply is, as we shall see, an insistence on critically understanding ideology as something that is parasitic on the real through which it is subsequently conditioned or mediated.

JÜRGEN HABERMAS

We can begin with Habermas's conception of the real. Put simply, Habermas provides us with a *communicative conception of social reality*. What does this mean? Habermas's claim is that the meanings we invest in the social world are mediated through our intersubjective use of language, being a product of what he famously calls 'communicative action oriented to mutual understanding' (1979: 1; 1984: 288). It is important to acknowledge that Habermas wants to defend this argument in the strongest possible terms. Philosophically speaking, we could say that Habermas is committed to the idea that social reality is *transcendentally conditioned* by communicative action, as the latter is taken to operate as an indispensable or, as Habermas would say, 'inescapable' feature of the former (Habermas 1990b: 82). One of the ways in which Habermas emphasises the transcendental importance or indispensability of communicative action is by insisting that it is vital and necessary in the formation of 'personal identity'. The implication and basis of Habermas's argument can be summed up thus: the process by which social actors collectively invest meaning in their shared social reality is only made possible by the fact that the respective identities of these actors are conditioned in and through communicative action. As Habermas himself puts it:

> The basic facts are the following: creatures that are individuated only through socialisation are vulnerable and morally in need of consider-ateness. Linguistically and behaviourally competent subjects are con-stituted as individuals by growing into an intersubjectively shared life-world, and the lifeworld of the language community is reproduced in turn through the communicative actions of its members . . . Unless the subject externalises herself by participating in interpersonal relation-ships through language, she is unable to form the inner centre that is her personal identity. This explains the almost constitutional insecu-rity and chronic fragility of personal identity – an insecurity that is antecedent to cruder threats to the integrity of life and limb. (1990b: 199)

The significance of Habermas's strong philosophical or transcendental commitment to a communicative conception of social reality is further re-flected in the fact that it can be used as a basis for a critical and normative theory of ideology. As we shall see below, by drawing on a strong claim con-cerning the fundamentally communicative nature of social reality, we are able, with Habermas, to engage in a critique of the forms of ideology that cast a morally or normatively questionable shadow over modern political or public life. In order to make this move from a theory of communica-tive action to a normatively grounded ideology critique, Habermas clearly needs to establish their linkage or relationship. And this is precisely what he does by emphasising that communicative action is necessarily governed by norms that have a distinctly moral resonance. Or, to develop the point slightly, Habermas wants to argue that communicative action oriented to mutual understanding is governed by a number of moral, or at least normatively constraining, assumptions (2000: 46). Four such normative assumptions or conditions are worth emphasising for illustrative purposes here. Firstly, there is a norm of *inclusiveness*. By this Habermas means that no relevant contribution made by speech actors during communicative action may be ignored by others. Secondly, there is a norm of *equal rights to participation*. By this Habermas means that communicative action must remain sufficiently open for all participants to freely or autonomously select and employ speech acts. Thirdly, there is a norm ensuring *immunisation against external compulsion*. By this Habermas means that communicative action must remain unencumbered by extra-discursive constraints such as threats or violence. Fourthly, there is a norm ensuring *the sincere expression of utterances*. By this Habermas means that communicative action between interlocutors be motivated by a genuine and serious concern to reach an intersubjective understanding. Again, it is imperative that we underline the *transcendental* weight that Habermas tries to lend to this argument. For these moral norms are, Habermas insists after a certain Kantian fashion, best thought of as necessary or 'unavoidable presuppositions' that invariably condition our communicative engagements with others (2000: 46).

Habermas's claim that communicative action is transcendentally governed by moral norms is undoubtedly a provocative one. Indeed, many critics and commentators have wondered whether the normatively textured picture of communicative action painted by Habermas is too rosy, idealised or impractical (See for example Rorty 2000: 2). Leaving aside the vexed question of whether Habermas's communication theory is ultimately susceptible to such a charge, it is imperative that we, in the limited space available to us here, focus on the issue of ideology. In essence, Habermas's normativism, his commitment to the idea that the communicative meanings we invest in social reality are normatively conditioned, can be employed as a critical standard against which to analyse the operation of ideology. Ideology, from a Habermasian perspective, functions by essentially repressing normativity: that is, by superimposing itself on social reality in a way that fails to take due regard of the communicative and normative structure of social relations. Consider, to take one of Habermas's own favoured examples, the ideological influence of money or economic power in modern public life (Habermas 1987: 363). In *The Structural Transformation of the Public Sphere*, one of his earliest works, Habermas provides an analysis of the influence of market forces, or what he would call 'commercialisation', in the modern public realm. That is to say, he emphasises how public institutions such as the modern press – 'the public sphere's pre-eminent institution' as he calls it – are ideologically circumscribed by commercial pressures, becoming, as it were, the mere consumptive vehicle for 'advertising' (1989: 181).

As a critic of this developing consumerism, Habermas is concerned, not unlike the young Karl Marx, to bring out the disparity between the terms on which it is justified and the actual consequences of its operation: that is, the contradiction between the 'idea' of consumerism and its 'ideology' (1989: 88–9). Generally speaking, the justification of the 'idea' of consumerism intuitively rests on an normatively inflected claim concerning its democratic responsiveness to the wants, desires and needs of the individuals who make up the public sphere. From a Habermasian perspective, though, this claim is inherently problematic, normatively deficient or ideological. The essence of Habermas's ideology critique is this: a public sphere governed by the dictates of the market is, in effect, a sham, normatively deficient and ideologically circumscribed to the extent that it stunts democratic conversation or what he calls 'rational-critical debate' on matters of shared public and political importance. One of the ways in which the dictates of the market or consumerist ideology stunt 'rational-critical debate' is by fostering a kind of atomism in social life. In a consumer society, debate and democratic conversation in the public sphere becomes increasingly difficult precisely because the forms of what Habermas calls 'public communication' facilitated through it are primarily directed at an atomised addressee. The 'web' of public communication, says Habermas, 'becomes unravelled into acts of individuated reception' (1989: 161). What Habermas means to say here is that the mass consumption of cultural products and public information – the consumption of newspapers, television, books, film, radio etc. – becomes so privatised and atomised that it radically curtails the possibility of individuals collectively engaging in a democratic conversation concerning issues of public and political significance (1989: 172).

Above we suggested that by drawing on a strong claim concerning the communicative nature of social reality, we are able, with Habermas, to engage in a critique of the forms of ideology that cast a morally or normatively questionable shadow over modern political or public life. We are now in a position to further clarify this crucial point. As we have seen, Habermas provides us with a communicative conception of social reality. Indeed, we saw how Habermas was concerned to mount a transcendental argument to the effect that the communicative nature of social reality is reflected in the way the self-conscious meanings we invest in the social world are inescapably conditioned in linguistically mediated interaction. Further, we saw that this transcendental feature of social life has, from a Habermasian perspective, a corresponding normative aspect precisely because communicative action is taken to be unavoidably governed by moral norms. Now, it is against this communicative and normative background that we must understand the status and function of ideology in social life. In terms used above, we can say that ideology functions by superimposing itself on social reality in a way that fails to take due regard of the communicative and normative social relations that sustain it. To put it another way, ideology operates under what we could call a *transcendental constraint*, or a set of communicative and normative conditions that indelibly leave their trace or mark on it. In a sense, this is what the Habermasian critique of consumerist ideology shows. Consumerism, from a Habermasian perspective, is justified by the normatively inflected claim that it represents a democratic form of social interaction between producer and consumer. Yet consumerism can be critically exposed as ideological to the extent that it fails, normatively speaking, to live up to this 'idea' in reality, being, as we implied a moment ago, the atomistic thorn in the side of democratic conversation.

Let us now bring our brief engagement with Habermas to a conclusion. From the perspective of a critical conception of ideology, the crucial point to emphasise is this: *ideology is to be critically analysed as something that is parasitic on the real in which it is invariably conditioned*. This amounts to saying, with Habermas, that we can only make sense of the operation of ideology by understanding it against the communicatively and normatively structured social relations through which it is mediated and given shape. It is best to think of the Habermasian image of communicatively and normatively structured social relations as importantly autonomous from the influence of ideology. Or, put in slightly different terms, the communicative and normative constraints that indelibly shape the meanings we invest in the contemporary social world are part of the constitutive fabric of a *non-ideological* or, better still, *pre-ideological* social reality onto which ideology is then grafted. Habermas refers to this as 'the normative content of modernity' (1987: 336–7).

Slavoj Žižek

Let us turn our attention to Žižek. Like Habermas, Žižek is keen to insist on the idea that a strong and substantive critical distinction can be drawn between the ideological and the real. But the manner in which he theorises this critical distinction is markedly different. Rather than drawing on language philosophy to argue for a communicative conception of the real, Žižek, *contra* Habermas, draws on the thought of Jacques Lacan to argue for what we can call a psychoanalytically inflected conception of 'the Real'. The importance of this notion of 'the Real' to Žižek is virtually impossible to overestimate, for it is the idea around which his theory of ideology – indeed all his thinking – so crucially turns. If this Lacanian notion of 'the Real' is the most crucial and significant of Žižek's conceptual lexicon, then this is clearly because it serves as a constant reference, permeating all his writing and argumentation. That this writing is thematically heterogeneous and constantly changing means that the concept of 'the Real' is forever being robbed of any settled meaning. Žižek adopts this style of writing about 'the Real' for a considered reason: namely, because he believes that a crucial way of coming into contact with 'the Real' is via the essentially negative experience that is the breakdown of shared, social and settled meanings. Crucial to Žižek's enterprise here is the development, and maintenance, of the distinction between 'the Real' and what he calls, again a Lacanian fashion, 'the symbolic'. We can, for our purposes, simply think of 'the symbolic' as a shared space of social meaning or, better still, as the sphere in and through which we invest sense and significance in the social world. Now, when 'the symbolic' breaks down, when the norms and values that sustain the shared space of social meaning are suspended, we, as Žižek would say, 'experience' the 'negativity' of 'the Real'. So, to reiterate this important point, the negative experience of 'the Real' is an experience of a breakdown or suspension of social meaning, a troubling gap or lack in the structure of 'the symbolic'. In *The Sublime Object of Ideology*, Žižek defines this resistance of 'the Real' to symbolic meaning in the following terms:

> The Real . . . is that which cannot be inscribed . . . the rock upon which every formalisation stumbles. But it is precisely through this failure that we can in a way encircle, locate the empty place of the Real. In other words, the Real cannot be inscribed, but we can inscribe this impossibility itself, we can locate its place: a traumatic place which causes a series of failures. And Lacan's whole point is that the Real is nothing but this impossibility of its inscription: the Real is . . . a void, an emptiness in a symbolic structure marking some central impossibility. (1989: 172–3)

What, we may be forgiven for asking, does this differentiation of 'the Real' from 'the symbolic' have to do with ideology? Put simply, the distinction that Žižek wants to maintain apropos 'the Real' and 'the symbolic' provides an important key to his understanding of how 'the Real' can be substantively distinguished from the ideological. Two points are worth broadly emphasising in order to clarify Žižek's thinking in this respect. Firstly, ideology circulates within the realm of 'the symbolic', essentially operating by structuring the meaning we invest in 'social reality'. One of the most crucial ways in which ideology can symbolically structure or project a certain image of 'social reality' is, Žižek never tires of pointing out, through the use of 'fantasy'. 'The fundamental level of ideology', he categorically asserts, 'is that of . . . fantasy structuring our social reality' (1989: 33). Consider, to use one of Žižek's favourite examples, the ideology of anti-Semitism, or what he also calls 'anti-Semitic paranoia'. Understood in the formal sense articulated by Žižek, the ideology of 'anti-Semitic paranoia' is predicated on the notion of a 'Jewish plot' that is taken to threaten the fabric of society; or, as that which precipitates the corrosion or corruption of the core values of the organic bond. The reason that this anti-Semitic ideology is, as Žižek says, an 'exemplary' case of 'social fantasy' is because it operates by influencing and shaping the desires of members of the body politic. Or, better still, anti-Semitism is ideologically effective to the degree that it literally teaches subjects to desire and 'enjoy' the purging of the 'Jew', a figure who is perversely assumed to be a clear threat to the organic well-being of the community (Žižek 1989: 126; 1997: 9).

Secondly, if ideology, for Žižek, can assume meaning and significance in 'the symbolic' by structuring or projecting a certain image of 'social reality', then it is in 'the Real' that this fixity of meaning will break down. What Žižek wants to argue for here is a notion of 'the Real' that is *immanent to*, and disruptive of, the symbolic operation of ideology. To say that 'the Real' is *immanent to* the symbolic functioning of ideology is, from a Žižekian perspective, to immediately suggest that the latter is indelibly marked by the prospect of failing to overwhelmingly fix social meaning and order social life. Žižek refers to this as the experience of 'the Real' as 'antagonism'. There is, Žižek says, a 'central antagonism' at the heart of all ideological discourses to the extent that they are 'doomed to fail' in their pursuit of symbolically imposing an unassailable meaning or order on 'the social' (1989: 127). Why, according to Žižek, does ideology fail in this way? It is because the meanings we attach to 'social reality', the meanings we invest in the symbolic realm, are essentially and forever contestable; and it is never possible to reach what Žižek calls 'a point of supreme density of Meaning' because meaning itself can never be assumed, but is always performed by the agent who posits it as such (1989: 99). So, and to reinforce Žižek's main point, 'the Real' immanently flows through and disrupts the symbolic functioning of ideology as an avoidable or necessary experience of 'antagonism', where 'antagonism' signifies or bears witness to the contingent and contestable meanings at play in all ideological discourses (1989: 163–4).

This experience of 'antagonism', this experience of the essential contestability or fragility of meaning, this experience of 'the Real' immanently resonating through 'the symbolic', is something that Žižek shows to be concretely mediated in the act of engaging in ideology critique. Consider, for instance, Žižek's own critique of the ideology of 'anti-Semitic paranoia'. Žižek's psychoanalytical and critical point here is that anti-Semitic ideology creates the fantasy figure of a threatening 'Jew' to act as a kind of scapegoat onto which the ills of society are projected. In a way, there is what he calls a form of 'displacement' at work whereby 'social antagonism' condenses around the figure of the 'Jew' who alone is offered as the source and reason for social strife and unrest. The clear consequence of this, for Žižek, is that the genuine sources or causes of antagonism in social life are removed from view, hidden, as they are, behind the smoke-screen of anti-Semitic paranoia (1989: 125). Framed in Žižek's terms, this ideology critique of anti-Semitism touches 'the Real', or bears witness to 'the Real' of 'antagonism', precisely through contesting and challenging the meaning of the fantasy figure of the 'Jew' (1994: 25). More generally, what we have emerging here is an image of 'the Real' that is importantly *autonomous from* the influence of ideology. That is to say, 'the Real' can be thought of as a critical space, or, as Žižek prefers, 'place', from which we can wrestle free from the grip of ideology: 'the Real' testifies to the prospect of gaining a critical 'distance' from the ideological (Žižek 1994: 17).

We are now in a position to sum up our engagement with Žižek. Four points are worth emphasising in this regard. Firstly, an adequate understanding of the operation of ideology in social life must, from a Žižekian perspective, proceed from an analysis of its 'symbolic function': that is to say, the critic of ideology must be sensitive to the ways in which ideology attempts to impose a certain fixity of meaning on 'social reality'. Secondly, by bringing into focus the contingent and contestable meanings or assumptions at play in such images of 'social reality', the critic of ideology bears witness to 'the Real', or, better still, 'the Real' of 'antagonism'. Further, and this is our third point, the space afforded to the critic by the existence of 'the Real' is at once a space, or 'place', that marks a distance from the grip or subjugating influence of ideology. Indeed, it is best to think of the 'place' of 'the Real' as a *non-ideological or pre-ideological site* which signifies the essential contestability and fragility of the meanings and assumptions that sustain ideological images of 'social reality'. Extrapolating from this, fourthly and finally, we can say that ideology is *parasitic on 'the Real'*, or is grounded in accordance with 'the Real', which immanently, and disturbingly, resonates through it.

GILLES DELEUZE AND FÉLIX GUATTARI

Let us now turn finally to Deleuze and Guattari. The first thing that we should acknowledge concerning Deleuze and Guattari's understanding of the concept of ideology is that they seem, at least at first sight, to express an open hostility concerning its critical utility. For example, in their delightfully baroque and provocative work *A Thousand Plateaus*, Deleuze and Guattari categorically assert: 'There is no ideology and never has been' (1988: 4). In light of such a remark it may seem strange to insist that we can garner a critical conception of ideology from Deleuze and Guattari, that Deleuze and Guattari can help us draw a substantive distinction between what we have been calling the ideological and the real. The irony or paradoxical nature of such an enterprise would not be lost on the commentators or Deleuze and Guattari scholars that take them at their word, assuming they are simply unconcerned with the problematic of ideology (See for example Colebrook 2002: 92). And yet, as we shall see in a moment, things are not quite as cut and dried as they may first appear. That is to say, Deleuze and Guattari can be shown to express a concern to critically employ the concept of ideology. A good example of this is when they critique the psychoanalytical theory of desire (1984: 101). Central to this critique is Deleuze and Guattari's insistence on the limitations of psychoanalytically theorising the origin and essence of desire in terms of the mythology of Oedipus. In essence, Deleuze and Guattari's argument is this: the drama or mythology of Oedipus does not explain or provide an adequate foundation for understanding the nature or origin of desire. On the contrary, the appearance and use of Oedipus mythology is something that must be explained, or critically accounted for. As Deleuze and Guattari put it in a crucial passage:

> Only in appearance is Oedipus a beginning, either as a historical or prehistorical origin, or as a structural foundation. In reality it is a completely ideological beginning, for the sake of ideology. Oedipus is always and solely an aggregate of destination fabricated to meet the requirements of an aggregate of departure constituted by a social formation. (1984: 101)

The significance of this passage – at least for our purposes – is obviously reflected in the fact that Deleuze and Guattari mobilise or use the concept of *ideology* to critically account for the 'fabricated' or constructed nature of Oedipus. What this clearly implies, of course, is that the concept of ideology still retains a specific critical purpose and utility in helping them come to terms with the way the psychoanalytical conception of desire is constituted. Two general points are worth emphasising in order to finesse and clarify the notion of ideology that Deleuze and Guattari are critically employing here. Firstly, if ideology refers to the 'fabricated' nature of social phenomena such as the 'oedipalisation' of desire, then a critique of this ideology obviously implies bringing into sharp focus its constructedness. In this sense, ideology critique implies what Deleuze and Guattari would call a 'constructivism', where 'constructivism' signifies a critical sensitivity to how supposedly universal, eternal or timeless concepts (for example the 'Oedipus complex') are, in reality, the product of specific 'fabrications' or 'creations' (Deleuze and Guattari 1994: 49). Now, this does not mean that the operation of ideology in social life is simply a matter of trickery, whereby the dominant elite deceive the duped masses with a lie which represses their interests and ensures their continuing servitude. Rather, ideology works through the structuring or fixation of desire, and the ideologically repressed, Deleuze and Guattari provocatively conclude, *remain in servitude precisely because they have been literally moved to desire it*. This is point that Deleuze and Guattari make apropos the ideology of fascism: that is to say, the historical success of fascism needs to be accounted for in terms of a manipulation or, as they say, 'perversion' of the desire(s) of the masses that were moved to crave it (1984: 29).

The second important point that needs to be emphasised in relation to the above passage is that Deleuze and Guattari explicitly ground their ideology critique (of Oedipus and the psychoanalytical theory of desire) with reference to the concept of 'reality'. Does this not suggest the clear possibility that, in our terms, a substantive distinction can be drawn between the ideological and the real? Of course, before we can begin to address this question we need to clarify precisely what the term 'reality' signifies in this context. Deleuze and Guattari are quite categorical on this issue, and are worth quoting accordingly:

> There is no such thing as the social production of reality on the one hand, and a desiring-production that is mere fantasy on the other... The truth of the matter is that *social production is purely and simply desiring-production itself under determinate conditions*. We maintain that the social field is immediately invested by desire, that it is the historically determined product of desire... *There is only desire and the social, and nothing else.* (1984: 28–9)

By insisting that desire importantly functions to produce the social field, Deleuze and Guattari clearly reserve a constitutive or constructive role for desire in the shaping of social reality. Now, ideology enters the frame here only through the fixation or repression of desire, or only when certain forms of desire belie their own 'fabricated' nature; being imbued, as they are, with an illusory universal, eternal or, as Deleuze and Guattari would also say, 'transcendental' status (1994: 73). So what can be emphasised here, with Deleuze and Guattari, is the emerging difference or distinction between 'the real' as constitutively anchored in desire, and 'the ideological' as operating through the fixation or repression of desire (1984: 26–9, 101). Before concluding our encounter with Deleuze and Guattari, it is necessary to emphasise the formal homology or similarity of their thinking with that of Žižek and Habermas discussed above. For, in a crucial sense, Deleuze and Guattari's notion of the real is autonomously *non-ideological* or *pre-ideological*, expressing the essentially 'fabricated' nature of the forms of desire that influence the meaning we invest in the social world. Ideology *parasitically* comes into being, and works its questionable magic, when the flow of desire is truncated: when we actively forget that desire is constructed, and, in this sense, open to reconstruction. And one of the critical dangers here, from Deleuze and Guattari's perspective, is that we may fail to see how the 'deliberate creation' of certain types of desire can be ideologically mobilised in order to serve the interests of a 'dominant' group or 'class' in the social order (Deleuze and Guattari 1984: 28).

CONCLUSION

Taken together, or understood in the formal sense articulated above, we can begin to see how Habermas, Žižek and Deleuze and Guattari provide us with a *critical conception of ideology*, where a 'critical conception of ideology' signifies or entails a belief in the autonomy of the real from the ideological. Whether we think of the real as constitutively anchored in desire (Deleuze and Guattari), as an experience of 'antagonism' (Žižek), or as mediated through communicative action (Habermas), the inference in each case is formally homologous: namely, *that ideology is parasitic on the real through which it is invariably conditioned*. Before concluding, or by way of conclusion, it is perhaps right to sound a note of caution concerning this image of ideology. The first, and perhaps most obvious, thing to say here is that the belief in the autonomy of the real over the ideological is hardly a universal article of faith among contemporary theorists of ideology. Indeed, the contemporary history of ideology theory has been increasingly marked by the refrain that any clear-cut distinction between the ideological and the real is problematic to the degree that the former conditions the latter. From this perspective, ideology is critically assumed to be an *inescapable* or *omnipresent* condition of social reality, as it is thought to be constitutively embedded in the sense-creating activities of social actors (see for example Althusser 1984 or Freeden 1996). In this way, we could think – somewhat ironically – of the belief in an autonomous or non-ideological real as decidedly ideological, or as particularly insensitive to the ideological influences or aspects implied therein.

The strength, provocation and merit of the kind of critical conception of ideology provided by Habermas, Žižek and Deleuze and Guattari is precisely reflected in its very resistance to the idea that ideology is an inescapable or omnipresent feature of social life. If we were to simply accept that the real is irreducibly ideological, that social reality is inescapably ideological, then this would mean that a critique of the forms of ideology we encounter in social life would be impossible to maintain. Why? Well, a critique of ideology (e.g. Habermas's critique of consumerism, Žižek's critique of 'anti-Semitic paranoia', or Deleuze and Guattari's critique of 'fascism') immediately implies that the critic is able to maintain some real or genuine distance over the thing criticised (i.e. that 'anti-Semitic' paranoia' is, in reality, displaced 'antagonism', that 'fascism' is, in reality, 'perverted' desire, that consumerism does, in reality, stunt the prospect of 'rational-critical' debate). To stress the inescapability or omnipresence of ideology in social life is to intuitively insist that the very act of engaging in critique is itself ideologically implicated. Therefore, the position of the critic is circumscribed as forever labouring under the grip of ideology. From the perspective of a critical conception of ideology, this conclusion lacks merit because it can all too easily end in a kind of quietism, or even cynicism, concerning the prospects of critically analysing the forms of ideology encountered in social life. Further, we could suggest, as Žižek explicitly does, that such quietism or cynicism serves a decidedly political purpose in reproducing the 'structuring power' of the ideological status quo (1989: 28–30).

QUESTIONS FOR DISCUSSION

- Habermas, Žižek and Deleuze and Guattari all implicitly or explicitly suggest that a substantive and critical distinction can be drawn between the ideological and the real. Do you agree?
- 'Ideology is an inescapable or omnipresent condition of social reality to the extent that it is embedded in the sense-creating activities of social actors'. Discuss.
- Is it possible to identify where ideology ends and where discourse begins? Or all are forms of discourse inevitably and irreducibly ideological?
- Implied in the different critiques of ideology advanced by Habermas, Žižek and Deleuze and Guattari (i.e. Habermas's critique of consumerism, Žižek's critique of anti-Semitism and Deleuze and Guattari's critique of fascism) is the notion that ideology compromises the freedom or liberty of subjects (i.e. subjects of consumerism, subjects of anti-Semitism or subjects of fascism). Does it make sense, then, to understand the critique of ideology in conjunction with a pursuit of liberty?

JÜRGEN HABERMAS
EXTRACTS FROM *THE PHILOSOPHICAL DISCOURSE OF MODERNITY*

THE NORMATIVE CONTENT OF MODERNITY

The radical critique of reason exacts a high price for taking leave of modernity. In the first place, these discourses can and want to give no account of their own position. Negative dialectics, genealogy, and deconstruction alike avoid those categories in accord with which modern knowledge has been differentiated – by no means accidentally – and on the basis of which we today understand texts. They cannot be unequivocally classified with either philosophy or science, with moral and legal theory, or with literature and art. At the same time, they resist any return to forms of religious thought, whether dogmatic or heretical. So an incongruity arises between these 'theories', which raise validity claims only to renounce them, and the kind of institutionalization they undergo within the business of science. There is an asymmetry between the rhetorical gesture with which these discourses demand understanding and the critical treatment to which they are subjected institutionally, for example in the framework of an academic lecture. No matter whether Adorno paradoxically reclaims truth-validity, or Foucault refuses to draw consequences from manifest contradictions; no matter whether Heidegger and Derrida evade the obligation to provide grounds by fleeing into the esoteric or by fusing the logical with the rhetorical: There always emerges a symbiosis of incompatibles, an amalgam that resists 'normal' scientific analysis at its core. Things are only shifted to a different place if we change the frame of reference and no longer treat the

Jürgen Habermas (1987), *The Philosophical Discourse of Modernity*, Cambridge: Polity Press. Notes not included.

same discourse as philosophy or science, but as a piece of literature. That the self-referential critique of reason is located everywhere and nowhere, so to speak, in discourses without a place, renders it almost immune to competing interpretations. Such discourses unsettle the institutionalized standards of fallibilism; they always allow for a final word, even when the argument is already lost: that the opponent has misunderstood the meaning of the language game and has committed a category mistake in the *sorts* of responses he has been making.

The variations of a critique of reason with reckless disregard for its own foundations are related to one another in another respect as well. They are guided by normative intuitions that go beyond what they can accommodate in terms of the indirectly affirmed 'other of reason'. Whether modernity is described as a constellation of life that is reified and used, or as one that is technologically manipulated, or as one that is totalitarian, rife with power, homogenized, imprisoned – the denunciations are constantly inspired by a special sensitivity for complex injuries and subtle violations. Inscribed in this sensitivity is the picture of an undamaged intersubjectivity that the young Hegel first projected as an ethical totality. With the counterconcepts (injected as empty formulas) of Being, sovereignty, power, difference, and nonidentity, this critique points to the contents of aesthetic experience; but the values derived therefrom and explicitly laid claim to – the values of grace and illumination, ecstatic rapture, bodily integrity, wish-fulfillment, and caring intimacy – do not cover the moral change that these authors tacitly envision in connection with a life practice that is intact – and not only in the sense of reconciling inner nature. Between the declared normative foundations and the concealed ones there is a disparity that can be explained by the *undialectical* rejection of subjectivity. Not only the devastating consequences of an objectifying relation-to-self are condemned along with this principle of modernity, but also the *other* connotations once associated with subjectivity as an unredeemed promise: the prospect of a self-conscious practice, in which the solidary self-determination of all was to be joined with the self-realization of each. What is thrown out is precisely what a modernity reassuring itself once meant by the concepts of self-consciousness, self-determination, and self-realization.

A further defect of these discourses is explained by their totalizing repudiation of modern forms of life: although they are interesting in regard to fundamentals, they remain undifferentiated in their results. The criteria according to which Hegel and Marx, and even Max Weber and Lukács, distinguished between emancipatory-reconciling aspects of social rationalization and repressive-alienating aspects have been blunted. In the meantime, critique has taken hold of and demolished the sorts of concepts by which those aspects could be distinguished from one another so that their paradoxical entanglement became visible. Enlightenment and manipulation, the conscious and the unconscious, forces of production and forces of destruction, expressive self-realization and repressive desublimation, effects that ensure freedom and those that remove it, truth and ideology – now all these moments flow into one another. They are not linked to one another as, say, conflicting elements in a disastrous functional context – unwilling accomplices in a contradictory process permeated by oppositional conflict. Now the differences and oppositions are so undermined and even collapsed that critique can no longer discern contrasts, shadings, and ambivalent tones within the flat and faded landscape of a totally administered, calculated, and power-laden world. To be sure, Adorno's theory of the administered world and Foucault's theory of power are more fertile, and simply more informative, than Heidegger's or Derrida's lucubrations on technology as an instrumental frame (*Gestell*) or on the totalitarian nature of the political order. But they are all insensitive to the highly *ambivalent* content of cultural and social modernity. This leveling can also be seen in the diachronic comparison of modern forms of life with pre-modern ones. The high price earlier exacted from the mass of the population (in the dimensions of bodily labor, material conditions, possibilities of individual choice, security of law and punishment, political participation, and schooling) is barely even noticed.

It is worthy of note that in the various approaches to the critique of reason, no systematic place is envisaged for everyday practice. Pragmatism, phenomenology, and hermeneutic philosophy have bestowed an epistemological status upon the categories of everyday action, speech, and common life. Marx even singled out everyday practice as the locus where the rational content of philosophy was supposed to flow into the life forms of an emancipated society. But Nietzsche so directed the gaze of his successors to the phenomena of the extraordinary that they contemptuously glide over the practice of everyday life as something derivative or inauthentic. [. . .] In communicative action the creative moment of the linguistic constitution of the world forms *one syndrome* with the cognitive-instrumental, moral-practical, and expressive moments of the intramundane linguistic functions of representation, interpersonal relation, and subjective expression. In the modern world, 'value spheres' have been differentiated out from each of these moments – namely, on the one hand, art, literature, and a criticism specialized in questions of taste, around the axis of *world-disclosure*; and, on the other hand, problem-solving discourses specialized in questions of truth and justice, around the axis of *intramundane learning processes*. These knowledge systems of art and criticism, science and philosophy, law and morality, have become the more split off from ordinary communication the more strictly and one-sidedly they each have to do with one linguistic function and one aspect of validity. But they should not be considered on account of this abstraction per se as phenomena of decline symptomatic of subject-centered reason.

To Nietzscheanism, the differentiation of science and morality appears as the formative process of a reason that at once usurps and stifles the poetic, world-disclosing power of art. Cultural modernity seems a realm of horrors, marked by the totalitarian traits of a subject-centered reason that structurally overburdens itself. Three simple facts are filtered out of this picture: first, the fact that those aesthetic experiences in the light of which true nature is supposed to reveal itself to an exclusive reason are due to the same process of differentiation as science and morality. Then the fact that cultural modernity also owes its division into special discourses for questions of taste, truth, and justice to an increase in knowledge that is hard to dispute. And especially the fact that it is only the modalities of interchange between these knowledge systems and everyday practice that determine whether the gains from such abstraction affect the lifeworld destructively.

From the viewpoint of individual cultural spheres of value, the syndrome of the everyday world appears as 'life' or as 'practice' or as 'ethos', over against which stands 'art' or 'theory' or 'morality'. We have already spoken about the mediating roles of criticism and philosophy in another context. For criticism, the relationship between 'art' and 'life' is just as problematic as the relationship between 'theory' and 'practice' or between 'morality' and 'ethos' is for philosophy. The *unmediated* transposition of specialized knowledge into the private and public spheres of the everyday world can endanger the autonomy and independent logics of the knowledge systems, on the one hand, and it can violate the integrity of lifeworld contexts, on the other. A knowledge specialized in only one validity claim, which, without sticking to its specific context, bounces across the whole spectrum of validity, unsettles the equilibrium of the lifeworld's communicative infrastructure. Insufficiently complex incursions of this sort lead to the aestheticizing, or the scienticizing, or the moralizing of particular domains of life and give rise to effects for which expressivist countercultures, technocratically carried out reforms, or fundamentalist movements can serve as drastic examples.

The profounder paradoxes of *societal* rationalization, however, are still not even touched by the complicated relationships between ordinary and expert *cultures*. They have to do with the systematically induced reification of everyday practice, to which I will return presently. However, the very first steps along the path to differentiation in the picture of the ambiguously rationalized lifeworld of modern societies already bring to our awareness the problem that will concern us in this last lecture.

De-differentiations are built into the leveling critique of reason only on the basis of descriptions that are guided in turn by normative intuitions. This normative content has to be acquired and justified from the rational potential inherent in everyday practice, if it is not to remain arbitrary. The concept of a communicative reason that transcends subject-centered reason, which I have provisionally introduced, is intended to lead away from the paradoxes and levelings of a self-referential critique of reason. On another front, it has to be upheld against the competing approach of a systems theory that utterly shoves the problematic of rationality aside, strips away *any* notion of reason as an old European drag, and then light-footedly takes over from the philosophy of the subject (as well as from the theory of power advanced by its sharpest opponents). This double battlefront makes the rehabilitation of the concept of reason a doubly risky business. It has to protect itself on both flanks from getting caught in the traps of the kind of subject-centered thinking that failed to keep the unforced force of reason free both from the *totalitarian* characteristics of an *instrumental* reason that objectifies everything around it, itself included, and from the *totalizing* characteristics of an *inclusive* reason that incorporates everything and, as a unity, ultimately triumphs over every distinction. Praxis philosophy hoped to derive the normative content of modernity from the reason embodied in the mediations of social practice. If the basic concept of communicative action replaces that of social labor, is the totality-perspective built into that concept radically altered?

[. . .]

The approach of communication theory seems to be able to salvage the normative content of modernity only at the cost of idealist abstractions. Once again suspicion is cast on the purism of a purely communicative reason – this time on an abstract description of rationalized lifeworlds that does not take into account the constraints of material reproduction. In order to defuse this suspicion, we have to show that the theory of communication can contribute to explaining how it is that in the modern period an economy organized in the form of markets is functionally intermeshed with a state that has a monopoly on power, how it gains autonomy as a piece of norm-free sociality over against the lifeworld, and how it opposes its own imperatives based on system maintenance to the rational imperatives of the lifeworld. Marx was the first to analyze this conflict between system imperatives and lifeworld imperatives, in the form of a dialectic of dead labor and living labor, of abstract labor and concrete labor; and he vividly illustrated it with materials from social history concerning the irruption of new modes of production into traditional lifeworlds. Meanwhile, the kind of system rationality that first became evident in the independent logic of capital self-realization has taken over other domains of action as well.

No matter how structurally differentiated lifeworlds may be, no matter whether they have developed highly specialized subsystems (and subparts of subparts of subsystems) for the functional domains of cultural reproduction, social integration, and socialization – the complexity of any lifeworld is narrowly restricted by the limits of the strain that can be placed upon the mechanism of mutual understanding. In the degree that a lifeworld is rationalized, the expenditure of understanding borne by the communicative agents themselves increases. This also increases the risk of dissent in a communication that generates a bonding effect only via the double negation of validity claims. Ordinary language is a risky mechanism for coordinating action; it is also expensive, immobile, and restricted in what it can accomplish. The meaning of the individual speech act cannot be detached from the lifeworld's complex horizon of meaning; it remains entwined with the intuitively present background knowledge of interaction participants. The plenitude of connotations, the functional richness, and the capacity for variation proper to the use of language oriented toward mutual understanding is only the reverse side of a relationship to totality that does not allow for any arbitrary expansion of the capacity to achieve understanding in everyday practice.

Because lifeworlds can afford only a restricted outlay for coordination and understanding, at a certain level of complexity ordinary language has to be disencumbered by the sorts of special languages that Talcott Parsons studied in connection with the example of money. When the medium for coordinating action no longer has to be called upon for *all* linguistic functions at once, then there is a disburdening effect. The binding of communicatively guided action to contexts of the lifeworld is also reduced by the partial replacement of ordinary language. Social processes set free in this way become 'de-worlded', that is, released from those relationships to the totality and those structures of intersubjectivity by which culture, society, and personality are interlaced with one another. Functions of material reproduction are especially open to this kind of disburdening because they do not per se need to be fulfilled by communicative actions. Changes in conditions in the material substrate can be traced back directly to the aggregate results and consequences of goal-directed interventions in the objective world. To be sure, these teleological actions need coordination too; they have to be socially integrated. But the integration can occur by way of an *impoverished* and *standardized* language that coordinates functionally specialized activities – for instance, the production and distribution of goods and services – without burdening social integration with the expense of risky and uneconomical processes of mutual understanding, and without connecting up with processes of cultural transmission and socialization through the medium of ordinary language. Evidently the medium of money satisfies these conditions for a specially encoded steering language. It has branched off from normal language as a special code that is tailored to special situations (of exchange); it conditions decisions for action on the basis of a built-in preference structure (of supply and demand), in a way that is effective for coordination but without having to lay claim to the resources of the lifeworld.

However, money makes possible not only specifically de-worlded forms of interaction, but the formation of a functionally specialized subsystem that articulates its relationships to the environment via money. Considered historically, capitalism saw the rise of an economic system that regulates internal exchanges as well as interchanges with its noneconomic environments (private households and the state) through monetary channels. The institutionalization of wage labor on the one hand, and that of a state based on taxation on the other, was as constitutive of the new mode of production as was the organizational form of the capitalist enterprise inside the economic system. Complementary environments were formed in the measure that the productive process was shifted over to wage labor and the apparatus of government was linked to production via taxes on those employed. On the one side, the state apparatus became dependent upon a media-steered economic system; this led, among other things, to the assimilation of official and personal power to the structure of a steering medium; that is, power became assimilated to money. On the other side, traditional forms of labor and of life broke down under the grip of gainful labor organized in business enterprises. The plebeianizing of the rural population and the proletarianizing of the labor force highly concentrated in cities became the first exemplary case of a systemically induced reification of everyday practice.

With exchange processes operating through media there emerges in modern societies a third level of autonomous functional contexts – above the level of simple interactions as well as beyond the level of forms of organization still bound to the lifeworld. Contexts of interaction that have gained autonomy as subsystems and that go beyond the horizon of the lifeworld congeal into the second nature of a norm-free sociality. This decoupling of system from lifeworld is experienced within modern lifeworlds as a *reification of life forms*. Hegel reacted to this basic experience with the concept of the 'positive' and the idea of a dirempted ethical totality; Marx started more specifically from alienated industrial labor and class antagonisms. Operating under premises of the philosophy of the subject, they both nevertheless underestimated the independent logic of systemically integrated domains of action that are dissociated from structures of intersubjectivity to such an extent that they no longer exhibit any structural analogies with socially integrated domains of action differentiated *within* the lifeworld. For Hegel and Marx, the system of needs or capitalist society arose from processes of abstraction that still pointed to ethical totality or rational praxis and remained subject to their structures. These abstractions constituted nonindependent moments within the self-relation and self-movement of a higher-level subject, into which they would flow once again. In Marx, this overcoming (*Aufhebung*) takes the shape of a revolutionary praxis, which breaks the systemic logic of capital's self-realization, brings the independent economic process back into the horizon of the lifeworld again, and frees the realm of freedom from the dictates of the realm of necessity. In attacking the private ownership of the means of production, the revolution simultaneously strikes at the institutional foundations of the medium through which the capitalist economy was differentiated out. The lifeworld rigidified under the law of value is to be given back its spontaneity; at that very moment, the objective illusion of capital will dissolve away into nothing.

As we have seen, this melting down of systemically reified domains of action into a spontaneous relation-to-self of spirit or of society already met with strong opposition from the Right Hegelians of the first generation. Against the de-differentiation of state and society, they insisted on the objective distinction between the societal system and the governmental subject. Their neoconservative successors gave this thesis an affirmative twist. Hans Freyer and Joachim Ritter saw in the dynamic of the reification of culture and society only the reverse side of the constitution of a realm of subjective freedom worth striving for. Arnold Gehlen criticized even the latter as an empty subjectivity released from all objective imperatives. Even those who, following Lukács, fastened upon the concept of reification came to agree more and more with their opponents in their description; they were increasingly impressed with the impotence of subjects in relation to the feedback processes of self-regulating systems, over which they could have no influence. It makes almost no difference whether the one indicts as a negative totality what the other celebrates as a crystallization; or whether the one denounces as reification what the other technocratically lays down as the law of reality. For decades, this trend in the social-theoretical diagnosis of the age has been heading toward the point that systems functionalism makes into its own point: it allows the subjects themselves to degenerate into systems. It tacitly sets a seal on 'the end of the individual', which Adorno encircled with his negative dialectic and protested against as a self-inflicted fate. Niklas Luhmann simply presupposes that the structures of intersubjectivity have collapsed and that individuals have become disengaged from their lifeworlds – that personal and social systems form environments for each other. The barbaric condition predicted by Marx in case revolutionary praxis failed is characterized by a complete subsumption of the lifeworld under the imperatives of a valorization process decoupled from use-values and concrete labor. Undisturbed by this, systems functionalism proceeds from the assumption that this condition has already set in – not merely at the entrance to the capitalist economy, but in the forecourts of *every* functional system. The marginalized lifeworld could survive only if it were to be transformed in turn into a media-steered subsystem and if it were to shed everyday communicative practice like a snakeskin.

On the one hand, Luhmann's version of systems functionalism takes up the heritage of the philosophy of the subject; it replaces the self-relating subject with a self-relating system. On the other hand, it radicalizes Nietzsche's critique of reason by withdrawing any kind of claim to reason along with the relationship to the totality of the lifeworld.

The fact that Luhmann draws upon the reflective content of these two opposed traditions and brings motifs from Kant and Nietzsche together in a cybernetic language game indicates the level at which he establishes social systems theory. Luhmann takes the same characteristics that Foucault attributed to discourse formations with the help of a transcendental-historical concept of power and transfers them to meaning-elaborating systems that operate in a self-relating fashion. Since he also relinquishes the intention of a critique of reason together with the concept of reason, he can turn all the statements that Foucault made by way of denunciation into descriptive ones. In this respect, Luhmann pushes the neoconservative affirmation of social modernity to a peak, and also to heights of reflection where everything the advocates of postmodernity could come up with has already been thought of – without any complaints and in a more differentiated manner. Moreover, systems functionalism is not open to the objection of being unable to give an account of its own status; it places itself without any hesitation within the system of science and comes forward with a claim to 'disciplinary universality'. Nor can it be charged with a tendency toward leveling. At most, Luhmann's theory, which is today incomparable when it comes to its power of conceptualization, its theoretical imaginativeness, and its capacity for processing information, raises doubts as to whether the price for its 'gains in abstraction' is not too high. The tireless shredding machine of reconceptualization separates out the 'undercomplex' lifeworld as an indigestible residue – precisely the realm of phenomena of interest to a social theory that has not burned all bridges to the prescientific experience of crisis.

In regard to the capitalist economy, Marx did not distinguish between the new level of system differentiation brought about by a media-steered economic system and the class-specific forms of its institutionalization. For him, abolishing class structures and melting down the independent systemic logic of functionally differentiated and reified domains of interaction formed a single syndrome. Luhmann commits a complementary error. Faced with the new level of the differentiation of systems, he overlooks the fact that media such as money and power, via which functional systems set themselves off from the lifeworld, have in turn to be institutionalized in the life-world. This is why the class-specific distributive effects of the media's being anchored in property laws and constitutional norms do not come into view at all. 'Inclusion', in the sense of the equal rights of all individuals to access to all functional systems, thus appears as a systemically necessary outcome of the process of differentiation. Whereas for Marx systemically autonomous functional contexts go up in smoke after a successful revolution, for Luhmann the lifeworld now has already lost all significance in the functionally differentiated societies of the modern world. What disappears from both perspectives is the mutual interpenetration and opposition of system and lifeworld imperatives, which explains the double-front character of societal modernization.

The paradoxes of societal rationalization, which I have developed elsewhere, may be summarized in an oversimplified way as follows. The rationalization of the lifeworld had to reach a certain maturity before the media of money and power could be legally institutionalized in it. The two functional systems of the market economy and the administrative state, which grew beyond the horizon of the political orders of stratified class societies, destroyed the traditional life forms of old European society to begin with. The internal dynamic of these two functionally intermeshed subsystems, however, also reacts back upon the rationalized life forms of modern society that made them possible, to the extent that processes of monetarization and bureaucratization penetrate the core domains of cultural reproduction, social integration, and socialization. Forms of interaction shaped by these media cannot encroach upon realms of life that by their function are dependent on action oriented to mutual understanding without the appearance of pathological side effects. In the political systems of advanced capitalist societies, we find compromise structures that, historically considered, can be conceived of as reactions on the part of the lifeworld to the independent systemic logic and growth in complexity proper to the capitalist economic process and a state apparatus with a monopoly on force. These origins have left their traces on the options that remain open to us in a social-welfare state in crisis.

The options are determined by the logic of a politics adjusted to the system imperatives of economy and state. The two media-steered subsystems, which constitute environments for one another, are supposed to be intelligently attuned to one another – and not simply to reciprocally externalize their costs so as to burden a total system incapable of self-reflection. Within the scope of such a politics, only the correctly dosed distribution of problems as between the subsystems of state and economy is in dispute. One side sees the causes of crisis in the unleashing of the dynamics proper to the economy; the other side, in the bureaucratic fetters imposed on the former. The corresponding therapies are a social subduing of capitalism or a displacement of problems from administrative planning back to the market. The one side sees the source of the systemically induced disturbances of everyday life in monetarized labor power; the other, in the bureaucratic crippling of personal initiative. But both sides agree in assigning a merely passive role to the vulnerable domains of lifeworld interaction as against the motors of societal modernization: state and economy.

[. . .]

I call those public spheres autonomous which are neither bred nor kept by a political system for purposes of creating legitimation. Centers of concentrated communication that arise spontaneously out of microdomains of everyday practice can develop into autonomous public spheres and consolidate as self-supporting higher-level intersubjectivities only to the degree that the lifeworld potential for self-organization and for the self-organized use of the means of communication are utilized. Forms of self-organization strengthen the collective capacity for action. Grassroots organizations, however, may not cross the threshold to the formal organization of independent systems. Otherwise they will pay for the indisputable gain in complexity by having organizational goals detached from the orientations and attitudes of their members and dependent instead upon imperatives of maintaining and expanding organizational power. The lack of symmetry between capacities for self-reflection and for self-organization that we have ascribed to modern societies as a whole is repeated on the level of the self-organization of processes of opinion and will formation.

This need not be an obstacle, if one considers that the indirect influence of functionally differentiated subsystems on the individual mechanisms of self-steering means something altogether different from the goal-oriented influence of society upon itself. Their self-referential closedness renders the functional systems of politics and economics immune against attempts at intervention in the sense of *direct* interventions. Yet this same characteristic also renders systems sensitive to stimuli aimed at increasing their capacity for self-reflection, that is, their sensitivity to the reactions of the environment to their own activities. Self-organized public spheres must develop the prudent combination of power and intelligent self-restraint that is needed to sensitize the self-steering mechanisms of the state and the economy to the goal-oriented outcomes of radical democratic will formation. In place of the model of society influencing itself, we have the model of boundary conflicts – which are held in check by the lifeworld – between the life-world and two subsystems that are superior to it in complexity and can be influenced by it only indirectly, but on whose performances it at the same time depends.

Autonomous public spheres can draw their strength only from the resources of largely rationalized lifeworlds. This holds true especially for culture, that is to say, for science's and philosophy's potential for interpretations of self and world, for the enlightenment potential of strictly universalistic legal and moral representations, and, not last, for the radical experiential contents of aesthetic modernity. It is no accident that social movements today take on cultural-revolutionary traits. Nonetheless, a structural weakness can be noticed here that is indigenous to all modern lifeworlds. Social movements get their thrust-power from threats to well-defined collective identities. Although such identities always remain tied to the particularism of a special form of life, they have to assimilate the normative content of modernity – the fallibilism, universalism, and subjectivism that undermine the force and concrete shape of any given particularity. Until now, the democratic constitutional nation-state that emerged from the French Revolution was the only identity formation successful on a world-historical scale that could unite these two moments of the universal and the particular without coercion. The Communist party has been unable to replace the identity of the nation-state. If not in the nation, in what other soil can universalistic value orientations today take root? The Atlantic community of values crystallized around NATO is hardly more than a propaganda formula for ministers of defense. The Europe of de Gaulle and Adenauer merely furnishes the superstructure for the basis of trade relations. Quite recently, left intellectuals have been projecting a completely different design as a counter-image to the Europe of the Common Market.

The dream of such a completely different European identity, which assimilates in a decisive way the legacy of Occidental rationalism, is taking shape at a time when the United States is getting ready to fall back into the illusions of the early modern period under the banner of a 'second American Revolution'. In the utopias painted in the old romances about the state, rational forms of life entered into a deceptive symbiosis with the technological mastery of nature and the ruthless mobilization of social labor power. This equation of happiness and emancipation with power and production has been a source of irritation for the self-understanding of modernity from the start – and it has called forth two centuries of criticism of modernity.

But the same utopian (in the bad sense) gestures of mastery are living on now in a caricature that moves the masses. The science fiction of Star Wars is just good enough for the ideology planners to spark – with the macabre vision of a militarized space – an innovative thrust that would give the colossus of worldwide capitalism sufficient footing for its next round of technological development. Old Europe could only find its way clear to a new identity if it opposed to this short circuit of economic growth, arms race, and 'traditional values' the vision of breaking out of these self-inflicted systemic constraints, if it put an end to the confused idea that the normative content of modernity that is stored in rationalized lifeworlds could be set free only by means of ever more complex systems. The idea that the capacity to compete on an international scale – whether in markets or in outer space – is indispensable for our very survival is one of those everyday certitudes in which systemic constraints are condensed. Each one justifies the expansion and intensification of its own forces by the expansion and intensification of the forces of the others, as if it were not the ground rules of social Darwinism that are at the bottom of the play of forces. Modern Europe has created the spiritual presuppositions and the material foundations for a world in which this mentality has taken the place of reason. That is the real heart of the critique of reason since Nietzsche. Who else but Europe could draw from *its own* traditions the insight, the energy, the courage of vision – everything that would be necessary to strip from the (no longer metaphysical, but metabiological) premises of a blind compulsion to system maintenance and system expansion their power to shape our mentality.

GILLES DELEUZE AND FÉLIX GUATTARI
EXTRACTS FROM *ANTI-OEDIPUS: CAPITALISM AND SCHIZOPHRENIA*

If desire produces, its product is real. If desire is productive, it can be productive only in the real world and can produce only reality. Desire is the set of *passive syntheses* that engineer partial objects, flows, and bodies, and that function as units of production. The real is the end product, the result of the passive syntheses of desire as autoproduction of the unconscious. Desire does not lack anything; it does not lack its object. It is, rather, the *subject* that is missing in desire, or desire that lacks a fixed subject; there is no fixed subject unless there is repression. Desire and its object are one and the same thing: the machine, as a machine of a machine. Desire is a machine, and the object of desire is another machine connected to it. Hence the product is something removed or deducted from the process of producing: between the act of producing and the product, something becomes detached, thus giving the vagabond, nomad subject a residuum. The objective being of desire is the Real in and of itself.[1] There is no particular form of existence that can be labeled 'psychic reality'. As Marx notes, what exists in fact is not lack, but passion, as a 'natural and sensuous object'. Desire is not bolstered by needs, but rather the contrary; needs are derived from desire: they are counterproducts within the real that desire produces. Lack is a countereffect of desire; it is deposited, distributed, vacuolized within a real that is natural and social. Desire always remains in close touch with the conditions of objective existence; it embraces them and follows them, shifts when they shift, and does not outlive them. For that reason it so often

Gilles Deleuze and Félix Guattari (1984), *Anti-Oedipus: Capitalism and Schizophrenia*, London: Athlone Press.

becomes the desire to die, whereas need is a measure of the withdrawal of a subject that has lost its desire at the same time that it loses the passive syntheses of these conditions. This is precisely the significance of need as a search in a void: hunting about, trying to capture or become a parasite of passive syntheses in whatever vague world they may happen to exist in. It is no use saying: we are not green plants; we have long since been unable to synthesize chlorophyll, so it's necessary to eat.... Desire then becomes this abject fear of lacking something. But it should be noted that this is not a phrase uttered by the poor or the dispossessed. On the contrary, such people know that they are close to grass, almost akin to it, and that desire 'needs' very few things – *not those leftovers that chance to come their way, but the very things that are continually taken from them* – and that what is missing is not things a subject feels the lack of somewhere deep down inside himself, but rather the objectivity of man, the objective being of man, for whom to desire is to produce, to produce within the realm of the real.

The real is not impossible; on the contrary, within the real everything is possible, everything becomes possible. Desire does not express a molar lack within the subject; rather, the molar organization deprives desire of its objective being. Revolutionaries, artists, and seers are content to be objective, merely objective: they know that desire clasps life in its powerfully productive embrace, and reproduces it in a way that is all the more intense because it has few needs. And never mind those who believe that this is very easy to say, or that it is the sort of idea to be found in books. 'From the little reading I had done I had observed that the men who were most *in* life, who were moulding life, who were life itself, ate little, slept little, owned little or nothing. They had no illusions about duty, or the perpetuation of their kith and kin, or the preservation of the State. . . . The phantasmal world is the world which has never been fully conquered over. It is the world of the past, never of the future. To move forward clinging to the past is like dragging a ball and chain'. The true visionary is a Spinoza in the garb of a Neapolitan revolutionary. We know very well where lack – and its subjective correlative – come from. Lack (*manque*)[2] is created, planned, and organized in and through social production. It is counterproduced as a result of the pressure of antiproduction; the latter falls back on (*se rabat sur*) the forces of production and appropriates them. It is never primary; production is never organized on the basis of a pre-existing need or lack (*manque*). It is lack that infiltrates itself, creates empty spaces or vacuoles, and propagates itself in accordance with the organization of an already existing organization of production.[3] The deliberate creation of lack as a function of market economy is the art of a dominant class. This involves deliberately organizing wants and needs (*manque*) amid an abundance of production; making all of desire teeter and fall victim to the great fear of not having one's needs satisfied; and making the object dependent upon a real production that is supposedly exterior to desire (the demands of rationality), while at the same time the production of desire is categorized as fantasy and nothing but fantasy.

There is no such thing as the social production of reality on the one hand, and a desiring-production that is mere fantasy on the other. The only connections that could be established between these two productions would be secondary ones of introjection and projection, as though all social practices had their precise counterpart in introjected or internal mental practices, or as though mental practices were projected upon social systems, without either of the two sets of practices ever having any real or concrete effect upon the other. As long as we are content to establish a perfect parallel between money, gold, capital, and the capitalist triangle on the one hand, and the libido, the anus, the phallus, and the family triangle on the other, we are engaging in an enjoyable pastime, but the mechanisms of money remain totally unaffected by the anal projections of those who manipulate money. The Marx–Freud parallelism between the two remains utterly sterile and insignificant as long as it is expressed in terms that make them introjections or projections of each other without ceasing to be utterly alien to each other, as in the famous equation money = shit. The truth of the matter is that *social production is purely and simply desiring-production itself under determinate conditions*. We maintain that the social field is immediately invested by desire, that it is the historically determined product of desire, and that libido has no need of any mediation or sublimation, any psychic operation, any transformation, in order to invade and invest the productive forces and the relations of production. *There is only desire and the social, and nothing else.*

Even the most repressive and the most deadly forms of social reproduction are produced by desire within the organization that is the consequence of such production under various conditions that we must analyze. That is why the fundamental problem of political philosophy is still precisely the one that Spinoza saw so clearly, and that Wilhelm Reich rediscovered: 'Why do men fight *for* their servitude as stubbornly as though it were their salvation?' How can people possibly reach the point of shouting: 'More taxes! Less bread!'? As Reich remarks, the astonishing thing is not that some people steal or that others occasionally go out on strike, but rather that all those who are starving do not steal as a regular practice, and all those who are exploited are not continually out on strike: after centuries of exploitation, why do people still tolerate being humiliated and enslaved, to such a point, indeed, that they *actually want* humiliation and slavery not only for others but for themselves? Reich is at his profoundest as a thinker when he refuses to accept ignorance or illusion on the part of the masses as an explanation of fascism, and demands an explanation that will take their desires into account, an explanation formulated in terms of desire: no, the messes were not innocent dupes; at a certain point, under a certain set of conditions, they *wanted* fascism, and it is this perversion of the desire of the masses that needs to be accounted for.

NOTES

1. Lacan's admirable theory of desire appears to us to have two poles: one related to 'the object small *a*' as a desiring-machine, which defines desire in terms of a real production, thus going beyond both any idea of need and any idea of fantasy; and the other related to the 'great Other' as a signifier, which reintroduces a certain notion of lack. In Serge Leclaire's article 'La réalité du désir', the oscillation between these two poles can be seen quite clearly.
2. The French word *manque* may mean both lack and need in a psychological sense, as well as want or privation or scarcity in an economic sense. Depending upon the context, it will hence be translated in various ways below. (*Translators' note.*)
3. Maurice Clavel remarks, apropos of Jean-Paul Sartre, that a Marxist philosophy cannot allow itself to Introduce the notion of scarcity as its initial premise: 'Such a scarcity antedating exploitation makes of the law of supply and demand a reality that will remain forever independent, since it is situated at a primordial level. Hence it is no longer a question of including or deducing this law within Marxism, since it is immediately evident at a prior stage, at a level from which Marxism itself derives. Being a rigorous thinker, Marx refuses to employ the notion of scarcity, and is quite correct to do so, for this category would be his undoing'. In *Qui est aliéné?* (Paris: Flammarion, 1970), p. 330.

2

DISCOURSE

James Martin

INTRODUCTION

To a great extent, politics is an activity conducted through language. Debating choices and acting collectively depends fundamentally on shared understandings of the meaning and use of certain words, for example 'freedom', 'power' or 'justice'. Without these shared understandings political life may well collapse into a struggle of brute force. Language is therefore both a medium and the substance of political life; it is simultaneously *how* we communicate and, often, it is *what* we communicate about. Consequently, disputes over the meanings of the words we use can all too easily become wider contests about how we co-exist as a community at all, who is part of the 'we' and who is not.

Discourse has emerged as a key concept in political theory as a result of a growing interest in the role of language in shaping human thought and action. Whilst this interest has existed within the arts and humanities for a very long time, it was only in the twentieth century that its significance for politics came overtly to the fore. Today, we are likely to come across reference to the term 'discourse', to specific discourses or even to the category of 'the discursive' across a range of disciplines from philosophy to social science, political theory to art history. Now, more than ever, the way social activities are mediated through language and other social systems of meaning is a primary preoccupation for those interested in revealing the operations of power and control in society. As a consequence, the concept of discourse has both expanded and enriched our understanding of politics and political life.

In what follows, we shall review the origins of discourse theory in the philosophy of language and its refinement in the poststructuralist analyses of Michel Foucault. Next we examine the political theory of discourse developed more recently by Ernesto Laclau and Chantal Mouffe. Finally, we consider the way discourse analysis itself illuminates what we might call a 'politics of politics' attuned to the intrinsically political effects of producing meaning.

Discourse and the philosophy of language

The term 'discourse' refers, broadly, to the languages, vocabularies and other symbolic systems we use to describe the world around us and to communicate to each other. Thinking of these languages as forms of discourse – rather than as, say, 'ideologies' or simply 'representations' – casts them in a particular light. To speak of discourse is to direct attention to the intrinsic, meaning-giving qualities of language itself as opposed to the interests it may serve or the objects it represents, however important those aspects may also be. For the term 'discourse' typically implies that the source of meaning lies not exclusively in the object being represented or the person or group doing the representation but in the social act of language use itself.

The origin of this focus on language is to be found in the so-called 'linguistic turn' in philosophy of the mid-twentieth century. This 'turn' had its precursors in philosophers such as Friedrich Nietzsche, John Dewey and Ludwig Wittgenstein, amongst others, who disputed the idea of language as a neutral medium for communicating meaning. The later Wittgenstein, for example, rejected the notion – which he himself previously held along with other 'ordinary language' philosophers – that words and concepts gain their validity from their correspondence with 'real' objects in the world. On the contrary, he argued, meaning (or semantics) is bound up with the use (or pragmatics) of words and concepts in practical contexts or 'language games' (Wittgenstein 1958). For example, the words 'watch out' make sense not because they describe the world but, rather, because I might say them loudly whilst pointing to a hole in the road just in front of you. Here meaning does not jump effortlessly from the sounds of the words themselves but is bound up with the act of pointing and the presence of a hole into which you might fall. If, however, you did not understand what pointing meant (that is, that you ought to follow the line of my finger out into space and eventually see that I was indicating something) or did not speak English, the act of warning might not have worked (and you would fall into the hole).

For Wittgenstein, it is this ability to 'follow a rule', or to participate in language games, that marks the *social* – rather than strictly individual, logical or descriptive – nature of language. There can be no private language, he argued, because language is a social act in which we can only participate with others. Moreover, he indicated, different societies and cultures (or 'forms of life') have their own, shared rules of meaningful behaviour which function as a 'grammar' to structure social meanings. Thus for one culture the meaning of a set of activities – for example, how to treat strangers – may differ vastly from another. In one society strangers may be viewed as hostile invaders or potential thieves, whilst in another they will be viewed as guests to whom there is an obligation of hospitality. Here the grammar that shapes the encounter is quite different.

The implications of views of language such as Wittgenstein's are profound indeed. As Richard Rorty (1989) puts it, the linguistic turn implied that 'truth' was not to be found – for example, through empirical or philosophical investigation – but rather *created* in social vocabularies. Language is not conceived here as a purely descriptive medium for representing truths 'out there' in a world of pre-linguistic facts; there is not an already constructed reality to which our words and phrases can 'correspond' with more or less accuracy, perhaps if we reduce them to purely descriptive or logical statements. On the contrary, the world is only knowable through the language games we inherit or ourselves construct. For Rorty, we can never get 'outside' this linguistic world and face reality without some means of symbolically constructing it. To imagine we can do so – as did philosophers of the Enlightenment and its heirs in modern scientific thought – is nonsense. Empiricists and rationalists of various sorts believed that it is possible to penetrate the world of interpretation and discover the essential nature of things as though the world itself spoke one language that we, too, might learn if we were to gauge our instruments accurately or find precise enough criteria against which to test our claims. But, claims Rorty,

> the world does not speak. Only we do. The world can, once we have programmed ourselves with a language, cause us to hold beliefs. But it cannot propose a language for us to speak. Only other human beings can do that. (1989: 6)

The claim that meaning is given in language rather than through direct experience undermines the possibility of purely 'objective' forms of judgement – that is, assertions justified by reference to an independent 'external reality' – that have been central to modern science and much philosophy for centuries. Instead, truth claims are conceived as relative to the linguistic contexts in which they are set. Different contexts will have different ways of conceiving and verifying what is regarded as true or false. Such a view goes against the thrust of much of modern science, which typically claims to base its superior knowledge on factual evidence, unmediated by the 'distortions' of language.

In the social sciences, the linguistic turn supported the (already held) view that the analysis of the social world cannot be modelled on the example of the natural sciences. To understand a society means understanding the grammar of its cultures, the distinctive 'self-understandings' and social practices that subjects in a culture share with each other (Winch 1958; Pitkin 1972). However, the linguistic turn had profound implications for understanding the natural sciences, too. As Thomas Kuhn (1970) argued, scientific claims are also premised on a wider framework of meanings and practices – what Kuhn calls 'paradigms' – that shape scientific enquiry, legitimise some approaches rather than others and determine the kind of knowledge it produces. Moreover, claimed Kuhn, when scientific paradigms change, they do not do so by incremental discoveries and the gradual extension of knowledge but by radical leaps – akin to social revolutions – that fundamentally restructure the nature of 'normal' inquiry and the legitimacy of certain kinds of truth claim.

The emphasis on language use made by philosophers of language such as Wittgenstein and J. L. Austin has been central to a currently influential strand of analysis of political thought. The so-called Cambridge school of historians – principally Quentin Skinner (2002) – have employed the argument that meaning can only be grasped by reference to the linguistic context within which it operates in order to study historical texts (see Tully 1988; Ball et al. 1989). For the Cambridge historians, placing a thinker's texts in relation to a wider web of concepts and arguments – or grammar – that the individual inhabited helps us make sense of what he or she is seeking to do with his/her own concepts. A text is not a series of ahistorical assertions about the world but, when placed within its original argumentative context, can be understood to be rhetorical, that is, as part of an effort within the social environment of language to actively redefine the meaning and/or application of concepts to produce significant effects. In this approach, an anachronistic reading of a text is one that ascribes to it meanings that the author could not possibly have known, often a contemporary meaning that was not part of its original linguistic context.

The wider implication here is that political concepts are intrinsically historical and that changes in political understandings and political vocabularies – what now we also call discourse – are integral to politics itself. It is this implication that has been pursued in the analyses of 'poststructuralist' thinkers and which has led to the emergence of theories that explicitly identify their object as discourse.

FOUCAULT: DISCOURSE, POWER AND SUBJECTIVITY

The idea that we gain meanings through our participation in discourse was radicalised from the 1960s and 1970s with a growing sensitivity to the role of language in structuring relations of power and setting limits to the way we conceive ourselves as subjects. It is no coincidence that this interest in power and language began at a time of growing tension between classes and other social groups in developed Western capitalist societies. Current uses of the term 'discourse' owe much to the sense that language is both a site of and a means for the control as well as contestation of forms of social subjectivity (or selfhood) and the enactment of power struggles. Here the scope of discourse is expanded beyond spoken language, texts or statements and conceived in terms of symbolic systems operative at various levels of society.

This expansion of discourse stems from the influence of structuralism on the social sciences. Structuralists followed the work of the Swiss linguist Ferdinand de Saussure (1983) in conceiving social practices as analogous to the relational pattern of language. For Saussure, language was a system of signs whose meanings are produced 'internally' through relations of difference rather than by direct reference to an external world. When we speak, we invoke a system of signs; that is, we employ words that supposedly signify something 'out there' in the world. But signification works by linking 'signifiers' (or sound images, such as 'dog') to 'signifieds' (or concepts, such as the idea of a dog); there is no natural relation between these two (there is nothing about a dog that necessitates it being referred to by the word 'dog'). The relationship between the signifier and the signified is simply a matter of arbitrary convention. Moreover, because real objects do not necessitate the words that signify them, meaning is conceived as a product of the internal structure of differences that mark out both the signifier and the signified from other signifiers and signifieds (for example, the sound image 'dog' is different from 'log' or 'fog'; and the concept of a dog is different from a cat or a mouse). It is these specific differences *within* language as it is constructed in individual sentences, rather than the object itself, that create meaning.

Structuralists followed Saussure by looking to internal relations of meaning rather than independent, external objects to understand social practices as diverse as social myths and customs (Lévi-Strauss 1963; Barthes 1993) or economic systems (Althusser and Balibar 1979). In so doing they disputed the claims of other scientific approaches (such as positivism or empiricism) that sought to identify the essential meanings of social phenomena by accurate analysis or measurement of things themselves. Instead, structuralists emphasised the way social entities were part of a wider system of associations, hierarchies, distinctions and so forth, just *like* language. Structuralists looked for the symbolic patterns or 'deep structures' upon which social relations were built. As such, they also undermined the 'humanist' claim that social practices gained their meaning exclusively from the intentions and choices of individuals. On the contrary, individuals unconsciously inherited and reproduced the structural patterns of economic relations, kinship systems or myths. Although not always their express intention, structuralists nevertheless tended to subsume subjectivity and the contingencies of individual and social existence within the wider pattern of structures under examination. Humans became passive supports for structures of meaning they reproduced regardless of their own intentions. Whilst most structuralists insisted that the structures they identified were not permanent and unchangeable, they failed to explain clearly how new structural patterns might come into effect and replace the old.

The work of Michel Foucault on discourse, power and subjectivity has been enormously influential in moving beyond the impasses of structuralism and generating a concept of discourse applicable in social science (Mills 1997; Howarth 2000). Foucault's early work in the 1960s sought out the discursive patterns that structured knowledge in the post-Renaissance period. In works such as *Madness and Civilization* (1965) and *The Order of Things* (1970) Foucault presented what he called his 'archaeological' method of examining the 'rules of formation' that governed a variety of systems of knowledge and, in particular, 'scientific' statements (see also Foucault 1972). These rules specify what can legitimately be said about a phenomenon, the ways in which it is said and who can say it. Like the structuralists, Foucault rejected humanism and looked to the ways in which unspoken rules determine the objects that science examines and how these rules shape 'truth claims' made about them. Human subjects enter into the structure of scientific discourses and follow a pattern of inquiry and knowledge generation that is to a great extent predetermined by discursive rules. These rules are not fixed and closed within one place but, rather, 'dispersed' across a range of sites, times and activities. For Foucault, examining discourses was less like defining deep structures of language applicable universally than digging up archaeological remains, that is, unearthing the surface-level principles that mark out ways of thinking and acting in a specific period.

For example, in examining the changing conceptualisation of madness, Foucault (1965) noted the shift from a discourse that constructed madness as a form of moral corruption – resolved at one point by expulsion of the mad from society – to a scientific practice in which madness was the obverse of 'reason', an internal dysfunction of the mind whose sufferers were best confined and, later, 'treated' as victims of 'mental illness' by 'experts' within medical institutions. In these shifts from one discourse to another, new forms of authority, power, social subjectivity and institutional organisation were fashioned. Thus discourses were not, in his view, simply isolated patterns of speech but organising principles embedded in wider patterns of social organisation and practice.

In his later work, Foucault modified his idea of discourse through 'genealogical' analyses of, for example, punishment (1977) and sexuality (1978). In this more nuanced approach, Foucault examined the complex and contingent emergence of contemporary systems of social discipline and knowledge. Here discourse was not conceived as autonomous formations of statements within specific settings but as a dynamic meeting point between power and knowledge. Power was understood by Foucault not as a repressive instrument of coercion but as productive of certain types of subjectivity around claims to 'truth' and knowledge. Foucault's genealogical method involved tracing the formation of and linkages between discrete discourses, their evolution and their deployment within institutional settings such as prisons, schools or medical practices. Thus, for example, he considered the way scientific discourses about sexuality set out to establish the 'true' nature of human bodies and to help promote 'normal' ways of conducting oneself. The nature of power here is not simply one of forcing people to act but of providing a vocabulary and a set of self-understandings that enable them to conceive themselves and their bodies in specific ways (and not in others). Nor is this a power that emanates from a central, unified source such as the state or a dominant class. On the contrary, discourses are formed and reformed, disseminated and modified in different institutional settings such that what emerges as a generalised 'truth' is the outcome of a multiplicity of discursive operations across numerous sites. In this attentiveness to the multiple accents and modalities of power we find in Foucault's later work the basis of a noticeably *post*-structuralist theory of discourse.

Michael Shapiro (1985) helpfully develops some of Foucault's (and, more broadly, poststructuralism's) insights by highlighting the use of metaphor in philosophies of social science. In so doing Shapiro discloses how these philosophies function discursively by imposing meanings on the social world. As he shows, the nature of social inquiry and explanation is not a neutral process but one that is constructed through the deployment of linguistic metaphors that frame and shape the objects under analysis and, consequently, this reveals different figurative techniques in making the social world knowable. Not all philosophies explicitly draw attention to these 'textual mechanisms' and Shapiro alerts us to the 'conservative' and 'radical' implications that arise from these mechanisms. Alternative epistemological metaphors position us as subjects towards our objects in different ways, sometimes passively, at other times more actively; they focus us on narrower or broader fields of historical inquiry; and they invite us to selectively acknowledge or occlude our relations with other subjects and identities. For Shapiro, these implicit choices embedded in the metaphors of knowledge testify to the intrinsically political character of social scientific discourse.

LACLAU AND MOUFFE: DISCOURSE AND POLITICAL STRUGGLE

Ernesto Laclau and Chantal Mouffe – the authors of the first extract – currently offer one of the most sophisticated and widely influential theories of discourse. Having emerged from Marxist debates on class and ideology in the 1970s and 1980s, Laclau and Mouffe's poststructuralism (sometimes termed 'post-Marxism') is more inclined to overtly political phenomena than was Foucault's; to 'macro' discourses rather than his 'micro' discourse analyses. In their key work of 1985, *Hegemony and Socialist Strategy* (second edition, 2001), they presented a highly abstract theory of political subjectivity combining Antonio Gramsci's concept of 'hegemony' with a post-structuralist theory of discourse inspired by Foucault, Jacques Derrida and Jacques Lacan. For Laclau and Mouffe, as we shall see, discourse is understood as the key to understanding the nature of social power, conflict and political struggles (see Torfing 1999).

Laclau and Mouffe build their discourse theory on the basis of an explicit rejection of Marxist 'economism', that is, a purported tendency amongst Marxists to identify an underlying, independent economic structure as the ultimate determinant of all social and political phenomena. Accordingly, all social identities would be linked to 'essential' class interests (the proletariat or the bourgeoisie), thereby implicitly (and often explicitly) minimising the significance of groups other than those of class in the social structure. The practical implication of this was to encourage Marxists to devalue non-class forms of oppression (such as environmental destruction, patriarchy or racism) and dismiss the need for a rigorously democratic politics to accommodate them. In rejecting this view, Laclau and Mouffe gave theoretical voice to the demands of new social movements and the desire for a radical democratic politics. To understand how political identities emerge out of social structures, they suggested, we need to conceive structures as complex, open-ended formations permeated by contingency and conflict. They did not renounce the importance of economic relations but, rather, underscored the way political discourses function to assemble and fix temporarily the identity of subjects within hegemonic formations.

For Laclau and Mouffe, all social relations are discursive. That is, all meaningful activity – linguistic or non-linguistic – is performed through patterns of symbolic differences that 'articulate' (or link together and differentiate) social agents, belief systems, vocabularies and institutions, even if these are unconscious or misrecognised. Thus, for example, a game of football is not an exclusively spoken activity but is performed as a series of different actions (for instance, being a member of a team, kicking the ball, scoring goals, blowing whistles, and so on) whose combination is understood as part of a meaningful whole or 'totality' (the game). Laclau and Mouffe conceive the realm of the discursive as co-extensive with society in general, spoken or otherwise. Rather than view discourses as entirely separate from a 'non-discursive' realm of social structures and institutions (as Foucault continued to suggest), they understand society as a primarily symbolic phenomenon, a dense ensemble of overlapping, contradictory and mutually modifying signifying practices from which it is impossible to escape and analyse in a purely objective way. For them, the social is not a discrete object about which we can distinguish neatly between its 'reality' and its 'appearance'. Discourses about society (and its various components) are part of what makes a society in the first place, in so far as these seek to impose on the so-called non-discursive some kind of structured meaning.

This argument is stated boldly at the beginning of the extract: ' "Society" is not a valid object of discourse', if by 'society' is meant a totality of relations with fixed limits that impose on it some kind of objective necessity free from discursive mediation. If, however, the articulation of society is understood as *symbolic* rather than 'natural' then the meaning of its various practices lack any final fixity: the arbitrariness of the link between signifier and signified renders the identity of objects and subjects infinitely variable and unstable, open to revision within an alternative set of differences. There is, as they say, always a 'surplus of meaning' that falls outside and never fully fits inside the discourses that govern any social practice. Thus 'any discourse is constituted as an attempt to dominate the field of discursivity, to arrest the flow of differences, to construct a centre' (Laclau and Mouffe 2001: 112). For example, whilst rules of football exist, there is nothing eternal or absolutely fixed about them. In principle, players are able to redesign the game as they wish, as children might when playing in a playground without goal posts or a referee. Whilst meaning and identity must have *some* degree of stability, they argue, the signifying 'elements' of any discourse are essentially 'floating' and 'polysemic' and their fixity is only partial. The effort to fix or stabilise symbolic differences within specified parameters is what they understand by the term 'hegemony'. This refers to a dominant discourse – or political ideology – that is fused with various ways of thinking and acting (that is, other discourses and discursive structures) that articulates them, if only momentarily, into a common project.

Laclau and Mouffe's extension of the discursive to social relations in general informs a particular approach to theorising politics that is radically anti-essentialist and anti-foundationalist. They are anti-essentialist because they view all identities as being formed through differences that vary depending on their contingent circumstances. Political identities are therefore effects of discourses that overlap and interplay in multiple and variable ways; that is, they are culturally determined and not 'natural' or automatic responses. Thus it is entirely plausible that some workers will identify as radical democratic subjects under anti-capitalist discourses whilst others may adopt more reformist or even anti-democratic, perhaps racist, identities. There is nothing intrinsic about being workers, therefore, that necessitates their adopting exclusively socialist, egalitarian or democratic political identities. These possibilities are a function of the context of competing discourses and the hegemonic discourses that prevail in any particular conjuncture.

This view of the discursivity of political identities also orients Laclau and Mouffe away from foundationalist arguments that presuppose a specific kind of political identity in politics. Both Marxist socialism and modern liberalism tend to presuppose that there is one specific, rational identity that subjects will inevitably adopt: either a class identity or an individual identity. Laclau and Mouffe, however, explain that political subjects form their identities in a particular way: through the process of 'antagonism'. It is this that explains why in reality political subjects take a number of diverse forms and none can be said to have automatic supremacy over any other (that is, to be rationally founded in the way others are not). In the second part of the extract they explain the distinctive logic of discursive antagonism.

Antagonism is the experience of being threatened or undermined by another subject or object. Laclau and Mouffe begin by distinguishing this from both conceptual contradiction and a real opposition. Unlike these easily 'definable' conditions, they claim, antagonism is the subversion of language, the marker of the limits of describing something, 'the negation of a given order' (2001: 126). When I experience antagonism, I may sense a potential breakdown in the sense of the world I occupy, a traumatic invasion of the irrational. Because identities 'make sense' discursively, what lies outside those discourses represents the limits of the social world, as we understand it.

Thus, with regard to modern political ideologies, the threat posed by capitalism is understood by socialists as an irrational force extinguishing human potential that must be overcome; or the danger of environmental degradation is for 'green' political subjects not just a discrete problem but a systemic threat that brings the future of the world and all life into doubt. In these discourses, the identification of an antagonist – a symbolic 'other' that subverts all reason and which cannot be incorporated into the political discourse – has the effect of unifying various discursive elements around a common 'frontier'. Different concepts and activities (for instance, the national flag, certain values and specific ethnic groups) come to be associated by virtue of their opposition to the other that purportedly prevents them from fully asserting themselves. Society, from this perspective, 'never manages fully to be society because everything in it is penetrated by its limits' (Laclau and Mouffe 2001: 127).

Political discourses, however, project the image of a future society that is no longer limited, a society that is fully itself once the antagonist has been overcome. As Laclau and Mouffe argue elsewhere in *Hegemony and Socialist Strategy* and in later work (see Laclau, 1990, 1996; Mouffe, 1993, 2000), this utopian vision is dangerous if understood as actually realisable. Instead, they argue, democratic politics requires that we grasp the contingency of our identities, and the negativity and conflict this throws up, as an ineliminable condition of political life.

DISCOURSE AND THE POLITICS OF POLITICS

For some, Laclau and Mouffe's expanded use of discourse goes too far in relinquishing the analysis of what are seen as determinate political conditions that materially influence our identities and choices. Their framework, it is sometimes said, is perilously close to a 'postmodern' relativism that overstates the 'floating' character of signifiers and consequently disregards 'real' constraints on discourses. Such a view is contested both by Laclau and Mouffe themselves (see Laclau and Mouffe 1987) and by those who have sought to apply their theory in relation to specific political contexts. In addition to studies that theorise identity we find discourse analyses of specific social and political movements (Howarth et al. 2000), changing political ideologies (Bastow and Martin 2002), institutional regimes (Norval 1996) and the developing structure of the contemporary capitalist state (Torfing 1998).

The continuing popularity and extension of Laclau and Mouffe's analyses testifies to a wider sense of the value of discourse in analysing political life. Increasingly, discourse analysis is being undertaken to examine how the terrain, the objects and the subjects of political action are partially determined through language, and how this determination itself involves power and conflict. In this sense, we might say discourse analysis encourages us to examine the politics *of* politics, that is, the power relations that generate the conditions for politics itself.

The second extract by, Gearóid Ó Tuathail and John Agnew, provides a practical example of a discourse analysis conceived as an inquiry into the politics of politics. The authors examine the geopolitical discourse of American foreign policy, the way international space was constructed in a quite specific way for the purposes of conducting policy. Whilst international politics often assumes that its objects are real and its reading of the situation is driven by a demand for 'truth', Ó Tuathail and Agnew indicate that discourses of geopolitics themselves bring into being certain dispositions and kinds of agency that render international space manageable for particular kinds of 'statecraft'. In the extract they examine the discursive conditions of the Cold War from the perspective of American intellectuals and policy-makers. They find that international space was constructed through forms of geopolitical reasoning that gave America a specific identity and responsibility in the world, one bound up with a self-conception as the universal defender of a form of civilization based on individual liberty. During the Cold War this conception was mobilised against the Soviet Union, the antagonistic 'other' of America's self-conception. The consequence of this preoccupation with one part of the world, paradoxically, was the simplification of real geographical space and the exclusion from public consideration of other areas of political significance. Here, then, we see how the analysis of discourse illuminates the choices that determine how the political environment is itself constructed.

CONCLUSION

If politics is typically conducted through language, the concept of discourse offers us a way of understanding the politics *in* language itself and hence of expanding our sense of the political as a domain of action. Here we should understand discourse not exclusively in textual terms – as a series of words and sentences – but rhetorically, too, as a kind of debate or argument that helps persuade ourselves and others to act in certain kinds of ways. If by speaking and communicating through discourse we are always already inside the space of a debate, it is difficult to imagine that we can climb out and make sense of it without abandoning communication altogether. The alternative perhaps, as the Greeks of ancient Athens realised, is to learn to excel in the arts of rhetoric, to understand the political effects, both beneficial and pernicious, of discourse on others, the wider community and ourselves. In this sense, the concept of discourse opens the way to a deeper engagement with politics than otherwise might be the case.

QUESTIONS FOR DISCUSSION

- In what ways do discourses of social science embody forms of power?
- What, according to Laclau and Mouffe, do antagonisms reveal about society?
- How might America's identity in the realm of global political economy be conceived discursively?
- In what sense is the state an object produced *through* discourse?

ERNESTO LACLAU AND CHANTAL MOUFFE EXTRACTS FROM *HEGEMONY AND SOCIALIST STRATEGY: TOWARDS A RADICAL DEMOCRATIC POLITICS*

Beyond the positivity of the social: antagonisms and hegemony

Articulation and discourse

[. . .]

The incomplete character of every totality necessarily leads us to abandon, as a terrain of analysis, the premise of '*society*' as a sutured and self-defined totality. 'Society' is not a valid object of discourse. There is no single underlying principle fixing – and hence constituting – the whole field of differences. The irresoluble interiority/exteriority tension is the condition of any social practice: necessity only exists as a partial limitation of the field of contingency. It is in this terrain, where neither a total interiority nor a total exteriority is possible, that the social is constituted. For the same reason that the social cannot be reduced to the interiority of a fixed system of differnces, pure exteriority is also impossible. In order to be *totally* external to each other, the entities would have to be totally internal with regard to themselves: that is, to have a fully constituted identity which is not subverted by any exterior. But this is precisely what we have just rejected. *This field of identities which never manage to be fully fixed, is the field of overdetermination.*

Thus, neither absolute fixity nor absolute non-fixity is possible. We will now consider these two successive moments, beginning with non-fixity. We

Ernesto Laclau and Chantal Mouffe (2001), *Hegemony and Socialist Strategy: Towards a Radical Democratic Politics*, 2nd ed., London: Verso.

have referred to 'discourse' as a system of differential entities – that is, of moments. But we have just seen that such a system only exists as a partial limitation of a 'surplus of meaning' which subverts it. Being inherent in every discursive situation, this 'surplus' is the necessary terrain for the constitution of every social practice. We will call it the *field of discursivity*. This term indicates the form of its relation with every concrete discourse: it determines at the same time the necessarily discursive character of any object, and the impossibility of any given discourse to implement a final suture. On this point, our analysis meets up with a number of contemporary currents of thought which – from Heidegger to Wittgenstein – have insisted on the impossibility of fixing ultimate meanings. Derrida, for example, starts from a radical break in the history of the concept of structure, occurring at the moment in which the centre – the *transcendental signified* in its multiple forms: eidos, arché, telos, energeia, ousia, alétheia, etc. – is abandoned, and with it the possibility of fixing a meaning which underlies the flow of differences. At this point, Derrida generalizes the concept of discourse in a sense coincident with that of our text.

> It became necessary to think both the law which somehow governed desire for a centre in the constitution of structure, and the process of signification which orders the displacements and substitutions for this law of central presence – but as a central presence which has never been itself, has always already been exiled from itself into its own substitute. The substitute does not substitute itself for anything which has somehow existed before it, henceforth, it was necessary to begin thinking that there was no centre, that the centre could not be thought in the form of a present-being, that the centre had no natural site, that it was not a fixed locus but a function, a sort of non-locus in which an infinite number of sign-substitutions came into play. This was the moment when language invaded the universal problematic, the moment when, in the absence of a centre or origin, everything became discourse – provided we can agree on this word – that is to say, a system in which the central signified, the original or transcendental signified, is never absolutely present outside a system of differences. The absence of the transcendental signified extends the domain and the play of signification infinitely.[1]

Let us move on to our second dimension. The impossibility of an ultimate fixity of meaning implies that there have to be partial fixations – otherwise, the very flow of differences would be impossible. Even in order to differ, to subvert meaning, there has to be *a* meaning. If the social does not manage to fix itself in the intelligible and instituted forms of a *society*, the social only exists, however, as an effort to construct that impossible object. Any discourse is constituted as an attempt to dominate the field of discursivity, to arrest the flow of differences, to construct a centre. We will call the privileged discursive points of this partial fixation, *nodal points*. (Lacan has insisted on these partial fixations through his concept of *points de capiton*, that is, of privileged signifiers that fix the meaning of a signifying chain. This limitation of the productivity of the signifying chain establishes the positions that make predication possible – a discourse incapable of generating any fixity of meaning is the discourse of the psychotic.)

Saussure's analysis of language considered it as a system of differences without positive terms; the central concept was that of *value*, according to which the meaning of a term was purely relational and determined only by its opposition to all the others. But this shows us that we are presented with the conditions of possibility of a *closed* system: only within it is it possible to fix in such a manner the meaning of every element. When the linguistic model was introduced into the general field of human sciences, it was this effect of systematicity that predominated, so that structuralism became a new form of essentialism: a search for the underlying structures constituting the inherent law of any possible variation. The critique of structuralism involved a break with this view of a fully constituted structural space; but as it also rejected any return to a conception of unities whose demarcation was given, like a nomenclature, by its reference to an object, the resulting conception was of a relational space unable to constitute itself as such – of a field dominated by the desire for a structure that was always finally absent. The sign is the name of a split, of an impossible suture between signified and signifier.[2]

We now have all the necessary analytical elements to specify the concept of articulation. Since all identity is relational – even if the system of relations does not reach the point of being fixed as a stable system of differences – since, too, all discourse is subverted by a field of discursivity which overflows it, the transition from 'elements' to 'moments' can never be complete. The status of the 'elements' is that of floating signifiers, incapable of being wholly articulated to a discursive chain. And this floating character finally penetrates every discursive (i.e. social) identity. But if we accept the noncomplete character of all discursive fixation and, at the same time, affirm the relational character of every identity, the ambiguous character of the signifier, its non-fixation to any signified, can only exist insofar as there is a proliferation of signifieds. It is not the poverty of signifieds but, on the contrary, polysemy that disarticulates a discursive structure. That is what establishes the overdetermined, symbolic dimension of every social identity. Society never manages to be identical to itself, as every nodal point is constituted within an intertextuality that overflows it. *The practice of articulation, therefore, consists in the construction of nodal points which partially fix meaning; and the partial character of this fixation proceeds from the openness of the social, a result, in its turn, of the constant overflowing of every discourse by the infinitude of the field of discursivity.*

Every social practice is therefore – in one of its dimensions – articulatory. As it is not the internal moment of a self-defined totality, it cannot simply be the expression of something already acquired, it cannot be *wholly* subsumed under the principle of repetition; rather, it always consists in the construction of new differences. The social *is* articulation insofar as 'society' is impossible. Earlier we said that, for the social, necessity only exists as a partial effort to limit contingency. This implies that the relations between 'necessity' and 'contingency' cannot be conceived as relations between two areas that are delimited and external to each other – as, for example, in Labriola's morphological prediction – because the contingent only exists within the necessary. This presence of the contingent in the necessary is what we earlier called *subversion*, and it manifests itself as symbolization, metaphorization, paradox, which deform and question the literal character of every necessity. Necessity, therefore, exists not under the form of an underlying principle, of a ground, but as an effort of literalization which fixes the differences of a relational system. The necessity of the social is the necessity proper to purely relational identities – as in the linguistic principle of value – not natural 'necessity' or the necessity of an analytical judgement. 'Necessity', in this sense, is simply equivalent to a 'system of differential positions in a sutured space'.

[. . .]

Antagonism and objectivity
[. . .]

It would [. . .] seem that the category of contradiction has an assured place within the real, and that it provides the basis from which to account for social antagonisms. But a moment's reflection is sufficient to convince us that this is not so. We all participate in a number of mutually contradictory belief systems, and yet no antagonism emerges from these contradictions. Contradiction does not, therefore, necessarily imply an antagonistic relation.[3] But if we have excluded both 'real opposition' and 'contradiction' as categories accounting for antagonism, it would seem that the latter's specificity cannot be apprehended. The usual descriptions of antagonisms in the sociological or historical literature confirm this impression: they explain the *conditions* which made antagonisms possible, but not the antagonisms as such. (The description proceeds through expressions such as 'this *provoked* a reaction' or 'in that situation X or Z *found itself* forced to react'. In other words, there is a sudden jump from explanation to an appeal for our common sense or experience to complete the meaning of the text: that is to say, the explanation is interrupted.)

Let us attempt to unravel the meaning of this interruption. First, we must ask ourselves whether the impossibility of assimilating antagonism to real opposition or to contradiction, is not the impossibility of assimilating it to something shared by these types of relation. They do, in fact, share something, and that is the fact of being *objective relations* – between conceptual objects in the second case, and between real objects in the first. But in both cases, it is something that the objects *already are* which makes the relation intelligible. That is, in both cases we are concerned with full identities. In the case of contradiction, it is because A *is fully* A that being-not-A is a contradiction – and therefore an impossibility. In the case of real opposition, it is because A is also fully A that its relation with B produces an objectively determinable effect. But in the case of antagonism, we are confronted with a different situation: the presence of the 'Other' prevents me from being totally myself. The relation arises not from full totalities, but from the impossibility of their constitution. The presence of the Other is not a logical impossibility: it exists; so it is not a contradiction. But neither is it subsumable as a positive differential moment in a causal chain, for in that case the relation would be given by what each force is and there would be no negation of this being. (It is because a physical force *is* a physical force that another identical and countervailing force leads to rest; in contrast, it is because a peasant *cannot be* a peasant that an antagonism exists with the landowner expelling him from his land.) Insofar as there is antagonism, I cannot be a full presence for myself. But nor is the force that antagonizes me such a presence: its objective being is a symbol of my non-being and, in this way, it is overflowed by a plurality of meanings which prevent its being fixed as full positivity. Real opposition is an *objective* relation – that is, determinable, definable – among things; contradiction is an equally definable relation among concepts; antagonism constitutes the limits of every objectivity, which is revealed as partial and precarious *objectification*. If language is a system of differences, antagonism is the failure of difference: in that sense, it situates itself within the limits of language and can only exist as the disruption of it – that is, as metaphor. We can thus understand why sociological and historical narratives must interrupt themselves and call upon an 'experience', transcending their categories, to fill their hiatuses: for every language and every society are constituted as a repression of the consciousness of the impossibility that penetrates them. Antagonism escapes the possibility of being apprehended through language, since language only exists as an attempt to fix that which antagonism subverts.

Antagonism, far from being an objective relation, is a relation wherein the limits of every objectivity are *shown* – in the sense in which Wittgenstein used to say that what cannot be *said* can be *shown*. But if, as we have demonstrated, the social only exists as a partial effort for constructing society – that is, an objective and closed system of differences – antagonism, as a witness of the impossibility of a final suture, is the 'experience' of the limit of the social. Strictly speaking, antagonisms are not *internal* but *external* to society; or rather, they constitute the limits of society, the latter's impossibility of fully constituting itself. This statement may seem paradoxical, but only if we surreptitiously introduce certain assumptions which must be carefully excluded from our theoretical perspective. In particular, two such assumptions would make absurd our thesis concerning the theoretical location of antagonism. The first is the identification of 'society' with an ensemble of *physically* existing agents who live within a given territory. If this criterion is accepted, it is obvious that antagonisms occur *among* those agents and are not external to them. But it does not necessarily follow, from, the 'empirical' coexistence of the agents, that the relations among them should be shaped according to an objective and intelligible pattern. (The price of identifying 'society' with the referent would be to empty it of any rationally specifiable content.) However, accepting that 'society' is an intelligible and objective ensemble, we would introduce another assumption incompatible with our analysis if we attributed to that *rational totality* the character of an underlying principle of the social conceived as an *empirical totality*. For there would then no longer be any aspect of the second which could not be reabsorbed as a moment of the first. In that case antagonisms, like everything else, would have to be *positive internal* moments of society, and we would have returned to the Hegelian cunning of reason. But if we maintain our conception of the social as a non-sutured space, as a field in which all positivity is metaphorical and subvertible, then there is no way of referring the *negation* of an objective position to an underlying positivity – be it causal or of any other type – which would account for it. Antagonism as the negation of a given order is, quite simply, the limit of that order, and not the moment of a broader totality in relation to which the two poles of the antagonism would constitute differential – i.e. objective – partial instances. (Let us be understood: the conditions which made the antagonism possible may be described as positivities, but the antagonism as such is not reducible to them.)

We must consider this 'experience' of the limit of the social from two different points of view. On the one hand, as an experience of failure. If the subject is constructed through language, as a partial and metaphorical incorporation into a symbolic order, any putting into question of that order must necessarily constitute an identity crisis. But, on the other hand, this experience of failure is not an access to a diverse ontological order, to a something beyond differences, simply because ... there is no beyond. The limit of the social cannot be traced as a frontier separating two territories – for the perception of a frontier supposes the perception of something beyond it that would have to be objective and positive – that is, a new difference. The limit of the social must be given within the social itself as something subverting it, destroying its ambition to constitute a full presence. Society never manages fully to be society, because everything in it is penetrated by its limits, which prevent it from constituting itself as an objective reality.

NOTES

1. J. Derrida, *Writing and Difference*, London 1978, p. 280.
2. A number of recent works have extended this conception concerning the impossibility of suturation and, therefore, of the ultimate internal intelligibility of every relational system, to the very system traditionally presented as a model of a pure structural logic: that is, language. F. Gadet and M. Pêcheux, for example, have pointed out concerning Saussure: 'Regarding the theories which isolate the poetic as a location of special effects, from language as a whole, the work of Saussure... makes the poetic a slipping inherent to every language: what Saussure has established is not a property of Saturnian verse, nor even of poetry, but a property of language itself' (*La langue introuvable*, Paris 1981, p. 57). Cf. F. Gadet, 'La double faille', *Actes du Colloque de Sociololinguistique de Rouen*, 1978; C. Normand, 'L'arbitraire du signe comme phénomène de déplacement', *Dialectiques*, 1972, no. 1–2; J. C. Milner, *L'amour de la langue*, Paris 1978.
3. On this point, our opinion differs with that expressed by one of the authors of this book in an earlier work, in which the concept of antagonism is assimilated to that of contradiction (E. Laclau, 'Populist Rupture and Discourse', *Screen Education*, Spring 1980). In rethinking our earlier position, the critical commentaries made by Emilio De Ipola in a number of conversations, have proved most useful.

GEARÓID Ó TUATHAIL AND JOHN AGNEW EXTRACTS FROM 'GEOPOLITICS AND DISCOURSE: PRACTICAL GEOPOLITICAL REASONING IN AMERICAN FOREIGN POLICY'

GEOPOLITICS AND DISCOURSE

[. . .]

By its own understandings and terms geopolitics is taken to be a domain of hard truths, material realities and irrepressible natural facts. Geopoliticians have traded on the supposed objective materialism of geopolitical analysis. According to Gray (1988: 93) 'geopolitical analysis is impartial as between one or another political system or philosophy'. It addresses the base of international politics, the permanent geopolitical realities around which the play of events in international politics unfolds. These geopolitical realities are held to be durable, physical determinants of foreign policy. Geography, in such a scheme, is held to be a non-discursive phenomenon: it is separate from the social, political and ideological dimensions of international politics.

The great irony of geopolitical writing, however, is that it was always a highly ideological and deeply politicized form of analysis. Geopolitical theory from Ratzel to Mackinder, Haushofer to Bowman, Spykman to Kissinger was never an objective and disinterested activity but an organic part of the political philosophy and ambitions of these very public intellectuals. While the forms of geopolitical writing have varied among these and other authors, the practice of producing geopolitical theory has a common theme: the production of knowledge to aid the practice of statecraft and further the power of the state.

Gearóid Ó Tuathail and John Agnew (1992), 'Geopolitics and discourse: practical geopolitical reasoning in American foreign policy', *Political Geography*, 11(2).

Within political geography, the geopolitical tradition has long been opposed by a tradition of resistance to such reasoning. A central problem that has dogged such resistance is its lack of a coherent and comprehensive theory of geopolitical writing and its relationship to the broader spatial practices that characterize the operation of international politics. This paper proposes such a theory by re-conceptualizing the conventional meaning of geopolitics using the concept of discourse. Our foundational premise is the contention that geography is a social and historical discourse which is always intimately bound up with questions of politics and ideology (Ó Tuathail 1989). Geography is never a natural, non-discursive phenomenon which is separate from ideology and outside politics. Rather, geography as a discourse is a form of power/knowledge itself (Foucault 1980; Ó Tuathail 1989).

Geopolitics, we wish to suggest, should be critically re-conceptualized as a discursive practice by which intellectuals of statecraft 'spatialize' international politics in such a way as to represent it as a 'world' characterized by particular types of places, peoples and dramas. In our understanding, the study of geopolitics is the study of the spatialization of international politics by core powers and hegemonic states. This definition needs careful explication.

[. . .]

Discourses are best conceptualized as sets of capabilities people have, as sets of socio-cultural resources used by people in the construction of meaning about their world and their activities. It is NOT simply speech or written statements but the rules by which verbal speech and written statements are made meaningful. Discourses enable one to write, speak, listen and act meaningfully. They are a set of capabilities, an ensemble of rules by which readers/listeners and speakers/audiences are able to take what they hear and read and construct it into an organized meaningful whole. Alker and Sylvan (1986) articulate the distinction this way:

> As backgrounds, discourses must be distinguished from the verbal productions which readers or listeners piece together. As we prefer to use the term people do not read or listen to a discourse: rather, they employ a discourse or discourses in the processes of reading or listening to a verbal production. Discourses do not present themselves as such; what we observe are people and verbal productions.

Discourses, like grammars, have a virtual and not an actual existence. They are not overarching constructs in the way that 'structures' are sometimes represented. Rather, they are real sets of capabilities whose existence we infer from their realizations in activities, texts and speeches. Neither are they absolutely deterministic. Discourses enable. One can view these capabilities or rules as permitting a certain bounded field of possibilities and reasoning as the process by which certain possibilities are actualized. The various actualizations of possibilities have consequences for the further reproduction and transformation of discourse. The actualization of one possibility closes off previously existent possibilities and simultaneously opens up a new series of somewhat different possibilities. Discourses are never static but are constantly mutating and being modified by human practice. The study of geopolitics in discursive terms, therefore, is the study of the socio-cultural resources and rules by which geographies of international politics get written.[1]

The notion of 'intellectuals of statecraft' refers to a whole community of state bureaucrats, leaders, foreign-policy experts and advisors throughout the world who comment upon, influence and conduct the activities of statecraft. Ever since the development of the modern state system in the sixteenth century there has been a community of intellectuals of statecraft. Up until the twentieth century this community was rather small and restricted, with most intellectuals also being practitioners of statecraft. In the twentieth century, however, this community has become quite extensive and internally specialized. Within the larger states at least, one can differentiate between types of intellectuals of statecraft on the basis of their institutional setting and style of reasoning. Within civil society there are 'defense intellectuals' associated with particular defense contractors and weapons systems. There is also a specialized community of security intellectuals in various public think-tanks (e.g. the RAND Corporation, the Hoover Institute, the Georgetown Center for Strategic and International Studies) who write and comment upon international affairs and strategy (Cockburn, 1987; Dalby, 1990b). One finds a different form of intellectualizing from public intellectuals of statecraft such as Henry Kissinger or Zbigniew Brzezinski who, as former top governmental officials, command a wide audience for their opinions in national newspapers and foreign-policy journals. Within political society itself there are different gradations amongst the foreign-policy community from those who design, articulate and order foreign policy from the top to those actually charged with implementing particular foreign policies and practicing statecraft (whether diplomatic or military) on a daily basis. All can claim to be intellectuals of statecraft for they are constantly engaged in reasoning about statecraft though all may not have the function of intellectuals in the conventional sense, but rather in the sense of Gramsci's 'organic' intellectuals (Gramsci, 1971).

[. . .]

PRACTICAL GEOPOLITICAL REASONING IN AMERICAN FOREIGN POLICY

Given our re-conceptualization of geopolitics, any analysis of American geopolitics must necessarily be more than an analysis of the formal geopolitical reasoning of a series of 'wise men' of strategy (Mahan, Spykman, Kissinger and others). American geopolitics involves the study of the different historical means by which US intellectuals of statecraft have spatialized international politics and represented it as a 'world' characterized by particular types of places, peoples and dramas.

[. . .]

The first of our three observations on practical geopolitical reasoning in American foreign policy is that representations of 'America' as a place are pervasively mythological. 'America' is a place which is at once real, material and bounded (a territory with quiddity) yet also a mythological, imaginary and universal ideal with no specific spatial bounds. Ever since early modern times, North America and the Caribbean have had the transgressive aura of a place 'beyond the line', as Dunn (1972, ch. 1) terms it, where might made right and the European treaties did not apply. By its own lore, the origins of the country are mythic and its location divine. In his famous pamphlet *Common Sense*, written in 1776 in support of the American rebellion, Thomas Paine wrote:

> This new world hath been the asylum for the persecuted lovers of civil and religious liberty from *every part* of Europe. Hither have they fled, not from the tender embraces of the mother, but from the cruelty of the monster . . . Everything that is right or natural pleads for separation. The blood of the slain, the weeping voice of nature cries 'TIS TIME TO PART'. Even the distance at which the Almighty hath placed England and America, is a strong and natural proof, that the authority of the one, over the other, was never the design of Heaven. The time likewise at which the continent was discovered, adds weight to the argument, and the manner in which it was peopled encreases [*sic*] the force of it. The reformation was preceded by the discovery of America, as if the Almighty graciously meant to open a sanctuary to the persecuted in future years, when home should afford neither friendship nor safety. (Paine 1969: 39, 40–1).

The dramatic hyperbole of Paine's geopolitical reasoning is part of the mythological origins of the American state. In the popular imagination 'America' was 'discovered'; it was a new, empty, pristine place, a New World. Despite the obvious inadequacies of this view, such an imaginary geography can still be found in contemporary American political culture and in the articulation of US foreign policy. Speaking over 210 years later on 2 February 1988 in an address to the nation supporting the Nicaraguan *contras*, President Ronald Reagan remarked:

> My friends, I have often expressed my belief that the Almighty had a reason for placing this great and good land, the 'New World', here

between two vast oceans. Protected by the seas, we have enjoyed the blessings of peace – free for almost two centuries now from the tragedy of foreign aggression on our mainland. Help us to keep that precious gift secure. Help us to win support for those who struggle for the same freedoms we hold dear. In doing so, we will not just be helping them; we will be helping ourselves, our children, and all the peoples of the world. We will be demonstrating that America is still a beacon of hope, still a light unto the nations. Yes, a great opportunity to show that hope still burns bright in this land and over our continent, casting a glow across centuries, still guiding missions – to a future of peace and freedom. (Reagan 1988: 35).

The continuity between the two texts is evidence of the durability of particular narratives in American political discourse. It is a structuralist fallacy to think of this narrative as having a 'deep structure' or a primordial set of binary oppositions – e.g., Old World: New World, despotism/totalitarianism: freedom – to which everything else can be reduced. As a discourse its existence is virtual not actual and is assembled and re-assembled differently by presidents and other intellectuals of statecraft: Such discourse freely fuses fact with fiction and reality with the imaginary to produce a reasoning where neither is distinguishable from the other.[2] Both narratives read like primitive ethnographic tales: the origins of a tribe from the wanderings of persecuted members of other tribes, the flight from persecution, the chosen land, divine guidance, blessings, precious gifts, beacons and monsters. America's first leaders are known even today in American political culture as the 'founding fathers'.

Secondly, there is a tension between a universal omnipresent image of 'America' and a different spatially-bounded image of the place. On one hand, American discourse consistenly plays upon the unique geographical location of 'America' yet simultaneously asserts that the principles of this 'New World' are universal and not spatially confined there. The geography evoked in the American Declaration of Independence was not continental or hemispheral but universal. Its concern was with 'the earth', the 'Laws of Nature and of Nature's God', and all of 'mankind'. In this universalist vision, 'America' is positioned as being equivalent with the strivings of a universal human nature. 'The cause of America', Paine (1969: 23) proclaimed, 'is in a great measure the cause of all mankind'. The freedoms it struggles for are, in Reagan's terms, the freedoms desired by 'all the peoples of the world'. 'America' is at once a territorially-defined state and a universal ideal, a place on the North American continent and a mythical homeland of freedom.

[. . .]

By the late nineteenth century, the increasing wealth and power of the US state, together with the scramble for colonies among the European powers, produced a foreign policy which subordinated the hemispheral identity of the United States to universalist themes and identities concerning race, civilization and Christianity. McKinley, acting under divine inspiration, saw it as the task of the United States to uplift and civilize the Philippines (while simultaneously preventing it from falling into the hands of commercial rivals France and Germany: Lafeber 1963) while Roosevelt's famous 'corollary' of 1904 declared:

> Chronic wrongdoing, or an impotence which results in a general loosening of the ties of civilized society, may in America, as elsewhere, ultimately require intervention by some civilized nation, and in the Western Hemisphere the adherence of the United States to the Monroe Doctrine may force the United States, however reluctantly, in flagrant cases of wrongdoing or impotence, to the exercise of an international police power. (Richardson 1905, vol. IX: 7053).

The geopolitical reasoning by which domestic slavery and continental US expansionism worked – i.e. those concerning civilized *versus* uncivilized territories, superior and inferior races, adult and child identifications of peoples with white Anglo-Saxon males as the adults – were drawn upon to help write global political space. The United States was beginning to consider itself a 'world power' with 'principles' that were no longer qualified as contingently applicable to the 'American hemisphere'. McKinley and Theodore Roosevelt's racial script was followed by Woodrow Wilson's crusade for what he and US political culture took to be democracy. That Wilsonian internationalism did not succeed was partly due to the re-invigoration of the mythology that an isolationist 'America' is the true and pure 'America'. Yet while the United States in the 1930s steered clear of political alliances with the rest of the world, its business enterprises continued their long-standing economic expansionism overseas. By the time of the Truman Doctrine, the US no longer conceptualized itself as *a* world power but as *the* world power. The geopolitical reasoning of Truman, as noted earlier, was abstract and universal. Containment had no clearly conceptualized geographical limitations. Its genuine space was the abstract universal isotropic plane wherein right does perpetual battle with wrong, liberty with totalitarianism and Americanism with the forces of un-Americanism.

A third feature of American discourse is the strong lines it draws between the space of the 'Self' and the space of the 'Other' (Todorov 1984; Dalby 1988, 1990a, 1990b). Like the cultural maps of many nations, American political discourse is given shape by a frontier which separates civilization from savagery in Turner's (1920) terms or an 'Iron Curtain' marking the free world from the 'evil empire'. Robertson (1980: 92) notes:

> Frontiers and lines are powerful symbols for Americans. The moving frontier was never only a geographical line: it was a palpable barrier which separated the wilderness from civilization. It distinguished Americans, with their beliefs and their ideals, from savages and strangers, those 'others' who could not be predicted or trusted. It divided the American nation from other nations, and marked its independence.

While such a point is valid, one can overstate the uniquely American character of this practice. Early European experiences, particularly the Iberian *reconquista* against the 'infidel' and the English colonial experience with 'heathens' in Ireland, were factors in the formation of imperialism as a 'way of life' in the United States (Meinig 1986; Williams 1980). European discourses on colonialism, we have already noted, found their way into US foreign-policy practice not only in Theodore Roosevelt's time but even in determining the shape of the post-war world.

[. . .]

CONCLUSION

The Cold War as a discourse may have lost its credibility and meaning as a consequence of the events of 1989 but it is clear from the Gulf crisis that intellectuals of statecraft in the West at least, and the military-industrial complex behind them, will try to create a 'new' set of enemies (the 'irrational Third-World despot') in a re-structured world order. The reductive nature of the practical geopolitical reasoning used in the 1990–91 Gulf crisis by President Bush and Prime Minister Thatcher looks all too familiar. The character of foreign places and foreign enemies is represented as fixed. In 1947 when George Kennan declared that 'there can be no appeal to common mental approaches' (1947: 574) in US dealings with the USSR he was effectively negating his own profession, namely diplomacy. The possibility of an open dialogue between the USSR and the United States was excluded *a priori* because the character of the USSR was already historically and geographically determined and thus effectively immutable. The irony of practical geopolitical representations of place is that, in order to succeed, they actually necessitate the abrogation of genuine geographical knowledge about the diversity and complexity of places as social entities. Describing the USSR then (or Iraq today) as Orientalist, is a work of geographical abstractionism. A complex, diverse and heterogeneous social mosaic of places is hypostatized into a singular, overdetermined and predictable actor. As a consequence, therefore, the United States was put in the ironic situation of being simultaneously tremendously geographically ignorant of the USSR (and today Iraq) yet fetishistically preoccupied with that state and its influence in world politics.

The global economic and political re-structuring of the contemporary age has been both a consequence and a generator of changing geographical sensibilities. The marked 'time-space compression' wrought by modern telecommunications and the globalization of capital, ideologies and culture has bound the fate of places more intimately together but has also opened up a series of possibilities for new types of subjectivities and new forms of political solidarity between places (Agnew and Corbridge 1989). Globalization has enabled certain critical social movements to make connections between their struggles and the struggles of other critical social movements in very different places (see, for example, Kaldor and Falk 1987; Walker 1988). Contemporary geography in deconstructing its own vocabulary and critically exploring the forms of practical geopolitical reasoning that circulate within states can be an ally to these critical social movements. It can help create descriptions of the world based not on reductive geopolitical reasoning but on critical geographical knowledge.

NOTES

1. In attempting to use Foucault and critical international-relations theories in political geography, there is a tendency to speak loosely of the 'discourse of geopolitics' or 'geopolitical discourse'. Such phrases can be unhelpful, for they suggest that geopolitics is a discrete discourse itself. This is not our contention. We prefer to use the term 'geopolitical reasoning' to describe the spatialization of international politics that results from the employment of discourses in foreign-policy practice.
2. Jean Baudrillard (1988: 7) has termed America 'the only remaining primitive society', a society of ferocious ritualism and hyperbolic primitivism that has 'far outstripped its own moral, social or ecological rationale'. For a discussion of the political and ecomomic realities of living in American mythology, see Davis (1986).

DIFFERENCE

Nathan Widder

INTRODUCTION

Difference is arguably the first concept of political thought, as it is only by virtue of differences (such as religious, ethnic, class or gender differences) that the problems of politics arise. One might imagine principles such as equality, justice, democracy and representation being realised in a homogeneous community. Yet in a society without differences these would not be *political* principles. In the history of Western political thought, the problem of difference appears already with Socrates, the thinker and critic whose difference and distance from Athenian politics made him a threat to his community.[1] From Plato onwards, numerous political philosophers have sought political principles to establish a harmonious community of different individuals and groups or at least to legitimate a neutral framework of laws and justice suitable to an inescapable 'fact of pluralism'. Their political problem, in short, has been to construct some form of unity, identity or agreement that is compatible with difference. Yet, as will be seen, these attempts have achieved their goals only by forcing difference to be compatible with unity, disregarding differences exceeding the terms of their proposed settlements and domesticating or simplifying the issues of difference they claim to confront. Ironically, while difference has given rise to political thinking, political thought has often ignored the full import of difference.

Several strands of recent political philosophy aim to reverse this trend, affirming the disruptive nature of difference and reconceptualising other political concepts through this affirmation. The following selections by William Connolly and Ernesto Laclau both express this aim. This introduction will set the stage for these selections by highlighting issues of difference emerging, first, in Plato's and Aristotle's philosophies, then in the debate between contemporary liberals and communitarians, and finally in 'postmodern' or 'poststructuralist' philosophies of difference.

COMPATIBLE AND DISRUPTIVE DIFFERENCES: PLATO AND ARISTOTLE

Plato's and Aristotle's philosophical conceptualisations of difference allow them to theorise ideal polities that harmoniously organise different groups. For Plato, the theory of Forms provides a foundation for difference and establishes the place of the three classes of his republic. For Aristotle, the *telos* of man as a political animal determines the place of the various members of the *polis* and makes them function together. Yet both thinkers also encounter differences that cannot be harmonised. The way each attempts to exclude or ignore these differences highlights the way difference is elided in traditional political thought.

In Plato's dialogues, Socrates consistently outwits his debating opponents by asking them questions in the form of 'what is justice?' or 'what is beauty?' When his interlocutors reply by citing, for example, specific instances of beauty, Socrates responds that these answers are inadequate, since the question calls not for an example of beauty but for a definition of beauty itself. No physical object is beauty itself, since any beautiful thing is, at certain times and places, ugly (Plato 1974: 139). Proceeding this way, Socrates implies the existence of something beyond the physical exemplars themselves – that there is a universal and unchanging Form of beauty, with different individuals being more or less beautiful according to their proximity to the Form. Differences of beauty are thus organised in relation to a fixed standard and the same is true of any other positive quality (there is no Form of a negative, such as ugliness; instead, ugliness is what is furthest removed from and thus most opposed to beauty). Such standards are indispensable, Plato argues, because otherwise differences remain ungrounded. Beauty, justice, honour etc. would not only be in the eye of the beholder, but, more significantly, opinions about them would always be open to manipulation, since no standard would exist to distinguish truth from falsity.[2]

In Book VI of *The Republic*, Plato establishes his metaphysical hierarchy, the Divided Line. The highest levels comprise the intelligible realm of unchanging Forms and mathematical realities, which are the objects of reasoning and knowledge. Beneath these are the varied and changing objects of the visible world – physical objects that copy Forms and images, artworks and simulations that copy or reflect physical things. Or, as Plato explains in Book X, there is the Form of a bed, the physical bed, and the painting of the bed, each having different degrees of reality and truth (1974: 240–2). One attains the highest levels of truth through wisdom and philosophical reasoning (dialectic) and therefore, Plato argues, philosophers should rule the *polis* while others who remain at the level of opinion should be led. This argument for philosopher-rulers reinforces the discussion in Books II–IV of the classes of the city and the components of the soul. Starting from the premises that 'not one of us is self-sufficient, but needs many things' and 'each one of us is born somewhat different from the others, one more apt for one task, one for another' (1974: 39–40), Plato constructs, first, a simple city where different producers supply the basic needs for survival and, later, a complex city composed of three classes: philosopher guardians, warrior auxiliaries and plebeian producers. When each class stays within its remit, so that the guardians, aided by the auxiliaries, rule the producers, the resulting harmony of differences constitutes justice in the city. Moreover, as these classes embody different character types, Plato asserts three analogous parts to the soul – wisdom, spirit and appetite – that when functioning harmoniously – reason, aided by spirit, ruling the appetites – constitute the just individual. In both soul and city, justice arises with the rule of that difference that can aspire to the truth.

Nevertheless, these orders exclude problematic differences. In Plato's metaphysics, the problem involves images or simulacra. Plato defines these as copies of copies – images copy physical objects, which copy Forms – arguing that, like all successive copies, they fade and become corrupted by errors the further they move from the original. Yet any good simulation *appears to be as real* as the physical thing it copies and this deceptiveness defies the definition of simulacra as copies twice removed. Simulacra in this way exceed their place, subverting the order of differences. Plato's resulting ambivalence towards simulacra and imitation appears as he dismisses the imitator as having 'neither knowledge nor right opinion' (1974: 246) while calling the sophist, 'the type of natures which imitate the philosophic' (1974: 148), the greatest threat to the philosopher. Similar ambivalence appears in his exclusion of actors from the ideal city. On the one hand, Plato, reasserting his postulate that each individual is best suited to one task, argues that no imitator can imitate two things equally well, and hence no actor can effectively perform both comic and tragic roles (1974: 65). On the other hand, he excludes actors because, being able to play many roles well, they undermine this premise and threaten the city where each must accept only one role.[3] Uncertain if they are a nuisance or a genuine threat, Plato's politics struggles with the existence of actors and sophists, depending as it does on differences resolving themselves into three reciprocally functioning classes. Plato can never fully explain the imitator and certainly cannot provide a structure of the imitator's soul like those he develops for the classes composing his ideal. Within the soul, city and Divided Line, Plato stumbles over excessive differences.

Rejecting the Forms, Aristotle turns to the idea of natural *telos*. A *telos* is an end or purpose and a natural *telos* is an end towards which a thing spontaneously moves – an acorn's natural *telos*, for example, is to become an oak. By contrast, a *telos* imposed on something – the way becoming a table might be imposed upon wood – is contingent or conventional. In either case, however, *telos* creates a unity of differences. The different parts of a table, and the roots and branches of an oak, are brought together and defined by their roles within an overall end which they achieve. Meanwhile, the *telos* itself, though only realised at the end, governs throughout the development of the parts towards their final goal.

Aristotle asserts that the *polis* is natural and that man is by nature a political animal. The *polis* thus develops by its own impetus instead of being imposed by some on others; moreover, its realisation enables different humans to fulfil their natural *telei*. By virtue of natural *telos*, the *polis* legitimately brings together a plurality of individuals. Man's natural potential for reason and speech, Aristotle argues, is realised only in deliberation on the good life, making his natural *telos* not merely to live but to live well in a *polis* (1988, esp. Book I). Aristotle, like Plato, holds that 'the individual, when isolated, is not self-sufficing' (1988: 4) and this necessitates that different members of the *polis* co-operate to fulfil various needs. But politics, being defined as a realm where equals take turns ruling and being ruled (Aristotle 1988: 51–9), must exclude many members of the *polis* from participation. Aristotle excludes women, children and slaves using natural *telos*. Natural slaves, he maintains, lack a capacity for rational judgement, so their *telos* is to obey well – that is, to be good slaves; women lack full rational capacities and their abilities are best realised when they remain in the household; and children have rational faculties but they are undeveloped (1988: 18–19). From these different *telei*, Aristotle organises household relations to provide freemen with the leisure time necessary to participate in politics as citizens.

Nature further assigns citizens roles appropriate to their abilities, the younger and stronger being warriors, the older and wiser being councillors (Aristotle 1988: 167–9). However, while nature provides sufficient reason to exclude women, children and slaves from politics, certain freemen are excluded only by the necessary work they perform. Farmers, artisans and mechanics, Aristotle maintains, perform work that 'makes the body or soul or mind of the freeman less fit for the practice or exercise of excellence' (1988: 186). He therefore suggests having the work done by slaves or barbarians (1988: 58, 170–1). Yet mechanical work is fundamentally different from slave work, as the latter fulfils the *telos* of the slave to serve well, while the former is self-directed work that fulfils no *telos* but deforms the capacities of the freeman. Indeed, this labour is simply unnatural, and so the basis for certain individuals being assigned these functions can only be convention and arbitrary social circumstance, the opposite of nature. Yet as the work is indispensable to the *polis*, Aristotle must accept the existence of these labourers while tightly restricting their influence. Non-citizens, he argues, should be prohibited from carrying arms (1988: 168) and citizens should not be taught mechanical skills (1988, Bk. VIII generally).

In aspiring to bring differences into harmony, then, both Plato and Aristotle exclude differences that they must nonetheless acknowledge in order to make their ideals function. Even while they articulate the compatibility of differences with one another, they also stumble across incompatibilities. Many contemporary theorists maintain that human plurality is too great to permit fully harmonious communities and modern political theory generally rejects Platonic and Aristotelian metaphysics. Yet difficulties with difference remain. The following section on the liberal–communitarian debate will demonstrate how difference remains a problem for political thought.

Difference and identity: the liberal–communitarian debate

So far this introduction has not made explicit the connections between identity and difference, though some aspects have been implied. If a thing's identity is comprised of those features that remain constant over time and define it, then Plato's Forms and Aristotle's *telos* can be seen to provide the stable markers necessary to anchor any thing's identity and differentiate it from others. If these metaphysical stabilities are rejected, a thing's identity – and, therefore, its difference from other things – might be considered something it has either positively in itself or only in relation to others. While liberal conceptions of toleration tend towards the former view, communitarian attempts to revive moral traditions tend towards the latter. However, the nature of identity and difference becomes problematic when considering the possibility that different identities might not only define themselves in relation to one another but also affirm themselves *only* through the deprecation of certain differences – that for an identity to affirm itself as good, for example, it must define some other as evil. This consideration is both a starting point for the two selections following this introduction and a stumbling point for liberal and communitarian theorists. For in so far as liberals and communitarians orient their politics towards harmonising differences, they must continue to emphasise compatibility over incompatibility, simplifying the differences they hope to bring together.

A defining feature of liberalism is its acceptance of the 'fact of pluralism' – the empirical reality that in modern society no single standard of the good can establish the kind of community sought by Plato and Aristotle,[4] making the search for this standard 'no longer a political possibility for those who accept the constraints of liberty and toleration embodied in democratic institutions' (Rawls 1988: 269). Liberal theory attempts to move from this acknowledgement to the ideal of a tolerant society where individuals, accepted as free and equal, can pursue different conceptions of the good life.

Liberalism thereby claims to be a more committed advocate of difference than classical political theories, but aspirations to unity remain. Defending and modifying his original theory of justice, John Rawls, for example, affirms that its principles apply to the basic structure of society understood as 'society's main political, social, and economic institutions, and how they fit together into one unified system of social cooperation' (1985: 225). Despite modern society's plurality, Rawls says, 'perhaps the divergence of opinion can be narrowed sufficiently so that a political cooperation on a basis of mutual respect can still be maintained' (1985: 226). This narrowing, however, cannot rely on metaphysical or epistemological claims to truth: 'Philosophy as the search for truth about an independent metaphysical and moral order cannot, I believe, provide a workable and shared basis for a political conception of justice in a democratic society' (Rawls 1985: 230).

The issue here is how this narrowing is achieved, for both Rawls and liberal advocates of toleration generally.[5] Rawls's early arguments from the original position and the veil of ignorance claim that hypothetical rational individuals, shorn of the particularities of their different identities, would choose his two principles of justice.[6] Replying to criticisms that this idea invokes an incoherent metaphysics of a self prior to and able freely to choose its identity,[7] the later Rawls argues that his original position is merely 'a device of representation' (1985: 236), but that it reflects 'one of the basic intuitive ideas which we take to be implicit in the public culture of a democratic society' (1985: 231). This is the idea of citizenship, a product of 'social and historical conditions [that] have their origins in the Wars of religion following the Reformation and the subsequent development of the principle of toleration, and in the growth of constitutional government and the institutions of large industrial market economies' (Rawls 1985: 225). According to it, individuals in their 'public identity' are regarded as free, equal, independent from any particular conception of the good, and able to revise the conception they may hold. Outside the public or political realm, individuals may consider themselves inseparable from their comprehensive identities, including their religious, ethnic, cultural or other differences and their conceptions of the good life, but this remains a private or 'nonpublic identity' (Rawls 1985: 241).

Rawls's route to political unity in light of the incommensurable differences in today's democracies thereby involves *depoliticising* these differences. Through this depoliticisation, differences are treated as a diversity of identities remaining *indifferent* to one another (see McClure 1990). This position on identity is indispensable to liberal toleration: if non-public differences were implicated in one another – if, for example, one's identity as Christian, male or middle class was constituted in relation to Muslim, female or working class – such identity matters could not be kept wholly private. Whether appealing to social contracts, original positions, principles of utility or, as with the later Rawls, publicly accepted intuitions of modern democratic society, liberal thinkers tend to see identities as separate positivities in this way. This allows liberals to accommodate still-existing intolerant identities (racist, sexist etc.) by circumscribing their influence over public and political life, while also proposing ways to press towards their elimination. Unsurprisingly, liberal theories view comprehensive identities as matters of either choice or socialisation and habituation. With respect to the latter, many liberals promote education so individuals can learn to tolerate differences by seeing them as matters of indifference and can avoid habituation into identities that exceed the tolerable. A tradition of liberal feminist thought, for example, views harmful gender stereotypes as being ingrained through social practices and calls for legislation and educational reform to eliminate them (Okin 1989; Wollstonecraft 1992). Similarly, Richard Rorty's 'bourgeois, postmodern liberalism', holding that 'the self, the human subject, is simply whatever acculturation makes of it', hopes to teach others through 'detailed descriptions of particular varieties of pain and humiliation' to promote 'the ability to see more and more traditional differences ... as unimportant when compared with similarities with respect to pain and humiliation – the ability to think of people wildly different from ourselves as included in the range of "us" ' (1989: 64, 192). The straightforward nature of the proposed solution, however, belies the difficulty in actually achieving it, and indicates a simplification of differences in the way they are treated as not only indifferent to each other but also malleable enough to be contained and socialised in this way.

Ironically, then, liberalism accepts the incompatibility of difference only if it can be bracketed off to establish public compatibility. Yet where liberals such as Rawls argue that the fact of pluralism requires the depoliticisation of different identities to establish a tolerant society, many communitarian thinkers argue that depoliticisation creates the very incommensurability that motivates liberal theory. Alasdair MacIntyre, for example, argues that liberal and Enlightenment rejections of the traditional philosophical search for teleological moral truths have severed contemporary life from the moral sources capable of establishing unity and harmony. Traditional morality determined what man ought to be from an idea of his purpose or end. Once this use of *telos* was dismissed, modern political philosophy could appeal only to rationality or human passions, which were inadequate to ground moral standards. The result, for MacIntyre, is that moral language, in the absence of publicly accepted standards, can only be manipulation. Liberal society becomes an emotivist society, where moral statements are '*nothing but* expressions of preference, expressions of attitude or feeling, insofar as they are moral or evaluative in character' (MacIntyre 1984: 12), and consensus is lacking even for the agreement over political principles desired by Rawls. Three character types now dominate: the bureaucrat, who administers through instrumental rationality with no reflection on the ends being served; the wealthy aesthete, who, absorbed in pursuing personal pleasure, finds nothing in society worthy of loyalty or respect; and the therapist, the ultimate manipulator, who turns neurotics into well-adjusted, productive members of society (MacIntyre 1984: 23–5). These characters, MacIntyre holds, arise in an atomised society devoid of genuine communal bonds and friendships, where individuals seek only their self-interest and cannot have commensurable notions of the good.

MacIntyre accepts that pre-modern understandings of human *telos*, especially if treated as universal and natural, are today unviable (1984: 111), but he nevertheless argues that a revised understanding, if made publicly viable, can bring differences into accord.[8] This alternative is found, first, in the idea of virtues linked to social practices. Such practices contain rules, including those governing relations between different practitioners, which must be followed to achieve the end of practising well. This end is internal to the practice and so opposes external goods or goals that may be achieved by cheating or not practising at all (MacIntyre 1984: 187–9). But affirming *telei* immanent to practices cannot alone recover moral standards, since these define only the 'good practitioner', not the 'good human'. Human life requires a unity that is fulfilled, for MacIntyre, by narrative and tradition. Narrative links together life's diverse events and experiences, giving them meaning and intelligibility in relation to long-term intentions and aspirations. Moreover, a narrative of an individual life necessarily links that life to its social context, as an individual's actions cannot be understood outside the individual's roles and practices or the traditions and history (both personal and social) that constitute the individual's situation. This, in turn, suggests a general formula of human purpose: 'Man is in his actions and practice, as well as in his fictions, essentially a story-telling animal. He is not essentially, but becomes through his history, a teller of stories that aspire to truth' (MacIntyre 1984: 216). Traditions are thereby indispensable for giving meaning and identity not only to a society as a whole but to its different individuals. Society's traditions, MacIntyre argues, are contingent on its time and place, even if the need for traditions is universal (1984: 220). Although traditions do not fully unify society, they make possible the narrowing of its incommensurabilities by linking together even its most opposing identities:

> For the story of my life is always embedded in the story of those communities from which I derive my identity. I am born with a past; and to try to cut myself off from that past, in individualist mode, is to deform my present relationships. The possession of an historical identity and the possession of a social identity coincide. Notice that rebellion against my identity is always one possible mode of expressing it. (MacIntyre 1984: 221)

It is therefore not by bracketing off the comprehensive aspects of identity but by recalling and reviving them that differences can come together.

MacIntyre is often criticised for praising the traditions of Homeric, ancient Greek and medieval Christian societies while breezing over their less desirable aspects, such as their acceptance of slavery, their subordination of women and their anti-Semitism. For liberals, this is precisely why comprehensive identities and conceptions of the good must not infiltrate political life. From the perspective of the kind of political philosophy of difference considered next, however, what makes MacIntyre's praise of the traditions and narratives that constitute social identity problematic is its lack of any consideration about how such an identity and its good are constituted through the definition of something else as inferior and evil. MacIntyre's communitarianism must avoid this issue, because it undermines the claim that identity harmonises differences. But liberal theories of toleration also avoid it by conceiving identity in ways that de-emphasise its relation to difference. This problem points to differences that, being incompatible with any notion of identity, disrupt the political goal of unity expressed in much political thought.

Different kinds of difference

At least since G. W. F. Hegel, it has been difficult to claim that identity is given in itself. A thing's identity is defined by properties that it holds over time, but properties are inherently relational. To say that something is green, for example, signifies a relation it has to a subject (it is green only *for* the subject perceiving it), but also to other objects having the same or different colours or even no colour. This makes identity necessarily relational and hence *constituted* by difference.[9]

But here we might distinguish two sorts of difference. If identity must delineate itself through differences, these differences must be stable enough to serve as markers against which an identity can be placed. Such differences can be localised, placed or *identified*, making them compatible with the establishment of identity. They can be organised, for instance, in terms of proximity or distance to the identity they anchor, the closer being more similar to and the further away being more different from and antithetical to that identity. We can therefore call these *oppositional* differences, which can be structured in binary categories of identity and opposition, good and evil etc., with any number of intermediate positions. Yet no matter how far removed, such differences could never be completely outside or alien to an identity: since an identity consolidates itself only by reference to these differences, these differences are in their own way *included* in that identity.

Another sort of difference, however, is like the simulacra exceeding their place and disrupting the order of Plato's Divided Line. These differences cannot be placed against identity in terms of proximity and distance, similarity and opposition, making their character inherently mysterious and deceptive. Rather than being oppositional, these differences might be called *other*. While being no less internal to identity, in so far as any identity is necessarily related to them, they are nevertheless 'outside' in the sense of exceeding any binary structure that would fix and identify them. They are therefore *neither* similar *nor* opposed, *neither* good *nor* evil, and in this way they can be identified only as *differing from themselves*. To the extent that identity depends upon these differences, it is related to something too fluid and unfixed to anchor it, and thereby risks becoming mysterious to itself. And to the extent that a politics of identity is oriented towards stability and unity, it is compelled to reduce the enigma of otherness, ignoring or excluding it.

Various political theories of difference, inspired by the likes of Friedrich Nietzsche, Michel Foucault, Jacques Derrida, Gilles Deleuze and Luce Irigaray, emphasise a triad of identity, opposition and otherness. They argue that if identity secures itself only within an oppositional schema, it necessarily collapses otherness into opposition, mapping this enigmatic difference onto the binaries that consolidate identity.[10] The result is a politics of either assimilation or antagonism. Otherness is defined as either like the self, but then necessarily in conformity with it, or antithetical to the self, but then necessarily an enemy to be conquered, an error to be corrected etc. It is either ignored in the name of a universal around which differences must coalesce or held as the contaminant preventing this universal from being realised. Political theorists of identity must either expel these differences, as Plato and Aristotle did with actors and mechanical workers, assume the possibility of circumscribing them within a private realm or aim to bring them into harmony in the public realm. None of these options acknowledge the enigma of otherness, yet it does not thereby disappear. Rather, precisely because enigmatic differences continue to circulate while exceeding the binaries into which they are placed, they deconstruct the dichotomies that work to fix identity, while the dichotomies themselves continue to invoke differences surpassing their terms.

Foucault's accounts (1977, 1978) of disciplinary and normalising society illustrate the continuing presence of excessive otherness within the binary categories governing modern life. For Foucault, the rise of liberal capitalist societies coincides with the need for new strategies of 'governmentality' more oriented towards the promotion of life and the efficiency of the body politic. Individuals must be constituted in certain ways to counterbalance the new economic and social freedoms (Foucault 1991: 171–2), and while this does not require individuals to become 'the same' as each other, it does necessitate their being constituted in relation to a norm that measures them. Various techniques arise to police this norm by delineating and gathering knowledge of various forms of deviancy that stand in opposition to it – the criminal delinquent opposing the law-abiding citizen, the sexual pervert opposing the monogamous heterosexual etc. Yet, ironically, no one ever quite lives up to the ideal of the 'normal individual', and those labelled deviants, despite all the efforts of observation, testing, classification and confession to comprehend and know them, remain mysterious. Unsurprisingly, Foucault concludes, an examination of the various criminal delinquents that modern society seeks to police reveals that they have always already passed through a myriad of institutions supposedly designed to normalise them (1977: 301). Yet these failures only reinforce the drive to secure the norm by policing difference even more intensely. Modern society, for Foucault, is thereby driven to generate otherness even while it seeks ever more stringently to reduce it to the kind of oppositional markers that can secure identity.

CONCLUSION

The critical task for these political philosophies of difference is to expose the way political thought and practice regularly iron out the discontinuities and strangeness of difference, refusing to acknowledge its disruptive character. Given how deeply notions of identity and stability, and corollary understandings of difference, have underpinned political ideals, this is a broad and varied task. Representation, for example, has usually assumed a stable subject whose interests can be brought to the political arena, while sovereignty, democracy and the nation-state have often presupposed a communal identity around which differences coalesce. The following selections, however, all aspire to reconsider the nature of politics and the various ways politics can be thought and practised by reading these off of difference rather than identity. Whereas political thought has regularly understood difference under the shadow of identity, they start with an affirmation of a difference that is strange, enigmatic and different from both identity and identity's concept of difference.

QUESTIONS FOR DISCUSSION

- Why is difference a core concept of political theory?
- Can we think about political differences without first prioritising political identities?
- Are current concerns with difference in political theory a reflection of capitalist ideologies of choice and consumption?
- Is a concept of difference central to our understanding of liberty?

NOTES

1. At his trial, Socrates maintained that his distinctive ethical stance required him to refrain from public political life in order to survive:

> If I had tried long ago to engage in politics, I should long ago have lost my life, without doing any good either to you or to myself... The true champion of justice, if he intends to survive even for a short time, must necessarily confine himself to private life and leave politics alone. (Plato 1993: 55–6)

2. 'As for those who contemplate many beautiful things but do not see Beauty itself and are incapable of following another who leads them to it, who see many just

actions but not Justice itself, and so with everything – these people, we shall say, opine everything but have no knowledge of anything they opine' (Plato 1974: 139).

3. 'It seems, then, that if a man who in his cleverness can become many persons and imitate all things should arrive in our city and want to give a performance of his poems, we should bow down before him as being holy, wondrous, and sweet, but we should tell him that there is no such man in our city and that it is not lawful that there should be' (Plato 1974: 68).

4. As John Rawls states in defining his own version of political liberalism:

> One of the deepest distinctions between political conceptions of justice is between those that allow for a plurality of opposing and even incommensurable conceptions of the good and those that hold that there is but one conception of the good which is to be recognized by all persons, so far as they are fully rational ... Plato and Aristotle, and the Christian tradition as represented by Augustine and Aquinas, fall on the side of the rational good. Such views tend to be teleological and to hold that institutions are just to the extent that they effectively promote this good ... Classical utilitarianism [also] belongs to this dominant tradition. By contrast, liberalism as a political doctrine presupposes that there are many conflicting and incommensurable conceptions of the good, each compatible with the full rationality of human persons, so far as we can ascertain within a workable political conception of justice. As a consequence of this supposition, liberalism assumes that it is a characteristic of a free democratic culture that a plurality of conflicting and incommensurable conceptions of the good are affirmed by its citizens (1985: 248).

5. The following argument is developed with respect to John Locke and early modern advocates of toleration by McClure (1990).

6. The principles, of course, being (1) 'Each person is to have an equal right to the most extensive total system of equal basic liberties compatible with a similar system of liberty for all' and (2) 'Social and economic inequalities are to be arranged so that they are both (a) to the greatest benefit of the least advantaged, and (b) attached to offices and positions open to all under conditions of fair equality of opportunity' (Rawls 1971: 302).

7. This criticism was most prominently put forward by Sandel (1982).

8. A similar view about a viable conception of *telos* is expressed by Charles Taylor and is examined in the selection by William Connolly following this introduction.

9. Friedrich Nietzsche puts the point far more succinctly than Hegel ever would when he writes: 'The properties of a thing are effects on other "things": if one removes other "things", then a thing has no properties, i.e., there is no thing without other things, i.e., there is no "thing in itself"' (1967: 302).

10. Connolly's selection uses the terminology somewhat differently. For Connolly, 'otherness' connotes difference that is congealed into a firm opposition to consolidate identity, while 'difference' connotes the wider sense of what exceeds the binary categories of identity: 'Identity requires difference in order to be, and it converts difference into otherness in order to secure its own self-certainty.'

ERNESTO LACLAU
EXTRACT FROM *EMANCIPATION(S)*

WHY DO EMPTY SIGNIFIERS MATTER TO POLITICS?

The social production of 'empty signifiers'

An empty signifier is, strictly speaking, a signifier without a signified. This definition is also, however, the enunciation of a problem. For how would it be possible that a signifier is not attached to any signified and remains, nevertheless, an integral part of a system of signification? An empty signifier would be a sequence of sounds, and if the latter are deprived of any signifying function the term 'signifier' itself would become excessive. The only possibility for a stream of sounds being detached from any particular signified while still remaining a signifier is if, through the subversion of the sign which the possibility of an empty signifier involves, something is achieved which is internal to significations as such. What is this possibility?

Some pseudo answers can be discarded quite quickly. One would be to argue that the same signifier can be attached to different signifieds in different contexts (as a result of the arbitrariness of the sign). But it is clear that, in that case, the signifier would not be *empty* but *equivocal*: the function of signification in each context would be fully realised. A second possibility is that the signifier is not *equivocal* but *ambiguous*: that either an overdetermination or an underdetermination of signifieds prevents it from being fully fixed. Yet this floating of the signifier still does not make it an empty one. Although the floating takes us one step towards the proper answer to our problem, the terms of the latter are still avoided. We do not

Ernesto Laclau (1990), *Emancipation(s)*, London: Verso.

have to deal with an excess or deficiency of signification, but with the precise theoretical possibility of something which points, from within the process of signification, to the discursive presence of its own limits.

An empty signifier can, consequently, only emerge if there is a structural impossibility in signification as such, and only if this impossibility can signify itself as an interruption (subversion, distortion, etcetera) of the structure of the sign. That is, the limits of signification can only announce themselves as the impossibility of realizing what is within those limits – if the limits could be signified in a direct way, they would be internal to signification and, *ergo*, would not be limits at all.

An initial and purely formal consideration can help to clarify the point. We know, from Saussure, that language (and by extension, all signifying systems) is a system of differences, that linguistic identities – values – are purely relational and that, as a result, the totality of language is involved in each single act of signification. Now, in that case, it is clear that the totality is essentially required – if the differences did not constitute a system, no signification at all would be possible. The problem, however, is that the very possibility of signification is the system, and the very possibility of the system is the possibility of its limits. We can say, with Hegel, that to think of the limits of something is the same as thinking of what is beyond those limits. But if what we are talking about are the limits of a *signifying system*, it is clear that those limits cannot be themselves signified, but have to *show* themselves as the *interruption* or *breakdown* of the process of signification. Thus, we are left with the paradoxical situation that what constitutes the condition of possibility of a signifying system – its limits – is also what constitutes its condition of impossibility – a blockage of the continuous expansion of the process of signification.

A first and capital consequence of this is that true limits can never be neutral limits but presuppose an exclusion. A neutral limit would be one which is essentially continuous with what is at its two sides, and the two sides are simply different from each other. As a signifying totality is, however, precisely a system of differences, this means that both are part of the same system and that the limits between the two cannot be the limits of the system. In the case of an exclusion we have, instead, authentic limits because the actualization of what is beyond the limit of exclusion would involve the impossibility of what is this side of the limit. True limits are always antagonistic. But the operation of the logic of exclusionary limits has a series of necessary effects which spread to both sides of the limits and which will lead us straight into the emergence of empty signifiers:

1. A first effect of the exclusionary limit is that it introduces an essential ambivalence within the system of differences constituted by those limits. On the one hand, each element of the system has an identity only so far as it is different from the others: difference = identity. On the other hand, however, all these differences are equivalent to each other inasmuch as all of them

belong to this side of the frontier of exclusion. But, in that case, the identity of each element is constitutively split: on the one hand, each difference expresses itself *as* difference; on the other hand, each of them *cancels* itself as such by entering into a relation of equivalence with all the other differences of the system. And, given that there is only system as long as there is radical exclusion, this split or ambivalence is constitutive of all systemic identity. It is only in so far as there is a radical impossibility of a system as pure presence, beyond all exclusions, that actual *systems* (in the plural) can exist. Now, if the systematicity of the system is a direct result of the exclusionary limit, it is only that exclusion that grounds the system as such. This point is essential because it results from it that the system cannot have a positive ground and that, as a result, it cannot signify itself in terms of any positive signified. Let us suppose for a moment that the systematic ensemble was the result of all its elements sharing a positive feature (for example that they all belonged to a regional category). In that case, that positive feature would be different from other differential positive features, and they would all appeal to a deeper systematic ensemble within which their differences would be thought of as differences. But a system constituted through radical exclusion interrupts this play of the differential logic: what is excluded from the system, far from being something positive, is the simple principle of positivity – pure being. This already announces the possibility of an empty signifier – that is a signifier of the pure cancellation of all difference.

2. The condition, of course, for this operation to be possible is that what is beyond the frontier of exclusion is reduced to pure negativity – that is to the pure threat that what is beyond poses to the system (constituting it that way). If the exclusionary dimension was eliminated, or even weakened, what would happen is that the differential character of the 'beyond' would impose itself and, as a result, the limits of the system would be blurred. Only if the beyond becomes the signifier of pure threat, of pure negativity, of the simply excluded, can there be limits and system (that is an objective order). But in order to be the signifiers of the excluded (or, simply of exclusion), the various excluded categories have to cancel their differences through the formation of a chain of equivalences to that which the system demonizes in order to signify itself. Again, we see here the possibility of an empty signifier announcing itself through this logic in which differences collapse into equivalential chains.

3. But, we could ask ourselves, why does this pure being or systematicity of the system, or – its reverse – the pure negativity of the excluded, require the production of empty signifiers in order to signify itself? The answer is that we are trying to signify the limits of signification – the real, if you want, in the Lacanian sense – and there is no direct way of doing so except through the subversion of the process of signification itself. We know, through psychoanalysis, how what is not direcly representable – the unconscious – can only find as a means of representation the subversion of

the signifying process. Each signifier constitutes a sign by attaching itself to a particular signified, inscribing itself as a difference within the signifying process. But if what we are trying to signify is not a difference but, on the contrary, a radical exclusion which is the ground and condition of all differences, in that case, no production of *one more* difference can do the trick. As, however, all the means of representation are differential in nature, it is only if the differential nature of the signifying units is subverted, only if the signifiers empty themselves of their attachment to particular signifieds and assume the role of representing the pure being of the system – or, rather, the system as pure Being – that such a signification is possible. What is the ontological ground of such subversion, what makes it possible? The answer is: the split of each unit of signification that the system has to construct as the undecidable locus in which both the logic of difference and the logic of equivalence operate. It is only by privileging the dimension of equivalence to the point that its differential nature is almost entirely obliterated – that is emptying it of its differential nature – that the system can signify itself as a totality.

Two points have to be stressed here. The first is that the being or systematicity of the system which is represented through the empty signifiers is not a being which has not been *actually* realized, but one which is constitutively unreachable, for whatever systematic effects that would exist will be the result, as we have seen, of the unstable compromise between equivalence and difference. That is, we are faced with a constitutive lack, with an impossible object which, as in Kant, shows itself through the impossibility of its adequate representation. Here, we can give a full answer to our initial question: there can be empty signifiers within the field of signification because any system of signification is structured around an empty place resulting from the impossibility of producing an object which, none the less, is required by the systematicity of the system. So, we are not dealing with an impossibility without location, as in the case of a logical contradiction, but with a *positive* impossibility, with a *real* one to which the x of the empty signifier points.

However, if this impossible object lacks the means of its adequate or direct representation, this can only mean that the signifier which is emptied in order to assume the representing function will always be constitutively inadequate. What, in that case, does determine that one signifier rather than another assumes in different circumstances that signifying function? Here, we have to move to the main theme of this essay: the relation between empty signifiers and politics.

Hegemony

Let me go back to an example that we discussed in detail in *Hegemony and Socialist Strategy:*[1] the constitution, according to Rosa Luxemburg, of the unity of the working class through an overdetermination of partial struggles over a long period of time. Her basic argument is that the unity of the class is not determined by an a priori consideration about the priority of either the political struggle or the economic struggle, but by the accumulated effects of the internal split of all partial mobilizations. In relation to our subject, her argument amounts to approximately the following: in a climate of extreme repression any mobilization for a partial objective will be perceived not only as related to the concrete demand or objectives of that struggle, but also as an act of opposition against the system. This last fact is what establishes the link between a variety of concrete or partial struggles and mobilizations – all of them are seen as related to each other, not because their concrete objectives are intrinsically related but because they are all seen as equivalent in confrontation with the repressive regime. It is not, consequently, something positive that all of them share which establishes their unity, but something negative: their opposition to a common enemy. Luxemburg's argument is that a revolutionary mass identity is established through the overdetermination, over a whole historical period, of a plurality of separate struggles. These traditions fused, at the revolutionary moment, in a ruptural point.

Let us try to apply our previous categories to this sequence. The meaning (the signified) of all concrete struggles appears, right from the beginning, internally divided. The concrete aim of the struggle is not only that aim in its concreteness; it also signifies opposition to the system. The first signified establishes the differential character of that demand or mobilization *vis-à-vis* all other demands or mobilizations. The second signified establishes the equivalence of all these demands in their common opposition to the system. As we can see, any concrete struggle is dominated by this contradictory movement that simultaneously asserts and abolishes its own singularity. The function of representing the system as a totality depends, consequently, on the possibility of the equivalential function neatly prevailing over the differential one; but this possibility is simply the result of every single struggle always being already, originally, penetrated by this constitutive ambiguity.

It is important to observe that, as we have already established, if the function of the differential signifiers is to renounce their differential identity in order to represent the purely equivalential identity of a communitarian space as such, they cannot construct this equivalential identity as something belonging to a differential order. For instance: we can represent the Tzarist regime as a repressive order by enumerating the differential kinds of oppression that it imposed on various sections of the population as much as we want; but such enumeration will not give us the specificity of the repressive moment, that which constitutes – in its negation – what is peculiar to a repressive relation between entities. Because in such a relation each instance of the repressive power counts as pure bearer of the negation of the identity of the repressed sector. Now, if the differential identity of the repressive action is in that way 'distanced' from itself by having itself transformed into the mere incarnating body of the negation of the being of another entity, it is clear that between this negation and the body through which it expresses itself there is no necessary relation – nothing predetermines that one particular body should be the one predestined to incarnate negation as such.

It is precisely this which makes the relation of equivalence possible: different particular struggles are so many bodies which can indifferently incarnate the opposition of all of them to the repressive power. This involves a double movement. On the one hand, the more the chain of equivalences is extended, the less each concrete struggle will be able to remain closed in a differential self – in something which separates it from all other differential identities through a difference which is exclusively its own. On the contrary, as the equivalent relation shows that these differential identities are simply indifferent bodies incarnating something equally present in all of them, the longer the chain of equivalences is, the less concrete this 'something equally present' will be. At the limit it will be pure communitarian being independent of all concrete manifestation. And, on the other hand, that which is beyond the exclusion delimiting the communitarian space – the repressive power – will count less as the instrument of particular differential repressions and will express pure anti-community, pure evil and negation. The community created by this equivalential expansion will be, thus, the pure idea of a communitarian fullness which is absent – as a result of the presence of the repressive power.

But, at this point, the second movement starts. This pure equivalential function representing an absent fullness which shows itself through the collapse of all differential identities is something which cannot have a signifier of its own – for in that case, the 'beyond all differences' would be one more difference and not the result of the equivalential collapse of all differential identities. Precisely because the community as such is not a purely differential space of an objective identity but an absent fullness, it cannot have any form of representation of its own, and has to borrow the latter from some entity constituted within the equivalential space – in the same way as gold is a particular use value which assumes, as well, the function of representing value in general. This emptying of a particular signifier of its particular, differential signified is, as we saw, what makes possible the emergence of 'empty' signifiers as the signifiers of a lack, of an absent totality. But this leads us straight into the question with which we closed the previous section: if all differential struggles – in our example – are equally capable of expressing, beyond their differential identity, the absent fullness of the community; if the equivalential function makes all differential positions similarly indifferent to this equivalential representation; if none is predetermined *per se* to fulfil this role; what does determine that one of them rather than another incarnates, at particular periods of time, this universal function?

The answer is: the unevenness of the social. For if the equivalential logic tends to do away with the relevance of all differential location, this is only a tendential movement that is always resisted by the logic of difference which is essentially non-equalitarian. (It comes as no surprise that Hobbes's model of a state of nature, which tries to depict a realm in which the full operation of the logic of equivalence makes the community impossible, has to presuppose an original and essential equality between men.) Not any position in society, not any struggle is equally capable of transforming its own contents in a nodal point that becomes an empty signifier. Now, is this not to return to a rather traditional conception of the historical effectivity of social forces, one which asserts that the unevenness of structural locations determines which one of them is going to be the source of totalizing effects? No, it is not, because these uneven structural locations, some of which represent points of high concentration of power, are themselves the result of processes in which logics of difference and logics of equivalence overdetermine each other. It is not a question of denying the historical effectivity of the logic of differential structural locations but, rather, of denying to them, as a whole, the character of an infrastructure which would determine, out of itself, the laws of movement of society.

If this is correct, it is impossible to determine at the level of the mere analysis of the *form* difference/equivalence which particular difference is going to become the locus of equivalential effects – this requires the study of a particular conjuncture, precisely because the presence of equivalential effects is always necessary, but the relation equivalence/difference is not intrinsically linked to any particular differential content. This relation by which a particular content becomes the signifier of the absent communitarian fullness is exactly what we call a *hegemonic relationship*. The presence of empty signifiers – in the sense that we have defined them – is the very condition of hegemony. This can be easily seen if we address a very well known difficulty which forms a recurring stumbling block in most theorizations of hegemony – Gramsci's included. A class or group is considered to be hegemonic when it is not closed in a narrow corporatist perspective, but presents itself as realizing the broader aims either of emancipating or ensuring order for wider masses of the population. But this faces us with a difficulty if we do not determine precisely what these terms '*broader* aims', '*wider* masses' refer to. There are two possibilities: first, that society is an addition of discrete groups, each tending to their particular aims and in constant collision with each other. In that case, 'broader' and 'wider' could only mean the precarious equilibrium of a negotiated agreement between groups, all of which would retain their conflicting aims and identity. But 'hegemony' clearly refers to a stronger type of communitarian unity than such an agreement evokes. Second, that society has some kind of preestablished essence, so that the 'broader' and 'wider' has a content of its own, independent of the will of the particular groups, and that 'hegemony' would mean the realization of such an essence. But this would not only do away with the dimension of contingency which has always been associated with the hegemonic operation, but would also be incompatible with the consensual character of 'hegemony': the hegemonic order would be the *imposition* of a pre-given organizational principle and not something emerging from the political interaction between groups. Now, if we consider the matter from the point of view of the social production of empty signifiers, this problem vanishes. For in that case, the hegemonic operations would be the presentation of the particularity of a group as the incarnation of that empty signifier which refers to the communitarian order as an absence, an unfulfilled reality.

How does this mechanism operate? Let us consider the extreme situation of a radical disorganization of the social fabric. In such conditions – which are not far away from Hobbes's state of nature – people need *an* order, and the actual content of it becomes a secondary consideration. 'Order' as such has no content, because it only exists in the various forms in which it is actually realized, but in a situation of radical disorder 'order' is present as that which is absent; it becomes an empty signifier, as the signifier of that absence. In this sense, various political forces can compete in their efforts to present their particular objectives as those which carry out the filling of that lack. To hegemonize something is exactly to carry out this filling function. (We have spoken about 'order', but obviously 'unity', 'liberation', 'revolution', etcetera belong to the same order of things. Any term which, in a certain political context becomes the signifier of the lack, plays the same role. Politics is possible because the constitutive impossibility of society can only represent itself through the production of empty signifiers.)

This explains also why any hegemony is always unstable and penetrated by a constitutive ambiguity. Let us suppose that a workers' mobilization succeeds in presenting its own objectives as a signifier of 'liberation' in general. (This, as we have seen, is possible because the workers' mobilization, taking place under a repressive regime, is also seen as an anti-system struggle.) In one sense this is a hegemonic victory, because the objectives of a particular group are identified with society at large. But, in another sense, this is a dangerous victory. If 'workers' struggle' becomes the signifier of liberation as such, it also becomes the surface of inscription through which *all* liberating struggles will be expressed, so that the chain of equivalences which are unified around this signifier tend to empty it, and to blur its connection with the actual content with which it was originally associated. Thus, as a result of its very success, the hegemonic operation tends to break its links with the force which was its original promoter and beneficiary.

Hegemony and democracy

Let us conclude with some reflections on the relation between empty signifiers, hegemony and democracy.

Consider for a moment the role of social signifiers in the emergence of modern political thought – I am essentially thinking of the work of Hobbes. Hobbes, as we have seen, presented the state of nature as the radically opposite of an ordered society, as a situation only defined in negative terms, But, as a result of that description, the order of the ruler has to be accepted not because of any intrinsic virtue that it can have, but just because it is *an* order, and the only alternative is radical disorder. The condition, however, of the coherence of this scheme is the postulate of the equality of the power of individuals in the state of nature – if the individuals were uneven in terms of power, order could be guaranteed through sheer domination. So, power is eliminated twice: in the state of nature, as all individuals equally share in it, and in the commonwealth, as it is entirely concentrated in the hands of the ruler. (A power which is total or a power which is equally distributed among all members of the community is no power at all.) So, while Hobbes implicitly perceives the split between the empty signifier 'order as such' and the actual order imposed by the ruler, as he reduces – through the covenant – the first to the second, he cannot think of any kind of dialectical or hegemonic game between the two.

What happens if, on the contrary, we reintroduce power within the picture – that is if we accept the unevenness of power in social relations? In that case, civil society will be partially structured and partially unstructured and, as a result, the total concentration of power in the hands of the ruler ceases to be a logical requirement. But in that case, the credentials of the ruler to claim total power are much less obvious. If partial order exists in society, the legitimacy of the identification of the empty signifier of order with the will of the ruler will have the further requirement that the content of this will does not clash with something the society *already* is. As society changes over time this process of identification will be always precarious and reversible and, as the identification is no longer automatic, different projects or wills will try to hegemonize the empty signifiers of the absent community. The recognition of the constitutive nature of this gap and its political institutionalization is the starting point of modern democracy.

NOTE

1. Ernesto Laclau and Chantal Mouffe, *Hegemony and Socialist Strategy*, London, Verso 1985.

WILLIAM E. CONNOLLY
EXTRACTS FROM
IDENTITY/DIFFERENCE: DEMOCRATIC
NEGOTIATIONS OF POLITICAL PARADOX

LIBERALISM AND DIFFERENCE

The paradox of difference

My identity is what I am and how I am recognized rather than what I choose, want, or consent to. It is the dense self from which choosing, wanting, and consenting proceed. Without that density, these acts could not occur; with it, they are recognized to be mine. *Our* identity, in a similar way, is what we are and the basis from which we proceed.

An identity is established in relation to a series of differences that have become socially recognized. These differences are essential to its being. If they did not coexist as differences, it would not exist in its distinctness and solidity. Entrenched in this indispensable relation is a second set of tendencies, themselves in need of exploration, to congeal established identities into fixed forms, thought and lived as if their structure expressed the true order of things. When these pressures prevail, the maintenance of one identity (or field of identities) involves the conversion of some differences into otherness, into evil, or one of its numerous surrogates. Identity requires difference in order to be, and it converts difference into otherness in order to secure its own self-certainty.

Identity is thus a slippery, insecure experience, dependent on its ability to define difference and vulnerable to the tendency of entities it would so define to counter, resist, overturn, or subvert definitions applied to them. Identity stands in a complex, political relation to the differences it seeks to fix. This

William E. Connolly (2002), *Identity/Difference: Democratic Negotiations of Political Paradox*, Minneapolis: University of Minnesota Press.

complexity is intimated by variations in the degree to which differences from self-identity are treated as complementary identities, contending identities, negative identities, or nonidentities; variations in the extent to which the voice of difference is heard as that with which one should remain engaged or as a symptom of sickness, inferiority, or evil; variations in the degree to which self-choice or cultural determination is attributed to alter-identities; variations in the degree to which one's own claim to identity is blocked by the power of opposing claimants or they are blocked by one's own power; and so on. The sensualist, the slut, the homosexual, the transvestite, the child abuser, and madness may merely suggest a few of these multifarious gradations at the level of the individual; the foreign, the terrorist organization, the dark continent, and the barbarian do so at the level of culture.

Such complexities suggest political dimensions in these relations. The bearer of difference may be one open to your appreciation or worthy of your tolerance, or an other whose claim to identity you strive to invert, or one who incorporates some of its own dispositions into her positive identity while you insist upon defining them as part of her negative identity, or one who internalizes the negative identity imposed upon it by others, or an impoverished mode of existence (e.g. 'madness') you refuse to recognize as an identity, or an anonymous self who resists the pressure to crystallize a public identity in order to savor the freedom of anonymity, and so on. Power plays a prominent role in this endless play of definition, counter-definition, and counters to counter-definitions.

What if the human is not predesigned to coalesce smoothly with any single, coherent set of identities, if life without the drive to identity is an impossibility, while the claim to a natural or true identity is always an exaggeration? And what if there are powerful drives, overdetermined by the very inertia of language, psychic instabilities in the human mode of being, and social pressures to mobilize energy for collective action, to fix the truth of identity by grounding it in the commands of a god or the dictates of nature or the requirements of reason or a free consensus?

If and when this combination occurs, then a powerful identity will strive to constitute a range of differences as *intrinsically* evil, irrational, abnormal, mad, sick, primitive, monstrous, dangerous, or anarchical – as other. It does so in order to secure itself as intrinsically good, coherent, complete or rational and in order to protect itself from the other that would unravel its self-certainty and capacity for collective mobilization if it established its legitimacy. This constellation of constructed others now becomes both essential, to the truth of the powerful identity and a threat to it. The threat is posed not merely by *actions* the other might take to injure or defeat the true identity but by the very visibility of its mode of *being* as other.

If there is no natural or intrinsic identity, power is always inscribed in the relation an exclusive identity bears to the differences it constitutes. If there is always a discrepancy between the identities a society makes available and that in human being which exceeds, resists, or denies those possibilities, then the claim to a true identity is perpetually plagued by the shadow of the other it constitutes. These 'ifs' are big and contestable – big in their implications and contestable in their standing. Anyone who thinks within their orbit, as I do, should periodically reconsider the strictness with which they apply and the status endowed upon them. So, too, should anyone who forsakes them in pursuit of more harmonious, teleological conceptions of identity and difference.

[. . .]

Individualism and individuality

Liberal individualism and liberal individuality are not equivalent. They converge in giving the individual moral primacy over the interests of the collectivity. But individualism presupposes a model of the normal or rational individual against which the conduct and interior of each actual self are to be appraised. This standard of the 'stiff, steadfast individual', as Nietzsche would characterize it, provides the ground for a theory of rights, justice, responsibility, freedom, obligation, and legitimate interests.

The doctrine of the steadfast individual (the autonomous agent, the self-interested agent, the normal individual) easily becomes – seen from the standpoint pursued here – a doctrine of normalization through individualization. Its tendency is to reduce the political to the juridical – to condense most issues of politics into the juridical categories of rights, justice, obligation, and responsibility and to treat the remaining issues instrumentally as contests in which individuals and aggregations compete within juridical rules to advance their 'interests' or 'principles' by rational means. Politics gets bifurcated into a dualism of principle and instrumentality, with one group of individualists (rights theorists, theorists of justice) celebrating the former and another group (utilitarians, pragmatists) insisting upon the incorrigibility of the latter. Neither faction comes to terms vigorously with the constructed character of *both* the virtuous self and the self-interested self or with the extent to which both constructions were valued by their early theoretical designers because of their calculability, predictability, and utility to sovereign power.

For these very reasons – the presentation of a single model of the generic individual, the minimalization of the contingent, constructed character of virtuous and self-interested individuals, and the reduction of politics to the juridical–theories of liberal individualism deflate the *politics* of identity and difference.

A theory of the normal individual establishes its parameters of normality not so much by specific argumentation as by omissions in its generic characterization of the individual. Certainly, once a general characterization of the rational agent as a bearer of rights, virtues, and interests is presented, the presenter is then free to contest a whole series of actual demands of normality imposed upon concrete selves but not required by the generic definition of the self. This, however, is not how such theories proceed. Rather, they insinuate a dense set of standards, conventions, and expectations into the identity of the normal self *by failing to identify or contest a constellation of normal/abnormal dualities already inscribed in the culture they idealize*. One can discern this tendency through retrospective exemplification and by comparing the rhetorical strategies of liberal texts defending the generic individual with those of critical texts interrogating the density of the normal individual.[1] I will merely offer one exemplification here.

In the 1950s in the United States, a topic of debate was whether 'homosexuality' (a medical term for a sexual disposition) was a moral fault (the then conservative view) or a personal sickness (the then liberal view). Neither party considered how both sides presupposed 'it' to be a defect in the self of one type or the other, or how their joint constitution of this disposition as a defect of one sort or the other protected the self-certainty of heterosexual identity. And this example could be replicated across a whole range of issues concerning the normal self. The usual mode of discourse governing individualist theory does not support a problematization of established standards of normal individuality; the narrative and rhetorical designs of its texts do not pose disturbing questions about the dense construction of the normal individual and its abnormalities.

The politicization of abnormality is made difficult in any event by the institutional silences and constraints that typically envelop the formation of normal identities. But the theory of individualism exacerbates these difficulties through its mode of theorization. It is pulled, by its minimalist understanding of how politics enters into the constitution of identity and difference, to consent tacitly to the politics of normal individualization.

A theory of liberal *individuality* is another kettle of fish. It gives primacy to the individual while qualifying or problematizing the hegemony of the normal individual. Here nonidentity with a normal or official self constitutes a sign of individuality. Individuality, indeed, comprises a range of conduct that is distinctive, stretches the boundaries of identity officially given to the normal self, reveals artifice in established standards of normality by superseding or violating them, and brings new issues into public life through resistances, eccentricities, refusals, or excesses that expose a series of contestable restraints built into fixed conventions.

George Kateb has done much, certainly the most in contemporary America, to clarify and advance this perspective. His version of the theory is inspired by Emerson, salted by Nietzsche. He celebrates 'democratic individuality', insisting, against Nietzsche, that the unsettled character of democratic politics and the enhanced institutional respect for the individual that tends to accompany the exercise of democratic citizenship together provide an institutional context in which any self may express its individuality. Democracy 'unsettles everything for everyone, and thus liberates democratic individuality'.[2]

Kateb strives to elicit from the lived experience of individuality both a public appreciation of diversity and an enhanced appreciation of the value of existence beyond its encapsulation in any particular network of identities, conventions, norms, and exclusions. For Kateb, those who express individuality and appreciate it in others tend, first, to say no to encroachments by the state into new areas of life, second, to accept responsibility for themselves and their life projects, and third, to 'acquire a new relation to all experience, which may be called either a philosophical or poetical relation to reality'.[3]

[. . .]

While Kateb emphasizes the roots of his philosophy in the American transcendentalists Emerson, Whitman, and Thoreau, one element in Nietzsche's articulation of individuality and the resistances to it is particularly pertinent to contemporary experience. This is the first point at which my solicitation of liberal individuality – its paradoxes and possibilities – diverges from Kateb's.

Consider three assertions: (1) Nietzsche is the philosopher who exposes the roots of resentment in theism and secularism and who seeks to elicit a nontheistic reverence for life to combat the subterranean politics of resentment. (2) Liberalism is a contemporary philosophy of rights and justice that has become an object of resentment in contemporary politics. (3) Most paradigmatic defenses of liberalism today refuse to ask whether its doctrine embodies and contributes to the resentment it encounters.

A reconstitution of liberal individuality might begin, then, by ascertaining whether there is something in liberal individualism that expresses resentment and something in it that tends to elicit resentment from many who receive its messages. Such an analysis, indebted to Nietzsche, may help to reveal traps liberal individuality must avoid and directions its supporters might consider.

That contemporary liberalism is an object of public resentment seems undeniable. This is so especially at those points where its welfarism and its individualism intersect, for these determine how freedom and responsibility are to be distributed among the various constituencies of the welfare state. Many liberal-welfare programs inaugurated in the 1960s to rectify injustice have been received by a variety of constituencies as the imposition of new injustices upon them. Programs in busing, aid to dependent children, affirmative action hiring, ecology, criminal parole and rehabilitation, and gun control often encounter virulent opposition, indicating that they touch the identities of the opponents even more than their interests. Juridical doctrines and judgments supporting civil liberties and civil rights encounter similar reactions.[4]

Of course these responses have several sources, but one of them is particularly pertinent here. Many of those asked to bear the immediate economic and psychic costs of ameliorative programs already resent some of the conditions of their own existence. But this resentment is not typically emphasized in the rhetoric or programs of liberalism: the resentment is accentuated by liberal programs and subdued in its rhetoric.

Think of white working-class males. They are subjected to a variety of disciplines and burdens that limit their prospects for life, but liberal programs devised since the 1960s tend to treat them as responsible for their own achievements and failures. And they are then told by liberals that many women and minorities suffer injustice if they do not rise to or above working-class levels of attainment.

Liberal representatives inadvertently manipulate the rhetoric of self-responsibility and justice in ways that assault the identity of this constituency. By implying that professional and corporate males have earned their position while asserting that women and minorities are victimized by discrimination, liberals imply that only one group *deserves* to be stuck in the crummy jobs available to it: white working-class males. The liberal glorification of self-responsibility, juridical justice, and welfare together thus accentuates the resentment of those whose identity is most immediately threatened by its ameliorative programs.

But why is this resentment often so virulent and volatile? Does liberalism today simply encounter a resentment it does not harbor? Or does liberal individualism help to dig a well of resentment that then flows into the culture in which it participates? I believe that any effort to reconstitute liberalism must explore this latter possibility. Nietzsche provides clues from which such an exploration might be launched.

From a Nietzschean perspective, the self constituted as a unified, self-responsible agent contains resentment within its very formation. The basic idea behind this formation is that for every evil there must be a responsible agent who deserves to be punished and that for every quotient of evil in the world there must be a corollary quotient of assignable responsibility. No evil without responsibility. No responsibility without reward or punishment according to desert. No suffering without injustice, and no injustice unless there is a juridical recipe for redressing it in life or afterlife. Life is organized around the principles of individual responsibility governing a baseball game.

A liberal might think that all freedom, responsibility, and justice must disappear if the ideals he endorses are linked to a subterranean demand that these equivalences be established. If the purity of these principles is sullied, everything else good and admirable will be soiled too. Perhaps. But to explore dangers and cruelties that may reside within these categories, it may be helpful to illuminate them from a different angle, to lower the source of illumination so that the shadows they throw become more discernible.

At the root of the demand for equivalence between evil and responsibility is a demand that the world contain agency in the last instance. Seen from this angle, these categories embody a modernized version of the traditional Christian demand that there be a responsible agent or purpose for suffering in the world, that human finitude and suffering be redeemed by an agency of responsibility. What Nietzsche called the slave revolt in morality – the formation and consolidation of a new set of equivalences–is not exhausted by the attempt of sufferers held in human bondage to invent a god to hold the masters responsible for their cruelty and indifference. Certainly the invention of this god involves an act of 'imaginary revenge' on the part of those whose social powerlessness makes actual revenge untenable. Certainly the habitual practice of this revenge eventually becomes consolidated into the creative demand that everyone acquire the honesty, meekness, industriousness, and virtue 'we' are already compelled to assume. Certainly weakness is here transformed into merit, so that what the slave *must be* becomes the standard against which every difference is defined as a deviation to be punished, reformed, or converted. But the early, intense transfiguration of overt resentment into the demand to convert or conquer the other for its own good exposes a more pervasive set of dispositions rooted in the human condition.[5] Otherwise, masters themselves would not become gripped by its attractions. Only a more pervasive human dream of a world without injustice seems sufficient to explain the appeal this system of equivalences exerts upon almost everyone. Humans resent the transiency, suffering, and uncertainty of redemption that mark the human condition. We suffer from the problem of our meaning, and we demand that meaning be given to existential suffering. So when the idea of a purpose in existence residing in nature or a god loses its credibility, the insistence that we are rational, responsible agents comes into its own. For if these previous sources of responsibility are dead, some new agency must be created. We give meaning to existential suffering, then, by holding ourselves responsible for it. 'Quite so my sheep', we say to one another, 'someone must be to blame for [suffering]; but you are this someone, you alone are to blame for it – *you alone are to blame for yourself*!'[6] It can't be a god who must be protected from responsibility for evil. It can't be nature. It will have to be us, if it is to be. We will have to be the responsible agents. 'Quite so my sheep'.

The modern normal, responsible individual can redirect resentment against the human condition into the self, first, by treating the rational, self-interested, free, and principled individual as morally responsible for willful deviations from normal identity and, second, by treating that in itself and other selves which falls below the threshold of responsibility as a natural defect in need of conquest or conversion, punishment or love. The modern individual, in short, contains resentment against the human condition in its own identity, and this comes out most clearly in the intensity of the resentment it expresses against any others who deviate significantly from that identity. For such deviations, if they proliferate, make the self-identical self appear to be a sucker for accepting the disciplines and restraints required to maintain itself in this way. Only if these deviations are false or evil can it see itself as true. Resentment against injuries to oneself flowing from the standard of self-responsibility becomes translated into rancor against those whom one construes as escaping the dictates of that standard.

On this interpretation, the modern ideal of the *unambiguous* agent is one of the costs we pay for the demand that there be an ethical life without paradox. And the demand for this set of equivalences, seldom stated overtly but working in the background of modern conceptions of self, justice, and responsibility, is itself nourished by a further set of insistences. The 'authoritarian personality' is thus not merely a personality type that threatens liberal tolerance. It is also an internal product of the *individualist* demand for a fixed and pure fundamental identity.

[. . .]

Individuality and difference

My first disagreement with Kateb, then, is a matter of emphasis. I place greater emphasis on the element of resentment already residing in the identity of the normal individual. Liberal individualism thus becomes a more ambiguous ally of liberal individuality than Kateb has acknowledged.

[. . .]

While Kateb advances a compelling ethic of individuality, the dilemmas and paradoxes within that ethic cannot be engaged until it is translated into a political theory. To put the point bluntly: *this theorist of liberal individuality offers an ethic of individuality in lieu of a political theory of individuality*, in lieu of a theory that confronts disjunctions between limitations on diversity intrinsic to a specific order and the demand for diversity that flows from an ethic of individuality. Once the outlines of such a theory are elucidated, one must either eliminate those disjunctions by making questionable teleological assumptions or confront a tragic element residing within the institutionalization of individuality itself. Engagement with institutional limits to individuality can be evaded either by succumbing to the teleological temptation or by restricting oneself to an *ethic* of individuality situated in a generically defined culture of liberal democracy.

Kateb pursues the second strategy. It finds expression mostly in silences with respect to the structural limits of late-modern liberal-capitalist society. To the extent that the state leaves the individual alone, Kateb is inclined to believe, to that extent individuality will flourish. And if we do not demand too much from the state, particularly in the area of economic life, it can afford to leave us pretty much alone. So, while democratic politics is a necessary precondition of individuality, a too active and organized democratic agenda will suffocate it. The individual's political involvement, therefore, should be limited, confined, episodic. Kateb quotes Whitman's advice to 'always vote', but to limit oneself with respect to other modes of political involvement: 'Disengage yourself from parties. They have been useful, and to some extent remain so, but the floating, uncommitted electors, farmers, clerks, mechanics, the masters of parties – watching aloof, inclining victory this side or that side – such are the ones most needed, present and future.'[7]

Notice the assumptions of early nineteenth-century America that form the silent background of this sentiment: 'floating, uncommitted electors', and so on, rather than role bearers whose conditions of daily existence enmesh them in corporate and bureaucratic structures imposing refined schedules and norms upon them; a self-subsistent state rather than one entangled in a global structure of interdependencies and conflicts that it is pressed to convert into disciplines for its most vulnerable constituencies; a domestic politics of 'parties' from which the individual can be 'disengaged' and 'aloof' without becoming an object of power struggles over norms, regulations, penalties, and incentives governing the details of life.

[. . .]

But the past ain't what it used to be. What's more, it probably never was. We do not reside today in a world where individuality can flourish if state, corporate, and associational institutions of normalization are left to their own devices except when they overstep clear constitutional boundaries or commit glaring atrocities. The atrocities that glare most brightly today are undergirded by everyday politics. Constitutional boundaries must be creatively redefined and enlarged through political pressures speaking to new circumstances.

The proliferation of drug tests; the extension of corporate codes into new corners of everyday life; credit tests; the increasing numbers of people subjected to security tests along with the increased number of criteria invoked in them; the bureaucratic definition and regulation of safe, healthy, normal sexuality; the introduction of home detention for convicted felons, allowing definitions of criminality to be extended indefinitely; the computerization of individual files, enabling a variety of authorities and semiauthorities to record the life history of each individual for multifarious uses; the militarization of welfare and scholarships; the refiguration of deviations construed in the nineteenth century as sins or moral faults into psychological defects of the self in need of correction or therapy; and most pervasively, the vague sense that each of one's actions today *might* form part of a record that *might* be used for or against one in the future – these signify a *regularized* politics of normalization through observational judgment and anticipatory self-policing.

Individuality secures space to be through resistance and opposition to these bureaucratic pressures. Gay rights movements; feminism; minority politics; emergent movements to attack the institutionalization of home-lessness; efforts on behalf of the elderly in nursing homes; movements to establish prisoners' rights; embryonic drives to resist the universalization of drug tests and other closures in codes of employee conduct; the political struggle to die on one's own terms rather than according to terms set by the state; periodic dissidence among young men and women in military, intelligence, and security agencies; localized pressures to roll back corpo-rate and state disciplines forged under the star of efficiency, productivity, and normality; antimilitarist movements to create alliances with dissidents in second- and third-world regions – these protests and movements, how-ever ineffective they may be on occasion, simultaneously signify a broad-ening and deepening of institutional investments in the life of the self and a corollary politics of resistances, disinvestments, and subversion on behalf of individuality.

[. . .]

When the paradox of difference is confronted in the context of late-modern society, it turns out that an ethic of individuality requires a multifarious politicization of difference in order to sustain itself.

Civic liberalism

Liberal individualism buries the paradox of difference first by insinuating too many dictates of a particular order into the identity of the normal indi-vidual and then by naturalizing the identity it has solidified. Liberal individ-uality evades the paradox by treating an ethic of individuality as if it were a political theory of identity/difference. A third scholarly version of liberal-ism completes the contemporary circle of evasions. Civic liberalism corrects defects in the first two positions by reminding us how a set of identities is defined and enabled within the context of institutionalized commonalities. It then naturalizes this insight by insisting that there must be a way of life, either now, in the past, or in a possible future, where established identities are harmonized through a politics of civic virtue.

Its strategy with respect to difference is this: the paradox of difference must be dissolved into a common good that both enables every form of otherness to reform itself until it fits into the frame of a rational commu-nity and enables the community to perfect its terms of inclusion so that excluded constituencies can find a home within it. Civic liberalism fosters normalization through a nonpolitics of gentle assimilation. That, at least, is its regulative ideal, the standard against which actuality is measured and through which it is authorized to characterize the present condition as one of fragmentation, loss of identity, and alienation.

'Civic liberalism' will seem like a category mistake to some. But most contemporary communitarian (or civic republican) theories are variants of liberalism because, first, they provide space for rights and individuality within the context of the harmonies they admire, second, they emphasize the juridical and communal sides of politics over its role in disturbing and unsettling established routines, third, they want the identities and commonalities endorsed to be brought to a peak of self-consciousness and rational legitimacy unimagined in traditional theories of community, and fourth, they maintain a corollary commitment to incremental change by democratic means as opposed to transformation by revolutionary or authoritarian means.

A communitarian strategy typically begins by trying to show how preunderstandings implicit in contemporary life point toward a coherent set of standards that justify a more inclusive and fulfilling good. We are already implicated in the circle of commitments communitarianism articulates and perfects, and our mutual rights, duties, and aspirations will be harmonized more effectively as we are brought to greater self-consciousness of their preconditions and implications.

But the question arises: what justifies the exclusions, penalties, restrictions, and incentives needed to sustain adherence to this common good on the part of those who might otherwise deviate from it? What if some would significantly shift priorities within the sanctified circle of implications if they had the power to do so? What if commonly established assumptions about the capacity for realization of the embodied self in a higher community encounter persistent resistances in many selves to these forms of self-organization? What if the circle of discourse in which these commonalities are articulated closes out other possibilities that would disturb, unsettle, fragment, ambiguate, politicize the achieved sense of unity if they were to find expression? When such questions are pursued persistently, the hermeneutic circle of mutual self-validation among interdependent components of the culture must have recourse to a supplement; it must appeal to a supplementary 'bent' or purpose or harmonious direction in being to which a community can become attuned.

The most reflective civic humanists endorse such a supplement, at least when faced by objections that require either that they do so or that they ambiguate more radically the good they endorse. Charles Taylor is exemplary here. In a recent exchange, while insisting that he rejects the strong teleological assumptions embodied in Hegelian theory, he affirms the presence of a principle of teleology in his political philosophy:

> For what is meant by a 'teleological philosophy'? If we mean some inescapable design at work inexorably in history, à la Hegel, then I am of course not committed to it. But if we mean by this expression that there is a distinction between distorted and authentic self-understanding, and that the latter can in a sense be said to follow from a direction in being, I do indeed espouse such a view. And that makes a big part of my 'ontology' of the human person.[8]

A 'direction in being'. Taylor proceeds from a rhetoric of self-realization within community, through a rhetoric of communal realization through harmonization of the diverse parts of an ongoing culture, to a rhetoric of progressive attunement to a harmonious direction in being. The latter is a requirement of his theory. But to say that 'we' need such a supplement to ground community, or, more strongly, that others who explicitly reject the ideal of harmonious community nonetheless presuppose a facsimile of this supplement in their own thinking, or, more strongly still, that such a supplement is an inescapable component of social thought as such, is still not to show that a supplemental direction (and a being who provides it?) is available to 'us'.

Taylor suggests that such a direction is needed if the civic ideal is to succeed, but he then exhibits the possibility of that direction, not through particular arguments, but through textual tropes that presuppose its availability. Taylor's Augustinianism emerges in this dimension of his texts. We are called upon to believe so that we can come to know. 'Lord', says Augustine, 'my faith calls upon you, that faith . . . which you have breathed into me'.[9] And Taylor breathes faith in the possibility of harmonious community into the rhetoric that governs his characterizations.

I do not mean to protest this dimension of Taylor's work as such, for no affirmative theory of politics can avoid some such strategy of reflective projection. But I do mean to call attention to the contestability of the projection he endorses and to note how communitarian texts typically fail to promote reflection on the rhetorical configurations through which they elicit faith in their highest ideals.

The problem is not only that this air is breathed into the narrative and rhetorical structure of communitarian texts, but that the realization of community itself requires that most of its members become attuned to the supplemental direction as a harmonious end that binds them together. The ideal of community itself presses its adherents to treat harmonious membership and consensus not as contestable ends to be interrogated by the most creative means at their disposal, but as vehicles of elevation drawing the community closer to the harmony of being. Communalization is harmonization and harmonization that is treated as contestable or deeply ambiguous is, well, no longer consonant with communalism.

But can't 'we' take this step of faith too? After all, it seems a small step, once the initial web of common preunderstandings governing the culture has been articulated. And the return seems so great: the paradox of difference becomes resolved into a project of assimilation in which those who now fall outside the range of communal identifications are drawn into the folds of a higher, more rational, and more inclusive community. Is it not time at last to be reasonable?

This step must be resisted by those who doubt the faith that sustains it. The gentle rhetoric of articulation, realization, community, purpose,

attunement, fulfillment, integration, and harmonization significantly rein-
scribes the common life, obligating people and institutions to reform and
consolidate themselves in ways that may be arbitrary, cruel, destructive, and
dangerous *if* the pursuit of consensus and commonality are not supported
by a harmonious direction in being. The gentle rhetoric of harmonization
must be ambiguated and coarsened by those who have not had its faith
breathed into their souls, particularly those moved by nontheistic reverence
for the rich ambiguity of existence. We thus return to the 'if' from which
we never actually departed.

The rhetoric of civic liberalism places too many possible disciplines outside its critical purview, revealing in its persistent folding of experience
into its specific modality that the supplement it invokes does not require
such a small step after all. It must constantly be tested and contested by
those whose hermeneutic draws supplemental sustenance from another social ontology, one in which the fit between human designs and the material
drawn into those designs is always partial, incomplete, and likely to contain an element of subjugation and imposition, in which the possibilities
of individuality and reverence for existence are enhanced when we refuse
to pretend that a god retains enough life to give supplemental direction to
late-modern existence, and in which democracy reaches its highest level of
achievement when agonistic respect is folded into its politics.

[. . .]

The politics of paradox

I have contended that liberal individualism, liberal individuality, and liberal
communitarianism generate complementary strategies to evade the paradox
of difference. How, then, might it be engaged? My response is to acknowledge it and to convert it into a politics of the paradoxical, into a conception
of the political as the medium through which the interdependent antinomies
of identity and difference can be expressed and contested. This orientation
is offered (again) not as a definitive *solution* to the paradox of difference,
but as a means by which to contest the affinities and closures shared by
dominant responses to that paradox.

This perspective on politics endorses dimensions from each of the theories criticized here. From liberal individualism and civic liberalism it draws
the understanding that any way of life that enables people to act collectively must embody a set of norms and commonalities that are given variable degrees of primacy in the common life. From the civic tradition alone
it draws appreciation of the hermeneutic character of ethical and political
discourse, wherein debate and argumentation proceed from preconceptions
and convictions already present in the life of the self and society. From the
theory of liberal individuality it draws the understanding that the claims
of individuality often clash with the claims of conventionality, order, and

normality, emphasizing more than theorists of individuality tend to that both sets of claims enter into the interior of the self as well as into public arenas of discursive engagement. And from the Nietzschean legacy it draws nontheistic reverence for the ambiguity of existence and the (iffy) idea that every identity is a contingent artifice that encounters resistances and recalcitrance to the pressures that form it. In each of these instances, though, it politicizes elements that the single-minded bearers of these insights tend to treat in unpolitical ways.

It may be pertinent to note how, according to the perspective advanced here, each of the other traditions repeals an essential element of politics. Kateb, Taylor, and Nietzsche provide excellent exemplifications. The first seeks to insulate the individual from political intrusions, endorsing minimalism in politics in the name of individuality. The second thematizes politics as a gathering together of disparate forces into a shared purpose realized in common, deflating the corollary idea of politics as a perpetual contestation of established commonalities that prevents injuries and injustices within them from becoming too thoroughly naturalized, rationalized, or grounded in a higher direction in being. The third projects an overman who engages the ambiguity of existence largely outside the reach of politics.[10]

On the model of liberalism projected here, the politicization of identities and commonalities is intrinsic to the ideal itself: the regulative ideal is one in which creative tension is generated between the claims of individuality and commonality, the claims of identity and that in the self which resists those claims, the drive to transcendence and that which is repressed by any particular claim to transcendence, the imperatives of the present and the claims of the future, the existing field of discourse and possibilities latent in its partially repressed history. From this perspective juridical politics, minimalist politics, and communitarian politics emerge as complementary apolitical ideals; each deflates one or more of the dimensions needed to keep the politicization of difference alive.

What, then, is the paradox of politics, and how does it relate to the politicization of identity? It can be given a variety of formulations. Here is one: a politics of the common good is essential both to sustain a particular set of identities worthy of admiration and to enable the public to act self-consciously in support of justice and the public interest as they emerge in the common life. But this politics of public rationality presents an ambiguous face. The very success in defining and enacting commonalities tends to naturalize them, to make them appear as unambiguous goods lodged in nature or consent or reason or the universal character of the normal individual or ideal dialogue or a higher direction in being. If humans are not predesigned, and if they therefore are ill suited to fit neatly into any particular social form, then any set of enabling commonalities is likely to contain corollary injuries, cruelties, subjugations, concealments, and restrictions worthy of disturbance and contestation. Each set of identities will generate differences that themselves need to find a political voice.

Another way to pose the paradox is this: the human animal is essentially incomplete without social form; and a common language, institutional setting, set of traditions, and political forum for enunciating public purposes are indispensable to the acquisition of an identity and the commonalities essential to life. But every form of social completion and enablement also contains subjugations and cruelties within it. Politics, then, is the medium through which these ambiguities can be engaged and confronted, shifted and stretched. It is simultaneously a medium through which common purposes are crystallized and the consummate means by which their transcription into musical harmonies is exposed, contested, disturbed, and unsettled. A society that enables politics as this ambiguous medium is a good society because it enables the paradox of difference to find expression in public life.

This perspective is, of course, a liberalism, an alternative, militant liberalism both indebted to and competitive with other liberalisms and nonliberalisms contending for presence in late-modern life. It is a liberalism in its refusal to choose between revolutionary overthrow and the idealization of traditional culture, in its appreciation of the claims of individuality, in its attentiveness to rights and constitutional protections, in its extension of these concerns to forces that would expand the dialectic of discipline and reactive disaffection to new corners of life, in its skepticism about any definitive resolution of the paradoxical relationship between identity and difference, in its radicalization of liberal battles against the hegemony of teleological and transcendental theories, in the ironic distance it insinuates into the identities it lives and modifies, in the ironic dimension in its politicization of difference in a world in which identity is essential to life, in its insistence on questioning fixed unities even while admiring some more than others.

It is not the best liberalism that can be dreamt, only the highest regulative ideal to pursue if we are incomplete without social form in a world not predesigned to mesh smoothly with any particular formation of personal and collective identity.

NOTES

1. Michael Shapiro examines the rhetorical strategies of some contemporaries in a way that is relevant to this issue. See 'Politicizing Ulysses: Rationalistic, Critical and Genealogical Commentaries', *Political Theory* (February 1989), 9–31, and *The Politics of Representation* (Madison: University of Wisconsin Press, 1988), especially chap. 1.
2. George Kateb, 'Democratic Individuality and the Claims of Politics', *Political Theory* (August 1984), 335.
3. Ibid., 343.
4. This portion of the argument is developed more extensively in William E. Connolly, *Politics and Ambiguity* (Madison: University of Wisconsin Press, 1987), especially chaps. 2 and 5.

5. The sources of closure and naturalization in identity are multiple and overdetermined as Nietzsche represents them. That is why it is so difficult and important to confront and contest those pressures. Nietzsche's treatment of language as a dense medium that condenses and consolidates values of the herd; of the limited capacity for consciousness and the extensive demands for social regularization that combine to drive many commonalities to the level of the tacit, the implicit, the unconscious, and the habitual; of the disturbance sown when a lived identity is exposed as conventional or artificial; of the limited capacity of each social order to tolerate diversity of identities – all of these themes must be considered when evaluating the quest to open up themes and norms that have become closed. For Nietzsche insists, first, that the sources of closure are powerful and, second, that no closed set of commonalities reflects a higher direction in being.

6. Friedrich Nietzsche, *On the Genealogy of Morals*, trans. Walter Kaufmann and R. J. Hollingdale (New York: Random House, 1967), 127.

7. Kateb, 'Democratic Individuality and the Claims of Politics', 355.

8. Charles Taylor, 'Connolly, Foucault and Truth', *Political Theory* (August 1985), 385. A more extensive comparison of Taylor and Foucault within the territory of language can be found in William E. Connolly, 'Where the Word Breaks Off', chap. 10 of *Politics and Ambiguity*. Taylor's book *Sources of the Self* (Cambridge, MA: Harvard University Press, 1989) appeared while the present book was in press. While harmonious community still seems to me to remain constant as his regulative ideal, the possibility of achieving a coherent unity in modern life that does not repress something essential and admirable is actively doubted in the new book. My discussion here is insufficient to that text. But the attribution of Augustinianism to Taylor's conceptions of identity and responsibility [...] hits the mark of this new book.

9. *The Confessions of St. Augustine*, trans. John K. Ryan (New York: Doubleday, 1960), 43.

10. Nietzsche does not always or consistently prove to be apolitical. But the presentation of the overman in *Thus Spoke Zarathustra*, trans. Walter Kaufmann (New York: Penguin, 1978), seems to me highly apolitical. Any other references to the overman, especially in the unpublished texts, might be referred to this foundational text for clarification and contextualization.

4

THE BODY POLITIC

Kieran Laird

INTRODUCTION

The human body: a skeleton of 206 bones; over 600 skeletal muscles; a central and a peripheral nervous system; a lymphatic system to stave off disease; a respiratory system which inhales and exhales an average of 500ml of air 12–17 times a minute; a 9m-long digestive tract; a hormone-producing endocrine system; a brain; five senses with their respective organs; cardiovascular, urinary and reproductive systems; all covered with two main layers of skin[1] and in a shape (and maybe for a duration) pre-programmed by an estimated 100,000 genes containing stretches of DNA code (Walker and McKay, 2000: 13). This mechanism is propelled through the world by a combination of instinct (such as the avoidance of danger), unconscious mechanical action (such as breathing and digesting) and (sometimes) conscious thought. Our life begins with the generation of cells and ends when the various important bodily functions cease to operate.

The body is that which things happen to. Whatever one experiences will happen to our bodies either in a physical way, impacting on the stuff of the body outlined above, or on the mental level, altering the neurochemistry and consequent electrical action of the brain. We are *embodied* beings. It is not surprising then that one may claim that the thoughts we have and the social systems we create are, to some extent, conditioned by our embodied experience. A simple example is mathematics. In Greenland there developed a base twenty number system 'divided into recurring five-base periods of reckoning referring to the fingers and toes of a person'. One begins counting on the fingers of one hand, moves to the other, then to the toes of the first foot and then to the toes of the second. So, for example, the number two is *mardluk*, the number seven is *arfineq-mardluk* (literally 'second hand, two'), the number twelve is *arkaneq-mardluk* (first foot, two) and seventeen is *arfersaneq-mardluk* (second foot, two) (Gullberg 1997: 7). One can also think of children learning our current base ten system by counting on their fingers.

The body has also been used as a metaphor throughout history for various feelings, events and ideas. The use of the heart as a metaphor for love is ever present, although, on the physical level, it is merely the organ which circulates the blood around the cardiovascular system of arteries and veins and the sight of the actual organ itself in all its red fleshy pulsating glory would not inspire thoughts of romance in the most ardent lover. The hand of history pushes humanity forward as the hand of destiny guides our individual paths and the invisible hand of the market regulates economics. It would seem perfectly natural to express our ideas in terms of the body, a lowest common denominator which we can all understand.

The use of the body in political thought is no exception and the idea of the 'body politic' is a recurring metaphor for the way in which we organise our social affairs. In this essay I shall trace the idea of the body in politics from being a metaphor for the state in early political thought to more recent ideas which see the body not as a metaphor for the political entity of the state, but as an important political site of action itself. As we progress through the essay we will be moving further and further from the description of the body with which we started, seeing it less as a purely given physical construction and more as a malleable political entity which can be formed and reformed by the exercise of social and political power. Consequently our bodies may also become sites of resistance to power. We shall wrap up by taking this line of thought to one of its conclusions, discussing the political possibilities of abandoning the body altogether, a prospect opened up to us with the advent of new technologies.

THE EMBODIED *POLIS*: PLATO

One of the first examples of the body as a metaphor for the political state is Plato's *The Republic*, written in the first half of the fourth century BC. Plato's aim in *The Republic* is to discover the principles of justice by elaborating the form that an ideal city-state would take. The underlying idea is that to define justice in the individual one may examine it in the community in order to find it on a larger scale (Plato 1987, Bk II, 368e–369b). The state for Plato is a kind of body writ large and what ties the two together in *The Republic* is the idea of balance: justice in the individual results from a balance of conflicting mental and physical attributes and justice in the state consists of a balance between all the different components of the *polis*, each knowing their place and acting within their own sphere of influence.

This can be seen clearly in Plato's discussion of the virtue of self-discipline (1987, Bk IV, 431–432b). Therein it is claimed that a person is 'master of himself' when the better element in one's personality controls the worse element. Likewise in the state 'the desires of the less respectable majority are controlled by the desires and wisdom of the superior minority' (Plato 1987, Bk IV, 431d). This self-discipline in the state 'produces a harmony between its strongest and weakest and middle elements... And so we are quite justified in regarding self-discipline as this unanimity in which there is a natural concordance between higher and lower about which of them is to rule in state and individual' (Plato 1987, Bk IV, 432–432b).

Further on in Book IV the connection between individual and state through the idea of harmony is directly stated. Plato identifies three elements in the human soul; appetite, reason and a more nebulous third element, *thumos* or *thomeides*, translated as 'anger', 'indignation' or 'spirit' according to context (1987, Bk IV, section 2; 207–8, trans. note). These elements are also claimed to be present in the order of the state and justice is defined as harmony between them. 'The state was just when the three elements within it each minded their own business... [and] each of us will be just and perform his proper function only if each part of him is performing its proper function' (Plato 1987, Bk IV, 441d–e). The individual and state are interconnected in this statement not only because they mirror each other but also because for the individual to perform his or her proper part in the state the internal elements of the body must be in harmony. Balance within leads to balance without and both are seen as forms of health, physical and political (Plato 1987, Bk IV, 444d–e).

THE EMBODIED *POLIS*: MEDIEVAL THOUGHT

The fully fledged metaphor of the embodied *polis* seems to have been born in medieval political thought. Political thought in Western Europe in the period succeeding the Roman Empire consisted in the study of preserved classical texts combined with an overriding concern to temper these essentially pagan works with the concerns of Christian dogma. No longer was the earthly *polis* an isolated phenomenon; it now took its place in a hierarchically ordered universe wherein human structures mirrored the ordering of the heavens under God's rule.

The hierarchy and interdependence of feudal society lent itself to explanation using the metaphor of the human body in an extended version of Plato's idea of harmony through the balance of different functions. One early example of this from the beginning of the twelfth century is Marie de France's *The Fable of a Man, His Belly, and His Limbs*. In this poem a man's head, hands and feet are said to have become disenchanted by the fact that his stomach reaped the benefit of all their hard work. To teach the stomach a lesson they deprive it of food but soon find that they themselves become weakened as a result. When they try to feed the stomach again they find it has become unaccustomed to food with the result that they all wither and die. The poem ends by relating this story to feudal society with the claim that a lord and his people are interconnected and 'If either one fails the other/Evil befalls them both' (Nederman and Langdon Forhan 1993: 25).

Other medieval writers concentrated on the idea of the sovereign as the head of the body politic, exercising control over its motions. We see, for example, John of Salisbury likening a well-ordered political community to a healthy body. He cites Plutarch's account of Roman society whereby the ruler functions as the head, the senate as the heart and the administrators and soldiers as the hands of the body politic with the peasants representing the feet (Nederman and Langdon Forhan 1993: 38–9). Similar accounts are found in Thomas Aquinas, John of Paris, Marsiglio of Padua and John Wyclif before getting their fullest medieval exposition in Christine de Pizan's *The Book of The Body Politic*, which uses both Marie's parable and John of Salisbury's organising theme of representing different state functionaries as different parts of the body (Nederman and Langdon Forhan 1993: 113, 162, 191, 225).

THE EMBODIED *POLIS*: THOMAS HOBBES

The vision of the state as an artificial person, a body made up of individual bodies is most famously exhibited and deeply elaborated in Thomas Hobbes's *Leviathan* (1651). The generation of political theory is, for Hobbes, intricately bound up with understanding how human beings operate on a physical level. This understanding and the generation of theory which flows from it are primarily mechanical processes. The first quarter of *Leviathan* is concerned with laying out a mechanistic account of human life and motivation, which is then used as the foundation and reason for the creation of the political state and each individual's subordination to it. Right from the introduction this method is made explicit:

> Life is but a motion of the limbs ... For what is the *heart*, but a *spring*; and the *nerves*, but so many *strings*; and the *joints*, but so many *wheels*, giving motion to the whole body, such as was intended by the artificer? *Art* goes yet further, imitating the rational and most excellent work of nature, *man*. For by art is created that great LEVIATHAN called a COMMONWEALTH, or STATE, ... which is but an artificial man (Hobbes 1996: 1).

Humans are but a created substance, a machine of component functional parts, much like the image with which this essay started. They are an artifice in the etymological sense of that word, from *ars*, 'art', and *facere*, 'make'. Just as the artificer created 'natural' humans, they in their turn can create an artificial human, the Leviathan. The idea is that one should flow from the other and that the essential mechanics should be the same: sovereignty is an artificial soul; the officers of the law represent joints; reward and punishment are nerves; wealth is the strength; memory, health, reason and even death in the form of 'sedition, sickness and civil strife' are mirrored (Hobbes 1996: 1). For each function in the natural body there is its correspondence in the artificial body of the state.

Hobbes's concern in the first part of *Leviathan* is then to elucidate the way in which humans work. In much the same way as one would dismantle a car engine in order to see if one could replicate its design he sets about theoretically dismantling the human being and setting out its component parts for examination. After discussions of sense, imagination, thought, speech and reason there comes in Chapter 6 of *Leviathan* one of the most important stages in Hobbes's argument, the consideration of what he terms 'vital' and 'animal', or 'voluntary', motion.

Vital motions are those mechanical processes of the body such as breathing, digestion or circulation 'to which motions there needs no help of imagination'. Animal or voluntary motions are those which are 'first fancied in our minds', they are conscious premeditated actions. The latter are, however, no less mechanical than the former; they are initiated by the motion of the mind in response to external objects. These imperceptible movements of the mind Hobbes calls 'endeavour' (1996, Pt I, ch. 6) and this mental action can, at its most basic, be subdivided into 'desire', movement towards an object, and 'aversion', movement away from an object (1996, Pt I, ch. 6). This is an important distinction for Hobbes because from these two he deduces all positive and negative emotions, even good and evil, and also founds the basis for humans resolving themselves into the political entity of *Leviathan*.

The basis for desire and aversion resolves itself into the concern each person has to preserve their life. We desire, and are attracted towards, things which we think will preserve or make our lives better, and we experience aversion towards that which will threaten our lives. Hobbes claims that it is a 'right of nature' for each person to 'use his own power, as he will himself, for the preservation of his own nature; that is to say, of his own life' (Hobbes 1996, Pt I, ch. 14). In a world not governed by the laws and regulations of society backed by some form of coercive power, the exercise of this right by each person will lead to a state of continual conflict and uncertainty and in Hobbes's famous words human life will end up 'solitary, poor, nasty, brutish, and short'.

The reason for the formation of a sovereign state is therefore primarily physical safety. Hobbes does claim that in the state of conflict which precedes the formation of government there would be none of the cultural progressions which flourish in a peaceful society, no industry, agriculture, navigation, building or knowledge generation, 'no arts; no letters; no society', but the reason for these absences is the uncertainty of the environment in which they would take place and the diversion of the energies which would be applied to these endeavours to the basic task of survival. It is made plain that at the root of all, and worst of all, is 'continual fear, and danger of violent death' (Hobbes 1996, Pt I, ch. 13). The reason for the creation of the artificial body of the state is the preservation of the natural body.

What we get, therefore, in Hobbes is an account of the body politic which is much more closely connected to the natural body of the individual. No longer, as in medieval thought, is the embodied *polis* merely a metaphor for political ordering; rather, the state itself comes into being because of the concerns of the natural body and the quest for its preservation. The Hobbesian state consciously mirrors the body because of the natural flow from one to the other: bodily motion leads to sensation which leads to desire and aversion which leads to both the war of all against all and the concern for physical safety which leads to the state in an unbroken chain of reasoning.

The next section will seek to problematise the idea of the 'natural body', which Hobbes uses as the basis of his reasoning. Rather than seeing the state as a function of bodily organisation we shall look at developments in political theory which claim that the individual physical body is a result of the functioning of state power. Following on from our investigation of the *polis* being embodied we shall now reverse the flow of that argument and look at the politicised body.

THE POLITICISED BODY: MICHEL FOUCAULT

Michel Foucault's book *Discipline and Punish: The Birth of the Prison* opens with a comparison of two different forms of punishment. In the first a regicide in 1757 has his flesh torn off with red-hot pincers, his hand burnt with sulphur, molten lead, boiling oil and burning resin poured on his wounds, and he is then drawn and quartered. In the second scenario from eighty years later a prison timetable is reproduced detailing the time prisoners shall rise, attend work, education, meals and washing, and go to bed. Every minute of the day is regimented (Foucault 1977: 1–7).

With the end of the corporal and capital emphasis in punishment and the reorganisation of punishment around ideas of reform the body becomes 'an instrument or intermediary: if one intervenes upon it to imprison it, or to make it work, it is in order to deprive the individual of a liberty that is regarded both as a right and as property. The body, according to this penalty, is caught up in a system of constraints and privations, obligations and prohibitions' (Foucault 1977: 11). Foucault's aim in this work is to 'study the metamorphosis of punitive methods on the basis of a political technology of the body in which might be read a common history of power relations and object relations' (1977: 24).

The main concern here is with the effects of power on the body and the idea of punishment is a very direct way of studying this. The punishment of the regicide serves as a very direct illustration: Damiens (the offender in question) had dared to kill the embodiment of the French state in the person of the king. The state then tore his body, quite literally, to shreds.

In times when this sort of extreme form of punishment is not carried out Foucault argues that it is still the body upon which punishment operates, even though the emphasis is on the reform of the criminal's psyche. In the prison timetable the body of the prisoner is told where to be at every time of the day and what acts to perform, even down to eating and sleeping. For Foucault the body is political not because a political entity mirrors the body but because the body is directly operated upon by the subtle effects of power. It is not just the power of the state which operates on the body, but that of the many social institutions and cultural webs which make up our everyday life. Our bodies have to be in certain places (school, church, workplace) and perform certain functions in society; the prison is simply an extreme case. 'The body is . . . directly involved in a political field; power relations have an immediate hold upon it; they invest it, mark it, train it, torture it, force it to carry out tasks, to perform ceremonies, to emit signs' (Foucault 1977: 25).

The body politic infests the body, penetrates and reforms it in certain ways. Power for Foucault is an essentially productive force – the prison regime is a set of ideas and practices (a *discourse* in Foucault's terms). It is a machine which takes criminals and produces useful members of society, people whose bodies will be at work or at home when they are meant to be; it renders 'individuals docile and useful, by means of precise work upon their bodies' (Foucault 1977: 231). Another good example of a discourse which operates upon bodies is the army: 'By the late eighteenth century, the soldier is something that can be made; out of a formless clay, an inapt body, the machine required can be constructed' (Foucault 1977: 135).

For Foucault the body is something which is extremely malleable; it is clay which can be formed, trained, manipulated into various shapes and patterns of behaviour. The idea of a 'natural' body is at any point in time merely the product of various social discourses. The vision of the body with which this chapter began (skeleton, veins, skin etc.) is a picture given by contemporary medicine, it was not always so and may be subject to change in the future. For Foucault this change is not about the perfection of scientific thought, it is about the interrelation of power and knowledge. The dominant social discourses produce knowledge and knowledge put into practice produces bodies. Again the penal system is a good example. Given the incarceration of inmates for periods of time in a given place, combined with the social concern which criminality causes in society, there has been a lot of time and effort devoted to the study of prisoners and to the effects which different forms of penal regimes have upon them. Knowledge is generated about what causes people to become criminals and what can be done to reform them back into docile and useful bodies. Given this knowledge the system changes, the bodies are put through different procedures and the effects are studied again.

The prison is a good example of a purely artificial system which manipulates bodies, but what about processes that we view as 'natural'? We may claim that it is all very well saying that prison requires bodies to act in certain ways but they still act in accordance with 'nature'. In *The History of Sexuality, vol. 1: An Introduction*, Foucault takes a 'natural' process/act/impulse to examine the effects of power on bodies. 'The purpose of … [this] study is … to show how deployments of power are directly connected to the body – to bodies, functions, physiological processes, sensations and pleasures' (1978: 151–2). In this study Foucault seeks to show how sexuality is operated upon by various discourses, including for example religious doctrine on sex, the scientific study of women, the study and regulation of children's sexuality and the birth of population control with the attendant study and manipulation of a nation's sexual practices. Our notions of sexuality, and consequently our practice of it, is therefore subject to change in different times and places. Sexuality is not 'natural', it is constructed according to time and place.

An important consideration when assessing a political concept is how useful it is in terms of resistance. An idea which allows no leverage and inspires no action by oppressed groups is not a very useful one in terms of the politics of resistance and change. Foucault's ideas of the malleability of the body and the productive nature of power are potentially of great use to those in society who suffer oppression through the action of dominant discourses on their bodies. If bodies are malleable and discourses changeable then oppressed groups can effect change. One feminist theorist who appropriates Foucault's ideas to open up cracks in dominant discourses is Judith Butler.

THE POLITICISED BODY: JUDITH BUTLER

In *Gender Trouble* Butler argues that there is no such thing as a naturally sexed body. She rejects the usual differentiation which claims that the distinction between the sexes is natural whereas that between genders or sexualities is cultural. For her the idea of sex is not tied to the body but is, like gender, a production of Foucaultian discourses (1990: 6–8). Butler argues that gender is a form of bodily signification. In other words the gender we adopt has an impact on the 'sexing' of our body. In this way gender is *performative*, a notion rooted in linguistic theory which claims that a speech act creates that which it names (Butler 1990: 25). One oft-used example of this in language is the marriage ceremony, wherein the pronouncement of the vows by bride and groom means they are married. In the same way that acting out a marriage constitutes (or creates) a married couple, the acting out of a gender will constitute the identity it is purported to be. This acting out takes place on the surface of the body – 'gender is the repeated stylization of the body, a set of repeated acts within a highly rigid regulatory frame that congeal over time to produce the appearance of substance, of a natural sort of being' (Butler 1990: 33). Gender is a set of 'acts, gestures, enactments, . . . [and] corporeal signs' (Butler 1990: 136). Once this is realised one can deconstruct the acts which constitute a particular gender and produce a sexed body and see them within the framework of the social discourses which produce them.

One can go further than this, however. One can use this knowledge to try and disrupt particular patterns of gender and sex by turning the acts which constitute these patterns against themselves. One way of doing this which Butler suggests, and which can be found in the second of the following reading selections, is drag. The performance of drag, for Butler, serves to highlight the difficulty of the notion of an original sex. It 'plays upon the distinction between the anatomy of the performer and the gender that is being performed' and uses the interplay of 'anatomical sex, gender identity, and gender performance' (Butler 1990: 137). Drag does not parody the original gender but parodies the very idea of an original.

Butler's ideas are of course controversial. She, like Foucault, in claiming that the body 'has no ontological status apart from the various acts which constitute its reality' (1990: 136) is criticised for denying the actual physical substance of the body. Critics suggest that there are physical limits to what the actual body can do and that it is not a blank sheet on which anything may be inscribed by discourse. In a later work Butler attempted to address these concerns by introducing the idea of 'materialisation'. This seems less a defence or a reworking of her beliefs than a restatement, however, in that again she claims that there is no natural body, only a process of 'materialization that stabilizes over time to produce the effect of boundary, fixity, and surface we call matter' (1993: 9).

THE BODY ELECTRIC

This may not seem such an odd idea given the technological innovation over the past years which has extended our idea of where the 'natural' body begins and ends. No longer can we view the physicality of our body as merely the sum of organic matter mentioned at the beginning of this chapter. Prosthetic limbs, pacemakers, cosmetic surgery and implants have meant that our natural body can be altered by technological means. In America about 10 per cent of the population are 'cyborgs' in the technical sense, incorporating these technologies in their bodies. 'Occupations make a much higher percentage into metaphoric cyborgs, including the computer keyboarder joined in a cybernetic circuit with the screen, the neurosurgeon guided by fibre-optic microscopy during an operation and the teen player in the local video-game arcade' (Hayles 1999: 158). One wonders how much altering a body can take before it ceases to be a 'natural' body and becomes a creation of science.

The idea of the cyborg, the marriage of human organic physicality and machine, is most famously explored by Donna Haraway in *A Cyborg Manifesto*. Haraway traces the rupture of three boundaries in contemporary

Western culture: between human and animal; between animal-human and machine; and between physical and non-physical (1991: 151–3). The cyborg is an entity 'committed to partiality, irony, intimacy, and perversity' (Haraway 1991: 151) which sheds the idea of a natural home on either side of these boundaries and exists by transgressing them. In terms of political possibilities 'cyborg unities are monstrous and illegitimate; in our present political circumstances, we could hardly hope for more potent myths for resistance and recoupling' (Haraway 1991: 154). Whereas Butler's ideas turn on the possibility of the body being infinitely malleable in itself, the cyborg can be seen as a way of extending this fluidity of form and substance and further problematising the idea of what constitutes our 'natural' bodies.

We have travelled a long way in our journey through the body politic. From a solid entity of skin, bone and blood which could serve as a metaphor for the sociopolitical reality of the state we have arrived at a blurred, fluid notion, a product of social discourses and gendered acts penetrated by technology and rendered thoroughly artificial.

Conclusion

A concluding thought may be the possibilities afforded by technologies which allow us to leave our bodies completely behind us. Technosocial spaces such as the Internet potentially allow us to float as pure consciousness and engage on disembodied terms with those we meet there. At the minute most people communicate online purely through typed language and this reduced sensory experience affords unique opportunities for the dissolution and recreation of online identities. One example from John Suler's fascinating study of cyberpsychology (1999) is gender-switching. As multimedia technologies, such as webcams, grow in sophistication and affordability some of these opportunities will be lost as we are forced back into our bodies during online communication by the reinstatement of the visual and auditory senses. Until then, however, cyberspace affords existence, and hence political possibility, at the furthest remove from the human body with which we began, one of words transmitted as binary digits.

Questions for discussion

- Do you think it was natural that people used the body as a starting point for thinking about politics? What other points of departure could they have taken?
- How convincing in our modern society is the medieval notion that the state should be ordered like a human body and why?
- How is our thinking about the body allied to the concept of 'discourse' discussed earlier?

- The criminal law sets down that an individual can not consent to certain acts being performed on his or her own body. It outlaws extreme forms of consensual torture and renders personal use of certain drugs illegal for example. Given what was discussed in the chapters on 'Liberty', 'Rights', 'Tolerance' and 'The Rule of Law', is this justified or should we be free to do whatever we like with our own bodies as long as it does not harm others?

NOTE

1. All information on the body is taken from *Gray* (2001) and Baggaley (2001).

JUDITH BUTLER
EXTRACTS FROM *GENDER TROUBLE: FEMINISM AND THE SUBVERSION OF IDENTITY*

The construction of coherence conceals the gender discontinuities that run rampant within heterosexual, bisexual, and gay and lesbian contexts in which gender does not necessarily follow from sex, and desire, or sexuality generally, does not seem to follow from gender – indeed, where none of these dimensions of significant corporeality express or reflect one another. When the disorganization and disaggregation of the field of bodies disrupt the regulatory fiction of heterosexual coherence, it seems that the expressive model loses its descriptive force. That regulatory ideal is then exposed as a norm and a fiction that disguises itself as a developmental law regulating the sexual field that it purports to describe.

According to the understanding of identification as an enacted fantasy or incorporation, however, it is clear that coherence is desired, wished for, idealized, and that this idealization is an effect of a corporeal signification. In other words, acts, gestures, and desire produce the effect of an internal core or substance, but produce this *on the surface* of the body, through the play of signifying absences that suggest, but never reveal, the organizing principle of identity as a cause. Such acts, gestures, enactments, generally construed, are *performative* in the sense that the essence or identity that they otherwise purport to express are *fabrications* manufactured and sustained through corporeal signs and other discursive means. That the gendered body is performative suggests that it has no ontological status apart from the various acts which constitute its reality. This also suggests that if that reality

Judith Butler (1990), *Gender Trouble: Feminism and the Subversion of Identity*, New York: Routledge.

is fabricated as an interior essence, that very interiority is an effect and function of a decidedly public and social discourse, the public regulation of fantasy through the surface politics of the body, the gender border control that differentiates inner from outer, and so institutes the 'integrity' of the subject. In other words, acts and gestures, articulated and enacted desires create the illusion of an interior and organizing gender core, an illusion discursively maintained for the purposes of the regulation of sexuality within the obligatory frame of reproductive heterosexuality. If the 'cause' of desire, gesture, and act can be localized within the 'self' of the actor, then the political regulations and disciplinary practices which produce that ostensibly coherent gender are effectively displaced from view. The displacement of a political and discursive origin of gender identity onto a psychological 'core' precludes an analysis of the political constitution of the gendered subject and its fabricated notions about the ineffable interiority of its sex or of its true identity.

If the inner truth of gender is a fabrication and if a true gender is a fantasy instituted and inscribed on the surface of bodies, then it seems that genders can be neither true nor false, but are only produced as the truth effects of a discourse of primary and stable identity. In *Mother Camp: Female Impersonators in America*, anthropologist Esther Newton suggests that the structure of impersonation reveals one of the key fabricating mechanisms through which the social construction of gender takes place.[1] I would suggest as well that drag fully subverts the distinction between inner and outer psychic space and effectively mocks both the expressive model of gender and the notion of a true gender identity. Newton writes:

> At its most complex, [drag] is a double inversion that says, 'appearance is an illusion'. Drag says [Newton's curious personification] 'my "outside" appearance is feminine, but my essence "inside" [the body] is masculine'. At the same time it symbolizes the opposite inversion; 'my appearance "outside" [my body, my gender] is masculine but my essence "inside" [myself] is feminine'.[2]

Both claims to truth contradict one another and so displace the entire enactment of gender significations from the discourse of truth and falsity.

The notion of an original or primary gender identity is often parodied within the cultural practices of drag, cross-dressing, and the sexual stylization of butch/femme identities. Within feminist theory, such parodic identities have been understood to be either degrading to women, in the case of drag and cross-dressing, or an uncritical appropriation of sex-role stereotyping from within the practice of heterosexuality, especially in the case of butch/femme lesbian identities. But the relation between the 'imitation' and the 'original' is, I think, more complicated than that critique generally allows. Moreover, it gives us a clue to the way in which the relationship between primary identification – that is, the original meanings accorded to gender – and subsequent gender experience might be reframed. The performance of drag plays upon the distinction between the anatomy of the performer and the gender that is being performed. But we are actually in the presence of three contingent dimensions of significant corporeality: anatomical sex, gender identity, and gender performance. If the anatomy of the performer is already distinct from the gender of the performer, and both of those are distinct from the gender of the performance, then the performance suggests a dissonance not only between sex and performance, but sex and gender, and gender and performance. As much as drag creates a unified picture of 'woman' (what its critics often oppose), it also reveals the distinctness of those aspects of gendered experience which are falsely naturalized as a unity through the regulatory fiction of heterosexual coherence. *In imitating gender, drag implicitly reveals the imitative structure of gender itself – as well as its contingency.* Indeed, part of the pleasure, the giddiness of the performance is in the recognition of a radical contingency in the relation between sex and gender in the face of cultural configurations of causal unities that are regularly assumed to be natural and necessary. In the place of the law of heterosexual coherence, we see sex and gender denaturalized by means of a performance which avows their distinctness and dramatizes the cultural mechanism of their fabricated unity.

The notion of gender parody defended here does not assume that there is an original which such parodic identities imitate. Indeed, the parody is *of* the very notion of an original; just as the psychoanalytic notion of gender identification is constituted by a fantasy of a fantasy, the transfiguration of an Other who is always already a 'figure' in that double sense, so gender parody reveals that the original identity after which gender fashions itself is an imitation without an origin. To be more precise, it is a production which, in effect – that is, in its effect – postures as an imitation. This perpetual displacement constitutes a fluidity of identities that suggests an openness to resignification and recontextualization; parodic proliferation deprives hegemonic culture and its critics of the claim to naturalized or essentialist gender identities. Although the gender meanings taken up in these parodic styles are clearly part of hegemonic, misogynist culture, they are nevertheless denaturalized and mobilized through their parodic recontextualization. As imitations which effectively displace the meaning of the original, they imitate the myth of originality itself. In the place of an original identification which serves as a determining cause, gender identity might be reconceived as a personal/cultural history of received meanings subject to a set of imitative practices which refer laterally to other imitations and which, jointly, construct the illusion of a primary and interior gendered self or parody the mechanism of that construction.

[. . .]

In what senses, then, is gender an act? As in other ritual social dramas, the action of gender requires a performance that is *repeated*. This repetition is at once a reenactment and reexperiencing of a set of meanings already socially established; and it is the mundane and ritualized form of their legitimation.[3] Although there are individual bodies that enact these significations by becoming stylized into gendered modes, this 'action' is a public action. There are temporal and collective dimensions to these actions, and their public character is not inconsequential; indeed, the performance is effected with the strategic aim of maintaining gender within its binary frame – an aim that cannot be attributed to a subject, but, rather, must be understood to found and consolidate the subject.

Gender ought not to be construed as a stable identity or locus of agency from which various acts follow; rather, gender is an identity tenuously constituted in time, instituted in an exterior space through a *stylized repetition of acts*. The effect of gender is produced through the stylization of the body and, hence, must be understood as the mundane way in which bodily gestures, movements, and styles of various kinds constitute the illusion of an abiding gendered self. This formulation moves the conception of gender off the ground of a substantial model of identity to one that requires a conception of gender as a constituted *social temporality*. Significantly, if gender is instituted through acts which are internally discontinuous, then the *appearance of substance* is precisely that, a constructed identity, a performative accomplishment which the mundane social audience, including the actors themselves, come to believe and to perform in the mode of belief. Gender is also a norm that can never be fully internalized; 'the internal' is a surface signification, and gender norms are finally phantasmatic, impossible to embody. If the ground of gender identity is the stylized repetition of acts through time and not a seemingly seamless identity, then the spatial metaphor of a 'ground' will be displaced and revealed as a stylized configuration, indeed, a gendered corporealization of time. The abiding gendered self will then be shown to be structured by repeated acts that seek to approximate the ideal of a substantial ground of identity, but which, in their occasional *dis*continuity, reveal the temporal and contingent groundlessness of this 'ground'. The possibilities of gender transformation are to be found precisely in the arbitrary relation between such acts, in the possibility of a failure to repeat, a de-formity, or a parodic repetition that exposes the phantasmatic effect of abiding identity as a politically tenuous construction.

If gender attributes, however, are not expressive but performative, then these attributes effectively constitute the identity they are said to express or reveal. The distinction between expression and performativeness is crucial. If gender attributes and acts, the various ways in which a body shows or produces its cultural signification, are performative, then there is no preexisting identity by which an act or attribute might be measured; there would be no true or false, real or distorted acts of gender, and the postulation of a true gender identity would be revealed as a regulatory fiction. That gender reality is created through sustained social performances means that the very notions of an essential sex and a true or abiding masculinity or femininity are also constituted as part of the strategy that conceals gender's performative character and the performative possibilities for proliferating gender configurations outside the restricting frames of masculinist domination and compulsory heterosexuality.

Genders can be neither true nor false, neither real nor apparent, neither original nor derived. As credible bearers of those attributes, however, genders can also be rendered thoroughly and radically *incredible*.

NOTES

1. See the chapter 'Role Models' in Esther Newton, *Mother Camp: Female Impersonators in America* (Chicago: University of Chicago Press, 1972).
2. Ibid., p. 103.
3. See Victor Turner, *Dramas, Fields and Metaphors* (Ithaca: Cornell University Press, 1974). See also Clifford Geertz, 'Blurred Genres: The Refiguration of Thought', in *Local Knowledge, Further Essays in Interpretive Anthropology* (New York: Basic Books, 1983).

MICHEL FOUCAULT
EXTRACTS FROM *DISCIPLINE AND PUNISH: THE BIRTH OF THE PRISON*

THE BODY OF THE CONDEMNED

[...]

Historians long ago began to write the history of the body. They have studied the body in the field of historical demography or pathology; they have considered it as the seat of needs and appetites, as the locus of physiological processes and metabolisms, as a target for the attacks of germs or viruses; they have shown to what extent historical processes were involved in what might seem to be the purely biological base of existence; and what place should be given in the history of society to biological 'events' such as the circulation of bacilli, or the extension of the life-span (cf. Le Roy-Ladurie). But the body is also directly involved in a political field; power relations have an immediate hold upon it; they invest it, mark it, train it, torture it, force it to carry out tasks, to perform ceremonies, to emit signs. This political investment of the body is bound up, in accordance with complex reciprocal relations, with its economic use; it is largely as a force of production that the body is invested with relations of power and domination; but, on the other hand, its constitution as labour power is possible only if it is caught up in a system of subjection (in which need is also a political instrument meticulously prepared, calculated and used); the body becomes a useful force only if it is both a productive body and a subjected body.

Michel Foucault (1991), *Discipline and Punish: The Birth of the Prison*, London: Penguin Books.

This subjection is not only obtained by the instruments of violence or ideology; it can also be direct, physical, pitting force against force, bearing on material elements, and yet without involving violence; it may be calculated, organized, technically thought out; it may be subtle, make use neither of weapons nor of terror and yet remain of a physical order. That is to say, there may be a 'knowledge' of the body that is not exactly the science of its functioning, and a mastery of its forces that is more than the ability to conquer them: this knowledge and this mastery constitute what might be called the political technology of the body. Of course, this technology is diffuse, rarely formulated in continuous, systematic discourse; it is often made up of bits and pieces; it implements a disparate set of tools or methods. In spite of the coherence of its results, it is generally no more than a multiform instrumentation. Moreover, it cannot be localized in a particular type of institution or state apparatus. For they have recourse to it; they use, select or impose certain of its methods. But, in its mechanisms and its effects, it is situated at a quite different level. What the apparatuses and institutions operate is, in a sense, a micro-physics of power, whose field of validity is situated in a sense between these great functionings and the bodies themselves with their materiality and their forces.

[...]

DOCILE BODIES

Let us take the ideal figure of the soldier as it was still seen in the early seventeenth century. To begin with, the soldier was someone who could be recognized from afar; he bore certain signs: the natural signs of his strength and his courage, the marks, too, of his pride; his body was the blazon of his strength and valour; and although it is true that he had to learn the profession of arms little by little – generally in actual fighting – movements like marching and attitudes like the bearing of the head belonged for the most part to a bodily rhetoric of honour; 'The signs for recognizing those most suited to this profession are a lively, alert manner, an erect head, a taut stomach, broad shoulders, long arms, strong fingers, a small belly, thick thighs, slender legs and dry feet, because a man of such a figure could not fail to be agile and strong'; when he becomes a pike-bearer, the soldier 'will have to march in step in order to have as much grace and gravity as possible, for the pike is an honourable weapon, worthy to be borne with gravity and boldness' (Montgommery, 6 and 7). By the late eighteenth century, the soldier has become something that can be made; out of a formless clay, an inapt body, the machine required can be constructed; posture is gradually corrected; a calculated constraint runs slowly through each part of the body, mastering it, making it pliable, ready at all times, turning silently into the automatism of habit; in short, one has 'got rid of the peasant' and given him 'the air of a soldier' (ordinance of 20 March 1764). Recruits become accustomed to 'holding their heads high and erect; to standing upright, without bending the back, to sticking out the belly, throwing out the chest and throwing back the shoulders; and, to help them acquire the habit, they are given this position while standing against a wall in such a way that the heels, the thighs, the waist and the shoulders touch it, as also do the backs of the hands, as one turns the arms outwards, without moving them away from the body ... Likewise, they will be taught never to fix their eyes on the ground, but to look straight at those they pass ... to remain motionless until the order is given, without moving the head, the hands or the feet ... lastly to march with a bold step, with knee and ham taut, on the points of the feet, which should face outwards' (ordinance of 20 March 1764).

The classical age discovered the body as object and target of power. It is easy enough to find signs of the attention then paid to the body – to the body that is manipulated, shaped, trained, which obeys, responds, becomes skilful and increases its forces. The great book of Man-the-Machine was written simultaneously on two registers: the anatomico-metaphysical register, of which Descartes wrote the first pages and which the physicians and philosophers continued, and the technico-political register, which was constituted by a whole set of regulations and by empirical and calculated methods relating to the army, the school and the hospital, for controlling or correcting the operations of the body. These two registers are quite distinct, since it was a question, on the one hand, of submission and use and, on the other, of functioning and explanation: there was a useful body and an intelligible body. And yet there are points of overlap from one to the other. La Mettrie's *L'Homme-machine* is both a materialist reduction of the soul and a general theory of *dressage*, at the centre of which reigns the notion of 'docility', which joins the analysable body to the manipulable body. A body is docile that may be subjected, used, transformed and improved. The celebrated automata, on the other hand, were not only a way of illustrating an organism, they were also political puppets, small-scale models of power: Frederick II, the meticulous king of small machines, well-trained regiments and long exercises, was obsessed with them.

What was so new in these projects of docility that interested the eighteenth century so much? It was certainly not the first time that the body had become the object of such imperious and pressing investments; in every society, the body was in the grip of very strict powers, which imposed on it constraints, prohibitions or obligations. However, there were several new things in these techniques. To begin with, there was the scale of the control: it was a question not of treating the body, *en masse*, 'wholesale', as if it were an indissociable unity, but of working it 'retail', individually; of exercising upon it a subtle coercion, of obtaining holds upon it at the level of the mechanism itself – movements, gestures, attitudes, rapidity: an infinitesimal power over the active body. Then there was the object of the control: it was not or was no longer the signifying elements of behaviour or the language of the body, but the economy, the efficiency of movements, their internal organization; constraint bears upon the forces rather than upon the signs; the only truly important ceremony is that of exercise. Lastly, there is the modality: it implies an uninterrupted, constant coercion, supervising the processes of the activity rather than its result and it is exercised according to a codification that partitions as closely as possible time, space, movement. These methods, which made possible the meticulous control of the operations of the body, which assured the constant subjection of its forces and imposed upon them a relation of docility-utility, might be called 'disciplines'. Many disciplinary methods had long been in existence – in monasteries, armies, workshops. But in the course of the seventeenth and eighteenth centuries the disciplines became general formulas of domination. They were different from slavery because they were not based on a relation of appropriation of bodies; indeed, the elegance of the discipline lay in the fact that it could dispense with this costly and violent relation by obtaining effects of utility at least as great. They were different, too, from 'service', which was a constant, total, massive, non-analytical, unlimited relation of domination, established in the form of the individual will of the master, his 'caprice'. They were different from vassalage, which was a highly coded, but distant relation of submission, which bore less on the operations of the body than on the products of labour and the ritual marks of allegiance. Again, they were different from asceticism and from 'disciplines' of a monastic type, whose function was to obtain renunciations rather than increases of utility and which, although they involved obedience to others, had as their principal aim an increase of the mastery of each individual over his own body. The historical moment of the disciplines was the moment when an art of the human body was born, which was directed not only at the growth of its skills, nor at the intensification of its subjection, but at the formation of a relation that in the mechanism itself makes it more obedient as it becomes more useful, and conversely. What was then being formed was a policy of coercions that act upon the body, a calculated manipulation of its elements, its gestures, its behaviour. The human body was entering a machinery of power that explores it, breaks it down and rearranges it. A 'political anatomy', which was also a 'mechanics of power', was being born; it defined how one may have a hold over others' bodies, not only so that they may do what one wishes, but so that they may operate as one wishes, with the techniques, the speed and the efficiency that one determines. Thus discipline produces subjected and practised bodies, 'docile' bodies. Discipline increases the forces of the body (in economic terms of utility) and diminishes these same forces (in political terms of obedience). In short, it dissociates power from the body; on the one hand, it turns it into an 'aptitude', a 'capacity', which it seeks to increase; on the other hand, it reverses the course of the energy, the power that might result from it, and turns it into a relation of strict subjection. If economic exploitation separates the force and the product of labour, let us say that disciplinary coercion establishes in the body the constricting link between an increased aptitude and an increased domination.

The 'invention' of this new political anatomy must not be seen as a sudden discovery. It is rather a multiplicity of often minor processes, of different origin and scattered location, which overlap, repeat, or imitate one another, support one another, distinguish themselves from one another according to their domain of application, converge and gradually produce the blueprint of a general method. They were at work in secondary education at a very early date, later in primary schools; they slowly invested the space of the hospital; and, in a few decades, they restructured the military organization. They sometimes circulated very rapidly from one point to another (between the army and the technical schools or secondary schools), sometimes slowly and discreetly (the insidious militarization of the large workshops). On almost every occasion, they were adopted in response to particular needs: an industrial innovation, a renewed outbreak of certain epidemic diseases, the invention of the rifle or the victories of Prussia. This did not prevent them being totally inscribed in general and essential transformations, which we must now try to delineate.

There can be no question here of writing the history of the different disciplinary institutions, with all their individual differences. I simply intend to map on a series of examples some of the essential techniques that most easily spread from one to another. These were always meticulous, often minute, techniques, but they had their importance: because they defined a certain mode of detailed political investment of the body, a 'new micro-physics' of power; and because, since the seventeenth century, they had constantly reached out to ever broader domains, as if they tended to cover the entire social body. Small acts of cunning endowed with a great power of diffusion, subtle arrangements, apparently innocent, but profoundly suspicious, mechanisms that obeyed economies too shameful to be acknowledged, or pursued petty forms of coercion – it was nevertheless they that brought about the mutation of the punitive system, at the threshold of the contemporary period. Describing them will require great attention to detail: beneath every set of figures, we must seek not a meaning, but a precaution; we must situate them not only in the inextricability of a functioning, but in the coherence of a tactic. They are the acts of cunning, not so much of the greater reason that works even in its sleep and gives meaning to the insignificant, as of the attentive 'malevolence' that turns everything to account. Discipline is a political anatomy of detail.

NOTES ON THE AUTHORS OF THE
SELECTED READINGS

John Agnew is Professor of Geography at the University of California, Los Angeles. He is the author and co-author of many books, including *Geopolitics: Re-visioning World Politics* (1998) and, with Stuart Corbridge, *Mastering Space: Hegemony, Territory and International Political Economy* (1995).

Benedict Anderson is currently the director of the Modern Indonesia Program and the Aaron L. Binenkorb Professor of International Studies at Cornell University, Ithaca, New York. Anderson's famous analysis of nationalism is presented in his book *Imagined Communities. Reflections on the Origin and Spread of Nationalism* (1983).

Isaiah Berlin was Chichele Professor of Social and Political Theory at the University of Oxford from 1957 to 1967. His main works include *Karl Marx: His Life and Environment* (1939), *The Crooked Timber of Humanity: Chapters in the History of Human Ideas* (1990) and *Freedom and Its Betrayal: Six Enemies of Human Liberty* (2002). One of the leading liberal thinkers of the twentieth century, Isaiah Berlin died in 1997.

Wendy Brown is Professor of Political Science and Women's Studies at the University of California, Berkeley. Her publications include *Manhood and Politics: A Feminist Reading in Political Theory* (1988), *Politics Out of History* (2001) and *Left Legalism/Left Critique* (2002), co-edited with Janet Halley.

Rogers Brubaker is Professor of Sociology at the University of California, Los Angeles and Recurring Visiting Professor in the Nationalism Studies

Program of the Central European University in Budapest. He has written on immigration, citizenship and ethnicity (e.g. *Citizenship and Nationhood in France and Germany*, 1992 and *Ethnicity without Groups*, 2004).

Judith Butler is Maxine Elliott Professor in the Departments of Rhetoric and Comparative Literature at the University of California, Berkeley. Her main publications include *Gender Trouble* (1990) and *Bodies That Matter* (1993).

G. A. Cohen is Chichele Professor of Social and Political Theory and a fellow of All Souls College at the University of Oxford. His work includes *Karl Marx's Theory of History: A Defence* (1978) and *Self-Ownership, Freedom, and Equality* (1995).

Joshua Cohen is Professor of Philosophy, Professor of Political Science and Leon and Anne Goldberg Professor of Humanities at the Massachusetts Institute of Technology. He has published extensively on theories of democracy, especially deliberative democracy.

William Connolly is Krieger-Eisenhower Professor of Political Science at Johns Hopkins University, Baltimore. His main publications include *Identity/Difference: Democratic Negotiations of Political Paradox* (1991), *The Ethos of Pluralization* (1995) and *Neuropolitics: Thinking, Culture, Speed* (2002).

Frederick Cooper is Professor of History at the Department of History at New York University. Together with Ann Stoler he is the editor of *Tensions of Empire: Colonial Culture in a Bourgeois World* 1997.

Gilles Deleuze was Professor of Philosophy at the University of Paris VIII, Saint Denis. He is the author (with Félix Guattari) of influential works such as *Anti-Oedipus* (1972), *A Thousand Plateaus* (1980) and *What is Philosophy?* (1991).

Ronald Dworkin is Professor of Philosophy and Frank Henry Sommer Professor of Law at New York University. Recent major publications include *Life's Dominion* (1993) and *Freedom's Law* (1996).

Amitai Etzioni is University Professor at The George Washington University, Washington, DC, the Director of the Institute for Communitarian Policy Studies and the author of *The New Golden Rule: Community and Morality in a Democratic Society* (1997).

Michel Foucault served as Professor of History of Systems of Thought at the Collège de France, Paris from 1970 until his death in 1984. His works include *The Archaeology of Knowledge* (1972), *Discipline and Punish* (1975) and three volumes of *The History of Sexuality* (1976, 1984, 1984).

Lon Fuller was a professor of law at the Universities of Oregon and Illinois and at Duke University, Durham, North Carolina between 1926 and 1939. From 1939 until his retirement in 1972 he was a professor of law at Harvard Law School. His major publications include *The Morality of Law* (1964) and *Anatomy of the Law* (1968).

Clifford Geertz is Professor Emeritus at the Institute for Advanced Study, Princeton. He is one of the world's leading anthropologists and in 2002 published an intellectual autobiography, *Works and Lives*.

Anthony Giddens was the director of the London School of Economics and Political Science until 2003, and is currently an advisor to Tony Blair. He participates in a number of public organizations, including the Institute for Public Policy Research, and was awarded a life peerage in 2004.

Félix Guattari was a practising psychoanalyst and writer who collaborated with Gilles Deleuze on a number of publications including *Anti-Oedipus* (1972), *A Thousand Plateaus* (1980) and *What is Philosophy?* (1991).

Jürgen Habermas is Professor Emeritus of Sociology and Philosophy at the Johann Wolfgang Goethe University, Frankfurt. He is the author of influential works such as *The Structural Transformation of the Public Sphere* (1962), *The Theory of Communicative Action* (1981), *The Philosophical Discourse of Modernity* (1985) and *Postmetaphysical Thinking* (1988).

Alan Hamlin is Professor of Economics at the University of Southampton. His extensive publications in economics and politics include *Democratic Devices and Desires* (2000) with Geoffrey Brennan.

Paul Hirst, until his death in 2003, was Professor of Social Theory at Birkbeck College, University of London. He published widely throughout his career on Marxism, law and democracy.

Will Kymlicka is presently Canada Research Professor in Political Philosophy at Queen's University, Kingston, Ontario. He has written extensively on multiculturalism. His books include *Liberalism, Community, and Culture* (1989), *Contemporary Political Philosophy* (1990), and *Politics in the Vernacular: Nationalism, Multiculturalism, and Citizenship* (2001).

Ernesto Laclau holds a chair in political theory and is Director of the Doctoral Programme in Ideology and Discourse Analysis at the University of Essex. He is also currently a distinguished visiting professor at the Department of Comparative Literature at the State University of New York at Buffalo. He is the author of *Hegemony and Socialist Strategy* (1985, with Chantal Mouffe), *Reflections on the Revolution of Our Time* (1990), and *Emancipation(s)* (1996).

Claude Lefort is Professor of Philosophy at the École des Hautes Études en Sciences Sociales, Paris. He was a co-founder of the prominent left-wing journal *Socialisme ou Barbarie*. His books in English translation include *Democracy and Political Theory* (1988) and *The Political Forms of Modern Society* (1994).

Doreen Massey is a professor of geography at the Open University. She writes widely on issues such as globalization, development, spatial theory, urbanization, gender and social justice. Her most recent book is *Cities for the Many not the Few* (2000).

Roger D. Masters is Research Professor in the Department of Government, Dartmouth College, Hanover, New Hampshire. As well as work on Rousseau, he has published and edited many books on the relation between biology and politics, including *Primate Politics* (1991).

Susan Mendus is a professor in the Department of Politics at the University of York. Her main research interests are in contemporary political philosophy, feminist theory and philosophy of education. In philosophy of education she is working on the role of education in developing toleration in multicultural societies. Amongst her recent publications is *Feminism and Emotion* (2000).

Chantal Mouffe is Professor of Political Theory in the Centre for the Study of Democracy at the University of Westminster, London. Her recent publications include *The Return of the Political* (1993) and *The Democratic Paradox* (2000).

Gearóid Ó Tuathail is Professor of Government and International Affairs at the Virginia Polytechnic and State University. He is author of *Critical Geopolitics: The Politics of Writing Global Space* (1996) and co-editor, with John Agnew, of *A Companion to Political Geography* (2003).

Michael Oakeshott was, from 1951 until 1969, Professor of Political Science at the London School of Economics and Political Science. His most important works were *Experience and its Modes* (1933), the long introduction to his edition of Hobbes's *Leviathan* (1946), *Rationalism in Politics* (1962), *On Human Conduct* (1975) and *On History and other essays* (1983).

John Rawls was James Bryant Conant University Professor of Philosophy at Harvard University, Cambridge, Massachusetts. His first book was *A Theory of Justice* (1971) and his other major works include *Political Liberalism* (1993), *The Law of Peoples* (1999) and *Justice as Fairness: A Restatement* (2001).

Michael Sandel is the Anne T. and Robert M. Bass Professor of Government at Harvard University, Cambridge, Massachusetts and the author of *Liberalism and the Limits of Justice* (1982).

John Schaar is Professor Emeritus of Political Philosophy at the University of California. Santa Cruz. He has written extensively on the topic of equality.

Carl Schmitt was a leading legal scholar and conservative nationalist during the Weimar Republic. Schmitt's decision to join the Nazi Party in 1933 is widely regarded as regrettable opportunism. His reputation barely survived that decision and it was only after his death, in 1985, that the merits of his critical reflections on liberal democracy were recognised again. Translations of his works include *Political Theology* (1985), *The Crisis of Parliamentary Democracy* (1985), *The Concept of the Political* (1996) and *Legality and Legitimacy* (2004).

James Tully is Distinguished Professor at the University of Victoria, British Columbia. Among his publications are two books on John Locke – *A Discourse on Property: John Locke and his Adversaries* (1980) and *An Approach to Political Philosophy: Locke in Contexts* (1993) – and an edited collection of essays on the work of Quentin Skinner (1988).

Voltaire (François-Marie Arouet) was born in 1694 and died in 1778. He was one of France's greatest writers and philosophers and a leading figure in the Enlightenment. He was an outspoken critic of religious intolerance and persecution, and served terms in the Bastille as well as having to live in exile on a number of occasions. In 1814 members of a right-wing religious group stole his remains from his sarcophagus in the Panthéon in Paris and dumped them in a rubbish heap, though no one noticed they were gone for fifty years. However, his heart had been removed from his body and lies in the Bibliothèque Nationale in Paris.

Kurt Vonnegut is a world-renowned author. His books include *Player Piano* (1952), *Cat's Cradle* (1963) and *Slaughterhouse Five* (1969).

Michael Walzer is based at the School of Social Science, Institute for Advanced Study, in Princeton, New Jersey. He has written extensively on political theory, especially on issues of pluralism, toleration and war. His most influential books have been *Just and Unjust Wars* (1977), *Spheres of Justice* (1983); and *On Toleration* (1997).

Iris Marion Young is Professor of Political Science at the University of Chicago. Her major publications include *Justice and the Politics of Difference* (1990), *Inclusion and Democracy* (2000) and *On Female Body Experience* (2004).

BIBLIOGRAPHY

Abramson, J., C. Arterton and G. Orren (1988), *The Electric Commonwealth: The Impact of New Media Technologies on Democratic Politics*, New York: Basic Books.

Abu-Laban, Y. and D. Stasiulis (1992), 'Ethnic pluralism under siege: popular and partisan opposition to multiculturalism', *Canadian Public Policy*, 18(4), 365–86.

Ackerman, B. (1980), *Social Justice in the Liberal State*, New Haven: Yale University Press.

Agamben, G. (1998), *Homo Sacer: Sovereign Power and Bare Life*, tr. D. Heller-Roazen, Palo Alto, CA: Stanford University Press.

Agnew, J and S. Corbridge (1989), 'The new geopolitics: the dynamics of geopolitical disorder', in R. Johnston and P. Taylor (eds), *A World in Crisis? Geographical Perspectives*, Oxford: Blackwell, pp. 266–88.

Ainslie, G. (1982), 'A behavioral economic approach to the defense mechanisms', *Social Science Information*, 21: 735–80.

Ake, C. (1999), 'Globalization, multilateralism and the shrinking democratic space', in M. Schechter (ed.), *Future Multilateralism: The Political and Social Framework*, Tokyo: United Nations University Press, pp. 179–95.

Albrow, M. (1996), *The Global Age: State and Society beyond Modernity*, Cambridge: Polity Press.

Alexander, T. (1996), *Unravelling Global Apartheid: An Overview of World Politics*, Cambridge: Polity Press.

Ali, Y. (1992), 'Muslim women and the politics of ethnicity and culture in northern England', in G. Sahgal and N. Yuval-Davis (eds), *Refusing Holy Orders: Women and Fundamentalism in Britain*, London: Virago Press.

Alker, H. and D. Sylvan (1986), 'Political disclosure analysis', paper presented at the Annual Meeting of the American Political Science Association, Washington, DC, September.

Althusser, L. (1984), *Essays on Ideology*, London: Verso.

Althusser, L. and E. Balibar (1979), *Reading Capital*, tr. B. Brewster, London: Verso.

Altmann, S. (1967), 'The structure of social communication', in S. Altmann (ed.), *Social Communication among Primates*, Chicago: University of Chicago Press, pp. 325–62.

Amnesty International (2004), *Amnesty International Report 2003*, London: Amnesty International. <http://web.amnesty.org/report2003/index-eng> [Accessed 25 October 2004]

Andersen, V. and K. Hansen. (2004), 'Deliberative democracy and the deliberative poll on the euro', *Scandinavian Political Studies*, 27(2): 261–86.

Anderson, B. (1983), *Imagined Communities: Reflections on the Origins and Spread of Nationalism*, London: Verso.

Anderson, B. (1991), *Imagined Communities: Reflections on the Origins and Spread of Nationalism*, 2nd ed., London: Verso.

Anderson, P. (1972), 'More Is Different', *Science*, 177: 393–6.

Appadurai, A. (1990), 'Disjuncture and difference in the global cultural economy', *Theory, Culture and Society*, 7: 295–310.

Araghi, F. (1995), 'Global depeasantization, 1945–1990', *Sociological Quarterly*, 36(2): 1–24.

Archibugi, D., D. Held and M. Köhler (eds) (1998), *Re-imagining Political Community: Studies in Cosmopolitan Democracy*, Cambridge: Polity Press.

Arendt, H. (1958), *The Human Condition*, Chicago and London: University of Chicago Press.

Arendt, H. (1970), *On Violence*, London: Allen Lane.

Arendt, H. (1973), *On Revolution*, Harmondsworth: Pelican.

Aristotle (1981), *The Politics*, ed. T. Saunders, rev. ed., Harmondsworth: Penguin.

Aristotle (1988), *The Politics*, ed. S. Everson, Cambridge: Cambridge University Press.

Aristotle (1996), *The Politics*, ed. S. Everson, rev. ed., Cambridge: Cambridge University Press.

Armijo, L. (ed.) (1999), *Financial Globalization and Democracy in Emerging Markets*, Basingstoke: Macmillan.

Arnhart, L. (1995), 'The new Darwinian naturalism in political theory', *American Political Science Review*, 89: 389–400.

Aronowitz, S. and W. DiFazio (1994), *The Jobless Future: Sci-Tech and the Dogma of Work*, Minneapolis: University of Minnesota Press.

Asch, S. (1956), 'Studies of independence and conformity: I. A minority of one against a unanimous majority', *Psychology Monographs*, 70(9): 1–70.

Aslanbeigui, N., S. Pressman and G. Summerfield (eds) (1994), *Women in the Age of Economic Transformation: Gender Impact of Reforms in Post-socialist and Developing Countries*, London: Routledge.

Attah, E. B. (1973), 'Racial aspects of zero population growth', *Science*, 180: 1143.

Bachrach, P. and M. Baratz (1962), 'Two faces of power', *American Political Science Review*, 56: 947–52.

Bachrach, P. and M. Baratz, (1963), 'Decisions and nondecisions: an analytical framework', *American Political Science Review*, 57: 632–42.

Bader, V. (1995), 'Citizenship and exclusion: radical democracy, community and justice', *Political Theory*, 23(2): 211–46.

Baggaley, A. (ed.) (2001), *Human Body*, London: Dorling Kindersley.

Baker, G. (2002a), *Civil Society and Democratic Theory: Alternative Voices*, London and New York: Routledge.

Baker, G. (2002b), 'Problems in the theorisation of global civil society', *Political Studies*, 50(5): 928–43.

Ball, T., J. Farr and R. Hanson (eds) (1989), *Political Innovation and Conceptual Change*, Cambridge and New York: Cambridge University Press.

Ballard, J. G. (1985), *Crash*, New York: Vintage.

Barash, D. (1977), *Sociology and Behavior*, New York: Elsevier.

Barber, B. (1984), *Strong Democracy: Participatory Politics for a New Age*, Berkeley: University of California Press.

Barber, B. (1996), *Jihad vs. McWorld*, New York: Ballantine.

Barkow, J, L. Cosmides and J. Tooby (1992), *The Adapted Mind: Evolutionary Psychology and the Generation of Culture*, New York: Oxford University Press.

Barlow, J. (1990), 'Being in nothingness: virtual reality and the pioneers of cyberspace', *Mondo 2000*, 2: 34–43.

Barry, B. (1989), *Theories of Justice*, Hemel Hempstead: Harvester Wheatsheaf.

Barry, B. (1991), 'Self-government revisited', in *Democracy and Power: Essays in Political Theory*, Oxford: Oxford University Press, pp. 156–86.

Barry, B. (1995), *Justice as Impartiality*, Oxford: Clarendon Press.

Barthes, R. (1993), *Mythologies*, tr. A. Lavers, London: Vintage.

Bastow, S. and J. Martin (2003), *Third Way Discourse*, Edinburgh: Edinburgh University Press.

Baudrillard, J. (1988), *America*, New York: Verso.

Baumeister, A. (2000), *Liberalism and the 'Politics of Difference'*, Edinburgh: Edinburgh University Press.

Baylis, J. and S. Smith (2001), *The Globalization of World Politics*, Oxford: Oxford University Press.

Beck, U. (1995), *Ecological Politics in an Age of Risk*, Cambridge: Polity Press.

Beetham, D. (1999), *Democracy and Human Rights*, Cambridge: Polity Press.

Bell, D. (1993), *Communitarianism and Its Critics*, Oxford: Oxford University Press.

Bell, D. (2000), *East Meets West: Human Rights and Democracy in East Asia*, Princeton, NJ: Princeton University Press.

Bellamy, R. (2000), *Rethinking Liberalism*, London: Pinter.

Benedict, R. (1934), *Patterns of Culture*, London: Routledge and Kegan Paul.

Beneria, L. and S. Feldman (eds) (1992), *Unequal Burden: Economic Crises, Persistent Poverty, and Women's Work*, Boulder, CO: Westview Press.

Benhabib, S. (1996), 'Toward a deliberative model of democratic legitimacy', in S. Benhabib (ed.), *Democracy and Difference: Contesting the Boundaries of the Political*, Princeton, NJ: Princeton University Press, pp. 67–94.

Bentham, J. ([1802] 1859), *Of the Influence of Time and Place in Matters of Legislation*, in *Works, vol. 1*, ed. J. Bowring, Edinburgh: William Tait, pp.171–94.

Bergsten, C. (1996), 'Globalizing free trade', *Foreign Affairs*, 75(3): 105–20.

Berlin, I. (1969), *Two Concepts of Liberty*, Oxford: Oxford University Press.

Berlin, I. ([1969] 2002), *Four Essays on Liberty*, in *Liberty*, ed. H. Hardy, Oxford: Oxford University Press.

Berry, C. (1986), *Human Nature*, Basingstoke: Macmillan.

Bessette, J. (1994), *The Mild Voice of Reason: Deliberative Democracy and American National Government*, London: University of Chicago Press.

Betzig, L. (1997), *Human Nature: A Critical Reader*, New York: Oxford University Press.

Beynon, J. and D. Dunkerley (eds) (2000), *Globalization: The Reader*, London: Athlone Press.

Binder, G. (1993), 'The case for self-determination', *Stanford Journal of International Law*, 29: 223–70.

Blank, R. (1981), *The Political Implications of Human Genetic Technology*, Boulder, CO: Westview Press.

Bobbio, N. (1987), *Which Socialism?*, tr. R. Griffin, Minneapolis: University of Minnesota Press.

Bohman, J. (1996), *Public Deliberation: Pluralism, Complexity and Democracy*, Cambridge, MA: MIT Press.

Bohman, J. (1998), 'The coming of age of deliberative democracy', *Journal of Political Philosophy*, 6(4): 400–25.

Bourdieu, P. (1996), *The State Nobility*, tr. L. Clough, Cambridge: Polity Press.

Bourdieu, P. (1998a), *Acts of Resistance*, Cambridge: Polity Press.

Bourdieu, P. (1998b), *Practical Reason: On the Theory of Action*, Cambridge: Polity Press.

Bouthoul, G. (1970), *L'Infanticide différé*, Paris: Hachette.

Boutros-Ghali, B. (1995), remarks to the World Summit for Social Development, Copenhagen, 5–12 March.

Bracton, H. de (1968), *On the Laws and Customs of England*, ed. S. Thorne, Cambridge, MA: Harvard University Press.

Brass, P. (1979), 'Elite groups, symbol manipulation and ethnic identity and the Muslims of South Asia', in D. Taylor and M. Yapp (eds), *Political Identity in South Asia*, London: Curzon Press, pp. 85–105.

Brass, P. (1991), *Ethnicity and Nationalism: Theory and Comparison*, New Delhi and Beverly Hills: Sage.

Brecher, J. and T. Costello (1994), *Global Village or Global Pillage: Economic Reconstruction from the Bottom Up*, Boston: South End Press.

Brennan, G. and A. Hamlin (1999), 'On Political Representation', *British Journal of Political Science*, 29.

Brennan, G. and L. Lomasky (1993), *Democracy and Decision: The Pure Theory of Electoral Preference*, Cambridge: Cambridge University Press.

Brennan, G. and P. Pettit (2003), *The Economy of Esteem*, Oxford: Oxford University Press.

Breuilly, J. (1993), *Nationalism and the State*, 2nd ed., Manchester: Manchester University Press.

Brown, W. (1995), *States of Injury: Power and Freedom in Late Modernity*, Princeton, NJ: Princeton University Press.

Brubaker, R. (1996), *Nationalism Reframed: Nationhood and the National Question in the New Europe*, Cambridge: Cambridge University Press.

Brubaker, R. (1998), 'Myths and misconceptions in the study of nationalism', in J. Hall (ed.), *The State of the Nation: Ernest Gellner and the Theory of Nationalism*, Cambridge and New York: Cambridge University Press, pp. 272–306.

Brubaker, R. (2002), 'Ethnicity without groups', *Archives Européennes de Sociologie*, 43(2): 163–89.

Bryan, L. and D. Farrell (1996), *Market Unbound: Unleashing Global Capitalism*, New York: John Wiley.

Brzezinski, Z. (1993), *Out of Control: Global Turmoil on the Eve of the Twenty-first Century*, New York: Charles Scribner's Sons.

Buchanan, A. (1991), *Secession: The Legitimacy of Political Divorce*, Boulder, CO: Westview Press.

Budge, I. (1996), *The New Challenge of Direct Democracy*, Cambridge: Polity Press.

Budge, I. (2000), 'Deliberative democracy versus direct democracy – plus political parties!', in M. Saward (ed.), *Innovations in Democracy*, London: Routledge, pp. 195–209.

Budhoo, D. (1990), *Enough Is Enough*, New York: Apex.

Burke, E. (1996a), 'Speech at the conclusion of the poll (3 November 1774)', in P. Langford (ed.), *The Writings and Speeches of Edmund Burke*, Oxford: Clarendon Press, pp. 63–70.

Burke, E. (1996b), 'Speech on conciliation with America (22 March 1775)', in P. Langford (ed.), *The Writings and Speeches of Edmund Burke*, Oxford: Clarendon Press, pp. 102–69.

Burtless, G. et al. (1998), *Globaphobia: Confronting Fears about Open Trade*, Washington: Brookings Institution.

Butler, J. (1990), *Gender Trouble: Feminism and the Subversion of Identity*, London: Routledge.

Butler, J. (1993), *Bodies That Matter: On the Discursive Limits of Sex*, London: Routledge.

Bygrave, M. (2002), 'Where did all the protestors go?', *Observer*, 14 July.

Caldwell, L. (1964), 'Biopolitics: science, ethics, and public policy', *Yale Review*, 54: 1–16.

Calhoun, C. (1997), *Nationalism*, Buckingham: Open University Press.

Camilleri, J. and J. Falk (1992), *The End of Sovereignty*, Aldershot: Edward Elgar.

Campbell, D. (1972), 'On the genetics of altruism and the counter-hedonic components in human culture', *Journal of Social Issues*, 28: 21–37.

Carens, J. (1987), 'Aliens and citizens: the case for open borders', *Review of Politics*, 49(3): 251–73.

Castles, S. and A. Davidson (2000), *Globalisation and Citizenship*, Basingstoke: Macmillan.

Chambers, I. (1986), *Urban Rhythms: Pop Music and Popular Culture*, London: Macmillan.

Chandler, D. (2003), 'New rights for old? Cosmopolitan citizenship and the critique of state sovereignty', *Political Studies*, 51(2): 332–49.

Chossudovsky, M. (1997), *The Globalisation of Poverty: Impacts of IMF and World Bank Reforms*, London: Zed.

Christiano, T. (1996), *The Rule of the Many: Fundamental Issues in Democratic Theory*, Oxford: Westview Press.

Christiano, T. (1997), 'The significance of public deliberation', in J. Bohman and W. Rehg (eds), *Deliberative Democracy*, Cambridge, MA: MIT Press, pp. 243–77.

Clark, K. (1971), 'The pathos of power', presidential address to the American Psychological Association Convention, Washington.

Cockburn, A. (1987), 'The defense intellectual: Edward N. Luttwak', *Grand Street*, 6(3): 161–74.

Cohen, G. A. (1983), 'The structure of proletarian unfreedom', *Philosophy and Public Affairs*, 12(1): 3–33.

Cohen, G. A. (1989a), 'On the currency of egalitarian justice', *Ethics*, 99.

Cohen, G. A. (1991), 'Capitalism, freedom, and the proletariat', in D. Miller (ed.), *Liberty*, Oxford: Oxford University Press.

Cohen, G. A. (1995), *Self-ownership, Freedom and Equality*, Cambridge: Cambridge University Press.

Cohen, G. A. (1997), 'Where the action is: on the site of distributive justice', *Philosophy and Public Affairs*, 26: 3–30.

Cohen, G. A. (2001), 'Freedom and money', *Revista Argentina de Teoría Jurídica*, 2(2): 1–32. <http://www.utdt.edu/departamentos/derecho/publicaciones/rtj1/pdf/finalfreedom.pdf> [Accessed 16 May 2005]

Cohen, J. (1989b), 'Deliberation and democratic legitimacy', in A. Hamlin and P. Pettit (eds), *The Good Polity: Normative Analysis of the State*, Oxford: Blackwell, pp. 17–35.

Cohen, J. (1998), 'Democracy and liberty', in J. Elster (ed.), *Deliberative Democracy*, Cambridge: Cambridge University Press, pp. 185–231.

Cohen, J. and A. Arato (1994), *Civil Society and Political Theory*, Cambridge, MA and London: MIT Press.

Cohen, J. and J. Rogers (1983), *On Democracy: Toward a Transformation of American Society*, New York: Penguin.

Cohen, J. and J. Rogers (1995), 'Secondary associations and democratic governance', in E. Wright (ed.), *Associations and Democracy*, New York: Verso, pp. 7–98.

Colás, A. (2002), *International Civil Society: Social Movements in World Politics*, Cambridge: Polity Press.

Colebrook, C. (2002), *Gilles Deleuze*, London: Routledge.

Commoner, B. (1972), *The Closing Circle: Confronting the Environmental Crisis*, London: Jonathan Cape.

Connolly, W. E. (1991), 'Democracy and territoriality', *Millennium*, 20(3): 463–84.

Connolly, W. E. ([1974] 1993a), *The Terms of Political Discourse*, 3rd ed., Oxford: Blackwell.

Connolly, W. E. (1993b), 'Beyond good and evil: the ethical sensibility of Michel Foucault', *Political Theory*, 21(3): 365–89.

Connor, W. (1972), 'Nation-building or nation-destroying', *World Politics*, 24: 319–55.

Connor, W. (1973), 'The politics of ethnonationalism', *Journal of International Affairs*, 27(1): 1–21.

Constant, B. ([1819] 1988), 'The liberty of the ancients compared with that of the moderns', in *Political Writings*, tr. and ed. B. Fontana, Cambridge: Cambridge University Press.

Cornell, D. (1998), *At the Heart of Freedom: Feminism, Sex, and Equality*, Princeton, NJ: Princeton University Press.

Cornia, G., R. Jolly and F. Stewart (1987–8), *Adjustment with a Human Face*, 2 vols, Oxford: Clarendon Press.

Corning, P. (1971), *Evolutionary Indicators*, Boulder: University of Colorado Institute of Behavior Genetics.

Corning, P. (1977), 'Human nature redivivus', in J. Pennock and J. Chapman (eds), *Human Nature in Politics*, New York: New York University Press, pp. 19–68.

Corning, P. and C. Corning (1972), 'Toward a general theory of violent aggression', *Social Science Information*, 11: 7–35.

Corover, S. (1973). 'Big Brother and psychotechnology', *Psychology Today*, October.

Crowder, G. (2002), *Liberalism and Value Pluralism*, London: Continuum.

Cvetkovich, A. and D. Kellner (eds) (1997), *Articulating the Global and the Local*, Boulder, CO: Westview Press.

Dahl, R. (1956), *A Preface to Democratic Theory*, Chicago: University of Chicago Press.

Dahl, R. (1961), *Who Governs? Democracy and Power in an American City*, New Haven: Yale University Press.

Dahl, R. (1968a), 'A critique of the ruling elite model', in R. Dahl and D. Neubauer (eds), *Readings in Modern Political Analysis*, Englewood Cliffs, NJ: Prentice Hall.

Dahl, R. (1968b), 'Power', in D. L. Sills (ed.), *International Encyclopaedia of the Social Sciences, vol. 12*, London: Cromwell Collier and Macmillan.

Dahl, R. (1971), *Polyarchy: Participation and Opposition*, New Haven: Yale University Press.

Dahl, R. (1989), *Democracy and Its Critics*, New Haven and London: Yale University Press.

Dahl, R. (1994), 'A democratic dilemma: system effectiveness versus citizen participation', *Political Science Quarterly*, Spring, 23–34.

Dalby, S. (1988), 'Geopolitical discourse: the Soviet Union as Other', *Alternatives*, 13: 415–442.

Dalby, S. (1990a), 'American security discourse: the persistence of geopolitics', *Political Geography Quarterly*, 9: 171–88.

Dalby, S. (1990b), *Creating the Second Cold War: The Discourse of Politics*, London: Pinter.

Daly, M. and M. Wilson (1992), 'The man who mistook his wife for a chattel', in J. Barkow, L. Cosmides and J. Tooby (eds), *The Adapted Mind: Evolutionary Psychology and the Generation of Culture*, New York: Oxford University Press, pp. 289–322.

Davis, M. (1986), *Prisoners of the American Dream*, London: Verso.

Dawkins, R. (1976), *The Selfish Gene*, New York: Oxford University Press.

De Waal, F. (1989), *Chimpanzee Politics*, Baltimore: Johns Hopkins University Press.

Deacon, B. (1997), *Global Social Policy: International Organizations and the Future of Welfare*, London: Sage.

Dearden, J. (1974), 'Sex linked differences of political behavior', *Social Science Information*, 13: 19–45.

Deleuze, G. and F. Guattari (1984), *Anti-Oedipus*, London: Athlone Press.

Deleuze, G. and F. Guattari (1988), *A Thousand Plateaus: Capitalism and Schizophrenia*, London: Athlone Press.

Deleuze, G. and F. Guattari (1994), *What is Philosophy?*, London:Verso.

Deutsch, K. (1963), *The Nerves of Government*, New York: Free Press.

DeVore, I. and S. Washburn (1967), 'Baboon ecology and human evolution', in N. Korn and F. Thompson (eds), *Human Evolution*, New York: Holt, Rinehart and Winston, pp. 137–60.

Diamond, L. and M. Plattner (eds) (1996), *The Global Resurgence of Democracy*, 2nd ed., Baltimore: Johns Hopkins University Press.

Dion, S. (1991), 'Le nationalisme dans la convergence culturelle', in R. Hudon and R. Pelletier (eds), *L'Engagement intellectuel: mélanges en l'honneur de Léon Dion*, Sainte-Foy, Que.: Presses de l'Université Laval, pp. 291–311.

Dion, S. (1992), 'Explaining Quebec nationalism', in R. Kent Weaver (ed.), *The Collapse of Canada?*, Washington: Brookings Institute.

Donnelly, J. (1982), 'Human rights as natural rights', *Human Rights Quarterly*, 4, 391–405.

Donnelly, J. (2003), *Universal Human Rights in Theory and Practice*, 2nd ed., Ithaca, NY: Cornell University Press.

Dreben, B. (2003), 'On Rawls and political liberalism', in S. Freeman (ed.), *The Cambridge Companion to Rawls*, Cambridge: Cambridge University Press, pp. 316–46.

Dryzek, J. (1990), *Discursive Democracy: Politics, Policy and Political Science*, Cambridge: Cambridge University Press.

Dryzek, J. (2000), *Deliberative Democracy and Beyond: Liberals, Critics, Contestations*, Oxford: Oxford University Press.

Dunleavy, P. and B. O'Leary (1987), *Theories of the State*, London: Macmillan.

Dunn, R. (1972), *Sugar and Slaves: The Rise of the Planter Class in the English West Indies 1624–1713*, New York: W. W. Norton.

Duso, G. (1988), *La rappresentanza: un problema di filosofia politica*, Milan: Franco Angeli.

Duso, G. (ed.) (1999), *Il potere: per la storia della filosofia politica moderna*, Rome: Carrocci.

Dworkin, R. (1977), *Taking Rights Seriously*, London: Duckworth.

Dworkin, R. (1985), *A Matter of Principle*, Cambridge, MA: Harvard University Press.

Dworkin, R. (1986), *Law's Empire*, Cambridge, MA: Harvard University Press.

Dworkin, R. (1988), *Law's Empire*, Oxford: Hart.

Dworkin, R. (1989), 'Liberal community', *California Law Review*, 77(3): 479–504.

Dyson, K. (1980), *The State Tradition in Western Europe*, Oxford: Martin Robertson.

Dyzenhaus, D. (ed.) (1998), *Law as Politics: Carl Schmitt's Critique of Liberalism*, Durham, NC and London: Duke University Press.

Eade, J. (1997), *Living the Global City: Globalization in Local Process*, London: Routledge.

Easton, D. (1965a), *A Framework for Political Analysis*, Englewood Cliffs, NJ: Prentice Hall.

Easton, D. (1965b), *A Systems Analysis of Political Life*, New York: John Wiley.

Edelman, M. (1964), *Symbolic Uses of Politics*, Urbana: University of Illinois Press.

Edwards, J. (1985), *Language, Society and Identity*, Oxford: Blackwell.

Ekeh, P. (1990), 'Social anthropology and two contrasting uses of tribalism in Africa', *Comparative Studies in Society and History*, 32(4): 660–700.

Elster, J. (1979), *Ulysses and the Sirens*, Cambridge: Cambridge University Press.

Elster, J. (1982), 'Sour grapes', in A. Sen and B. Williams (eds), *Utilitarianism and Beyond*, Cambridge: Cambridge University Press, pp. 219–38.

Elster, J. (1983), *Sour Grapes*, Cambridge: Cambridge University Press.

Elster, J. (1986), 'The market and the forum: three varieties of political theory', in J. Elster and A. Hylland (eds), *The Foundations of Social Choice Theory*, Cambridge: Cambridge University Press, pp. 103–32.

Elster, J. (1998), 'Introduction', in J. Elster (ed.), *Deliberative Democracy*, Cambridge: Cambridge University Press, pp. 1–19.

Elstub, S. (2004), 'Cultivating autonomy: a case for deliberative and associational democracy', unpublished Ph.D. thesis, University of Sheffield.

Estlund, D. (1997), 'Beyond epistemic fairness and deliberation: the epistemic dimension of democratic authority', in J. Bohman and W. Rehg (eds), *Deliberative Democracy*, Cambridge, MA: MIT Press, pp. 3–33.

Etzioni, A. (1993), *The Spirit of Community: Rights, Responsibilities, and the Comm-unitarian Agenda*, New York: Crown.

Etzioni, A. (ed.) (1995), *New Communitarian Thinking: Persons, Virtues, Institutions, and Communities*, London: University Press of Virginia.

Etzioni, A. (1997), *The New Golden Rule: Community and Morality in a Democratic Society*, New York: Basic Books.

Etzioni, A. (2000), *The Third Way to a Good Society*, London: Demos.

Etzioni, A. (2001), *The Monochrome Society*, Princeton, NJ: Princeton University Press.

Evans, P., D. Rueschemeyer and T. Skocpol (1985), *Bringing the State Back In*, Cambridge: Cambridge University Press.

Falk, R. (1992), *Explorations at the Edge of Time: The Prospects for World Order*, Philadelphia: Temple University Press.

Falk, R. (1993), 'Global apartheid', *Third World Resurgence*, 37: 15–16.

Fearon, J. (1998), 'Deliberation as discussion', in J. Elster (ed.), *Deliberative Democracy*, Cambridge: Cambridge University Press, pp. 44–68.

Featherstone, M. (1991), *Consumer Culture and Postmodernism*, London: Sage.

Femia, J. (1996), 'Complexity and deliberative democracy', *Inquiry*, 39: 361–97.

Festenstein, M. (2002), 'Deliberation, citizenship and identity', in M. Passerin d'Entrèves (ed.), *Democracy as Public Deliberation: New Perspectives*, Manchester: Manchester University Press, pp. 88–111.

Fields, A. B. (2003), *Rethinking Human Rights for the New Millennium*, New York: Palgrave Macmillan.

Finley, M. (1973), *Democracy: Ancient and Modern*, London: Chatto and Windus.

Finnis, J. (1979), *Natural Law and Natural Rights*, Oxford: Clarendon Press.

Fishkin, J. (1991), *Democracy and Deliberation*, New Haven and London: Yale University Press.

Fishkin, J. and R. Luskin (2000), 'The quest for deliberative democracy', in M. Saward (ed.), *Innovations in Democracy*, London: Routledge, pp. 17–27.

Flora, C. (1990), 'Rural peoples in a global economy', *Rural Sociology*, 55(2): 157–77.

Føllesdal, D. and R. Hilpinen (1971), 'Deontic logic: an introduction', in R. Hilpinen (ed.), *Deontic Logic: Introductory and Systematic Readings*, Dordrecht: Reidel, pp. 1–35.

Forgacs, D. (ed.) (1988), *A Gramsci Reader: Selected Writings 1916–1935*, London: Lawrence and Wishart.

Fortes, M. and E. E. Evans-Pritchard (1940), *African Political Systems*, London: Oxford University Press.

Foucault, M. (1965), *Madness and Civilization: A History of Insanity in the Age of Reason*, London: Routledge and Kegan Paul.

Foucault, M. (1970), *The Order of Things: An Archaeology of the Human Sciences*, London: Tavistock Press.

Foucault, M. (1972), *The Archaeology of Knowledge*, London: Routledge and Kegan Paul.

Foucault, M. (1977), *Discipline and Punish: The Birth of the Prison*, London: Allen Lane/New York: Vintage.

Foucault, M. (1978), *The History of Sexuality, vol. 1: An Introduction*, Harmondsworth: Penguin/New York: Vintage.

Foucault, M. (1979), *The History of Sexuality, vol. 1: An Introduction*, London: Allen Lane.

Foucault, M. (1980), *Power/Knowledge*, ed. C. Gordon, Brighton: Harvester Press/New York: Pantheon.

Foucault, M. (1983), 'The subject and power', in H. Dreyfus and P. Rabinow, *Michel Foucault: Beyond Structuralism and Hermeneutics*, Chicago: University of Chicago Press.

Foucault, M. (1986), *The History of Sexuality, vol. 2: The Use of Pleasure*, Harmondsworth: Viking.

Foucault, M. (1988a), *The History of Sexuality, vol. 3: The Care of the Self*, London: Allen Lane.

Foucault, M. (1988b), 'The political technology of individuals', in L. Martin, H. Gutman and P. Hutton (eds), *Technologies of the Self: A Seminar with Michel Foucault*, London: Tavistock.

Foucault, M. (1991a), 'Governmentality', in G. Burchell, C. Gordon and P. Miller (eds), *The Foucault Effect: Studies in Governmental Rationality*, Hemel Hempstead: Harvester Wheatsheaf.

Foucault, M. (1991b), *Remarks on Marx: Conversations with Duccio Trombadori*, tr. J. Goldstein and J. Cascaito, New York: Semiotext(e).

Foucault, M. (1997), *The Essential Works of Michel Foucault, vol. 1: Ethics*, ed. P. Rabinow, Harmondsworth: Penguin.

Fox, R. (1967), 'In the beginning: aspects of hominid behavioral evolution', *Man*, 2: 415–33.

Fraser, N. (1989), *Unruly Practices: Power, Discourse and Gender in Contemporary Social Theory*, Cambridge: Polity Press.

Fraser, N. (1992), 'Rethinking the public sphere: a contribution to the critique of actually existing democracy', in C. Calhoun (ed.), *Habermas and the Public Sphere*, Cambridge, MA: MIT Press, pp. 107–42.

Frazer, E. (1999), *The Problems of Communitarian Politics: Unity and Conflict*, Oxford: Oxford University Press.

Frederick, H. (1993), 'Computer networks and the emergence of global civil society', in L. Harasim (ed.), *Global Networks: Computers and International Communication*, Cambridge, MA: MIT Press, pp. 283–95.

Freeden, M. (1996), *Ideologies and Political Theory: A Conceptual Approach*, Oxford: Oxford University Press.

Freedom House (2004), *Freedom in the World 2003: The Annual Survey of Political Rights and Civil Liberties*, Lanham, MD: Rowman and Littlefield. <http://www.freedomhouse.org/research/freeworld/2003/index.htm> [Accessed 25 October 2004]

Freeman, M. (2002), *Human Rights: An Interdisciplinary Approach*, Cambridge: Polity Press.

Frost, M. (2002), *Constituting Human Rights: Global Civil Society and the Society of Democratic States*, London: Routledge.

Fuentes, A. and B. Ehrenreich (1983), *Women in the Global Factory*, Boston: South End Press.

Fukuyama, F. (1992), *The End of History and the Last Man*, London: Hamish Hamilton.

Fuller, L. (1969), *The Morality of Law*, rev. ed., New Haven and London: Yale University Press.

Galle, O., W. Gove and J. McPherson (1972), 'Population density and pathology: what are the relations for man?', *Science*, 176: 23–30.

Gallie, W. E. (1956), 'Essentially contested concepts', *Proceedings of the Aristotelian Society*, 56: 167–98.

Gal-Or, B. (1972), 'The crisis about the origin of irreversibility and time anistropy', *Science*, 176: 11–17.

Gambetta, D. (1998), '"Claro!": an essay on discursive machismo', in J. Elster (ed.), *Deliberative Democracy*, Cambridge: Cambridge University Press, pp. 19–43.

Gamble, A. (1994), *The Free Economy and the Strong State: The Politics of Thatcherism*, Basingstoke: Macmillan.

Garner, R. (2003), 'Animals, politics and justice: Rawlsian liberalism and the plight of non-humans', *Environmental Politics*, 12(2): 3–22.

Gaus, G. (1997), 'Reason, justification, and consensus: why democracy can't have it all', in J. Bohman and W. Rehg (eds), *Deliberative Democracy*, Cambridge, MA: MIT Press, pp. 205–42.

Geertz, C. (1963), 'The integrative revolution: primordial sentiments and civil policies in the new states', in C. Geertz (ed.), *Old Societies and New States: The Quest for Modernity in Asia and Africa*, New York: Free Press, pp. 107–13.

Geertz, C. (1972), *The Interpretation of Cultures: Selected Essays*, New York: Basic Books.

Geertz, C. (1993), *The Interpretation of Cultures: Selected Essays*, London: Fontana Press.

Gellner, E. (1983), *Nations and Nationalism*, Oxford: Blackwell.

Gellner, E. (1996), *Conditions of Liberty*, Harmondsworth: Penguin.

Geras, N. (1983), *Marx and Human Nature*, London: Verso.

Ghai, D. (ed.) (1991), *The IMF and the South: The Social Impact of Adjustment*, London; Zed.

Giddens, A. (1984), *The Constitution of Society: Outline of the Theory of Structuration*, Cambridge: Polity Press.

Giddens, A. (1988): *The Third Way: The Renewal of Social Democracy*, Cambridge: Polity Press.

Giddens, A. (1990), *The Consequences of Modernity*, Cambridge: Polity Press.

Giddens, A. (1999), 'Globalisation', in *Runaway World: How Globalisation is Reshaping Our Lives*, London: Profile Books.

Gill, S. (1995), 'Globalisation, market civilisation, and disciplinary neoliberalism', *Millennium*, 24(3): 399–423.

Gill, S. (1996), 'Globalization, democratization, and the politics of indifference', in J. Mittelman (ed.), *Globalization: Critical Reflections*, Boulder, CO: Rienner, pp. 205–28.

Gilligan, C. (1982), *In a Different Voice*, London: Harvard University Press.

Gills, B. (ed.) (1997), 'Globalisation and the politics of resistance', special issue, *New Political Economy*, 2(1).

Gills, B., J. Rocamora and R. Wilson (eds) (1993), *Low Intensity Democracy: Political Power in the New World Order*, London: Pluto Press.

Gleick, J. (1987), *Chaos*, New York: Viking.

Godwin, W. ([1798] 1976), *Enquiry Concerning Political Justice*, ed. I. Kramnick, Harmondsworth: Penguin.

Golding, P. and P. Harris (eds) (1997), *Beyond Cultural Imperialism: Globalization, Communication and the New International Order*, London: Sage.

Goldman, A. (1972), 'Toward a theory of social power', *Philosophical Studies*, 23: 221–68.

Goodin, R. (1989), 'The state as a moral agent', in A. Hamlin and P. Pettit (eds), *The Good Polity: Normative Analysis and the State*, Oxford: Blackwell.

Goodin, R. (2003), 'Democratic deliberation within', in J. Fishkin and P. Laslett (eds), *Debating Deliberative Democracy*, Oxford: Blackwell, pp. 54–79.

Gould, C. (1988), *Rethinking Democracy: Freedom and Social Co-operation in Politics, Economics, and Society*, New York: Cambridge University Press.

Gramsci, A. (1971), *Selections from the Prison Notebooks*, New York: International.

Gray, C. (1988), *The Geopolitics of Superpower*, Lexington: University of Kentucky Press.

Gray, H. ([1858] 2001), *Anatomy: Descriptive and Surgical*, facsimile of 1858 ed., London: Grange.

Gray, J. (1998), *False Dawn: The Delusions of Global Capitalism*, London: Granta.

Gray, J. (2000), *Two Faces of Liberalism*, Cambridge: Polity Press.

Green, L. (1988), *The Authority of the State*, Oxford: Clarendon Press.

Green, P. and M. Walzer (eds) (1969), *The Political Imagination in Literature*, New York: Free Press.

Green, T. H. ([1885] 1927), *Lectures on the Principles of Political Obligation*, London: Longmans, Green and Co.

Green, T. H. ([1888] 1991), 'Liberal legislation and freedom of contract', in D. Miller, (ed.), *Liberty*, Oxford: Oxford University Press.

Greenfeld, L. (1992), *Nationalism. Five Roads to Modernity*, Cambridge, MA: Harvard University Press.

Greider, W. (1997), *One World, Ready or Not: The Manic Logic of Global Capitalism*, London: Allen Lane.

Gruter, M. and R. Masters (eds) (1986), *Ostracism: A Social and Biological Phenomenon*, New York: Elsevier.

Gullberg, J. (1997), *Mathematics: From the Birth of Numbers*, New York and London: W. W. Norton.

Gundersen, A. (2000), *The Socratic Citizen: A Theory of Deliberative Democracy*, Oxford: Lexington.

Gutmann, A. and D. Thompson (1996), *Democracy and Disagreement*, London: Harvard University Press.

Haas, P., R. Keohane and M. Levy (eds) (1993), *Institutions for the Earth: Sources of Effective International Environmental Protection*, Cambridge, MA: MIT Press.

Habermas, J. (1975), *The Legitimation Crisis of Late Capitalism*, tr. T. McCarthy, Boston: Beacon Press/London: Heinemann.

Habermas, J. (1977), 'Hannah Arendt's communications concept of power', *Social Research*, 44(1): 3–24.

Habermas, J. (1979), *Communication and the Evolution of Society*, tr. T. McCarthy, London: Heinemann.

Habermas, J. (1984), *The Theory of Communicative Action, vol. 1: Reason and the Rationalization of Society*, tr. T. McCarthy, Boston: Beacon Press.

Habermas, J. (1987a), *The Philosophical Discourse of Modernity*, Cambridge: Polity Press.

Habermas, J. (1987b), *The Theory of Communicative Action, vol. 2: Lifeworld and System*, tr. T. McCarthy, Cambridge: Polity Press.

Habermas, J. (1989), *The Structural Transformation of the Public Sphere*, Cambridge: Polity Press.

Habermas, J. (1990a), 'Discourse ethics: notes on a program of philosophical justification', in J. Habermas, *Moral Consciousness and Communicative Action*, tr. C. Lenhardt and S. W. Nicholsen, Cambridge, MA: MIT Press, pp. 43–115.

Habermas, J. (1990b), *Moral Consciousness and Communicative Action*, Cambridge: Polity Press.

Habermas, J. (1994), 'Struggles for recognition in the democratic constitutional state', in C. Taylor, *Multiculturalism: Examining the Politics of Recognition* (ed. A. Gutmann), Princeton, NJ: Princeton University Press.

Habermas, J. (1996a), *Between Facts and Norms: Contributions to a Discourse Theory on Law and Democracy*, Cambridge: Polity Press.

Habermas, J. (1996b), 'Three normative models of democracy', in S. Benhabib (ed.), *Democracy and Difference: Contesting the Boundaries of the Political*, Princeton, NJ: Princeton University Press, pp. 21–30.

Habermas, J. (2000), 'Richard Rorty's pragmatic turn', in R. Brandom (ed.), *Rorty and His Critics*, Oxford: Blackwell.

Hall, J. (1985), *Powers and Liberties*, Oxford: Blackwell.

Hall, J. (ed.) (1986), *States in History*, Oxford: Blackwell.

Halton, E. (1995), 'The modern error: or, the unbearable enlightenment of being', in M. Featherstone, S. Lash and R. Robertson (eds), *Global Modernities*, London: Sage.

Hamilton, A., J. Madison and J. Jay (1948), *The Federalist*, ed. M. Beloff, Oxford: Blackwell.

Hamlin, A. and P. Pettit (eds), *The Good Polity: Normative Analysis and the State*, Oxford: Blackwell.

Hansson, B. (1970), 'An analysis of some deontic logics', *Nous*, 3: 373–98.

Haraway, D. (1985), 'A manifesto for cyborgs: science, technology and socialist feminism in the 1980s', *Socialist Review*, 15: 65–107.

Haraway, D. (1991), *Simians, Cyborgs and Women: The Reinvention of Nature*, London: Free Association.

Harcourt, W. (ed.) (1999), *Women@Internet: Creating New Cultures in Cyberspace*, London: Zed.

Harlow, H. (1971), *Learning to Love*, New York: Ballantine.

Harlow, H. and M. Harlow (1963), 'A study of animal affection', in C. Southwick (ed.), *Primate Social Behavior*, Princeton, NJ: Van Nostrand Reinhold, pp. 174–84.

Hart, M. and A. Negri (2001), *Empire*, Cambridge, MA: Harvard University Press.

Hartsock, N. (1990), 'Foucault on power: a theory for women?', in L. Nicholson (ed.), *Feminism/Postmodernism*, London: Routledge.

Harvey, D. (1989), *The Condition of Postmodernity: An Enquiry into the Conditions of Cultural Change*, Oxford: Blackwell.

Harvey, R. (1995), *The Return of the Strong: The Drift to Global Disorder*, London: Macmillan.

Hawking, S. (1988), *A Brief History of Time*, New York: Bantam.

Hayek, F. (1960), *The Constitution of Liberty*, London: Routledge and Kegan Paul.

Hayek, F. (1979), *The Political Order of a Free People, vol. 3: Law, Legislation and Liberty*, London: Routledge and Kegan Paul.

Hayles, N. (1999), 'The life cycle of cyborgs: writing the posthuman', in J. Wolmark (ed.), *Cybersexualities: A Reader on Feminist Theory, Cyborgs and Cyberspace*, Edinburgh: Edinburgh University Press.

Held, D. (1995a), *Democracy and the Global Order: From the Modern State to Cosmopolitan Governance*, Cambridge: Polity Press.

Held, D. (1995b), 'Democracy and the new international order', in D. Archibugi and D. Held (eds), *Cosmopolitan Democracy: An Agenda for a New World Order*, Cambridge: Polity Press, pp. 96–120.

Held, D. (1996), *Models of Democracy*, 2nd ed., Cambridge: Polity Press.

Held, D. (ed.) (2000), *A Globalizing Word? Culture, Economics, Politics*, London: Routledge.

Held, D. and A. McGrew (1993), 'Globalization and the liberal democratic state', *Government and Opposition*, 28(2): 261–85.

Held, D. and A. McGrew (eds) (2000), *The Global Transformations Reader: An Introduction to the Globalization Debate*, Cambridge: Polity Press.

Held, V. (1984), *Rights and Goods: Justifying Social Action*, New York: Free Press.

Hemphill, M. (1973), 'Pretesting for Huntington's disease', *Hastings Center Report*, 3: 12–13.

Hewison, K. (1999), *Localism in Thailand: A Study of Globalisation and Its Discontents*, Coventry: University of Warwick Centre for the Study of Globalisation and Regionalisation.

Hill, K. and J. Hughes (1998), *Cyberpolitics: Citizen Activism in the Age of the Internet*, Lanham, MD: Rowman and Littlefield.

Hirst, P. (1993), 'Associational Democracy', in D. Held (ed.), *The Prospects for Democracy: North, South, East, West*, Cambridge: Polity Press, pp. 112–35.

Hirst, P. (1994), *Associative Democracy: New Forms of Economic and Social Governance*, Cambridge: Polity Press.

Hobbes, T. ([1651] 1968), *Leviathan*, ed. C. B. Macpherson, Harmondsworth: Penguin.

Hobbes, T. ([1640] 1969), *The Elements of Law: Natural and Politic*, ed. F. Tönnies, 2nd ed., London: Frank Cass.

Hobbes, T ([1651] 1985), *Leviathan*, ed. C. B. Macpherson, Harmondsworth: Penguin.

Hobbes, T. ([1679] 1990), *Behemoth*, ed. F. Tönnies, Chicago: University of Chicago Press.

Hobbes, T. ([1651] 1996), *Leviathan*, ed. J. Gaskin, Oxford: Oxford University Press.

Hobsbawm, E. (1990), *Nations and Nationalism since 1780*, Cambridge: Cambridge University Press.

Hofmann, H. (1974), *Repräsentation, Studien zur Wort- und Begriffsgeschichte von der Antike bis ins 19. Jahrhundert*, Berlin: Duncker & Humbolt.

Hogarth, R. M. (1977), 'Methods for aggregating opinions', in H. Jungermann and G. de Zeeuw (eds), *Decision Making and Change in Human Affairs*, Dordrecht: Reidel, pp. 231–56.

Holden, B. (ed.) (2000), *Global Democracy: Key Debates*, London: Routledge.

Holland, H. Jr (ed.) (1968), *Politics through Literature*, Englewood Cliffs, NJ: Prentice Hall.

Hollis, M. (1997), *Invitation to Philosophy*, 2nd ed., Oxford: Blackwell.

Holm, H. and G. Sørensen (1995), 'International relations theory in a world of variation', in *Whose World Order? Uneven Globalization and the End of the Cold War*, Boulder, CO: Westview Press, pp. 187–206.

Holmes, S. (1995), *Passions and Constraint: On the Theory of Liberal Democracy*, Chicago: University of Chicago Press.

Honohan, I. (2002), *Civic Republicanism*, London: Routledge.

Hoogvelt, A. (1997), *Globalisation and the Postcolonial World: The New Political Economy of Development*, Basingstoke: Macmillan.

Howarth, D. (2000), *Discourse*, Buckingham: Open University Press.

Howarth, D., A. Norvall and Y. Stavrakakis (eds) (2000), *Discourse Theory and Political Analysis*, Manchester: Manchester University Press.

Howes, D. (ed.) (1996), *Cross-cultural Consumption: Global Markets, Local Realities*, London: Routledge.

Hudson, J. (1986), 'The philosophy of immigration', *Journal of Libertarian Studies*, 8(1): 51–62.

Hughes, G. and A. Little (1999), 'The contradictions of New Labour's communitarianism', *Imprints*, 4(1): 37–62.

Hume, D. ([1739] 1978), *A Treatise of Human Nature*, ed. L. A. Selby-Bigge, Oxford: Clarendon Press.

Hume, D. ([1739] 2002), *A Treatise of Human Nature*, ed. D. Norton and M. Norton, Oxford: Oxford University Press.

Hummel, R. (1973), 'A psychology of charisma', paper presented to the 9th Congress of the International Political Science Association, Montreal, August.

Hunter, F. (1953), *Community Power Structure: A Study of Decision-Makers*, Chapel Hill: University of North Carolina Press.

Huntington, S. (1991), *The Third Wave: Democratization in the Late Twentieth Century*, Norman: University of Oklahoma Press.

Hurrell, A. and N. Woods (eds) (1999), *Inequality, Globalization, and World Politics*, Oxford: Oxford University Press.

Hutton, W. (1996), *The State We're In*, rev. ed., London: Vintage.

Hyland, J. L. (1995), *Democratic Theory: The Philosophical Foundations*, Manchester: Manchester University Press.

ICFTU (1998), 'Globalisation on trial', statement of the International Confederation of Free Trade Unions to the Annual Meetings of the IMF and World Bank.

Ignatieff, M. (1993), *Blood and Belonging: Journeys into the New Nationalism*, New York: Farrar, Straus and Giroux.

Ignatieff, M. (2000), *The Rights Revolution*, Toronto: Anansi Press.

Ihde, D. (1990), *Technology and the Lifeworld: From Garden to Earth*, Bloomington: Indiana University Press.

Isaac, G. (1978), 'The food-sharing behavior of protohuman hominids', *Scientific American*, 238: 90–108.

Issues Deliberation Australia (1999), 'Australia deliberates: a republic, yes or no?'. <http://www.ida.org.au/republic.htm>

Jameson, F. (1991), *Postmodernism or the Cultural Logic of Late Capitalism*, London: Verso.

Janis, I. (1972), *Victims of Group-Think*, Boston: Houghton Mifflin.

Jefferson, T. ([1774] 1999), *Summary View of the Rights of British America*, in *Political Writings*, ed. T. Ball and J. Appleby, Cambridge: Cambridge University Press.

Jessop, B. (1990), *State Theory: Putting Capitalist States in Their Place*, Cambridge: Polity Press.

Joekes, S. and A. Weston (1994), *Women and the New Trade Agenda*, New York: UNIFEM.

Johnson, J. (1998), 'Arguing for deliberation: some skeptical considerations', in J. Elster (ed.), *Deliberative Democracy*, Cambridge: Cambridge University Press, pp. 161–84.

Kaldor, M. (2003), *Global Civil Society: An Answer to War*, Cambridge: Polity Press.

Kaldor, M. and R. Falk (1987), *Dealignment: A New Foreign Policy Perspective*, New York: Blackwell.

Kant, I. (1983), 'To perpetual peace: a philosophical sketch', in I. Kant, *Perpetual Peace and other essays*, tr. T. Humphrey, Indianapolis: Hackett.

Kaplan, R. (1994), 'The coming anarchy', *Atlantic Monthly*, 273(2): 44–76.

Kapstein, E. (1996), 'Workers and the world economy', *Foreign Affairs*, 75(3): 16–37.

Kaul, I., I. Grunberg and M. Stern (eds) (1999), *Global Public Goods: International Cooperation in the 21st Century*, New York: Oxford University Press.

Kaviraj, S. and S. Khilnani (eds) (2001), *Civil Society: History and Possibilities*, Cambridge: Cambridge University Press.

Keane, J. (ed.) (1988), *Civil Society and the State: New European Perspectives*, London and New York: Verso.

Keane, J. (1989), 'Introduction', in N. Bobbio, *Dictatorship and Democracy*, tr. P. Kennealy, Cambridge: Polity Press.

Keane, J. (1998), *Civil Society: Old Images, New Visions*,

Keane, J. (2003), *Global Civil Society?*, Cambridge: Cambridge University Press.

Kempadoo, K. and J. Doezema (eds) (1998), *Global Sex Workers: Rights, Resistance, and Redefinition*, London: Routledge.

Kennan, G. (1947), 'The sources of Soviet conduct', *Foreign Affairs*, 25: 566–82.

Kennedy, E. (1985), 'Introduction', in C. Schmitt, *The Crisis of Parliamentary Democracy*, tr. E. Kennedy, Cambridge, MA: MIT Press.

Kenny, M. (2003), 'Communitarianism', in A. Finlayson (ed.), *Contemporary Political Thought: A Reader and Guide*, Edinburgh: Edinburgh University Press.

King, A. (1995), 'The times and spaces of modernity (or who needs post-modernism?)', in M. Featherstone, S. Lash and R. Robertson (eds), *Global Modernities*, London: Sage.

King, T. (1983), 'Immigration from developing countries: some philosophical issues', *Ethics*, 93(3): 525–36.

Kitcher, P. (1985), *Vaulting Ambition: Sociobiology and the Quest for Human Nature*, Cambridge, MA: MIT Press.

Klein, N. (2001), *No Logo*, London: Flamingo.

Knight, J. and J. Johnson (1994), 'Aggregation and deliberation: on the possibility of democratic legitimacy', *Political Theory*, 22(2): 277–96.

Köhler, W. (1959), *The Mentality of Apes*, New York: Vintage.

Kolm, S.-C. (1977), *La transition socialiste*, Paris: Editions du Cerf.

Kolm, S.-C. (1981a), 'Altruismes et efficacités', *Social Science Information*, 20: 293–354.

Kolm, S.-C. (1981b), 'Efficacité et altruisme', *Revue Economique*, 32: 5–31.

Korten, D. (1995), *When Corporations Rule the World*, West Hartford, CT: Kumarian Press.

Kramer, M. (2004), 'On the moral status of the rule of law', *Cambridge Law Journal*, 63(1): 65–97.

Kramer, M. (forthcoming), 'The big bad wolf: legal positivism and its detractors', *Cambridge Law Journal*.

Kuhn, T. (1970), *The Structure of Scientific Revolutions*, London: University of Chicago Press.

Kukathas, C. (1995), 'Are there any cultural rights?', in W. Kymlicka (ed.), *The Rights of Minority Cultures*, Oxford: Oxford University Press, pp. 228–56.

Küng, H. (1991), *Global Responsibility: In Search of a New World Ethic*, London: SCM.

Kymlicka, W. (1989), *Liberalism, Community, and Culture*, Oxford: Clarendon Press.

Kymlicka, W. (1990), *Contemporary Political Philosophy: An Introduction*, Oxford: Oxford University Press.

Kymlicka, W. (1995), *Multicultural Citizenship: A Liberal Theory of Minority Rights*, Oxford: Clarendon Press.

Kymlicka, W. (2002), *Contemporary Political Philosophy: An Introduction*, 2nd ed., Oxford: Oxford University Press.

Lacarrieu, M. and L. Raggio (1997), 'Citizenship within the globalization context: an analysis of trends within Mercosur', *Mankind Quarterly*, 37(3): 263–81.

Laclau, E. (1990), *New Reflections on the Revolutions of Our Time*, London: Verso.

Laclau, E. (1996a), 'Deconstruction, pragmatism, hegemony', in C. Mouffe (ed.), *Deconstruction and Pragmatism*, London: Routledge.

Laclau, E. (1996b), *Emancipation(s)*, London: Verso.

Laclau, E. (2000), 'Identity and hegemony: the role of universality in the constitution of political logics', in J. Butler, E. Laclau and S. Žižek, *Contingency, Hegemony, Universality: Contemporary Dialogues on the Left*, London: Verso.

Laclau, E. (2001), 'Democracy and the question of power', *Constellations*, 8(1): 3–14.

Laclau, E. and C. Mouffe (1985), *Hegemony and Socialist Strategy: Towards a Radical Democratic Politics*, London: Verso.

Laclau, E. and C. Mouffe (1987), 'Post-Marxism without apologies', *New Left Review*, 166.

Laclau, E. and C. Mouffe (2001), *Hegemony and Socialist Strategy: Towards a Radical Democratic Politics*, 2nd edn, London: Verso.

Laclau, E. and L. Zac (1994), 'Minding the Gap: The Subject of Politics', in E. Laclau (ed.), *The Making of Political Identities*, London: Verso.

Lafeber, W. (1963), *The New Empire: An Interpretation of American Expansionism 1860–1898*, Ithaca, NY: Cornell University Press.

Langlois, A. J. (1998), 'Redescribing human rights', *Millennium Journal of International Studies*, 27(1): 1–22.

Langlois, A. J. (2004), 'The elusive ontology of human rights', *Global Society*, 18(3): 243–61.

Laponce, J. (1987), *Languages and Their Territories*, Toronto: University of Toronto Press.

Larsen, R. R. (1973), 'Leaders and non-leaders: speculation on charisma', paper presented to the 45th Meeting of the Southern Political Science Association, Atlanta, November.

Lash, S. and J. Urry (1994), *Economies of Sign and Space*, London: Sage.

Laxer, G. and S. Halperin (eds) (2003), *Global Civil Society and its Limits*, Basingstoke: Palgrave Macmillan.

Lee, E. (1997), *The Labour Movement and the Internet: The New Internationalism*, London: Pluto Press.

Lefort, C. (1986), *The Political Forms of Modern Society: Bureaucracy, Democracy, Totalitarianism*, Cambridge: Polity Press.

Lefort, C. (1988), *Democracy and Political Theory*, Cambridge: Polity Press.

LeHeron, R. (1993), *Globalized Agriculture: Political Choice*, Oxford: Pergamon Press.

Lehrer, K. (1978), 'Consensus and comparison: a theory of social rationality', in C. Hooker, J. Leach and E. McClennen (eds), *Foundations and Applications of Decision Theory, vol. 1: Theoretical Foundations*, Dordrecht: Reidel, pp. 283–310.

Leibniz, G. W. (1988), *Political Writings*, ed. P. Riley, Cambridge: Cambridge University Press.

Lenihan, D. (1991), 'Liberalism and the problem of cultural membership', *Canadian Journal of Law and Jurisprudence*, 4(2): 401–19.

Lévi-Strauss, C. (1963), *Structural Anthropology*, tr. C. Jacobson and B. Schoepf, New York: Basic Books.

Lévi-Strauss, C. ([1944] 1967), 'The social and psychological aspects of chieftainship in a primitive tribe', in R. Cohen and J. Middleton (eds), *Comparative Political Systems*, Garden City, NY: Natural History Press, pp. 5–62.

Lewontin. R., R. Rose and L. Kamin (1984), *Not in Our Genes*, New York: Pantheon.

Lindblom, C. (1965), *The Intelligence of Democracy*, New York: Free Press.

Linklater, A. (1998), *The Transformation of Political Community: Ethical Foundations of the Post-Westphalian Era*, Cambridge: Polity Press.

Lipsey, R. G. and K. Lancaster (1956–7), 'The general theory of the second-best', *Review of Economic Studies*, 24: 11–32.

Little, A. (2002a), 'Community and radical democracy', *Journal of Political Ideologies*, 7(3): 369–82.

Little, A. (2002b), *The Politics of Community: Theory and Practice*, Edinburgh: Edinburgh University Press.

Little, A. (2002c), 'Rethinking civil society: radical politics and the legitimization of unpaid activities', *Contemporary Politics*, 8(2): 103–15.

Little, A. (2004), *Democracy and Northern Ireland: Beyond the Liberal Paradigm?*, London: Palgrave.

Loader, B. (ed.) (1998), *Cyberspace Divide: Equality, Agency, and Policy in the Information Society*, London: Routledge.

Locke, J. ([1690] 1963), *Two Treatises of Civil Government*, ed. P. Laslett, New York: Cambridge University Press.

Locke, J. ([1690] 1965), *Two Treatises of Government*, ed. P Laslett, New York: New American Library.

Locke, J. ([1690] 1988), *Two Treatises of Government*, ed. P. Laslett, Cambridge: Cambridge University Press.

Locke, J. ([1689] 1990), *A Letter Concerning Toleration*, New York: Prometheus.

Locke, J. ([1690] 1993), *Two Treatises of Government*, London: Orion.

Lorenz, K. (1967), *Evolution et modification du comportement*, Paris: Payot.

Lorenz, K. ([1931–63] 1970–1), *Studies in Animal and Human Behavior*, 2 vols, Cambridge, MA: Harvard University Press.

Lukes, S. (1974), *Power: A Radical View*, London: Macmillan.

Lukes, S. (ed.) (1986), *Power*, Oxford: Blackwell.

Lyons, D. (1965), *Forms and Limits of Utilitarianism*, Oxford: Oxford University Press.

MacCallum, G. C. (1967), 'Negative and positive freedom', *Philosophical Review*, 76(3): 312–34.

McClure, K. (1990), 'Difference, diversity, and the limits of toleration', *Political Theory*, 18(3): 361–91.

McCormick, J. (1989), *Reclaiming Paradise: The Global Environmental Movement*, Bloomington: Indiana University Press.

McGrew, A. (ed.) (1997), *The Transformation of Democracy? Globalization and Territorial Democracy*, Cambridge: Polity Press.

McGrew, A. (2000), 'Power shift: from national government to global governance?', in D. Held (ed.), *A Globalizing World? Culture, Economics, Politics*, London: Routledge.

McGuire, M. and M. Raleigh (1986), 'Behavioral and physiological correlates of ostracism', in M. Gruter and R. Masters (eds), *Ostracism: A Social and Biological Phenomenon*, New York: Elsevier, pp. 39–52.

MacIntyre, A. (1981), *After Virtue: A Study in Moral Theory*, London: Duckworth.

MacIntyre, A. (1984), *After Virtue: A Study in Moral Theory*, 2nd ed., Notre Dame, IN: University of Notre Dame Press.

MacKinnon, C. (1987), *Feminism Unmodified: Discourses on Life and Law*, Cambridge, MA: Harvard University Press.

Maclay, G. and H. Knipe (1972), *The Dominant Man*, New York: Delacorte.

MacLean, P. (1983), 'A triangular brief on the evolution of the brain and law', in M. Gruter and P. Bohannan (eds), *Law, Biology, and Culture*, Santa Barbara, CA: Ross-Erikson, pp. 74–90.

McLuhan, M. (1964), *Understanding Media*, London: Routledge.

McMichael, P. (1993), 'World food system restructuring under a GATT regime', *Political Geography*, 12(3): 198–214.

Mc Michael, P. (ed.) (1994), *The Global Restructuring of Agro-Food Systems*, Ithaca, NY: Cornell University Press.

McMichael, P. (1996a), *Development and Social Change: A Global Perspective*, Thousand Oaks, CA: Pine Forge Press.

McMichael, P. (1996b), 'Globalization: myths and realities', *Rural Sociology*, 61(1): 25–55.

Macpherson, C. B. (1977), *The Life and Times of Liberal Democracy*, Oxford: Oxford University Press.

Madison, J., A. Hamilton and J. Jay (1987), *The Federalist Papers*, ed. I. Kramnick, Harmondsworth: Penguin.

Madson, D. (1985a), 'A biochemical property related to power-seeking in humans', *American Political Science Review*, 79: 448–57.

Madson, D. (1985b), 'Power seekers are (biochemically) different: further evidence', paper presented to the Meeting of the International Political Science Association, Paris, July.

Mander, J. and E. Goldsmith (eds) (1996), *The Case against the Global Economy and the Turn to the Local*, San Francisco: Sierra Club.

Manin, B. (1987), 'On legitimacy and political deliberation', *Political Theory*, 5(3), 338–68.

Mann, M. (1986), 'The autonomous power of the state', in J. Hall (ed), *States in History*, Oxford: Blackwell.

Mann, M. (1997), 'Has globalization ended the rise and rise of the nation-state?', *Review of International Political Economy*, 4(3): 472–96.

Mansbridge, J. (1980), *Beyond Adversary Democracy*, London: University of Chicago Press.

Marchand, M. and A. Runyan (eds) (2000), *Gender and Global Restructuring: Sightings, Sites and Resistances*, London: Routledge.

Margalit, A. (1983), 'Ideals and second bests', in S. Fox (ed.), *Philosophy for Education*, Jerusalem: Van Leer Foundation, pp. 77–90.

Margalit, A. and M. Halbertal (1994), 'Liberalism and the right to culture', *Social Research*, 61(3): 491–510.

Margalit, A. and J. Raz (1990), 'National self-determination', *Journal of Philosophy*, 87(9): 439–61.

Markus, R. (1988), *Saeculum: History and Society in the Theology of Saint Augustine*, rev. ed., Cambridge: Cambridge University Press.

Marshall, P. (1993), *Demanding the Impossible: A History of Anarchism*, London: Fontana.

Martin, H.-P. and H. Schumann (1997), *The Global Trap: Globalization and the Assault on Prosperity and Democracy*, London: Zed.

Martin, R. (1985), *Rawls and Rights*, Lawrence: University of Kansas Press.

Martin, R. (1988), 'Truth, power, self: an interview with Michel Foucault', in L. Martin, H. Gutman and P. Hutton (eds), *Technologies of the Self: A Seminar with Michel Foucault*, London: Tavistock.

Martin, R. (2003), 'Rawls', in D. Boucher and P. Kelly (eds), *Political Thinkers: From Socrates to the Present*, Oxford: Oxford University Press, pp. 496–515.

Marx, K. (1975), *Early Writings*, tr. R. Livingstone and G. Benton, Harmondsworth: Penguin.

Marx, K. (1977), *Selected Writings*, ed. D. McLellan, Oxford: Oxford University Press.

Marx, K. (2000), 'On the Jewish question', in *Selected Writings*, ed. D. McLellan, 2nd ed., Oxford: Oxford University Press, pp. 46–64.

Massey, D. (1994), *Space, Place and Gender*, Cambridge: Polity Press.

Masters, R. (1964), 'World politics as a primitive political system', *World Politics*, 16: 595–619.

Masters, R. (1977), 'Nature, human nature, and political thought', in R. Pennock and J. Chapman (eds), *Human Nature in Politics*, New York: New York University Press, pp. 69–110.

Masters, R. (1978), 'Classical political philosophy and contemporary biology', paper presented at the Conference for the Study of Political Thought, Chicago, April.

Masters, R. (1983), 'The duties of humanity: legal and moral obligation in Rousseau's thought', in F. Eidlin (ed.), *Constitutional Democracy: Essays in Comparative Politics*, Boulder, CO: Westview Press, pp. 83–105.

Masters, R. (1989), *The Nature of Politics*, New Haven: Yale University Press.

Maynor, J. (2003), *Republicanism in the Modern World*, Cambridge: Polity Press.

Mayr, E. (1958), 'Behavior and systematics', in A. Roe and G. Simpson (eds), *Behavior and Evolution*, New Haven: Yale University Press, pp. 341–62.

Mayr, E. (1974), 'Teleological and teleonomic: a new analysis', *Boston Studies n the Philosophy of Science*, 14: 91–117.

Mazrui, A. (1994), 'Global apartheid: structural and overt', *Alternatives*, 19(2): 185–7.

Meadows, D. H, D. L. Meadows and J. Randers (1992), *Beyond the Limits: A Global Collapse or a Sustainable Future*, London: Earthscan.

Meadows, D. H, D. L. Meadows, J. Randers and W. Behrens (1972), *The Limits to Growth*, New York: Signet.

Meinig, D. (1986), *The Shaping of America, vol. 1: Atlantic America 1492–1800*, New Haven: Yale University Press.

Michels, R. ([1911] 1959), *Political Parties*, tr. E. and C. Paul, New York: Dover.

Midgaard, K. (1980), 'On the significance of language and a richer concept of rationality', in L. Lewin and E. Vedung (eds), *Politics as Rational Action*, Dordrecht: Reidel, pp. 83–97.

Mill, J. ([1818] 1975), *The History of British India*, ed. W. Thomas, Chicago: University of Chicago Press.

Mill, J. S. ([1859] 1969), *On Liberty*, in *On Liberty and Utilitarianism*, Oxford: Oxford University Press.

Miller, D. (1989), *Market, State, and Community: The Foundations of Market Socialism*, Oxford: Oxford University Press.

Miller, D. (1991), 'Introduction', in D. Miller (ed.), *Liberty*, Oxford: Oxford University Press.

Miller, D. (1993a), 'Deliberative democracy and social choice', in D. Held (ed.), *Prospects for Democracy*, Cambridge: Polity Press, pp. 74–92.

Miller, D. (1993b), 'In defense of nationality', *Journal of Applied Philosophy*, 10(1): 3–16.

Miller, D. (1995), *On Nationality*, Oxford: Clarendon Press.

Miller, D. (2000a), 'Is deliberative democracy unfair to disadvantaged groups?', in *Citizenship and National Identity*, Cambridge: Polity Press, pp. 142–160.

Miller, G. (2000b), *The Mating Mind*, London: Heinemann.

Mills, C. (1956), *The Power Elite*, New York: Oxford University Press.

Mills, S. (1997), *Discourse*, London: Routledge.

Mingst, K. (1999), *Essentials of International Relations*, London: W. W. Norton.

Mittelman, J. and R. Johnston (1999), 'The globalization of organized crime, the courtesan state, and the corruption of civil society', *Global Governance*, 5(1): 103–26.

Monbiot, G. (2003), *The Age of Consent: A Manifesto for a New World Order*, London and New York: Flamingo.

Montaigne, M. de (1991), *The Complete Essays*, ed. M. A. Screech, London: Penguin.

Moon, G. (1995), *Free Trade: What's in It for Women?*, Fitzroy, Vic.: Community Aid Abroad.

Moravec, H. (1988), *Mind Children: The Future of Robot and Human Intelligence*, Cambridge, MA: Harvard University Press.

Morin, E. (1973), *Le Paradigme perdu*, Paris: Editions du Seuil.

Mouffe, C. (1993), *The Return of the Political*, London: Verso.

Mouffe, C. (2000), *The Democratic Paradox*, London: Verso.

Murphy, L. (1998), 'Institutions and the demands of justice', *Philosophy and Public Affairs*, 24(3).

Musonda, R. (1991), 'The significance of modern hunter-gatherers in the study of early hominid behaviour', in R. Foley (ed.), *The Origins of Humans*, London: Unwin Hyman, pp. 39–51.

Muzaffar, C. (1993), *Human Rights and the New World Order*, Penang: Just World Trust.

Nagel, T. (1979), *Mortal Questions*, Cambridge: Cambridge University Press, reprinted in M. Clayton and A. Williams (eds) (2000), *The Ideal of Equality*, Basingstoke: Palgrave Macmillan.

Nagel, T. (2003), 'Rawls and liberalism', in S. Freeman (ed.), *The Cambridge Companion to Rawls*, Cambridge: Cambridge University Press, pp. 62–85.

Nederman, C. and K. Langdon Forhan (1993), *Medieval Political Theory: A Reader: The Quest for the Body Politic 1100–1400*, London: Routledge.

Negus, K. (1996), *Popular Music in Theory*, Cambridge: Polity Press.

Nickel, J. (1995), 'The value of cultural belonging: expanding Kymlicka's theory', *Dialogue*, 33(4): 635–42.

Niebuhr, R. (1932), *Moral Man and Immoral Society*, New York: Scribner's.

Nietzsche, F. ([1901] 1967), *The Will to Power*, tr. W. Kaufmann and R. J. Hollingdale, New York: Vintage.

Nordlinger, E. (1981), *On the Autonomy of the Democratic State*, Cambridge, MA: Harvard University Press.

Norval, A. (1996), *Deconstructing Apartheid Discourse*, London: Verso.

Nozick, R. (1974), *Anarchy, State, and Utopia*, New York: Basic Books/Oxford: Blackwell.

Nussbaum, M. (2003), 'Rawls and feminism', in S. Freeman (ed.), *The Cambridge Companion to Rawls*, Cambridge: Cambridge University Press, pp. 488–520.

Ó Tuathail, G. (1989), 'Critical geopolitics: the social construction of place and space in the practice of statecraft, unpublished PhD thesis, Syracuse University.

Ó Tuathail, G. (1996), *Critical Geopolitics: The Politics of Writing Global Space*, London: Routledge.

Oakeshott, M. (1946), 'Introduction', in T. Hobbes, *Leviathan*, ed. M. Oakeshott, Oxford: Blackwell.

Oakeshott, M. (1975), *On Human Conduct*, Oxford: Clarendon Press.

Oakeshott, M. (1993), *Religion, Politics, and the Moral Life*, New Haven and London: Yale University Press.

O'Byrne, D. J. (2003), *Human Rights: An Introduction*, Harlow: Pearson Education.

O'Donovan, O. (1996), *The Desire of the Nations: Rediscovering the Roots of Political Theology*, Cambridge: Cambridge University Press.

Offe, C. (1996), *Modernity and the State: East, West*, Cambridge: Polity Press.

Ohmae, K (1996), *The End of the Nation State*, New York: HarperCollins.

Okin, S. (1989), *Justice, Gender, and the Family*, New York: Basic.

O'Neill, O. (2000), *Bounds of Justice*, New York: Cambridge University Press.

Ophuls, W. (1973), 'Leviathan or oblivion?', in H. E. Daly (ed.), *Toward a Steady-State Economy*, San Francisco: W. H. Freeman, pp. 215–30.

Ophuls, W. (1977), *Ecology and the Politics of Scarcity*, San Francisco: W. H. Freeman.

Orend, B. (2002), *Human Rights: Concept and Context*, Toronto: Broadview Press.

Paine, T. (1969), *The Essential Thomas Paine*, New York: Mentor.

Parekh, B. (ed.) (1973), *Bentham's Political Thought*, London: Croom Helm.

Parfit, D. (2000), 'Equality or priority?', in M. Clayton and A. Williams (eds), *The Ideal of Equality*, Basingstoke: Palgrave Macmillan.

Parsons, T. (1967), *Sociological Theory and Modern Society*, New York: Free Press.

Pateman, C. (1986), *Participation and Democratic Theory*, Cambridge: Cambridge University Press.

Pateman, C. (1988), *The Sexual Contract*, Cambridge: Polity Press.

Pateman, C. (1989), *The Disorder of Women: Democracy, Feminism and Political Theory*, Cambridge: Polity Press.

Patrick, M. (2002), 'Rights and recognition: perspectives on multicultural democracy', *Ethnicities*, 2(1): 31–51.

Peccei, A. (1969), *The Chasm Ahead*, London: Macmillan.

Penley, C. and A. Ross (1991), 'Cyborgs at large: interview with Donna Haraway', *Social Text*, 25/26: 8–23.

Perczynski, P. (2000), 'Active citizenship and associative democracy', in M. Saward (ed.), *Democratic Innovation: Deliberation, Representation and Association*, London: Routledge, pp. 161–71.

Peterson, V. and A. Runyan (1999), *Global Gender Issues*, 2nd ed., Boulder, CO: Westview Press.

Peterson, W. (1975), 'On the subnations of Europe', in N. Glazer and D. Moynihan (eds), *Ethnicity: Theory and Experience*, Cambridge, MA: Harvard University Press, pp. 117–208.

Petras, J. (1993), 'Cultural imperialism in the late 20th century', *Journal of Contemporary Asia*, 23(2): 139–48.

Pettit, P. (1997), *Republicanism: A Theory of Freedom and Government*, Oxford: Oxford University Press.

Pettman, J. (1996), 'An international political economy of sex?', in E. Kofman and G. Youngs (eds), *Globalization: Theory and Practice*, London: Pinter, pp. 191–208.

Phillips, A. (1993a), 'Must feminists give up on liberal democracy?', in D. Held (ed.), *The Prospects for Democracy: North, South, East, West*, Cambridge: Polity Press, pp. 93–111.

Phillips, D. (1993b), *Looking Backward: A Critical Appraisal of Communitarian Thought*, Princeton, NJ: Princeton University Press.

Piccone, P. and G. Ulmen (1987), 'Introduction to Carl Schmitt', *Telos*, 72: 3–14.

Pieterse, J. (1995), 'Globalization as hybridization', in M. Featherstone, S. Lash and R. Robertson (eds), *Global Modernities*, London: Sage, pp. 45–68.

Pietilä, H. and J. Vickers (1994), *Making Women Matter: The Role of the United Nations*, rev. ed., London: Zed.

Pitkin, H. (1972), *Wittgenstein and Justice*, Berkeley: University of California Press.

Pittendrigh, C. (1958), 'Adaptation, natural selection, and behavior', in A. Roe and G. Simpson (eds), *Behavior and Evolution*, New Haven: Yale University Press, pp. 390–416.

Plant, R. (1985), 'Welfare and the value of liberty', *Government and Opposition*, 20(3): 297–314.

Plato (1974), *The Republic*, tr. G. M. A. Grube, Indianapolis: Hackett.

Plato (1987), *The Republic*, tr. D. Lee, London: Penguin.

Plato (1993), 'The apology', in *The Last Days of Socrates*, tr. H. Tredennick and H. Tarrant, London: Penguin.

Pocock, J. (1975), *The Machiavellian Moment*, Princeton, NJ: Princeton University Press.

Podelech, A. (1984), 'Repräsentation', in R. Koselleck (ed.), *Geschichtliche Grundbegriffe: historisches Lexikon zur politisch-sozialen Sprache in Deutschland*, Stuttgart: Klett-Cotta, pp. 509–48.

Portmann, A. (1961), *Animals as Social Beings*, London: Hutchinson.

Poulantzas, N. (1969), 'The problem of the capitalist state', *New Left Review*, 58: 67–78.

Poulantzas, N. (1978), *State, Power, Socialism*, tr. P. Camiller, London: Verso.

Prakash, A. and J. Hart (eds) (2000), *Globalization and Governance*, London: Routledge.

Przeworski, A. (1998), 'Deliberation and ideological domination', in J. Elster (ed.), *Deliberative Democracy*, Cambridge: Cambridge University Press, pp. 140–60.

Raghavan, C. et al. (1996), 'Globalisation or development', *Third World Resurgence*, 74: 11–34.

Rajput, P. and H. Swarup (eds) (1994), *Women and Globalisation: Reflections, Options and Strategies*, New Delhi: Ashish.

Rawls, J. (1964), 'Legal obligations and the duty of fair play', in S. Hook (ed.), *Law and Philosophy*, New York: New York University Press.

Rawls, J. (1982), 'The basic liberties and their priority', in S. McMurrin (ed.), *Tanner Lectures on Human Values, vol. 3*, Salt Lake City: University of Utah Press.

Rawls, J. (1985), 'Justice as fairness: political not metaphysical', *Philosophy and Public Affairs*, 14(3): 223–51.

Rawls, J. (1987), 'The idea of an overlapping consensus', *Oxford Journal of Legal Studies*, 7: 1–25.

Rawls, J. (1988), 'The priority of the right and ideas of the good', *Philosophy and Public Affairs*, 17(4): 251–76.

Rawls, J. (1993a), 'The law of peoples', in S. Shute and S. Hurley (eds), *On Human Rights: The Oxford Amnesty Lectures*, New York: Basic Books, pp. 41–82.

Rawls, J. (1993b), *Political Liberalism*, New York: Columbia University Press.

Rawls, J. (1997), 'The idea of public reason revisited', *University of Chicago Law Review*, 94(3): 765–807.

Rawls, J. (1999a), *The Law of Peoples*, Cambridge, MA: Harvard University Press.

Rawls, J. (1999b), *A Theory of Justice*, rev. ed., Oxford: Oxford University Press.

Rawls, J. (2001), *Justice as Fairness: A Restatement*, Cambridge, MA: Harvard University Press.

Raz, J. (1979), 'The rule of law and its virtue', in *The Authority of Law: Essays on Law and Morality*, Oxford: Clarendon Press.

Raz, J. (1986), *The Morality of Freedom*, Oxford: Clarendon Press.

Reagan, R. (1988), 'Peace and democracy for Nicaragua: address to the nation on February 2, 1988', *Department of State Bulletin*, 88(2133): 32–5.

Reed, D. (ed.) (1996), *Structural Adjustment, the Environment and Sustainable Development*, London: Earthscan.

Reinicke, W. (1998), *Global Public Policy: Governing without Government?*, Washington: Brookings Institution.

Renan, E. (1996), *Was ist eine Nation? Rede am 11. März 1882 an der Sorbonne*, Hamburg: Europäische Verlagsanstalt.

Reynolds, V. (1966), 'Open groups in hominid evolution', *Man*, 1: 441–52.

Rheingold, H. (1993), *The Virtual Community: Homesteading on the Electronic Frontier*, Reading, MA: Addison-Wesley.

Rich, B. (1994), *Mortgaging the Earth: The World Bank, Environmental Impoverishment and the Crisis of Development*, London: Earthscan.

Richardson, J. (ed.) (1905), *A Compilation of Messages and Papers of the Presidents 1789–1902*, 12 vols, Washington: Bureau of National Literature and Art.

Ridley, M. (1996), *The Origins of Virtue*, London: Viking.

Rifkin, J. (1983), *Algeny*, New York: Viking.

Rifkin, J. (1995), *The End of Work: The Decline of the Global Labor Force and the Dawn of the Post-market Era*, New York: Putnam.

Riker, W. (1982), *Liberalism against Populism: A Confrontation between the Theory of Democracy and the Theory of Social Choice*, San Francisco: W. H. Freeman.

Ritzer, G. (1996), *The McDonaldization of Society*, Thousand Oaks, CA: Pine Forge Press.

Roberts, D. E. (1991), 'Punishing drug addicts who have babies: women of colour, equality, and the right of privacy', *Harvard Law Review*, 104(7): 1419–82.

Robertson, J. (1980), *American Myth, American Reality*, New York: Hill and Wang.

Robertson, R. (1992), *Globalisation*, London: Sage.

Robinson, W. (1996a), 'Globalisation: nine theses on our epoch', *Race and Class*, 38(2): 13–31.

Robinson, W. (1996b), *Promoting Polyarchy: Globalization, US Intervention and Hegemony*, Cambridge: Cambridge University Press.

Roe, A. and G. Simpson (eds) (1958), *Behavior and Evolution*, New Haven: Yale University Press.

Rorty, R. (1979), *Philosophy and the Mirror of Nature*, Princeton, NJ: Princeton University Press.

Rorty, R. (1982), *The Consequences of Pragmatism*, Brighton: Harvester Press.

Rorty, R. (1989), *Contingency, Irony, and Solidarity*, Cambridge: Cambridge University Press.

Rorty, R. (1993), 'Human rights, rationality and sentimentality', in S. Shute and S. Hurley (eds), *On Human Rights: The Oxford Amnesty Lectures*, New York: Basic Books, pp. 111–34.

Rorty, R. (1998), *Achieving Our Country*, Cambridge, MA: Harvard University Press.

Rorty, R. (2000), 'Universality and truth', in R. Brandom (ed.), *Rorty and His Critics*, Oxford: Blackwell.

Rosenau, J. (1990), *Turbulence in World Politics*, Princeton, NJ: Princeton University Press.

Rosenblum, N. and R. Post (eds) (2002), *Civil Society and Government*, Princeton, NJ: Princeton University Press.

Rousseau, J.- J. ([1762] 1968), *The Social Contract*, ed. M. Cranston, Harmondsworth: Penguin.

Rousseau, J.-J. ([1762] 1973), *The Social Contract and the Discourses*, London: Campbell.

Runciman, W. G. and A. Sen (1965), 'Games, justice, and the general will', *Mind*, 74: 554–62.

Runyan, A. (1996): 'The places of women in trading places: gendered global/regional regimes and inter-nationalized feminist resistance', in E. Kofman and G. Youngs (eds), *Globalization: Theory and Practice*, London: Pinter, pp. 238–52.

Russell, B. (1952), *Sceptical Essays*, London: Allen and Unwin.

Ruthven, M. (2000), *Islam in the World*, Harmondsworth: Penguin.

Sandel, M. (1982), *Liberalism and the Limits of Justice*, Cambridge: Cambridge University Press.

Sandel, M. (1984), 'The procedural republic and the unencumbered self', *Political Theory*, 12(1): 81–96.

Sanders, L. (1997), 'Against deliberation', *Political Theory*, 25(3), 347–76.

Saussure, F. de (1983), *Course in General Linguistics*, ed. C. Bally and A. Sechehaye, tr. R. Harris, London: Duckworth.

Saward, M. (2000a), 'Democratic innovation', in M. Saward (ed.), *Innovations in Democracy*, London: Routledge, pp. 3–13.

Saward, M. (2000b), 'Less than meets the eye: democratic legitimacy and deliberative theory', in M. Saward (ed.), *Innovations in Democracy*, London: Routledge, pp. 66–77.

Scalia, A. (1989), 'The rule of law as a law of rules', *University of Chicago Law Review*, 56.

Scanlon, T. (1982), 'Contractualism and utilitarianism', in A. Sen and B. Williams (eds), *Utilitarianism and Beyond*, Cambridge: Cambridge University Press, reprinted in T. Scanlon (2003), *The Difficulty of Tolerance: Essays in Political Philosophy*, Cambridge: Cambridge University Press.

Scanlon, T. (1998), *What We Owe to Each Other*, Cambridge, MA: Belknap Press.

Scanlon, T. (2003), *The Difficulty of Tolerance: Essays in Political Philosophy*, Cambridge: Cambridge University Press.

Schmitt, C. (1993), *Verfassungslehre*, 8th ed., Berlin: Duncker & Humbolt.

Schmitt, C. (1996), *The Concept of the Political*, tr. G. Schwab, Chicago: University of Chicago Press.

Scholte, J. (2000), *Globalization: A Critical Introduction*, London: Palgrave.

Scholte, J. (2001a), 'Beyond the buzzword: towards a critical theory of globalization', in E. Kofman and G. Youngs (eds), *Globalization: Theory and Practice*, London: Pinter.

Scholte, J. (2001b), 'The globalization of world politics', in J. Baylis and S. Smith (eds), *The Globalization of World Politics*, Oxford: Oxford University Press.

Schotter, A. (1981), *The Economic Theory of Social Institutions*, Cambridge: Cambridge University Press.

Schubert, G. (1966), 'Politics as a life science', in A. Somit (ed.), *Biology and Politics*, The Hague: Mouton, pp. 155–95.

Schubert, G. (1985), 'Sexual differences in political behavior', *Political Science Review*, 15: 1–68.

Schubert, G. (1986), 'Primate politics', *Social Science Information*, 25: 647–80.

Schumpeter, J. (1987), *Capitalism, Socialism and Democracy*, London: Counterpoint.

Schwarzmantel, J. (1994), *The State in Contemporary Society: An Introduction*, Hemel Hempstead: Harvester Wheatsheaf.

Scott, A. (ed.) (1997), *The Limits of Globalization*, London: Sage.

Sen, A. K. (1997), 'Equality of what?', in R. Goodin and P. Pettit (eds), *Contemporary Political Philosophy*, Oxford: Blackwell, pp. 476–86.

Shapiro, M. (1985), 'Metaphor in the philosophy of the Social Sciences', *Culture and Critique*, 2: 191–214.

Shapiro, M. and H. Alker (eds) (1996), *Challenging Boundaries: Global Flows, Territorial Identities*, Minneapolis: University of Minnesota Press.

Shaw, K. and W. Magnusson (2003), *A Political Space: Reading the Global through Clayoquot Sound*, Minneapolis: University of Minnesota Press.

Shaw, M. (1994), *Global Society and International Relations*, Cambridge: Polity Press.

Shelley, L. (1995), 'Transnational organized crime: an imminent threat to the nation-state?', *Journal of International Affairs*, 48(2):463–89.

Shestack, J. (2000), 'The philosophical foundations of human rights', in J. Symonides (ed.), *Human Rights: Concepts and Standards*, Aldershot: Ashgate, pp. 31–66.

Shils, E. (1981), *Tradition*, Chicago: University of Chicago Press.

Shin, D. (1994), 'On the third wave of democratization: a synthesis and evaluation of recent research and theory', *World Politics*, 47(1): 135–70.

Shore, B. (2000), 'Human diversity and human nature', in N. Roughley (ed.), *Being Humans*, Berlin: De Gruyter, pp. 81–103.

Silverman, I. and M. Eals (1992), 'Sex differences in spatial abilities', in J. Barkow, L. Cosmides and J. Tooby (eds), *The Adapted Mind: Evolutionary Psychology and the Generation of Culture*, New York: Oxford University Press, pp. 533–53.

Simmonds, N. (2002), *Central Issues in Jurisprudence: Justice, Law and Rights*, 2nd ed., London: Sweet and Maxwell.

Simmonds, N. (2004), 'Straightforwardly false: the collapse of Kramer's positivism', *Cambridge Law Journal*, 63(1): 98–131.

Simmonds, N. (forthcoming a), 'Jurisprudence as a moral and historical inquiry'.

Simmonds, N. (forthcoming b), 'Wicked justice: a reply to Kramer', *Cambridge Law Journal*.

Simmons, A. (1979), *Moral Principles and Political Obligations*, Princeton, NJ: Princeton University Press.

Simpson, J. A. and Weiner, E. S. C. (eds) (1989), *Oxford English Dictionary*, 2nd ed., Oxford: Clarendon Press.

Sivaraksa, S. (1999), *Global Healing: Essays and Interviews on Structural Violence, Social Development and Spiritual Transformation*, Bangkok: Sathirakoses-Nagaradipa Foundation.

Skinner, B. F. (1965), *Science and Human Behavior*, New York: Free Press.

Skinner, Q. (1989), 'The state', in T. Ball, J. Farr and R. Hanson (eds), *Political Innovation and Conceptual Change*, Cambridge: Cambridge University Press.

Skinner, Q. (2002), *Visions of Politics, vol. 1: Regarding Method*, Cambridge: Cambridge University Press.

Skocpol, T. (1979), *States and Social Revolutions*, Cambridge: Cambridge University Press.

Skrobanek, S., N. Boonpakdee and C. Jantateero (1997), *The Traffic in Women: Human Realities of the International Sex Trade*, London: Zed.

Smith, A. (1986), *The Ethnic Origin of Nations*, Oxford: Blackwell.

Smith, A. (1991), *National Identity*, London: Penguin.

Smith, A. (1994), 'Gastronomy or geology? The role of nationalism in the reconstruction of nations', *Nations and Nationalism*, 1(1): 3–23.

Smith, A. (1998), *Nationalism and Modernism*, London and New York: Routledge.

Smith, G. (2000), 'Toward deliberative institutions', in M. Saward (ed.), *Innovations in Democracy*, London: Routledge, pp. 29–39.

Smith, P. (1993), 'Feminist jurisprudence and the nature of law', in P. Smith (ed.), *Feminist Jurisprudence*, New York: Oxford University Press.

Smouts, M.-C. (1999), 'Multilateralism from below: a prerequisite for global governance', in M. Schechter (ed.), *Future Multilateralism: The Political and Social Framework*, Tokyo: United Nations University Press, pp. 292–311.

Smullyan, R. (1980), *This Book Needs No Title*, Englewood Cliffs, NJ: Prentice Hall.

Sobchack, V. (1995), 'Beating the meat/surviving the text, or how to get out of this century alive', in M. Featherstone and R, Burrows (eds), *Cyberspace/Cyberbodies/Cyberpunk: Cultures of Technological Embodiment*, London: Sage.

Sobel, J. H. (1967), '"Everyone," consequences, and generalization arguments', *Inquiry*, 10: 373–404.

Somit, A. (1968), 'Toward a more biologically oriented political science', *Midwest Journal of Political Science*, 12: 550–67.

Somit, A and S. Peterson (1997), *Darwinism, Dominance, and Democracy*, Westport, CT: Praeger.

Sparr, P. (ed.) (1994), *Mortgaging Women's Lives: Feminist Critiques of Structural Adjustment*, London: Zed.

Sprout, M. and H. Sprout (1971), *Ecology and Politics in America*, New York: General Learning Press.

Spuhler, J. (1959), 'Somatic paths to culture', in J. Spuhler (ed.), *The Evolution of Man's Capacity for Culture*, Detroit: Wayne State University Press, pp. 1–13.

Squires, J. (2002), 'Deliberation and decision-making: discontinuity in the two-track model', in M. Passerin d'Entrèves (ed.), *Democracy as Public Deliberation: New Perspectives*, Manchester: Manchester University Press, pp. 133–56.

Stalin, I. ([1913] 1954), *Marxism and the National Question*, in *Works, vol. 2*, Moscow: Foreign Languages Publishing House, pp. 300–81.

Stauffer, R. (1971), *The Role of Drugs in Political Change*, New York: General Learning Press.

Steenbergen, B. van (ed.) (1994), *The Condition of Citizenship*, London: Sage.

Stienstra, D. (1994), *Women's Movements and International Organizations*, Basingstoke: Macmillan.

Strange, S. (1986), *Casino Capitalism*, Oxford: Blackwell.

Strange, S. (1998), *Mad Money*, Manchester: Manchester University Press.

Strauss, L. (1953), *Natural Right and History*, Chicago: University of Chicago Press.

Strauss, L. (1965), *Hobbes politische Wissenschaft*, Neuweid-Berlin: Luchterhand.

Suler, J. (1999), 'Do boys (and girls) just wanna have fun? Gender-switching in cyberspace', in *The Psychology of Cyberspace*. <http://www.rider.edu/~suler/psycyber/genderswap.html>

Sullivan, D. and R. Masters (1988), 'Happy warriors: leaders' facial displays and viewers' emotions, and political support', *American Journal of Political Science*, 32: 345–68.

Sunstein, C. (1984), 'Naked preferences and the constitution', Columbia Law Review, 84: 1689–1732.

Sunstein, C. (1986), 'Legal interference with private preferences', *University of Chicago Law Review*, 53: 1129–84.

Symons, D. (1979), *The Evolution of Sexuality*, New York: Oxford University Press.

Tamir, Y. (1993), *Liberal Nationalism*, Princeton, NJ: Princeton University Press.

Tanner, S. (1997), 'Healing the sky to survive globalization: a gender analogy', in T. Schrecker (ed.), *Surviving Globalism: The Social and Environmental Challenges*, Basingstoke: Macmillan, pp. 141–57.

Taylor, C. (1979), 'What's wrong with negative liberty', in A. Ryan (ed.), *The Idea of Freedom*, Oxford: Oxford University Press.

Taylor, C. (1985), 'Atomism', in *Philosophical Papers, vol. 2: Philosophy and the Human Sciences*, Cambridge: Cambridge University Press, pp. 187–210.

Taylor, C. (1986), 'Human rights: the legal culture', in P. Ricoeur (ed.), *Philosophical Foundations of Human Rights*, Paris: UNESCO, pp. 49–57.

Taylor, C. (1990), *Sources of the Self*, Cambridge: Cambridge University Press.

Taylor, C. (1991), 'Shared and divergent values', in R. Watts and D. Brown (eds), *Options for a New Canada*, Toronto: University of Toronto Press, pp. 53–76.

Taylor, C. (1992), 'The politics of recognition', in A. Gutmann (ed.), *Multiculturalism and the 'Politics of Recognition'*, Princeton, NJ: Princeton University Press, pp. 25–73.

Taylor, C. (1994), 'The politics of recognition', in A. Gutmann (ed.), *Multiculturalism: Examining the Politics of Recognition*, Princeton, NJ: Princeton University Press.

Taylor, C. (1995a), 'Heidegger, Language and Ecology', in *Philosophical Arguments*, Cambridge, MA: Harvard University Press, pp. 100–26.

Taylor, C. (1995b), 'Liberal politics and the public sphere', in *Philosophical Arguments*, Cambridge, MA: Harvard University Press, pp. 257–87.

Taylor, C. (1997), 'Invoking civil society', in R. Goodin and E. Pettit (eds), *Contemporary Political Philosophy: An Anthology*, Oxford: Blackwell, pp. 66–77.

Taylor, C. (1998), 'The dynamics of democratic exclusion', *Journal of Democracy*, October: 143–56.

Taylor, C. (1999), 'Conditions of an unforced consensus on human rights', in O. Savié (ed.), *The Politics of Human Rights*, London: Verso, pp. 101–19.

Taylor, C. (2003), 'Cross-purposes: the liberal–communitarian debate', in D. Matravess and J. Pike (eds), Debates in Contemporary Political Philosophy, London: Routledge.

Taylor, G. (1968), *The Biological Time-Bomb*, New York: Mentor.

Teeple, G. (1995), *Globalization and the Decline of Social Reform*, Atlantic Highlands, NJ: Humanities Press.

Thomas, C. and P. Wilkin (eds) (1997), *Globalization and the South*, Basingstoke: Macmillan.

Thomas, C. and P. Wilkin (eds) (1999), *Globalization, Human Security, and the African Experience*, Boulder, CO: Rienner.

Thompson, P. (1976), 'A behavior model for *Australopithecus africanus*', *Journal of Human Evolution*, 5: 547–58.

Tiger, L. (1969), *Men in Groups*, New York: Random House.

Tilly, C. (1992), *Coercion, Capital, and European States*, Oxford: Blackwell.

Tilly, C. (1995), 'Globalization threatens labor's rights', *International Labor and Working Class History*, 47: 1–23.

Todorov, T. (1984), *The Conquest of America: The Question of the Other*, tr. R. Howard, New York: Harper and Row.

Tomasi, J. (1995), 'Kymlicka, liberalism, and respect for cultural minorities', *Ethics*, 105(3): 580–603.

Tomlinson, J. (1991), *Cultural Imperialism: A Critical Introduction*, London: Pinter.

Tooby, J. and L. Cosmides (1992), 'The psychological foundations of culture', in J. Barkow, L. Cosmides and J. Tooby (eds), *The Adapted Mind: Evolutionary Psychology and the Generation of Culture*, New York: Oxford University Press, pp.19–136.

Torfing, J. (1998), *Politics, Regulation and the Modern Welfare State*, Basingstoke: Macmillan.

Torfing, J. (1999), *New Theories of Discourse*, Oxford: Blackwell.

Tully, J. (ed.) (1988a), *Meaning and Context: Quentin Skinner and his Critics*, Cambridge: Polity Press.

Tully, J. (1988b), 'The pen is a mighty sword: Quentin Skinner's analysis', in J. Tully (ed.), *Meaning and Context: Quentin Skinner and his Critics*, Princeton, NJ: Princeton University Press.

Tully, J. (1995), *Strange Multiplicity: Constitutionalism in an Age of Diversity*, Cambridge: Cambridge University Press.

Tully, J. (1999), 'The agonic freedom of citizens', *Economy and Society*, 28(2): 161–82.

Turner, F. (1920), *The Frontier in American History*, New York: Henry Holt.

Tylor, E. (1871), *Primitive Culture*, London: John Murray.

Van Creveld, M. (1999), *The Rise and Decline of the State*, Cambridge: Cambridge University Press.

Vandenberg, A. (ed.) (2000), *Citizenship and Democracy in a Global Era*, Basingstoke: Macmillan.

Vickers, J. (1991), *Women and the World Economic Crisis*, London: Zed.

Virilio, P. (1986), *Speed and Politics: An Essay in Dromology*, tr. M. Polizzotti, New York: Semiotext(e).

Viroli, M. (2002), *Republicanism*, New York: Hill and Wang.

Vlastos, G. (1962), 'Justice and Equality', in R. Brandt (ed.), *Social Justice*, Englewood Cliffs, NJ: Prentice Hall.

Vonnegut, K. (1979), 'Harrison Bergeron', in *Welcome to the Monkey House*, pb. ed., St Albans: Triad/Granada, pp. 19–25.

Waldron, J. (1992), 'Minority cultures and the cosmopolitan alternative', *University of Michigan Journal of Law Reform*, 25(3): 751–93.

Waldron, J. (1993a), 'Homelessness and the issue of freedom', in *Liberal Rights: Collected Papers 1981–1991*, Cambridge: Cambridge University Press.

Waldron, J. (1993b), *Liberal Rights: Collected Papers 1981–1991*, Cambridge: Cambridge University Press.

Waldron, J. (1999), *Law and Disagreement*, Oxford: Oxford University Press.

Waldron, J. (2002), *God, Locke, and Equality: Christian Foundations in Locke's Political Thought*, New York: Cambridge University Press.

Walker, M. and D. McKay (2000), *Unravelling Genes: A Layperson's Guide to Genetic Engineering*, St Leonards, NSW: Allen and Unwin.

Walker, R. (1988), *One World, Many Worlds: Struggles for a Just World Peace*, Boulder, CO: Lynne Rienner.

Wallerstein, I. (1974), *The Modern World-System*, New York: Academic Press.

Wallerstein, I. (1979), *The Capitalist World Economy*, Cambridge: Cambridge University Press.

Wallerstein, I. (1980), *The Modern World-System II*, New York: Academic Press.

Wallerstein, I. (1989), *The Modern World-System III*, New York: Academic Press.

Walton, J. and D. Seddon (1994), *Free Markets and Food Riots: The Politics of Global Adjustment*, Oxford: Blackwell.

Walzer, M. (1981), 'Philosophy and democracy', *Political Theory*, 9(3): 379–99.

Walzer, M. (1983), *Spheres of Justice*, Oxford: Blackwell.

Walzer, M. (1997), 'Complex equality', in R. Goodin and P. Pettit (eds), *Contemporary Political Philosophy*, Oxford: Blackwell, pp. 487–503.

Warnock, M. (2002), *Making Babies: Is There a Right to Have Children?*, Oxford: Oxford University Press.

Warren, M. (2001), *Democracy and Association*, Princeton, NJ: Princeton University Press.

Washburn, S. and F. C. Howell (1960), 'Human evolution and culture', in S. Tax (ed.), *Evolution of Man*, Chicago: University of Chicago Press, pp. 33–56.

Waterman, P. (1998), *Globalization, Social Movements and the New Internationalisms*, London: Mansell.

Waters, M. (1995), *Globalization*, London: Routledge.

Watts, M. (ed.) (1984), *Biopolitics and Gender*, New York: Haworth Press.

Weale, A. (2000), 'Conversations and democracy', *CSD Bulletin*, 7(2), 1–2.

Weber, M. (1948), *From Max Weber: Essays in Sociology*, ed. H. H. Gerth and C. Mills, London: Routledge and Kegan Paul.

Weber, M. ([1922] 1964), *Wirtschaft und Gesellschaft*, ed. J. Winckelmann, Cologne: Kiepenhauer & Witsch.

Weber, M. (1968), *Economy and Society: An Outline of Interpretative Sociology, vol. 1*, New York: Bedminster Press.

Wenman, M. (2003a), '"Agonistic pluralism" and three archetypal forms of politics', *Contemporary Political Theory*, 2(2): 165–86.

Wenman, M. (2003b), 'Laclau or Mouffe? Splitting the difference', *Philosophy and Social Criticism*, 29(5): 581–606.

Whatmore, S. (1994), 'Global agro-food complexes and the refashioning of rural Europe', in A. Amin and N. Thrift (eds), *Globalization, Institutions, and Regional Development in Europe*, Oxford: Oxford University Press, pp. 46–67.

Wheeler, N. (2000), *Saving Strangers: Humanitarian Intervention in International Society*, Oxford: Oxford University Press.

Willhoite, F. Jr (1976), 'Primates and political authority: a biobehavioral perspective', *American Political Science Review*, 70: 1110–26.

Williams, B. (1985), *Ethics and the Limits of Philosophy*, London: Collins/Cambridge, MA: Harvard University Press.

Williams, B. (1995), *Making Sense of Humanity and other philosophical papers*, Cambridge: Cambridge University Press.

Williams, P. (1994), 'Transnational criminal organisations and international security', *Survival*, 36(1): 96–113.

Williams, W. (1980), *Empire as a Way of Life*, Oxford: Oxford University Press.

Williamson, J. (1990), 'What Washington means by policy reform', in J. Williamson (ed.), *Latin American Adjustment: How Much Has Happened?*, Washington: Institute for International Economics.

Wilson, E. (1978), *On Human Nature*, Cambridge, MA: Harvard University Press.

Wilson, R. and W. Dissanayake (1996), *Global–Local: Cultural Production and the Transnational Imaginary*, Durham, NC: Duke University Press.

Winch, P. (1958), *The Idea of a Social Science and Its Relation to Philosophy*, London: Routledge and Kegan Paul.

Winston, K. (2001), 'Fuller, Lon Luvois', in L. Becker and C. Becker (eds), *Encyclopedia of Ethics*, 2nd ed., New York and London: Routledge.

Wittgenstein, L. (1958), *Philosophical Investigations*, tr. G. E. M. Anscombe, Oxford: Blackwell.

Wolff, J. (1998), 'John Rawls: liberal democracy restated', in A. Carter and G. Stokes (eds), *Liberal Democracy and Its Critics*, Cambridge: Polity Press, pp. 118–34.

Wollstonecraft, M. ([1792] 1992), *A Vindication of the Rights of Woman*, London: Penguin.

Woodward, K. (1994), 'From virtual cyborgs to biological time bombs: technocriticism and the material body', in G. Bender and T. Druckrey (eds), *Culture on the Brink: Ideologies of Technology*, Seattle: Bay Press.

Wriston, W. (1992), *The Twilight of Sovereignty: How the Information Revolution Is Transforming Our World*, New York: Charles Scribner's Sons.

Young, I. (1996), 'Communication and the other: beyond deliberative democracy', in S. Benhabib (ed.), *Democracy and Difference: Contesting the Boundaries of the Political*, Princeton, NJ: Princeton University Press, pp. 120–35.

Young, I. (1997), 'Difference as a resource for democratic communication', in J. Bohman and W. Rehg (eds), *Deliberative Democracy*, Cambridge, MA: MIT Press, pp. 383–406.

Young, I. (2000), *Inclusion and Democracy*, Oxford: Oxford University Press.

Young, O., G. Demko and K. Ramakrishna (eds) (1996), *Global Environmental Change and International Governance*, Hanover, NH: University Press of New England.

Žižek, S. (1989), *The Sublime Object of Ideology*, London:Verso.

Žižek, S. (1994), 'Introduction' and 'The spectre of ideology', in S. Žižek (ed), *Mapping Ideology*, London:Verso.

Žižek, S. (1997), *The Plague of Fantasies*, London:Verso.

Zolo, D. (1992), *Democracy and Complexity: A Realist Approach*, University Park, PA: Penn State University Press.

FURTHER READING

Some of the contributors to this book have recommended works for further study. They are listed here, section by section.

POLITICAL PRINCIPLES: EQUALITY

Dworkin, R. (2000), *Sovereign Virtue: The Theory and Practice of Equality*, Cambridge, MA: Harvard University Press.
Kymlicka, W. (2000), *Contemporary Political Philosophy*, Oxford: Clarendon Press.
Nagel, T. (1991), *Equality and Partiality*, Oxford: Oxford University Press.
Pojman, L. and R. Westmoreland (eds) (1997), *Equality: Selected Readings*, Oxford: Oxford University Press.
Sen, A. (1992), *Inequality Reexamined*, Oxford: Clarendon Press.
Swift, A. (2001), *Political Philosophy: A Beginners' Guide for Students and Politicians*, Cambridge: Polity Press.
Williams, B. (1997), 'The idea of equality', in R. Goodin and P. Pettit (eds), *Contemporary Political Philosophy: An Anthology*, Oxford: Blackwell, pp. 465–75.

POLITICAL PRINCIPLES: RIGHTS

Appiah, K. (2003), 'Citizens of the world', in M. Gibney (ed.), *Globalizing Rights: The Oxford Amnesty Lectures 1999*, Oxford: Oxford University Press, pp. 189–232.
Hobbes, T. ([1651] 1974) *Leviathan*, Glasgow: Collins.
Nozick, R. (1974), *Anarchy, State, and Utopia*, New York: Basic Books / Oxford: Blackwell.

POLITICAL LEGITIMACY: TOLERATION

Appignanesi, L. and S. Maitland (1989), *The Rushdie File*, London: Fourth Estate.
Cook, J. (1999), *Morality and Cultural Differences*, Oxford: Oxford University Press.
Heyd, D. (1996), *Toleration: An Elusive Virtue*, Princeton: Princeton University Press.

Horton, J. (ed.) (1993), *Liberalism, Multiculturalism and Toleration*, Basingstoke: Macmillan.

Horton, J. and S. Mendus (eds) (1991), *John Locke: 'A Letter Concerning Toleration' in Focus*, London: Routledge.

Horton, J. and P. Nicholson (eds) (1992), *Toleration: Philosophy and Practice*, Aldershot: Ashgate.

Howarth, A. (1998), *Free Speech*, London: Routledge.

Kernohan, A. (1998), *Liberalism, Equality, and Cultural Oppression*, Cambridge: Cambridge University Press.

King, P. (1998), *Toleration*, London: Frank Cass.

Kymlicka, W. (1989), *Liberalism, Community, and Culture*, Oxford: Clarendon Press.

Kymlicka, W. (ed.) (1995), *The Rights of Minority Cultures*, Oxford: Oxford University Press.

Leigh, R. A. (1979), *Rousseau and the Problem of Tolerance in the Eighteenth Century*, Oxford: Clarendon Press.

Levine, A. (ed.) (1999), *Early Modern Skepticism and the Origins of Toleration*, Lanham, MD: Lexington.

Locke, J. (1993), 'A letter concerning toleration', in *Political Writings*, London: Penguin.

Macedo, S. (1993), 'Toleration and fundamentalism', in R. Goodin and P. Pettit (eds), *A Companion to Contemporary Political Philosophy*, Oxford: Blackwell.

Marcuse, H. (1969), 'Repressive tolerance', in R. Wolff, B. Moore and H. Marcuse (eds), *A Critique of Pure Tolerance*, London: Jonathan Cape.

Mendus, S. (1989), *Toleration and the Limits of Liberalism*, Basingstoke: Macmillan.

Mendus, S. (ed.) (1999), *The Politics of Toleration: Tolerance and Intolerance in Modern Life*, Edinburgh: Edinburgh University Press.

Mendus, S. and D. Edwards (eds) (1987), *On Toleration*, Oxford: Clarendon Press.

Mill, J. (1998), *On Liberty and other essays*, Oxford: Oxford University Press.

Nederman, C. and J. Laursen (1996), *Difference and Dissent: Theories of Toleration in Medieval and Modern Europe*, London: Rowman and Littlefield.

Newey, G. (1999), *Virtue, Reason and Toleration*, Edinburgh: Edinburgh University Press.

Oberdiek, H. (2001), *Tolerance: Between Forbearance and Acceptance*, London: Rowman and Littlefield.

Parekh, B. (1995), 'The Rushdie affair: research agenda for political philosophy', in W. Kymlicka (ed.), *The Rights of Minority Cultures*, Oxford: Oxford University Press.

Rawls, J. (1972), *A Theory of Justice*, Oxford: Oxford University Press.

Rawls, J. (1995), *Political Liberalism*, New York: Columbia University Press.

Rawls, J. (2001), *The Law of Peoples*, Cambridge, MA: Harvard University Press.

Raz, J. (1986), *The Morality of Freedom*, Oxford: Clarendon Press.

Razavi, M. and D. Ambuel (eds) (1997), *Philosophy, Religion, and the Question of Intolerance*, Albany: State University of New York Press.

Tan, K.-C. (2000), *Toleration, Diversity, and Global Justice*, University Park, PA: Penn State University Press.

Walzer, M. (1983), *Spheres of Justice*, Oxford: Martin Robertson.

Walzer, M. (1997), *On Toleration*, New Haven: Yale University Press.

POLITICAL LEGITIMACY: MULTICULTURALISM

Barry, B. (2001), *Culture and Equality: An Egalitarian Critique of Multiculturalism*, Cambridge: Polity Press.

Fernandez, J. (1986), *Persuasions and Performances: The Play of Tropes in Culture*, Bloomington: Indiana University Press.

Okin, S. (1999), *Is Multiculturalism Bad for Women?*, Princeton: Princeton University Press.

Parekh, B. (2000), *Rethinking Multiculturalism: Cultural Diversity and Political Theory*, Basingstoke: Macmillan.

GOVERNING THE POLITICAL: CIVIL SOCIETY

Bauböck, R. (2000), 'Social and cultural integration in civil society', in C. McKinnon and I. Hampsher-Monk (eds), *The Demands of Citizenship*, London and New York: Continuum, pp. 91–119.

Bobbio, N. (1988), 'Gramsci and the concept of civil society', in J. Keane (ed.), *Civil Society and the State: New European Perspectives*, London and New York: Verso, pp. 73–99.

Brown, W. (1995), *States of Injury: Power and Freedom in Late Modernity*, Princeton: Princeton University Press.

Burchell, G., C. Gordon and P. Miller (eds) (1991), *The Foucault Effect: Studies in Governmentality*, Hemel Hempstead: Harvester Wheatsheaf.

Deakin, N. (2001), *In Search of Civil Society*, Basingstoke: Palgrave.

Edwards, M. (2004), *Civil Society*, Cambridge: Polity Press.

Flyvbjerg, B. (1998), 'Habermas and Foucault: thinkers for civil society?', *British Journal of Sociology*, 49(2): 210–33.

Gill, S. (2003), *Power and Resistance in the New World Order*, Basingstoke: Palgrave Macmillan.

Goodin, R. and P. Pettit (eds.) (1997), *Contemporary Political Philosophy: An Anthology*, Oxford: Blackwell.

Hall, J. (ed.) (1995), *Civil Society: Theory, History, Comparison*, Cambridge: Polity Press.

Hardt, M. and A. Negri (2000), *Empire*, Cambridge, MA: Harvard University Press.

Havel, V. (1988), 'Anti-political politics', in J. Keane (ed.), *Civil Society and the State: New European Perspectives*, London and New York: Verso, pp. 381–98.

Hegel, G. W. F. (1991), *Elements of the Philosophy of Right*, Cambridge: Cambridge University Press.

Held, D. and A. McGrew (2002), *Globalization/Anti-globalization*, Cambridge: Polity Press.

Hobbes, T. ([1651] 1968), *Leviathan*, ed. C. B. Macpherson, Harmondsworth: Penguin.

Keane, J. (1988), 'Despotism and democracy: the origins and development of the distinction between civil society and the state 1750–1850', in J. Keane (ed.), *Civil Society and the State: New European Perspectives*, London and New York: Verso, pp. 35–71.

McKinnon, C. and I. Hampsher-Monk (eds) (2000), *The Demands of Citizenship*, London and New York: Continuum.

McLellan, D. (ed.) (2000), *Karl Marx: Selected Writings*, Oxford: Oxford University Press.

Mouffe, C. (ed.) (1992), *Dimensions of Radical Democracy: Pluralism, Citizenship, Community*, London and New York: Verso.

Muetzelfeldt, M. and G. Smith (2002), 'Civil society and global governance: the possibilities for global citizenship', *Citizenship Studies*, 6(1): 55–75.

Pateman, C. (1988), *The Sexual Contract*, Cambridge: Polity Press.

Rousseau, J.-J. ([1762] 1968), *The Social Contract*, ed. M. Cranston, Harmondsworth: Penguin.

Seligman, A. (1994), 'The fragile ethical vision of civil society', in B. Turner (ed.), *Citizenship and Social Theory*, London: Sage, pp. 139–61.

Taylor, C. (1990), 'Modes of civil society', *Public Culture*, 3(1): 95–118.

Turner, B (ed.) (1994), *Citizenship and Social Theory*, London: Sage.

Walzer, M. (1992), 'The civil society argument', in C. Mouffe (ed.), *Dimensions of Radical Democracy: Pluralism, Citizenship, Community*, London and New York: Verso, pp. 89–107.

POLITICAL IDENTITIES: NATION

Brubaker, R. and F. Cooper (2000), 'Beyond identity', *Theory and Society*, 29(1): 1–47.

Gellner, E. (1996), 'Do nations have navels?', in *Nations and Nationalism*, 3(2): 366–70.

Hall, J. (ed.) (1998), *The State of the Nation: Ernest Gellner and the Theory of Nationalism*, Cambridge and New York: Cambridge University Press.

Smith, A. (2001), *Nationalism: Theory, Ideology, History*, Cambridge: Polity Press.

POLITICAL IDENTITIES: GLOBALISATION

Bauman, Z. (1998), *Globalization: The Human Consequences*, Oxford: Blackwell.

Featherstone, M. (1995), *Undoing Culture: Globalization, Postmodernism and Identity*, London: Sage.

Featherstone, M., S. Lash and R. Robertson (eds) (1995), *Global Modernities*, London: Sage.

Fukuyama, F. (1992), *The End of History and the Last Man*, London: Hamish Hamilton.

Hirst, P. and G. Thompson (1996), *Globalization in Question: The International Economy and the Possibilities of Governance*, Cambridge: Polity Press.

Kofman, E. and G. Youngs (eds) (2001), *Globalization: Theory and Practice*, London: Pinter.

Robins, K. (1997), 'Global times: what in the world is going on?', in P. Du Gay (ed.), *The Production of Culture/Cultures of Production*, London: Sage/Open University Press.

COPYRIGHT ACKNOWLEDGEMENTS

INDEX